RUSSIA'S
COLD WAR

RUSSIA'S
COLD WAR

From the October Revolution to the Fall of the Wall

Jonathan Haslam

Yale
UNIVERSITY
PRESS
New Haven & London

Published with assistance from the Mary Cady Tew Memorial Fund.

Yale University Press books may be purchased in quantity for educational, business,
or promotional use. For information, please e-mail sales.press@yale.edu (U.S. office)
or sales@yaleup.co.uk (U.K. office).

Set in Electra type by Newgen North America
Printed in the United States of America by Sheridan Books, Ann Arbor, Michigan.

Library of Congress Cataloging-in-Publication Data

Haslam, Jonathan.
Russia's Cold War : from the October Revolution to the fall of the wall /
Jonathan Haslam.
p. cm.
Includes bibliographical references and index.
ISBN 978-0-300-15997-4 (cloth : alk. paper)
1. Soviet Union—Foreign relations—1917–1945. 2. Soviet Union—Foreign relations—
1945–1991. 3. Cold War. I. Title.
DK266.45.H37 2011
327.47009'04—dc22

2010026281

A catalogue record for this book is available from the British Library.

This paper meets the requirements of ANSI/NISO Z39.48–1992 (Permanence of Paper).

10 9 8 7 6 5 4 3 2 1

For Karina and Timothy

When Napoleon I conducted war under the slogan liberation from serfdom, he found support, had allies and was successful.

When Napoleon I shifted to wars of conquest, he multiplied his enemies and met with defeat.

—Stalin, 5 May 1941

CONTENTS

Contents

PREFACE

The term "Cold War" was coined by George Orwell in describing the impact of the atom bomb on world politics in October 1945, at a time of tension with Russia. "We may be heading not for general breakdown but for an epoch as horribly stable as the slave empires of antiquity," he wrote. The Soviet Union was "a state . . . at once unconquerable and in a permanent state of 'cold war' with its neighbours."[1] Of course, those relations were never good since the foundation of the Bolshevik regime. Thus our story properly begins in 1917.

Any serious account of foreign policy conducted beyond American shores is above all concerned with high politics, attenuated or enhanced, of course, by macroeconomic, domestic political, social, ideological, and cultural determinants that either confine or motivate policy in one direction or another. In this sense the USSR was little different from its European neighbors whose foreign policies were traditionally "crown prerogative," of which France under the Fifth Republic is a prime example. Moreover, although the Bolsheviks did not believe in reasons of state as such — because Marxism-Leninism dictated goals that stood above and beyond merely the state — they did practice realpolitik: they were realists in terms of means, though utopians in terms of ends.[2] From the outset Soviet foreign policy was tightly controlled at the center, initially by Lenin and subsequently by the senior Party secretary, but always — excepting the years of extreme terror under Stalin (1936–41 and 1948–53) — within a broad consensus forged among dominant figures in the Politburo on the basis of the Leninist inheritance.

At one level below, Party and state organs with access to classified documents and the foreign press could propose but not dispose. The numbers of Soviet missiles and other armaments were, for example, pencilled into the documents at the Party's Military-Industrial Sector, information available to no one other

than a handful of officials serving the leading secretary of the Party. Even someone as high up as Alexander Yakovlev was given the wrong figures, and Margaret Thatcher had occasion to correct Mikhail Gorbachev on the data he had
been given.

Moreover — and this is crucial — it is hard for those in the West to understand
without direct experience the degree to which the most privileged Soviet citizen in the metropolis was almost totally cut off from all objective information
and alternative viewpoints from abroad, even after the Helsinki Final Act (1975)
and well into the Gorbachev era. The Westerner visiting and living in Russia
even for brief periods suffered sensory deprivation, particularly acute when the
authorities were jamming broadcasts from outside. Information is power. And
without it no amount of democratization — and there was none until spring
1988 with partially representative elections and finally the release of "trouble-
makers" from special psychiatric hospitals — could seriously affect the conduct
of foreign policy. One cannot therefore sensibly find among the Russian people
an explanation of foreign policy under Soviet rule, let alone the end of the Cold
War. It is for these reasons that the Cold War could draw to an end as the direct
result of decisions essentially by one man, Gorbachev.

Understanding events at the time they occurred was hard enough. But even
historians with the inestimable advantage of hindsight have found it difficult.
Parallel to the Cold War we have also faced a historiographical Cold War, not
so much between East and West — since what we would regard as scholarly history was impermissible in Russia until 1992 due to the most rigorous censorship
and punishment for "anti-Soviet" activity in any form — as between academics
within the West. The war in Vietnam broke a social contract within the US
elite in the most painful manner. Thereafter few fields of historical inquiry as
Cold War history have been so beset by political dispute in open and covert
form. Moreover, resolution of factual accuracy even about Western policy was
hindered by the fact that archives in the West were combed by the authorities to
remove items which were not merely those vital to state security but also those
that exposed the hypocrisy of government or embarrassed allied regimes.

Much undoubtedly still remains hidden. For these and no doubt other reasons, we are unlikely for many years to see the kind of objective history one
has learned to expect for World War I. But official censorship should never be
allowed to determine the writing of history.

So what of Soviet sources? A complaint commonly levied with justification
against histories of the Cold War is that the scholars concerned neither read
nor speak Russian.[3] It was once plausible to plead that records were closed. But
this excuse no longer stands since much has been released following German
reunification (1990) and the collapse of the Soviet Union (1991). Relying solely

on Western sources amounts to taking testimony from one side only in an unpleasant divorce. Under the rule of law no court would seriously allow such a
practice.

Non-Russian speakers have partial access to archival documents. A great deal
is available translated by the Cold War International History Project, in the
National Security Archive, and from the Parallel History Project. Invaluable
though it may be, the material is uneven. Little is offered on the earliest phase
of the Cold War. And the focus is on dramatic episodes rather than policy over
time. It excludes most memoirs and all secondary works, which — given continued censorship in Moscow — are critical on military matters.

A further charge is that historians focus excessively on Soviet-American relations to the exclusion of Europe.[4] The assumption all too often holds that the
Cold War was generated and sustained by Washington and Moscow alone. It
is perhaps inevitable that history has been tilted in this direction because by far
the greater number of specialists — with such notable exceptions at the senior
level as Marc Trachtenberg and William Hitchcock — are Americans with little
direct experience of Europe or knowledge of European languages. And even
respected scholars born and bred in Europe have dismissed its role in the emergence (Vojtech Mastny) and continuation (Arne Westad) of the Cold War. Yet
how can one understand the *grand peur* of 1947 or the furore over the SS-20
without direct access to West European archives? And the archives of at least
one key Communist Party — that of Italy — are completely open to research.

This work is thus intended to fill both lacunae by highlighting Russia while
giving Europe its due. No consecutive narrative yet exists that uses Russian-
language archives throughout from 1945 to 1989. The most recent works present
only isolated episodes in Cold War history and do so with a broad brush. They
undoubtedly contribute greatly to our understanding but they are ultimately
unsatisfactory because consecutive narrative is critical to causal explanation
in the writing of history. Moreover, detailed research at firsthand in the original language does matter. *Fingerspitzengefühl* is hard enough to acquire even
when directly immersed in the primary sources of one's own country, let alone
in alien archives. This was hitherto impossible without selective opening of
documents in Moscow; the rich array of top secret Soviet documents held by
the Bundesarchiv (notably the SED archive in Berlin); and the extraordinary
Russian collections at the Hoover Institution archive at Stanford (the Kataev
Papers on military matters, for instance); the Volkogonov Papers in the Library
of Congress; and the National Security Archive in Washington DC.

The specialist reader will immediately note that references to secondary
sources are few and far between. This is because I have tried to rely as far as
possible on declassified documents and interviews. To do this would have been

impossible if required to weave through the narrative a running commentary on all prior interpretations of Soviet policy. So readers will have to bear with me, assume that I am familiar with what has gone before, and judge my interpretation against existing knowledge of events derived from my predecessors. Moreover, aggrieved historians should recall that the mass of pioneering research conducted by such political scientists as Alex Dallin and Adam Ulam years before any archive was open has largely been neglected by historians of the Cold War, as has much of the pioneering work in any language other than English where not available in translation.

Archives were critical to this book: Birmingham University Library Archive; Churchill College Archives (Cambridge); CIA Electronic Reading Room (Internet); Eisenhower Library and Archive (Abilene, Kansas); Quai d'Orsay archive (Paris); Fondazione Gramsci (PCI) archive (Rome); Hoover Institution archive (Stanford, California); Library of Congress (Washington DC); Liddell Hart Archive (King's College, London); National Security Archive (Washington DC); Kennedy Library and Archive (Boston, Massachusetts); Labour Party Archives (Manchester University); Lyndon Johnson Library and Archive (Austin, Texas); National Archives (Kew); Library of Congress Manuscripts Division (Washington DC); Firestone Memorial Library (Princeton University); Russian Centre for the Preservation and Study of Documents of Contemporary History (RTsKhIDNI), now the Russian State Archive of Socio-Political History (RGASPI); Russian Foreign Ministry Archive (AVPRF, Moscow); SAPMO (Bundesarchiv, Berlin); Truman Library and Archive (Independence, Missouri); US National Archives (College Park, Maryland); the Widener Library (Harvard University).

Without direct access to some of those involved in policy making and execution, however, it would have been difficult to make full sense of events so distant from us now. I would therefore like to acknowledge crucial assistance from the following on key points of detail over the past twenty years, some befriended and some now unfortunately deceased (in italics): Egon Bahr, Lucius Battle, Tony Bishop, Sir Rodric Braithwaite, Harold Brown, Mary Acheson Bundy, Sir Bryan Cartledge, Anatoly Chernyaev, Vyacheslav Dashichev, Vladimir Erofeev, Dr. Stefan Halper, *Sir Nicholas Henderson*, John Hines, Viktor Israelyan, *the Kennans, Sir John Killick*, Tatyana Litvinova, *Paul Nitze, William ("Bill") Odom, Baroness Park of Monmouth*, Phillip Petersen, Lord Powell of Bayswater, James Schlesinger, Brent Scowcroft, *Georgii Shakhnazarov*, Sir John Thomson, George Walden, and others who have preferred to remain anonymous.

The following kindly read and commented on all or part of the manuscript in its various guises: *Sir Nicholas Henderson*, Peter Hennessy, David Holloway,

Mark Kramer, *Baroness Park*, Silvio Pons, Lord Powell, David Reynolds, Brendan Simms, Sir John Thomson, and Marc Trachtenberg. And I should record here belated recognition of the late Alex Dallin of Stanford University, who counselled me judiciously on elements of this work even before it had been fully conceived. Time spent at Stanford, Berkeley, Yale, and Harvard greatly illuminated my understanding, as did a two-year appointment at the Johns Hopkins University School of Advanced International Studies at the height of the Reagan administration, just down embassy row. Others whom I should thank for directing me to sources include Lloyd Gardner, Gordon Barrass, and Timothy Garton-Ash. Of course, no one bears responsibility for the following other than myself.

Acronyms and Abbreviations

ABM	Antiballistic Missile (System)
BBC	British Broadcasting Corporation
BMEWS	Ballistic Missile Early Warning System
BRUSA	Britain–United States of America Agreement
Cab	British Cabinet papers
CCP	Chinese Communist Party
Cheka	Chrezvychainaya Komissiya
CDU	Christlich Demokratische Union Deutschlands
CGT	Confédération National de Travail
CIA	Central Intelligence Agency
Cominform	Communist Information Bureau
Comintern	Communist International
CPSU	Communist Party of the Soviet Union
CSCE	Conference on Security and Co-operation in Europe
CSU	Christlich Soziale Union
DDR	Deutsche Demokratische Republik
DIA	Defense Intelligence Agency
DRV	Democratic Republic of (North) Vietnam
DST	Direction de la Surveillance Territoire
EAM	Ethnikón Apeleftherotikón Métopon
EDC	European Defence Community
EEC	European Economic Community
ELAS	Ethnikón Laïkós Apeleftherotikós Strátos
FBS	(US) Forward-Based Systems
FCO	Foreign and Commonwealth Office
FDP	Freie Demokratische Partei

FNLA	Frente Nacional de Libertação de Angola
FO	Foreign Office
FRG	Federal Republic of (West) Germany
FSLN	Frente Sandinista de Liberación Nacional
GCHQ	Government Communications Headquarters (UK)
GDR	(East) German Democratic Republic
GLCM	Ground-Launched Cruise Missile
GRU	Glavnoe Razvedyvatel'noe Upravlenie
IBM	International Business Machines Corporation
ICBM	Intercontinental Ballistic Missile
IEMSS	Institut Ekonomiki Mirovoi Sotsialisticheskoi Sistemy
IMF	International Monetary Fund
INF	Intermediate-Range Nuclear Forces
INR	(US Bureau of) Intelligence and Research
IRBM	Intermediate-Range Ballistic Missile
KGB	Komitet Gosudarstvennoi Bezopasnosti
KKE	Kommounistikó Kómma Elládes
KMT	Kuomintang
MCP	Malayan Communist Party
MFA	Movimento do Forças Armadas
MI5	British secret service (domestic)
MI6	British secret service (overseas); otherwise SIS
MPLA	Movimiento Popular de Libertação de Angola
MVD	Ministerstvo Vnutrennykh del
Narkomindel	Narodnyi Komissariat Inostrannykh Del
NATO	North Atlantic Treaty Organization
NKGB	Narodnyi Komissariat Gosudarstvennoi Bezpasnosti
NKVD	Narodnyi Komissariat Vnutrennykh del
NSA	National Security Agency
NSC	National Security Council
NSDD	National Security Decision Directives
NSDM	National Security Decision Memorandum
PCF	Parti Communiste Français
PCF	Partito Comunista Italiano
PCP	Partido Comunista Português
PKI	Partai Komunis Indonesia
Politburo	Political Bureau of the Central Committee
PPR	Polska Partia Robotnicza (Communist)
PRC	People's Republic of China

Prem	British Prime Minister's papers
PSF	Parti Socialiste Français
PSI	Partito Socialista Italiano
PUWP	Polish United Workers' Party (Communist)
Razvedupr	Razvedyvatel'noe Upravlenie, forerunner to GRU
RYAN	Raketno-Yadernoe Napadenie
SALT	Strategic Arms Limitation Talks
SAM	Surface-to-Air Missile
SDI	Strategic Defense Initiative
SED	Sozialistische Einheitspartei Deutschlands (Communist)
SIOP	Single Integrated Operational Plan (US)
SLBM	Submarine-Launched Ballistic Missile
SPD	Sozialistische Partei Deutschlands
SSBN	Ship Submersible Ballistic Nuclear (Submarine)
TASS	Telegrafnoe Agenstvo Sovetskogo Soyuza
UAR	Egypt
UKUSA	UK-USA Agreement
UN	United Nations
UNEF	United Nations Emergency Force
UNITA	União Nacional para Independência Total de Angola
USA	United States of America
USAF	US Air Force
USSR	Union of Soviet Socialist Republics
VPK	Voenno-Promyshlennyi Komitet

Underlying Antagonisms

Without international revolution neither the Soviet Union nor any other [socialist] country can triumph. Without international revolution no one can triumph. We have to increase the number of our friends.

—*Molotov, 26 August 1979*

The Cold War did not, of course, burst in suddenly onto an entirely harmonious world. But there was something peculiar about it—and not merely the fact that nuclear weapons deterred open warfare between Superpowers. The conflict had deep-seated ideological foundations that outlasted leaders who differed in the degree of attachment to fundamental principle in the conduct of foreign policy. On the grand scale of history the Cold War stemmed directly from a thoroughgoing revolt against Western values established since the Enlightenment, a wholesale rejection of an entire way of life and its economic underpinnings increasingly dominant since the seventeenth century, and the substitution of something new and entirely alien in terms of culture and experience. That revolt began with the October Revolution in 1917.

It was largely because of a recent history of deep suspicion and mutual hostility that common cause was never recognized in confronting Hitler before the war and that the United States never actually signed an alliance with the USSR during World War II. Indeed, a veritable cold war prevailed between Britain and Russia through most of the 1920s. George Kennan attacked the view that the "state of sharp conflict and tension" between East and West began only in 1945 as "erroneous." "Never were American relations with Russia at a lower ebb than in the first sixteen years after the Bolshevik seizure of power in 1917."[1] Thus even when German aggression temporarily brought the two camps together in joint opposition to Hitler's bid for global supremacy in 1941, those relations were never as good in private as they were represented in public.

Furthermore, they were regarded with far greater suspicion from Moscow than Western leaders ever imagined. It therefore makes sense to seek the roots of the Cold War in the fetid undergrowth of relations mired in mistrust well before 1945.

THE OCTOBER REVOLUTION

The Bolshevik seizure of power in November 1917 launched in the name of an Enlightenment philosophy was implemented in one of the most backward countries in Europe. Thus from the very beginning the gap between vision and reality, dream and nightmare, already wide under Lenin, very soon stretched to breaking point under Stalin. The revolution threatened chaos to an international system already shaken by an unexpectedly long and destructive war. Since the French revolutionary wars the European states system had reasserted the principle that the preservation of that system was the paramount objective and that within it foreign policy should be conducted on the principle known as "reasons of state": whereby the safety of the state far outweighed any other value, whether religious or ideological. The secular universalist goals of the French Revolution that challenged this idea had been successfully contained by war and postwar diplomacy. The United States, never fully committed to this doctrine, self-consciously excluded itself from the system; and thereby represented no challenge to it. But from 1917 in both domestic and foreign policies Soviet Russia mounted a fearsome front to a world based on capitalist foundations which the Great Powers were determined to protect.

The comprehensive nationalization of industry involved the expropriation of foreign capital without compensation. And even before the regime took this unprecedented measure, it had antagonized the West by refusing to recognize treaties previously concluded in secret by the tsarist and provisional governments. Soviet Russia then affronted the world by publishing those treaties. This was a symptomatic challenge to practices long established in European diplomacy since the inception of the modern state. On seizing power, the Bolsheviks also offered an immediate ceasefire to the belligerents in World War I, with conditions for a general peace that included liberation of colonies and dependant, oppressed, and deprived nations. And, absent any response, they concluded a separate peace with Berlin, thus closing the Eastern Front. They called on workers of all lands to bring down bourgeois governments and install soviets. They refused to recognize all debts contracted by the Russian government from other governments as well as private banks.

The states system had not witnessed such a wholesale threat to its integrity and customs — commonly proclaimed as Western civilization — since the revolution in France of 1789. And that threat had by 1794 precipitated military intervention, led thereafter by Britain, whose publicly expressed concerns for the balance of power were inextricably enmeshed in privately articulated fears of insurrection at home. For the Bolsheviks, hostility from the capitalist world was only to be expected, not least because the parallels with 1789 were to the forefront of their minds, as was the brutal fate of the Paris Commune in 1871. "The Russian working class will win their freedom and give an impetus to Europe by their revolutionary action," Lenin had promised in 1907.[2] Indeed, "the Russian revolution can achieve victory by its own efforts," Lenin wrote, "but it cannot possibly hold and consolidate its gains by its own strength. It cannot do this unless there is a socialist revolution in the West. Without this condition restoration is inevitable."[3] "The Russian revolution has a great international ally both in Europe and in Asia, but, at the same time, and *for that very reason*, it has not only a national, not only a Russian, but also an *international* enemy. Reaction against the mounting proletarian struggle is inevitable in all capitalist countries, and it is uniting the bourgeois governments of the whole world against every popular movement, against every revolution both in Asia and, particularly, in Europe."[4]

After the Bolsheviks seized power in November 1917, conflict with the capitalist world arose persistently over backing for revolution abroad, refusal to recognize and repay debts incurred prior to the revolution, and Lenin's resolute opposition to compensation for assets. Britain was most disturbed by revolutionary propaganda; France and the United States were initially most concerned about monetary loss. These differences and the deeply entrenched reservations about cooperation that arose from them were later merely suppressed by the exigencies of war in 1941–45, not completely expunged.

From 1917 Moscow's continued support for world revolution drove it headlong into collision with the swollen and tottering British Empire, now at its height. In Europe, too, the spectre of revolution stalked the streets. The high point of misplaced euphoria on the part of the Bolsheviks occurred when the prospect of conquering Poland emerged in July 1920. Lenin declared "the situation in Comintern" to be "superb." "My personal opinion," he wrote, "is that for this we need to sovietise Hungary, and perhaps, also Czechoslovakia and Romania."[5] Only Karl Radek voiced skepticism. It was, he agreed, entirely possible that a revolution in Italy would transform the scene. "But in any case we must refrain from the method of sounding out the international situation with the aid of bayonets. The bayonet would be good if it were necessary to aid a particular revolution, but for seeing how the land lies in this or that country we have another weapon—Marxism, and for this we do not need to call upon Red Army soldiers."[6]

Some even saw support for foreign revolution as a bargaining chip. After the Red Army evacuated Poland, First Deputy Commissar for Foreign Affairs Lev Karakhan pressed for the invasion and occupation of Persia so that, in his words, "we become for England a serious and immediate menace and that we place our aggression in the East in direct dependence on England's policy toward us: we respond blow for blow." Lenin sensibly rejected the advice, and in fact Russia dropped its armed support for revolutionaries in northern Iran (Ghilan) within a year.[7] They retreated without a quid pro quo. But the surrender to common sense was hard to accept. A bitter Azeri communist leader, Narimanov, protested to Stalin: "And where would we have stood now with the Entente, had we not killed the liberation movement in Persia through Rothstein [the Soviet envoy in Tehran]?" "We would have the power to dictate to the Entente! Two critical places—the Straits [the Bosphorous] and the gates to India—would stand within our immediate influence."[8]

Revolutionary war no longer an immediate option, Lenin separated out the organization and pursuit of world revolution from day-to-day diplomacy. The Commissariat of Foreign Affairs (Narkomindel) handled the latter. Revolution was promoted by the Communist International, or Comintern. Having failed to expunge the revolution in 1918–19, Britain under liberal Prime Minister David Lloyd George naïvely assumed that Moscow would adjust to the prevailing world order run by the Great Powers in a capitalist international states system. These moves were also determined by the dual need to revive trade and settle the peace of Europe, which would in turn improve dismal economic prospects. Thus in March 1921 Britain reluctantly signed a trade agreement with Moscow effectively establishing diplomatic relations with the new regime.[9]

To meet British anxieties, each signatory agreed to refrain "from hostile action or undertakings against the other and from conducting outside of its own borders any official propaganda direct or indirect against the institutions of the British Empire of the Russian Soviet Republic." For Moscow this was a dead letter on signature, since it maintained that Comintern was unconnected with the Soviet government and was therefore not bound by such terms: "I think we shall ultimately emerge on top as a result of our firm stand that the Communist International is not a governmental institution," Lenin wrote, adding that "any attempt to present us seriously with an ultimatum that we get rid of the Communist International is inexcusable. However, the emphasis laid on the matter shows where the shoe pinches and what displeases them in our policy."[10]

This dual policy, which epitomized the distance between the need for Bolshevik accommodation to failed world revolution and the belief that this revolution was not only essential but inevitable disrupted relations with all the

Powers in the following decades; indeed, until the very end of the regime. But at any given moment a Power divided against the rest would need a measure of alignment with Moscow, albeit merely for short-term purposes.[11] Lenin reminded his followers, "We have often said that an alliance with one imperialist state against another to consolidate the socialist republic is not objectionable in point of principle."[12] This was known as the exploitation of inter-imperialist contradictions.

Moscow engaged in a risky gamble. Chief of Staff Mikhail Tukhachevsky argued that "neither the Red Army nor the country is ready for war."[13] The risk was by no means as great as the Russians imagined, though the fact that the Red Army comprised a mere 610,000 men along more than 50,000 kilometers of frontier from Leningrad to Vladivostok, and the absence of an independent arms industry to secure the country's borders against any combination of adversaries at the level of technology of the Great Powers, certainly gave them good reason to be nervous. Yet the idea that Moscow should therefore stand back and avoid trouble prompted contempt from most if not all, including the rising figure in the Soviet regime, Stalin: "Would it not be dangerous to support the liberation movement in China? Does this not set us at loggerheads with other countries?" he said, responding to questions from an audience at Sverdlovsk University. "Would it not be better to establish for ourselves 'spheres of influence' in China in common with other 'leading Powers'" and gain something to our advantage in China? It would be both useful and safe," he suggested ironically.[14] Naturally, the Bolsheviks hoped to win China entirely for themselves. Only when that failed, in the spring of 1927, and London broke off diplomatic relations did lesser options appear acceptable — indeed, essential — in the belief that part of China was better than none. The war scare that resulted — to which Stalin was indifferent — was fuelled, though not caused, by these events. But the drama highlighted the urgency of rapid and forced industrialization, without which the USSR would sooner or later fall prey to its enemies. And it was the hard man of the regime, Stalin, who lashed himself irrevocably to that towering mast in 1929.

STALIN IN POWER

Iosif Stalin (Dzhugashvili), self-styled "man of steel," was born on 21 December 1879 in Gori, Georgia. A member of the Party (then the Russian Social Democratic Labor Party) from 1898, for which expulsion from his seminary was an inevitable result, he did not come into prominence until well after the October Revolution. A man in the shadows, who consistently voiced skepticism of foreign revolutions, whose only foreign language was Russian, instead he took to committee work. And on 3 April 1922 he assumed the unglamorous and apparently unrewarding task of becoming General Secretary of the Party, a purely bureaucratic position. It was, however, by means of organization and unrelenting control over the apparatus, including personnel, that he secured an indirect path to power. Lev Trotsky, a much more brilliant man and the second great figure of the revolution, never understood how such a mediocrity could triumph; but then Trotsky made others nervous, while Stalin put them at ease; Trotsky could not be bothered to attend meetings even of crucial importance out of impatience or pique, whereas Stalin never missed one. And of course Trotsky was the cosmopolitan Jew—a man of culture fluent in several languages, whereas Stalin at times struggled with comprehensible Russian pronunciation. It was as though the Party favored someone more reassuringly familiar, with all the traits Trotsky lacked and who was deprived of all the qualities Trotsky possessed.[15]

A handsome Caucasian as a young man—swarthy, black-haired, moustached, with seductive dark eyes—Stalin was nevertheless deeply troubled. And to the surprise of the unsuspecting visitor he was small—no more than five feet four at most, his left lower arm incapacitated from a childhood accident, the torso too short for his arms and legs. As he aged, his eyes took on a yellowish appearance, perhaps from gallstones or jaundice, his faced pockmarked, his poor teeth discolored by tobacco, his thinning hair increasingly gray, a paunch emerging under the colorless costume. And like those who worked for him, that Kremlin pallor—white-faced with a strange touch of red on the cheeks—resulting from working long hours late at night and into the early morning, a demanding requirement that created a tortuous schedule for subordinates with families they scarcely saw.

Stalin was the great dissimulator: in public the modest, thoughtful, shrewd, self-controlled, benign figure, willing to listen while he walked the room and puffed on his pipe or doodled wolves on a pad with a red crayon, yet capable of tough decisions. Stalin the modernizer of backward Russia: this was the statesman gullible foreigners, such as Lady Astor, were pleased to meet; the familiar face of reason who charmed them all. Yet he epitomized backwardness in its Eurasian form, as distant from the Enlightenment as the Byzantine church that educated him was from the nonconformist congregations of New England. Away from prying eyes the ever-brooding, sometimes brutal, vindictive, psychopathic and occasionally paranoid mind-set of a tribal chieftain familiar to the mountains of the Caucasus or, indeed, tsar and executioner in early Russia: reminiscent of Ivan the Terrible in Sergei Eisenshtein's dark film portrayal. The habit of solitude acquired in exile appealed to him as he aged. Those around noticed that the closer he came to supreme power the more dark suspicion predominated. Like Oscar Wilde's Dorian Gray, while the public image remained ever untouched by age and the scars of life, the true portrait in the attic showed the true horror of depravity.

COLLECTIVE SECURITY FAILS

In January 1929 Stalin embarked on the first five-year plan of industrialization. His immediate obsession was with the maintenance and amplification of the state. "The Russian tsars did a great deal that was bad," he acknowledged. "They robbed and enslaved the people. They waged wars and seized territories in the interests of the landowners. But they did one thing that was good—they amassed an enormous state, all the way to Kamchatka. We have inherited that state."[16] But survival and expansion required rapid industrialization. The irony was that this was to be obtained through extensive importation of capital goods and know-how from the West. Indeed, Stalin later freely acknowledged "that the United States had greatly assisted Soviet industry—perhaps two-thirds of all large plants in the Soviet Union had been constructed with American help or experience."[17]

While domestic construction was advancing at breakneck speed, the need to ensure that capitalists were at one another's throats instead prompted Stalin to bet on German nationalism, however extreme, against France.[18] Comintern thus sustained its attacks on social democracy even when it was obvious that this would open the path to power for Hitler.[19] The real price for participating in schemes to destroy the British and French empires would be billed later. Once Hitler attained power, he turned against Moscow and attempted to build a coalition against the Bolsheviks in an anticommunist front.

By the time Stalin was fully conscious of the danger, fundamental ideological differences made a coalition between West European democracies and Russia impossible despite the best efforts of Commissar for Foreign Affairs Maxim Litvinov, who somehow hoped against hope that reasons of state would win out. On 13 September 1938 Prime Minister Neville Chamberlain wrote to King George VI of his trip to see Hitler. The purpose was Anglo-German understanding. Chamberlain intended to outline "the prospect of Germany and England as the two pillars of European peace and buttresses against Communism."[20] Indeed, "One of Neville Chamberlain's motives," recalled parliamentary private secretary, Lord Home, who was with him at Munich, "in trying to dissuade Hitler from war and in doing so to risk slipping over the edge of reconciliation into the pit of appeasement, was that he felt certain in his mind that if Europe weakened itself in another war, Russia would try to dominate the continent of Europe."[21]

After the turn of the tide in the war against Germany, the sinister Deputy Commissar for Foreign Affairs Andrei Vyshinsky commented that "if only England had invited Russia to Munich the result might have been the happy position obtaining to-day, and, who knows, perhaps no war."[22] Having led the anti-Bolshevik cause in 1918–19, by the end of 1933 Winston Churchill resolved that Hitler's Germany for the time being constituted the immediate threat to the British Empire. Russia was thus a necessary ally. Churchill was prepared to take whatever terms were on offer. Watched by Stalin for his potential as Prime Minister and therefore ally against Germany, Churchill, however, never commanded sufficient support in his own party to take power in time of peace, despite repeated predictions of a coup from the Soviet ambassador in London, Ivan Maisky.[23] According to Lev Helfand who defected as ambassador in Rome (July 1940), Stalin appears to have been willing to reach agreement with London up to mid-June 1939. But Chamberlain began maneuvering to prevent any westward expansion of Soviet forces.[24] This matches Molotov's ultimatum to Foreign Secretary Lord Halifax on 10 June: "We consider that without a guarantee for the security of the northwestern boundaries of the USSR by means of a decisive countermeasures of the three treaty partners against direct or indirect attack by the aggressor on Estonia, Latvia, or Finland, it will be impossible to satisfy public opinion in the Soviet Union."[25]

FROM PARIAH TO RELUCTANT ALLY

Helfand told the British that Stalin had been "nibbling" for an agreement with Hitler for quite some time. The search for an understanding with Britain was nothing more than a consequence of deep-seated and sustained Nazi hostility to Moscow. The change of line thus depended entirely on Berlin. Finally, the Germans moved. The Nazi-Soviet pact that resulted on 23 August 1939 and the friendship pact on 30 September divided Poland and placed the fate of the Baltic states in Soviet hands. Stalin saw this as preempting a further division of Eastern Europe along the lines of the Munich settlement. "In Moscow," Maisky surmised, "they are not expecting war; they are counting on a new Munich."[26] And once war did break out, Maisky the former Menshevik (moderates of the revolution) believed capitalism could not survive.[27] Stalin welcomed war between Britain, France, and Germany in September 1939: "We can see nothing wrong in their having a good hard fight and weakening each other," he said. "It would be fine," he added, "if at the hands of Germany the position of the richest capitalist countries (especially England) were shaken." Hitler was thereby "without understanding it or desiring it, shaking and undermining the capitalist system." Russia could "maneuver, pit one side against the other to set them fighting with each other as fiercely as possible."[28]

Hard though it may be to believe, prospects for revolution in Germany had yet to be extinguished.[29] At Comintern headquarters Secretary-General Georgi Dimitrov told subordinates that the Nazi-Soviet pact exerted "revolutionary influence" on Germany, where the Nazi Party was "not homogenous but a heterogeneous party." Socialism was once again on the agenda. The most likely scenario was "victory of the Anglo-French imperialists underpinned by America" which would "mean the exhaustion of all the Powers. In such a scenario the outlook for the working-class in Germany would not be so bad."[30]

It is, moreover, worth remembering that the USSR fought Germany only as a result of invasion on 22 June 1941, and that the United States did so only as a result of Japan's attack on Pearl Harbor and Hitler's declaration of war on 7 and 8 December 1941 respectively. What was the first item of Stalin's instructions to his new intelligence chief in Washington that December? "See to it that Churchill and the Americans do not conclude a separate peace with Hitler and that they don't jointly move against the Soviet Union."[31]

On the eve of Germany's invasion of Russia, Rudolf Hess, Hitler's deputy, had flown to Britain. Soviet spy Kim Philby reported that Hess had "brought peace proposals with him."[32] Hess claimed to have come to England "to conclude a compromise peace that must put an end to the increasing exhaustion of the two warring countries and prevent the final liquidation of the British Empire as a stabilising force." He also claimed continuing loyalty to Hitler and believed "that in England there is a strongly anti-Churchill party standing for peace, which with his [Hess's] arrival will receive powerful stimulus in the struggle for the conclusion of peace." Philby considered "that the time for peace negotiations has not yet come, but that in the course of the further progress of the war Hess could become the centre of intrigues for the conclusion of a compromise peace and will be of value to the peace party in England and to Hitler."[33]

At this stage Stalin saw raw intelligence. An analytical service designed to check and filter what came in was not established until the end of 1943.[34] Its absence meant that Stalin was free to pick and choose among its products without restraint for what fitted in with his prejudices.

Philby's unfortunate warning was to haunt Stalin after the invasion, particularly when Russia was on its knees at Stalingrad. The invasion took Stalin entirely by surprise. He secretly initiated peace feelers to Germany in a futile effort to stem the tide of Russian blood and the humiliating loss en masse of

Russian territory. Pavel Sudoplatov of the NKVD was summoned to see Beria and told that Moscow had decided to clarify the terms Germany might accept for a compromise peace. It would give space to maneuver and allow time to recuperate. This was to be done through the Bulgarian ambassador whose outgoing telegrams were monitored by the NKVD. The meeting took place at the Aragvi restaurant and at a particular table wired by the services.[35] It was not known what, if anything, resulted, but it showed just how desperate Stalin had become, even if subsequently he drew back from the likely consequences.

After catastrophic defeats in the summer of 1941, Soviet forces finally recovered the initiative. Stalin emphasized how important it was "to know whether we shall have to fight at the Peace Conference in order to get our western frontiers." He warned Foreign Secretary Anthony Eden that "our people who are fighting with such heavy losses at the front, losses in blood and tears, if they were to hear this bargaining that is going on as to the restoration of our legitimate frontiers, it would make my position and . . . Molotov's extremely difficult. We are fighting," Stalin emphasized, "not for the interests of the *Roi de Prusse*, but for our own frontiers."[36] But all was lost by late March 1942 when Stalin overreacted and exposed his men to devastating counterattacks.

Indeed, the greatest danger appeared to be a Russian defeat at the hands of Germany. Churchill wrote to Eden: "No one can foresee how the balance of power will lie or where the winning armies will stand at the end of the war. It seems probable, however, that the United States and the British Empire, far from being exhausted, will be the most powerfully armed and economic bloc the world has ever seen, and that the Soviet Union will then need our aid in reconstruction far more than we shall need theirs."[37] A degree of complacency about Russia lingered. Thus even though from the outset of the alliance a sense of rivalry with Moscow persisted in London, it was assuaged at the top by the illusion that Russia would emerge from war far weaker than at the outset.

Barely a week later Maisky had informed his superiors that although Britain was relieved at the opening of the Eastern front, "for many this feeling is mixed with the secret thought that now it would be possible to dump the main weight of the struggle with the German military machine onto the shoulders of others." The most reactionary elements hoped that "England will by some means or another come out of the game without serious loss and, perhaps, even with profit."[38] Stalin, not needing encouragement, informed Maisky: "In essence, the English government is helping the Hitlerites by its passive policy of waiting. The Hitlerites want to beat their opponents one by one—today the Russians, tomorrow the English. The fact that England is applauding us and uses foul language against the Germans in no way changes the situation. Do the English understand this? I think they understand. What do they want? It seems they want us to be weakened," Stalin concluded.[39]

Circumstantial information was sufficient to set Stalin glooming. Britain's Minister of Aircraft Production, John Moore-Brabazon, indiscreetly expressed the wish that Russia and Germany wipe one another out, leaving Britain the opportunity to hold the balance (almost exactly Stalin's calculation in the autumn of 1939 with regard to Britain and Germany).[40] Germany, Stalin claimed, hoped "to set up a general coalition against the USSR, draw Great Britain and the United States into this coalition, intimidating the ruling circles of these countries beforehand with the spectre of revolution, thereby completely isolating our country from the other Powers." Hess had been sent to Britain in May 1941, he argued, "to convince England to join in a general attack on the USSR."[41]

These suspicions submerged when fighting was going relatively well for Moscow. Correspondingly, like unexploded ordnance buried beneath a thin layer of soil, they burst to the surface when the Soviet counteroffensive launched in the autumn of 1941 broke by the spring of 1942. Furthermore, the failure to predict correctly the direction of the German spring offensive—which, instead of aiming at Moscow, targeted Stalingrad to the southeast—nearly cost Russia the war. Stalin lost battle after battle. And on 20 May the Kerch peninsula fell again to Germany. The failure of Soviet arms heightened Stalin's barely contained suspicions of Churchill's intentions. The absence of a second front in France appeared deliberately calculated to ensure the further weakening of Russia. Even war correspondent Ilya Ehrenburg "was convinced that the British would only establish a second front if it became clear that the Russians were either being defeated or were about to be victorious. He said that in pursuing such a policy Britain was running the risk of incurring the lasting hatred not only of the Russians but of all Europe no matter which side won the war."[42]

Maisky told Eden that "it seemed to his Government, they had been fighting for 16 months practically alone. By a superhuman effort they had repelled the German attack and had even passed to the offensive. They were now on the eve of further great trials . . . what they hoped for was that we should take off their shoulders the burden of 30 to 40 divisions. . . . While . . . Maisky said he understood the difficulties that confronted us in the creation of a second front, I would understand that the fact that Russia had to bear virtually the whole burden created a measure of resentment, even bitterness, in Moscow."[43] By the time Molotov opened negotiations for a full alliance on 21 May 1942, Stalin's reckless military gambling on a massive series of counteroffensives had failed. The collapse of the front on the Kerch peninsula a day earlier had further undermined his waning diplomatic leverage. Moscow was once again staring in the face the prospect of complete collapse. Thus, although the treaty was not without significance, it was the opening of a second front in France that was the primary Soviet goal.

Accordingly, when Molotov was denied Britain's recognition of the enlarged Soviet frontiers as of 21 June 1941, Stalin unexpectedly told him to settle on the basis of the British draft that left frontier recognition aside. The Anglo-Soviet treaty was therefore speedily concluded on 26 May 1942. Signs of desperation on Molotov's part were no less evident in his insistence that "the weeks and months ahead will be an especially difficult time," when Hitler would make a desperate attempt to wipe out the Red Army. Hence the immediate need for a second front. The question was now "more severe" than ever before. The forces of the Germans "surpass our forces," Molotov emphasized.[44] The balance of power lay with the enemy. Hitler could draw on reserves throughout the European subcontinent. Molotov thus proposed that Anglo-American troops draw off at least forty divisions from the Russian front that summer and autumn. If the allies were determined to lock Russia into a particular postwar framework, surely now was the time to have done it.

US President Franklin Roosevelt refused to sign anything, even in secret, that recognized Soviet annexation of the Baltic states, and in the Balkans Bessarabia and Bukovina, on the grounds that public opinion was not ready for this.[45] Moreover, a Soviet defeat seemed all too likely. In Washington on 29 May Molotov bluntly warned that "the Red Army might not be able to hold out against the Nazis."[46] Although the final communiqué implied that full agreement had been secured to launch a second front, this was done at Soviet request largely for its impact on Berlin.

The acute problem of securing the second front remained, however. The military in both Britain and the United States insisted that the logistics were not yet available, landing craft in particular. Moscow now had an alibi against the West in the event of German forces inflicting further serious defeats, which now occurred and to a degree unimaginable in the fevered optimism of the previous winter. As far as the Russians were concerned this was the turning point of the war. A revealing echo of suspicions can be found in Andrei Gromyko's comment to his son many years later. In 1941–42 Gromyko—whose spoken English was then incomprehensible—had been deputy head of mission at the Soviet embassy in Washington. He told his son that the Cold War "began as 'the secret cold war,' accompanying the 'hot' war, as the allies at Churchill's insistence without justification delayed the opening of the second front in Europe."[47] Certainly Moscow acted on that assumption. The degree of anxiety in the Kremlin is captured in Stalin's candid acknowledgment at Tehran a year later "that had

Russia not had at her disposal such a vast territory the Germans would have probably won the victory."[48]

The true extent of Stalin's suspicions is revealed in an extraordinary telegram to Maisky. Hess was being held in reserve: "All of us in Moscow have gained the impression that Churchill is aiming at the defeat of the USSR, in order then to come to terms with the Germany of Hitler or Brüning at the expense of our country."[49] These unfounded allegations did not disappear entirely as Soviet troops finally burst through German lines and pushed the Wehrmacht back from Stalingrad; defeating it at Kursk in July 1943 due largely to knowledge of Hitler's plans via military intelligence (Razvedupr) residents in London—Ivan Sklyarov ("Briand")—and New York—Pavel Melkishev ("Molière").[50] Crucially, from January 1942 the Razvedupr had been receiving from agent "Dolly" at the War Office copies of decrypted German diplomatic and military telegrams. They arrived in such quantity that "Briand" asked permission to send it by "normal mail" to avoid overloading wireless transmissions.[51]

PREPARING FOR TEHRAN

En route to Tehran in November 1943 former ambassador Maisky, now deputy commissar, warned the British that a winter offensive in December might drive Germany out of Russia altogether. "If this happened before the second front opened, it would crystalise Russian opinion that they had beaten Germany and would create [a] difficult post-war position."[52] The opening of a second front in France was still Stalin's first priority. Thanks to "Briand" he knew in detail of Operation Overlord but had no indication when it would come into effect. Moreover, on 9 October "Briand" reported, "The second front in Western Europe is not being opened for purely political reasons. . . . Above all our allies fear a Russian invasion of Germany as this could, they think here, precipitate communist revolutions in every country of Europe."[53]

Other factors also weighed in the balance of mistrust. Before the allied summit Moscow faced the prospect of a postwar federation in Europe. This had been encouraged from London and Washington, spurred on by Irish Catholic Owen O'Malley who had served in Moscow and currently was liaising with the émigré Poles. Moscow negotiated a separate treaty with the Czech government-in-exile to block such a federation, signed on 12 December 1943.[54] British anxiety to contain postwar Soviet expansion was equally evident in the gathering of ambassadors and foreign ministers to prepare the agenda for Tehran in a series of meetings at the Tripartite (Moscow) Conference which ran from 18 October to 11 November 1943.

Concerned that Moscow was misreading signals from the democracies, London drew up a "Note on Declaration about Joint Responsibility for Europe" aimed at forestalling Soviet temptation to carve out their exclusive sphere of influence in Eastern Europe:

> If the three great powers had separate areas of responsibility or influence in Europe, there would be grave danger that they would tend to organise these areas, or suspect each other of organising them, against one another. This might very quickly lead to friction and the division of Europe into separate armed camps. . . . The effect of separate spheres of responsibility would also cause acute nervousness among the smaller powers. This would apply particularly in Eastern Europe, where the smaller countries are naturally terrified of Russian power.[55]

The trouble was that no alternative structure of international security had been fully identified, let alone tested as workable, and the ideological divisions between East and West were deeply rooted, making impossible the level of trust required to dispense with traditional spheres of influence.

Molotov "stated that he knew of no reason to believe that the Soviet Government would be interested in separate zones or spheres of influence and he could guarantee that there was no disposition on the part of the Soviet Government to divide Europe into such separate zones."[56] Moscow nevertheless worked to have the British proposal withdrawn, and Litvinov, now deputy commissar, insisted that "since there was no evidence that any of the three Powers here was seeking special areas of responsibility or influence he felt that to make a special declaration denying this would give rise to the belief that there had been some such intention on the part of one of the three countries here represented. He also inquired why it was confined only to Europe."[57]

Only recently Litvinov had served in Washington at the request of the Americans (1942–43). In January his wife Ivy wrote to lover Joe Freeman: "A great crisis is approaching. . . . It is possible that in a very short time I (we) shall be leaving." Maxim was dictating his memoirs at increasing speed.[58] When instructed to return in April, Litvinov complained to Under Secretary Sumner Welles "that he was unable to communicate with Stalin, whose isolation then bred a distorted view of the West." He tried to talk Ivy into staying, but for fear of what would doubtless happen to the children they returned.[59] On 4 September the Politburo handed Litvinov and Maisky pro forma responsibility for postwar planning.[60]

Litvinov believed in spheres of influence but not in the manner of Stalin and Molotov. Part of Litvinov's reasoning related to his position on Poland. Having

grown up as a Jew along the anti-Semitic marches of the Russian Empire popu-
lated by Poles, and having seen Poland wreck his collective security proposals
in the 1930s, he entirely shared the Kremlin's determination not to allow any future Poland the luxury of choosing its enemies. Indeed, Litvinov erupted into

> a torrent of abuse against the Poles, the gist of it being that they would have to
> learn to live within their ethnographical boundaries as a small nation and give
> up the idea that they were a great power. They were arrogant people without
> the ability or power to carry out their extreme nationalism. They had ab-
> surdly thought they could beat the Germans alone. . . . They were historically
> antagonistic to Russia and they had always created trouble for the peaceful
> Russians. They had to be taught a lesson or they would continue to be trouble
> makers. It was unreasonable to consider the interests of a small nation like
> the Poles when they opposed the interests of 180 million Russians. . . . Litvi-
> nov talked as if he were antagonistic not only to the Government in exile in
> London but to the Poles in general. He said that, fortunately for us, Molotov
> did not feel as extremely as he did. He said the Poles were the most difficult
> people in the world, and then corrected himself and said "next to the Japs."[61]

THE PRICE OF WESTERN IGNORANCE

Neither Britain nor the United States knew what was happening behind the
scenes, nor could they place Litvinov's outburst in the larger context. Intelligence sources were minimal and woefully insufficient. Britain had decrypted
Comintern communications in the 1930s but attention to Russia diminished
substantially after June 1941. In 1942, however, discovery of a widespread illegal
Soviet network by the Radio Security Service and Scotland Yard led MI6 to
renew efforts against NKVD, Razvedupr, and Comintern communications.[62]
In the United States a two-member section opened on 1 February 1943 and
expanded in August on the back of knowledge about Soviet codes from intercepted Japanese communications. Thereafter the army and navy worked together on the problem. The surreptitious training of Russian linguists also began
in 1944.[63] Progress was extremely slow, however, because Moscow used onetime
pads. Not until the end of the war did Washington realize that some had been
duplicated. Moreover, British efforts were substantially offset after Moscow was
alerted to what was going on by agents within MI5. On 17 March 1943 head of
the NKVD fifth department—foreign intelligence—Pavel Fitin notified Dimitrov of MI5's systematic monthly surveys of international communist activities.
He warned Dimitrov on 18 May 1944 that "according to information received
by us from completely reliable sources, English counterintelligence has set up

microphones in the premises belonging to the Communist Party of England. As a result of this measure counterintelligence receives transcripts of conversations that are conducted in these premises by the leading officials of the CC of the CP of England."[64]

The occasional clue as to what Moscow was intending therefore usually left London and Washington alike innocently uncomprehending. On 30 October 1943, "Stalin said that he was sure [US Secretary of State] Mr. [Cordell] Hull and [British Foreign Secretary] Mr. [Anthony] Eden had arrived with the idea that the Soviets were going to make a separate peace with Germany and he hoped that they had found out this was not going to be done."[65] This had been his obsession from the outset. Eden protested but failed to see what this demonstrated about Stalin's state of mind. It was as gloomy as in November 1942. Few understood. Charles (Chip) Bohlen came close, later emerging as a leading Sovietologist in the Foreign Service.[66] At Harriman's right hand on the eve of Tehran, he warned that Litvinov's remarks indicated trouble and therefore wanted the forthcoming summit to settle the future of Finland, Poland, the issue of federations in East-Central Europe, and the 1941 borders of the USSR.[67] Had this proved possible, the Cold War would certainly not have emerged as and when it did. Bohlen, however, was both junior and isolated. He could scarcely influence let alone determine the course of policy.

Allied leaders finally met in Tehran from 28 November to 1 December. Stalin arrived serviced by Molotov's team under the head of the Sovnarkom secretariat, Ivan Lapshov, and for the Narkomindel, Boris Podtserob and Vladimir ("Pinky") Pavlov. His train from Moscow put into Baku on the evening of 26 November, and the group flew into Tehran on the following morning in a four-engine SI-47.[68] He came knowing in detail the position papers of Churchill and Roosevelt.[69] At Tehran the White House preoccupation with the next election made havoc of attempts to limit Soviet expectations. Moreover Roosevelt held to the view "that this Russian dictatorship is less dangerous to the safety of other nations than is the German form of dictatorship. The only weapon which the Russian dictatorship uses outside of its borders is communist propaganda."[70] He was therefore inclined to wishful thinking where Stalin was concerned. Dining on 28 November 1943, Roosevelt blurted out "that he had only envisaged the sending of American planes and ships to Europe, and that England and the Soviet Union would have to handle the land armies in the event of any future threat to the peace. He went on to say that if the Japanese had not attacked the United States he doubted very much if it would have been possible to send any American forces to Europe."[71] Given Stalin's belief that "unless prevented, Germany would completely recover within 15 to 20 years,"[72] and given also his morose suspicion of the allies, certain conclusions were bound to be drawn from Roosevelt's careless musings. London and Moscow were to arrange the affairs of postwar Europe.

This pro-Soviet stance could not have surprised Stalin. He knew from Razvedupr agent "Sonya" (Ursula Kuczynski) in London that Roosevelt and Churchill agreed at Quebec on joint efforts for an atomic bomb. But he also knew from "Molière" in New York that at the same meeting Roosevelt had insisted on the forthcoming summit with Stalin "without delay." But that "Churchill suggested waiting until the situation on the Eastern front stabilized."[73] Moreover, "Molière" added, "Roosevelt's stance in favour of the establishment of good relations with the USSR has strengthened above all after breaking the German offensive at Kursk and the Red Army's shift to the counteroffensive. Roosevelt has convinced Hull that a realistic agreement with the USSR must be concluded because the previous policy of temporizing was bankrupt due to Red Army victories. The Americans are very worried about the position of the English after the war and wish to use the USSR as a barrier to the reinforcement of their influence in Europe, especially in the Balkans."[74]

Stalin thus aired anti-British sentiments in full expectation of US approval. He insisted to Churchill that "just because Russians are simple people, it was a mistake to believe that they were blind and could not see what was before their eyes."[75] When he argued that "really effective measures" had to be adopted to control postwar Germany and proposed liquidating 50,000 to 100,000 of the officer corps, Churchill spoke out against, prompting a malicious jibe about "Mr. Churchill's secret liking for the Germans." Harriman noted that Stalin "did not let up on the Prime Minister through the entire evening." Even when Churchill attempted to appease by suggesting that the USSR needed warm-water ports and that Britain would be happy to see its fleet on the world's oceans, Stalin—with the Dardanelles in mind—"said that Lord Curzon [Foreign Secretary in 1923 at the time of the Lausanne Treaty, which cut Russia out] had had other ideas."[76]

Stalin argued that in victory the allies "must retain possession of the important strategic points in the world so that if Germany moved a muscle she could be rapidly stopped."[77] When directly challenged as to what territorial claims he might have in mind, Stalin was coy. But what he said was ominous in retrospect: "There is no need to speak at the present time about any Soviet desires, but when the time comes, we will speak."[78] Similarly when Roosevelt's foreign policy aide Harry Hopkins raised the issue of strategic bases, Molotov held back.

The problem was that Roosevelt complicated his proposal on bases by referring to management by a new "sovereign" body—the projected United Nations.

Uneasy at any delegated sovereignty, Molotov indicated that those states "responsible for securing the peace will have to see to it that the main strategic bases will be in their control."[79] At dinner Stalin's dislike of the British resurfaced, chiding Field-Marshal Alan Brooke not inaccurately and repeatedly in a "pointed and rough" manner for being still "grim and distrustful of the Russians."[80] The British should have considered what access Stalin had to top-level memoranda within Whitehall that showed this to be on target, but entirely unprepared for the task of dealing with Stalin, they gave it not a moment's thought.

Roosevelt told Stalin that territorial concessions were not possible because of the émigré electorate within the United States. He acknowledged that "he fully realized the three Baltic Republics [whose future independence had blocked the signature of a treaty of alliance with Moscow in 1942] had in history and again more recently been a part of Russia and added jokingly that when the Soviet armies re-occupied these areas, he did not intend to go to war with the Soviet Union on this point." He just wanted some ex post facto legitimation of the takeover through a referendum and he "personally was confident that the people would vote to join the Soviet Union." Roosevelt then suggested that he agreed with Stalin on moving Poland westwards even to the Oder. But he could not participate in decisions on this either at Tehran or even, after re-election, the following winter.[81]

Thus Roosevelt simultaneously counted himself out of the fate of Europe, dropped heavy hints that Stalin could have his way, and left London alone with Moscow, deprived of any understanding as to how the president's world security organization would be realized. Roosevelt's priorities were apparent from his casual disregard for his ambassador to Moscow, Harriman, who had arrived with personal access but soon found himself at the mercies of a none-too-benign State Department. It left him isolated and despairing. Bohlen was the only specialist he had, and Bohlen was recalled to Washington. Young diplomats were in great demand. Those with the Russian language were a tiny minority. Harriman had only Llewellyn ("Tommy") Thompson, a young and inexperienced third secretary. He therefore called for the most experienced Russianist in the service, the tall, emotionally sensitive yet intellectually hard-headed George Kennan, of whom he had good report; but in utter ignorance and woefully short of talent, State assigned Kennan to Winant on the advisory commission in London.[82] These arrangements left Harriman virtually paralyzed, with no command of Russian and reliant entirely on interpreters. This was surely no way to conduct relations with what was shortly to become the second most important Power in the international system. It accounted for many difficulties that arose later.

THE POLISH QUESTION

Molotov once told Dimitrov: "As long as we are being pressed by the Germans, we should avoid any major, serious actions abroad," but that "when things start looking up for us, that is the time to deploy everything we have."[83] That time had now arrived. Signs all was not well in relations with the allies were already emerging by the end of January 1944. *Pravda* published rumours of a British peace offer to Germany. The reaction was one of "bewilderment and serious concern." Harriman read it as a retreat from the spirit of cooperation evidenced at Tehran.[84] Yet he never seriously entertained the thought that this symbolic retreat toward isolationism could have originated with Stalin, returning to an accustomed level of mistrust after excessive exposure to the allies at Tehran. The issue was Poland.

Moscow's discontent arose from the émigré refusal to reach agreement on the future. The liquidation of an entire section of the elite at Katyn in 1940 was Stalin's answer to Piłsudski's men,[85] who had consistently favored Germany over Russia from 1926 to 1939 with disastrous consequences for all (in the East, at least) concerned. Polish intransigence reflected two substantial concerns: first, ever since 1917 Moscow had sought to overthrow the Polish regime and replace it with communists; second, the division of Poland between Nazi Germany and the USSR had removed whatever small potential for cooperation that remained. Indeed, the Polish prime minister-in-exile told Harriman (and members of the press in London) "that the only thing that will settle Polish relations with the Soviet Union will be a war between the Soviet Union and the United States and Great Britain, with the latter countries on Poland's side."[86]

This belligerence effectively blocked prospects for resolving matters amicably. Moreover, it poisoned relations between Moscow and the allies; worse than that, as London and Washington continued at an arithmetic rate to try to salvage something for an ever more demanding émigré government, Stalin's morbid suspicions grew geometrically. Apart from Stalin's firm indication that postwar Russia must have a "friendly" Poland, Moscow withdrew under a cloak of ambiguity as to the details of its preferred solution. Harriman complained: "Soviet officials have not been accustomed to talking things out frankly with us as we do with the British. They often talk by indirection and it is hard to know at times what is in their minds." But for some reason, no doubt due entirely to

native optimism and his ignorance of Stalin's Russia, the ambassador drew unwarranted conclusions worthy of an amateur: "I do not believe that the Soviet
leaders wish to communize Poland or set up a puppet state. They are ready to
let the Poles work out their own problems provided this results in a Poland that
is basically friendly to the Soviet Union and is not opposed to the major foreign
policies of the Soviet Union."[87]

Such optimism proved ill placed after the uprising launched on 31 July in
Warsaw by the London Poles in anticipation of the Red Army's arrival. They
hoped to have the city substantially in their own hands and failed. Moreover,
this proved a disaster when the Red Army suffered defeat at Radzymin on
4 August and, with the uprising well under way and its larger political purpose
obvious to Stalin, assistance was withheld by Moscow until it was too late.[88]

Harriman had no sooner arrived in the spring of 1944 than Litvinov warned
him of the trend in Soviet policy. But Harriman dismissed it (until reiterated by
Ivy a year later, making it obvious that he should have paid attention earlier).
His stubborn reluctance to face the worst in Moscow contrasts with Kennan,
who finally returned following six years' absence at the beginning of July 1944
briefed, as Harriman before him, by the increasingly pessimistic and powerless
Litvinovs. He was also given an envelope (which may have contained reminiscences damaging to Stalin) for Meyer—a friend of the Litvinovs, owner of the
Washington Post. He was told that Maxim slept with a pistol under his pillow,
intending to shoot himself and his wife in the event of the police arriving to
take him.[89] Whereas Harriman took so little notice of what Ivy had said that
he failed even to record it at the time, Kennan, who understood the Soviet
system, having served in Moscow through the terror, reacted very differently.
In a memorandum composed that September, he recalled that "the men in
the Kremlin have never abandoned their faith in that program of territorial
and political expansion which had once commended itself so strongly to Tsarist diplomatists, and which underlay the German-Russian nonaggression pact
of 1939." This program, he continued, "was intended not only to increase the
physical military strength of Russia. It was intended to prevent the formation
in central and eastern Europe of any power or coalition of powers capable of
challenging Russian security." The reversals suffered to these plans at the hands
of Hitler "failed to shake Russian confidence in the ultimate efficacy of this
policy of expansion. The Russian conclusion was not that the policy had been
unsound. It was rather that it had not been carried far enough."[90]

Kennan had already seen the delight with which the arrival of Soviet forces
in Poland was greeted in Moscow.[91] More important, he foresaw with unusual
clarity what would occur when they reached Germany. The allies envisaged

postwar Soviet occupation of the entire northeastern segment. "As originally conceived," Kennan wrote on 3 July 1944, "this was to have been part of a joint allied occupation, coordinated by a tripartite over-all administration of Berlin. Germany will, for all practical purposes, be partitioned between the Anglo-American and Russian forces." Nevertheless, he added, "the Russian commander will administer his zone not as an integral part of Germany, in accordance with a joint plan coordinated with Anglo-American commanders, but as an outlying province of Russia. And in the absence of agreement with other powers on the political future of Germany, I cannot see these Russian occupation forces being withdrawn at an early date."[92]

BRITAIN SEEKS AN ACCOMMODATION

Shorn of complacency as to the likely postwar balance of power in Europe, Churchill watched anxiously the extraordinary pace of Red Army progress into the Balkans in the spring of 1944. This was a region vital to the security of British shipping lanes in the eastern Mediterranean and the Suez Canal. Yet he had been unable to persuade Roosevelt that this was the best site for the second front. Having reactivated MI6 operations in the area, Churchill instructed Eden to sound out Moscow on spheres of influence. This was done on 5 May. A fortnight later Moscow proved willing if Washington did not object. The initiative leaked, however. Lincoln MacVeagh, US ambassador to the exiled Greek and Yugoslav governments in Cairo, waxed indignant and briefed Sulzberger of the *New York Times*. Censorship prevented publication.[93] But Churchill was furious. Cordell Hull's objections then further delayed matters until resolved by Roosevelt.[94] Finally, in frustration, Churchill took himself off to Moscow.

A number of minds in distant capitals had separately converged around the idea of dividing Europe into spheres of influence. In London on 10 March 1943, assistant editor of the *Times* E. H. Carr expressed the belief that Russia had forsaken Bolshevism for reasons of state, that Eastern Europe would inevitably fall to Russian arms and remain a Soviet responsibility after the war, just as the postwar security of Western Europe would remain primarily in British hands. "If Britain's frontier is on the Rhine," he wrote, "it might just as pertinently be said—though it has not in fact been said—that Russia's frontier is on the Oder, and in the same sense." The governments in Eastern Europe could not be hostile to Moscow. "The sole interest of Russia is to assure herself that her outer defences are in sure hands; and this interest will be best served if the lands between her frontiers and those of Germany are held by governments and peoples friendly to herself. That is the one condition on which Russia must and will insist." Moscow had the power, anyway. "But," Carr argued, "it will make all the difference for the future of Anglo-Russian friendship whether these lines have been freely approved and welcomed by Britain in advance, or whether they are grudgingly accepted as a fait accompli after the victory has been won."[95] This leader and similar were quoted by Litvinov in a memorandum on "The Question of Joint Responsibility for Europe in Contrast to Separate Regions of Responsibility."[96]

The assumption throughout was that spheres of influence were as tradition-ally understood, as expressed by Lord Curzon in his study of *Frontiers*. They did not mean colonization and social transformation patterned according to the dominant Power. Carr argued that only the foreign and defense policies of those states falling under the neighboring Great Power would be determined by that Power, leaving the domestic framework intact. In Washington, journalist Walter Lippmann said the same. Meanwhile Litvinov, quoting Carr, produced a report for Stalin on the postwar shape of Europe in like manner.

Stalin was cautiously opportunistic within the emerging allied sphere of in-fluence. The Anglo-American occupation of southern Italy and the existence of a regime under General Badoglio, formerly a fascist, created particular difficul-ties. Palmiro Togliatti, leader of the Communist Party (PCI), finally obtained permission to return to Italy six months after the Americans landed in Salerno. He outlined his program to Dimitrov just as though Comintern still existed. In turn Dimitrov obtained a meeting with Stalin for the night of 3–4 March 1944. Here Stalin reduced expectations for a major advance by the left and insisted the hard line of opposition to Badoglio be dropped in favor of unity among antifascist parties. Indeed the PCI could even join the Badoglio regime if the opportunity arose.[97] The French were similarly instructed. Elsewhere it made sense to limit spheres of influence by express agreement.

Litvinov assumed that Britain would resume its prewar role as the leading Western Power. He discounted the United States, which he expected to return to isolation as it had after World War I.[98] This position was strongly contested by Deputy Commissar Solomon Lozovskii, quondam General Secretary of Profintern, a fundamentalist. Lozovskii assailed "all our diplomats who think that if in notes and memoranda we do not mention classes, then one can also get by without a Marxist analysis in one's internal reports to the Narkomindel. I hold to the modest opinion," he sermonized, "that Marxist-Leninism is also obligatory even for diplomats, and that without the Marxist-Leninist approach to events in each country we are likely to make political mistakes."[99] A skeptic about Litvinov's whole approach, he also pointed out, "We communists should know that anything which holds together the USSR, England, America, plus

China after the war is an extremely difficult business."[100] In brief, he did not see that any kind of international relations could transcend the class barrier.

Litvinov, of course, believed otherwise. Written between 4 August and 15 November 1944, his report arising from discussion at the committee, "On the Prospects and Possible Basis for Soviet-British Co-operation," argued that an agreement "can be brought about only on the basis of an amicable delimitation of spheres of security in Europe on the principle of the closest neighbourly relations. The Soviet Union can consider as its maximum sphere of interests Finland, Sweden, Poland, Hungary, Czechoslovakia, Romania, the Slavic countries of the Balkan peninsula, and Turkey as well. Holland, Belgium, France, Spain, Portugal and Greece can undoubtedly be included in the English sphere."[101]

Stalin, however, never discussed such matters with Litvinov who, denied the diplomatic traffic, was obliged "to confine himself to matters of general forecasting."[102] Even while working on the report, he asked to see US journalist Edgar Snow in private to warn Washington. On 6 October Litvinov, who for Snow "personified the hope that a means might yet be found, after the war, to reconcile the 'absolute' truth, the infallible Stalinist truth, in some workable compromise with the West," proceeded to shatter this illusion.[103] "What he really saw ahead was heavy trouble for us," Snow recalled. "Events were clearly placing Russia in the position of the strongest power in Europe," Litvinov said. The British had always sought to counterbalance any preponderance of power on the Continent and would use to Americans to do so. The German problem divided both sides. "We will not be able to agree on a common program for Germany." And in respect to Litvinov's bugbear Poland, "The British and the Americans don't even want to throw out the old crowd there!" By the time they sat down as allies to discuss to fate of Europe, it would be too late. And as to Litvinov and the few like him who remained, "We're on the shelf. . . . This commissariat is run by only three men and none of them knows or understands America and Britain." These people saw the nonaggression pact with Germany (1939) as the right move; they saw no fundamental differences between fascist and democratic states. Matters could have been different, Litvinov professed: "If we had made clear the limits of our needs, to each other, good diplomacy might have been able to avoid the conflict. Now it is too late. Suspicions are too rife." Roosevelt had to be told of all this, but no one else.[104] The battle between fundamentalists and revisionists that had been played out in the 1930s over whether collective security against Nazi Germany was feasible was thus played out again over the fate of the postwar settlement, but on this occasion with Litvinov in opposition.

Arriving in Moscow on 9 October to propose a division according to spheres of interest, Churchill knew none of this. What he had in mind was what Litvinov had hoped for, but on a limited scale because this was all that Washington could swallow.[105] Churchill pressed for predominance over not only postwar Greece but the Mediterranean as a whole. Moreover he asked that Moscow "soft-pedal the Communists in Italy and not to stir them up." To which request Stalin was characteristically evasive. Nevertheless he described Togliatti as "a wise man, not an extremist," who "would not start an adventure in Italy."[106] Here Churchill stepped in where Roosevelt feared to tread, and it was evidently this that reinforced Stalin in his initial view that Washington did not have the will to world power which London, long accustomed to the role, forcefully exhibited under the incumbent prime minister. What neither Carr nor Lippmann nor Litvinov had suspected, but Kennan had immediately assumed, was that spheres of influence would be interpreted as colonization: Bolshevization rather than merely the formation of old-fashioned protectorates. Just as the isolationist Stalin surprised the internationalist Trotsky in 1939–40 with the sovietization of part of Poland and the Baltic states, so too did he confound his allies by seeking to extend that model throughout Russia's sphere of influence and, where practicable, beyond.

Kennan, alarmed at Litvinov's warnings, immediately began sending worrying dispatches when Harriman left town. State appeared uninterested. Yet, unknown to Kennan in brooding isolation, Roosevelt was increasingly resigned to a showdown with Moscow, though he felt that it would have to be avoided until Japan was defeated. On the evening of 4 November Hopkins spoke to British diplomat Michael Wright: Roosevelt "believes there is going to be another war, and he has made up his mind that in that war there will be a strong Britain on the side of the United States. He wants you strong and will help you to be so."[107] That this was not merely diplomatic flattery soon became apparent (see below). Unaware of the president's foreboding, on the eve of the Yalta conference Kennan characterized the Soviet Union bluntly as a "jealous Eurasian land power, which must always seek to extend itself to the West and will never find a place, short of the Atlantic Ocean, where it can from its own standpoint safely stop."[108]

Averse to focusing on personalities or ideology, Kennan insisted that the Russian problem was "the product of tradition and environment and should be beyond the scope of moral judgement." Here he unknowingly echoed others in despairing the lack of realism in American thinking about foreign affairs: "If we insist at this moment in our history in wandering about with our heads in the clouds of Wilsonian idealism and universalistic conceptions of world collaboration, if we continue to blind ourselves to the fact that momentary peaceful intentions of the mass of inhabitants of Asia and eastern Europe are only the products of their misery and weakness and never the products of their strength, if we insist on staking the whole future of Europe on the assumption of a community of aims with Russia for which there is no real evidence except in our own wishful thinking, then we run the risk of losing even that bare minimum of security which would be assured to us by the maintenance of humane, stable and co-operative forms of human society on the immediate European shores of the Atlantic." His thinking at this stage was closer to that of Churchill (shorn of Churchillian lapses into credulity). "Although it was evident that the realities of the after-war were being shaped while the war was in progress we have consistently refused to make clear what our interests and our wishes were, in eastern and central Europe. We have refused to name any limit to Russian expansion and Russian responsibilities, thereby confusing the Russians and causing them constantly to wonder whether they are asking too little or whether it was some kind of trap. We have refused to face political issues and have forced others to face them without us."[109]

The argument made was that Europe should be divided into spheres of influence. From his vantage point, Kennan pleaded that if Washington was not ready to go the whole hog and oppose with all the physical resources at American disposal the domination of Eastern Europe by a single Power "we should write it off, frankly acknowledge the division of Europe into spheres of influence, and have nothing to do with the Declaration on Liberated Europe." Similarly, in London on the eve of Yalta, Churchill shared Kennan's bleak pessimism. He asked Eden: "Why are we making a fuss about Russian deportations in Roumania of Saxons and others? It is understood that the Russians were to work their will in this sphere. Anyhow we cannot prevent them."[110] It was worse than that. As he told Colville: "Make no mistake, all the Balkans, except Greece, are going to be bolshevised; and there is nothing I can do to prevent it. There is nothing I can do for poor Poland either."[111]

Stalin's approach to the implementation of the precentages agreement was that of inertia. He would not go out of his way to help Greek communists against Britain. But neither would he rein them in. Greece may have been allocated to Britain under the agreement sketched out by Churchill to Stalin in October, yet the communists (KKE), heading a broad left coalition (EAM) and an army serving it (ELAS), knew nothing of it. They refused to disarm once the Germans were expelled. But Moscow was not about to countenance direct aid. "Taking into account the complex international position of Greece," Dimitrov informed Molotov, "direct aid on the part of the Soviet Union to the

Greek national liberation movement in the form of EAM and ELAS is scarcely possible." All that could be suggested was "moral support" in press coverage.[112] Despite this setback, on 1 December 1944 EAM ministers resigned from the Papandreou government which, in turn, issued a decree declaring their army, ELAS, dissolved. Churchill's anxiety lest ELAS seize power prompted him to reinforce troops in Athens and instruct the officer commanding, General Scobie, to restore order "without bloodshed if possible, but also with bloodshed if necessary."[113]

The fighting that escalated thereafter was never explicitly sanctioned by Moscow though supported in the press. In June 1945 its informal mouthpiece *New Times* (formerly *The War and the Working-Class*) referred to Greece not being "allowed to breathe freely and enjoy the fruits of victory" and went on to attack the British explicitly for sustaining terror in power.[114] When Polychronidis of the KKE asked for assistance, however, he was promptly informed "that in the current situation our Greek friends will not be able to count on active intervention and assistance from here." They were also told that Bulgaria would not do so either.[115] Stalin informed the Yugoslavs that the Greeks "did not ask us about this."[116] "I advised not starting this fighting in Greece. The ELAS people should not have resigned from the Papandreou government. They've taken on more than they can handle," Stalin noted on 10 January 1945. "They were evidently counting on the Red Army's coming down to the Aegean. We cannot do that. We cannot send our troops in to Greece, either. The Greeks have acted foolishly," he concluded.[117] Answering a further enquiry to Moscow, the Greeks were "recommended" to follow a dual strategy of mobilizing the people politically while also organizing their own self-defense. Preparations for "an armed uprising" were discouraged.[118]

Few in Washington were yet listening to voices of concern. Soviet entry into the Pacific war was critical to an early end to the struggle in the Pacific that was costing too many American lives, and to secure Soviet entry Washington not only bamboozled China into major territorial and extraterritorial concessions but also took a softer line on European issues. It was, after all, Japan that brought the United States into the war, however much Roosevelt accorded Europe the first priority. Indeed the second front had been delayed in part because landing craft became a priority for the Pacific theater. Moreover, although Washington undoubtedly had the power, one should not assume that it had a clear and coherent policy. Roosevelt was a distant dreamer as well as a ruthless political tactician.

The allies did not discuss the fate of Japan again until mid-October 1944. Major General John Deane, secretary of the US Joint Chiefs of Staff, bluntly put several questions to Stalin. When would he enter the war against Japan? How long would the operations take to prepare? And what could he do to provide support for US forces in the Pacific? To Deane's surprise, Stalin responded positively: it would take three months to prepare; supplies would have to be stockpiled to enable forces to fight for two or three months, as it would be impossible for the trans-Siberian to supply sixty divisions on a day-to-day basis (it was currently supplying thirty divisions in the Far East); Russia would allow the United States to use air bases in the maritime province and on Kamchatka. Stalin insisted that the terms for entry had to be clarified: "The Russians . . . had certain claims against Japan."[119] They "would have to know what they were fighting for."[120] On 14 December Stalin fetched a map from the room next door, drew a circle around the Liaodong peninsula, including Port Arthur and Dairen. Working down Malik's checklist, Stalin told ambassador Harriman that he wanted to lease these areas and to control the Chinese eastern and south Manchurian railways. Arguing, inter alia, that "all outlets to the Pacific Ocean are now held or blocked by the enemy," he also made the case for additional acquisitions further east.[121] "The Soviet Union," Stalin added, "would like to receive South Sakhalin, i.e., restitution of what was handed over to Japan in the Portsmouth Treaty, and also to receive the Kurile Islands."[122] The full account was presented at Yalta.

Up to the US presidential elections in November 1944, it was entirely plausible for Stalin—like Litvinov—to see Britain as the effective future leader of the Western Europe. And those London backed, such as General Charles de Gaulle, who led the main resistance against the Nazis in France, were to be sustained in power against the communists. On 19 November Stalin broke the bad news to PCF General Secretary Maurice Thorez: "The situation is now new, different. It has afforded de Gaulle the opportunity. Now the Communist Party is not strong enough to knock out the government."[123]

That winter a crucial sea change took place in Stalin's thinking. From sharing a core Litvinovian assumption that Washington would remain aloof with respect to Europe and that out of concern for rising American power Britain, leading Western Europe, would necessarily come to terms with Moscow, Stalin became convinced that the United States would displace British preeminence in Western Europe and unseat the USSR as a leading Power. When Edvard Kadelj visited Moscow on behalf of Yugoslav communist leader Tito in November 1944, barely a month after the percentages agreement between Stalin and Churchill, he presented notes on the international situation to Lozovskii. In these notes Kardelj assumed US predominance in the West after the war. "I don't know what the old man [Stalin] will say to it all," Lozovskii said. "You see, he still thinks that England is the centre of world imperialism, the main enemy of the proletariat, and that America plays a secondary role."[124] Between then and the Yalta conference, however, Stalin changed his mind. His unrelenting mistrust of American intentions then mounted with frightening rapidity even under Roosevelt. Signs of such moods had been intermittently apparent vis-à-vis Britain in 1938 and in 1942, but not yet toward the United States and only toward Britain at moments of acute Soviet vulnerability. Yet victory was now in sight. Soviet forces were entering the heart of Europe. Washington was counting on help against Japan. How could such fears be justified? Even Stalin's right-hand man Molotov clung to the belief that some kind of modus vivendi could be worked out with the West; so much so as to arouse Stalin's deepest distrust. Of course, unlike Britain the United States had never signed an alliance with Russia. And there were those in Washington deeply unhappy at the prospect of postwar aid to Moscow.

IDEOLOGY TRIUMPHANT

Our main enemy is America. But the basic thrust must not be delivered against America itself.

—Stalin

The bleak contrast between glowing public affirmations of allied solidarity and the growing mistrust of Washington and London toward Moscow was deeply disturbing. The comforting assumption that, in the end, Stalin would be prepared to settle the peace of Europe along lines dictated by traditional reasons of state inevitably succumbed to ideological priorities resurgent in Moscow: nourished by Stalin's sullen suspicions of American aims and ambitions, heightened by the euphoria of victory, and augmented by the unprecedented might of the Red Army—eleven million strong—to dictate events on the ground.

On the eve of war Stalin had annihilated or imprisoned most serving Soviet diplomats as well as half his officer corps, with equally damaging results. And whereas the destruction of so many men in command can be quantified to the extent of losses in battle, the sudden disappearance of diplomats who had lived and worked abroad in exile and then as diplomats for the regime was bound to cost Russia dear in a manner impossible to enumerate yet no less harmful. In their place, Molotov's foreign policy assistant Vladimir Erofeev recalls, "Stalin and Molotov created the Ministry of Foreign Affairs [Minindel] along their own lines, in their own likeness, inculcating it with imperial ambitions, a strongly ideological orientation and a tough spirit of battle."[1]

"Despite close cooperation with the allies in the years of war," Erofeev writes, "Stalin and Molotov did not for one moment drop their guard. All actions, proposals and statements from the leadership of Great Britain and the United States were closely analyzed; everything was searched top to bottom for dirty tricks and secret *arrières pensées*. They demanded from the entire state and party apparatus a class approach to international phenomena and, above all, to the activities of the allies."[2] Molotov routinely lectured leading diplomats that the Minindel was not only "a political ministry" but also a "Party" institution.[3] Moreover, being on guard was not just an instruction, it was a cast of mind. Stalin was obsessed with what was hidden from him. At Yalta he made a pointed remark to Roosevelt: "I as a naïve person think that the best for me is not to deceive my ally, even if he is stupid. It is possible that our alliance is strong precisely because we do not deceive one another, or because it is not so easy to deceive one another."[4]

Moreover, mistrust only encouraged the Kremlin into expanding control over others, and that meant the Marxist-Leninist incentive to take over neighboring states was to be driven further than reasons of state would have implied. It also meant taking the offensive. Military power would now be used to further political objectives that went beyond merely defense of the motherland. Stalin enunciated the new spirit at a meeting with the General Staff and the editors of two military journals, *Voennaya Mysl'* and *Voennyi Vestnik*, on 5 March 1945. What kind of military ideology did the country need?

> We began the war essentially without a military ideology. Our slogan was: we don't want the land of others, but we will not give up one inch of our own land. This is in essence a defensive ideology. This is a civilian form of ideology. The army must not only defend but it has also to attack, to defend the interests of the state by all means. We established such an ideology at a time of war. Now we have our own military ideology. . . . We need an ideology of preparedness not only for defense but also for attack. Our army must be in a position to defend any of our state's interests by all means at its disposal.

Stalin repeated the point several times.[5] It was "good that the Russian tsars took so much land by force," Molotov believed, and for a simple reason: "now it is easier to fight capitalism." Former conquests were thus celebrated as expansion was on the agenda. Molotov saw his task "to expand the frontiers of our motherland." And it later seemed to him that "Stalin and myself did not do such a bad job."[6] At a price, of course; paid in decades of costly confrontation with the United States that ultimately ended in humiliating collapse of the USSR from within.

Another unambiguous indicator that Moscow had not been transformed from its prewar incarnation as a citadel of revolution—despite Comintern's abolition—appeared with an attack on the American communist leader Earl Browder in April 1945. It took the form of an article, "Au sujet de l'Association

Politique Communiste des États-Unis," signed by deputy head of the PCF Jacques Duclos in *Cahiers du Communisme*. Browder was reprimanded for abolishing the US Communist Party at its twelfth congress in May 1944 and for turning it into a political association; for having "declared, in effect, that at Teheran capitalism and socialism had begun to find the means of peaceful coexistence and collaboration in the framework of one and the same world"; and for asserting "that the Teheran accords regarding common policy similarly presupposed common efforts with a view to reducing to a minimum or completely suppressing methods of struggle and opposition of force to force in the solution of internal problems of each country." "By transforming the Teheran declaration of the Allied governments, which is a document of a diplomatic character, into a political platform of class peace in the United States in the postwar period, the American Communists are deforming in a radical way the meaning of the Teheran declaration and are sowing dangerous opportunist illusions." This had resulted in the dissolution of the American Communist Party and had led in France to a similar line of argument.[7]

The document originated in Moscow and had followed attempts by Dimitrov nearly a year earlier to dissuade Browder from adopting "new theoretical, political, and tactical positions," including "denial of the theory and practice of class struggle."[8] It went into page proof on 19 January 1945 and was then translated into French before publication.[9] The attack reasserted the class basis of Soviet foreign policy and the line demarcating peaceful coexistence between states and between societies: whereas the former was acceptable to Moscow, if not desirable, the latter was utterly unacceptable, as it would amount to a denial of Marxism-Leninism in the international sphere. It affirmed an abyss in East-West relations that even Stalin would not cross and it predated the summit between allied leaders at Yalta from 4 to 11 February. Churchill was "all set for the worst."[10]

Thus Moscow was already committed to continuing the prewar struggle over the ultimate fate of the states system and to that end further territorial expansion where practicable; albeit Molotov more cautiously so than Stalin.[11] The West was ill prepared, however, on either front. The energy that had characterized the victors at Paris in 1919 was nowhere evident. At the Livadia Palace under an azure sky overlooking a clear blue sea Roosevelt seemed exhausted and unfocused. Others appeared to be there for the purpose of putting words into his mouth. Churchill's interpreter, Major Arthur Birse, noted: "The former self-confidence and firmness of tone, so evident at Tehran, seemed to have gone. His voice was that of a man weary in spirit."[12] When, for instance, Roosevelt opened a rambling intervention about the United Nations as a potential solution to the poverty of other less fortunate countries such as Iran and spoke of "the need to liquidate favoritism between countries," Maisky for one "listened and couldn't believe his ears." Stalin, meanwhile, doodled distractedly in his notebook.[13]

Britain was poorly equipped to cope with resurgent Russia, even at the most basic level of professional competence. When Tom Brimelow returned to the Foreign Office from Moscow he was astonished to find no one in the appropriate department proficient in Russian: Brimelow was alone. And Geoffrey Wilson who ran the department without any Russian to his name was much influenced by Carr at the *Times* in the reassuring but unwise assumption that Stalin was governed by reasons of state not Bolshevik conviction.[14] Wilson, a forgiving quaker and socialist, habitually "gave the Russians the benefit of the doubt whenever there was any doubt."[15]

The timing of the Yalta conference itself proved a serious misjudgment. Whereas Tehran had been preceded by foreign ministerial negotiation, Yalta opened after no horse trading and lasted an extraordinarily brief span which, British ambassador to Moscow Sir Archibald Clerk Kerr noted, inevitably meant "a tendency to scramble over and to skimp the all important business of drafting, with the result that ambiguous texts get us into trouble afterwards."[16] Moreover, Moscow had purloined a copy of London's position paper through one of its leading agents, the notoriously indiscreet Guy Burgess. Burgess obtained a job in the press department of the Foreign Office after Donald Maclean, another member of the group, took up the post of first secretary at the British embassy in Washington in October 1944.[17] There, as head of chancery he was responsible for the coderoom.[18] Moscow thus received a windfall with his arrival at a key moment.

What kept Stalin cooperating was his pessimistic judgment that "the war will not end before summer." He told allied military chiefs: "It is proper and also sound selfish policy that we should help each other in time of difficulty. It would be foolish for me to stand aside and let Germany annihilate you; they would only turn back on me when you were disposed of. Similarly it is to your interest to do everything possible to keep the Germans from annihilating me."[19] Such cool logic was never sufficient, however, to remove lingering suspicions of imminent betrayal. And as victory loomed within reach all pretense was dropped. Stalin came to Yalta convinced that sooner or later another war would erupt: "We are now with one faction [of capitalists] against another [Britain and the United States versus Germany and Japan]; and in the future we will also be against this faction of capitalists [Britain and the United States]."[20] Given this bleak outlook, nothing would be conceded except under duress. A further deterioration in relations was to be expected as far as Stalin was concerned.

On 6 February, Stalin was at his most obdurate to the visible consternation of Roosevelt as much as Churchill.[21] Furthermore, and this mattered because it altered any assessment of Churchill's percentages deal the previous October, Stalin had now changed his mind as to which English-speaking Power would be the main adversary. Instead of Britain's faltering extra-European empire, he now faced the dismal prospect of a challenge to Soviet predominance in Europe from a burgeoning commercial empire backed by formidable military might on land, at sea, and in the air; moreover committed to framing the European peace in its own image—that of the United States. "Whoever dominates Europe will dominate the world," Stalin had said only five years earlier. And what was particularly pertinent to the United States, now indisputably the world's greatest naval Power, was his view that Europe could not be dominated "without command of the seas."[22]

THE MAIN ADVERSARY

For Moscow, working out who in the West would predominate after hostilities had not been as easy as it would appear with hindsight. For Washington it was choice rather than necessity, as it had been after World War I—or so it seemed to many. At Tehran Roosevelt had horrified Churchill with the suggestion that Britain and Russia alone would settle the fate of postwar Europe. Whether Washington would now override London and bid against Moscow for predominance in Europe thus for a time remained an open question. The attitude taken on the crucial issue of Poland was a litmus test. An American challenge would make all the difference. In January 1944 it was reported to Moscow that Roosevelt's rival for re-election, Republican Thomas Dewey, governor of New York, was drawing around him Polish figures in the United States to guarantee the ethnic vote at the elections forthcoming.[23]

Though wary of Moscow, London proved anxious to compromise where necessary with Moscow, as Churchill showed through his percentages deal. This, however, was understood as a necessary response to fear of American power. The empire was in decline. The United States was at the cusp of world supremacy. Washington had hitherto studiously left open every option regarding the peace in Central and Eastern Europe. Whether from electoral considerations or from naïveté, the apparent advantage in sustaining a free hand with regard to Europe could be exploited in a manner at odds with Soviet ambitions. Stalin was therefore most anxious to fix the realities on the ground before

Washington changed its mind and decided to have a say in what those realities should be.

Stalin's reassessment of the main adversary did not turn upon personalities. He preferred the coolly urbane Roosevelt to the more combustible Churchill, who had committed himself only for the time being against Germany as the greatest threat to the British Empire, a position hitherto occupied by the USSR. But within the Marxist-Leninist vision "subjective" factors such as character were ultimately less important than "objective" factors dictated by the nature of the socioeconomic system: in this case capitalism in its imperialist and final phase. "It would be incorrect to think that the second world war arose by chance or as a result of the mistakes of this or that statesman, although mistakes were made," Stalin insisted. "In actual fact war occurred as the inevitable result of the development of world economic and political forces on the basis of contemporary monopoly capitalism."[24] Even Roosevelt, who had since 1933 tirelessly accumulated an unprecedented extension of power, was by no means a free agent. His behavior was not implausibly assumed to reflect, albeit indirectly, larger elements at work, even if mitigated by the cosmopolitan, patrician emollience of his character, as against the awkward, provincial angularity of his untried successor, then Vice President, Harry Truman. It was crucially a question of the balance of forces within the United States.

Having bet on rapid industrialization of the economy from 1929, and having done so largely on the back of American technology (*amerikanomania*), Stalin did not underestimate the economic weight of the capitalist colossus that had emerged across the Atlantic. Moreover, his own economy had been severely damaged by war. Losses were estimated by Gosplan at no less than 679 million rubles: double the amount of investment made in all prewar five-year plans. The costs of war and associated losses to national income stood at 1,890 million rubles. Loss of population alone—some twenty-five million—was estimated to cost the country 1,664 million rubles. Overall, Russia had been deprived of some 4,734 million rubles: $893 million.[25]

It was only a matter of time before consciousness of power caught up with the unprecedented accumulation of American strength in wartime. That awareness was sharpened in Moscow by the extent of aid from Washington. "Stalin more than once said that without Lend-Lease we could not have won the war," Khrushchev recalled.[26] The experience of 1929–32 had, however, also shown that the United States lay along a financial fault line that could without warning jolt the country back into self-absorbed political isolation: a repeat of the Great Crash of 1929 was a recurring nightmare and not just on Wall Street. Evidence was not hard to find that the US market would have to continue to expand overseas if full employment were to be sustained into the peace. Sooner or later the country's elite would realize how precarious was the new prosperity, and this would inevitably determine foreign policy.

Stalin was well aware of the link between US needs for overseas markets and Soviet purchasing power postwar. Moscow managed a number of agents within the Treasury and related departments, including Harry Dexter White, Secretary Morgenthau's right-hand man.[27] When Eric Johnston, president of the US Chamber of Commerce, visited to discuss trade credits on 26 June 1944, Stalin told him "that the task confronting the American Government was to avoid unemployment and to assist returning soldiers in finding work, thus preventing depression."[28] This fast became an idée fixe in Moscow, so much so that three years later the US ambassador rightly commented that "the Russians count a great deal on an American economic crisis."[29] It played a significant role in resistance to compromise with Washington in the years to come.

There, lobbying from the private sector had already begun to make itself felt. In late October 1944 at the House of Representatives Subcommittee on Foreign Trade, the executive vice president of Stein, Hall and Co. and the vice president of the National Council of American Importers testified to "general agreement on the need of expanding world trade in the post-war era in order to assure our own American system of doing business with the full employment of our population and a decent standard of living for all the people."[30] Similarly the president of US Steel demanded "free access to world trade."[31] George Wolf argued that postwar tariffs from Europe should be resisted. "I don't believe," he said, "there are any trade spheres of influence—I don't think that any country has the right to set up a sign and say 'This is our backyard, and the rest of you keep out.'"[32] John Otterson of the American Maritime Council pointed out that the US merchant fleet would at the end of the war amount to one-half the world's tonnage and double that of Britain. He insisted: "From the standpoint of our own economy we shall be confronted with the simple fact that we can produce more than we can consume under a peacetime economy. We are in danger of having unemployment as a permanent part of our national economy."[33] This was a very real fear. Vice President Chenea of Pan-Am Airways similarly pointed out by letter to Secretary of War Henry Stimson that fifty million jobs were required to sustain full employment postwar. And to meet that target, ten million had to be created. His conclusion was that "several million of these new jobs will be found in the wide expansion of our foreign trade, and in the rapid development of global air transport."[34]

The needs of commerce were inevitably bound up with political necessity. The two came to complement one another in a manner that to distinguish between the interests of business and the "national interest" in the emerging conflict with Moscow appeared superfluous. Conflict arose only over the degree to which excessive federal expenditure in support of foreign policy would simultaneously overinflate the economy and deflate financial markets by squeezing private investment. This became a serious bone of contention in the second half of the decade as shares underperformed relative to treasuries because of pessimism about the inflationary outlook.

Full employment also came to be essential to presidential prospects, and full employment turned on foreign trade. Fred Vinson succeeded Henry Morgenthau at Treasury on 5 July 1945. "Our own program of maintaining high levels of production, employment and national income is dependent on our success in expanding world trade," he argued two days later. "For trade is an important factor in our economy. We need markets abroad."[35] Prewar statistics show that only certain sectors of the US economy were trade dependent. But, electorally as well as economically, these were sectors of significance: in 1937–38, they included 31 percent of raw cotton, 30 percent of leaf tobacco, 12 percent of wheat flour, 54 percent of refined copper, 15 percent of farm equipment and machinery, 14 percent of autos and trucks, 14 percent of industrial machinery, and 11 percent of refined oil. Vinson therefore took the view that "for large segments of agriculture and industry, exports mean the difference between prosperity and depression."[36] The conclusions were inescapable. The United States had little choice but to become a global Power. Otterson was certainly not alone in the belief that "the development of ourselves as a great foreign trading nation involves radical and extensive changes in our national philosophy and psychology and in our economic, financial, and political structure."[37]

THE UNITED STATES AND WORLD POWER

When Churchill reached Moscow on 9 October 1944 to negotiate an agreement on the division of the Balkans and the rest of the Danube basin, Stalin still assumed that Britain would return to hold the balance of postwar Europe as it had repeatedly since the War of the Spanish Succession (1701–14). Yet Roosevelt's foreswearing of US interest in Europe at Tehran lasted only so long as re-election on 7 November. *The War and the Working-Class* was the sole informal mouthpiece of the Kremlin on foreign affairs, created by Stalin and edited by Molotov—a former editor of *Pravda*—at the Narkomindel.[38] Just over a week later it appeared with a belated review of Joseph Jones, *A Modern Foreign Policy for the United States.*

The delay is interesting because the substance of the book had appeared previously in *Fortune* magazine prior to the Tehran conference in August, September, and October 1943. Moscow had discounted its significance no doubt as a result of Roosevelt's explicit personal abnegation of interest in postwar Europe. Two other significant works on the future of US foreign policy also emerged in 1943—*America's Strategy in World Politics* by Nicholas Spykman, the Dutch-American at Yale, and *U.S. Foreign Policy: Shield of the Republic* by the popular columnist Walter Lippmann. Yet neither had contradicted what Roosevelt said in private to Stalin about Europe; indeed, Lippmann effectively argued for what Stalin saw as minimal: the Soviet right to Eastern Europe as a sphere of influence/protectorate.

What was unusual about Jones was the peremptory assertion of American primacy, that "no country but the United States is equal to the task of leadership in organizing world power for peace-keeping purposes";[39] the emphasis on the importance of "a living principle" for US foreign policy;[40] and the link established between that principle ("freedom") and the need for "expanding markets" for the United States.[41] Indeed, the anonymous Soviet reviewer—certainly approved by Molotov if not by Stalin—seized upon these ideas, summing it all up in Jones's bold claim for the United States that "the moment is ours." Leadership would go to Washington above all because of its massive industrial and technological power and the immense increase in its air force. The review concluded, "Jones's judgments about the 'leadership' of the USA, although in a less acute form, in essence reproduced the stance of those American circles which are very vociferously laying claim to the domination of the United States in the postwar world."[42]

Jones's theses emerged from the stables of publishing magnate and activist Henry Luce, owner of *Time, Life,* and *Fortune* magazines, the most influential American journals of the day. Writing before Pearl Harbor Luce had expressed deep regret: "In the field of national policy, the fundamental trouble with America has been, and is, that whereas their nation became in the 20th Century the most powerful and the most vital nation in the world, nevertheless Americans were unable to accommodate themselves spiritually and practically to that fact. Hence they have failed to play their part as a world power—a failure which has had disastrous consequences for themselves and for all mankind. And the cure is this: to accept wholeheartedly our duty and our opportunity as the most powerful and vital nation in the world and in consequence to exert upon the world the full impact of our influence, for such purposes as we see fit and by such means as we see fit."[43] Furthermore, the vision was that of bourgeois democracy: "It is for America and America alone to determine whether a system of free economic enterprise—an economic order compatible with freedom and progress—shall or shall not prevail in this century."[44] The United States would become the "dynamic center of ever-widening spheres of enterprise."[45]

Luce had employed the formidable Raymond Buell to write weekly memoranda on foreign affairs throughout the war and to chair a series of roundtable
study groups to which the great and the good were invited, at the Council on
Foreign Relations. Buell's preliminary task lay in defining "what America herself
intends to be or will be or might be—or contra."[46] He shared Luce's conviction
that "so few intellectuals these days understand the concept of the free market
and its relation to democracy."[47] A core assumption was the "widespread fear
in many circles that at the end of this war the U.S. will suffer a depression even
more serious than in 1930."[48] Buell also believed that peace in postwar Europe
needed an American presence "because of an inherent power disequilibrium."
Without the Americans, Russia or Germany would tend to predominate.[49] Instead he and others believed the United Staes should take and hold the balance
of Europe as Britain had done since 1701.

Roosevelt's victory by no means dispelled Kremlin concern. On the contrary.
Shortly thereafter, NKVD resident in New York, Vladimir Pravdin (Roland Ab-
biate), sent a report "on the outlook for the domestic and foreign policies of
the USA" after the elections. Although Roosevelt had won, Pravdin argued, his
success in establishing international cooperation was by no means guaranteed.
"The re-election of the Roosevelt administration has put off for several years the
serious threat of the rise to power of fascism, but not liquidated it. It would be a
mistake to underestimate the actual strength of American reactionaries. Despite
the selection by the Republican apparatus of the unpopular candidate Dewey,
whose isolationist ties are widely known, through its organization, discipline,
and capable propaganda the Republican Party has succeeded in attracting to
itself a vast mass of voters and to a significant extent reducing Roosevelt's majority in comparison with previous elections. It has also to be borne in mind,"
Pravdin emphasized, "that in contrast to previous years, when the industrial and
financial magnates supported Roosevelt, this year economic groupings almost
exclusively supported Dewey." Crucially, isolationism was effectively dead and
buried. But this was not entirely good news. "The old isolationists have turned
into expansionists and will be the initiators of an adventurist and aggressive policy. Instead of a policy of international cooperation they will aim at establishing
American domination of the world, and their policy will in this first instance be
directed against the USSR."

Pravdin also expressed the view that as a result of Germany's defeat and the
fundamental shift in the European balance of power "only one Great Power
remains—the USSR." Moreover Britain, which traditionally pursued a policy
of balancing the Powers on the Continent, could "no longer" do so since all
the forces they would rely upon were extinguished. Thus the United States was

left facing only the USSR in Europe and only the British Empire — "seriously weakened but still sufficiently powerful" — beyond. Britain was the "natural" ally of the United States but also, as a result of its global interests, "the main rival" and the likely victim of US economic expansion. The key point, however, and this is where Stalin came around to Pravdin's viewpoint, was that "such fundamental alterations in the balance of world power has driven the ruling class of the USA, independently of party affinity, to the conclusion that the interests of the USA demand continuous and direct participation in the resolution of international issues. Otherwise, the course of world events would be decided exclusively by the USSR and England which, for understandable reasons, the USA cannot permit. This is understood by both the isolationist Republicans and the anti-Roosevelt Democrats." The transformation of public opinion has played its part in this.[50]

Moscow was thus alert to Washington infighting. Control of the State Department was naturally seen as symptomatic of changes in the offing. Hull headed the department only because, as a former senator (for Tennessee), his presence would silence criticism from Capitol Hill.[51] At the Moscow conference he had injudiciously told reporters: "While we were signing these declarations, I could give them no assurances whatever that the American people could in the long run support the aims of these documents. I told them that I knew the American people at the moment were fully in support of the principles and these declarations, but that I just could not say how long they would feel that way about them."[52] Not surprisingly Roosevelt cut him out of Tehran to Moscow's astonishment.[53] Buell brutally commented: "Hull is himself senile. He never has an idea of his own."[54] His ideas were a collection of core liberal beliefs held with a rigidity never fully shared by his patron, Roosevelt. When he retired in November 1944 Hull told a joint session of Congress: "There will no longer be need for spheres of influence, for alliances, for balance of power, or any other of the special arrangements which, in the unhappy past, the nations strove to safeguard their security or to promote their interests."[55] It was no accident that Luce's contacts with State ran through Welles rather than through Hull. And that Welles, the experienced Under Secretary "cut from the same cloth of Groton, Harvard, and the Eastern establishment,"[56] was Roosevelt's conduit to the department until exposure as a homosexual and his resignation on 16 August 1943.[57] And Welles had, by the time of his forced retirement, come to see the Russian problem with more realism than he had at the outbreak of war and, indeed, into 1942, having been warned by Litvinov on 7 May 1943 that Stalin's aims were alarmingly uncertain and uninformed by any real understanding of US opinion or regard for it.[58]

Quondam vice president of US Steel, Hull's successor Edward Stettinius, a salesman by nature as much as by trade, was scarcely any better regarded. Bohlen scorned him as "a decent man of considerable innocence" with "a Boy Scout enthusiasm."[59] Moscow understood from decrypting Lord Halifax's telegrams from Washington that he represented a victory of Harry Hopkins over "Jimmy" Byrnes, who had been backed by Senators Connelly and George, both fellow southerners. The choice of Stettinius as against Byrnes, an independent figure in his own right, cemented State to the White House.[60] The Kremlin cannot have been displeased. In late November 1944, Buell attacked Stettinius's irresponsible statement to the press "that this government's traditional policy of not guaranteeing specific frontiers of Europe is well known." Buell rightly regarded this as an open invitation for Moscow to expand at will.[61]

Buell was anxious for "some counterpoise to the divisive forces in the postwar world, one of which would probably be Russian imperialism in Europe and in the Orient." At the Council on Foreign Relations Anglo-American study group, British diplomat Michael Wright "concurred in the necessity of charting our course prior to the collapse of Germany. If we did this, remarked Mr. Buell, we could say to Russia that we intended to build a barrier in the West against economic chaos. Then there might be some hope that Russia would join our Atlantic Union as a second line of defense." Another member insisted that the Atlantic powers had first to put their own house in order or "Russia was likely to take advantage of the situation. Indeed, said Mr. Wriston [president of Brown University], Russia is doing that very thing now."[62]

Luce and Buell were by no means voices in the wilderness. Others now shared their concern lest US naïveté cost them the peace, economically as well as politically. Floyd Blair, vice president of National City Bank "thought it foolish to approach the problem of a world organization in idealistic terms. Russia would be bound by her own interests and the foreign policy of the United States would be designed to protect the interests of the American people." Should Britain and the United States cooperate, "Western Europe, he felt sure, would fall within our orbit." And publisher of the *Washington Post*, the formidable Eugene Meyer—a confidant of Litvinov when the latter was ambassador to Washington—expressed the view that "Americans, on the whole, were illiterate as regards foreign affairs. They were sensitive to strong leadership, but except in the military departments of the Government strong leadership was now lacking—in the White House, in the State Department, and in Congress."[63] Buell's ideas were for a foreign policy in the waiting, of which Jones's book was the most coherent outward projection. Moscow had good reason to take notice, not least because an anti-Soviet headwind was blowing through Washington.

FAR EASTERN PROMISES

At the close of December 1944 Stettinius learned "that the revolt against the administration now brewing in the Senate was based largely on the feeling that whereas we are fighting this war to destroy German and Japanese totalitarianism, what we are really doing is to substitute Soviet totalitarianism." Rebel senators, numbering some twenty-seven, included "an astonishing cross-section . . . including both isolationists and reactionaries."[64] The increasingly weary president was not helped by the fact that public opinion polls simultaneously revealed rising disquiet lest the country was being taken advantage of in its foreign relations.[65] The tide thus appeared to turn in favor of those who had long pressed for a more confrontational foreign policy than Roosevelt had been willing to implement; in particular, against the USSR. Like it or not, Luce and Buell were the shape of things to come. The newly assertive stance adopted by Roosevelt after re-election—opposing Russian recognition of a communist regime in Poland—symptomized a harder line against Moscow's growing unilateralism.[66]

The Far East, however, was one area where agreement proved easier to obtain and was vital if many more American lives were to be saved. As Litvinov indicated at the Moscow conference, Japan had long been a problem, and not just for the United States. But Soviet victory against Germany at Kursk in July 1943 turned Japan from threat to suitor. On 6 March 1944 the assertive young ambassador to Japan, Yakov Malik, a Stalin favorite, noted the impact made by "the victorious successes of the Red Army" and "the deterioration in the military circumstances of Japan in the Pacific Ocean" on the stance of "hostile armed neutrality" in prompting "a qualitative change in the nature of Japanese-Soviet relations." Malik concluded that "from the vantage point of the future . . . independently of the outcome of the current mortal combat between Japan and the Anglo-Saxons in the Pacific Ocean, the USSR must and will have its weighty word to add on Far Eastern questions too."[67] Japan offered to reopen talks that had led to the compromise neutrality pact of April 1941, now hoping for the full nonaggression pact it had denied Russia on the eve of the German invasion.[68]

Recalled, Malik was instructed to formulate proposals for negotiations that required clarification of Soviet goals for the postwar Pacific. "On the Issue of Japanese-Soviet Relations" was ready within a month, on 21 July 1944. Unaware of Stalin's commitment to enter the war against Japan, Malik paid particular attention to the hope that Moscow mediate with Washington. "Without doubt," wrote Malik, "to the degree that the allies increase their attacks on Japan, the

Japanese will be forced to become all the more 'soft and polite' in relations with the USSR." Yet Tokyo knew that, still engaged in Europe, Moscow would not wish to fight in Asia; it was this that had prevented Japan making far-reaching concessions. The key was power. "One must always take into account and never forget that Japan more, if you like, than any other country in the world takes notice only of strength."[69]

The memorandum is striking in a number of respects. Throughout, Malik used the term "Russia" interchangeably with the USSR: heresy to all but Stalin, who surprised Georges Bidault by referring to "Russia," whereas Molotov referred to the Soviet Union.[70] Malik went further in attributing to geography the decisive factor in Russian history. This was also unusual and provoked Molotov's blue crayon into action. But when Malik went on to say that Russia should not stand aside while Britain and the United States destroyed the Japanese Empire, Molotov was delighted. He underscored the following: "in no way can we allow territories contiguous to Soviet Far Eastern possessions (Manchuria, Korea, Tsushima, the Kurile Islands) [to] pass from the hands of the Japanese into the hands of some other strong power."

Malik went on to list questions of importance for a settlement. This was compiled from a classified US State Department assessment of likely Soviet aims in the region, purloined from the Office of Pacific Affairs within the month, likely as not from GRU agent Alger Hiss who worked there.[71] For instance, with respect to Manchuria, Malik took into account that Washington was considering the region for joint Chinese and Soviet control. Malik also assumed Moscow would take possession of the Kurile island chain, "blocking as they do Russia's route for egress into the Pacific Ocean." He also suggested neutralization of the straits of Tsushima or a Soviet naval base to guard the entry points for the purpose, inter alia, of keeping the British out. "Russia must expunge the black stain of the Portsmouth Treaty," Malik insisted; and, in contrast to 1905, the United States should be excluded from the matter. The list went on to some twenty-seven points. The only other items worthy of note are the possible strengthening of national liberation movements in Southeast Asia, the need to secure a friendly and "democratic" China, and payment by the Japanese of reparations to the USSR.

Summing up, Malik wrote: "The days of the Washington conference, when Soviet representatives were not even allowed into this conference, have long since passed." He added, "Circumstances and the array of forces in the Pacific Ocean after the defeat of Japan will evidently take shape in such a way that the Soviet Union must have and will have, as I see it, sufficient moral and legal bases to sustain for itself a weighty if not decisive voice in the examination of the majority of international problems in the Pacific Ocean and especially of those of them which directly relate to the question of measures for the maintenance and defense of the security of the USSR."[72] Stalin needed little convincing. At Tehran he had responded to allied requests with the complaint that the only warm water port he possessed—other than Murmansk—was Petropavlovsk on Kamchatka.[73]

Stalin pretended that his only reason for intervening in the Pacific war was to please the West and that unless his conditions were met, the people would not understand "the national interest involved."[74] Finally, at Yalta on 11 February it was agreed that "two or three months after the capitulation of Germany," the USSR would enter the war against Japan. Roosevelt's only caveat with regard to Stalin's terms was that those relating to China had to be made conditional upon the consent of Chiang Kai-shek.[75] Stalin had waited impatiently for news of presidential agreement. When a special messenger arrived, he excitedly asked young Gromyko to translate word for word. Every so often Gromyko was told to repeat the occasional phrase. "He [Stalin] paced up and down the study and repeated out loud: 'Good. Very good!' . . . Several times he passed through the room serving as the study with it in his hands, as though he did not want to let go of what he had received." Gromyko adds, "He was still holding the letter in his hand at the moment I left him."[76] Roosevelt had granted Stalin by promissory note the territorial gains in the Far East sought in return for a Soviet war against Japan. But that was music of the future until Russian troops had advanced and made promise fact, which was not likely until 1946. This much is evident from internal documentation. Stalin thereafter suspected that the Americans might meanwhile secure a separate peace with Japan and deprive Russia of the ability to secure a *place d'armes* in northeast Asia at Japanese expense.

DOMINATION OF POLAND

At Yalta the tacit quid pro quo for entering the war in Asia was that Moscow should effectively have most but not all of its way on Poland, which was largely in Soviet hands by virtue of victory in the field; so the democracies could effectively change matters only through hard bargaining. Harriman later summed up the position: "Though it may be difficult for us to believe, it still may be true that Stalin and Molotov at Yalta considered that by our willingness to accept a general wording of the Declaration on Poland and Liberated Europe, by our recognition of the need of the Red Army for security behind its lines, and of the predominant interest of Russia in Poland as a friendly neighbor and a corridor to Germany, we understood and were ready to accept Soviet policies as they had already made them known."[77]

Poland long held the focus of attention in Moscow. An alliance, Stalin had asserted back in August 1944, was "the basis of our policy." The rationale was simple: "Whatever restrictions are place on Germany, it will regenerate regardless and stand on its own two feet. After the Franco-Prussian War in 1870 Germany took little more than forty years to attack again in 1914. In 1939 Germany once again succeeded in attacking; this time the interval that it required for preparation was reduced to twenty-five years. We reckon that Germany will regenerate once more after the present war within twenty to twenty-five years."[78] Poland was thus the frontline for the containment of Germany. It did not come quietly. Resistance to Soviet occupation began with the abortive Warsaw Uprising in August 1944, which, as we have noted, was launched to preempt the arrival of the Red Army and continued sporadically throughout the rest of the decade.

One straw appeared in the wind on 25 January 1945 when Czech envoy Zdeněk Fierlinger was bluntly informed "that there had been enough delay and that the Soviet Government expected the Czechs to recognize [the Lublin regime] without more ado."[79] After Yalta an allied commission was formed in Moscow to reconstitute the provisional Polish government. On 2 March Harriman's reporting from Moscow indicated growing pessimism born of unrealistic expectations—for the simple reason that it was entirely Eurocentric: "The Russians cannot afford to let the Crimea declaration break down is still my conviction. It is apparent, on the other hand, that Molotov is under instructions from Stalin and his associates to fight every inch of the way and to give as little ground as possible in the direction of bringing in elements not under Soviet control."[80] Yet whereas Moscow decided that the Yalta formula on Poland was effectively a face-saving gesture for their allies, Washington began pressing for genuine implementation of the compromise obtained and thus ran into an impenetrable barrier.

Matters were further complicated by the fact that Stalin now also suspected the allies of overturning understandings tacitly agreed at Tehran. Thus when the United States and Britain took the surrender of German forces in Italy, he sensed collusion and demanded Soviet participation. Roosevelt was furious. Amidst this unpleasantness, on 13 March he met an old friend he had not seen for many years and alarmed him by his gloomy outlook on relations with Moscow. Roosevelt told Leon Henderson that the Western allies would abide by the agreements on Germany. But when asked whether Moscow would be meticulous in this respect, Roosevelt said "'yes'—on protocols, on anything that would show, but anywhere else, they would go their own way."[81] Yet even this proved too optimistic. Ten days later Roosevelt was more depressed and correspondingly more negative: "Averell [Harriman] is right," he told Anna Rosenberg at lunch. "We can't do business with Stalin. He has broken every one of the promises he made at Yalta."[82]

The point of contention on Poland was that at Yalta Stalin dropped a demand that the communist government should merely be "enlarged" in favor of the Western stance that it be "reorganized." But now Molotov, on Stalin's instructions, insisted that he "be shown one sentence which says that the Warsaw Government would not be taken as the basis for the future government." Moreover, Moscow demanded the right to veto noncommunist Poles for consultations on reforming the government: "If Poles are hostile to the Soviet Union they are not suitable for consultation even if they call themselves democrats and are not members of the émigré government."[83]

Roosevelt was reluctant to press matters, however, not least because the Red Army occupied Poland in its entirety en route to Berlin, but also because he was ever anxious to lock Moscow into the world security organization negotiated into being at Dumbarton Oaks the previous autumn as well as to hold them in reserve against Japan. Roosevelt found it hard to scale down grand universalist aspirations to the grim reality of bargaining with Stalin. Amateurism, idealism, and naïveté were still evident in the most unusual quarters of the US government. Ill-informed comment reflected either an unbounded sense of American power or genuine innocence, sometimes both. General William Donovan, head of the OSS (US intelligence), was reported to have "told the Polish Ambassador in Washington that he should not worry about the Russians in Poland because we will straighten all of that problem at the San Francisco Conference next month."[84] But Molotov's bottom line, with which even Litvinov agreed and which Churchill clearly understood, was "that according to the map Mexico is nearer to the United States than Poland, but since Poland according to the map is nearer to the Soviet Union, what transpires there is more important to the Soviet Union than to the United States."[85] At this stage Litvinov was rather more careful talking to newspapermen than diplomats. He was nevertheless "obviously pessimistic about the world situation" when Cyrus Sulzberger of the *New York Times* talked to him on 5 April. Litvinov was "a regular Jeremiah, full of gloom. He didn't say so outright, but he seemed to think worse trouble was coming."[86]

Increasingly depressed and soon fatally ill, Roosevelt lost his grip. His foreign policy in Europe was adrift in uncertain waters, kept afloat on unfounded hopes but doomed to wreckage on the rocks of Stalin's sullen suspicions. He believed still that the Red Army was vital to defeat Japan and save further American lives. The atomic bomb now being engineered had yet to prove itself. Meanwhile, in late February Moscow learned that leading representatives of the Polish government-in-exile from London had reached Poland. A trap was set once their whereabouts had been established. It was laid by Red Army Colonel-General Ivanov—Deputy Commissar Ivan Serov of the NKVD—as a result of which the sixteen disappeared from circulation on 27 March. They included Jan-Stanisław Jankowski and General Leopold Okulicki, who had formally dissolved the underground army in his command but had ordered the formation of small fighting cells to remain ready for future instructions.[87] On 31 March former Prime Minister Wincenty Witos was also tricked into NKVD custody. Interrogation of the sleep-deprived prisoners then proceeded for the preparation of an indictment, a trial, and long sentences for incarceration. In this matter Stalin was acting on intelligence information from London as to the intentions of the Polish government-in-exile.

Thus were the last months of the war in Europe overshadowed by growing acrimony in relations between London and Washington on one side and Moscow on the other. Stalin still seriously suspected a separate peace to be in the offing. On 21 March word came in from the London residency of a telegram from Ribbentrop to the German ambassador in Dublin. "I do not know," Ribbentrop wrote, "which Englishmen or Americans you can count on in the current situation. If the opportunity presents itself, I would ask you to convey these instructions via an agent of very special authority among English or American circles. Nothing on paper must in any circumstances originate with us." What the war had demonstrated was "the military might of the Soviet Union," which had now taken over Eastern Europe in its entirety. Even in France and Italy, communists were especially active.[88]

After news arrived of the arrests in Poland, Churchill took heed and advised Roosevelt that they must shake hands with the Russians "as far to the East as possible."[89] At the Foreign Office, arch-realist and Deputy Under-Secretary Orme ("Moley") Sargent brooded on Soviet obstructionism, and not merely in Poland. Given the sudden rapidity of the breakthrough on the Western front, it looked as though they "were resolved to give nothing away a moment sooner than they need, because they now find that in view of the sudden increase in strength of our military position they will need all the bargaining counters they can lay their hands on in the coming struggle for position in the political field."[90] Stalin was well aware of the sentiments expressed. This document reached Soviet intelligence and was dispatched to Moscow on 22 April, together with minutes from Permanent Under-Secretary Alec Cadogan and Eden dated 4 April.[91]

PRESSURE ON THE NEAR EAST

Stalin then compounded concern by pressing Ankara to revise the foundation of relations with Moscow that were settled at a time of chronic Soviet weakness in December 1920. In both 1923, at Lausanne, and 1936, at Montreux, Moscow failed to obtain a treaty that placed control over access to the Black Sea solely in the hands of the riparian Powers. In 1939 negotiations between Ankara and Moscow stumbled because Stalin saw London's influence gaining at Russian expense. He therefore demanded a military base on the Straits and failed to obtain it. In negotiating with Berlin in 1940 Russia was keen to establish predominance over Bulgaria and influence over the fate of Romania given the proximity of both—one hundred miles and two hundred miles—to the Straits in an age of airpower. Lack of sympathy for a state that failed to commit against Germany left Turkey isolated and therefore vulnerable. Churchill had repeatedly and foolishly promised Stalin during the war that this anomaly would be rectified to Soviet advantage. Nothing had been done, however. The fate of Turkey had arisen in Molotov's talks with Hitler on 13 November 1940.[92] At that time Stalin could not contain his distaste and his corresponding determination not merely to master the Straits. "We will drive the Turks into Asia," he fulminated. "*What is Turkey? There are two million Georgians there, one and a half Armenians, a million Kurds, and so forth. The Turks amount to only six or seven million.*"[93]

Thus after Turkey's belated declaration of war against Germany—received with derision in the Soviet press—on 19 March 1945, the Kremlin, in defiance of advice from its diplomats,[94] informed Ankara that the treaty of neutrality and friendship signed twenty years before would lapse. But Stalin expected much more than Churchill had anticipated. He was pressing not merely for control over the Straits but also responding, as in the case of Iran, to irredentist ambitions from within Soviet republics in the region (Armenia, Georgia, and Azerbaijan). He therefore pressed for realignment of the Turkish-Soviet frontier. Molotov strongly objected to what he regarded as a Great Power chauvinist policy,[95] but Stalin's Caucasian instincts won out, encouraged no doubt by deputy foreign commissars Vladimir Dekanozov and Sergei Kavtaradze plus Beria (all from Georgia) and Anastas Mikoyan (from Armenia).

In the knowledge that Moscow was insisting on revision of the Straits convention, the leaders of Armenia turned to Stalin on 6 April making the case for retrocession of territory lost to Turkey during the Russian civil war and its aftermath. That Stalin then chose publicly to receive Archbishop Gevorg Cheorekchiyan of the Armenian Church on 19 April indicated open sympathy for Armenian nationalism.[96] Thus on 7 June Molotov presented the Turkish ambassador, Selim Sarper, with a set of demands, including joint control over the Straits, naval bases in the Bosphorous and Dardanelles, plus retrocession of Kars and Ardagan. It was clear that "should the territorial side of the question, which in the Soviet-Turkish treaty was decided to the disadvantage of the Soviet Union, including Armenia and Georgia, be settled, that would have great significance for the strengthening of friendly relations for many years between the Soviet Union and Turkey."[97] The demands were reiterated on 18 June in no uncertain terms.[98] And a further note on 7 August 1946 restated the insistence that the riparian Powers alone settle the fate of the Straits, including their joint defense (a point reiterated on 24 September).

The Caucasian lobby had made themselves felt but had been suppressed after a collision with Lenin in 1920–21.[99] It was here, however, with respect to Iran rather than Turkey that the greatest disagreement arose. In 1942 London and Moscow divided the country between them for the duration of hostilities. This then presented Stalin with an ideal opportunity to bring about the formation of a separatist movement identical to that of the fetal Ghilan republic, which Lenin had ruthlessly aborted for reasons of state in 1921. As early as 6 March 1944 the Kremlin decided to extend its influence throughout occupied northern Iran for the indefinite future. All key officials in the area were replaced by Azeri officials. Molotov emphasized in his briefing to those appointed that they work all out "for the purpose of reinforcing our influence among the population."[100] As we have seen, Molotov never cared much for this policy. One obvious source of influence on Soviet policy came from rival Beria who, noting Anglo-American interest in postwar Iran for its oil, emphasized the importance of northern Iran as a contiguous source.[101] To these ends a front organization was established, the separatist Democratic Party, at the initiative of Bagirov, secretary of the Azerbaijan Central Committee. This was decided on 6 July 1945 at a Politburo meeting "on measures for the organization of a separatist movement in southern Azerbaijan and other provinces of northern Iran."[102]

Meanwhile Moscow tried to extract from Tehran agreement to exclusive rights for oil exploration and extraction in northern Iran. Instead of withdrawing when it was time to leave in March 1946, Stalin sent in a further 15,000 troops to augment the 60,000 already there while Azeris and Kurds clamored for independence from Tehran.[103] As he openly admitted, there was no "deep revolutionary crisis"; the success of the separatists was due entirely to the presence of Soviet forces.[104] A pattern of territorial expansion that was by no means restricted to Europe thus began to emerge as the war reached its close in Europe.

The Near East had its importance in illustrating the blatant use of local revolutionaries for national objectives. This was equally evident in the Middle East, instanced by Soviet support for Zionist terrorism. The first contacts between Moscow and the Jewish Agency representing the community in Palestine (*Yishuv*) occurred in October 1940 between Dr. Nahum Goldman and ambassador Konstantin Umansky, himself a Russian Jew and protégé of Litvinov, in Washington. The second took place at the end of January 1941 at a meeting between Dr. Chaim Weizmann and Maisky, also Jewish, in London. In discussing whether Palestine was the only likely future solution for the diaspora of the capitalist world, Maisky said that if this were so, then populations would have to be moved. In the words of the Jewish Agency record of the conversation, Weizmann "said that if half a million Arabs could be transferred, two million Jews could be put in their place. That, of course, would be a first instalment; what might happen afterwards was a matter of history."[105] The meeting was followed up by David Ben-Gurion, chairman of the Jewish Agency executive, in early October. He called in ostensibly to ask what help the Jewish community globally could do for the war effort. It soon became apparent he was disturbed that the Arab-Jewish Communist Party of Palestine had before the war supported the Arabs against Jewish colonization. He clearly wanted that policy changed and suggested a delegation be sent to Moscow.[106] But Stalin was too preoccupied with repelling Germany to look so far from the field of battle and into so distant a future.

When, however, the tide of war began to turn to allied advantage following the battle of Kursk, it occurred to the more extreme element within the *Yishuv* that Moscow might see them as a convenient instrument with which to undermine British power in the postwar Middle East. A breakthrough occurred when Maisky stopped over in Palestine en route from London to Moscow as part of his duties as deputy commissar. There, despite the best efforts of the British authorities, Maisky managed to see Ben-Gurion, visit Jerusalem and a few settlements, and probe the intentions of the agency for their plans.[107] Encouraged as a result of Moscow's evident interest, by the end of the year one terrorist group, the Stern Gang (*Lohamei Herut Yisrael*, or "*Lehi*"), recommended collaboration with Moscow in view of its rivalry with London in the region.[108]

On 1 November 1944, the other terrorists, led by Menachem Begin, "*Etzel*" (*Irgun Tzva'i Le'umi*), assassinated the British resident minister in Palestine, Lord Moyne, who was vocally anti-Jewish. Vyshinsky was one of two senior Soviet officials who expressed a positive view of the struggle in conversation with the Jewish Agency representative in Bucharest, Joseph Clarman.[109] Such sentiments arose from assumptions that Arab "efforts to unite and to create a United Arab Federation are incited and supported by the British insofar as it suits their plans to reinforce their influence in the Middle East and to establish a barrier against any possible penetration of Soviet influence there." As "none of the Arab countries is really an independent state," Moscow estimated, "any sort of unification among them is possible only under the aegis of a ruling power, which at present is Britain."[110]

ANGLO-AMERICAN DIFFERENCES

Anxious at the prospect of Stalin making impossible a postwar balance of Europe, Churchill attempted to persuade General Dwight Eisenhower, commanding allied forces in the West, that troops press ahead to take both Berlin and Prague before Moscow did so. Stalin was aware of this. Churchill's message to Eden concerning Prague reached Soviet intelligence and was copied to Stalin on 26 April 1945.[111] But neither the trusting Eisenhower, an increasingly despondent Roosevelt, nor his untutored successor Truman showed that they really understood the crucial importance of the battlefield in defining of the territorial settlement following war. Only Stalin and Churchill did so, conscious of precedent; Stalin tutored by the historian Yevgenii Tarle, Churchill something of an historian himself.

Washington was at this early stage much lower down the learning curve in realpolitik. Kennan, writing to a former colleague two decades hence, reflected on the "naïve assumptions about the personality of the Stalin regime and the prospects for postwar collaboration which permeated our entire policy-making at that time."[112] A few years and a growing conviction that Stalin was taking the United States insufficiently seriously were to make all the difference. A note to Moscow on 6 July 1948, for instance, claimed the right of Americans to be in Berlin as a consequence of withdrawing its forces from the region in 1945 to cede it to Russia. The note also stated that, had it known of what was to come in respect of the Soviet blockade of Berlin, the United States would not have done so.[113] It was unquestionably a failure of statesmanship not to have realized this sooner. Clausewitz's dictum *On War* as the continuation of politics through other means was evidently read neither extensively nor deeply at West Point. General Walter Bedell Smith, as ambassador to Moscow and later head of CIA, had good cause for rueful regret at the "great mistakes . . . made during the war because of American failure to realize that military and political action had to go hand in hand."[114] Stalin, however, knew all too well. He had absorbed Clausewitz via Engels and Lenin. "This war is not as in the past; whoever occupies a territory also imposes on it his own social system. Everyone imposes his own system as far as his army can reach. It cannot be otherwise," Stalin famously told Yugoslav communist leader Milovan Djilas.[115] And extravagant hopes of reaching as far as Denmark excited the Soviet mind. At discussions on postwar planning in June 1944 Lozovskii insisted on the need for military bases on Bornholm at the gates of the Baltic Sea. The problem was that Denmark was not an enemy state. The argument made to Dekanozov by the head of the fifth European department was that Russia had "special interests . . . in Denmark which controls egress from the Baltic Sea."[116]

Few were in a position to enlighten Washington for fear of rapid and fatal retribution. The Litvinovs were a notable exception; the only problem being that Maxim's warnings were easily brushed aside as the grievances of a senior official passed over for the highest office.[117] The fact that Litvinov had to emphasize the responsibility of Molotov rather than Stalin (the necessary fiction of the evil counselors advising the innocent monarch) certainly did not help advance the credibility of his position. It was during the spring of 1945 that his garrulous wife asked Harriman whether he remembered the unsolicited advice she had offered a year before. "At that time," Harriman recalled, "she had told me that it was her opinion that efforts on our part to ingratiate ourselves with the Soviet authorities were only interpreted as weakness on our part and that if we wished to establish our relations on a satisfactory basis we should be firm in all our dealings with them. In commenting on the fact that Molotov was not going to San Francisco and the present very unsatisfactory state of our relations, she chided me for not having followed her advice of last year. She said that this advice still held true and that it was not too late to put it into practice if we desired to have our relations with the Soviet Union placed on a satisfactory basis."[118]

UNCERTAIN SUCCESSION

Roosevelt finally died of a stroke at 4:35 p.m. on 12 April. The bewildered and entirely uninformed Harry Truman found himself in power two and a half hours later, at a crucial moment for the United States, with the world confronting an uncertain, unsettled, and therefore troubled peace. Vice President less than three months before, Truman had attended cabinet meetings and had seen Roosevelt once or twice since then. "But he never did talk to me confidentially about the war," Truman recalled, "or about foreign affairs or what or what he had in mind for the peace after the war."[119]

Those at the White House were so disoriented on 12–13 April that no one got up when Truman walked into the Oval Office. This instinctive lack of respect lingered. That it would take time to adjust was inevitable. Yet time was short.

Washington paralyzed by grief, Churchill wasted not a moment reassessing Britain's position. Immediately he resolved to take preemptive action where nothing had been agreed in advance with Moscow. "It is in our interests," he wrote, "to prevent the Russian submergence of Central and Western Europe as far as possible."[120] To this end British forces were told to take northeastern Italy, Venezia Giulia, as speedily as possible in order to deny the key port of Trieste to the irredentist and communist Yugoslavs, who had signed a mutual assistance pact with Stalin on 11 April, thus breaching the letter of the percentages agreement of October 1944; and to hold open the possibility of granting possession to Italy in order to throw the local Communist Party into confusion by raising aloft the banner of Italian nationalism above the red flag. Churchill's message to Eden in Washington that it was now a waste of time to fritter away British efforts in a lost cause with Yugoslavia was sent to Stalin by the London residency of the NKVD/NKGB on 5 May.[121]

Churchill acted swiftly because the death of Roosevelt prompted a new sense of uncertainty that Moscow might quickly exploit. He understood "that the new man [Truman] is not to be bullied by the Soviets."[122] This assessment was also read by Stalin,[123] as was a telegram insisting that Britain and the United States had to stop the USSR absorbing Central and Western Europe.[124] But Churchill also knew Truman had been kept in the dark by Roosevelt. Predictions of US policy were thus hard to make. Litvinov's successor as ambassador and Molotov's protégé, the dullard Gromyko, found it "difficult to judge what domestic and foreign policy Truman will carry out."[125]

Stalin, however, appears to have found intelligence assessments more penetrating. He immediately made a show of force on 21 April by signing a mutual assistance pact with a Polish communist government as yet unrecognized in by the West. The omens were therefore not propitious when Molotov met Truman for the first time on 22 April—only ten days after Roosevelt's death. Harriman had warned Truman that "in effect what we were faced with was a 'barbarian invasion of Europe,' that Soviet control over any foreign country did not mean merely influence on their foreign relations but the extension of the Soviet system with secret police, extinction of freedom of speech, etc." Stalin had the impression that he did not have to heed US opinion and that "some quarters in Moscow believed erroneously that American business needed as a matter of life and death the development of exports to Russia."[126]

Stalin had originally refused to allow Molotov to go to the United States for the opening of the UN. Indeed a TASS communiqué on 29 March had stated that Gromyko would attend instead. Stalin and Molotov had argued. On 19 April, however, having won out, Molotov left, traveling via Anchorage, Alaska, and then on to San Francisco before a hasty departure for Washington to see Truman. Erofeev noted: "Molotov's participation in the San Francisco conference turned out to be very important, and he understood this from the very beginning, but had to take Stalin's opinion into account. This was yet another instance of disagreements with Stalin, which increasingly became exacerbated and took on an increasingly severe form. In these disputes Beria played his part; he was no friend of Molotov's."[127]

Stalin's actions the day before Molotov's meeting with Truman consciously poured fuel on the flames. But Truman remained studiously cool, and the meeting, a preliminary before the foreign ministers began working on Poland, was brief and cordial. Matters were to prove different on the following day, however. Alerted that Moscow's position had moved not one iota, Truman told Molotov that "our agreements with the Soviet Union so far had been a one-way street and that could not continue; it was now or never. He intended to go on with the plans for San Francisco and if the Russians did not wish to join us they could go to hell." But this was only one side of the coin. Those advising him most concerned with the campaign to defeat Japan were not at all enthusiastic for a showdown.

Indeed, Stimson had no knowledge of Poland and, like the Chairman of the Joint Chiefs of Staff, General George Marshall, he was inclined to forgive Moscow anything on the grounds that they succeeded in battle. "He said we must understand that outside the United States with the exception of Great Britain there was no country that understood free elections."[128] The overall impression Truman received, however, was "that the time has arrived to take a strong American attitude toward the Soviet, and that no particular harm can now be done to our war prospects even if Russia should slow down or even stop its war effort in Europe and in Asia."[129] On this occasion, therefore, he sided with James Forrestal, Admiral William Leahy (now presidential chief of staff), Stettinius, and Harriman, venting his fury at Molotov when they met later that day, on 23 April. This much is evident even from the toning down of the record by note-taker Bohlen.

Taking up Harriman's suggestion of Lend-Lease as a stick with which to threaten Moscow, Truman insisted that failure to reach agreement on Poland would damage public opinion; that popular support was vital to economic appropriations for overseas projects; and that Moscow should consider this in weighing his own and Churchill's proposals on Poland. When Molotov countered that Moscow was interested in cooperation, Truman snapped back that this was of course true, "otherwise, they would not be talking today." When Molotov went on to say observance of the Yalta decisions was for him a matter of honor, Truman "replied with great firmness that an agreement had been reached on Poland and that it only remained for Marshal Stalin to carry it out in accordance with his word."[130] "I have never been talked to like that in my life," Molotov objected. "Carry out your agreements and you won't get talked to like that," Truman responded.[131] The president "used plain American language" (only retrospectively cleaned up for the record), Leahy noted, adding "language that was not at all diplomatic."[132]

Present, Gromyko characteristically omitted all mention of this disagreeable exchange in his memoirs—themselves a monument to discretion (and trivia)—but more than once confided what had taken place to Oleg Troyanovsky, Molotov's foreign policy assistant on the United States. According to him, "Truman immediately took the offensive, accusing the Soviet Union of various mortal sins. The onslaught was indeed so unexpected that Molotov was taken aback, which rarely happened to him. After Truman's tirade he readied himself to reply, but the President thereupon gave to understand that the conversation was at an end and, excusing himself, left."

Molotov was patently alarmed. He foresaw that Truman's conduct would draw an extremely negative response from Moscow, and he feared Stalin would hold him responsible for everything. Back at the embassy a palid Molotov began putting together an account of the meeting for dispatch to Moscow. "He spent a long time writing. Evidently he completely failed to recast the dark tones of the discussion into brighter colors. Finally he called over Gromyko, and together they set to softening the sharp edges."[133] From Molotov's standpoint, however, this was a risky procedure. Sooner or later Stalin would find out what had really happened. Molotov was not Caesar's wife; Stalin, as he was soon to be reminded, was much given to fatal suspicion even of his closest brother-in-arms, with Beria's encouragement, of course.

TRUMAN BACKS OFF

The first skirmishes over Truman's attention had thus been won by Harriman, who said nothing to Kennan. But as the war against Japan drew to a climax, Truman muted his assertiveness against Moscow in deference to the military. Litvinov correctly advised Molotov that the allies were "interested in our entering the war with Japan. . . . For this very reason they will be more inclined to be accommodating than after their victorious conclusion of the war in the East."[134] He was right. On further reflection Truman "felt that agreements made in the war to keep Russia fighting should be kept and I kept them to the letter." He added, "All of us wanted Russia in the Japanese war."[135] Indeed, the Kremlin was conscious that Washington refrained from exacerbating the relationship still further.[136] Intelligence information reaching Stalin from San Francisco noted that, although sent by Roosevelt to mediate between the Chinese nationalists and the communists, General Patrick Hurley had forbidden US officials to have anything to do with the Mao Tse-tung and that London and Washington were agreed on liquidating communism in China. Yet, and this was the material issue for Stalin, Truman was nevertheless bent on defeating Japan.[137]

The end of the war in Europe thus sounded an inconclusive note in East-West relations. In Moscow on the evening of 11 May, Marshal Georgii Zhukov, Commander-in-Chief of Soviet forces in Germany, was summoned to Stalin, who suggested that the British were colluding with the Germans to use them against the Russians. Molotov expressed the view that with the death of Roosevelt, Truman would soon come to terms with the British. And the Americans appeared to be lingering in Thuringia to snap up what they could lay their hands on in terms of technology. On Stalin's view they were trying to improve their bargaining position vis-à-vis the Russians. "If you live with wolves, you have to howl like a wolf," Stalin quipped.[138] Meanwhile, on the following day in a telegram to Truman, Churchill expressed alarm "that half the American air forces in Europe has already begun to move to the Pacific theatre. The newspapers are full of the great movements of the American Armies out of Europe. Our Armies also are under previous arrangements likely to undergo a marked reduction. The Canadian Army will certainly leave. The French are weak and difficult to deal with. Anyone can see that in a very short space of time our armed power on the Continent will have vanished except for moderate forces to hold down Germany." What, then, "is to happen about Russia?" "I have always worked for friendship with Russia but," Churchill emphasized, "like you, I feel deep anxiety because of their misinterpretation of the Yalta decisions, their attitude towards Poland, their overwhelming influence in the Balkans excepting Greece, the difficulties they make about Vienna, the combination of Russian power and the territories under their control or occupied, coupled with the Communist technique in so many other countries, and above all their power to maintain very large Armies in the field for a long time. What will be the position in a year or two, when the British and American Armies have melted and the French have a handful of divisions, mostly French, and when Russia may choose to keep two or three hundred on active service?" Churchill saw an "iron curtain . . . drawn down upon their front. We do not know what is going on behind."[139] It was this that led the prime minister plan for the possibility of war with Russia.

Churchill was right to worry. Having condemned Browder for ignoring the class struggle, Moscow now openly reasserted revolutionary solidarity with regard to the working class in the West facing "the looming danger of mass employment" and "the struggle which the peoples of the colonial countries are waging for their freedom and independence," adding that it was "not surprising that the striving of the peoples in dependent countries for liberation flared up with new force during the struggle against fascist aggression."[140]

In ignorance, Washington was unreceptive when asked to exploit military dispositions in the field. Hopkins insisted to Truman that delaying withdrawal was "certain to be misunderstood by the Russians."[141] Truman sent Hopkins to see Stalin in late May. He returned early June via Frankfurt where he spoke at allied headquarters, "bubbling with enthusiasm about his meetings with Stalin." And whereas those he addressed naturally saw Germany as "the most difficult problem in Europe," Hopkins "made it clear that Germany was pretty far down on Washington's priority list." He said with "obvious sincerity" that "we can do business with Stalin! He will co-operate!"[142] Truman shared this naïveté: the Russians had "always been our friends and I can't see why they shouldn't always be."[143] Thus when Truman and Churchill requested "free access" to Berlin "by air, road and rail" and failed to obtain it, the president let the matter drop. Harriman, however, still shared Churchill's concern. Newly appointed Under Secretary of State Dean Acheson wrote to daughter Mary a few days later: "Averell is furious about the Rouskis—an attitude which is OK for those who can handle it but dangerous medicine for those who want to be ineffectively anti-Russian. He says rightly that they are behaving badly and running out of arguments and attempting to dominate Europe and elsewhere. With this I agree and I am for a policy of firmness. . . . He sees lots of trouble ahead and fears that San Francisco lulls people into a false sense that we don't have to stand up to Stalin."[144]

Acheson, however, had no intention of remaining in government.[145] He had what his latter-day special assistant Lucius ("Luke") Battle affectionately referred to as only "a veneer of Eastern seaboard polish."[146] Along with Marshall, whom Truman revered, Acheson rather than the president was to give intellectual cohesion and steadfast purpose to US conduct of the Cold War in its crucial phase. For the moment, however, his views had yet to cohere. Acheson refused to see conflict with Moscow as inevitable. Thus the only apparent by-product of "crocodile" Harriman's gruff lobbying was the decision encouraged by Leahy to cut Lend-Lease completely—leaving Britain in the same empty boat as Russia. Stalin had by then reached stark conclusions. He refused to contemplate a division of Germany on the grounds that it would lead to "American domination" of that country.[147]

In the West a fundamental problem lay with a president entirely unaccustomed to dealing with other societies. A natural, prickly, and provincial isolationism pervaded Truman's early decisions. On 20 July, for instance, he wrote of his having "to make it perfectly plain to them [Churchill and Stalin] at least once a day that so far as this President is concerned Santa Claus is dead and that my first interest is [the] U.S.A."[148] He also tended to project his own personal experience onto alien political cultures. After the Potsdam summit he wrote: "I like Stalin. He is straightforward." Stalin, indeed, reminded him of his sponsor, the corrupt Tom Pendergast of Missouri.[149] Thus the dispatch of Hopkins to negotiate a compromise on Poland made sense if one were dealing with Pendergast; yet Stalin was ill suited to the role assigned to him. Given his outlook, any compromise was bound to be a victory of form over substance.

In Poland, communists headed by Władisław Gomułka who had led a guerrilla struggle against Germany amounted to a mere 140,000.[150] Without the Red Army they were powerless. On the other hand the behavior of the NKVD made ever more problematic attempts to win over the population. Gomułka therefore pleaded with the Kremlin to release some of those taken in the hope that they could be won over to widen the basis of support for the communist cause. Stalin was persuaded to release many from the underground army who had been swept up in mass arrests that followed the entry of the Red Army into most of Poland.[151] But, unable to secure freedom for leading émigré Poles imprisoned in March and ever anxious that Moscow be kept onside for the defeat of Japan, which Hopkins discussed with Stalin, Washington conceded without consulting London and accepted communist predominance.

Churchill had little choice but to accept US concessions, though no more than that. "We desire the entry of the Soviets into the war against Japan at the earliest possible moment," he wrote. However, Churchill continued, "Having regard to their own great interests in the Far East, they will not need to be begged, nor should their entry be purchased at the cost of concessions prejudicing a reign of freedom and justice in Central Europe or the Balkans."[152] In a sop to Truman, Stalin allowed Stanisław Mikołajczyk, formerly leader of the London Poles and head of the Smallholders' Party, to join the Polish government as deputy chairman of the Council of Ministers on 28 June. On 5 July, the defeat of Japan in sight but with Soviet assistance still assumed vital, the United States and Britain swallowed hard and recognized the new Polish government.

Stalin had thereby secured Poland as a fiefdom with window dressing. But he knew that resistance was growing. Moscow had long been reading the secret correspondence between the president and prime minister. On 4 June Churchill reiterated to Truman the "profound misgivings" with which he viewed "the retreat of the American Army to our line of occupation in the central sector, thus bringing Soviet power into the heart of Western Europe and the descent of an iron curtain between us and everything to the eastward." He had "hoped that this retreat, if it has to be made, would be accompanied by the settlement of many great things which could be the true foundation of world peace." However, "nothing really important has been settled yet, and you and I will have to bear great responsibility for the future."[153] With this approach, had he known of it, which doubtless he did not, Litvinov was entirely out of sympathy. Still reacting to the preceding period of tension following Molotov's visit to Washington, Litvinov asked Edgar Snow: "Why did you Americans wait till right now to begin opposing us in the Balkans and Eastern Europe? You should have done this three years ago. Now it's too late, and your complaints only arouse suspicion here."[154] Before long, however, when he came to realize the full extent of what lay behind Moscow's behavior, he was to press for ever greater firmness from the West.

What flowed out of London did nothing to reduce Stalin's suspicions. From the NKVD residency on 3 August arrived the copy of a memorandum by Under-Secretary Sargent dated 11 July. It argued that, although Britain had had to come to come to terms with Russia in the diplomatic arena, the time had come to throw down the gauntlet over Finland, Poland, Czechoslovakia, Austria, Yugoslavia, and Bulgaria instead of waiting for Moscow to threaten British interests in Germany, Italy, Greece, and Turkey. London's policy should be to turn Italy, Greece, and Turkey into bastions of liberalism. The battle for Germany, however, would not only be more difficult but also more decisive for the whole of Europe.

The trouble was, and here Stalin's ears will have pricked up, Britain could not count on continuing cooperation from the United States. Too many Americans considered Britain dangerous and reactionary, just as the British had seen the French in the 1920s. Only on the problem of economic revival, which touched core interests, did they seem likely to collaborate. Once it had given material aid to countries in difficulty, Washington was more likely to show an interest in their politics. As to Britain, it should challenge communist penetration in the majority of Eastern Europe and resist communism in Germany, Italy, Greece, and Turkey even if the Americans refuse assistance or embark on the appeasement of the Soviet Union. It was very much in terms of an economic counterweight that Sargent saw the security of British and American political interests in Europe: the earliest sign of the thinking that led eventually to the Marshall Plan.[155]

A crucial exception to US misgivings about Britain occurred in the field of intelligence cooperation that had begun in February 1941 with the gift of the Purple Analog machine—a machine that broke the Japanese diplomatic code—to the British. This gesture was eventually rewarded with the sharing of the efforts to break the German Enigma codes in June 1942.[156] In June 1945 the US Army and Navy Communications Intelligence Board (ANCIB) suggested that London and Washington extend their collaboration after the war but against the USSR. This became project Bourbon. Arrangements remained informal, with the exchange of liaison units.[157] Stalin will have known since Philby was building up the counterintelligence Soviet section of MI6.

RUSSIA ATTACKS JAPAN

Meanwhile, the sudden end to war in Europe had caught Moscow short. Germany's defeat was not expected until much later. Throughout, Stalin had been rotating units between the Far East and the European front. Signs of a shift of air forces eastwards became apparent as early as October 1944. Previous air strength was calculated at around 1,770 aircraft. But between October 1944 and July 1945 about 2,000 additional plans were moved east and between mid-April and mid-June heavy military traffic was observed along the trans-Siberian railroad, which was working to full capacity.[158] From April to September an average of 10 trainloads were transported in twenty-four hours, peaking at 22 in July.[159] From May to 9 August 136,000 carriage loads of materiel had been transported.[160] The number of men moved amounted to 33,465 in May, rising to 152,408 in June and 206,042 in July, dropping to 11,449 between 1 and 8 August.[161]

Lozovskii, supervising Soviet policy in the East, wrote to Molotov on 10 January 1945 anxious lest the neutrality pact with Japan be extended. Russia needed "a free hand." At the same time Moscow had to be careful to rid itself of the pact in such a way "that the Japanese hope through serious concessions on their part to see the neutrality pact extended for another five years."[162] Thus it was duly denounced in the press on 6 April.[163] Plans for the attack on Japan were not complete until the end of the month.[164] But the need to catch up in planning as well as logistics inevitably heightened Stalin's anxiety lest Washington jeopardize his prospective share in the Far Eastern settlement. Suspicions were easily aroused. A dispatch from Malik in Tokyo on 7 June reported an approach by former Prime Minister Hirota. Malik noted, "Throughout my discussion with Hirota, not only did he not once attack the USA and England, but he did not even direct a sharp remark at them. Doubtless the story about talks with the USSR is needed by the Japanese for peace soundings that could lead to negotiations with the USA and England."[165] Later Stalin acknowledged that "the deterioration in relations . . . was due to an accumulation of facts antedating the return of the Labour Government to power."[166] Since Labour came to power during the course of the Potsdam summit in July, it is fair to conclude that in Stalin's mind, at least, a cold war was by now certain.

Stalin's greatest concern, evidenced by his encrypted correspondence with the embassy in Tokyo, was lest Japan, fearing an attack and a vengeful settlement, sought a separate peace with the United States and thereby forestalled Russian entry into the war and its share of the fruits. From Lisbon US diplomats reported an approach from the Japanese legation expressing interest in conditional terms of peace and arguing in strongly anti-Soviet terms similar to those used by Himmler in negotiations with Sweden for a separate peace. Japan was said to be useful in keeping Russia out of China. Washington stood to lose the Chinese market if Russia came in.[167] Moscow learned of this *ballon d'essai*. Early in June the Soviet political representative in Budapest, Pushkin, asked his American opposite number, Schoenfeld, for information about such peace feelers. But he was told nothing was known. Pushkin thanked him, adding by way of explanation that "the Soviet Union had a bone to pick with Japan."[168] Stalin's concern was made apparent when Hopkins saw him in May: "Stalin," Hopkins noted, "expressed the fear that the Japanese will try to split the allies."[169] Attempts by Hirota to lure Moscow into negotiation were thus firmly rebuffed.

Goodwill naturally counted for nothing. As in Europe, so in Asia, Russia was dissatisfied with what had been formally agreed with the allies. At a meeting with the Politburo, leaders of the state apparatus, and senior officers on 26–27 June, veteran of the Far Eastern army Marshal Kirill Meretskov proposed the occupation of Hokkaido, Japan's largest island to the north, along with territory agreed at Yalta. Young Nikita Khrushchev spoke in favor. Molotov, however, consistently Eurocentric and anxious to pace Soviet expansionism, spoke against on the grounds that it would breach the Yalta agreements; as did Marshal Georgii Zhukov, who dismissed it as an escapade.[170] Stalin split the difference. He instructed the military to plan for the occupation of Hokkaido and then asked Washington to consent, fully expecting Truman to agree.[171] Just as Litvinov feared and had warned, as with respect to Hitler, the appetite was growing with the eating. And it was not merely Stalin who had exaggerated expectations of the fruits of victory that he was reluctant to disappoint.

On 30 June Stalin appointed army Chief of Staff Marshal Aleksander Vasil'evsky commander-in-chief for the war. Negotiations now opened with China to secure what Roosevelt had promised on their behalf. On 2 July Stalin outlined the geopolitical rationale for his demands in terms strikingly similar to that deployed with respect to Europe: "We are closed up. We have no outlet. One should keep Japan vulnerable from all sides, north, west, south, east, then she will keep quiet." "Japan will be crushed," he continued, "but she will restore her might in 20, 30 years," Stalin told Soong, Chiang Kai-shek's Foreign Minister and brother-in-law. "The whole plan of our relations with China is based on this."[172]

In conversation with Hopkins, Stalin appeared unduly anxious for a peace conference to close matters in Europe. Only this would consolidate the gains of war and translate them into legal form. He was lucky. British anxiety to settle matters before American forces demobilized and left them alone facing the mass of Russian troops worked precisely in the same direction. It was thus agreed to hold a summit that opened in the outskirts of Berlin at the Cecilien-hof in Potsdam on 17 July. By agreeing to Berlin against Churchill's wishes, Washington effectively placed the West once again — as at Yalta — in Soviet hands. Moscow made full use of the opportunity by delaying the opening of the conference until all US troops had been hurried out of the Soviet zone.[173] Here Truman reiterated the wish that Russia enter the war against Japan.[174] "At the time," Truman later confessed, "we were anxious for Russian entry into the Japanese war. Of course we found later that we didn't need Russia there and the Russians have been a headache to us ever since."[175] After the plenary session on 17 July, as everyone was dispersing, Truman ran after Stalin to say something. Soviet interpreter Pavlov hurried over and translated the president's news that on the previous day the United States had tested a bomb of unusual destructive power. Stalin just listened and said nothing. Not a muscle moved on his face. He turned on his heels and departed. Taken aback by the reaction, or lack of it, Truman was at a loss for words, gazing after the disappearing Stalin.[176] "Believe the Japs will fold up before Russia comes in," Truman wrote in his diary on 18 July. "I am sure they will when Manhattan appears over their homeland."[177] "Had we known what the Atomic Bomb would do we'd have never wanted the Bear in the picture," Truman wrote later.[178]

On the successful atomic test, Churchill said he "now thought it a good thing that the Russians knew about it and it may make them a little more humble."[179] But ham-fisted attempts by Truman and his new and independent-minded Secretary of State, Irish-American southern segregationist Byrnes, to highlight the atom bomb in order to intimidate Russia backfired badly, instead reinforcing Stalin's suspicions about the breadth of US ambitions. He commented: "They slay the Japanese, and bully us. Once more everything is done in secret."[180] The Soviet military were horrified at developments. Gromyko recalls: "The military in our General Staff had their heads in their hands. The Soviet Union, having only just beaten the fascist armies, once again faced the threat of attack. There sat people who, having passed through the hell of a fearful war, had not yet re-covered from the '22 June' syndrome and seriously considered that the USA, as soon as it had to its credit 10–15 atomic bombs, could in a possible war with the USSR deploy them against the major cities and industrial centers. The Kremlin and the General Staff were nervous; mistrust of the allies now mounted. Opinions were expressed in favor of the preservation of a mass land army, the establishment of control over great expanses as a counter to possible losses from atomic bombers. In other words, the atomic blows against Japan forced us yet again to evaluate the significance for the USSR of the entire East European bridgehead."[181]

Stalin knew an atomic bomb had been tested. On 8 August 1941 an officer in Soviet military intelligence (Razvedupr) in London, Semyon Kremer (codename "Barch"), formally the military attaché's secretary since January 1937, made the acquaintance of one Klaus Fuchs. Fuchs, a German refugee, was then working on the theoretical side of the British atomic bomb project at Birmingham University. The practical application was done at Oxford. It was expected work would be complete in three months. Thereafter everything would go to Canada for industrial production.[182] On 16 September 1941 the British Uranium Committee chaired by Lord Hankey but led by physicist Sir George Thomson convened and agreed that a uranium bomb was feasible in a few years. This information from spy John Cairncross was sent in to Moscow on 25 September by NKVD resident in London Anatolii Gorskii along with the news that on 20 September the Chiefs of Staff had agreed to proceed with its speedy construction.[183]

Not until 10 March 1942, however, did Commissar of Internal Affairs Lavrenty Beria present the state defense committee chaired by Stalin with this vital information, the significance of which had evidently eluded him.[184] Fuchs handed over about 246 pages of secrets between August 1941 and October 1942, when Kremer returned to Moscow, and contact was taken over by Kuczynski by whom a further 324 pages were obtained through to November 1943. Meanwhile Yan Chernyak (codename "Jack") recruited Alan Nunn May at the Cavendish Laboratory in Cambridge in 1942 obtained some 142 pages on the bomb in several months' work. The activities of both Razvedupr and the NKVD were coordinated on this issue under the control of Sudoplatov's section "S" at the NKVD. Early in 1944 everything—including the handling of Fuchs—was transferred to NKVD foreign intelligence. Nevertheless important progress was made in the United States by Arthur Adams, a Swede, who headed the Razvedupr's illegal residency. He recruited a key scientist codenamed "Kemp" in February 1944 who supplied more than 5,000 pages of secret documents in that year alone.[185]

The atomic bomb destroyed Hiroshima on 6 August. Two days later Russia hurriedly declared war on Japan. Another bomb fell on Nagasaki the day after.

Tokyo surrendered on condition that the emperor remain in place. Meanwhile Stalin, sending his forces across the borders into China and Korea against Japan's occupation troops, had his eyes focused on the not-so-distant past as well as the future when Japanese forces on the mainland finally laid down their arms: "The defeat of Russian forces in 1904 in the period of the Russo-Japanese War left painful memories in the consciousness of the people. It left a black stain on our country. Our people believed and waited for the day when Japan would be beaten and the stain would be liquidated. We waited forty years, the people of the old generation, for this day. And here we are, this day has come."[186]

The subordinate position of the USSR in the region was, however, underlined when Molotov suggested that several commanders-in-chief receive Japan's surrender. "Besides General MacArthur there could be Marshal Vasil'evsky," he suggested. Ambassador Harriman erupted in indignation: "The Soviet Union cannot present such demands after a total of two days at war with Japan. The United States, in tying up Japanese forces, did not give the Japanese the possibility of attacking the Soviet Union at the most critical time for the Soviet Union."[187] Moscow had thereby been served notice that this was exclusively an American sphere of influence. Stalin was beside himself with fury. Japan was a direct neighbor. Unpleasant memories of Russia's humiliation at the hands of Japan at Tsushima still rankled even among Bolsheviks and imperial Japan had subsequently held a gun to Moscow's head for over a decade. Now Russia might be denied satisfaction. On 16 August Stalin had asked that Soviet forces occupy the northern half of Hokkaido, the main northern island of Japan, thus bisecting the country in the manner of Korea and Germany. Given Truman's bitter experience of noncooperation with Stalin, this was hardly likely to be accepted, despite Stalin's pleas. In reply on 18 August Truman rejected Stalin's suggestion outright.[188] Plans to land forces on the main northern island of Hokkaido were nevertheless confirmed by Stalin on 20 August, only to be abruptly curtailed on the morning of 22 August. That day Stalin complained, "I and my colleagues did not expect from you such a response."[189]

Moreover the US request for temporary landing rights on the Kuriles, territory explicitly allocated to Russia, was viewed with suspicion. Five days later Harriman clarified that Washington was not seeking a permanent military base. Stalin received him coldly: "He was astounded to have received Truman's original request."[190] That same day the Chief of Staff Soviet forces in the Far East, Colonel-General Ivanov, circulated an advisory: "In order to avoid creating conflicts and misunderstandings with the allies, it is categorically forbidden to send any kind of ship or plane whatever in the direction of Hokkaido."[191] For its part, Washington saw no reason why Stalin should be allowed more say in the fate of Japan than Truman had in Eastern Europe under Soviet occupation. Even allies like Britain were effectively excluded from the process of occupying Japan.[192] These differences between Washington and Moscow were to come to a head when the foreign ministers of Britain, the United States, and the USSR met in London that September.

Stalin's position prior to the conference was undoubtedly reinforced by surreptitious receipt on 7 September of yet another memorandum purloined from the Foreign Office: a record of Foreign Secretary Ernest Bevin's views. Here the veteran of trades union clashes with British communists and staunch opponent within the cabinet of extensive wartime aid to Russia said that the previous government had made too many concessions to Moscow and that these had led to the division of Europe into spheres of influence, which the Labour government opposed. Bevin wished to proceed with the bases of a Western bloc, but not officially or in any haste. Bevin felt that Eden, who poorly understood economics, had underestimated what an understanding of economies and social democracy could do for the future of Europe.[193] Britain was thus ready and waiting for what became the Marshall Plan at least two years before Marshall or anyone else in Washington had heard of it. They were therefore more than prepared to assist in conception and aid delivery when eventually the waters broke.

STALIN AND MOLOTOV FALL OUT

Molotov represented the USSR at the Council of Foreign Ministers in London, but he was on a tight leash. Milovan Djilas contrasts him with Stalin: "With Molotov not only his thoughts but also the process of their generation was impenetrable. Similarly his mentality remained sealed and inscrutable. Stalin, however, was of a lively, almost restless temperament."[194] Molotov had differed with Stalin during the 1920s, insisting on the importance of the expanding the revolution worldwide.[195] Yet as Stalin consolidated his power among equals Molotov became the loyal, indispensable, though never unquestioning, adjutant. In 1930 he was put in as Chairman of the Council of People's Commissars. In 1939 he took over from rival Litvinov whom he hated. "Molotov doesn't know how to charm foreigners," commented Alexandra Kollontai, ambassador to Sweden, "as the clever Litvinov did."[196]

Molotov did, however, represent a safe pair of hands, staying in his office into the early hours of the morning—with his staff—until the signal came that Stalin had retired for the night, which often meant he did not himself sleep until 4:00 a.m. The difference was made up in catnapping. He used to tell the head of his own bodyguard: "Wake me up in fifteen minutes," and he was asleep as soon as his head hit the pillow.[197] His office as chairman and, after 1941, deputy chairman, was on the same floor of the Kremlin government house building as Stalin's, at the end of another wing.[198] His other office, from May 1939 until April 1949, was at Kuznetsky Most, the Narkomindel (which from 1946 became the Minindel). It was effectively "on wheels" to and from the Kremlin as occasion demanded. Among his many subordinates Molotov used to be known as "the boss"; Stalin, "the big boss."[199]

Generally Molotov stood proudly in Stalin's all-encompassing shadow. He was more moderate, though extremely tough, highly efficient, slow, plodding, dull, unrelenting, always in control. Being Georgian and of a more mercurial temperament, Stalin, however, had great difficulty in containing the darker side of his own emotions and not infrequently fell victim to a terrifying paranoia that resulted in the deaths of intimates and the imprisonment of the wives of immediate subordinates, let alone the millions of wretches rounded up in early morning raids and shot or starved to death in labor camps at the hands of the NKVD.

Throughout, Molotov was also undeniably loyal — unhesitatingly he went along with every death sentence Stalin proposed. Molotov protected his own, but to work for him was no privilege. He never obtained special treatment for subordinates. Duty was everything. The diplomatic traffic delivered, half a dozen diplomats who worked in his secretariat would have to sort out what was important or vital from what was not; then they annotated the documents with recommendations. This meant that Molotov saw only a small percentage of materials and these had been assessed for action. He would then correct the annotations and admonish his subordinates for every kind of mistake, real or imagined.[200] It was, moreover, impermissible to fall ill. "He was verbally abusive. And if someone did not match up in his work Molotov replaced him without further ado. Moreover, former service was not taken at all into account."[201] As Erofeev recalls, in justified exasperation, everyone suffered from high blood pressure working in Molotov's office except Molotov.[202]

Differences with Stalin nevertheless arose over policy that sorely tested his temper because of Molotov's notorious stubbornness, long ago noted with exasperation by Lenin. "Molotov was far from being the obedient executor all the time," recalls Mikhail Smirtyukov, who worked under him at Sovnarkom from 1930.[203] Molotov had strongly pressed for an understanding with Germany in opposition to Litvinov. Even before the invasion Stalin showed his annoyance at Molotov by demoting his wife, Polina Zhemchuzhina, from membership of the Central Committee at the Eighteenth Party Conference (15–20 February 1941); Molotov then openly abstained from voting, in defiance of Stalin.[204]

Once the Nazi-Soviet pact was shown to be disastrous in June 1941, as Litvinov had predicted it would be, "albeit unofficially, Stalin put the blame for its conclusion on Molotov."[205] Stalin's irritation showed with the evacuation of the government to Kuybishev in October 1941 entrusted to the more junior deputy chairman of Sovnarkom Nikolai Voznesenskii instead.[206] Molotov's status within the tight inner circle never fully recovered from his fundamental misjudgment in the foreign policy of the 1930s most probably because, rather than despite the fact that, Stalin had listened to him but bore the ultimate responsibility for these errors. What is remarkable, perhaps, given Molotov's evident limitations was Stalin's tolerance of him. Khrushchev has pointed out that "Molotov . . . displayed incredible stubbornness to the point of stupidity." And for Stalin this was a word of last resort in arguments with Molotov.[207]

The common portrayal of Molotov as invariably obedient is thus misleading, though the innocent view taken by a high US official in the spring of 1945—that "Uncle Joe is all right—a straight shooter. It's that double-crossing little Molotov who causes all the trouble"—was equally misleading.[208] Molotov later lashed out at the presumption that he had been merely Stalin's lapdog. "I more than any among you, above all you, comrade Khrushchev, sometimes argued with comrade Stalin and as a consequence of this faced great unpleasantness."[209] One core difference in emphasis with Stalin apparent in the mid-1920s over the USSR's internationalist revolutionary duty came to light again indirectly after the war. Whereas Molotov, self-consciously the old Bolshevik, spoke of "the Soviet Union," Stalin increasingly referred to "Russia."[210] And whereas Stalin was willing to take the occasional risk, assistant Smirtyukov noted that "Molotov always knew that in any matter limits existed beyond which even he should not go."[211] Foreigners generally expected Molotov to succeed Stalin. And as the war drew to a close Stalin had talked of retirement: "Let Vyacheslav [Molotov] do some work!" he declared.[212] "Age has taken its toll," Stalin, now merely sixty-five, confessed to the US ambassador.[213]

This was not surprising. Stalin had not had a holiday for nine years. Some time from mid-October 1945 he "became ill, seriously so and for a long time."[214] Rumors of illness leaked out. Yet handing over the reins was impossible. He became fearfully jealous when Molotov failed properly to consult him. Molotov recalls: "In my opinion the last years Stalin began to weaken . . . sclerosis comes to all with age to various degrees. . . . But in him it was noticeable."[215] Indeed, arteriosclerosis figured prominently in Stalin's postmortem. He now spent a number of months toward the end of each year secluded on the Black Sea, where self-imposed isolation relieved only by the occasional visitor and a mass of incoming intelligence information fed morose and, indeed, lethal suspicions. Here differences in temperament, reflected in a greater willingness on the part of Molotov to compromise with the West and a reluctance to expand Soviet territory too far, which had previously been forgiven when overlain with absolute loyalty, now appeared threatening to Stalin's ultimate authority.

When allied foreign ministers gathered in London in September 1945, common adversity that had held together this fragile wartime alliance against the onset of deep-seated mistrust was now a rapidly fading memory. Yet Truman hastened demobilization, a move he later conceded to have been premature.[216] The international situation remained fragile, and the domestic economy could not easily absorb the return of jobless GIs in the absence of burgeoning wartime production. "The people and Congress are so intent on demobilising and getting the boys home to the farm and to the country store and to the city barber shop that the question of what is to be done with him when he arrives has not been made too full an impression," complained Major General Fred Anderson at US Army headquarters.[217]

US dependence for the credibility of its power thus pivoted upon atomic bombs that had yet to be stockpiled. At Molotov's side, Troyanovsky noted a distinct cooling of the atmosphere.[218] For the first time an allied summit was to close without any decisions. Two critical factors were at work. First, Stalin believed Russia had to stand firm against the United States—not only had Washington challenged hegemony over Eastern Europe, it was now cutting Moscow completely out postwar Japan. Was not unilateral possession of the atomic bomb going to their heads? Second, Byrnes ineptly left everything to the full sessions, which were conducted morning and afternoon without allowing for quiet soundings and coordination in informal gatherings that could normally take place when meetings were restricted to half the day. Trouble thus could not be correctly anticipated and proved impossible to head off in private with minimal fuss.

At the beginning of the conference Molotov conceded to a request that France and China be admitted to the negotiations for peace treaties with the former Axis Powers, in this case Finland and the Balkans. Summing up the first week of talks in a telegram to Stalin on 19 September, Molotov mentioned the presence of the France and China, which were backing the Anglo-American position against Moscow. Carelessly overconfident, Molotov predicted a deal as the search for compromise gained pace. Through Vyshinsky, Stalin, encouraged if not incited by Beria, pointed out that according to the Potsdam agreements only the big three could negotiate the treaties of peace. Molotov confidently replied that because this was not "particularly important" and because Bevin and Byrnes were insistent, he had given way. There followed a brutal response on 21 September, dropping the familiar form of address (*ty*) and instructing Molotov in no uncertain terms to follow the decisions of the Potsdam conference. "While the Anglo-Saxon states—the United States and England—stood in opposition to the Soviet Union, no one raised the question of majorities or minorities. Now that, in violation of the decisions of the Berlin conference and in the face of your connivance, the Anglo-Saxons have succeeded in bringing in the Chinese and the French as well, Byrnes has found a way of raising the question of majorities and minorities."[219]

Molotov immediately fell into line. He still favored following through with a proposal from Byrnes concerning the demilitarization of Germany for a twenty- to thirty-year period, "without displaying any special interest." But Stalin again drew him up short. "Byrnes's proposal," he wrote, "has four objectives in mind: first, distract our attention from the Far East, where America is behaving like a latter-day friend of Japan's, and by that means creating the impression that all is well in the Far East; second, to obtain from the USSR formal agreement that the USA will play the same role in the affairs of Europe as the USSR, in order then, in a bloc with England, to take the fate of Europe into its hands; third, to devalue the alliances already concluded by the USSR with European states; fourth, to render pointless all future alliances of the USSR with Romania, Finland, and others."[220]

This rebuke affords a fascinating glimpse into Stalin's thinking. Whereas Litvinov always favored an overarching international security framework, Stalin's instincts were unilateralist. His priority was to create a Russian-dominated system of alliances in Eastern Europe justified by the danger of a German revival. A US proposal to forestall such a revival would undermine the core rationale for that system. It would make Soviet security dependent, albeit in part, on Washington. This mattered because Stalin's security priorities were not in effect directed at Germany at all, but aimed primarily at the United States. Stalin's position thereby matched the demands of the international communist movement in standing up to the leading capitalist Power. Moscow still harbored hopes for, rather than fears of, postwar Germany. Prior to the rise of Hitler, the German Communist Party (KPD) had been the largest in Europe outside Russia. At the outbreak of war, as already noted, even ex-Menshevik Maisky believed in the potential of revolution.

During the war, resident for Razvedupr in London Sklyarov claimed: "Above all our allies fear the entry of Russians into Germany, since this could, they believe, prompt communist revolutions throughout the countries of Europe."[221] Khrushchev also tells us that with the advent of peace, "initially Stalin along with the other leaders of the CPSU presupposed that a strong Communist Party would reemerge in Germany, that the entire working class would unite around it, and that it would take a fitting place in the construction of a new Germany."[222] Meeting German communist leaders on 4 June 1945 Stalin made clear that he expected them to work toward "an antifascist democratic Germany" in the form of a parliamentary democratic republic; that they should "not transpose the Soviet system to Germany"; thus all talk of socialism had to be put aside. At the same time, however, "the hegemony of the working class and its revolutionary party" had to be assured.[223]

It was the dashing of such hopes through the Marshall Plan that made Stalin more pessimistic about prospects in Europe. There was also more to the clash between Stalin and Molotov than policy. Behind the scenes, Soviet diplomat Erofeev learned, "Beria, who hated Molotov, began to play upon these disagreements."[224]

The US pursuit of predominance in the Far East in fact left Britain no happier than Russia. The difference was that, in desperate need of Washington to counterbalance Moscow, London knew it had no choice. Bevin wistfully noted in November 1945: "The United States have long held, with our support, to the Monroe Doctrine for the Western Hemisphere and there is no doubt now that, notwithstanding all the protestations, they are attempting to extend this principle financially and economically to the Far East to include China and Japan."[225] Similarly Bevin told Harriman that "the United States already had their 'Monroe' on the American continent and were extending it to the Pacific."[226] But, as we have already noted, the issue for Stalin amounted to more than merely Japan.

STALIN TIGHTENS THE SCREW

The reign of repression now gripping Poland made a mockery of the Yalta decision on free and unfettered elections. "You keep conducting a defensive policy," Stalin told Gomułka in mid-November. "You behave as if you were sitting in the dock." The time for appeasement was over. "You don't need to worry so much about the bloc disintegrating. If you are strong they are going to come to you." Weakness was relative. The fact that the PPR—as the communists called themselves—were a tiny minority should not worry Gomułka. "A membership of 200,000 is a force which can overturn a whole country if it is well organized, well managed and controlled, and if it has instructions as to what to say and how to say it." He advised: "Do not believe in divergences between the English and the Americans. They are closely connected to each other." As to rumors of a war with the USSR, "They are not capable of waging a war against us. Their armies have been disarmed by agitation for peace and will not raise their weapons against us." And as to the atomic bomb: "Not atomic bombs, but armies decide war." As to their aims: "First of all, they are trying to intimidate us and force us to yield in contentious issues concerning Japan, the Balkans, and reparations. Secondly, to push us away from our allies—Poland, Romania, Yugoslavia, and Bulgaria. I asked them directly when they were starting a war against us. And they said '*Chto vyi? Chto vyi?*' [What on earth do you mean?]. Whether in thirty years or so they want to have another war is another issue. This would make them great profits, especially America, which is overseas and couldn't care less about the effects of a war. Their policy of sparing Germany testifies to that. He who spares the aggressor wants another war."[227]

The West had no grounds for complacency. What followed only reinforced the conviction that in this Britain was correct. An important indicator was the suggestion that the United States continue intelligence cooperation "in view of the disturbed conditions of the world and the necessity of keeping informed of the technical developments and possible hostile intentions of foreign nations," a proposal to which Truman responded positively.[228] At the theater on 21 November 1945 Harriman encountered Litvinov, who told him "that he was disturbed by the international situation, that neither side knew how to behave towards the other, and that this was the underlying reason for the breakdown of the London Conference and the subsequent difficulties." Litvinov was not to be palmed off with the comment that time would heal the wounds. "He replied that in the meantime, however, other issues were developing. I suggested that it might clear the atmosphere if we came to an understanding about Japan. He replied that other issues would then confront us." When asked whether he was deeply pessimistic, he responded, "Frankly, between us, yes." But, as before, "crocodile" Harriman—never notably perceptive about human nature—was unfortunately still inclined to discount the warnings on the grounds that Litvinov was personally out of sorts, "obviously antagonistic to Molotov, and his advice has evidently been disregarded by the Soviet Government."[229]

LITVINOV PROPOSES CONTAINMENT

With ever greater pessimism Litvinov lobbied nevertheless for a settlement. Just as in 1944 he had pressed for a division of spheres of influence with Britain, so now he argued the same with the United States. "The strategic appetite of the United States, encompassing the entire Atlantic and almost all the Pacific oceans, West Africa and the countries of the Near East, makes possible at the appropriate moment an approach to the American Government with the offer of 'revealing one's cards.'" Nothing, however, came of this suggestion, even had Molotov wished to risk Stalin's wrath once more on behalf of a longstanding rival.[230] On 22 February 1946, Kennan, by now utterly exasperated and enervated, sent a long telegram to Washington that outlined his solution to the Soviet problem and in so doing echoed that of Litvinov. He differed, however, in having resolved that Marxism in Russia was merely a "fig leaf," a "guise" that overlay "the steady advance of uneasy Russian nationalism," whereas Litvinov saw ideology as a force in and of itself. Yet both diagnoses led to the same conclusions. Highlighting an "instinctive Russian sense of insecurity," Kennan emphasized, that "they have learned to seek security only in patient but deadly struggle for total destruction of rival power, never in compacts and compromises with it." This was "a political force committed fanatically to the belief that with [the] US there can be no permanent modus vivendi, that it is desirable and necessary that the internal harmony of our society be disrupted, our traditional way of life be destroyed, the international authority of our state be broken, if Soviet power is to be secure." The answer was to resist: "Impervious to [the] logic of reason," it was "highly sensitive to [the] logic of force. For this reason it can easily withdraw—and usually does—when strong resistance is encountered at any point." He concluded, "If the adversary has sufficient force and makes clear his readiness to use it, he rarely has to do so."[231]

Despite their differences, it is no accident that the strategy advocated by Kennan was identical to Litvinov's: containment of burgeoning Soviet power. In February the usually cautious Molotov boasted publicly, "It is now impossible to resolve the serious questions of international relations without the participation of the Soviet Union or without listening to the voice of our motherland."[232] The problem was that in alienating the Western Powers to the point where they were coalescing against the USSR, Stalin's behavior would result in Moscow being cut out of any say in the settlement of issues within an exclusively Western sphere of influence. And as if to underline Kennan's worrying message, Stalin, who had raised control of the Dardanelles at Yalta and made demands for territorial concessions on Turkey in June 1945, once again turned up the heat on Ankara. Moreover, when incoming US ambassador Bedell Smith visited the Kremlin on 4 April 1946 he asked, in part with reference to Turkey, how much further Stalin intended to go. Looking the ambassador directly in the eye, Stalin coolly and provocatively parried: "We're not going much further."[233]

This attitude of mind was precisely what drove Churchill, now in opposition, to speak out at the hitherto little-known Westminster College in Fulton, Missouri—Truman's bailiwick—on 5 March. Here he repeated in public that an iron curtain had been drawn across Europe. "I do not believe that Soviet

Russia desires war," he intoned, also echoing Litvinov. "What they desire is the fruits of war and the indefinite expansion of their power and doctrines."[234] The reaction from the Kremlin was forceful; as Stalin freely confessed, "crude." But there was no danger of war, he insisted. "The aim was to intimidate us."[235]

In March 1946 London and Washington finally cemented intelligence cooperation with the UK-USA agreement which updated its predecessor, BRUSA, concluded in 1943.[236] Kennan's long telegram relaunched his idling career. It arrived just as the White House had to make sense of continued failure to redress the relationship with Moscow along American lines. Clark Clifford drew it to Truman's attention. Before long Kennan was recalled to Washington; though it was not until 5 May 1947 that General Marshall made him the first director of policy planning in the State Department, a post that handed him the construction of strategy and tactics in US foreign and intelligence policies against the expansion of Soviet power and communist power in general. He returned from Russia "disgusted with our defeatism and hysteria, in the face of the Soviet political onslaught: disgusted with the attitude of 'collaboration with Russia is impossible; therefore there must be a war.' I was conscious of the weakness of the Russian position, of the slenderness of the means with which they operated, of the ease with which they could be held and pushed back."[237]

Meanwhile, ignorant of the shift that Kennan's arrival in Washington signified and despairing lest no one important was listening, Litvinov raised the risk to his own life and that of his family by briefing others, including Kennan's counterpart at the British embassy, Frank Roberts, in the deputy commissar's office. The briefing was presumably intercepted by Beria and the transcript read by Stalin and Molotov, as was the case with Litvinov's warnings to the US journalist Hottelet on 18 June.[238]

Although no Russianist, the diminutive but quick-minded Roberts—"the wicked wizard"—needed no prodding on Litvinov's part; but, just in case he did, Litvinov spelled out matters with characteristic bluntness. If concessions were granted in reaction to Moscow's entreaties, Litvinov emphasized, it "would lead to the West being faced, after a more or less short time with the next series of demands."[239] When asked whether he meant to compare the USSR with Nazi Germany, Litvinov said, "Hitler probably felt sincerely that his demands were justified that he was entitled to Lebensraum. Hitler was probably genuinely convinced that his actions were preventive and forced on him by external circumstances."[240]

This came as something of a shock. Bevin might, in a moment of peevishness, liken Moscow's behavior to that of the Nazis, but for Litvinov to do so was truly astonishing. Roberts noted that "Litvinov himself was less outspoken than his wife, but he has consistently taken the line that a fundamental decision had been taken in the Kremlin which precluded the development of friendly relations on the basis of our joint war effort, and that this decision made increasing suspicion and friction inevitable. When I have suggested to him that the Soviet rulers in the Kremlin could not want war, Litvinov has agreed but has usually added: 'Neither did Hitler, but events became too strong for those who should control them, if they have set a wrong course.'"[241]

At home Litvinov paced the house in frustration with little to do, knowing it to be bugged, muttering, "You have got to bully the bully."[242] And he left no doubt whom he meant by the bully, though in conversation with foreigners he was very careful never to mention Stalin's name, only Molotov's; the more perceptive understood what he meant, however. Nevertheless, "Mrs. Litvinov herself talks to us quite openly about the possibility of their being sent to Siberia," Roberts wrote.[243] Anything in writing that could incriminate them in Stalin's eyes had to be destroyed. "Never mention to anyone," Ivy had written to the Meyers in mid-November 1943, "but I have left behind a document in ms. which might one day (in about 10 yrs is my guess) be of the greatest interest."[244] In January 1946 she wrote to Freeman asking him to destroy the memoir that by then lay in the vaults of a New York bank. "I cannot live in peace till I know it no longer exists," she wrote, adding, "These last two years have been full of struggle and anxiety."[245] Freeman consigned it to the furnace in the basement of the building.

To Hottelet in June a resigned and fatalistic Litvinov suggested that relations between East and West had deteriorated beyond the point of recovery. The root cause was the ideological conception prevailing in Moscow that conflict between capitalism and communism was inevitable. Peaceful coexistence no longer seemed practicable. Asked why the existing leadership should cling to the acquisition of natural frontiers to ensure security, Litvinov said that Russia had returned to an outmoded concept of geopolitics to assure their security through territorial expansion and they had done so "because they are conservative in their thinking and still follow old lines." And he was pessimistic whether a younger generation would make any difference given that they would be indoctrinated as was the old. Unfavorable comparisons with Hitler's search for Lebensraum were again made, as with Roberts, and he did not see any chance of changing a totalitarian state from within.[246] When the subject of Germany arose in conversation with Hottelet, Litvinov expressed the view that each side wanted Germany as a whole. Thus it would be broken in two. It remained the greatest problem outstanding between East and West. Molotov's comments later left no doubt where he stood. "Litvinov was completely hostile to us . . .

we received a transcript of the conversation by the usual means. . . . A complete betrayal."[247] For his outspokenness Litvinov merely lost his job and not his life or his freedom.

In London, by April 1946 spy Burgess was assistant private secretary to the Minister of State at the Foreign Office, Hector McNeill, with access to everything Moscow needed. McNeill was a clever and tough-minded thirty-six-year-old Scot, but he was also a lazy man who gave Burgess free run of his office and had him draft his papers.[248] By no means all Stalin's questions were answered, however. The key question was whether the US quest for predominance would result in an early collision with Britain or whether, ever mindful of reduced resources, Britain would seek to harness the United States to its own advantage and therefore abrogate understandings already made with Russia.

The response in Moscow to rising hostility from Washington was twofold. When the Americans showed every sign of resolute resistance to Soviet encroachment in areas marginal to Russian security—Turkey, Manchuria, Denmark, and Iran—Stalin had taken a step back. With respect to Iran his reasoning is available and of great interest. The withdrawal of troops was completed on 9 May 1946, a move that prompted complaint from the head of the so-called democratic party of Azerbaijan (northern Iran). Stalin did not think highly of foreign communists unable to achieve what the Bolsheviks had achieved. But he generously outlined his reasoning: "We cannot leave them any longer in Iran mainly because the presence of Soviet forces in Iran has undermined the bases of our liberation policy in Europe and Asia. The English and the Americans have told us that if Soviet forces remain in Iran, then why should English forces not remain in Egypt, Syria, Indonesia, Greece; and American forces as well—in China, Iceland, Denmark." Nevertheless in rebuke he saw fit to add: "While Soviet forces were in Iran, you had the chance of furthering the struggle in Azerbaijan and of organizing a broad democratic movement with far-reaching demands. But our forces had to leave Iran."[249]

On crucial issues, however, the dominant line was to offer stubborn resistance to US solutions, notably to the German problem, on equitable terms. Thus, when allied foreign ministers met, Stalin seemed more intent on confrontation rather compromise. Twice, on 30 April and 2 May, he reprimanded Molotov for not exposing US expansionism in spreading military bases around the globe.[250] Molotov duly obliged on 5 May.[251] "Across the globe," Molotov argued, "there is not one corner that has not attracted the gaze of the United States. The USA is organizing its air bases everywhere: in Iceland, Greece, Italy, Turkey, China, Indonesia, and other places; there are a great number of naval and air bases in the Pacific Ocean. Up to now the USA has maintained its forces in Iceland in spite of protests from the Iceland government, and also in China."[252]

At home, Stalin simultaneously cracked down on the limited degree of cultural and literary pluralism unleashed in time of war. The so-called Zhdanovshchina was inaugurated at a meeting on 18 August 1946, to which representatives of the creative intelligentsia were summoned.[253] And in a parting gesture of indifference to Western opinion, on 24 August Litvinov was finally dismissed from the Minindel. The last time he had been sacked was a matter of months before the Nazi-Soviet pact. Stalin's action was thus resonant with symbolism. It indicated that he was now dispensing with even the appearance of acting in concert with the democracies. Anti-American polemics were discharged with virulence from the pages of a press controlled absolutely by party and state, even while a noticeable lightening of attacks on Britain indicated that Stalin believed he could encourage a measure of Western disunity. But, contrary to nonsense spread by Mikoyan and reiterated by Valentin Berezhkov, Litvinov was never murdered. Indeed, Maxim—no sentimentalist—told his daughter that Stalin was holding him in reserve in the event of the need to heal relations with the West.[254] Ivy recalled that he "was still going to the Kremlin every day for dinner and to mix with former colleagues." And in the last months of his life he had "round-the-clock nurses, weekly consultations by the first [best] heart specialists in the country . . . anti-biotics . . . sedatives . . . at last the oxygen tent."[255]

Struggling to meet popular demand for greater welfare, Britain faced humiliating conditions for a loan from Congress, mediated by the sympathetic figure of Acheson—convinced by Truman of the need to stay in government. Meanwhile, as the Labour backbenches in Britain reacted to worsening East-West relations by sympathizing with Moscow, Stalin saw an opportunity to drive a wedge between London and Washington. He attributed any attempt at rapprochement to weakness. On 4 September Andrei Zhdanov—now overseeing relations with fraternal parties—briefed Dimitrov, former head of the defunct Comintern. Stalin thought "that a new war in the immediate future is out of the question. He is," Zhdanov assured Dimitrov:

> completely calm about the way things are developing. If in our analysis of the present situation we base our judgement *not on form* but *on the content of what is going on,* we can say with confidence that from our point of view *everything is in order.* All the noise made by the Anglo-Ameri[cans] and the threats of a new war are nothing but blackmail. They want to discredit the Soviet Union in the eyes of their workers. But this is already evidence that our influence in their countries is strong enough. The contradictions between England and America are still to be felt. The social conflicts in America are increasingly unfolding. The Labourites in England have promised the English workers so much concerning socialism that it is hard for them now to

step back. They will soon have conflicts not only with their bourgeoisie, but also with the American imperialists. It was not by chance that [Labour Party chairman Harold] *Laski* came to us with his delegation. All the time he was justifying himself and the Labour Party and reported what they had done. He declared that they would not give in to the imperialists. They will follow their own parliamentary path to socialism. Stal[in] told him: We consider the Soviet way to be a better one, but if you think that the parliamentary way is more suitable for England, we will not object to that. It is obvious that Laski was trying to find out whether Moscow would conduct a policy of "societiz-ing" [socializing] England. . . . It was also clear that the Labourites wanted to prepare the ground for the moment when, should they be in a tight spot, they would have some support from the Sov[iet] Union.[256]

In conducting a policy of expansion predicated on a degree of risk carefully calibrated, Stalin was inadvertently hastening the very outcome he had always dreaded: the emergence of the United States as a formidable force to reckon with that would challenge Russia for predominance. To gird itself for the con-frontation ahead, Washington had to mobilize public opinion along ideologi-cal lines according to the values, both capitalist and democratic, that had long inspired the Republic. Here Kennan, for one, was soon at variance with the struggle under way. From being a conflict over the balance of Europe, the Cold War now also became preeminently a clash of values. And before long the two had become so interwoven as to make any degree of separation invisible to the casual onlooker.

3

3

COMINFORMITY

The entire question is one of the balance of power. If you are in the right condition, attack. If not, do not take to the field. We do not go into battle when our enemy wishes, but when it is in our interests.

—*Stalin*

It has been assumed by some that because Trotsky berated Stalin for betraying the revolution and that because Stalin butchered so many revolutionaries, he had no commitment to the Leninist heritage. Yet Trotsky himself expressed surprise and, indeed, satisfaction in 1940 that, in occupying territories obtained through the Nazi-Soviet pact, Stalin eviscerated the old order and installed the new on the Soviet model:

> In the regions which must become a component of the USSR, the Moscow government will take measures to expropriate the big property owners and to nationalize the means of production. Such action is more likely not because the bureaucracy is true to the socialist program, but because it does not wish to and is unable to share power and the privileges connected with the old ruling classes of the occupied regions. Here an analogy presents itself. The first Bonaparte brought the revolution to a halt with the aid of military dictatorship. However, when French forces invaded Poland, Napoleon signed a decree: "Serfdom is abolished." This action was not dictated by Napoleon's sympathy for the peasants, but by the fact that the Bonapartist dictatorship rests not on private but on state property. The Red Army's invasion of Poland must virtually bring with it the liquidation of capitalist private property, in order thereby to bring the regime of the occupied territories into line with the regime in the USSR.[1]

This assessment would apply equally to Central or Eastern Europe under Soviet occupation from 1945. In this sense Stalin's own preferences are irrelevant: he was as driven as Napoleon by forces much greater than his own. If one instead concedes Stalin's preferences to have been Bolshevik, then he and Trotsky differed rather more over means than ends.

Stalin outlined his position regarding revolution abroad in 1925. He never foreswore international revolution, but he certainly doubted the ability of others to accomplish it alone. Soviet military assistance was essential:

> Linked to the fact that the preconditions for war are growing and war could certainly come if not tomorrow or the day after tomorrow but after some years, it is an inevitable concomitant that war cannot but exacerbate a domestic, revolutionary crisis; in connection to which we could not but face the question of our involvement in these affairs. I suggest that the strength of the revolutionary movement in the West is great; it could lead to the fact that somewhere the bourgeoisie are removed, but they are unlikely to be able to hold their ground without our help. . . . This does not mean that we are under any obligation to take direct action against anyone. That is not the case. . . . Should war break out we, of course, would enter into it last, at the very last, in order to throw our weight on the scales, a weight that could tip the scales.[2]

Whereas for other Soviet leaders, notably Lenin and Trotsky, the revolution could succeed elsewhere by its own efforts, for Stalin the exertion of external military power was vital. The acquisition of more than 11 million men in uniform as a by-product of beating the Germans thereby put on the agenda the prospect of aiding others to revolution in a manner unthinkable prior to 1939. Whether to intervene was, of course, a matter of judgment as to the prevailing balance of power and how the West was likely to react. Given Western sensitivities, in the case of Germany and the lands between, it was deemed wise to "mask" the process of domination. Around the summer of 1944 Leningrad Party secretary Andrei Zhdanov, a Stalin favorite, noted that the USSR's neighbors — Austria, Hungary and Germany — would likely as not make "a peaceful transition to socialism." In the spring of 1945 he explained to Finnish Party leaders that "certain commanding positions" had to be taken, the state apparatus had to be penetrated, and its orientation adjusted.[3]

Thus the entire process of absorbing Eastern Europe within the Soviet sphere had been orchestrated to lull Western public opinion into believing that a spirit of compromise had taken hold: between Soviet security, the ambitions of local communist movements, and the demands of bourgeois as well as social democratic parties.[4] Stalin himself recognized that "during the first three to four years after the war in Hungary, Czechoslovakia, and Poland nationalist sentiment will predominate."[5] A degree of national autonomy had therefore initially been sanctioned, varying from country to country, that allowed local rulers to determine how far, how fast, and in what form communist practices were introduced. Hungary even had free parliamentary elections on 4 November 1945 until, that is, the communists lost to the Smallholders' Party.

The narrow margin of tolerance enabled Moscow to embed what were largely alien elements into national soil. This process would take time. Stalin was therefore initially unconcerned that the East European Parties rejected the Soviet model. The Red Army's presence and the weakness of the opposition sufficed: "The advantage of the Soviet form is that it solves the problems quickly—by shedding blood; but you can do without it because the capitalists in your country surrendered immediately. In other words, you were lucky, and we are responsible for your luck, as we readily admit."[6] By the time this was said, however, relative autonomy had gone, policies rammed into reverse, and Soviet control rigidly enforced when national resistance appeared.

Molotov and Beria had said that the coalition governments in Eastern Europe would not last long.[7] Later Molotov recalled their caution. "For this reason it was people's democracy and not dictatorship of the proletariat; what was needed took transitional form." But it was nonetheless "in essence" a "tough line" leading to the "construction of socialism in these countries."[8] Stalin's advice to the Yugoslav communists was in this respect instructive:

It is a general rule that if you cannot attack, defend yourself, gather your strength, and then attack. In relation to bourgeois politicians one has to be cautious. They, bourgeois politicians, are quick to take offense and are vengeful. You need to keep your feelings to yourself; if sentiment takes over, you will lose. In his day Lenin could not conceive of the correlation of forces that we have obtained in this war. Lenin reckoned that everyone would attack us; and the best that could happen would be if some distant country, America, for example, were neutral. And now it has turned out that one group of the bourgeoisie moved against us, and another—with us. In the past Lenin did not think it possible to ally with one wing of the bourgeoisie and fight with the other. We succeeded in doing this; we are ruled not by sentiment but by common sense, analysis, calculation.[9]

Given the tentative hold the Polish Communist Party—now called the United Workers' and Peasants' Party—had on the sentiments of the population, only rigged elections and the use of terror could ensure that Moscow's friends remained in power. On 19 January 1947 the legislative elections were won overwhelmingly by the peasant party, Polskie Stronnictwo Ludowe, but the result was a crushing victory for the communists and their allies.[10] Thus a

memorandum of April 1948 from the foreign policy department of the Soviet
Central Committee rightly accused the nationalist Gomułka of underestimat-
ing "the decisive role of the Soviet Union and the Soviet army in guaranteeing
favorable preconditions for the victory of the forces of Polish democracy over
reaction and the strengthening of the democratic system in Poland."[11]

TROUBLE IN GREECE

Stalin said in May 1946, "We do not intend to attack England and America;
they would not take the risk. No war is possible for at the very least twenty
years."[12] He thus ratcheted up the tension to force the other side to back down
through territorial demands to Turkey; claims to Norwegian soil (Bear Island
and Spitsbergen); occupation of Danish Bornholm; resistance to withdrawing
troops from Manchuria and northern Iran. All raised serious questions about
Soviet intentions. But Stalin also called a tactical retreat along many fronts
in March 1946 after Kennan's long telegram. One area in particular was a significant test of Stalin's respect for his adversaries. This was Greece, which had
clearly been designated a British sphere in the negotiations of October 1944.

Here Stalin moved with great caution. The idea of a communist Greece
was inherently desirable. The question was whether it was attainable without
directly confronting Britain. The latter had hoped the return to Athens in May
1945 of Party General Secretary Nikos Zachariadis from internment in Dachau
would consolidate a moderate line.[13] Zachariadis, however, defended the December revolt, though acknowledging an opportunity had been lost to negotiate with Churchill. He also spoke of Greece balancing between the north
(Russia) and the south (Britain).[14] But comment in the Soviet press indicated
Moscow's support against British "occupation" of the country.[15] And asked in an
interview with the *Manchester Guardian* on 27 August whether Britain should
leave Greece, Zachariadis replied: "When you go there will be civil war for two
months. Then everything will be all right."[16]

On 31 March 1946 the KKE boycotted the parliamentary elections. Moscow believed this an error of judgment. When the Greek comrades had asked
whether they should "prepare for an armed uprising," they were told instead to
"organize their self-defense, combined with the political mobilization of the
pop[ular] masses."[17] Had they participated, Molotov maintained, it "would have
permitted the KKE to evaluate the situation continuously and, depending upon
developments, to throw its weight sometimes into legal forms of mass struggle,
and other times into armed struggle."[18] This much will have been made clear
to Zachariadis on 2 April 1946 when he visited Dimitrov in Sofia, Bulgaria.[19]

Later Stalin "stressed the fact that the Greek Communists earlier made an error with the boycott of the parliamentary elections." "Boycotting makes sense when it brings about the failure of elections," he advised. "Otherwise, a boycott is a foolish thing."[20]

Josip Broz ("Tito"), who had liberated most of Yugoslavia independently of Moscow and was soon to collide headlong, was an unusual, oddly feminine but charismatic figure. In contrast to Russia, and this is where Moscow and Belgrade came to blows, Tito supported the boycott and promised comprehensive moral and material support.[21] Having rejected the ballot, the KKE now embarked on armed struggle, but of independent bands of partisans rather than regular military detachments. Throughout late summer the leadership bid for material support from both Yugoslavia and Bulgaria, trying and failing to obtain permission to argue their case in Moscow. At the end of August Zachariadis told Dimitrov that civil war was a fact in Thessaly, Macedonia, and Thrace; to a lesser extent also in the Peloponnese. In a transparent attempt to deceive, Zachariadis argued, somewhat implausibly, no doubt to appeal to the cautious Stalin, that the fighting under way was not for military victory but to provoke international opinion into forcing a British withdrawal, opening the path to power.[22] A fortnight later, on 12 September, Iannis Ioannidis, now KKE permanent representative in Belgrade, arrived in Sofia with a memorandum for fraternal parties calling for extensive aid, including munitions.[23]

Belgrade was always more responsive to Greek communists than Sofia. Dimitrov balanced precariously between Moscow and Belgrade. On 14 October Macedonian partisan units of the Yugoslav army were transferred to the so-called Democratic Army of Greece, which consolidated communist ranks into a single entity on 27 December with its own general staff under Markos Vafeiadis. Thereafter KKE demands for aid were inexhaustible. Bulgaria, however, persistently held back, initially on the plausible grounds that it was awaiting settlement of peace treaties with Britain and the United States. Thereafter, reflecting Stalin's view, Dimitrov was openly discouraging: the encroaching winter conditions and the international situation overall were not conducive to operations on a broad scale. A radiogram on 10 November from the KKE to Zhdanov thus went unanswered, as did a further message on 20 December calling for aid.[24] With some 20,000 under arms by January 1947, the KKE was not downhearted. "The Bulgarians themselves promise and later refuse," the KKE complained on 28 November.[25] They had nevertheless given generous financial support in dollars from Party reserves some two years before.[26] Zachariadis, as determined as ever, then visited Moscow to plead with Zhdanov on 22 May, requesting heavy artillery. He received a lecture on Soviet priorities.

"The big reserve" had to be retained for the future: "Not everybody realizes that one has to pick a moment to unleash all the forces of the USSR," Zhdanov said.[27] Moscow did, however, give $100,000 after Dimitrov subsequently interceded on behalf of the KKE.[28]

THE TRUMAN DOCTRINE

By February 1947 the White House had no illusions. "I went to Potsdam with the kindliest feeling toward Russia," Truman noted; "in a year and a half they cured me of it."[29] And a new crisis loomed. The pound sterling was collapsing. With troops on the line and financial support to Athens straining the Treasury, London insisted Washington shoulder the protection of the eastern Mediterranean. Little advance notice had been given, and Congress had to be brought alongside. Truman seized the initiative, issuing a melodramatic declaration elaborated by Joseph Jones (now in the Office of Public Affairs), Acheson, and Clark Clifford, a clever young and ambitious lawyer from Missouri.[30]

The Truman doctrine was thus proclaimed in "a panic move."[31] Addressing Congress on 12 March, Truman anathematized communism in general on the false assumption that it was entirely directed from the Kremlin as it had been before 1941.[32] Truman promised to contain its advance. Sustaining the case, the US ambassador to Greece outlined a domino theory: "What is going on in Greece now," Lincoln MacVeagh argued, "is the efforts of the successful revolution in the bordering countries to bring about a successful revolution in the next country. When that is successful in the next country, it is the doctrine of international communism to breed [sic] into the next country as it goes along. The same line has to be drawn, and Greece and Turkey are a strategic line. If they break that down, the whole Near East falls and they pick the lock of world dominion. . . . In our own interests the thing to do is to hold them before they get to a critical line."[33]

British diplomats dismissed all this as an instance of Truman's "sudden and self-contradictory flashes of 'inspiration.'"[34] In late March before the Senate Foreign Relations Committee, Acheson had to backtrack and denied this was "an ideological crusade."[35] He need not have bothered. The newly enunciated doctrine caused no alarm in Moscow, which was reading the British ambassador's dispatches. Zhdanov scoffed at the "embarrassment even among capitalist circles accustomed to anything."[36] "It's all over," a Red Army general boasted. "It is no longer possible to encircle Russia, far less extinguish it. It is too powerful! And for their part the capitalist states cannot prevent the rise of democratic forces in all countries."[37]

By now British and American intelligence were already active within the Russian zone of Germany: establishing the Red Army's order of battle, disrupting its activities and those of local communist administrations.[38] From 25 March to 30 July 1947 Stalin was "generally unwell," suffering uncomfortable bouts of "chronic dysentery" that cannot have improved his mood nor kept him on top of events as they unfolded.[39] Of immediate concern was the unaccustomed disarray evident in the world communist movement where initiatives were seized on the ground, and some to Stalin's acute discomfort. The resignation of communist ministers from the French coalition government on 4–5 May 1947 was prompted by their failure to persuade the rest of the coalition to halt the embarrassing war against the Vietminh in revolt against recolonization since 1946, and the attempt to stem pent-up demand for wage rises at home that was itself stimulated by the communist-dominated trades union movement, the CGT. Zhdanov, with a command of French and charged with management of foreign Communist parties, wrote to Thorez on 2 June 1947. Moscow, he noted, "is worried by recent political events in France as a result of which the French communists were heaved overboard from government."[40]

Zhdanov wanted to know what was going on. The PCF was not keeping Moscow informed. The Soviet leadership thus found it "difficult" to give "a clear response" to anxieties expressed by the "workers" of the USSR: "*We do not know how to respond since we ourselves do not understand what happened in France.*" "Many suppose," Zhdanov continued, "that French communists agreed their moves with the CC RCP (b). You yourselves know that this is untrue, that to the CC RCP (b) the steps you took came as a complete surprise."[41] On 13 May Christian Democratic Prime Minister of Italy Alcide de Gasperi, sensitive to American goodwill and mindful of the French example, dismissed his own cabinet coalition, thereby depriving the PCI of power. This occurred barely a week after Togliatti held talks with de Gasperi and drew the conclusion that the determined exclusion of the PCI from government was not on the cards.[42] Togliatti had expected a crisis on the prime minister's return from Washington in January. Because nothing happened, he concluded that de Gasperi wished to delay until the peace treaty had been signed so that blame could be shared.[43] The other basic assumption that turned out to be equally flawed was that "without us government is not possible."[44] This had become a mantra, reiterated by others in the leadership, who served in the government.[45] Reality now dawned that his calculations were badly wrong.

"This is the way it will be for at least twenty years," Togliatti confided to Giulio Cerreti; "any kind of participation in government is out of the question."[46] Resort to arms was ruled out, however: "We do not have the faintest possibility of making a revolution to liquidate de Gasperi. The Americans will not permit us to do so. We would risk ending up like Greece." "I fear that we have missed the bus," he added bitterly.[47] Togliatti was most anxious lest the Party overreact. He was concerned above all not to alienate "the middle strata" of Italy. "Let there be no doubt. We must base ourselves on the following points: the exclusion of any possibility of moving to violence; the maintenance, though in a different tone, of the duplicity of our political behavior." For those reluctant to foreswear violence, one had only to observe events in France, where the strikes and growing class struggle was alienating the population. The PCF had already lost 250,000 members.[48]

Pressure from Moscow, however, began to make itself felt. Barely a week after the PCI was ejected from office, Molotov advised Hungarian Party leader Mátyás Rákosi "to adopt the line of a stronger class struggle."[49] Communists behind the iron curtain became concerned that they too could be maneuvered out of governments in Eastern Europe. "Hungary will not be Greece," Rákosi assured one and all. "It will not be France either."[50] Within a week the prime minister representing the Smallholders' Party was overthrown in a communist coup. Now only Czechoslovakia remained a weak link in the chain of East European satellite states buffering Russia from the West.

THE MARSHALL PLAN

Proposals for a European recovery program brought matters to a head. Here the intersection between US commercial self-interest and West European needs became explicit. John Hickerson, director for European affairs at the State Department (1947–49) readily agreed that the Marshall Plan was needed for domestic economic reasons, "even if the Soviet Union had not existed." The existence of the USSR and Stalin's behavior aggravated a problem in its own right.[51] The precedent was the US loan to Britain, subjected to a fierce debate on Capitol Hill in March 1946. Credit would not be granted without British policy restructured. The US Treasury "stood for and . . . advocated, a definite international policy." That policy was "to restore world trade, to free it from the restrictions that isolate countries and from the discrimination that divide nations into conflicting economic blocs." Here the lesson learned from the Great Depression was that protectionism provoked war.[52] A logical corollary was to break down, where possible, existing empires that were closed trading blocs. And the largest was the British Empire, which operated on the basis of monetary inconvertibility throughout the war. If that system continued to exist,

Treasury Secretary Fred Vinson predicted, "Our position in world trade would be threatened."[53]

Vinson echoed strong sentiment in the Senate, which legally shared foreign policy making with the executive and sought to recover much that it had lost under Roosevelt in depression and war. The chamber was united against facilitating any revival of British dominance in world trade: "You say she [the British Empire] has a dominating position," the universally popular Senator Alben Barkley (Dem., Kentucky), later Vice President (1949–53), noted. "It is the very dominating position, it seems to me, that we are trying to get her out of." "So that we might have a chance to do some dominating in those regions ourselves," Barkley added.[54] Vinson readily agreed. The linkage between principles and self-interest was also made clear by Acheson: "We are interested not primarily in lending money to keep good relations with the British, but in an economic system which is the very basis of our life—the system of free, individual enterprise. We are interested tremendously in maintaining that way of life in all of the world which depends on it."[55] It was thus improbable that the Marshall Plan could be ratified on any other basis,

Unlike the Truman doctrine, the European Recovery Program (ERP) announced by Marshall on 5 June 1947 was a product of sustained thought. It emanated not from the White House but State, where from January the steady and independent hand of General Marshall predominated. "He gave a sense of purpose and direction," Bohlen recalled.[56] Everyone knew exactly where they stood and who was in charge. Furthermore, the respect in which Marshall was held clearly helped on the Hill. In late February Republican Arthur Vandenberg, Chairman of the Senate Foreign Relations Committee, and the columnist Lippmann had privately raised the idea of a dramatic initiative, including "the revival of some such schemes as Lend-Lease."[57]

Meeting Stalin for the first time on 18 April to impress upon him the urgency of resolving the German question and utterly unaware of Stalin's chronic discomfort, Marshall was taken aback by his cool indifference. "We may agree the next time," Stalin said with studied detachment, "or if not then, the time after that." The continued deterioration in economic conditions, Marshall calculated, could only work to Soviet advantage. On return he instructed Kennan to get to work on European recovery.[58] The failure of the UN Economic Committee for Europe to make any progress in the presence of a massive and obstructive Soviet delegation meant that another forum had to be created from which Russia could be excluded if required.[59] Kennan, who played a crucial role, had very soon after Yalta dismissed any chance of Soviet cooperation: "The idea that

Soviet representatives can be induced to sit down at a table with us and face the problem of relief in Europe as a technical international problem, divorced from national interests and from the struggle for political power, has no basis in past experience. It presumes a fundamental change in the motives and methods of Soviet foreign policy for which we have no evidence."[60] Indeed, in private officials drew attention "to Mr. Marshall's accompanying warning that any Government which manoeuvres to block the recovery of other countries cannot expect United States aid," the British embassy noted.[61] Western Europe was to take the initiative. Now more securely anchored close to US waters, France, nudged by Britain with Bevin to the fore, extended invitations on 19 June for a conference to discuss implementation of the American proposals.

Stalin was suspicious. Molotov nevertheless saw a possibility of obtaining aid through reducing "all the negative aspects . . . so that they did not encumber us with any kind of conditions."[62] That this might prove practicable was encouraged by economist Eugene Varga. It had nothing to do with altruism: the United States was destined for another great depression; the health of the economy requiring a higher level of exports, which could only be financed by dollar credit. "The decisive factor in the advancement of the Marshall plan was the USA's economic situation," Varga informed Molotov. It was a way of easing the forthcoming economic crisis that everyone was expecting. Nevertheless several issues remained of particular concern. One was the apparent intention to reunify Germany economically on a capitalist basis. Another was the possibility of the Americans insisting on opening the "iron curtain" as a precondition for aid. A third consideration was that were the USSR to refuse participation, the rest of Europe might be under pressure to form a bloc "under the hegemony of the USA."[63]

Confirmation was not hard to find. The *Wall Street Journal* had appeared with a leader on 5 June—the very day of Marshall's speech—predicting "The Coming "Recession." It argued, "The stock market has flown the warning flag for nearly a year. It is longer than that since economists of greater or less distinction began demonstrating with complicated charts that a post-war slump was inevitable and telling us what to do about it." The clarion call was followed a day later with the reminder that US exports made up nearly 10 percent of national income and "the top 10% that could mean the difference between prosperity and trouble." This was not least because "purchases by foreign customers are nearly five times the 1936–40 average, dollar-wise."[64] Published at a time when Marshall's proposals were discreetly canvassed, the editorial went on to explain that it was "this fear of the dollar shortage, as much as political considerations, that is sparking the gigantic foreign trade pump-priming program now being brewed in the State Department." It added: "The public arguments for this multi-billion dollar foreign aid program have been on a 'stop Communism' basis. But underlying these arguments is the economists' theory that the U.S. must keep its foreign trade booming to keep prosperity at home." "U.S. booms and depressions, the chartists note, can be measured by the rise and fall of the nation's overseas commerce."[65] Moreover, Kennan noted that European views of the aid were colored by the assumption that "we can't afford not to give it."[66]

STALIN OVERREACTS

Despite the gloomy prognosis offered by the *Journal*, the contrast between economic conditions in the United States and the USSR could not have been greater. Molotov was only too aware of his country's dire economic plight after a devastating war—with some 25 million dead: he was deputy chairman of the Council of Ministers with responsibility for the economy among other matters. Molotov therefore brought to the Politburo proposals for the Marshall Plan summit.[67] Moscow stayed silent for a full eleven days for good reason. The proposition had excited "great debate" within the leadership.[68] It was, moreover, a subject about which Molotov felt strongly. The arguments developed at the Minindel that he pressed upon Stalin were to a large extent his own inspiration.[69] On 21 June Molotov briefed the Politburo, which agreed to his attending the preliminary meeting in Paris.[70] Moscow was anxious to ensure that the East European satellites also be invited and called on them to ensure their presence.[71]

A meeting of the allied foreign ministers was held on 27 June. Two days later Stalin's worst prognosis was confirmed when British and French statements appeared to indicate that assistance would mean meddling in the internal economic affairs of other countries. This alone was as yet insufficient to prompt Moscow to withdraw. On 30 June, however, Molotov received intelligence via Vyshinsky from Maclean, first secretary at the British embassy in Washington, as well as from Burgess in London.[72] Bevin had told Under Secretary William Clayton that the plan proposed "is the quickest way to break down the iron curtain. My recent experience in France shows that Russia cannot hold its satellites against the attraction of fundamental help toward economic revival in Europe."[73]

Molotov was "indignant" to learn that he had been duped.[74] Vyshinsky informed him, "Any organization created to put the Marshall Plan into effect must stand outside the UN. The reason for this is that Germany is not a member of the United Nations." "England and the USA consider that Germany

still remains the key to the European economy. Therefore it is de facto one of
the bases of any plan for putting the continent back on its feet." Furthermore,
"England and America will oppose [German] payments to the Soviet Union of
reparations from current production."[75]

If this were not bad enough for Moscow, any hope that Anglo-American
squabbles would lead to a nasty divorce—a distant aspiration since 1944—
proved demonstrably unrealistic. "Both England and France find themselves in
very difficult circumstances and do not have in their hands any serious means
of overcoming their economic problems. Their only hope is the United States,
which demands of England and France the establishment of some kind of all-
European structure that will facilitate the interference of the United States in
both the economic and political affairs of European countries. Both Great Britain and, to some degree, France are counting on using this structure in their
own interests."[76] Stalin instructed Molotov to return home immediately. Russia's new allies were then expected to follow suit. All the signs now pointed to
the emergence of a Western bloc under US auspices with the Western zone of
Germany at its center.

Moreover Stalin now faced resistance from within his own camp. The satellite states looked to a bleak future without US aid. Eugen Loebl, a leading
Czech economist, recalls: "As far as the Marshall Plan is concerned, there were
two views in our Politburo and also in the Polish Politburo. At that time by
chance Mr. Minc (who was the economic dictator of Poland) was in Czechoslovakia, and he was all for the Marshall Plan being accepted." Loebl himself
"was asked by [Prime Minister and Communist Party Chairman Klement] Gottwald to work out an analysis of our future economic development; I advocated
close cooperation with the West and Gottwald was very, very much in favor of
that."[77] Only 24 hours after Warsaw assured the US ambassador that Poland
would participate, this position was entirely reversed.[78]

Stalin was thus certain to face a struggle to sustain a unanimous veto. On
4 July the Czech Social Democrats under Beneš in coalition with the communists decided to attend the conference implementing the Marshall Plan when it
formally opened on 12 July. On 5 July, however, Moscow informed Prague that
they would not attend. On 30 June Zhdanov had lambasted Finnish communist
leaders for being too moderate and insufficiently critical of partners in government. "From the Finnish Communist Party we expected offensive battles," he
argued.[79] By 7 July it was clear that Helsinki would reject the Anglo-French
invitation to attend the Paris conference. A phrase in the statement issued, however, left no one in any doubt but that this was under duress: "Finland's position as a state has not yet been established in the form of a permanent peace

treaty."[80] Moscow was now turning the screw. The contrast between Czech recalcitrance and Finnish acquiescence reinforced Stalin's determination to discipline Prague. Astonishment was expressed that the Czechs had decided to go ahead regardless. "You are objectively helping to isolate the Soviet Union, whether you want to or not," Stalin accused Gottwald and Foreign Minister Jan Masaryk at a meeting on 9–10 July. They were obliged to rescind their decision (unanimously made by all parties) despite the fact that industry was dependent upon the Western market. It had to be done that very day.[81]

COMINFORM

Planning a conference of Communist parties was the next step. Proposed by Belgrade in 1945, it was discussed once again in June 1946. Stalin asked Tito if he still thought a new Comintern—to exchange ideas and experiences— should be established. When he agreed, Stalin suggested that Tito take the initiative.[82] Subsequently Zhdanov took up the idea of resuscitating Comintern but Stalin decided to delay.[83] Now, however, the need was urgent. Stalin inveigled Gomułka into hosting a meeting in Poland for what purported to be a simple exchange of views and information: a ruse in order to avoid prompting suspicion that the intention was to recreate Comintern that ran on orders from Moscow. In mid-August 1947 the directives for the Soviet delegation had been drafted. The first item on the agenda (concealed from other participants) revealed its core purpose: "The task of democratic organizations in the struggle against attempts by American imperialism to enslave economically the countries of Europe ('Marshall Plan')." Another purpose that was bound to give rise to concern was the third item treating "relations between communist parties and the Soviet Union and the Soviet Communist Party," added to the fact that the meeting was to be "closed."[84]

When unsuspecting delegates arrived at the Silesian resort of Skłarska Poręba (until recently Schreiberschau), for the conference (22–26 September 1947) inaugurating a Communist Information Bureau (Cominform), they were surprised to find Moscow in control of security.[85] At the conference, held over the course of a week in the dining room of a small country inn, the Yugoslavs— Milovan Djilas and Edvard Kardelj—sat with the Russians, Zhdanov and Malenkov, whispering loudly among themselves and passing notes throughout the proceedings as East Europeans tend to do.[86] The conference was opened by Gomułka at 6:15 p.m. on 22 September. Taking advantage of his position as host and chairman, he brazenly lauded "the Polish peaceful road of social change." Gomułka casually commented, "Our party has, for a long time, renounced the

organization of collective farms," and he bluntly insisted that shortages in agriculture made "inevitable and even, in a certain sense, desirable the development, within certain conditions and limitations, of kulak properties in the
countryside."[87] Heresy was compounded by complete silence on the subject of
the hard-fought and costly Soviet victory against German occupation. At this
Kardelj, leading the bullish Yugoslav team, muttered to Zhdanov: "A 'Polish'
road to socialism—why, it was the Red Army that liberated them!"[88]

Poland was exceptionally privileged by Moscow. After the Red Army arrived,
it received extensive economic assistance including grain at a time when Ukrai-
nians were starving. Yet ordinary Poles had no idea, since this was censored.
After refusing the Marshall Plan, Poland also received $450 million in cred-
it.[89] Gomułka, however, was in a fighting mood and notoriously bad tempered.
Jakub Berman recalls that in private he "began to get agitated: Stalin had deceived him, he said; we would vote against the creation of the Information
Bureau."[90] Berman was horrified. He did his best to dissuade Gomułka and
ultimately succeeded.

The Yugoslav delegates, still ruinously intoxicated by the monopolization of
power obtained largely, though by no means entirely, through their own efforts,
were then encouraged by Moscow to voice in public their disdain of the PCF
and PCI for operating within the parliamentary framework. Kardelj was particularly fierce, calling for "a resolute course toward the total seizure of power."[91]
He attacked the Italians for saying "that they do not want what they call 'the
Greek situation' to be created in their own country." Kardelj, speaking for radical Belgrade, made the reckless suggestion that "the 'Greek situation' is at the
present time an incomparably better situation than what prevails in France or
Italy."[92] But what Belgrade did not know, but which became clear by the end of
the year, was that Stalin did not want another Greece on his doorstep. Berman
recalls that in attacking the French and the Italians Djilas was also "terribly
eager to oblige."[93] And Moscow made no attempt to restrain them—evidently
with an ulterior motive. In August Stalin had already voiced his displeasure at
moves by Belgrade and Sofia toward a Balkan federation. And when, after the
attack on the PCF in Poland, Thorez came to Moscow complaining to Stalin,
he found him supportive. Indeed, Stalin went further, openly disowning Yugoslavs who all too easily "engage in criticism on such matters."[94] It is striking that
when the Cominform committee was set up on 27 September, no Yugoslav was
selected for membership. By then few wished to speak to them. With his own
score to settle with Belgrade, Stalin no doubt intended that these high-handed
onslaughts encouraged by Moscow would win Yugoslavia few friends.

The attacks inflicted predictable damage on the prospects of nonruling Communist parties. A signal went out that the insurrectionist wing was now back in favor. Stalin had depressed the revolutionary accelerator. Yet he was not really interested in risking another Greece within the Western sphere of influence. He would thus soon have to squeeze the brakes. Sufficient chaos in the streets, on the docks, and in the factories was required to destabilize social peace and economic growth in Western Europe but without actually touching off open revolt that might play into the hands of those looking for an obvious reason to crush Moscow's fifth column and outlaw Communist parties, as Kennan wished to do.

Stalin repeated that he did not fear war. Moscow considered it neither "imminent nor near. The United States is not in a position to provoke one. It is conducting a cold war, of nerves, with the aim of 'blackmail.' The Soviet Union will not allow itself to be intimidated and will persist in its policy."[95] One Soviet diplomat said of the Americans in France: "in a few years they will be kicked out of here" (*ils seront fichus d'ici quelques années*).[96] Meanwhile Moscow carefully ensured that treaties of defense between the satellite states of Eastern Europe also included provision not merely against Germany but "against aggression from any state joining with it in a policy of aggression."[97] And Germany did not even exist, reconstituted, as an independent entity, let alone have any armed forces.

At the Politburo on 14 October the Minindel was nevertheless directed to ensure alliances were concluded between the various countries of Eastern Europe.[98] Stalin also boosted defense expenditure. Between 1945 and 1947 men in uniform were cut from 11 million to 3,929,000.[99] Direct military outlays dropped from 54.3 percent of the budget in 1945 to 24 percent in 1946 and then to 18 percent in 1947 as production shifted to meet civilian needs.[100] This shift was needed badly because of the fall in output, the growth of inflation, and the shortage of food supplies and raw materials for production. However, in November 1947 proposals were accepted to raise tank production, for example, for 1948 from 1,150 to 4,350; likewise artillery from 2,061,000 to 6,519,000 pieces.[101] Moreover, toward the end of 1948 five more parachute divisions and two air transport divisions were added.[102] This process was to continue. By 1950 the net weight of military expenditure in the national economy stood above 20 percent, excluding outlays on military-scientific research and experimentation.[103] The impact on the economy was predictably negative.

Stalin was gambling with high stakes. Certainly hopes of precipitating a breakdown in West European recovery seemed plausible, and not only from

Moscow, where economic conditions were appalling. To make up the vast losses in capital equipment and agricultural production, Moscow took reparations by rail from Central and Eastern Europe in massive amounts. In 1945 alone more than 400,000 wagons carried goods to the East, of which one-half went to the USSR, the rest servicing occupation forces scattered between Brest and Helmstedt.[104] Entire plants from over five and a half thousand enterprises—ranging from meat and milk production to aviation and artillery—were taken to the USSR from Germany, Poland, Austria, Hungary, Manchuria, and North Korea. In addition came a vast quantity of individual capital goods plus supplies of industrial raw materials.[105] But even the special shipments bleeding white the Russian zone of Germany were insufficient to stave off famine throughout the Soviet Union after a severe drought in 1946, not least because Stalin exported grain needed desperately at home to pay for machinery imports and more than 2.5 million tons went to appease political sentiment in Eastern Europe.[106]

Despite this Stalin was determined to concede nothing to Washington in return for assistance. Foreign policy and defense priorities far exceeded the needs of ordinary Russians. This forced Truman to act. Clayton advised, "The emergency needs of western Europe cannot be met without immediate action on the part of the United States. These countries, particularly Italy and France, are without adequate food and fuel supplies for the fall and early winter and have no dollars with which to buy them. They cannot, by their own efforts, survive the major crisis which is already upon them. . . . Totalitarian forces are engaged in a concerted effort to capitalize on the deteriorating situation and to overthrow democratic governments before American aid can be forthcoming."[107]

The Marshall Plan was thus vital to Western Europe and not merely economically. The bill went to Congress on 19 December 1947 during the worst winter in recent memory. Waves of strikes organized by Communist parties engulfed the region. But the bill had also to be sold in terms of US economic self-interest. US exports to Europe had dropped below the figure for 1946 or before the war. Marshall argued that, if the plan were not adopted, "we would find the European situation—certainly from our point of view—in a process of disintegration, which would quickly permit development of the police-state regime. We ourselves would be confronted across the Atlantic with, if not a trade barrier, certainly with a great detriment to our ordinary business, or commerce and trade."[108] Harriman echoed these sentiments: "I am not suggesting that the United States could not endure the loss of European markets. However, our output of many industrial and agricultural products and that of other countries has been developed on the basis of European participation in international multilateral trade. The decline of Europe would require far-reaching adjustments of agricultural and industrial production and distribution in this country and in other areas."[109] Similarly Secretary of Agriculture Clinton Anderson pointed out that since 1900, 60–75 percent of food exports had gone to Western Europe.[110] Thus the ability of the Europeans to pay in dollars was vital.

The role of the plan and its antecedents in forestalling depression was tacitly underlined on the eve of completion early in 1950 when Acheson, now Secretary of State, warned: "United States exports, including the key commodities on which our most efficient agriculture and manufacturing industries are heavily dependent, will be sharply reduced, with serious repercussions on our domestic economy."[111] Indeed, between 1946 and 1948 the US export surplus stood at $25 billion, paid almost entirely from US government grants and loans.[112] This highlights the fact that Washington was already supplying large amounts of foreign aid before the plan was announced, mainly but not wholly in the form of emergency relief—not merely in Europe, but China, the Philippines, Turkey, Latin America, and so on. In the first nine months of operation the ERP amounted to only one-third of all aid for 1948; not until the last quarter, in supplanting previous aid programs, did it reach two-thirds of the total ($5.5 billion). Of ERP aid, about one-third was made up of grants and two-thirds in credits. In 1948 the total of loans issued amounted to some $1,670 million, of which about $1,000 million went to ERP countries. In return, recipients had to agree to balance budgets, sustain acceptable rates of exchange, stabilize the currency, reduce barriers to trade, prevent the growth of cartels, and give US access to strategic raw materials on terms Washington deemed reasonable.[113] These concessions were clearly advantageous to US companies in expanding foreign trade and investment. US economic needs dovetailed with the reinforcement of European markets to contain communist power. The Plan thus represented enlightened self-interest on a large scale for the world's bastion of capitalism. Kennan, however, also insisted that the United States "manipulate our aid program dexterously for political purposes."[114]

Khrushchev was impressed: "The entire might of the USA was mobilized to sustaining the ravaged countries of Europe from mass revolt. The USA put into play its capital, tried to feed the hungry and to keep them in check, in order to secure the mass of the people and sustain the local economy on the basis of capitalism. This is what took place . . . it did not turn out as we had supposed. Capitalism showed its vitality and put a stop to what had been going on. We were disappointed."[115] That the Marshall Plan did not entirely meet the demands of US business either was apparent from commentary in the *Wall Street Journal*. Head of the American mission to Greece, Paul Porter, was quoted as saying that the supplies would be used for "economic security and political liberty. We will not use them in an effort to impose *laissez-faire* capitalism upon Europe." "Well," the *Journal* commented tartly, "there appears one reason— perhaps the principal reason—why American foreign policy is not more effectual. The people who are trying to carry it out either do not understand or they dislike the American social and economic system."[116] Matching the needs of US capitalism to Cold War policy was thus not always as friction-free as some might have assumed. Truman, moreover, had a fight on his hands to create and sustain a bipartisan foreign policy with a presidential election looming in November 1948. Either way, from Stalin's viewpoint, defeating the Marshall Plan could be expected to accomplish two objectives simultaneously: blocking West European economic recovery and in so doing hasten a US depression. Great hopes rested on the assumption that both could be expected to assure Soviet predominance in the balance of Europe.

NO MORE COMMUNIST UPRISINGS FOR NOW

One of the side effects of criticizing PCF and PCI policy at Cominform was to tilt the balance of influence to the left within both parties. Thorez had to shift policy to neutralize rivalry for leadership of the Party. An about-face drove the PCF back into the self-defeating policy of the "third period" (1928–34), when socialists were ostracized as social fascists. Strikes were used extensively, particularly in the mines, to demonstrate that France was ungovernable without communists in power.[117] The left in the PCF thus seized the initiative and launched disruption nationwide on a scale that put the Party's very existence in jeopardy. Washington was alarmed. Kennan noted that as a result of the disruption "a full two months was knocked out of our aid program."[118] Moscow then unexpectedly called the PCF to order. Thorez was suddenly summoned to Stalin at one of the "distant" datchas on the Black Sea coast to have his ears boxed. On return at the beginning of December, he warned the Politburo that the Party was fast losing ground. "We must not give the government an excuse to outlaw the Party," he pleaded, adding: "Stalin said to me without any attempt to be diplomatic that, if we carry on like this, he would calmly wash his hands of us."[119]

An adjustment had been anticipated by the PCI leadership just before September 1947, with greater emphasis on strikes.[120] But that made them no less a target. And even after the condemnation, some remained defiant. The most independent minded, Umberto Terracini, much respected by Togliatti, spoke out fervently against radicalizing policy. "With respect to our party," he declared, "the comrades of other parties . . . theorize about the political behavior of their organizations without taking into account the fact that it is determined by the presence of Soviet occupation forces; that is to say, they reason in strictly local terms." "Thus," he continued, "they are bringing the situation to a head. But should we, today, radically change our policy, we will lose contact with the other strata, even if the working class and the peasantry can be temporarily reinforced." Terracini's direct opposite was the leftist Pietro Secchia who chafed under Togliatti's cautious, constitutionalist approach. He stood firmly behind the Cominform critique. "I believe," he said, "that the lack of an organized partisan movement is our big mistake. After liberation the government was unresponsive to our effective power and to our position." In other words, elections meant little or nothing, when the Party had the organized strength, including the weapons, to enforce its will on the population. And as to anxieties about alienating the middle class, "we have worried too much about breaking with the middle strata."[121]

The clash between Secchia and Terracini enabled Togliatti to hold the center of gravity within the leadership, arguing firmness of principle but retaining residual tactical flexibility. Terracini was attacked for questioning loyalty to Moscow: "On the issue of the Bolshevik party," Togliatti intoned, "it must be stated clearly that the dissolution of the Communist International has not put an end to the leading role of the Bolshevik Communist Party [sic]." On the other hand, "does there exist an immediate prospect of insurrection? I maintain that it is incorrect to pose the question in this way; though, certainly, a communist cannot exclude it indefinitely."[122] Terracini thus stood condemned yet remained within the ranks. Nothing better reflected Togliatti's determination to have his cake and eat it: aligning securely with Stalin in order to retain freedom of maneuver on the ground.

Unsurprisingly, Stalin never considered Togliatti a revolutionary; more an intellectual, a theoretician.[123] But he was safe, unlike Secchia, a self-appointed man of action destined to supplant his chief. On 13 December Secchia came to Moscow to discuss matters with Zhdanov clearly hoping for Soviet blessing. Three days later he also met Stalin and Molotov to discuss the strategy paper he had been asked to write. Secchia advocated greater economic and political struggle: "We must orient ourselves toward harder, wider, and more decisive battles." These included "a violent battle against reactionary groups."[124] In response to objections that Italy was not ready for insurrection, Secchia implausibly denied that this was ever his intention. Utterly unconvinced, the Russians insisted that "in substance what I said would inevitably lead to such an outcome. Today this is not possible. You should instead reinforce yourselves, make good preparation, etc."[125] Stalin thus depressed the brake in Italy as well as France.

PUTTING YUGOSLAVIA IN ITS PLACE

Yugoslavia and its neighbors were acting independently. On the signing of the Romanian-Bulgarian mutual assistance pact, Dimitrov was asked by journalists about prospects for a Balkan federation. Believing himself on solid ground, he told them, "It is not the right time for us to discuss the question of creating a federation or confederation. When the time is ripe, and without doubt, it will some time be so, our nations, the countries of popular democracy—Romania, Bulgaria, Yugoslavia, Albania, Czechoslovakia, Poland, Hungary, and Greece— notice, Greece as well!—will make a decision." The interview appeared in the Bulgarian daily, *Rabotnichesko delo,* after three days and in *Pravda* on 23 January 1948. Extraordinarily, five days later *Pravda* published a disclaimer, saying that what these countries needed was not federation, confederation, or a customs union, but "reinforcement and defense of their independence and sovereignty through the mobilization and organization of internal national democratic forces, as was correctly mentioned in the well-known declaration of the nine communist parties."[126]

Stalin was incensed, not merely because everyone would think it his idea, but because Bevin rose in the House of Commons just five days later to propose an alliance against the USSR encompassing most of Western Europe and its colonies as well.[127] The *ballon d'essai* let aloft by Dimitrov had unknowingly given Bevin justification for his own initiative, thus depriving Moscow of a propaganda advantage. *Pravda* had therefore appeared to the puzzlement of many with an editorial brusquely disowning the Dimitrov project. A disclaimer was dispatched from Sofia to Moscow immediately at 1:30 a.m. on the following morning by the "VCh"—the special high frequency telephone line linking the Kremlin with senior officials in Russia and within the bloc.[128]

Dimitrov was summoned to Moscow. Yugoslavia was also in the dock, for having initialled an alliance with Bulgaria without consulting the Kremlin. On 12 August 1947 Stalin had telegraphed his displeasure to both.[129] Now Belgrade was attempting to take over Albania by moving in Yugoslav forces, also without consulting Moscow. Tito had been surreptitiously trying to absorb less developed Albania piece by piece working through his "adviser" to the Albanian Party, Savo Zlatić, who behaved more like a viceroy, and Koçi Xoxe and Pandi Kristo, among others in the Politburo. Where possible, nothing was put on paper except the Albanian record of the meetings. The first signs of trouble emerged after Kardelj met Stalin on 19 April and was startled to learn that Albanian General Secretary Enver Hoxha had complained of the Yugoslav military advisers in his country.[130] Once Hoxha visited the USSR in June 1947, however, those in Belgrade became ever more suspicious and ever more critical of Tirana. The ostensible grounds for sending in a division and support units were that the Greeks would attack with Anglo-American backing: "In case of a provocation," Tito wrote, "our units will be able to intervene more quickly."[131] Hoxha reported all this to Moscow and was relieved to find Stalin supporting his opposition to Tito.[132] It gave Stalin yet one more argument against Belgrade and, by extension, Sofia.

"You are giving the reactionary elements in America ammunition with which to convince public opinion that America is doing nothing special in creating a Western bloc," Stalin berated Dimitrov on 10 February 1948. "At this time in America a major electoral struggle is in progress. To us, what government there is has great significance."[133] Yet it was less detail than principle that concerned Stalin. This was really all about reestablishing his authority over the entire international communist movement, Eastern Europe in particular. Belgrade had become accustomed to doing what it wanted regardless of Moscow. Kardelj lamely attempted to mollify: "We consider that there is no essential disagreement between us. This is a matter of individual mistakes." Stalin, irate, tersely retorted: "These are not individual mistakes, but a system."[134] His finger-pointing fooled no one. The following day Dimitrov told Kardelj and Djilas: "It's not a matter of criticizing my statements, but of something else."[135]

A further difference between Belgrade and Moscow concerned Greece. Here Stalin's restraining hand on the PCI and PCF fitted into a larger pattern. It is likely word had reached him of the US National Security Council report that treated Greece as a test case in respect of Soviet intentions. "The Communists," it noted, "under the leadership of the USSR, seek world domination and to this end are making piecemeal advances, principally by aggression through indigenous Communist movements within other countries." Should the partisans succeed, an example would be set for the PCF and PCI; resistance elsewhere to communism would be undermined; the success of the Marshall Plan would be jeopardized; Russia might be emboldened to take further action; and Britain might reconsider their stance in the region. The conclusions were uncompromising: "The United States should, therefore, make full use of its political, economic and, if necessary, military power in such manner as may be found most effective to prevent Greece from falling under the domination of the USSR."[136]

Stalin thus argued: "Recently I have come to doubt victory for the partisans. If we are not sure that the partisans will win, we need to wind up the partisan movement." The United States and Britain were very interested in the Mediterranean, wanting bases in Greece. They could sustain Greeks that would listen

to them. "If the partisan movement is removed, they will have no grounds for attacking us."[137] When Traicho Kostov, number two in the Bulgarian leadership,
insisted that the partisans be supported because their defeat would create "a very
serious situation for other Balkan countries," Stalin agreed, only to contradict
himself entirely by adding: "But if the prospects for the partisan movement are
deteriorating, then it would be better to postpone the struggle for better times.
What is lacking in respect of countervailing power cannot be made up for with
bawling and wailing. What is needed is a rational assessment of the forces in
play." He accused Kostov of thinking in terms of a moral debt: "We have no
categorical imperatives. The entire question is one of the balance of power. If
you are in the right condition, attack. If not, do not take to the field. We do not
go into battle when our enemy wishes, but when it is in our interests."[138] Thus
when Rákosi, Secretary General of the Hungarian Party, asked whether they
should formally recognize the Greek partisans as the government of Greece
under General Markos (on Yugoslav territory), head of the Central Committee foreign policy department Mikhail Suslov advised him: "Isn't it too early?
Would this not reinforce Anglo-American intervention in Greece?"[139]

COUP IN PRAGUE

For all his caution over Greece, where Stalin saw the opportunity to strike
a decisive blow, he did so. A speech drafted for Molotov in April 1948 argued
that Moscow "will now have pacts with all its European neighbours from the
Black to the Barents sea, firmly closing the path to this part of Europe for the
aggressor."[140] Yet despite its treaty of mutual assistance with the USSR, Czechoslovakia represented a gap in the defensive perimeter. It was understood that
"events at the end of 1947 and early 1948 showed that reactionary forces in
Czechoslovakia have become significantly more active in the struggle against
progressive forces in the country led by the communists; that these reactionary
forces still have the support chiefly among a significant section of the intelligentsia, bureaucracy and students, and also among a certain section of petit bourgeois elements—artisans, tradesmen, peasants, etc." Prague claimed to be heading for socialism on their "own path" and that "the experience of the USSR" was
"scarcely appropriate for Czechoslovakia," while also underlining the country's
historic links to the West. For the previous six months Britain and the United
States had been particularly active in spreading their views with the cooperation
of Czech political parties and had "established their own centers of influence
in Czechoslovakia." Moscow had even added up the number of American as
against Soviet films being shown in Prague and the number of books sold.[141]
Concern had also been expressed by General Shatilov, officer commanding

the political directorate of the Red Army. Czech Minister of Defense Ludvig Svoboda supported the communists but was under pressure from the right and worked toward close cooperation with Beneš's private office, which "was de facto in charge of the army and pursues the national socialist line, increasingly commandeering leading posts in the army for his own people."[142]

The fate of Czechoslovakia was significant and not merely because of common borders with the Ukraine and the Western zones of Germany but also because here lay the main source of uranium for the Soviet atomic bomb project. The British consul in Karlovy Vary (formerly Karlsbad) had reported in the autumn of 1946 on the arrival of some sixty Russian families, specialists destined to work in the Jáchymov mines, where ore production was being directed by one Krivonosov, with extensive construction undertaken in the neighborhood. Similar reports had come in from Schönficht, eighteen kilometers east of Cheb.[143]

Moreover, reports had emerged that the Czech army was drifting from Soviet influence. On the eve of the Cominform meeting Molotov wrote: "To comrades Zhdanov and Malenkov. This question needs to be addressed with the Czechs at the meeting in P[oland]."[144] By the end of the year the Soviet embassy in Prague was reporting that "the parties of the right are putting the communists in constant fear of isolation" and that in order to escape the Party tended to ever-greater concessions.[145] It added, "Reactionary elements within the country, actively supported by representatives of the West, continue to consider that in Czechoslovakia there is every reason that the parties of the right will receive a majority at the forthcoming elections and that the communists will be thrown out of the government."[146]

Whereas Moscow blamed Party leaders in Prague, some of them wanted the Kremlin to take charge and put an end to the stream of concessions required by parliamentary democracy. Indeed, one wrote to Moscow in January 1948 complaining that if the Party met the same fate as the PCF and PCI the responsibility would lie entirely with Moscow.[147] Finally, Stalin had had enough: on 19 February Deputy Foreign Minister Valerii Zorin arrived in Prague, ostensibly to inspect the supply of grain to Russia — an implausible duty for so senior an official from such a department and the man who ran the intelligence committee as Molotov's deputy. That very day he told Gottwald "to be firmer, not to make concessions to those on the right and not to waver."[148] Zorin reported that there was "no doubt at all" Gottwald "understood" what was meant.[149]

Communist Minister of the Interior Václav Nosek had been substituting subordinates with members of the Party. Resistance to these measures finally prompted twelve coalition ministers representing the national socialists, Catholics, and Slovak democrats to resign on 20 February. Meeting with Party General Secretary Rudolf Slánský and Chairman Gottwald that day, Zorin impressed upon them the need "to be ready for decisive action and for the possibility of breaching the formal stipulations of the constitution and laws as they stand." This they had a terrible fear of doing. Zorin later reported, "Gottwald started to say that for the time being it was not necessary to move against the President, but it was another question if they had to move against him. I responded that he was needlessly exaggerating the difficulties and that the authority of the president to a significant extent depends upon their support. Gottwald appeared to have made up his mind to act more decisively, but the idea of a normal, parliamentary path of development for Czechoslovakia without any collisions still had its hold on him."[150]

Gottwald wanted Red Army maneuvers along the frontier to exert pressure and deter Western retaliation for a communist coup. Though Soviet tanks crossed into Slovakia to influence the national assembly elections in 1946, on this occasion Moscow, intent on concealing its hand, refused. The following day mass meetings of the Party faithful were organized and telegrams were dispatched to Beneš insisting he accept the resignations of other ministers. Gottwald had taken Stalin's advice. In a meeting on 21 February, Beneš asked, "What if I don't accept the resignations?" Gottwald threatened a general strike and the presence of the workers' militia on the streets. He added, "Then there is also the Soviet Union!" Beneš subsequently gave others to understand he believed that the Red Army might invade. He had no idea that Moscow was in fact holding back and cautioning Zorin to wait for further instructions before visiting Beneš.[151] A *Pravda* editorial on 22 February then backed up Zorin's position, as he had requested. On the following day "action committees" suddenly appeared; armed trades unionists emerged onto the streets. Two days later Beneš asked Gottwald to form a government. The communists soon had sole power in their hands and rapidly sealed the borders. On the night of 9–10 March it appears that Foreign Minister Masaryk fell from a window to his death either in despair or assisted by unknown hands. Arrests followed in April to silence political opposition preparatory to the rigging of national assembly elections on 30 May.

Truman reacted gloomily. He wrote to daughter Margaret on 3 March: "Now we are faced with exactly the same situation with which Britain and France were faced in 1938/39 with Hitler." "Things look black," he added. "A decision will have to be made. I am going to make it."[152]

BELGRADE CAST OUT

Following West European alliance negotiations, on 6 March head of the third European department of the Foreign Ministry Andrei Smirnov reported:

"The Western Powers are transforming Germany into their stronghold and will include it in the formation of a politico-military bloc directed against the Soviet Union and the countries of the new democracy."[153] On 17 March, Britain, France, Belgium, the Netherlands, and Luxembourg signed the Western Union in Brussels. It was described at the Foreign Ministry as the first "treaty of alliance in the creation of a 'Western bloc' under the leadership of the USA."[154] Reactions were predictable. Tito responded with open defiance. "We must be unyielding in respect to the line we have taken, in respect of reinforcing the role of Yugoslavia in the world, which in the final analysis is in the interests of the USSR."[155]

The closer the Western Powers drew together, the tighter Stalin clasped the East to his side. Yugoslavia had to be called to order. Despite Stalin's view that the civil war should be wound up, at a summit with Zachariadis on 21 February Tito, Kardelj, and Djilas agreed to continue backing the partisans in defiance of the Kremlin.[156] Inevitably the news leaked to Moscow because at least one Yugoslav Politburo member, Sreten Žujović-Crni, was spying for Russia.[157] By 1 March, Tito told the Politburo, relations with the USSR were "in deadlock." He had every intention of sending a division of troops to Albania, which faced retaliation as a result of aiding the Greek rebels. "We would like the Greeks to understand that our alliance with Albania is unbreakable. They are not prepared for war though capable of provocations." He described Molotov's latest telegram of reprimand as "quite uncouth" and Stalin's recent drubbing of Dimitrov as equally "uncouth."[158]

At the suggestion of Anatolii Lavrent'ev, Soviet ambassador in Belgrade, the foreign policy department of the Central Committee presented Suslov on 18 March with a comprehensive survey of "serious political mistakes" committed by Yugoslavia. One particular objection was that of *lèse-majesté* toward the USSR, long accustomed to be lauded as "the fundamental and decisive force" for "all progressive and democratic forces of the world." Given war preparations by "the Anglo-American imperialists," the Yugoslavs were "obliged to use all the strength and means in their power to support and reinforce the authority of the Soviet Union." It was "in this light" that Moscow viewed Yugoslavia's belittling of the Soviet contribution to the country's liberation and postwar construction. The memorandum quoted Kardelj, Djilas, and, above all, Tito to this effect.[159]

The policy of reining in Belgrade was applied elsewhere. Autonomous revolutionary activity was now unacceptable. It was clear by December 1947 that the communists would never win the Greek civil war. And, if they could not win, it was most unlikely those in Italy had any hope of so doing. After Secchia returned from Moscow, Togliatti duly promoted him to join Luigi Longo as

deputy general secretary.[160] But Secchia remained virulently assertive at meetings of the leadership.[161] With elections in the offing on 18 April 1948, Togliatti
sought to neutralize him by tackling Soviet ambassador Mikhail Kostylev with
an ingenious question to be settled once and for all. Kostylev was gently asked
"if, in the event of provocation on the part of the Christian Democrats and
other reactionaries, armed insurrection should be initiated by the forces of the
democratic popular front for the seizure of power." No doubt as Togliatti expected, on 26 March Molotov, clearly alarmed, instructed Kostylev, "Regarding
the seizure of power by means of armed insurrection: the PCI must not undertake one for any reason whatever."[162]

The disappointing election results then exacerbated differences still further. These were the first elections where CIA played a role in subsidizing the
anticommunist vote, backed by psychological warfare from MI6 (the creation of
the Don Camillo stories being the most successful example).[163] But Sereni, very
much of the Terracini mold, argued forcefully: "The cause of our failure is not
to be found merely in the intervention of priests, of America, etc. Foreign intervention has had its impact because the policy of the Front [PCI plus the socialists under Nenni] did not succeed in advancing [*fare argine*] against them."[164]
Togliatti firmly rejected the French example advocated by Noce, Secchia, and
Negarville of taking up the offensive *à l'outrance*.[165] The attempt on Togliatti's
life on 14 July 1948 then threatened to tilt the balance toward insurrection. A
general strike was called. But the PCI leadership soon brought it to an end for
fear that events would get out of control. Secchia, aware of Moscow's stance,
now acknowledged that "the Italian situation today is not prerevolutionary, nor
ready for insurrection." He did "not share optimistic statements concerning a
balance of power in our favor. The adversary has yet to engage all the strength
at his disposal."[166] The PCI thus teetered back from the precipice.

SUPPRESSING DISSENT

The Kremlin's sense of caution with respect to the Western sphere of influence was evident equally in the Far East, where Stalin rejected Kim Il Sung's
proposals for war, repeatedly delayed a visit to Moscow by Mao Tse-tung for fear
he would be identified wholly with the USSR, and obliged the Soviet embassy
in Nationalist China to stick like glue to Chiang Kai-shek when he abandoned
Nanking, even when the Western Powers refused to do so.

Naturally Mao's concern to sort out his ambivalent relations with Stalin was
due not least to the fact that Moscow had launched not just an anti-Yugoslav
campaign, but a more general attempt to reestablish rigid conformity. A second
memorandum emerging from the Soviet Party's foreign policy department at-

tacked "the anti-Marxist ideological positions" of the Polish comrades, Gomułka in particular.[167] It was also clear that the problem Moscow faced was even more widespread. When Dimitrov passed through Belgrade on 19 April, he squeezed Djilas's hand and said with feeling, "Hold fast, hold fast!" adding: "You must remain steadfast. The rest will follow."[168] Moreover, in the privacy of the Bulgarian leadership Dimitrov told his colleagues that they should not forget that Yugoslavia was a friendly country.[169] Elsewhere support for Moscow's stance was also weak. Gomułka was already known to MI6 and the Foreign Office as *"the only one* [of the communists in government] *who was mentally genuinely a Pole."*[170] He had received a copy of Moscow's letter to Tito on 4 April but did not respond. Two weeks later Molotov instructed ambassador Lebedev in Warsaw to have a reply produced "as the Hungarian Communist Party had done." Gomułka was reticent. The matter went to the Politburo the following day. The resulting letter to Moscow was supportive but expressed concern at the negative impact of the dispute on relations within the bloc and on the international communist movement in general.[171] On 21 August Gomułka was told Stalin agreed he ought to step down as General Secretary. This took place at a plenum on 31 August–3 September. It was a decision confirmed despite an appeal directly and in person to Stalin on 19 December.[172] The trials of East European leaders of suspect loyalty to Moscow followed not long thereafter, beginning in Hungary with László Rajk (16–24 September 1949).[173]

The difference between Belgrade and the rest, however, was that when the pressure proved unremitting everyone else gave way, even Gomułka. That Yugoslavia did not do so was essentially due to the undiminished self-confidence of having liberated most of the country with little help from outside. Matters came to a head when secret policeman Vasilii Moshetov from the foreign policy department in Moscow arrived in Belgrade on 19 May requesting—to no avail—that Tito appear in person at the next Cominform meeting, which was to be held in Romania on 19–23 June.[174] Even then, Yugoslavia persisted in its determination to absorb Albania as a protectorate in the face of Hoxha's increasingly willful resistance. On 27 May, well after the Soviet summons had been delivered, Yugoslavia insisted that Albania come to Belgrade cap in hand to resolve the differences between them.[175]

Despite chaos within the Soviet delegation to Bucharest as a result of fierce rivalry between Zhdanov and Malenkov, reflected in the very different tone of their speeches—the more restrained line coming from Zhdanov mirrored statements from the reluctant among the East European delegations—round condemnation of Yugoslavia was followed by expulsion of their party from "the family of fraternal communist parties."[176] Yet even after this, Dimitrov took on the role of mediator at his own request.[177] Stalin was now beside himself with fury, wreaking his worst on Zhdanov, who was unceremoniously removed from his posts and replaced by rival Malenkov, less inhibited at Bucharest in attacking Yugoslavia. Stalin's onetime favorite then disappeared off to a sanatorium, where he died in dubious circumstances—his illness was misdiagnosed by the majority of Kremlin doctors—on 31 August.[178] And when one broke ranks and disputed the diagnosis, her complaints went unheeded before he died and after. She was then banished from the prestigious Kremlin hospital. Stalin's only reaction to her protest was to have her letter archived.[179] Yet he would normally have suspected a plot where there was none.

The Greeks, who had flirted with Belgrade, were not admitted to Cominform; in this Moscow was guided by "the current international situation" (another sign of Stalin's concern to retain formal acceptance of the Western sphere of influence even while undermining it from within).[180] Where no obvious gains could be made and where relations were needlessly exacerbated, Stalin brutally cut his losses. The converse was, however, that now he had no hesitation in striking where the adversary was weak.

BLOCKADING WEST BERLIN

Neither the Western Powers nor Russia had been willing to concede the possibility of dominating postwar Germany. Khrushchev claimed that Stalin

> was convinced (and I too shared this opinion) that after the defeat of the Germans and the destruction of their state, the German working class, the peasantry, and the whole of society would want to escape the political and social conditions in which Germany found itself before the war. We presupposed that a social revolution would take place there, the capitalist state would be liquidated, a proletarian state would emerge, which would be guided by Marxist-Leninist doctrine and establish the dictatorship of the proletariat. This was our dream. We thought that this would be the simplest solution to the German question. As a result Germany would cease to be a militaristic state and would cease to threaten Europe with war, which it had already unleashed several times. It seemed to us that such a renaissance of the country was inevitable. . . . With respect to Germany, we had no doubts. We were absolutely sure that it would become a socialist state.[181]

Khrushchev continued: "Stalin spoke out for a unified Germany. He imagined that a unified Germany would be socialist and would become an ally of the USSR. This is the conception that Stalin held and we, too, the whole of his entourage."[182]

This may well have been the "dream," but Stalin's tactics indicate a more prosaic and realistic assessment. By January 1947, with unification of the Western occupation zones into Bizonia a reality and a separate West Germany in prospect, he was banking more on German nationalism than socialist sentiment just as he had done in 1930–33. He startled Otto Pieck, Walter Ulbricht, and Otto Grotewohl with the following questions: "Are there many fascist elements in Germany? In what proportion, percentage-wise? What kind of power do they have? Can one say approximately? In the Western zones in particular?" By the same token there would also be fascists in the Soviet zone. "Can one not allow them to organize their own party under another name?' He later suggested the title "National Democratic Party." One did not want them all driven into the hands of the Americans. "In relation to the fascists, you (the leaders of the SED) are following a course of exterminating the fascists." Instead, perhaps a different line was in order: one of "winning them over" so that not all former Nazis ended up in the rival camp. They would not be attracted to the SED, but as a separate party they could work together with it as a bloc. "Former fascists live in fear. They must be neutralized. This is a tactical problem. This is not lack of principle." One should not forget, he added, that "elements of Nazism exist not merely among bourgeois strata but also in the working class and petite bourgeoisie." To reassure Grotewohl and others, he insisted that this would not mean taking reactionaries on board "but only patriots and not active fascists."[183]

Nothing came of this idea. But the sentiment behind it came to dominate Stalin's thinking. Marshal Vasilii Sokolovskii, Commander-in-Chief of the Soviet Group of Forces in Germany, told Chairman of the SED Wilhelm Pieck that "the English and the Americans will try to buy off the Germans, placing them in a privileged position. Against this one option remains—to turn people's minds toward unification."[184] At a further meeting on 18 December 1948 Stalin argued "For the Soviet zone an 'opportunistic policy' is proposed. Otherwise the coalition of democratic forces will break up and the influence of [Kurt] Schumacher [leader of the SPD in the Western zone] and his masters ['Herren'] will be strengthened among the workers. The people will not win as a result." There was, Stalin insisted, no direct route to socialism, only via "zig-zags and evasive maneuvers" as "the circumstances in Germany are difficult and dictate a more cautious policy." Stalin, laughingly, pointed out that "that in this instance in his old age he had become an opportunist."[185]

By then Stalin had also tried, by the threat of force, to break allied unity and forestall the formal division of Germany. On 14 March 1948 the US Senate had passed the Marshall Plan overwhelmingly 69 votes to 17; the House of Representatives followed suit on 2 April with even greater enthusiasm: 318 votes to 75.

The success of the Plan depended upon the incorporation of the Western zone into the West European trading community. Failure to reach agreement with Moscow on the fate of Germany therefore prompted Washington and London to create Bizonia. On 3 October 1947 Smirnov warned Molotov, "This is a matter not of propaganda or political blackmail but a real threat of the political and economic division of Germany and the inclusion of western Germany with all its resources in a western bloc created by the United States."[186]

The complete failure of the London conference of allied foreign ministers (25 November–15 December 1947) to agree on Germany led the State Department on 19 December to announce an end to reparations payments for Russia from Bizonia. The next stage was to introduce currency reform. In Moscow it was soon confirmed that Washington and London were "carrying out measures toward the creation of a West German state, with whom they are determined to conclude a separate peace treaty or peace accord."[187] Smirnov advised Molotov: "We therefore need to take such measures that would not only limit the separate activities of the USA, England, and France in Germany, but also actively disrupt their plans for the formation of a western bloc, including Germany within it."[188]

Since the Anglo-American zones of occupation in Berlin (along with that of France) lay deep within the Soviet zone and because no provision had been made to ensure rights of access on land, Stalin moved to squeeze the allies out of the city through blockade. This was despite the fact that West Berlin had been swapped for Thuringia-Saxony. On 12 March 1948 Marshal Sokolovskii was summoned to Moscow. On 15 March Washington adopted an embargo on the export of strategic goods to the USSR and demanded that recipients of the Marshall Plan follow suit. Just under a week later Sokolovskii walked out of the allied control council, with the result that it ceased to function. And on 25 March he issued an order "on the reinforcement of the security and control of the demarcation line of the Soviet zone of occupation of Germany." The head of the transportation directorate of the Soviet Group of Forces in Germany was told to cut to a minimum the movement of passenger trains and transporters of western forces.[189]

An instruction went out to strengthen control over the movement of people and goods through greater Berlin. On 1 April further measures were taken to reduce communications from Berlin to the Western zone. Confidence was high at the Russian headquarters in suburban Karlshorst: "Our control restrictions have delivered a serious blow to the prestige of the Americans and the English in Germany. The German population reckon that the 'Anglo-Americans have retreated in the face of the Russians' and that this demonstrates the strength of the Russians." They rushed to the premature conclusion that "the attempts of [General] Clay to establish 'an air bridge' between Berlin and the Western zones has failed. The Americans have recognized that this is too expensive an undertaking."[190] It looked likely that Stalin had every chance of success; in which case the consequences for the West were bleak.

As anticipated in Moscow, on 18 June the military governor of the American zone, General Lucius Clay, announced by letter to Sokolovskii the currency reform to be instituted in the Western zones. Two days later Moscow insisted that the reform was illegal and that the Soviet government would act to protect the Soviet zone (including greater Berlin) from its effects. On the night of 19 June it closed traffic along the autobahn entirely and reduced railway passage to a trickle. On 22 June the US Air Force began the airlift of supplies for the American garrison in Berlin. Two days later Moscow suspended all transportation by land to and from the city. On 25 June the Royal Air Force began missions to Berlin for the British garrison. Coal came in for the first time on 7 July. Initially Moscow held strongly to the belief that the West could not hold out. In negotiations with an obdurate Molotov, it rapidly became clear that the sine qua non for lifting the blockade was an end to plans for a separate Western Germany. And pressure not to give way came from those in the field, not just from Stalin.

On 30 August Sokolovskii urged Molotov against appeasing to the West: "further concessions would not be expedient as (1) . . . significant changes in the mood of the population in Berlin are working to our advantage; and (2) the West is now interested in hastening an agreement."[191] By 5 November, however, a new airfield at Tegel was operational. In January 1949 the airlift reached its peak in terms of deployment (225 C-54s for the US Air Force), and on 16 April, 1,398 sorties carried a record delivery of 12,940 short tons of supplies. One plane landed every minute and kept the Russian garrison awake as the aircraft flew just above the rooftops. By the time Moscow lifted the blockade as a failure on 12 May, some 2,326,406 short tons of supplies had been brought in by air alone in 278,228 sorties. It was an extraordinary display of air power, ingenuity, and determination.

Up to now Truman had steadfastly resisted planning for war against the USSR using the atomic bomb. Rather, all planning for possible war was predicated on air supremacy. This was only one glaring contradiction in White House thinking. The number of atomic weapons had grown slowly but steadily: two by the end of 1945, nine in July 1946, thirteen in July 1947, and fifty in July 1948. By then only thirty B-29s, all held at the 509th bombing group at Roswell, New Mexico, had been modified to carry these weapons. Under the impact of the blockade, however, White House opinion shifted. Contingency planning followed suit.

Finally on 28 July the Joint Chiefs of Staff were instructed by Secretary of Defense Forrestal to institute contingency plans for an atomic offensive, and on 16 September Truman approved use of the bomb in directive NSC-30. A follow-up directive on 23 November, NSC-20/4, provided for a general war to reduce or eliminate communist control of the Soviet Union and the satellites, with no need for subsequent occupation. Then in December the joint war plan Trojan was approved for assaults on 70 Soviet cities with 133 atomic bombs.[192] Up to this point, the British ambassador noted, in the Soviet capital "hardly any air raid precautions" had been taken.[193]

For the Kremlin much rested on the outcome of the US presidential elections that November. Before the campaign was over, on 26 October a Five-Power invitation went out to the United States and Canada to join Western Europe in a North Atlantic treaty. Yet Molotov is reported to have persisted in believing that Dewey would win—in this he was scarcely alone—and that therefore the isolationist streak epitomized in the person of Senator Robert Taft would gain foothold. But Molotov was also somehow convinced the pro-Soviet former vice president Henry Wallace would obtain more than 6 million votes; that he would in due course become the major contender in 1952; and that by then the United States would have succumbed to a major economic depression (a belief shared by the British ambassador to Washington).[194] He was wrong. Moscow had badly miscalculated and not for the first time since the war. Some plausibility was lent to such wild notions when news leaked out on 8 October that Truman was planning to authorize Vinson, now Chief Justice, to see Stalin in Moscow in vain pursuit of a solution to Soviet-American differences: a very Wallace-like gesture and a gaffe of major proportions at a time of the Berlin blockade that utterly undermined US foreign policy. This was a trial moment for Marshall who was then in Paris. He began a dispatch to the effect that "never in the history of diplomatic bungling," but when Bohlen read it back to him instead he asked Truman for an urgent meeting. Marshall then threatened to resign if the Vinson mission proceeded. Embarrassed, Truman promptly backed off.[195] News of the gaffe did not pass unremarked in Moscow, which subsequently claimed "how important to the success of Truman's 1948 campaign was the election stunt of spreading the rumour that the President was about to dispatch a representative to Moscow for talks with the Soviet Government."[196] But Wallace's Progressive Party platform was effectively a creature of the US Communist Party, and as a result he won a paltry 2.4 percent of the vote. Truman squeezed back into office with 49.5 percent against rival Dewey's 45.1 percent. The president thus won *faute-de-mieux*. As Dewey's equally dull and disconsolate running mate Governor Warren of California whined in exasperation: "the President got too many votes."[197]

A SECRET COUNTEROFFENSIVE

Hitherto Bevin had adopted lofty restraint in retaliating against Soviet attempts to disrupt economic recovery. "We have been scrupulously careful," he wrote, "not to encourage subversive movements in Eastern European countries or anti-Russianism, or to lead the anti-Communists to hope for support which we cannot give."[198] Not for the first or the last time, the Kremlin had underestimated the negative impact of its own provocative behavior in mobilizing adversaries and undermining allies. Moscow was now to be challenged on its own terms. Both Britain and the United States had been caught napping by Tito's break with Stalin. McNeill at the Foreign Office liaising with MI6, scoffed at their lack of knowledge.[199] But a lesson had been learned, certainly in Britain, which saw Titoism as a useful means of pulling the rug from under Russia, not just in Eastern Europe but also in China. The attempt now made was to use subversion to undermine Soviet rule, building on the experience of the Special Operations Executive and the OSS during the war but also adding from textbook communist practice. Second, an alliance committing the United States explicitly to the defense of Western Europe was now entirely practicable. At a stroke Stalin had united Americans and West Europeans as never before.

In Washington covert operations were run from Frank Wisner's Office of Policy Coordination (OPC), formally under State Department tutelage but transferred to the new Central Intelligence Agency (CIA), now headed by Bedell Smith, on 12 October 1950. Prior to this, the passage of NSC-10/2 was the first major step in toward a full-scale strategy, followed in London on 14 December 1948 by proposals for a "counteroffensive" to Soviet political warfare. First, by "making the Soviet Orbit so disaffected that in the event of war it would become a dangerous area requiring large armies of occupation, and not a source of useful manpower for Russia." Second, prizing "the Soviet hold on the Orbit countries, and ultimately enabling them to regain their independence." Third, "seizing every opportunity of discrediting the Soviet regime or weakening its position within the frontiers of the Soviet Union." And finally, "frustrating the Soviet effort to build up the economic war potential of the Soviet Union and the satellites."

These goals were to be accomplished "by all available means short of war" and with no expectation of immediate war until 1956. The expectation was that the West could take advantage of the Yugoslav split to create chaos within the Soviet bloc. "The first rift in the Orbit has already been created by Tito's quarrel with the Kremlin; and this has provided us with an opening which we should be able to exploit. If this opportunity is thus exploited, a sort of chain reaction among the satellites might be started."[200] The means by which this could be done included the "spreading of rumours and the sowing of suspicion among Communists."[201] The subsequent show trials suggest this policy may have had some success. The only immediate opportunity for overturning a communist regime, however, was Albania where, after the Yugoslav split, the leadership were reported to be in chaos. Germany was the next target. There were obvious risks to this policy, which meant a price would have to be paid. "The consolidation of the Orbit is so important to Russia that they must be expected to react vigorously to any attempt to disrupt it. If plans on the lines contemplated are put into operation, we must suppose that their existence will soon become known to the Russians, and when this happens the tension between the Soviet Union and the Western Powers must be expected to increase considerably."[202]

The second major effect was the North Atlantic treaty signed on 4 April 1949. Despite the fact that within State both Kennan and Bohlen believed the treaty to be mistaken and Under Secretary Robert Lovett was skeptical that it would be acceptable to Congress,[203] the Senate ratified it on 21 July by an overwhelming vote of 82 to 13. All thanks to the fearsome visage Stalin projected.

It was now time to retreat. By February 1949 the failure of the blockade and the announcement of the intended pact alone had prompted Moscow to seek a dignified exit from the Berlin crisis. Poland acted as go-between. Deputy head of the Polish mission Colonel Gebert made a sounding. Moscow, he said, was "desperately anxious" to have a meeting of the Council of Foreign Ministers. They were above all keen to preserve at least the appearance of a unified Germany, perhaps with a loose federal structure within which the Länder could reflect the current balance between East and West.[204] No meeting was convened. The West had successfully defended the status quo. On 10 May Stalin asked the Politburo to end the blockade.[205]

The West now hastened to alter the postwar status quo. Covert action in Albania began with an uprising attempted in December 1949. It was led on the British side by David Smiley.[206] It proved a disaster as it had been revealed at planning stage by Philby, then in Washington.[207] This left the West without any effective offensive capability vis-à-vis Moscow short of preemptive war, for which contingency plans existed in Washington but which inevitably threatened to devastate most of Europe. The explosion of an atomic device by the USSR at the end of August then exposed the inadequacy of US military planning based entirely on nuclear warfare against an adversary not so armed. The pressure was therefore on in Washington from Acheson and his new head of policy planning Paul Nitze to beef up conventional warfare capabilities to meet Soviet levels. The result was NSC-68 proposing a massive commitment to contain Russia by military means.[208] Truman, however, had appointed as Secretary of Defense

Louis Johnson, "a bastard," in the words of Luke Battle.[209] But he had also been a major contributor to Truman's re-election, and Truman was a man with loyalties that sometimes overrode common sense. In April–May 1949 Johnson began slashing the burgeoning military budget in the belief, shared by Truman, that waste was rife and in order to prevent growth of government expenditure from squeezing private investment by raising the cost of borrowing.[210] Cutting the budget may seem incongruous for a president who had signed the North Atlantic Treaty. Truman, however, never saw the alliance "as anything but a gamble, a deterrent to war provoked by Russia, not a 'blueprint' that would take form in detail."[211] The British were well aware of this. "I feel the President while not disapproving of the present firm Russian policy of the State Department feels that the ultimate objective should be to reach some accommodation with the Soviet Government," wrote ambassador Oliver Franks in a dispatch to London.[212]

The outbreak of war in Korea in June 1950 then rid all but the most trusting of any further doubts about Stalin and forced upon Western Europe a process of rearmament long demanded by Congress. This held back economic recovery by several years. The outlook from London at the beginning of 1952 thus came to be largely one of weary resignation to a cold war of indefinite duration. "So long as the Communist régime exists in Soviet Russia in its present form we cannot expect to enjoy peace in the full sense of the word. We shall only be able to stem Soviet Russia's encroachment by active and ceaseless vigilance over a long period of time, backed by armed strength. But the present state of affairs—an uneasy absence of war—is not the only form of accommodation with Soviet Russia to which Western policy should aspire. Efforts must be made to find a firmer footing." No indication, however, was given as to what would secure such a footing; presumably yet further increases in military capability. Despite the Albanian fiasco, MI6 hoped against hope that the West could still "cause trouble and disturbance in the satellite countries, and these measures could be stepped up in proportion to the increase in our strength." This was not, however, a cost-free option, and the caveat now inserted anticipated the dilemma shortly to be faced in all its brutality: Berlin (June 1953) and Hungary (October 1956). "There are evident risks that subversive activities involving anti-Soviet elements in the satellite countries may at a certain stage get out of control. We might then be faced with a choice between supporting the revolutionary movement by force of arms or abandoning the revolutionaries to their fate—an alternative which would inevitably lead to a strengthening of the Soviet hold over the whole of the Soviet empire and the liquidation of all potential supporters of the West."[213]

4

ON THE OFFENSIVE IN ASIA

The center of the revolution . . . has shifted to China and East Asia.

—*Stalin, July 1949*

Contained across Europe, by now disappointed in the new state of Israel, neutralized by Gandhi in India, and shut out of occupied Japan, Stalin inevitably sought egress elsewhere and found it where least expected: in China.

NO PREFERENCE FOR MAO

China proved a major instance where the inclinations of the Russians were, for reasons of realpolitik, statist rather than revolutionary, but where events proved stronger than preferences. "They [the Russians] did not let us make a revolution: that was in 1945," Mao recalled. "Stalin wanted to prevent China from making revolution, saying we should not have a civil war and should cooperate with Chiang Kai-shek, otherwise the Chinese nation would perish. But we did not do what he said."[1] Stalin insisted that Mao visit Chungking in order to talk peace with Chiang.[2] He came, reluctantly. The negotiations took place from 28 August. The Chinese Communist Party (CCP) had been taking a military offensive in order to make Chiang more accommodating, Mao told diplomats at the Soviet embassy on 10 October 1945 when an agreement was signed. But it afforded merely a breathing space. Mao said Chiang insisted that the Red Army subordinate itself to Nationalist control and demanded that it be reduced in size.[3]

Reflecting obliquely on his own position, Mao told ambassador Petrov that "Chiang Kai-shek thus far has no deep ideological sense of direction or, as we would say, focal point around which everything else could revolve. Chiang Kai-shek himself doesn't know what road to follow: dictatorship or democracy. In foreign policy Chiang Kai-shek doesn't know whether to orientate toward the United States or the USSR. He has decided not to orient himself entirely on the United States because of the USSR's international influence; and fears orienting toward the USSR. His attitude toward the CCP is determined by such factors as the strength of the CCP, the international weight of the USSR, the situation in Sinkiang and the presence of the Soviet army in Manchuria."[4] According to Mikhail Kapitsa, present as third secretary, Mao emphasized: "We do not fear war; provided the Americans do not intervene—that would worry us."[5]

By the time he saw Harriman on 23 January 1946, Stalin appeared to have given up all hope of forcing compromise between the Kuomintang and CCP. He refused to place Moscow in the position of mediator. The main obstacle was, he claimed, personal mistrust. "Chiang Kai-shek does not trust Mao, and Mao does not trust Chiang."[6] Though viewed with a certain contempt as incapable of attaining national supremacy, the CCP was, however, indispensable to Stalin as a means of limiting the scope of the American reach into China. This had been most apparent in Manchuria where Japanese aggression began in 1931; even so, the Soviet army ripped out all the factory equipment practicable, as they did in the Eastern zone of Germany, before leaving on 3 May 1946.

On 29 December 1945 Lozovskii, responsible for the Far East, produced a memorandum for Molotov and Stalin. He pointed out that "whereas before the war the English and in part the Japanese were the masters of China, now the master in China is the United States of America." Moreover, "the United States is laying claim to ground not only in northern China but also in Manchuria. For the Soviet Union this is a most important problem. We have removed our Japanese neighbor from our borders; and we should not allow Manchuria to become the *mise-en-scène* for the economic and political influence of another Great Power."[7] Between September and November 1945, Russia therefore handed over to the local Red Army 327,877 rifles, 5,207 machine guns, 5, 219 pieces of artillery, 743 tanks and armored cars, 612 planes, and 1,224 vehicules.[8] Yet its forces pillaged systematically. In Mukden (Shenyang) "the Red Army blasted holes in the walls of factories to drag machinery out and load it onto trains."[9] The continued existence of the CCP in this part of China, at least, became a firm Soviet strategic interest once the Red Army had been withdrawn to appease Washington. As to the fate of the remainder of the country, however, Stalin was skeptical.

China led the way. But Moscow stood ostentatiously aloof. Early in 1947 Mao telegraphed his wish to visit Stalin. In mid-June the wish was granted but rescinded two weeks later.[10] The same happened the following year—an April invitation withdrawn in May.[11] This was repeated in July 1948, when the trip was postponed until November.[12] The last excuse—Soviet leaders would be too involved in the harvest—seemed particularly implausible; indeed, his bags already packed, a baffled and downhearted Mao subjected his two Soviet doctors, Orlov (GRU) and Melnikov (MVD), to close questioning on the matter.[13] This no doubt dampened still further his confidence in Stalin. Thus on 21 November Mao himself postponed traveling until the end of December. The visit did not take place even then. At this stage Soviet relations with the West had deteriorated to its lowest ebb as a result of the Berlin blockade. Further, unnecessary risks were evidently to be avoided. Washington was now planning for the prospect of nuclear war, and Stalin still possessed no means of retaliation.

On 14 January 1949 the Politburo again delayed a visit for the same underlying reasons as before—Mao was still only the leader of a guerrilla force and the purpose of the trip would be seen in the West as receipt of instructions from Moscow.[14] Instead Stalin "insisted" on delaying the visit and proposed instead sending Mikoyan (rather than Molotov) to see Mao.[15] This was bound to provoke concern. Mao's anxiety was to tie down Soviet relations with the CCP on a new basis that would underscore Chinese sovereignty once the communists were in power, thereby ruling out any chance that Washington restore the status quo. The bottom line in Moscow, however, was Stalin's continued reluctance to make public acknowledgement of CCP primacy. News of a visit by Mao, though cloaked in secrecy, might leak out, thus compromising relations with the Chinese Nationalists and perhaps also precipitating US military intervention in a last-ditch attempt to avert the loss of China. The dispatch of troops to North China from General Douglas MacArthur's forces occupying Japan suggested that an option such as this was not entirely foreclosed. The fact that Mao's ideological credentials were still viewed with suspicion doubtless further reinforced Stalin's reluctance to take risks for what was as yet an uncertain return.

Mikoyan arrived on 30 January and stayed until 8 February.[16] Mao said it would take one to two years to complete the takeover of China, including such cities as Nanzhing and Shanghai, and outlined his traditional preference for taking the countryside first and the cities only when sure that they could be adequately supplied. Old Bolshevik Mikoyan expressed the view shared by Stalin that the sooner the cities were taken the better. Mao stoutly defended his position, boasting that "the Chinese peasants are more [politically] conscious than all American workers and many English workers." When Mikoyan urged upon him the early formation of a coalition government, Mao was equally unyielding. It rapidly became clear that Mao's request for "directives" from the Stalin was window dressing. A deeply insincere game was then played on the issue of the Soviet base at Port Arthur—Russia offering to return it, China insisting they stay—that was repeated when Mao eventually came to Moscow in December. Mao also feared Soviet expansionist aims to the West, in Sinkiang, a province only nominally Chinese. Mikoyan was reassuring. But when Mao proposed uniting Chinese Inner Mongolia with the People's Republic of Mongolia and that both then form a part of the new China, Stalin, by telegram, insisted that independence was not up for discussion.

Subsequent Soviet advice to avoid a directly communist platform for revolutionary change was ignored, as was the advice on a peace offensive against elements of the Nationalists eager to split the difference between Chiang and Mao. All the CCP did was to lead Washington astray with the idea that some Chinese communists were not entirely sympathetic to Moscow; this, though true, was not a genuine indication of CCP orientation but essentially designed to neutralize any possibility of US military intervention.[17] Mikoyan wisely concluded that all talk of "directives" and backwardness was a display of oriental modesty not to be taken literally. Mao ended by reassuring Stalin that he would hold to "a pro-Soviet orientation," but his declaration of sympathy for Stalin's condemnation of Yugoslav nationalism indicated that what lay at the back of his mind was an attempt to allay Stalin's likely suspicions that he could shortly have another Tito on his hands.[18]

In April–May 1949 Chinese communist armies crossed the Yangtze and took Nanzhing and Shanghai. The end of the civil war lay in sight. Only the extensive but less populous outlying regions—Sinkiang, Tibet, etc.—lay beyond reach. American aid to Chiang was never sufficient because the Nationalist cause was inefficiently organized, poorly led, badly corrupted, and judged unsustainable to merit a more ambitious and more generous outlay of men as well as money. Truman scorned the Nationalists: "All the money we had given them is now invested in United States real estate," he declared in 1950.[19] The USSR nevertheless sustained diplomatic relations with Chiang to the very end. Even while the ambassadors of the capitalist Powers refused to move from Nanzhing as Nationalist forces were routed from the region, ambassador Nikolai Roshchin in February 1949 meekly followed Chiang to Canton.[20] Even when the communists crossed the Yangtze in April, Stalin still warned lest Britain and the United States resort to military intervention by landing in the rear of Mao's forces while they drove southwards. To Mao this underlined the importance of direct access to Stalin. Once again he asked to visit. Once more Stalin replied on 26 May: "We do not consider the present moment suitable."[21]

Instead, on 26 June a delegation led by Liu Shao-ch'ih arrived, focusing on technical aid and financial credit ($300 million). Received by Stalin late the following night, Liu said disingenuously that the CCP had "in the course of a prolonged period been located in the countryside, that it had conducted guerrilla warfare and was therefore very little acquainted with foreign affairs." This led to the assertion, hitherto honored only in the breach that, being merely a branch of the world communist movement, the CCP would naturally subordinate itself to Soviet wishes and "*decisions.*" To which Stalin responded with a firm "no!" Mao's projected visit Moscow toward the end of the year once diplomatic relations were established met with no objection.[22] Stalin did, however, break with custom in making something of an apology: "We have been a hindrance to you, and for this I am very regretful."[23] He had already told Kardelj: "I also doubted that the Chinese could succeed, and I advised them to come to a temporary agreement with Ch[i]ang Kai-shek. Officially, they agreed with us, but in practice they continued mobilizing the Chinese people. . . . The Chinese proved to be right, and we were wrong."[24]

But the distance separating the two sides persisted. Moscow saw the revolution as sui generis but simultaneously refused to acknowledge what flowed from this in terms of leadership in East Asia. When Liu asked Stalin if China could join the Cominform, he replied that this was "not so necessary. Why? Because there is a basic difference between the situations of the new democratic countries of Eastern Europe and China." First, imperialism "has still not abandoned its threats against China. . . . China has to put an enormous effort to resist the pressures from imperialism." Second, because the bourgeoisie of China "stood up in the struggle against America and Chiang Kai-shek," the revolutionary government had "no grounds" for repressing it. It was thus "still not possible to establish the revolutionary power of the proletarian dictatorship." On the other hand, the "situation in the countries of East Asia has a lot in common with the situation in China and creates the possibility of organizing a Union of East Asian Communist Parties." But this "may still be premature"; furthermore, because the USSR spanned Eurasia, "it would take part in the Union of East Asian Communist Parties."[25]

SOUTHEAST ASIA

Increasingly the forced radicalization of Communist parties under Cominform direction spread to the East. It was the second congress of the Indian Communist Party (28 February–6 March) and a meeting of the World Federation of Democratic Youth in Calcutta preceded by a symbolic attack on Prime Minister Pandit Nehru in *Pravda* that provided the forum for extending more aggressive tactics from Europe to the Asian subcontinent.[26] A year later the

World Federation *Bulletin* heralded the conference as a "call to intensified action," taken up by the "active liberation movements in Vietnam, Burma, Malaya, Indonesia, and particularly China."[27] "The militant policy which emerged from these conferences," CIA concluded, "is believed to have been the basis for the near-simultaneous Communist-inspired uprisings in Burma, Indonesia, and Malaya."[28] Only a year before British diplomats in Washington noted with regret that there was "no sense of a community of Anglo-American interests . . . we and other colonial powers are thought to be on the way out, assisted by Russian intrigue." No support to sustain them was therefore forthcoming.[29] Washington had to be shaken out of its disdain for allied colonialism. Until then a policy of containment in the Far East did not really exist.

Of those succumbing to revolt, Malaya was of the greatest significance commercially and strategically. It was the world's largest producer of both rubber and tin. It was also the source for most of US rubber and about one-third of its tin. The Malayan Communist Party (MCP) had been set up by Ho at the end of April 1930, its First Secretary a Chinese-speaking Vietnamese (half of the population of Malaya were Chinese);[30] Lai Te was later assassinated in Bangkok, having spied for Britain. The new Secretary of the Party from 6 March 1947, Chin Peng took the Calcutta conference to mean that insurrection was the order of the day. Moscow pointed out: "The national-liberation movement in Malaya is . . . integrally linked with the liberation struggle of the other Asiatic peoples."[31] By the end of March 1948 the MCP had embarked on a policy of selectively assassinating strikebreakers, a nucleus was established for guerrilla warfare, and fighting broke out in June.[32] A month later, anticipating a full-scale uprising then only planned, the British formally outlawed the Party with the introduction of Emergency Regulation 17b. The insurrection thus became known as the Malayan Emergency. In September some twenty members from the South China branch of the CCP left Hong Kong for Singapore to help the MCP organize the Party for insurrection.[33]

Even though China was aiding revolution elsewhere in Asia, Stalin still suspected Mao could turn to Washington. Vyshinsky emphasized to Liu the importance of China "showing particular caution and vigilance" toward them.[34] "After the victory of our revolution, Stalin had doubts about its character," Mao told Khrushchev nearly a decade later. "He thought China was a second Yugoslavia."[35] Stalin need not have worried, however. Under growing domestic pressure, Washington gave up attempts at a rapprochement with the CCP. Mao therefore announced that China would "lean to one side" (*yibiandao*). "Sitting on the fence will not do," he declared; "nor is there a third road."[36] According to Wu Xiuquan, head of the Chinese Foreign Ministry Soviet department, Stalin "continued to worry that China might also follow the road of Yugoslavia and become independent from him . . . a national policy of 'leaning to one side,' that is, to the side of the Soviet Union, was put forward by Chairman Mao, so as to allay their worries."[37]

For Mao and Liu Shao-Ch'ih similar worries emerged. At a meeting with the Soviet Politburo on 27 July, Kao Kang, leader of the Party in Manchuria, suggested declaring the region the seventeenth Soviet socialist republic and deploying Soviet forces so as to deter Washington. This proposal was greeted with applause. But Liu's face darkened menacingly. He telegraphed Beijing demanding that Kao Kang be recalled immediately for treachery.[38] Despite Stalin's call for toleration, Kao's fate was sealed. On return Liu and Chou continuously tormented him until he was finally demoted in 1954.

MAO FINALLY REACHES MOSCOW

Moscow formalized recognition of the People's Republic of China (PRC) on 2 October 1949. Yet Stalin's suspicions and reservations were evident in the poverty of Soviet press coverage, including the absence of a *Pravda* editorial and the use of the term "Mr." in the exchange of letters with Chou En-lai, China's new Foreign Minister and Chairman of the Council of Ministers.[39] The new regime was welcomed as a part of the broader struggle for national liberation against imperialism rather than as a victory for socialism, and in Soviet statements it ran behind Eastern Europe and even the new East German state as an achievement for social progress. The "unofficial" *New Times* ran an editorial, "The Chinese People's Great Victory," with emphasis on national liberation with no mention of socialism. It also tactlessly attributed a large part of the victory to the Bolshevik revolution having plunged the colonial system "into a state of crisis and debilitation," to the Soviet victory over Germany and Japan in World War II, and to "Stalin's genius."[40]

On 5 November Mao expressed a wish to visit Moscow on the occasion of Stalin's seventieth birthday, adding that he also hoped to take a break and medical treatment. Three days later this was reiterated through diplomatic channels. On 10 November Chou visited ambassador Roshchin, a GRU officer, now in Beijing, having been pragmatically but insensitively switched from one administration to the other, to reinforce the request.[41] Moscow acquiesced. Mao's purpose was to enhance the status of the Chinese People's Republic, thereby obliging "the capitalist countries to play by rules that will be set by us, it will be favorable for the unconditional recognition of China by various countries, [it will lead to] the cancellation of the old treaties and the conclusion of new ones, and it will also deter the capitalist countries from reckless undertakings."[42] He left Beijing on 7 December. His uncertain state of mind was apparent from an incident en route, when he passed through Manchuria, where he stopped to see the sights. Finding the streets of Mukden festooned with portraits of Stalin and only a few of himself, he abruptly cancelled his schedule, hastened back to the station and took off for the Soviet frontier.[43]

Mao thus arrived in Moscow on 16 December by train at Yaroslavskii station with rather mixed emotions. That day Stalin along with Molotov, Malenkov, Bulganin, and Vyshinsky received him. Mao was clearly anxious to establish personal rapport without the interference of other Chinese leaders, who were notable for their absence. Moreover he excluded China's ambassador from all discussions. But at every meeting with Stalin any attempt he made to raise all the traumas of the past in his relations with Moscow was skillfully deflected by his host. Little time was wasted on small talk. The first question Mao raised concerned the prospects for peace.[44] But a vast distance separated him from Stalin. Throughout, the "big boss" persisted in addressing Mao as "Mr." instead of "comrade." When the visit concluded in February, Mao's interpreter Shi Zhe finally asked Stalin why he did so; to which Stalin is said to have reluctantly conceded, "He is indeed a comrade. Let us say comrade."[45] Yet persistent reluctance to use normal communist nomenclature said much about Stalin's reservations toward this idiosyncratic new regime.

THE KOREAN TEMPTATION

Washington now could agree on no China policy at all — except waiting for the dust to settle. Instead, the Chinese revolution "makes it vital that, with or without a peace treaty, the orientation of Japan toward the West be assured."[46] For this reason the Americans were holding back on a peace treaty with Japan: Tokyo had to be securely in the Western camp before the risk of allowing it the independence to choose. In the meantime the construction of military, communications, and naval bases proceeded apace — notably at Yokusaka[47] — as they were across the Baring Straits from Alaska and down to Guam. Stalin could therefore expect that the future Japan could be counted into the American camp with little expectation that it might be lured away.

Meanwhile, the supreme commander of allied forces in the Far East, General MacArthur, guided by his enlightened political adviser William Sebald, molded imperial Japan as best he could to US values. Thus Stalin had every reason not to wait. Soviet eyes naturally turned to Korea. Divided in two by Moscow and Washington at the 38th parallel in 1945, the northern half was effectively a Soviet protectorate. Kim Il Sung, a Korean serving as captain in the Red Army, was placed in charge of the country. He had not been a heroic guerrilla fighter against Japan but had headed a unit operating out of Vyatskoe in the Soviet maritime province across the Manchurian border for the purposes of gathering field intelligence.[48] Kim was thus entirely a Soviet creation. In the ensuing administration Koreans with a Soviet background held more senior posts than those trained locally or in China. Russian troops were pulled out in December 1948 but a four- to five-thousand man team of advisers remained behind scattered throughout the administration to guarantee the regime's subordination to Moscow's wishes.[49] Soviet interest stemmed from a common border, flanking communications by land and sea separating Vladivostok from Port Arthur, plus a long common frontier with Manchuria. Furthermore, Korea had always represented a knife pointed at the heart of Japan.

If Japan were revived as a military Power for the capitalist cause or, at the very least, became a permanent staging area for the United States in the northwest Pacific, it made strategic sense to hold the Korean peninsula in its entirety. Without Soviet permission, nothing could be done of substance in North Korea any more than in the Eastern zone of Germany. As in the case of Germany, this certainly did not prevent hopes ever present on both sides of the divide to recover the other half. In the case of Korea, Russian and American forces of occupation withdrew but left behind a mirror image of their own dispute exacerbated by inflamed nationalist sentiment easily channeled against the other side.

Kim first proposed an invasion of South Korea to Moscow on 11 March 1949. The response was not encouraging. The Berlin blockade had failed and Stalin was scarcely of a mind to open a new chapter in confrontation until CCP victory was assured without US intervention and until an atomic test had been successfully completed. The North Korean army was not obviously superior to the South and the North could not count on Soviet participation since Washington and Moscow had agreed that the 38th parallel demarcated the line between the two. The only legitimate grounds for attack would arise if the South attacked the North.[50] An echo of Kim's request and underlying Soviet sympathy nonetheless found its way into *New Times*, where a promissory note in the form of a leader on "Soviet-Korean Relations" passed unnoticed in the West: "Korea will exist as a united and independent people's democratic state, such as all the Korean people want their country to be! In this the Korean people have, and will have, the all-round assistance of the Soviet Union."[51]

Kim was not about to give up, however. The Soviet ambassador, General Terentii Shtykov, had been a protégé of Zhdanov. His role in Pyongyang was more that of proconsul than diplomat. Nothing of any importance in North Korea happened without his permission; even the Communist Party in the South answered to him.[52] On 12 and 14 August, about to leave for Moscow and his holidays, Shtykov was again pressed for permission to invade.[53] To the chagrin of the northern leadership, the South not only failed to move toward an invasion of the North but went so far as to decide on the construction of a Maginot Line to ensure its defense along the 38th parallel.[54] Absent the virtues of self-defense, Kim now claimed that in recent border skirmishes, Pyongyang demonstrated its superiority against its opponents: invasion was therefore less of a risk. Shtykov, who carried Stalin's authority and was therefore not averse to expressing his own mind in blunt terms to a regime wholly dependent on Moscow for its very existence, pointed out that the North's leaders were excessively optimistic. As though it somehow lessened the significance of the action, Kim suggested that they just launch a local invasion on the Ongjin peninsula, with a view to using this as a base for further operations later.

Shtykov made short work of Kim's arguments. In the event of military action Washington "could intervene"; he thought it might ship in Japanese forces. Shtykov also dismissed the idea that the North was superior to the South. Evidently loath to appear wholly negative, however, he did support the idea of a limited operation against the Ongjin peninsula. No sooner had Shtykov left than Kim's personal secretary Mun Il told chargé d'affaires Tunkin that according to reliable sources the South would in the near future attack that part of the peninsula on the northern side of the parallel.[55] How this squared with Kim's assertions of the North's military superiority is hard to say. Moscow inevitably suspected that Kim was in desperate search of a casus belli to support his arguments for invasion.

Loath to take a decision that could have momentous consequences, Stalin was characteristically evasive. Instead he played for time and demanded more detailed information: not least what Kim thought Washington could do if the North attacked.[56] Kim replied that the United States might send in Japanese and Chinese troops, deploy their own instructors with the South Korean army, and use their own sea and air power.[57] Of course, Kim had no idea whether in saying this he was ensuring Soviet support—since someone would have to counter Washington: Pyongyang had no air or sea power at its disposal—or deterring Stalin. Tunkin was certain that no invasion should take place. The North's army was "insufficiently strong for launching successful and speedy operations against the South." A drawn-out war could not be won either, for both military and political reasons.[58] It would give more time for the Americans to come in. "After its failures in China," Tunkin wrote, reading the American mind with some perspicacity, "the Americans are more likely to intervene in Korean affairs more decisively than they have done in China." Moreover, he added, a drawn-out civil war in Korea "could be used by the Americans with the aim of agitation against the Soviet Union and for further exacerbation of war hysteria." Only a blitzkrieg could work, and the requirements for one in Pyongyang simply did not exist. Tunkin also dismissed the idea of a minor campaign as a Trojan horse for a full-blooded civil war by the North and would only be "used to reinforce US and international intervention in Korean affairs in the interests of the South."[59]

These sentiments were reflected in a Politburo resolution concerning the Korean question on 24 September. Shtykov was told to communicate this to Kim. Interestingly in one of the final drafts of the resolution, apparently involving Gromyko, it was prophetically pointed out that "an attack by the People's army against the South may give the Americans grounds for putting the issue to a session of the UN, accusing the KPDR [Korean People's Democratic Republic] of aggression and obtaining from the General Assembly agreement to the entry of American forces into south Korea."[60] Stalin was at this stage very reluctant to leave any door open for Kim to launch an attack on spurious evidence of an attack from the South. One draft that left this as a possibility met with Stalin's censure. In place of the text proposed, he suggested evasively, "In the event that the South Koreans begin offensive operations, you must remain ready to act in the future according to the circumstances."[61]

Pyongyang persisted, however, and its ambitions collided with those of Beijing. Here the priorities did not include war for anything except domestic objectives: first and foremost seizure of Taiwan (Formosa), allocated to China by wartime allied agreement. When Mao arrived in Moscow, this was the first point he raised in his first discussion with Stalin. China, Mao said, needed "a peaceful breathing space lasting 3–5 years which could be used to reestablish the prewar level of the economy and stabilize the overall situation in the country." The resolution of China's most important issues hinged on the international situation. Stalin sounded optimistic. No direct threat to China existed. "Japan is not yet on its feet and is therefore not ready for war; America, although it shouts about war, above all fears war; Europe is intimidated by war; in essence China has no one to fight, unless Kim Il Sung has a go at China." Peace depended on what Russia and China did: "If we are friends, peace could be guaranteed not only for 5–10 but also for 20–25 years; and, possibly, for an even longer time."[62]

Notwithstanding the expression of interest in peace, Mao sought help to seize Taiwan. On 25 July he had instructed the delegation in Moscow to request such aid over six months to a year through the training of 1,000 pilots and 300 ground crew, plus the sale of 100 to 200 fighter-planes and 40 to 80 bombers.[63] In Moscow Mao repeated the request but in even more provocative form. He asked Stalin "to send volunteer fighter pilots or secret military units to speed up the seizure of Taiwan." Yet it was the United States that had ferried Chiang and his remaining troops to safety on the island. Stalin was therefore not eager to get embroiled in a shooting match with Washington in what was seen as a residual US sphere of influence.

On 21 December CCP intelligence in Hong Kong reported conditions demanded by the US government for preserving Chiang's base in Taiwan; and they included control over both civil and military administrations on the island.[64] The Kremlin was undoubtedly aware of this. Although apparently sympathetic to Mao's request, Stalin was bound to disappoint. He insisted: "The main thing is not to give grounds for US interference. As to those at staff level and instructors, they can be contributed at any time. We will think about the rest." He suggested instead that Mao infiltrate former Nationalist troops into the island and prompt an uprising from within.[65] It was entirely acceptable, however, for Stalin to send a bomber squadron to airlift CCP troops into Sinkiang and, later, at the alliance negotiations, to agree to have them used to attack Tibet.[66]

Stalin's suspicions about Mao had been nourished by Kovalev, his emissary to the CCP. Mao, who pronounced himself in good health by the end of the first week in January, was left cooling his heels in a datcha outside Moscow and made no moves toward negotiation. Instead it was suggested he travel around. Some unpleasant conversations took place with Kovalev and orientalist Nikolai Fyodorenko. "All this offended me," Mao later complained.[67] The bleak contrast between the magnitude of his hard-won victory, attained despite rather than because of Russia, and the cool treatment he received in Moscow was hard to accept. Stalin retained serious reservations about the CCP and saw it as a force for national liberation rather than for socialism. The camp led by Moscow nevertheless now had a massive bridgehead in mainland Asia; and the North Koreans were not alone in hoping to profit by it.

Doubting Stalin's commitment, Kim tried to play off Beijing against Moscow. At a dinner in honor of both Chinese and Soviet guests in Pyongyang on 17 January 1950, he hinted that Mao was his friend and disposed to help against South Korea.[68] Insisting that if unification failed, he would personally "forfeit the trust of the people of Korea," Kim dutifully accepted that he was a communist and a disciplined man and that for him Stalin's instructions were law. But, he added, if it were impossible to see Stalin, then he would attempt to see Mao after his return from Moscow. Kim emphasized that Mao had—apparently at their meeting in June 1949—promised to render assistance after the end of the war in China, a promise which, if indeed given, Mao would later have good reason to regret.[69] Shtykov, responding to this blatant attempt at extortion, retorted that Kim had never raised the issue of meeting Stalin and that if he requested it, then something would be arranged.[70]

The greatest objection against facilitating an attack on South Korea was fear lest it provoke World War III, for which, all sides accepted, Moscow was not yet prepared. Yet the danger of general war seemed slim if not negligible. The assumption in the West was that Russia would not risk World War III; the corollary was that it would therefore not risk local war because that could escalate into major war. The Americans thus saw no need for containment to be watertight and sealed with military power forward-based. The disposition of forces on the ground was therefore dictated by long-term planning for major war, not likely until the mid-fifties, rather than limited war. The lessons from Clausewitz had again been forgotten, if ever learned. Britain's embassy in Washington read the situation better, pointing to the impact of the revolution in China in September 1949: "The impending defeat of the Nationalist forces there forced a change in American strategy in the Far East which had its most noticeable effect in Korea. A natural consequence of the fact that the success of the Communists in China left the Korean peninsula an isolated beach-head on the Asiatic continent highly vulnerable to Soviet attack, was an American willingness to withdraw."[71]

Stalin was thus not irrational in assuming that an attack by the North could conceivably be accomplished speedily and at low risk. Yet his concern lest China come to terms with the United States had not been relieved by Mao's determination to sign a new alliance. These residual anxieties may well have played a role in his decision to grant Kim's wishes. In the unlikely event that Washington was drawn in, Stalin was keen to ensure, first, that Mao had agreed on war in principle; second, that details be withheld from him until action was imminent; and, third, that if the United States entered the war, China be pressed to back up North Korea. Indeed, when the Korean War broke out, the Yugoslav ambassador to Washington, Bebler, warned that the conflict had been engineered by Moscow "in order thoroughly to embroil the United States with Communist China. Russia was, according to Bebler, apprehensive of the growth of Communist China's power and determined not to have the latter in the United Nations. It was for this reason," he continued, "that the Russians had recognised Ho-Chi-minh [sic]. Now by prevailing on the United States to take action in respect of Formosa they had effectively embroiled the Americans with the Chinese communists and put a stop to any likelihood of the latter's early admission to the United Nations."[72]

Stalin's suspicions of Mao grew rather than diminished on the eve of talks for the alliance. When Acheson spoke at the National Press Club on 12 January 1950 he defined "the [US] defensive perimeter" running "from the Ryukyus to the Philippine Islands" in such a way as to exclude South Korea, making clear that "so far as the military security of other areas in the Pacific is concerned, it must be clear that no person can guarantee these areas against military attack." He saw it "a mistake . . . in considering Pacific and Far Eastern problems to become obsessed with military considerations." Acheson also asserted the symbiotic nature of Chinese and American interests and attacked Russia for "detaching the northern provinces of China from China and . . . attaching them to the Soviet Union." In a blatant appeal to Chinese nationalism, he referred to Outer Mongolia as a former possession—the implication being that Washington might recognize it as such, which Moscow could not and would not do—and suggested that the fate of Inner Mongolia and Sinkiang would be similar. Acheson reassured Beijing that Washington would reject "foolish adventures" advocated by some on the grounds that Americans "must not undertake to deflect from the Russians to ourselves the righteous anger, and the wrath, and the hatred of the Chinese people which must develop." The stance he struck could not be read as anything other than a discreet overture for a new relationship with Beijing: "We must take the position we have always taken— that anyone who violates the integrity of China is the enemy of China and is acting contrary to our own interest."[73] The speech was thus carefully crafted to provoke problems in relations between Mao and Stalin, and given the underlying tension in relations between the two, it did.

Five days later, on 17 January, Molotov and Vyshinsky went to see Mao and proposed that the USSR, the PRC, and Outer Mongolia issue "official statements" denouncing the "shameless lie" issued by Acheson.[74] These denunciations were published on 21 January. Vyshinsky duly issued an official attack on Acheson's "slander."[75] But instead of issuing an official statement, Mao issued a lesser declaration under the name Hu Qiaomu, the head of the PRC information department; not only that, the condemnation liberally quoted Acheson's allegations and thereby made them freely available to the Chinese population.[76] Mao and Chou—who had arrived in Moscow on 20 January to negotiate the treaty of alliance—were then invited in to see Stalin and Molotov, with only the interpreters present, for a private meeting.

The atmosphere at this tête-à-tête soon clouded. Shi Zhe, Mao's interpreter, recalls Stalin turning to Molotov, who promptly quizzed Mao about the statement issued and the identity of Hu Qiaomu. Molotov attacked: "The Chinese side has failed to act in accordance with what we agreed upon, which is a violation of our agreement. As a result, China's statement fails to get the effect as we have expected. . . . To observe what we have promised is an important part of our cooperative relationship." Stalin could therefore sound more moderate, though no less offensive: "I believe that we must keep the promise we have made, cooperate with each other, and coordinate our steps. This will make us more powerful. . . . This is not a big matter. But because we have failed to act in accordance with the original arrangement, our steps become confused, leaving space for the enemy to maneuver." The subsequent ride to see Stalin did nothing to ease Mao's suppressed anger, nor did the ensuing banquet.[77]

On 30 January, with the Sino-Soviet talks proceeding slowly, Stalin sent via Shtykov a reassurance that he understood Kim's "dissatisfaction," but that he had raised an important proposal requiring serious preparation. "Matters had so to be organized that there would be not too great a risk."[78] Kremlin anxiety lest word leak out through North Korean indiscretion resulted in a further message on 2 February: "Explain to Kim Il Sung that at present the question he wishes to discuss with me must remain in confidence. There is no need to disclose it to others in the North Korean leadership, nor to the Chinese comrades." All that had been agreed with Mao in Moscow was to augment military aid to Pyongyang.[79]

After much hard bargaining by Chou, in which Chinese determination to sustain a semblance of equality, was strikingly evident (in respect of the Chinese Eastern Railway and control over joint enterprises),[80] the alliance was finally signed on 14 February[81] and an exchange of notes abrogating the Sino-Soviet treaty of 1945. Mao left Moscow three days later, his basic task achieved. To the outer world China and the USSR were now as one. Yet those privy to the actual state of relations understood that this was inherently an unstable relationship. In talks with Liu, Stalin had earlier undertaken that all Soviet intelligence agents in China make themselves known to the authorities.[82] This was confirmed in Moscow during the alliance negotiations. Yet, as Mao told Soviet ambassador Pavel Yudin in October 1957, "intelligence operations were conducted." Indeed, Roshchin (GRU) recruited at least one foreign service official, who came to Chou En-lai to inform him of the fact.[83]

ATTACK

From 30 March to 25 April Kim and his delegation stayed in Moscow to plan the attack on the South. At these talks, to which China was not invited and about which they were never consulted, Stalin said that in extremis Beijing could help Kim with their own forces. The Americans had retreated from China and would not dare fight the People's Republic. Moreover, with the conclusion of the Sino-Soviet treaty Washington was in even less of a position to crush communism in Asia. Within the United States, Stalin asserted, the dominant sentiment was to stay out of Korea because the USSR had become an atomic power (the bomb was tested at the end of August). Nevertheless, he insisted that they had to be absolutely sure Washington would not get involved.[84] What Stalin did not add was that although he had the bomb, there was as yet no means of delivery. It was also essential to have support from Beijing.

Kim argued that Washington would not risk being drawn into a major war faced, as it was, with a Sino-Soviet alliance. He also argued that China would help even to the point of sending in troops. But Stalin warned Kim that he should not count on direct participation from the USSR.[85] Not until 14 May did Stalin inform Mao that execution of the plans in train would depend upon Beijing's approval (sought by Pyongyang), and even this was prompted by news that Kim was arranging a meeting with the Chinese.[86] Mao approved the plans but offered his own advice, stemming from his civil war strategy, not to concentrate the attack on the cities. He also expressed concern lest Washington send in Japanese forces. The presence of such troops, he warned, could extend the conflict; and even the Americans themselves might get involved.[87] Kim rashly dismissed such fears out of hand.[88] It should at this point have been apparent to all that China was scarcely 100 percent behind the war and that its complete support was a matter of doubt.

Kim informed Moscow on 27 May that he preferred to invade at the end of June for two reasons: first, military preparations would become apparent if they delayed any longer; and, second, the rainy season began in July. Shtykov spoke to those Soviet generals advising the Koreans, Vasil'ev and Postnikov. They took a dim view of the likelihood that the armies would be fully ready by then.[89] All the Soviet armaments arrived by the end of May, by which time the plan of attack detailed by the Koreans in conjunction with Vasil'ev was in his hands.[90] The final plan was completed only on 15 June. The attack would take place nine days later. It must have disturbed Moscow to learn at the last minute of a request for landing craft manned by Russians to enable an encirclement of enemy forces from east and west.[91]

Mao was reluctant to have an official summit with Kim if war were imminent.[92] Nevertheless Kim arrived in Beijing on 13 May. The war was an immediate prospect, but Mao treated with some caution the assertion that Stalin approved an invasion but expressed his full support when assured that this was correct. A full discussion between Mao and Kim took place two days later. Although supportive in principle, Mao expressed concern lest Japanese forces (which did not officially exist) be sent in by Washington along with US troops.

Kim insisted the United States showed no sign of readiness to fight in the Far East, adding that just as they left China without fighting, they were also proving cautious in Korea.[93] Mao warned: "Should the Americans leave and the Japanese not turn up, in this situation we would not advise the Korean comrades to undertake an attack on South Korea, but to wait for more suitable circumstances because in the course of this offensive MacArthur could swiftly deliver Japanese units and weapons to Korea."[94] Mao was very nearly entirely correct.

The attack took the South by surprise on Sunday 25 June at 4.00 a.m. Korean time with an artillery barrage. And aside from a general warning from the US army that military action was a possibility, intelligence was unprepared for what followed.[95] Two hours later infantry and tanks crossed the 38th parallel from the North into Ongjin near Kaesong and Chunchon while landings were made along the coast. Truman was at home in Independence, Missouri. On receiving the news of this "all out offensive" by telegram that evening (still Saturday, US time) between 10.00 and 10.30 p.m., Acheson immediately telephoned the president.[96] By the following evening Truman was back for a meeting with the secretaries of state and defense and the Joint Chiefs of Staff on the Korean situation. By then Acheson had persuaded the UN Security Council to adopt a resolution condemning North Korea and calling for immediate withdrawal to the 38th parallel. It passed without opposition, Yugoslavia abstaining. The Soviet representative was not present, at Stalin's stubborn insistence, because the UN refused to recognize Communist China. Thus Washington had a free hand. General Omar Bradley "said that Russia is not yet ready for war" and that the "Korean situation offered as good an occasion for action in drawing the line as anywhere else." He also "said we should act under the guise of aid to the United Nations." Admiral Sherman echoed these sentiments, saying "that the Russians do not want war now but if they do they will have it. The present situation in Korea offers a valuable opportunity for us to act." Only General Vandenberg said "he would not base our action on the assumption that the Russians would not fight."[97]

At this stage Truman held back MacArthur's forces in Japan until it was clear to all that North Korea had ignored the Security Council resolution. Finally on Monday, 26 June, he issued a statement to the effect that "the United States will vigorously support the effort of the Council to terminate this serious breach of the peace."[98] Up to this point US action against the North Koreans by air and sea had been restricted to avoid combat. That evening at a further session with Truman, Acheson argued and received agreement for "an all-out order . . . to the Navy and Air Force to waive all restrictions on their operations in Korea and to offer the fullest possible support to the South Korean forces, attacking tanks, guns, columns, etc., of the North Korean forces." This was to be done exclusively south of the 38th parallel. When Truman said no action was to be taken north of the line, he also added "not yet." These decisions were taken in the knowledge that State had prepared a second UN resolution and that it counted on full support. Acheson "noted that even the Swedes were now supporting us."[99] The resolution duly passed by the Security Council on 27 June recommended that North Korea having failed to comply with the previous resolution, "the Members of the United Nations furnish such assistance to the Republic of Korea as may be necessary to repel the armed attack and to restore international peace and security in the area."[100] MacArthur simultaneously established a command post in Seoul.

Stalin now realized his mistake in boycotting the Security Council to force the diplomatic recognition of Communist China. Permanent representative Malik returned early July to block progress. The Americans then moved to the General Assembly, where they commanded an automatic majority. It issued the "Uniting for Peace" resolution, and in so doing circumvented the Soviet veto effectively ignored the UN charter. Stalin had long before become concerned lest the North held back from completing its mission. On 1 July he telegraphed Shtykov that he had heard nothing about current plans of the Korean command. Were they going to continue the advance or had they decided to call a halt where they were? "In our opinion," he advised, "the attack must unquestionably be continued and the sooner South Korea is liberated, the less the chances of intervention." Stalin also wanted to know how the North was responding to US air attacks behind the 38th parallel.[101] Shtykov immediately saw Kim, who not only asked for more munitions but also attempted to find out whether Moscow would intervene more directly.[102]

On 8 July Kim asked Stalin for permission to make use of twenty-five to thirty-five Soviet military advisers at the front because of the shortage of skilled personnel. But Stalin was extremely reluctant to risk Soviet personnel falling into American hands. At the same time, in spite of the difficulties that Pyongyang was increasingly meeting, Kim dismissed out of hand Britain's proposal that he withdraw behind the parallel to speed a peaceful resolution of the conflict. Stalin intended to give the perverse reply that "the Korean question has become too complicated after armed foreign intervention and that such a complex question could be resolved only by the Security Council with the participation with the USSR and China and with the Korean representatives called in so that their opinion can be heard."[103] As the situation worsened, however, the North began to lose its nerve. Stalin tried to reassure Pyongyang. On 28 August he sent his congratulations, saying that there were allies who would assist them and that the situation during the allied war of intervention in Russia in 1919 had been a good deal worse.[104]

MacArthur's bold and successful landing at Inchon on 15 September made possible by breaking enemy codes and ciphers spliced the armies of the North; the worst fears on the Communist side were now realized. Three days later the Soviet ambassador and two military advisers were called in to see Chou. Chou asked if they were aware of the landing and went on to complain that Pyongyang left Beijing uninformed. The North Koreans had never even replied to a Chinese request to send military observers from their frontier regions.[105] At this stage Beijing was fairly sanguine that Washington might seek compromise to avoid an extended war. This is certainly what Mao told Pavel Yudin. Yudin was in Beijing to edit Mao's works, but he also acted as an unofficial emissary for Stalin.[106] The conversation took place on 22 September.

Moscow, on the other hand, had become seriously alarmed at MacArthur's thrust and warned Kim to withdraw at least four divisions northward to avoid being cut off from the rear. The first and second army groups disobeyed Kim's orders to retreat, with disastrous consequences. Stalin was probably as much alarmed at Chinese sangfroid as he was at the circumstances in which the North Koreans now found themselves. And since he had no intention of directly embroiling Soviet forces in the conflict, he now worked hard to get China involved.

Like a rabbit hypnotized in the middle of the road by the lights of oncoming traffic, Pyongyang now panicked. Not merely were its forces being sliced in two but US air power was bringing home the war to those who had launched it. At Moscow's instruction Marshal Vasil'evsky finalized a plan for the deployment of Soviet air force squadrons primarily to defend Pyongyang and other cities and communications from air attack.[107] Indeed, the situation deteriorated to the point where on 29 September Shtykov asked Moscow for the evacuation of the majority of advisers and embassy personnel from North Korea.[108] The following day Kim wrote to Stalin: "We cannot but ask for special assistance from you. In other words at the moment hostile forces cross the 38th parallel we will very much need direct military aid from the Soviet Union."[109]

CHINA CROSSES THE YALU

From a datcha in distant Sochi on 1 October Stalin sent an urgent dispatch calling on China to send in five to six divisions immediately to hold back the American advance and allow North Korea to pull in reserves behind them. "The Chinese divisions could take the form of volunteers, of course, with Chinese commanders in charge."[110] Replying two days later Mao said China had originally thought of sending in volunteers when "the enemy" breached the 38th parallel. "However, thinking matters through, we now consider that this kind of action could prompt the most serious consequences." Several divisions would be insufficient. Not only was China no match for the Americans — "the enemy might force us to retreat" — but "it is most likely that it would precipitate an open conflict between the United States and China, as a consequence of which the Soviet Union also might be drawn into war, and thereby become a question of great moment." Many comrades, he emphasized, considered that caution was required. He also added that an open conflict with the United States threatened to wreck the plan for peaceful construction at home and that the people needed more time to recover from the strains of war. Mao did, however, emphasize that a final decision had yet to be taken and that an expanded plenum of the Central Committee would meet to discuss the matter.[111]

Roshchin reported that he had no idea what had shifted opinion in Beijing: possibly the Anglo-American soundings through Nehru warning against disaster.[112] In a gloomy state of mind, on 5 October the Politburo took a decision to withdraw from North Korea some of its advisers and employees.[113] Stalin steadfastly held to the view that "the USA, as the Korean events have shown, is not ready at present for a big war." This had consistently been his view since 1945 yet doubtless said at this point to encourage Mao into battle. As was the assurance that "the USA will be obliged to concede on the Korean question to China, behind which stands its ally the USSR, and will agree to such conditions for the regulation of the Korean question that would be favorable to Korea, and which would not give enemies the possibility of transforming Korea into its *place d'armes*." "For the same reasons," Stalin continued, "the USA will be obliged not only to renounce Taiwan but also renounce a separate peace with the Japanese reactionaries, renounce the restoration of Japanese imperialism and the transformation of Japan into its *place d'armes* in the Far East." But, Stalin insisted, "China cannot receive these concessions as a result of passive temporizing." Even if the Americans ended up causing a great war "from prestige," the USSR and China together were stronger than the United States and Britain, the only capitalist states that counted. "If war is inevitable," Stalin boasted, "then let it be now and not after a few years when Japanese militarism is restored as an ally of the USA and when the USA and Japan have a *place d'armes* ready on the continent in the form of Li Syn Man's Korea."[114]

The pressure continued. But Stalin seemed to be getting nowhere. On 12 October he told Kim: "The Chinese have again refused to send forces. In this connection you must evacuate North Korea and move Korean forces northwards."[115]

A day later the message was further reinforced: "We consider the continuation of resistance pointless. The Chinese comrades refuse to participate militarily. In these circumstances, you will have to prepare full evacuation to China or the USSR." The message came as a shock to the North Korean leadership; they nonetheless agreed to set about planning the evacuation.[116] But no sooner had spirits reached their lowest point than a further telegram completely altered the situation. Yudin reported a conversation with Mao. The Central Committee had again discussed the matter and had finally decided on military assistance.[117] What made the decisive difference was the Soviet commitment to Chou in Moscow that Russia would provide air support (a promise they promptly reneged on once China went in).

Stalin's war by proxy against the West in Korea came to have catastrophic results for Sino-American relations and did no small damage to Korea itself. Whether intended or not, the war tied Beijing to Moscow until the armistice at Panmunjon on 27 July 1953. Thereafter China remained alienated from the United States for nearly two decades, despite falling out with Russia in the early 1960s. The Korean War thus worked to Moscow's advantage despite ending in stalemate. The Sino-Soviet alliance held together for negative rather than positive reasons, although the underlying friction between Beijing and Moscow was barely concealed beneath the surface of comradeship, even in war. Late in the autumn of 1950 Sir Gladwyn Jebb, Britain's permanent representative to the UN, gave a ride to Malik, his Soviet counterpart, after a cocktail party. "On the way," Jebb recalls, "he [Malik] expanded at length on the tendency of the Chinese to regard *all* foreigners as devils, not only those who 'come by sea' but also those who 'come by land' as well."[118] It proved greatly to the disadvantage of the United States not to recognize and act on this truth as the shortsighted policy of the incoming Eisenhower administration was to demonstrate.

5

THAW

It would be a pity if a sudden frost nipped spring in the bud, or if this could be alleged, even if there was no real spring.

—Winston Churchill

Stalin died on 5 March at 9:50 p.m., sprawled across a sofa bed in the big hall at the "near" datcha within the Moscow suburb of Kuntsevskaya, Volynskaya or, to the security organs, "Object 001." He had lost consciousness four days earlier; it is reported that no one dared approach because of previous false alarms that had aroused his fury.[1] The doctors had finally arrived at 7:00 a.m. on 2 March. His condition was "extremely serious": a brain hemorrhage on top of hypertension and general arteriosclerosis.[2] Survival appeared unlikely.

If the Cold War could be attributed largely to the person of Stalin, now an end to it could have been expected. "After the death of Stalin our country underwent a serious test," Khrushchev said later.[3] Stalin never believed his successors would be able to cope. He scorned their chances of survival: "When I die," Stalin admonished them, "you will perish; the enemy will smother you as they would partridges."[4] It may be hard to see his successors as almost tame, unintelligent and overfed birds, but perhaps in comparison with the big boss they were. "Right up to his death Stalin tried to convince us that we, his fellow Politburo members, were worthless people, that we would not be capable of withstanding the forces of imperialism, that at the first personal contact we would not know how to be worthy of representing our country and how to defend its interests," recalled Khrushchev.[5] Stalin "underestimated people who worked around him. We had nothing to do with foreign policy. Only he and Molotov handled that." Khrushchev claims he himself "didn't even see the documents."[6] Indeed, at Politburo meetings Stalin wandered the room smoking his pipe while members argued out a foreign policy issue, then on occasion turned and stopped in front of Khrushchev to ask what "our Mikita" thought, prompting smiles and chuckles—the very idea of which seemed comical.[7] Not surprisingly, Khrushchev recalled, when Stalin died it was "a very hard time" for those remaining.[8]

HOW MUCH CHANGE?

Stalin's dominance had also blocked any prospect of détente, having extended communism across one-third of the world's surface. His role in the emergence of the Cold War was freely acknowledged within the leadership. "Stalin did not always approach an evaluation of the international situation soberly; he overestimated the role of our armed forces," Khrushchev noted.[9] Both he and Mikoyan recalled that Stalin also "changed greatly in the latter years of his life, becoming more suspicious and intolerable [intolerant?]."[10] Deputy Chairman of the Council of Ministers Maxim Saburov, a Party member from 1920, commented that "in the postwar period they [Stalin and Molotov] ruined relations with all nations." "We lost a great deal from a stupid policy (the war with Finland, Korea, Berlin)," he added.[11] Defense Minister Nikolai Bulganin said Stalin had spoiled the USSR's relations with neighbors Turkey and Iran.[12] Yet criticism remained tactical rather than strategic, marginal rather than fundamental. Moreover, Stalin's legacy also meant that his successors felt pressured to disprove by example his accusations of weakness. This necessarily meant standing up to the West. Doing so in the Eisenhower-Dulles era when Americans were fiercely anticommunist and possessed strategic military supremacy was, however, even less likely to succeed than under Truman. The omens were thus not good.

Since the Cold War began over Stalin's threat to the balance of Europe, his death raised the possibility of resolving the German problem. But the Cold War was not so simply packaged. It represented two conflicts conflated into one; and the second element, the global ideological struggle between the United States and USSR, ran along a dynamic entirely of its own to which even Stalin had had to adjust. The threat to the balance of Europe had been accelerated if not originally prompted by Stalin's abiding concern to preempt US global dominance. Stalin's line also stemmed from a dangerous and visceral sentiment epitomized in Molotov but shared by his successors that somehow victory in World War II gave Moscow the moral right to determine the fate of Europe unilaterally. Moreover, when in 1945–46 the West was ready for accommodation to settle the affairs of Europe, Stalin had held to unilateral expansion at the expense of his neighbors. Now, with Stalin gone and the Kremlin apparently more willing to deal, Western resolve, itself a consequence of Soviet obduracy but reinforced by ignorance, was not easily abated.

Eisenhower's administration had come to power in January 1953 on a wave of anticommunist sentiment that held policy hostage not merely on China but also on the USSR. "Rollback" was a Republican election slogan and the policy adopted, albeit cautiously, in the years to come. Senators William Knowland, Styles Bridges, and Joseph McCarthy rose to toast the Chinese Nationalists with the slogan "Back to the mainland."[13] Doctrinal assumptions were, however, firmly underpinned by interests. To have accepted the potential for change in Moscow would have jeopardized German rearmament, were reunification on offer in return for renunciation of NATO membership. The plain fact was that the Eisenhower administration had no interest in détente.

The degree to which American thinking had become warlike in reaction to strategic intelligence assessments that were little more than guesses even before the Korean War illustrates the dangers that the Kremlin now faced with Stalin's demise. On 29 April 1950 General George Kenney of the USAF wrote to Chief of Staff Hoyt Vandenberg: "By all previous definitions, we are now in a state of war with Russia. Whether we call it a cold war or apply any other term, we are not winning. We are not seriously mobilizing to start winning or to undertake the offensive between now and mid-summer 1952. When a state of war exists, it is not necessary to tell out opponent what our next move is going to be. It seems to me," he concluded, "that almost any analysis of the situation shows that the only way that we can be certain of winning is to take the offensive as soon as possible and hit Russia hard enough to at least prevent her from taking over Europe."[14]

A further problem arose in that the "early days of the new Eisenhower administration represented the blackest period for U.S. intelligence on Soviet forces and strategic capabilities."[15] In the absence of adequate secret intelligence, a tendency had entrenched itself to exaggerate Soviet strength and willpower. Russia was reaping what it had sown by concealing so completely its serious vulnerabilities from prying eyes. Yet important though lack of direct access was, even where expertise existed—analysts within CIA; Bohlen and Louis Joxe, his French counterpart in Moscow; Robert Conquest in Whitehall; and journalists like the Marxist Isaac Deutscher—it was carelessly tossed aside. The line that nothing substantial *would* change because nothing substantial *could* change thus became something of a self-fulfilling prophecy. The doctrine of totalitarianism refurbished at Harvard by Carl Friedrich and the ambitious young Zbigniew Brzezinski, just when some argued it was reaching its sell-by date in 1956, was a lesson too recently learned to be casually abandoned.[16]

SUCCESSION

On the eve of Stalin's death, 4–5 March, Malenkov had already emerged as the leading figure in the Kremlin, initially as both leading Party secretary and Chairman of the Council of Ministers. Short—only about five feet four inches—eunuch-like, plump, flabby, with a full head of dark hair, a cherubic but sallow complexion and an expressive face with finer features than those of his colleagues, Georgii ("Yegor") Maximilianovich Malenkov was born in Orenburg on 8 January 1902.[17] Malenkov's father was from the hereditary nobility, of Macedonian descent, who had served as colonel in the tsar's army. He married a blacksmith's daughter and was as a consequence alienated from the family. Thus when Maximilian died of pneumonia, leaving the children behind, Malenkov's mother had to work hard as a midwife to sustain the family. Malenkov joined the Bolsheviks in the civil war, entered the Party in 1920, took higher education on demobilization, but was recruited to serve in the Central Committee apparatus before completing his degree. Here he became a technical secretary to the Politburo before being assigned a senior job in the Moscow Party. Malenkov worked closely with secret police chief Yezhov from 1936. Yezhov was eventually arrested in Malenkov's own office when Beria became head of the secret police. Malenkov was elected to the Central Committee on 22 March 1939, becoming a secretary, member of the organization bureau, and head of the personnel directorate.[18] On 18 March 1946 he joined the Politburo. A setback arose on 6 May: on the grounds of faults in the aviation industry, for which he had been in theory responsible, Malenkov was suddenly demoted, a position not restored until 1 July 1948 when he outmaneuvered rival Zhdanov who fell into disgrace for being too lenient over rebel Yugoslavia. After Zhdanov died, Malenkov never looked back.

Following Molotov's removal from the Foreign Ministry, Malenkov effectively became second secretary to Stalin. He therefore held the reins of power on Stalin's death. "At that time Malenkov was the main figure" despite never having actually headed a Party organization, Molotov complained.[19] At the Central Committee plenum on 14 March 1953, however, Malenkov offered to relinquish one of his two positions. He stepped down as the senior Party secretary while retaining chairmanship of the Council of Ministers. And as chairman he also continued to chair meetings of the Party Presidium (Politburo) as had Lenin, Rykov, Molotov, and Stalin before him. Even though no longer Party secretary he also continued—until September—to control the Party secretariat.[20] So he had every reason for believing himself secure. Yet Malenkov had been nominated by the one man all others feared equally: chief of the secret police, the sinister Beria.[21] And the semi-literate Nikita Khrushchev, thus far much underestimated, though a member of the Presidium, continued as Party secretary but now chaired meetings of the secretariat.

The son of a Mingrelian peasant, who sacrificed much for his son's education, Beria was born near Sukhumi in Abkhazia on 29 March 1899. He was "rather a stout man, with a fleshy face and blue ice-cold staring eyes . . . always on the alert."[22] Beria once dreamed of becoming an architect and was a passable artist. After technical education, however, he was rapidly drawn into the secret police in 1921 where his analytical mind was put to ruthless work. He was good at the job. Within three years he was deputy head of the Cheka in Georgia. Head of the NKVD from 24 November 1938, Beria moved to become chief of strategic intelligence during World War II. From 20 August 1945 he chaired a special committee supervising the atomic bomb project.[23] His path to power paralleled that of Malenkov in the latter phases, becoming a Politburo member at the very same time on 18 March 1946.[24] More than that: "Malenkov and Beria appeared to be great friends," Molotov noted;[25] Malenkov, he pointed out in 1955, had been "tied to that rascal Beria for a decade."[26]

Just hours before Stalin's death, at 8:00 p.m. on 5 March, a joint meeting of the Central Committee in plenum, the Council of Ministers, and the Presidium of the Supreme Soviet gathered for a forty-minute meeting to rubber-stamp what had been agreed in an informal gathering of the old guard in the room above Stalin. At that gathering, and to the astonishment of all, Malenkov and Beria suddenly appeared with "pre-prepared suggestions, Central Committee declarations, proposals for the Presidium of the Supreme Soviet—the composition of the government, heads of government, ministries."[27] This included Malenkov's appointment as chairman of the Council of Ministers. Malenkov, Beria, and Khrushchev were to take charge of Stalin's papers, both current and past.[28]

The preeminence of Malenkov was bound to cause alarm sooner or later because he seemed infinitely pliable. Not a natural leader, by nature a trimmer, he was viewed by Molotov as bereft of ideology: "very active, lively, evasive. On key questions he fell silent."[29] He was "not . . . independent-minded."[30] Mikoyan also believed "Malenkov was a weak-willed individual."[31] He had two pejorative nicknames: "tumbleweed"[32] (according to Khrushchev) and "telephone man"[33] (according to Molotov). "He's a clerk," Khrushchev scoffed, quoting Stalin. "He can compose a resolution quickly, not always himself, but he can organize people. He can do it faster and better than others, but he is not capable of any kind of independent thought or independent initiative."[34] Malenkov's repetition at a Kremlin banquet of the phrase *"Terpeniya, terpeniya i terpeniya"* (patience,

patience, and again patience) epitomized his approach to politics.[35] Clearly, this was not a man with the strength of character to set post-Stalinist Russia on a new course.

No one disputed Malenkov's intelligence, however. Indeed, Bohlen was pleased that "he at least seemed to perceive our position and, while he did not agree with it, I felt he understood it. With other leaders, [however,] particularly Khrushchev, there was no meeting point, no common language. Like trains on parallel tracks, we went right by each other."[36] The obvious danger, though, was that the impressionable Malenkov would do Beria's bidding and before long the rest of the leadership would face an untimely end. After the death of Stalin, Beria set up a special group, headed by his assistant Mamulov, charged with the preparation of "an agenda for initiatives."[37] He thus showed an unhealthy eagerness to lead on policy, though later the plea came that he was merely acting like the others. "I, also, like all of you tried to bring forward proposals to the Presidium directed toward the correct resolution of questions such as on Korea and Germany. Replies to Eisenhower and Churchill, the Turkish and Iranian questions, etc."[38] Molotov concurred: Beria was "a very able man possibly"; however, he wanted "to make decisions along his own lines."[39] Doubtless the defection of Burgess and Maclean from Britain in May 1951 made available a great deal of information about the substance as well as the making of British and American policy toward the USSR. It also provided a unique source of advice upon which the post-Stalin policies could be based.[40] What is surprising, however, is how little constructive use was made of them in the Khrushchev era or, indeed, thereafter.

Initially Khrushchev "befriended Beria and Malenkov."[41] Indeed, Mikoyan remembered his recurrent anxiety at seeing the three of them leave at the end of each day closeted at the back of Beria's car in deep discussion. It was only later and to their surprise that the others learned how greatly Khrushchev feared Beria and how determined he was to dispose of him once and for all.[42] Born in the Kursk region—the Don basin—on 17 April 1894, a member of the Party from 1918, Khrushchev rose rapidly through the ranks during Stalin's terror.[43] He stood at a mere five feet four inches (all Stalin's lieutenants had to be smaller than his five feet six inches) but weighed around 220 pounds with a 49-inch waist, protruding ears, and several chins. He had kidney problems, liver problems, and high blood pressure and, typically, ignored doctors just as he was to ignore most other professional advice.[44]

"One can never forget that tubby little figure," recalled ambassador Sir Humphrey Trevelyan, "showing on his face the emotions of the moment, either happy, amused and showing off or bored and depressed, waddling into a party with supreme self-confidence. And when he let himself go even Mrs. Khrushchev was heard to remark that she wished he would stop."[45] A member of the Central Committee from 10 February 1934, Khrushchev joined the Politburo as a nonvoting member at the height of the terror on 14 February 1938, becoming a full member from 22 March 1939 and a secretary of the Central Committee on 16 October 1952. He never succeeded in learning how to write. Former chairman of the KGB Semichastny recalled that he could not even put decisions on paper. The only item in his own hand was his signature; even the word "agreed" was recorded by aides.[46] Khrushchev did, however, learn to read fluently.[47] "This was a man of natural talents," reflected Mikoyan, "who can be compared to a diamond in the rough. In spite of his very limited education he quickly caught the point; he learned quickly. He had leadership qualities: persistence, unyielding in pursuit of his objectives, courage and readiness to go against convention. Granted, he was inclined to extremes. . . . Attracted to a new idea, he knew no limit, didn't want to listen to anyone and drove ahead like a tank."[48] Their relationship grew when Khrushchev took on board the need for de-Stalinization, a policy originating with Malenkov but backed by Mikoyan.

A slim build, his swarthy face dominated by a powerful-looking hooked nose, bridged by glittering dark eyes, a Hitler moustache, and a cleft chin, Mikoyan was a man widely acknowledged to have great ability; uniquely within the Soviet leadership he had an instinctive understanding of international relations, though still recognizably a Leninist. He was undoubtedly the best foreign minister Moscow never had. "Diplomacy is a means that must be deployed across the board," he argued, largely in vain.[49] Born on 25 November 1895, into a working-class household in the village of Sanain, Allahverdi, now part of Armenia, like Stalin Mikoyan received his education in a seminary and even advanced from secondary level to the theological academy. He was, however, a member of the Party from 1915 and served with the Red Army from its formation in 1918. Mikoyan became part of the Central Committee early, from 26 April 1923, a candidate member of the Politburo on 19 December 1927, but not a voting member until 22 March 1939. His expertise was foreign trade and light industry, both low priorities on the Stalinist list and therefore politically a safe cul-de-sac that kept him out of the cemetery. A survivor par excellence—Stalin used to joke that for some reason only hinted at he was the only Baku commissar left alive by a British-sponsored firing squad—Mikoyan nonetheless openly sympathized with Litvinov's pro-British foreign policy (along with Voroshilov) as against Molotov's German preferences in the 1930s.[50]

Mikoyan and Beria had worked together in their youth. "They hated one another," says Molotov, invariably correct on such matters.[51] "After the death of

Stalin," Molotov recalls, "[Mikoyan] became strongly linked to Khrushchev."[52] But this was by no means happened immediately after Stalin's death. Mikoyan was well aware that "at first Khrushchev had little ability in foreign policy but he quickly mastered it."[53] And US intelligence later concluded that in foreign affairs "Mikoyan appears to have been the originator of his [Khrushchev's] principal concepts."[54] But the relationship grew only once Malenkov's star visibly faded in the autumn of 1954. It was then increasingly reinforced by Molotov's stubborn if not obtuse resistance to foreign policy initiatives in 1955.

Not all ran smoothly, however. Mikoyan's younger son notes that his father and Khrushchev developed a "curious relationship. They were friends, but Khrushchev was envious of my father's background and education."[55] Moreover, Mikoyan recalled it "difficult to imagine just how careless and disloyal to people Khrushchev could be. . . . He was jealous of me; he frequently attacked me. . . . I wasn't silent on any issue. I never engaged in intrigue but argued openly. . . . This made him angry." At least twice Mikoyan nearly resigned: first, over the occupation of Hungary in 1956 after he had negotiated a peaceful solution; second, over the ultimatum on Berlin in 1958.[56] But though clearly irritated by Mikoyan's obvious intellectual superiority, Khrushchev valued his "penetrating intelligence" and his "ability to generalize from facts. It was interesting to exchange ideas with him," Khrushchev noted, "and at other times argue about international affairs and domestic problems."[57] In the end, Khrushchev could not do without him. It was like Stalin and Molotov in the latter days: complementarity rather than similarity with an undertone of rivalry.

Restored to the Foreign Ministry, now inhabiting a Stalinist gothic skyscraper towering over Smolenskaya Square, in his early sixties Molotov proved "incapable of innovation."[58] "After Stalin they [Malenkov, Beria, Khrushchev, and Mikoyan] tried to break our policy," Molotov recalls.[59] The claims made by Alexandrov-Agentov, later Brezhnev's senior foreign policy aide, that it would be "unjust to present Molotov's actions in this period as unremittingly conservative and opposed to flexibility (as it was in the Austrian and Yugoslav questions and certain others)" lacks credibility, not least because the only instances he cites of Molotov's initiatives are the amelioration of relations with Iran (Molotov anyway never approved of Stalin's expansionism to the south) and the Korean truce, which Stalin had opposed for fear of admitting he had been wrong in going ahead with the invasion of South Korea.[60]

The Soviet leadership was thus in some disarray while Molotov obdurately refused to turn back the Stalinist wheel. Malenkov reflected a pervasive anxiety when he said that on Stalin's death "the whole of the world hostile to us counted on a struggle within the leadership of our C[entral] C[ommittee]."[61] Defense Minister Bulganin recalled that "in the last years before Stalin's death we faced a very serious international situation. In relations with the Western Powers and [*sic*] the USA we were on the verge of war."[62] This is a claim repeated by First Deputy Foreign Minister Vasily Kuznetsov.[63]

NATO PARALYZED

Ironically at a time when Russia was nervous of exposing differences to NATO, now a full-fledged organization, the West was also paralyzed by the thought of dropping its guard vis-à-vis Moscow. Stalin had done all he dared to overturn German rearmament with the proposal for neutralization and re-unification on 10 March 1952. It served a double purpose: first, in purporting to render rearmament unnecessary; and second, in reminding the troublesome and headstrong Walter Ulbricht that he and his regime were ultimately dispens-able.[64] On 2 April Stalin told East German leaders "that, whatever proposals on the German question we may bring forward, the Western Powers will not come to an understanding and in any event will never leave West Germany. To think that a compromise will result or that the Americans will accept the draft of a peace treaty is to make a mistake. The Americans need an army in Germany to keep Western Europe in their hands." They had "Adenauer in their pocket." He did not want the East Germans heralding socialism. That would continue to be built economically but under "a mask" so as "not to scare off the middle strata in West Germany." Stalin summed it up: "In the beginning was the fact, and then came the word." Instead "the propagation of German unity must be con-tinued the whole time"; that has great significance for those in West Germany. "Now that you have these weapons in your hands, you must keep it in your hands the whole time." "We will go further in making proposals for the unity of Germany to expose the Americans."[65]

Even though the West demonstrated in the subsequent "battle of the notes" that Moscow had no real interest in delivering on this promise, it feared any ap-peasement given the credulity of public opinion founded on fears of Germany rearmed. The United States finally induced France into signing up to the Eu-ropean Defense Community (EDC) on 26 May 1952. It did so by offering finan-cial aid, continued backing for colonial wars in Indochina and North Africa, and a more prominent role in NATO decision making. Thereafter, however, Paris hesitated to bring forward ratification in the face of Gaullist opposition and from fear of having to depend on the socialists as a quid pro quo to muster sufficient votes in parliament.[66]

On Stalin's death the fate of the EDC thus still hung in the balance. The rapid emission of overtures from Moscow made all recipients in the West un-easy, evident at the NATO Council on 24 April 1953. The argument made was to build up greater power as a prelude to some distant negotiation: in short, negotiation from strength.[67] At a special meeting of the National Security Council (NSC) on 31 March, Secretary of State Foster Dulles "turned to ways and means of ending the peril represented by the Soviet Union. This, he said, could be done by inducing the disintegration of Soviet power. This power is already overextended and represents tyrannical rule over unwilling peoples. If we keep our pressure on, psychological and otherwise," he continued, "we may either force a collapse of the Kremlin regime or else transform the Soviet orbit from a union of satellites dedicated to aggression, into a coalition for defense only. Of course, said the secretary of state, no one can surely tell, but Stalin's death certainly marked the end of an era. There is no real replacement for Stalin the demi-god. The current peace offensive is designed by the Soviets to relieve the ever-increasing pressure upon their regime. Accordingly, we must not relax this pressure until the Soviets give promise of ending the struggle. The amount of dollars this will take will certainly fluctuate, but the American effort must not now be abandoned."[68]

Returned to power on 26 October 1951, Churchill was not entirely alone in seeing an opportunity on Stalin's death.[69] But he was isolated in his enthusiasm and his determination. "The PM feels that Stalin's death may lead to a relaxation of tension," Churchill's doctor noted. "It is an opportunity which will not recur and with [Foreign Secretary] Anthony [Eden] away he is sure he can go straight head. He seems to think of little else."[70] Eden "did not share the optimism of those who saw in this event an easement of the world's problems."[71] But Eisenhower buried the idea. A summit was not scheduled until January 1954, by which time the delicate configuration of power in the Kremlin had shifted to the disadvantage of more thorough-going reform in both domestic and foreign policy. The momentum was thus lost. Dulles, Konrad Adenauer, and Molotov had won.

DISSOLUTION OF THE GDR?

The only real opportunity to end the European Cold War was unwittingly forestalled by a proposal hastily prepared by Beria and Malenkov. The ideas behind it had been brewing for months. But its unexpected appearance broke the coalition. It had been prompted by fear of collapse in the German Democratic Republic (GDR.) Under Ulbricht's utterly unimaginative direction the country had taken a leap toward a command economy by forcing the development of heavy industry and the collectivization of agriculture at the expense of the population's poor standard of living. This was approved by the Politburo on

8 July 1952. The net result was to prompt a wave of refugees—above all the most skilled—fleeing the country through West Berlin. Between January 1951 and April 1953 more than 447,000 escaped.[72] The regime was in crisis.

Proposals were prepared initially on 18 May 1953 for consideration by the Council of Ministers' committee of three—Molotov, Malenkov, and Beria. In drafting the proposals on "Questions about the GDR," however, Beria—backed by the pliant Malenkov—took advantage of the occasion to propose dissolving the regime in the GDR: in framing proposals "we should start from the fact that the basic reason for the unsatisfactory situation in the GDR is the course, mistaken in current circumstances, toward the construction of socialism carried out in the GDR." Beria went on to suggest they reconsider government measures to restrict the activity of capitalist elements in the economy, notably in trade and agriculture.[73]

On receiving his copy, Molotov asked Malenkov whether this meant that movement toward the construction of capitalism *was* correct since "there was no other course." Malenkov's answer was "I don't know." When Beria was asked him whether "the course toward forcing the construction of socialism" was incorrect, he bluntly retorted, "Of course, it is incorrect; then shall we take a course toward capitalism? I agree."[74] At a meeting of the Presidium of the Council of Ministers the majority agreed on rejecting plans for socialist construction and agricultural collectivization. At which point Beria then insisted on German demilitarization and reunification as a neutral democratic state.[75] This position was shared by Malenkov, who, in the words of his personal assistant Dmitrii Sukhanov, thought that "we have to have a united Germany, because Germany divided was fraught with the possibility of confrontation and even the possibility of military conflict."[76] But on the following day Molotov proposed changing the phrase about "rejected the course toward socialist construction" and inserting in its place rejection of "a rapid course toward." This would effectively forestall any movement in the direction of reunification.[77] All other members of the Presidium present led by Molotov expressed their support for this. Malenkov fought on,[78] but resistance increased, as a result of which his authority was badly dented and Beria's fatally undermined. Kaganovich later asked in some alarm: "What would have happened to Czechoslovakia, to Hungary, to Poland, had we given up the GDR?"[79] Indeed, the entire empire would have collapsed sooner rather than later and thereby the very bases for the European Cold War.

The Beria-Malenkov proposals thus had every prospect of ending one Cold War, though leaving open the question of the other—over global predominance. But Khrushchev now sided with Molotov. After intense discussion, on

2 June 1953 the Council of Ministers chaired by Malenkov resolved on measures "to improve the health of the political situation in the GDR."[80] Typically East Berlin was told only after the fact. At meetings on 2–4 June, Otto Grotewohl, Ulbricht, and others were castigated by Malenkov: "If we don't correct now, a catastrophe will happen. . . . One has to act *quickly*."[81] The resulting adjustments were too little and came too late. On the morning of 16 June construction workers in East Berlin gathered to demonstrate against increased output quotas. By the evening larger crowds had formed and stones were thrown at the statue to Stalin on Stalinallee at 9:30 p.m. Meanwhile in West Berlin *Der Abend* called for a general strike in the East on seventeenth.[82] Strikes and demonstrations followed, resulting in an assault on government buildings. Martial law was instituted at 1:00 p.m. that day.[83] Washington was satisfied that hardening the line against Moscow were delivering results. "This pressure," Harold Stassen told the NSC on 18 June, "which had begun to be applied by the President and Secretary Dulles five months ago, was really beginning to hurt, and cracks in the Soviet edifice were beginning to be visible."[84] Moreover, on 29 June the NSC resolved "to nourish resistance to communist oppression throughout satellite Europe, short of mass rebellion in areas under Soviet military control, and without compromising its spontaneous nature."[85] Yet it is striking that despite the electoral rhetoric of rolling back communism, the United States left Russia to suppress the Berlin uprising unopposed as it did the Hungarian rising more than three years later. Acquisition of power had inevitably induced a sense of caution and Eisenhower was, unlike Dulles, politically not a betting man. Whenever the Cold War appeared in immediate peril of becoming a real war, one side or other backed away: a pattern to be repeated until the very end.

NEGOTIATION RENEWED

Foreign ministers of the Four Powers eventually met as scheduled in Berlin from 25 January to 18 February 1954. But Beria's execution on 23 December 1953 had buried the possibility of resolving the German question. Britain tried to outflank attempts to capitalize on possible rejection of the EDC by proposing German reunification through free elections.[86] Molotov had already ruled out neutralization of a bourgeois Germany as "an illusion . . . a position alien to Communism."[87] His undiplomatic response was: "We cannot permit Fascist degenerates again to occupy the dominating position in the central organs of power in Germany by some means or other—including the help of parliamentary procedure." Instead Molotov suggested a provisional government that would ban "fascist, militarist and other organizations hostile to democracy and the preservation of peace."[88] The draft included the right of the allies "to call in their troops." This went hand in hand with a clumsy proposal for the liquidation of NATO and the equally absurd suggestion that with respect to the treaty on European security the United States be involved merely on a par with China, as an observer.[89] The Americans "laughed out loud and the Russians were taken completely by surprise at our reaction . . . the Russian momentum was gone." Molotov appeared "drawn, gray and angry." When Foster Dulles said that classifying the United States as observers may seem a "poor joke" but that this was an affront to Washington "after the blood and treasure the U.S. had expended in Europe, Molotov actually went white and then red."[90]

Molotov was still completely in charge of policy on Germany. Dulles noted that he scarcely reported back to Moscow for instructions as discussions continued.[91] That was soon about to change; yet too late to have a decisive impact on the German question. The failure to forestall Bonn's incorporation into the Western camp—the *Gleichberechtigung*—and thereby solve the German question on terms favorable to Moscow was to haunt Khrushchev to the very end. He was to have every reason to regret his betrayal of Beria and Malenkov in 1953 though, typically, this remained unacknowledged to the very grave.

At Soviet bidding the former allied foreign ministers reconvened at Geneva from 26 April to 19 June 1954. Whereas Berlin was taken up with European questions (the fate of Germany and Austria), Geneva focused on Asia (Korea and Indochina). Discussion of Korea degenerated into a propaganda exercise on both sides. With regard to Indochina, the kind of movement the Americans sought was not quite what others wanted: freedom from communist control. The oft-repeated phrase from the US ambassador in Saigon was that the "French would not be allowed to skedaddle unless China gave absolute guarantees."[92] With the fall of Dien Bien Phu inevitable, Assistant Secretary of State Walter Robertson, drunk and emotional, told Sulzberger on 21 April that the United States had to intervene because the loss of Southeast Asia would follow the loss of Indochina. "What is the difference, Robertson asked, whether the Communists start a war of aggression or we lose our civilization because we have failed to take a sufficiently powerful stand?"[93] On 7 May Ho Chi Minh was victorious. "One must not forget," said Molotov, "the fact that the fall of Dien Bien Phu in North Vietnam brought a new upsurge in the national liberation movement in Vietnam. . . . In addition this day of defeat for colonial politics in Vietnam had deep resonance in other of France's colonies, in North Africa, for example."[94]

OPENING TO THE THIRD WORLD

In the eyes of states newly emergent in the region—notably Ceylon, India, Pakistan, Burma, and Indonesia—the security of the subcontinent was jeopardized by the Cold War. Khrushchev was itching for movement, and Mikoyan offered sage advice, particularly in respect of activism toward what had recently become known as the Third World. Whereas Europe had relapsed into a theater of battle for influence from a fixed position, the postcolonial countries held open possibilities for a war of movement not entirely contingent on the prospects for communist revolution. This was a fast expanding field almost entirely neglected by Stalin who, from the moment he held supreme power in 1929, dispensed with the complications of dealing with regimes whose socioeconomic identity failed to fit the Marxist-Leninist model. Expertise covering these regions withered on the vine. The original Leninist policy of supporting national liberation from imperialism by backing bourgeois nationalism in the colonial world had been unceremoniously dumped. The death of Stalin thus finally presented possibilities for real change.

Early shoots sprung up in 1952 as heir apparent Malenkov, presumably with Beria, delicately began to unpick policies hitherto woven into a seamless tapestry and start the delicate process of cautious innovation. At the second congress of the Indian Communist Party in Calcutta a call had gone out to overthrow the Nehru government by force. Disturbances followed and Nehru responded by extending emergency powers.[95] The communists were nevertheless admonished by Moscow for not taking the violent path to power after the Chinese example. In June 1951, however, Moscow publicly applauded the Party's rejection of peasant revolt and its extension of a broad front to encompass "progressive" sections of the bourgeoisie. A year later other Asian parties followed India rather than China's example. But by ceaseless rejection of Nehru's attempts to intercede between Moscow and Washington for peace in Korea, impossible for Stalin because to accept would mean recognition of his catastrophic error, Moscow had unnecessarily tied hands that could usefully have achieved a great deal—as future relations with India were to show.

Nehru had for some time been under pressure from Indonesia to consolidate an Asian-African group that emerged at the UN now that it had expanded to include Thailand, the Philippines, Ethiopia, and Liberia. To this he objected that "the larger the number of countries in the group, the vaguer would be their common ground." But what he had in mind was that "some countries were very closely tied up with the US, such as the Philippines and Thailand. Others [meaning himself] wanted to adopt a more or less independent foreign policy."[96] Instead, heads of government from Ceylon, Burma, India, Pakistan, and Indonesia gathered in Colombo from 28 April to 2 May 1954 in parallel to the proceedings in Geneva.

Nehru's naïveté toward Moscow and Beijing contrasted with stark realism about Washington and lingering mistrust of imperial Britain. Belief that China, in particular, was interested in a stable modus vivendi was apparently cemented by bilateral summits, reassurances on frontiers followed by treaties, and a common antipathy toward the Eisenhower administration. Beijing, fronted by agile tactician Chou, had embarked on an astute diplomatic game, and Moscow was on side. The negotiations between Beijing and New Delhi on the Tibet region of China begun on 31 December 1953 had led to agreement on 29 April 1954.

The verbose preamble to the Sino-Indian treaty referred loftily to "mutual respect for each other's territorial integrity and sovereign, mutual non-aggression, mutual non-interference in each other's internal affairs, equality and mutual benefit and peaceful co-existence."[97] But what Nehru did not seem to realize was that the Leninist term "peaceful coexistence" between states did not restrict interference in other states by the CCP as a nongovernmental institution and the furtherance of world revolution by other means. Moreover, though admirable in principle, respect for territorial integrity failed to deal with the McMahon Line, a frontier not demarcated on the ground. This was a problem that was to arise in the severest form in March 1959 when the Dalai Lama fled to India and a border war broke out as Chinese troops sought to secure the frontier. In fact, even at the time of signature Beijing's meddling in Burma, where Chinese Nationalists were still operating against the communists, already indicated that in practice Mao's policy would remain effectively unchanged by declarations of high principle.[98]

Dulles abandoned the Geneva conference soon after it opened, ostentatiously refusing even to shake hands with Chou: echoing Curzon's shunning of the Soviet delegation in London over three decades before. Business was left to Bedell Smith instead. Moscow had the compromise solution up their sleeves for some time. At the beginning of March in London a diplomat from the Soviet embassy, Rodionov, had suggested that if it were not possible for Ho to join a coalition government in a unified Vietnam, "the solution might be a partition of the country on the sixteenth parallel."[99] In fact the agreements on Indochina signed on 21 July 1954 divided Vietnam along the 17th parallel, leaving Ho with only the northern half of the country. Washington refused to sign, agreeing only to respect the agreement, which provided for elections within two years to reunite both territories. Yet they had no intention of doing so and within a year this had become self-evident, thereby creating a problem that seriously undermined the United States just over a decade later. When Hanoi asked for advice as to the future, Moscow argued for coexistence with the noncommunist south. Beijing, however, had other ideas. The Vietnamese were told to "work underground for a long period, maintain ties with the masses, accumulate strength and bide our time."[100] This advice was followed.

To offset what it saw as appeasement at Geneva, the United States mobilized Britain, France, Australia, New Zealand, the Philippines, and Thailand to sign the Manila treaty on 8 September 1954 setting up the Southeast Asia Treaty Organization (SEATO). The Geneva agreements suffered from rapid drafting because of the deadline of 20 July that the French imposed upon themselves. As a result the fate of Laos and Cambodia remained somewhat indeterminate because both royal armies refused to abide by the agreements. And the accords themselves were fatally undermined when US protégé, prime minister of South Vietnam, Ngo Dinh Diem defiantly announced on 16 July 1955 that they had been signed against the will of the people and would therefore not be observed.

MALENKOV OUTMANEUVERED

Signs were already emerging in Moscow that the ebullient Khrushchev was advancing on the pliable Malenkov. After Beria's downfall, Khrushchev snatched chairmanship of the Presidium from Malenkov, and at a plenum of the Central Committee on 7 September 1953 he secured the title First Secretary, with control of the party apparatus. The omens were not good and were visible in Malenkov's declining authority. On 12 March 1954 Malenkov delivered an election address highlighting the dangers of nuclear war for the survival of civilization. He was merely expressing what others were thinking. But saying so was an entirely different matter. It was regarded as the most sensitive subject of comment, confined entirely to closed quarters and those with security clearance. Indeed, Molotov regarded Malenkov's statement not as inaccurate but as "a very dangerous mistake from a theoretical point of view."[101] A month later, at the Supreme Soviet, Malenkov effectively recanted by reverting to the standard position that socialism would triumph nonetheless. In June 1955 Zhukov, now Defense Minister, "said he had made a special study of [the] effect of atomic weapons, and in his 8 May article on [the] anniversary of [the] end of [the] war published in Pravda, he originally had several paragraphs giving [a] graphic description in understandable local terms of their power of destruction. However, "the editors" had felt it unwise to publish these paragraphs since they might "frighten" people."[102] In 1955 Voroshilov retorted: "We must not intimidate ourselves with fables that in the event of a new war world civilization will be destroyed. We know that should the imperialists once again unleash a world war, then civilization will not be destroyed but the capitalist system moribund."[103] The Soviet public was to be denied all knowledge of the dangers the country faced in confronting the West to the verge of war.

In the process of outflanking and usurping Malenkov, Khrushchev set himself up as spokesman for heavy industry. At a rally in Prague on 15 June Khrushchev abandoned his set text. But the BBC, along with the US intelligence services at Caversham, monitored the original. "When we sincerely declare that we wish and desire peace," Khrushchev declared, "our enemies frequently interpret our wish and desire as weakness; therefore, comrades, peace can be won only by toil, the upsurge of our industry, our agriculture and the daily strengthening of our armed forces." Citing Churchill as having favored negotiation from strength, Khrushchev argued: "The bourgeoisie knows us well and understands only strength . . . we have created atomic energy in our country, we have created atomic bombs, we have outstripped the capitalist camp and have created hydrogen bombs before it did. Bourgeois politicians point their finger at us and think of intimidating us. But we cannot be frightened, because they know, as well as we do, what the bomb means." Referring to the failed Berlin summit, he added: "As long as our enemies do not want to conclude a treaty with us we must be strong, so that they should know 'that the horse cannot be held back.' The last of Hitler's wars should have taught certain people some sense. Hitler also thought that the Soviet Union had feet of clay, but we are still alive whilst Hitler has rotted in his grave. If we are strong[,] all the enemies who raise their hands against us will follow Hitler's and Mussolini's examples."[104] Stalin could not have put it better.

Khrushchev moved decisively against Malenkov in September 1954 while on holiday at the Black Sea where, unlike Stalin, he favored dipping into the water and later built a villa at Pitsunda near the beach, much used by his successors. At one fell swoop Malenkov lost his right to chair the Presidium and was relieved of the General Department that serviced the Presidium.[105] From November all documents from the Council of Ministers were formulated in the name of Bulganin, Malenkov's deputy.[106]

Malenkov's decline paralleled the dwindling prospects for détente between East and West. The London conference and the Paris accords signed on 23 October 1954 had ensured Bonn's admission to NATO. They were "a matter of reality from which the corresponding conclusions must be drawn."[107] These accords effectively sealed Malenkov's fate and that of the more moderate line. Greater military expenditure, which had been kept in check hitherto, would inevitably mean downgrading consumer goods, Malenkov's priority. At a plenum of the Central Committee on 29–31 January Malenkov was finally forced out of office, roundly condemned for having counterposed the progress of heavy industry to the pace of light industry in order to press for the interests of consumers. This was alleged to be "anti-Marxist, anti-Leninist" and "right opportunist."

Malenkov was further condemned for warning that world civilization would be destroyed through atomic war. This undermined "the mobilization of public opinion in the active struggle against the criminal designs of the imperialists for unleashing atomic war." It encouraged "the emergence of a feeling of hopelessness in the efforts of the people to foil the plans of the aggressor, which works to the advantage only of the imperialist advocates of a new world war, counting on intimidating the people through 'atomic' blackmail." And in a further blow against any lingering prospect of compromise on German reunification at the forthcoming Geneva summit (July 1955), Malenkov was excoriated for supporting "Beria's proposals for the complete rejection of the course toward the construction of socialism in the GDR and hold to a course of leaving Germany, opening up the possibility of establishing a united bourgeois Germany in the form of a 'neutral' state. When these capitulationist proposals were rejected by the overwhelming majority of members of the CC Presidium, after the meeting Beria and Malenkov pounced upon individual members of the Presidium with threats, trying to intimidate them with the aim of bringing into effect their capitulationist line."[108]

Positioning himself closer to the center of opinion in the Presidium, Khrushchev now became increasingly critical of Molotov "for sluggishness, insufficient initiative in European, Asian, and disarmament matters."[109] Officials in the United States now noted that Molotov did not appear "as self-confident or as completely in command of the situation as when he [Foster Dulles] had last seen the Soviet Foreign Minister at the Berlin conference. Indeed, he seemed a little shrunken and shrivelled."[110] Once Mikoyan was at Khrushchev's elbow, Washington rapidly found itself targeted by the most sustained diplomatic offensive since the war: the Americans found themselves simultaneously pressed for neutralization of Central Europe (ironically with support from Kennan, now retired) facing the possible loss of Japan (which Dulles blocked in 1956), overtures to win over Egypt through arms sales, and the courting of India.[111]

The Americans suddenly found themselves on the back foot. It was not communism as a creed but planned industrialization that attracted the underdeveloped world. At the 273rd meeting of the NSC in January 1956 Dulles confessed "that the United States had very largely failed to appreciate the impact on the underdeveloped areas of the world of the phenomenon of Russia's rapid industrialization. Its transformation from an agrarian to a modern industrialized state was an historical event of absolutely first class importance." All the underdeveloped countries saw were "the results of Russia's industrialization and all they want is for the Russians to show them how they too can achieve it."[112] Encouraged by Mikoyan, Khrushchev eagerly pressed ahead into uncharted territory.

STATISM RATHER THAN REVOLUTION

Soviet policy in 1955 thus became more realistic about what could be expected merely from relaxation of tension. What Moscow settled for in Vienna, Bonn, and Tokyo partook of that greater realism and willingness to compromise, though it fell far short of the kind of dramatic initiative that could have scooped the pool from the American alliance and forced an abrupt end to the Cold War by depriving them of a common enemy. In Asia willingness to accept nonalignment as an asset also indicated a sober assessment of realities on the ground rather than the will-o'-the-wisp of revolution. The statement Khrushchev made to Indonesia's ambassador in August 1955 caught the new spirit. He indicated that "Moscow had counted too much on the action of 'peoples' alone and that henceforth one had to pay more attention to relations with foreign governments."[113] This applied to both East and West.

It also meant realigning the focus of Soviet diplomacy toward those in the Third World openly hostile to the West. Here Israel no longer qualified. After the UN decision to partition Palestine, when embattled Israel eventually came into being on 14 May 1948, it was recognized by Moscow de jure on the third day of its existence. Stalin sent the first foreign diplomatic mission to Tel Aviv (even Washington at this stage accorded only de facto recognition). Despite the UN embargo on arms exports to the region decided upon only a few days before (29 May 1948), in June 1948 Russia told Czechoslovakia and Yugoslavia to sell arms to Israel, both planes and artillery.[114] By August bombers and fighter-bombers piloted by Israelis were en route.[115]

At the UN, ambassador Malik "expressed his deep admiration for Israel's military effort. The Soviet view had always been that the Arabs were overrated as a military power, due to what they had regarded as the social weaknesses of the Near East and of the essential disunity amongst the various elements of the Arab League. Nevertheless, they had never expected any such debacle." Foreign Minister Abba Eban read this and more to mean that Moscow "believed they had made a correct analysis and taken the correct decision, of which they now expected to reap the fruits. He hinted that he assumed our appreciation of the fact that the various forms of assistance which we had received from East European and Balkan countries were in the final analysis, a consequence of Russia's favourable attitude." He also "hinted that the British position had been undermined, not merely in Palestine but throughout the Near East, and that this too represented success for the Soviets' Palestine policy."[116] The issue of heavy weaponry for the army was followed up in late November by ambassador

Golda Meir—herself a Ukrainian Jew by birth—and military attaché Colonel Yohanan Ratner, who added tanks to the shopping list.[117]

Yet even while backing Israel, Moscow feared that a Jewish state could side with the West.[118] And knowledgeable Jewish officials were themselves fully aware of the opportunism underpinning Soviet policy.[119] Crucially, an unspoken anxiety haunted Moscow lest Zionism undermine the regime's iron grip on the people, given that the second largest diaspora was in the USSR and Meir was all too explicit demanding mass immigration. Indeed, while Moscow and Tel Aviv were embracing, forces at the root of the relationship had already begun tearing them apart.

When Golda Meir arrived in Moscow she attracted a public display of affection from tens of thousands of Jews and also from Polina, Molotov's wife.[120] Her mother, who lived with them and whom Molotov called "babushka" (granny), was herself rigidly orthodox, so her sympathies were scarcely surprising.[121] On 17 December 1948 head of state security Viktor Abakumov handed Stalin compromising testimony on Polina—she had expressed the belief at the funeral of Jewish leader Mikhoels that he had been assassinated. Moreover when in the summer of 1946 Mikhoels came and asked whether he should approach Malenkov or Zhdanov for help in maintaining the Jewish Antifascist Committee, under attack from within the apparat, she bluntly said that he was wasting his time since "all the power in this country is concentrated in the hands of Stalin alone. And he is not positively disposed toward Jews and, naturally, would not support us." She was excluded from the party on 29 December 1948. Molotov again abstained, as in 1941, but on 20 January 1949 he formally acknowledged his "mistake" and she was taken to the Lubyanka the following day. Molotov was nevertheless dismissed as foreign minister.[122]

Contacts with the Israelis were thus lethal, and although they remained formally nonaligned, as early as August 1950 Soviet intelligence learned that Tel Aviv was conducting joint operations in the region as well as exchanging information with the United States.[123] Moreover, as an Israeli politician pointed out: "We depend upon the USA twice over—on the government of the USA and on American Jews, who give us aid." The Israeli Foreign Minister added that the state was effectively bankrupt and without US aid the country would go hungry, quite literally.[124]

In such circumstances it is surprising how long it took for Moscow to turn to the Arabs. Following the institution of an arms embargo in the Middle East by the United States, Britain, and France—the Tripartite Declaration of 25 May 1950—Arab states had been unable find supplies. On 11 September 1951 a representative of a major Egyptian company—El Alamiya—approached the trade counselor at the Soviet mission in Cairo. He was interested in equipping two armored divisions, either directly from Russia or via a third party, such as Czechoslovakia. Although Alekseenko said he had no authority to discuss such matters, he was presented with the request in writing. Ambassador Kozyrev believed Cairo was behind it and would not rule out the possibility that this was an attempt to exert pressure on Britain to review the Anglo-Egyptian treaty of 1936. Alekseenko was instructed to say that such proposals were normally discussed government-to-government.[125]

Nothing more was heard from Egypt until after 23 July 1952 when a more momentous event occurred fraught with consequences for the future of the Middle East over the next several decades. In Egypt Naguib seized power with the assistance of the young, charismatic, and ambitious colonel Gamal Abdul Nasser and proclaimed a republic. Finally on 29 January, Naguib came to see Kozyrev, with one aim in view: "Is Russia ready to give Egypt tanks and aeroplanes?" Kozyrev was somewhat taken aback and too mistrustful to respond adequately.[126] For his crass ineptitude, he was rapped firmly over the knuckles. Vyshinsky instructed him to respond to any further request by saying that Moscow was uninterested in selling weapons but would consider any such request.[127] In the USSR anti-Jewish sentiment had risen with the announcement of the so-called doctors' plot to murder Stalin. The day before Kozyrev's telegram, a bomb exploded at the Soviet legation in Tel Aviv seriously wounding the minister, Yershov, and others. The apology for the incident had no effect, and two days later Moscow broke off diplomatic relations.[128] Relations were, however, duly restored within months of Stalin's death, after anti-Semitism diminished and the doctors' plot was revealed as fiction.[129]

In mid-October Naguib, now president but ill, received Kozyrev at his private residence on his departure from Cairo. Naguib said he wished to see relations develop in the long term through expansion of trade. Reminding the ambassador of their conversation in January, he suggested trading cotton for armaments.[130] Suspicion lingered, however, tainted by ideological considerations. From Cairo the new minister, Solod, took the view that "in fact the entire set of military rulers of Egypt copies German and Italian fascism in everything." The Minister for Social Affairs even told Solod that he considered Hitler "the greatest leader of the century."[131] But Syria now also asked for armaments, either directly from the USSR or via Czechoslovakia.[132] And in June 1954 Nasser, now Prime Minister of Egypt, received Solod and "began to complain at the fact that Egypt is essentially an occupied country and in existing circumstances can in reality do nothing to rid itself of occupation as the Egyptian army does not have the necessary armaments." London turned them down and Washington required impossible conditions. Solod reiterated that the USSR was prepared to help build up industry to produce their own, but Nasser said that this would take too long. He went directly to the point: how would the Soviet government respond in principle to a request to buy armaments? When asked, he insisted it was an official request.[133]

On 8 July Solod informed Nasser that Moscow was ready to consider a detailed proposal.[134] At this point Soviet policy looked toward a major reorientation of some 180 degrees. But, as ever, progress was by no means certain. On 19 October Egypt secured agreement to evacuate British troops from their base on the Suez Canal, though the waterway itself remained in Anglo-French hands: a compromise between irreconcilable positions. This eased tension between Cairo and London as well as between London and Washington.

RUSSIA GOES WITH EGYPT

Dulles was working toward the Baghdad pact. This drove Moscow into a corner. Zorin argued, "Taking into account that renewed activity of the Americans and the English in the Near and Middle East is of hostile intent toward the USSR, we need to find means of blocking the realization of American and English plans for the creation of an aggressive bloc of Near Eastern countries, to this end exploiting both Anglo-American friction as well as disagreements within the Arab League."[135] Russia had to raise its profile in the Arab world. A plausible rationale for the new line in Moscow appeared in a position paper for the Foreign Ministry collegium on Soviet-Israeli relations dated 10 March 1955.

The head of the Near and Middle Eastern Department, Zaitsev, pointed out that Israel received 34.5 percent of its budgetary income from abroad, mainly the United States; Israeli indebtedness to Washington exceeded $400 million; there were more than fifty US advisers in Israeli ministries; in the UN Israel voted with the United States; and the United States "looks upon Israel as one of its bases in the Middle East."[136]

Before Nasser headed out to the conference for nonaligned countries at Bandung in Indonesia (18–24 April 1955), he instructed Deputy War Minister Hasan Raguib to talk to Moscow about arms supplies. On 6 April Raguib raised the matter with the Soviet military attaché, and five days later was told Russia was ready for negotiations. It was agreed that they be held in Prague rather than Moscow. Nasser promised to follow through.[137] The assumption was that little would in fact be lost by supplying Egypt with arms because Israel would sooner or later break out of their neutralist stance.[138] The Foreign Ministry's department for the Near and Middle East stated: "In spite of the Nasser government's inconsistency . . . and the possibility of a change in foreign policy toward closer cooperation with the USA and England, the present stance of Egypt's nonparticipation in aggressive blocs to a certain extent counteracts the attempts of the USA and England to put together a bloc hostile to the USSR in the Near and Middle East and objectively facilitates the realization of our measures counteracting such intrigues."[139] Dulles's activities in trying to mediate a settlement between Israel and the Arabs were seen as a particular threat to Moscow.[140]

Nasser was extremely nervous lest Washington discover the arms sales before they were complete. He insisted on strict secrecy, fearing a coup orchestrated by Washington from within the Egyptian officer corps.[141] London had already warned that sanctions would follow the purchase of arms from Moscow,[142] as had Washington.[143] Kermit Roosevelt was dispatched as a special emissary to Cairo by CIA in late September 1955 to warn Nasser that buying Soviet arms might lead to the blockading of Alexandria and prompt Israel to attack Egypt, but that if Cairo broke off its deal with Moscow, Washington would supply all the arms Nasser needed. Britain followed suit by offering arms on its own account.[144] Meeting the Soviet ambassador on 29 September Nasser requested "the supply to Egypt in the shortest time possible of the armaments they had bought. Now was not the time to stick to the schedule agreed. Each day was costly. Initially weapons could be supplied in small quantities. The arrival of Soviet arms in Egypt will put an end to the opinions on this issue and will raise the morale of the Egyptian army which fully supports the Egyptian government's purchase of armaments in the USSR and Czechoslovakia. The army has to see these weapons, the planes and tanks in particular."[145]

Nasser remained anxious about likely Western reactions, however. He rejected Soviet proposals to send in 130 Soviet specialists along with the weaponry and suggested 20 instead.[146] In fact Moscow was just as anxious to avert any open confrontation with Washington, given the dominance of the Mediterranean by the Sixth Fleet and their concern to sustain the "spirit of Geneva."[147] On 18 October Solod informed Nasser that on 20–21 October the Soviet vessel *Krasnodar* would arrive at the port of Alexandria laden with armaments. Moscow insisted once more on absolute secrecy.[148] Loose threats from Israel of a preventive war against Egypt boosted the level of tension.[149] Soviet relations with Israel were already at a parting of the ways; so if anything these threats reinforced their concern to back the Arabs. Now Syria was also seeking weapons systems—sixty T-34 tanks, eighteen artillery pieces, thirty-two antiaircraft guns, eighteen MiG fighters and small arms.[150]

On 14 April 1956 the new Soviet ambassador to Cairo, Kiselev, received a request for two squadrons of MiG-17s on the grounds that Israel received the Mystère-4 from France, inferior to the MiG-17 but superior to the MiG-15 that Egypt already possessed.[151] Washington's reaction to Egyptian arms purchases was to refuse backing vital to financing the Aswan Dam project that was supposed to transform Egypt. The French ambassador, Maurice Couve de Murville, recalls this decision as "stupid—for various reasons. One was that clearly it was an affair of domestic politics . . . a combination of the cotton-growing states who were frightened that the Aswan Dam would lead Egypt to produce more cotton; of the Zionists, of course—and it was not long before the elections—and of the so-called Formosa lobby, because Egypt had just before recognized the Peking regime." Moreover, the assistant secretary for the region, Allen, did not believe there would be a price to pay.[152]

In a whirlwind tour of the Middle East, Molotov's replacement as Foreign Minister, Dmitrii Shepilov, spent six days in Cairo (16–22 June), where he tried to talk Nasser into a friendship and cooperation treaty but failed. The Egyptians at this stage still feared "an excessive rapprochement with Moscow." They were, however, much more receptive toward the offer of help with the Aswan Dam, a metallurgical plant, and a machine-tools industry.[153]

Further East, Nehru had been doing his sums. "Our foreign policy," he noted with satisfaction, "has helped us internally as well in that it has completely confused the Communist Party of India. In view of the appreciation shown by the Soviet leaders of our foreign policy, Indian communists find it difficult to criticise the Government."[154] Nehru thus anticipated de Gaulle. And, having failed to dissuade Indonesia from summoning a full Afro-Asian conference in Bandung from 18 to 24 April, he made virtue of necessity once aware of US pressure to forestall it.[155] The Colombo Powers (Burma, Ceylon, Indonesia, Pakistan, and India) funded the venture. The twenty-nine countries that gathered heard Nehru reject proposals by the pro-American wing (Turkey, Pakistan, Iraq, Lebanon, Philippines, and Thailand) to condemn the "new colonialism" of the USSR in Eastern Europe along with the old colonialism of the West European Powers.[156] Moscow had no illusions concerning the bourgeois identity of the leaders in the postcolonial world. But that was no longer of any concern, except perhaps for Molotov. Khrushchev led a Soviet delegation to India, Burma, and Afghanistan from 18 November to 19 December 1955. "Look at our Party's policy of splitting the bourgeois world. Our comrades went to India, to Burma, and succeeded in disrupting the influence of the imperialist Powers upon the countries of Asia," boasted Mikoyan proprietorially.[157]

AUSTRIAN STATE TREATY

The last productive Soviet initiative in Europe before Khrushchev's supremacy destroyed the tentative détente was the Austrian state treaty. Neutralization also matched the pattern of accepting nonalignment in Asia and the Middle East.

The first signs of Soviet movement on the Austrian question since the onset of the Cold War had emerged after a brief in August 1952 from the Committee of Information in Moscow reporting US attempts to draw Austria into the Western bloc.[158] On 26 September Nikolai Grigoriev from the Soviet embassy in Washington had suggested to his Austrian counterpart that the allies could withdraw their forces provided Austria did not then join NATO. "Austria must follow a policy of strict neutrality similar to that of Sweden or Switzerland." This would have to apply to trade as much as politics (that is to say, ignore the NATO embargo on the sale of strategic goods to the Eastern bloc). It was up to Austria to seize the initiative, however.[159] Nothing happened for two years and for good reason. Molotov's aide Erofeev recalls: "No one suspected that . . . he [Molotov] put the brakes on preparation of this treaty for a long time, not wishing to hasten the withdrawal of Soviet forces from Austria."[160]

Soon after Stalin's death Khrushchev raised the idea of evacuating Austria but met fierce resistance from Molotov. With Mikoyan's support, however, Khrushchev persisted.[161] Finally, on the eve of Bonn's entry into NATO (23 October 1954) at dinner on 13 October third secretary Gorinovich and military attaché Beletskii sounded an Austrian diplomat on troop withdrawal and neutralization of Austria. "Both of the gentlemen again and again insisted on the necessity of an Austrian initiative."[162] Again, nothing happened. Finally, on 8 February 1955 Molotov publicly offered neutralization of Austria following the withdrawal of allied troops. Although he implied that this was conditional upon a satisfactory German settlement, the proposal in fact reflected a belief that Moscow had lost the battle to forestall German rearmament. It was made in the hope of forestalling the possibility of Anschluss between the rump of Austria and the rump of Germany.

This proposal was followed up by direct contact with the Austrian ambassador to Moscow, Norbert Bischoff, on 25 February 1955.[163] Thereafter negotiations resulted in signature of a treaty neutralizing Austria on a basis similar to that of Switzerland (1815), thereby securing US/UK and Soviet military withdrawal. Dulles was unhappy but offered no opposition despite the fact that it cut directly across his objections to nonalignment.[164] It was signed on 14 May and in force on 27 July 1955. Meanwhile the formal establishment of a multilateral alliance in Eastern Europe—the Warsaw Treaty Organization (usually known in the West as the Warsaw Pact)—announced on 21 March registered Moscow's abiding concerns about German rearmament.

The state treaty thus marked not just the high point of Russian attempts at détente in Europe but also its resting point for some time to come. The fact that détente had no further to go at a time of Khrushchev's personal ascendancy was not accidental. As First Secretary, Khrushchev was indisputably the substantive source of policy, though he was not entitled by office to attend the summit of heads of government that gathered at Geneva on 18–23 July 1955. Bulganin had replaced Malenkov as Chairman of the Council of Ministers, not Khrushchev. The only way Khrushchev could go was under transparent guise: membership of the Supreme Soviet's Presidium.[165] On arrival in Geneva, however, the delicate veil kept slipping as the bullish Khrushchev interrupted Bulganin in private discussions "and took over completely at dinners and receptions."[166]

Neither side had a realistic agenda for serious negotiation anyway. Moscow could not be said to have approached the summit constructively. Khrushchev recalled: "The meeting of heads of government of the four Great Powers was Churchill's venture merely to sound us out. It stemmed from the fact that in Russia after the death of Stalin new people came into the leadership, whom he evidently considered insufficiently competent in international political questions, before they were firmly established. Thus he decided that it was necessary to sound us out, exert pressure on us and obtain concessions required by the imperialist Powers."[167] Khrushchev personally felt the leadership was under intense scrutiny.[168] He therefore vigorously resisted progress on the German question; treated the French with calculated disdain; and noted, with a certain superiority, that Dulles wrote notes on his pad and handed them to Eisenhower, who then read from these notes word for word "like a dutiful schoolboy."[169]

Eisenhower still had no interest in détente. Dulles "said he believed that we were now confronting a real opportunity in the present situation for a rollback of Soviet power. Such a rollback might leave the present satellite states in a status not unlike that of Finland. He, for one, said Secretary Dulles, would not object to such a development. The big idea is to get the Russians out of the satellite states and to provide these states with a real sense of their freedom. Now for the first time this is in the realm of possibility."[170] Indeed, just before the summit Dulles impressed upon Adenauer "the importance of not selling out too cheaply to the Russians. He had outlined his view that the Russians were under some strain economically and politically at home: we should therefore set ourselves objectives which are inherently reasonable and pursue them firmly and patiently. Our position had much improved already, but the Russians would 'later' feel more need to fall in with our wishes than they do now. In other words, Mr. Dulles felt that the tensions in Europe were probably hurting the Russians more than us."[171] Eisenhower saw the German question as effectively concluded and instead emphasized the importance to US opinion of "the two subjects that I brought up, the Satellites [Eastern Europe] and international Communism."[172]

Geneva thus yielded no agreement. Moscow took consolation in the fact that it "broke the isolation that had hitherto surrounded us." And the invitation from Eden to visit Britain in 1956 was regarded as something akin to a breach in the adversarial front.[173] It also proved something of an education for Khrushchev: "Our trip to Geneva once more convinced us that we were not then on the eve of war, and that our undoubted opponents feared us just as we feared them."[174] The summit had, however, delayed Adenauer's official visit to Moscow. An invitation was received on 7 June. The visit began just over three months later on 8 September. In a speech after dinner on the following day, Khrushchev greeted the delegation bluntly with the demand: "What do you Germans want—friendship or enmity?"[175] Although diplomatic relations between Bonn and Moscow were established at the end of Adenauer's visit on 13 September, the Chancellor was now certain that Khrushchev was not about to concede reunification. Instead Bonn settled for relations based on *Sachlichkeit*—the facts as they stood—in the words of States Secretary Walter Hallstein.

The visit did, however, have a curious side effect. In anticipation of a further meeting of foreign ministers in Geneva (27 October–16 November), Molotov, no doubt conscious of his declining authority, decided on a radical gesture. He called Khrushchev's bluff with startlingly radical proposals on Germany: an offer of mutual military withdrawal plus free elections for reunification contingent upon abrogation of the Paris accords of 23 October 1954 that brought Bonn rearmed into NATO. Khrushchev, however, took fright and immediately spoke against. There was no need to go this far: "There are many rocks under the water." Others spoke in a similar vein, including Mikoyan, Malenkov, Voroshilov, Kaganovich, Pervukhin, and Saburov. "Howls will go up that negotiation from strength is winning out," Khrushchev insisted. "The Germans from the GDR will say, 'You are selling us out.' There is no way we will take the risk." "We have to show patience and pertinacity. There should be no change of position," Khrushchev concluded, to the satisfaction of all but Molotov.[176]

Somehow Khrushchev had convinced himself that the tide would turn to his advantage in Germany; and even when events undermined this unfounded assumption, he persisted. Zorin, who launched the Prague coup in 1948, was tactlessly sent from Moscow as a top-level ambassador to Bonn. Unsurprisingly he made no progress at all and was eventually recalled in July 1956. His counterpart, the unknown Dr. Haas, did not even arrive in Moscow until March and then found himself bogged down in administrative complications. Washington certainly had no need to worry about an imminent German defection from NATO.

The Adenauer formula, following the state treaty, thus punctuated the new line of accommodation from Moscow. The open question was what might happen if the leadership succumbed completely as it had before to one-man predominance, under Khrushchev. To CIA director Allen Dulles he was "the most dangerous person to lead the Soviet Union since the October Revolution. He was not a coldly calculating person, but rather one who reacted emotionally. . . . Stalin always calculated the results of a proposed action."[177] On the core issue of the German question anxiety was bound to arise given Khrushchev's illusions. He told French Foreign Minister Christian Pineau that if the cards were played right, Germany as a whole would eventually land in the Soviet lap "like a ripe plumb."[178] There was thus every reason to expect trouble further down the road.

LAND OF EARTHQUAKES AND VOLCANOES

That other former enemy, Japan, stood on the sidelines after signing peace with the Western Powers on 8 September 1951.[179] Moscow foolishly excluded itself from the treaty negotiations at Stalin's obdurate insistence. Japan had soon become a source of sustained anxiety in Washington, however. The NSC affirmed "the critical importance" of Japanese economic survival to "the security of the United States." But it simultaneously argued that "this viability will be extremely difficult to achieve."[180] Japan was still "a desperately poor country."[181] After a visit, Vice President Richard Nixon fretted that as "one of the best fronts in Asia," Japan's foundations were "very weak and terribly unsound."[182] During the Korean War, which boosted Japan's economy as a base area, traditional racist sentiment found the killing of whites on the peninsula no bad thing. Strikes were all too common and fully exploited by the Communist Party. The leadership that emerged into power was formed of ex-war criminals. And there was a distinct trend toward recognizing Communist China for reasons of trade and maintaining a neutralist stance in the Cold War proper.

Washington was worried: "The long-term alignment of Japan with the free world has become less certain."[183] Dulles saw a "weak and vacillating" government in Tokyo.[184] He was equally convinced that "we should not build up Japanese military strength unless we need confidence that Japan's future political orientation would be toward the West. Japan was the heart and soul of the situation in the Far East. If Japan is not on our side our whole Far Eastern position will become untenable."[185] Yet Japan was still a major host to US air power: the island of Okinawa was a sovereign base area all of its own — "our great bastion of defense for the Pacific."[186] Xenophobia was never far beneath the surface, and Japan wanted the security treaty negotiated in 1951 renegotiated to restore sovereignty over these bases. Dulles therefore sought desperately to buy it off by obtaining special unilateral trading privileges for exporters to the US market as the best means of offsetting aspirations to the Chinese market. The situation was thus ripe for a carefully calibrated Soviet initiative to upset the American applecart.

Finally Moscow moved in response to an unexpected announcement from Foreign Minister Shigemitsu on 11 December 1954, expressing interest in normalizing relations with the USSR and China "on mutually acceptable terms."[187] Molotov, "opposed to the normalization of relations with Japan,"[188] grudgingly retorted that Moscow was "prepared to discuss the question of practical measures to bring about the normalization of relations . . . if the government of Japan is really determined to undertake steps in this direction."[189] The problem was not merely Molotov, however. Peace with Moscow became embroiled in Japanese domestic politics — as a result of which Shigemitsu began to back away — and Washington was opposed to a successful outcome. The US ambassador to Japan, John Allison, saw his basic task as "to deter . . . the drift of the Japanese Government toward some degree of political and economic accommodation with the Soviet Union and Communist China."[190]

On 25 January 1955 the Russians delivered an undated and unsigned "*bout de papier*" to the office of the new Japanese Prime Minister, Ichiro Hatoyama, repeating Molotov's response. The two sides agreed to negotiate in London on 1 June. The timing was propitious to Moscow. In Washington a good deal of anxiety was expressed that Japan was "beginning to display a desire for greater freedom of international action. This tendency reflects a national trend, rooted in racial pride, a longing for national prestige and a desire for greater maneuverability in the event of conflict between Communist China or the USSR and the United States." As to US sovereign bases: "While the Japanese look upon U.S. bases in Japan as protection for Japan, they also regard them as serving U.S. strategic interests and as dangerously exposing Japan to nuclear attack in the event of war. Furthermore, Japanese policy is colored by serious doubts as to whether an acceptable defense of Japan is possible in the event of nuclear war." The United States was thus pressing Tokyo not to concede "the Soviet Union's claim to sovereignty over the Kurile Islands and Southern Sakhalin."[191]

At the London talks Russia was represented by Malik who under Molotov's instructions on 14 June presented Matsumoto with proposals virtually recapitulating the entirely unproductive stance at San Francisco in 1951. Britain was both astounded and relieved. "To me the most interesting feature of this whole business is that the Russians should have been stupid enough to stand pat on the position they took up in S[an] F[rancisco] four years ago," commented Sir Esler Denning, ambassador in Tokyo.[192] Japan's main demand was territorial:

the Habomais, Shikotan, Kunashiri, and Etorofu, islands south of the main Kurile chain extending from Kamchatka down to Hokkaido. It was presented to Malik on 16 August. By now Khrushchev had taken a more direct role, and on 6 September Malik was able to express interest in a deal surrendering the Habomais and Shikotan only, with the proviso that the Sea of Japan be neutralized and the islands be demilitarized. This came as "a complete surprise," according to Ohtaka of the Japanese embassy, "and Mr. Matsumoto wanted to settle the territorial question on that basis soon after. However Mr. Shigemitsu intervened and insisted that a strong demand should be made for the return of Etorofu and Kunashiri also. This had irritated Mr. Matsumoto and even more the Russians."[193] And once the two parties, Liberals and Democrats, amalgamated in December this became the policy agreed between two factions of the Liberal Democratic Party. Instead of settling on the terms of either side, after desultory further negotiation Moscow and Tokyo retreated to the Adenauer formula of reopening diplomatic relations and delaying a treaty of peace sine die. This was agreed by Tokyo on 2 October 1956, and a joint declaration was issued to that effect on 19 October.

London concluded: "the Japanese deceived themselves into thinking they might have gained more than they did in their talks with the Soviet Union. In fact, considering how weak their bargaining position was, they did better than any outsider expected."[194] Paris, however, took another view: "In offering to return them [all four sets of islands requested], Moscow would have placed the government of Japan in a delicate position vis-à-vis America, obliging it to call for the return of Okinawa."[195] Heading internal security, Seki "stated that the greatest fear of officials like himself before the talks began was that the Russians would be willing to give more than the Japanese asked for." Indeed, "the Japanese Communist Party issued statements endorsing the Russian stand, but there was an immediate adverse reaction within the party itself which is eliciting criticism from the members and has caused party leaders to think about the possibility of announcing an independent line of thought for Japanese consumption, reversing their previous stand in support of Russia's attitude."[196]

Washington noted with some surprise that "Japan's alignment with the United States . . . in some respects has been strengthened, rather than weakened, as a result of the solution of several outstanding problems and as a reaction to recent Communist pressure tactics aimed at stimulating a neutral policy. . . . The consistently 'tough' Soviet policy toward Japan—rejection of Japanese territorial claims to the Kurils, restrictions on fishing in the Northwestern Pacific, and continued Soviet accusations of Japanese subservience to the United States—has impeded [a] Japanese rapprochement with the USSR."[197] That Moscow failed to press its advantage is no mystery: "For us the solution of this question is a question of prestige," Khrushchev acknowledged.[198] Washington had every reason to be delighted. Elsewhere, however, his personal qualities were to prove alarming, particularly when he inadvertently undermined his own standing at home through jeopardizing the security of the empire in Eastern Europe.

6

SUDDEN FROST

So, as you understand it, the United States, not we, are to blame for the events in Hungary? . . . You should understand that we had an army in Hungary; we supported that fool Rákosi. That was our mistake, and not the mistake of the United States.

—*Khrushchev to Mao, August 1958*

The détente epitomized in the "spirit of Geneva" was severely circumscribed. Moscow exploited friction between capitalist countries—"wedge-driving" as it became known in NATO—while highlighting the need to relax international tension. Washington and Bonn argued against concessions on the grounds that détente was merely a pause convenient to the reinforcement of Soviet power in a continuing conflict. They saw the USSR as inherently weak at home and unsteady in Central and Eastern Europe. A reduction of international tension was thus not a benefit in its own right but a means to ending the Cold War. That "culminating point of victory" was not yet in sight.

Dulles insisted: "We are in the situation of being prepared to run a mile in competition with another runner whose distance suddenly appears to be a quarter mile. At the quarter mile mark, the Russian quarter miler says to the American miler, 'This is really a quarter of a mile race, you know, and why don't we call it off now?'" To the Senate he "emphasized and reemphasized that what Russia had predicted for our system—namely, collapse—was precisely what appeared to be about to happen to them."[1] Not fully accounted for, however, was the extent to which limited détente was contingent not on Russian weakness so much as a thaw in Moscow that could end abruptly. The uncertain progress of de-Stalinization was continually called into question by active opponents in the leadership. Unrest in Eastern Europe consequent upon further de-Stalinization would play into their hands. The thaw could thus at any time be cut short by sudden frost. Ironically, it was Khrushchev who precipitated the prospect of collapse unwittingly, as usual, and in impetuously blind pursuit of personal and domestic political goals.

DENUNCIATION OF STALIN

Khrushchev's speech to a closed session of the Twentieth Party Congress on 25 February 1956 proved a turning point for both the Soviet bloc and for East-West relations as a whole. He highlighted the consequences of "unlimited power in the hands of one figure." "These negative characteristics grew and grew, and in recent years assumed a character of complete intolerance." Brute force was used against those that stood up to him and "that seemed to him, capricious and despotic as he was, to be contradicting the positions he took." If prior to the Seventeenth Party Congress in 1934 "he still recognized the opinions of the collective," after that point "Stalin increasingly ceased to take into account members of the Party Central Committee and even members of the Politburo." Worse still, Stalin took the view that the closer they came to socialism, "the more enemies there would be." Hence the "mass repressions," including destruction of the officer corps on the eve of war (1937–41). And not long after the USSR was attacked in June 1941, Stalin fell into a blue funk. "Everything that Lenin created we have obliterated forever," Khrushchev quoted him as having said. Thereafter the Cold War followed on the steps of victory, and not by chance: "Under Stalin's leadership our peaceful relations with other countries were frequently placed under threat, as a result of which decisions made by one man could lead and at times did lead to great complications."[2]

Of course, no reference was ever made to the likely international impact of such dramatic revelations. But they threatened to undercut foreign communists and fellow travellers who had steadfastly denied these facts. And word of Khrushchev's secret speech soon began to leak out. On 12 March the French ambassador to the USSR summarized the broad outlines in a dispatch to Paris.[3] Pietro Nenni, leader of the PSI, broke cover on 25 March in his party's daily *Avanti!* with "Light and Shadow in the Moscow Congress," printed in the socialist journal *Mondo Operaio* later that month. Worse was to follow. Stefan Staszewski, First Secretary of the Warsaw committee of the Polish Workers' Party (PUWP), "personally handed a copy, hot off the press, to Philippe Benn, the *Le Monde* correspondent, and to Gruson from the *Herald Tribune* and Flora Lewis from the *New York Times*."[4] By the end of May CIA had a complete copy. Only after considerable debate, however, did the US government finally print it with massive publicity on 4 June.[5]

POLAND REVOLTS

As late as 11 July, even after a massacre of workers demonstrating in Poznán on 28 June—150 were killed, 500 wounded[6]—Khrushchev expressed himself blithely optimistic about the international situation. In Europe he did "not see any country sufficiently militaristic that it could be turned against us by America." And the United States talked of war only because it was afraid. Underlying concerns were nevertheless raised by others about stability in Eastern Europe.[7] Moreover, at a time of West German rearmament, Khrushchev had embarked upon a steady reduction in the size of the army which underpinned hegemony over Central Eastern Europe. Marshal Georgii Zhukov, appointed Defense Minister in place of Bulganin in February 1955, presided over a massive cut reducing numbers from 5,396,038 on 1 March 1953 to 3,986,216 in December 1956.[8] Where possible he did so by axing as many men superfluous to actual war fighting as possible, including—and this ultimately led to his downfall in October 1957—those political officers overseeing the armed forces at all levels, whom he generally described as useless. Moreover, Order 0090 forbade officers to appeal over his head to the Central Committee on pain of severe retribution. And, in Khrushchev's words, he "extorted" money for the military-industrial system by giving a "defeatist speech" to the effect that the United States could tear them to pieces.[9]

First Secretary of the PUWP Edward Ochab was involved in "an acrimonious discussion" with Moscow, which "before the July plenum had suggested to us that the bloody Poznan clashes had been provoked by the imperialists. I told them there was no proof," he said, "and that I couldn't make a claim of that kind at the Central Committee plenum."[10] The resolutions of the Polish Politburo on 28–29 June and 3 July thus made no mention whatever of imperialist subversion.[11]

The accusations against "imperialism" were of course a fig leaf conveniently brandished by Moscow, behind which lay a double crisis equally evident in the repression of the rebels in East Berlin during 1953: in the illegitimacy of communist regimes originating in Red Army occupation, and their evident failure to sustain a decent standard of living for the working class. The people were told they had forfeited the confidence of their government. Playwright and poet Bertolt Brecht had asked, not unreasonably: "Would it not be easier in that case for the government to dissolve the people and elect another?"[12]

Not unexpectedly Poland's complications grew rather than diminished as, not only within the Party but also public opinion at large, a groundswell arose in favor of Gomułka: the same man removed from office in 1948 for national deviation in opposing the collectivization of agriculture and incipient Titoism in his resistance to copying all Soviet practices. Ochab later noted with some bitterness and obvious envy, "They [the Poles] fell for those phrases . . . about patriotism and independence,"[13] which were precisely what worried Moscow.

On 19 October a delegation led by Khrushchev hurriedly left for Warsaw to forestall the election of Gomułka at a Central Committee plenum to which Khrushchev had not been invited. His presence—marked by abusive and bullying behavior in public and in private—made no difference anyway, and he returned to face the dilemma of what to do next in the face of Polish recalcitrance. The Poles had robustly asserted their right to determine their own affairs—not least the composition of the leadership in Party and state (including the army)—though they were sufficiently cautious to reassure Moscow that they would remain allies.[14] The Soviet Presidium considered whether "to put an end to what is going on in Poland."[15] No conclusion was reached. On 21 October they considered two options: "to influence and watch events" or "go the road of intervention." Khrushchev—despite the rancor of his conversations with Gomułka—came down in favor of "refraining from military intervention" and "showing patience." All were agreed. They simultaneously called a meeting of other fraternal parties, "given that the European parties have been expressing considerable anxiety, as political and economic problems have arisen in Poland in a severe form."[16]

Poland was helped by having Chinese support. Ochab—intending to draw Gomułka back into the leadership—had made it his business to attend China's Party congress at the end of September where, in extensive discussions with and without the presence of the inquisitive Soviet ambassador, he emphasized the urge to greater independence within the bloc.[17] On the Polish issue at the interparty discussions in Moscow on 24 October the "weight" lay with China.[18] So misgivings such as those of the GDR's dour diehard Ulbricht—"They are opening the doors to bourgeois ideology, a leadership in drift"[19]—were more easily dismissed. Henceforth something of a special relationship emerged between Warsaw and Beijing. Moscow, however, was nothing if not grudging. Zhukov later said, with customary brutal candor, that "what we had at our disposal would have been enough to wipe them out like flies."[20]

But Warsaw's nouvelle cuisine soon influenced impressionable chefs in Budapest, even though more was promised on the menu than ever appeared on the plate. Imre Nagy—willing informer for the NKVD as agent Volodya from 1933 to 1945 and therefore not an unnatural choice for Beria[21]—was deposed as Chairman of the Council of Ministers in 1955 when Khrushchev defeated Malenkov and the reformers in Moscow. He was now hailed as "the Hungarian

Gomułka."[22] The circumstances of his reemergence were even more startling. Indeed, well before the events of 1956 US intelligence had noted the high levels of passive resistance to communism in Hungary.[23] But they had wrongly concluded that open conflict was most unlikely.[24] As events gathered pace, all eyes gravitated toward Poland. But Hungary never lay far behind. Moscow, hoping to salvage the situation, had brusquely dismissed Rákosi, but in his place sat the equally diehard but less sadistic Ernö Gerö.

The self-exculpatory Soviet analysis of the problem was that everything could be attributed to "the errors committed by the leadership of the workers' party and of the government of Hungary" in respect of economic development. Added to this was "the distance of the party from the masses of the people." And the Party itself, with a mere 900,000 members, was "from the ideological and organizational point of view weak, crumbling." Apart from anything, discontent within the Party and among the working class was due to "the gross violation of socialist legality and repression against the innocent (in the years 1949–52)." Although Russia was ultimately responsible, and in the case of the repression directly culpable, it was congenitally incapable of acknowledging this—at least on paper.[25] So, having failed to take an objective view of how things came to crisis, it is not surprising, perhaps, that they were repeatedly caught by surprise.

HUNGARY RESISTS

Plans for the worst had been laid. Moscow was already disturbed by the direction of events in Budapest in the summer of 1956. This is evident from the review conducted by First Deputy Chief of the Soviet General Staff and Chief of Staff of the Warsaw Pact General Alexei Antonov. On 20 July corps commander Lieutenant-General Petr Lashchenko produced a plan of action—codenamed "Wave"—"for the establishment of public order on the territory of Hungary." This identified areas of occupation and designated units for action by which control over the country could be obtained in just three to six hours.[26]

Writers naturally led the drive for freedom of speech. At first they gave the government under Gerö time to meet their demands. But this grace came to a decisive end on 8 September when Gyula Hay published an article calling for full freedom of expression, a position echoed by speaker after speaker at the Hungarian Writers' Association on 17 September.[27] A further sign that the government was gradually giving way to demands from below came on 14 October when Nagy was readmitted to the Party, having refused to recant much of his criticism of its conduct in the past.

From 6 to 19 October Soviet ambassador Yuri Andropov kept the military advised in detail on developments within Hungary and urged them to raise their level of readiness. By 19 October the 108th guards parachute regiment of the 7th guards parachute division was put on alert, ready for airlift from air bases in Kaunas and Vilnius in Lithuania. Two days later troops in Hungary were inspected with a view to implementation of operation "Wave."[28] The upsurge of discontent then reached a peak on 23 October when a demonstration banned by the authorities of writers, students—who had formed an organization independent of communist control a week before—and off-duty soldiers took place regardless. They demanded a new government under Nagy and the immediate withdrawal of forces based in Hungary, amounting to some 27,000 ground troops.[29]

By nightfall the ranks of the demonstration were swollen with angry government employees and impatient workers from the surrounding factories. Up to this point the Presidium was entirely taken up with Poland, which was to be discussed by leaders of fraternal parties in Moscow on the following day. Gerö decided he could not risk further absence, having been with Tito when the troubles began—and instead rushed back. It is variously claimed that he phoned Moscow and Andropov in panic at 7:00 p.m. that evening and immediately requested forces to put down the troubles or that he was called to the phone by the Russians and pressed to request troops.[30] Given that Moscow later attempted to extort from various figures a predated letter requesting military intervention,[31] it was doubtless Khrushchev who took the initiative. It is agreed, however that Gerö inflamed opinion at home with an ill-considered, intemperate, and insulting radio broadcast an hour later. Speaking in the same language as that used to denounce Nagy in 1955, he attacked the leaders of the demonstration for "chauvinist incitement" and "nationalism."[32] This led directly to an assault by demonstrators on the radio station on Sándor Street staunchly defended by the AVO, the political police. To the sound of calls such as "Russians, go home" and "Death to Gerö," the battle for Budapest thus began with what American intelligence described as "large-scale, armed violence."[33]

Despite persistent references to imperialist involvement, the revolt was spontaneously generated. Once it was under way, however, Washington did much to accelerate the speed of progress toward open rebellion by rebroadcasting local Hungarian radio programs calling for insurrection.[34] Eisenhower's right-hand man in the White House, General Andrew Goodpaster, recalls: "later he [Eisenhower] was very conscious that there might have been previous inducements and enticements held out to the Hungarians to lead them to think that if they took this action that we would intervene to support them. We had a couple of surveys and examinations made, investigations really, of what had been beamed out to them over Radio Free Europe and other ways."[35] These were the actions of Frank Wisner, conducting covert operations for CIA. He is reliably reported to have attempted and been refused permission to fly in weapons and men.[36]

That evening—23 October—between about 10:00 and 11:00 p.m. Moscow time, Zhukov reported to the Presidium on the 100,000 demonstrators in Budapest, the attack on the radio station, and the seizure of the headquarters of the regional Party and the Ministry of Interior. Whereupon Khrushchev suggested moving Soviet troops into the capital. Bulganin spoke out in support, as did almost everyone else present. Mikoyan alone opposed: let the Hungarians restore order, he insisted. Sending in Soviet forces would only "make things worse." "Try political measures and then bring in the troops," he suggested instead. Mikoyan argued for Nagy's appointment as head of the regime: it would be "cheaper for us." Molotov, however, saw Nagy as useless and spoke in favor of troops. Kaganovich was even more blunt: "It is a question of overthrowing the government. There is no comparison with Poland." Zhukov also pressed for troops, a state of emergency with curfew, and the dispatch of a Presidium member. Nagy did, indeed, emerge as Chairman of the Council of Ministers early on the morning after the demonstration at a time when events were already running out of control. In summing up, however, Khrushchev accepted the need for Nagy in government but not as chairman. Mikoyan and Suslov would be sent to take charge of affairs on the ground.[37]

From the outset, therefore, with the single exception of Mikoyan, Moscow chose a military solution, immediately effected. When the meeting opened at 10:00 p.m., Chief of the General Staff and First Deputy Minister of Defense Sokolovskii were already placing the special corps in Hungary on alert.[38] Immediately after the Presidium dispersed, Zhukov formally mobilized the special corps in Hungary and units from Ukraine (a rifle brigade) and Romania as planned.[39] At 12:30 a.m. on the following day, 24 October, the 2nd guards mechanized division of the Soviet army stationed at Kecskemét, fifty miles southeast of Budapest, rolled forward into the capital in some urgency, arriving at 4:00 a.m.[40] The instructions were to fire with cannon to clear the streets of rioters.[41] An hour later two detachments from the 33rd mechanized division forming a seventy-six-truck artillery convoy left Timisoara in western Romania for Hungary. At 11:28 a.m. the 17th guards mechanized division at Szombathely, more than one hundred miles due east of Budapest, was also called into action.[42] The commanders of its 83rd tank and 1043rd artillery regiments were ordered to Budapest.[43] Fighting continued across the country through the 25 October. That morning at Mikoyan's suggestion Gerö was removed as First Secretary by János Kádár, once severely tortured by the previous regime but now rehabilitated.[44]

After a moment of calm, the situation further worsened when at midday a massive crowd emerged onto the square outside parliament refused to disperse on orders from Soviet forces, who opened fire and killed sixty. There was more shooting just outside the Central Committee building where Mikoyan and Suslov were negotiating. Nagy requested a reinforcement of Soviet troops. Only József Këbël, a recent entry into the Politburo, called on Moscow to withdraw its forces. "We stated," Mikoyan and Suslov reported to the Presidium, "that it was impossible to raise the question of removing Soviet forces from Hungary because this will mean the entry of American forces." Instead all they promised was that once order was restored, Soviet forces would return to their bases. The others agreed.[45] Thereafter, Mikoyan and Suslov pressed for the slimming down of the Politburo to a "directorate" and, when anyone spoke out of line, they talked ominously of "taking measures."

"Some Hungarian troops have joined the insurgents and legation officers personally witnessed on the afternoon of the 25th some Soviet tanks and their crews who had also joined the rebels," CIA noted. Soviet forces continued to be mobilized for transfer across the frontier. Following talks with Mikoyan and Suslov, Nagy announced at 3:30 p.m. (Budapest time) that the "Hungarian government is initiating negotiations on relations with the USSR on the basis of national independence and equality between Communist parties and will ask for the withdrawal of Soviet forces stationed in Hungary when order is restored."[46] Yet this was not what the Presidium had agreed with Mikoyan and Suslov, who received a verbatim translation of Nagy's speech only later that night. Indeed, it was precisely the reverse (in fact Nagy had the meeting reconvened after Mikoyan and Suslov left the building in order to obtain agreement to the speech which contradicted what had been agreed with the Russians).[47]

On 26 October the 70th guards rifle division in the Trans-Carpathian military district was mobilized to reach northeastern Hungary two days later.[48] Large-scale fighting had spread to the countryside, with much of western Hungary in the hands of the rebels. As a consequence the frontier with Austria was now open to traffic in both directions.[49] A hole had effectively been punched through the Warsaw Pact. CIA reported: "The government of Premier Imre Nagy . . . apparently does not exercise real authority." At least one regional administration emerged independently in Miskolc and Borsad, in northeastern Hungary. Such autonomous entities were demanding concessions from the center in return for subordination.[50] There were now four Soviet divisions in the country, totaling some 40,000 men.[51]

By 28 October it was clear that all attempts to put down the rebellion had failed despite headlines in *Izvestiya* that morning arguing "The Organizers of the Counterrevolutionary Putsch in Hungary Have Failed." According to US intelligence, "rebel forces, acting independently with no central leadership" were "in control of most of Hungary outside of Budapest." Nagy, evading Politburo meetings at which Mikoyan and Suslov were present, was calling for a cease-fire on the basis of the new status quo, ordering troops not to fire unless fired upon.[52] At noon that day the 31st guards parachute division of the Red Army was also mobilized for airlift from air bases in Lvov and Khel'nitskii.[53] As of 2:00 p.m. on 29 October CIA reported that Nagy's government had identified itself with the rebel cause—*Szabad Nép* was calling on Soviet troops to withdraw—and that "the Soviet forces in Hungary have largely disengaged themselves from the fighting in order to await further orders from Moscow." Moreover, in contrast to other neighboring parties, the Central Committee of the Polish Party echoed the demand.[54] That evening at 10:00 p.m. Soviet forces in Budapest were ordered to cease fire.[55] A straw in the wind was that two Romanian officials told Thayer, minister at the US embassy in Bucharest, that "things were just as they should be" in Poland and Hungary.[56] Clearly the infection of national liberation from the Soviet empire was spreading.

As of 2:00 p.m. Budapest time on 30 October, with the population reported as in a state of "psychological frenzy" and the lynching of AVO personnel increasingly evident, having disengaged from street fighting, Soviet forces were withdrawing from the capital. The crowds marching on the parliament that afternoon demanded that Soviet troops leave Hungary by mid-November. Nagy stated that the provisional regional administrations that had emerged had to maintain order. He announced the abolition of the one-party state. A multiparty government came into being.[57] Radio Budapest now denied that Nagy had ever called in the Soviet military, blaming former Chairman of the Council of Ministers András Hegedüs and Gerö.[58]

That day, 30 October, the Presidium agreed on a declaration on relations between the USSR "and other socialist countries," which, it claimed, were founded on "the immutable basis of respect for the full sovereignty of each socialist state." It explained that "the future stationing of Soviet military units in Hungary may serve as grounds for an even greater worsening of the situation" and that these forces would be withdrawn from Budapest at the wish of the Hungarian government. It also announced the willingness of the Soviet government to discuss the "presence of Soviet forces on the territory of Hungary" and its willingness to do so with all members of the Warsaw Pact.[59] Yet no sooner had this appeared in the editorial column on the front page of *Pravda* the following day than the Presidium reversed the decision and set about the final liquidation of the Hungarian revolt.

SUEZ SHIFTS THE BALANCE

The trigger was the Anglo-French invasion of Egypt—operation Muscateer—which began at 7:44 a.m. Moscow time. Moscow plausibly but mistakenly understood that Washington was implicated. Khrushchev announced that the situation in Hungary had to be reviewed, that forces would not be withdrawn but would instead "take the initiative in restoring order." The reason given was entirely new: "If we leave Hungary, this will encourage the Americans, the English, and the French—the imperialists." They would "understand us to be weak and will attack." The Party would not understand. "Together with Egypt we would then add Hungary. We have no other choice."[60] Had Moscow known that Washington was unconnected and, indeed, utterly opposed to the Suez adventure, it is doubtful whether the Kremlin would have gone ahead, particularly once Britain and France were in the dock for aggression at the UN Security Council. Out of premature fear and alarm the Moscow leadership allowed themselves to be panicked into hasty action. A week later the uprising had been crushed.

The revolt stirred discontent even among those at Moscow State University: "Many of them hostile to Khrushchev," a KGB veteran recalls, "called for demonstrations in support of the Hungarians and to protest against the actions of the Soviet government. At these meetings there were a number of anti-Soviet slogans and placards."[61] This implied that the USSR could be subverted via Eastern Europe: a lesson not lost in 1968. The United States and Britain had since 1948 been committed to rolling back Soviet control over Eastern and Central Europe through covert action, now supervised by the "54–12 group." Hungary therefore represented opportunity, but not one that they had been expecting. The evidence is that much was done to encourage the revolt but without hard thought about where this would lead. CIA was not always fully controlled in these years with forceful personalities like Wisner in the field. Director Allen Dulles disliked personal confrontation. For this a price was paid on the ground. Eisenhower thereafter believed that "elements in our government—and specifically the CIA—had gone beyond their authority and in fact had carried out a line of propaganda of their own which was not in accord with his policy."[62]

The dramatic events of 1956 had clearly demonstrated certain core facts: the close interconnection between attempts to reform Soviet society and the fate of fraternal Communist parties both in and out of power; the underlying fragility of the bloc in Eastern Europe; the international price of using force to sustain that hegemony; and the deep insecurities at the roots of Soviet power. A further and critical weakness was that Moscow stood at a grave disadvantage with respect to US strategic nuclear power. This fact was as yet unknown to the world at large, including Washington. It was essential for Khrushchev to create and sustain the illusion that the reverse was the case, and this was made possible by continued secrecy and the fortuitous gift of winning the race into outer space in the following year.

TAKING THE WORLD TO THE BRINK

Soon all hell will break loose.

—Khrushchev, end of September 1962

In the mid-seventies General Secretary Leonid Brezhnev reflected that the USSR had since Khrushchev conducted a consistent foreign policy that had won trust. "If we had taken this line from the very beginning then Adenauer would not have been able to hang on so long, and the whole process up to 1964 would have been better than that which we inherited. . . . With Cuba— [Marshal Sergei] Biryuzov [officer commanding Strategic Missiles Forces] said palm trees were there: 'I can put the missiles under palms.' But if you had seen what happened at the datcha in [Novo-] Ogarevo [just outside Moscow] when the Americans launched the blockade."[1]

It was not just the Cuban missile crisis that jeopardized peace. In October 1964 Khrushchev was also indicted over the Berlin crisis: "Comrade Khrushchev wished to frighten the Americans; however, they were not scared, and we had to retreat." Khrushchev, the indictment continued, menaced Britain and France at the time of Suez. All this amounted to "a system, a special 'medium' of conducting foreign policy by means of threatening the imperialists with war." And by such "adventurism," he succeeded in binding the West together, when "our job required . . . making use of dissension and contradictions within the camp of imperialism." Khrushchev also "brought the world to the brink of nuclear war; which struck terror into the very organizer of this dangerous fantasy."[2] This was what Brezhnev and the rest of the leadership had experienced at Novo-Ogarevo on Sunday 28 October 1962.

Arraigned before the Central Committee, Khrushchev disingenuously insisted that "all these measures were good, and they were all at their time approved, so why now raise the question and hold me personally responsible for all this?"[3] Marshal Rodion Malinovsky became Defense Minister after Khrushchev's summary dismissal of Zhukov on 26 October 1957, a surprise move prompted partly as a result of Malinovsky's own warnings as to how dangerous Zhukov was.[4] Brezhnev, in a moment of inspired eloquence, warned Zhukov to be "quieter than water, lower than the grass."[5] General Dmitrii Yazov was a regimental commander intimately involved in the Cuban gambit. He recalls no prior consultation with Malinovsky and Chief of the General Staff Matvei Zakharov. "After the decision was taken, only then were Malinovsky and Zakharov asked for advice about the planning: that you must do this, that, and the other. This is not advice," Yazov recalls, "it is the implementation of instructions. That is how it was."[6] Such practices were no less true of the second Berlin crisis. Furthermore, Khrushchev's close confidant in foreign policy, Mikoyan, "spoke out against" provoking the Berlin crisis and "argued" with Khrushchev against placing missiles in Cuba.[7]

THE SECOND CRISIS OVER BERLIN

Failure to resolve the German question had left the contours of Europe's political map in dispute since the end of World War II. The rearmament of West Germany and its inclusion within NATO in 1955 were rapidly followed by Adenauer's wish expressed on 19 September 1956 that Bonn obtain "as speedily as practicable the possibility of itself producing nuclear weapons."[8] Khrushchev felt impelled to cut across such unsettling ambitions by forcing the West to accept the postwar territorial status quo.

From 27 March 1958, now Chairman of the Council of Ministers as well as First Secretary, he pressed ahead with Stalin's solution. The vulnerability of West Berlin was only too apparent and all too tempting. Soviet plans indicated that the Red Army could take the city in six to eight hours.[9] Khrushchev decided on an ultimatum: the allies had to abandon West Berlin within six months. Mikoyan recalled: "Khrushchev also displayed astonishing lack of understanding of the entire complex of questions; he was prepared to renounce the Potsdam agreements and he stated all this in the autumn of 1958 in a speech without prior discussion in the Presidium and the Council of Ministers. This was in itself the most blatant breach of Party discipline." Mikoyan asked if Gromyko had a view. "He murmured something inarticulate. I repeated the question—once again he murmurs: it was evident that he did not dare contradict Khrushchev." Mikoyan suggested discussion be adjourned for a week while a Foreign Ministry memorandum was prepared. Khrushchev accepted this. Yet he did not find support even within the Central Committee Information Department under

Georgii Pushkin. Up-and-coming Germanist, the former lathe worker Valentin Falin argued that the ultimatum would lead to military conflict, a point of view brusquely dismissed by Khrushchev on the grounds that the Americans would never risk war over West Berlin.[10] Falin's judgment was shared by other Soviet officials.[11] Yet the worst Khrushchev expected was increased international tension. "West Berlin is after all a splinter in a healthy body that must be removed," he later assured US ambassador "Tommy" Thompson.[12]

Mao's attempt to force American diplomatic recognition by bombarding islands offshore (Quemoy and Matsu) in August played a role. Reacting to it, Dulles had declared that force might have to be used to prevent their capture from Chiang, adding that the same applied to West Berlin.[13] Ulbricht brought this to Khrushchev's attention. Why, if China, in a much more precarious situation, could rebuff the United States, was the USSR, militarily so powerful, unable to do the same in Europe? On 2 October Ulbricht and Grotewohl called for the deployment of "an offensive against West Germany." In response to Bonn's rearmament and bid for nuclear weapons, "we should also act from a position of strength," Ulbricht insisted. "It must be borne in mind," he continued, "that as soon as the question of the Chinese islands goes onto the back burner, it is Germany's turn."[14]

"Between ourselves," Khrushchev told Mao on 3 August, "we will not fight for the sake of Taiwan." But "in the event of a deterioration in the situation as a result of Taiwan, the USSR will defend the CPR. In turn the USA will declare that it will defend Taiwan. Thus a situation is created that verges on war."[15] Yet Khrushchev also knew from decrypted communications between Chiang and Dulles that Washington would not fight for the offshore islands.[16] Returning home, Khrushchev decided to test Dulles's courage: let China take the islands and Dulles can be given what he deserves in Berlin (expletives deleted relating to the Secretary's mother).[17] The combination of Beijing's pinpricks and accusations of appeasement from Ulbricht with Khrushchev's intemperate character thus launched the world headlong into another crisis.

When on 10 November Gomułka read the draft of Khrushchev's note, he asked whether the aim was ousting the West from Berlin. Khrushchev corrected him: "It is not that simple."[18] The priority was to secure Western recognition of the GDR and thereby the postwar frontiers of Central and Eastern Europe. Furthermore, in the Central Committee apparatus where he managed relations with fraternal parties, Andropov was responsive to East German anxieties at the unending flow of skilled labor westward and had urged a solution for some time. Moreover, by signing a separate peace treaty with East Germany and handing over Soviet rights within Berlin as a whole, Moscow would force the West to recognize the East merely for access to the city. This, of course, was bound to conflict with the policy of dividing NATO. It cut directly across attempts to win over France, where the logical consequences of Khrushchev's policy spelt disaster for national security: "If the West abandons Berlin," Foreign Minister Maurice Couve de Murville insisted, "it runs the risk that Germany will turn toward Russia."[19] Khrushchev evidently thought the price worth paying. Were he to succeed, then Bonn was more likely to fall into his hands.

Moscow thus issued a note on 27 November 1958 accusing Washington, London, and Paris of grossly violating the Potsdam agreement on Germany. They were "turning it [Berlin] into a kind of state within a state and using it as a center from which to pursue subversive activity against the GDR, the Soviet Union, and the other parties of the Warsaw Treaty." They were simultaneously sabotaging the reunification of Germany. This was intolerable. The USSR could not put up with the situation "any longer." Moscow regarded "as null and void" the protocol on the occupation and administration of Berlin originally agreed on 12 September 1944 and related supplementary agreements. The USSR would therefore transfer its rights under those agreements to the GDR. This included the possible transformation of West Berlin into a "free city." If the receiving governments did not agree to renegotiate the above, then the USSR would unilaterally agree terms with the GDR.[20]

The note created the crisis intended. In order to push matters along, Mikoyan was sent to the United States for consultations on 4–20 January 1959, later described as "useful." Yet nothing was achieved. Moscow thus decided to go ahead and sign a peace treaty with the GDR alone.[21] A further meeting on 11 February resolved that Western forces in the city would be left untouched but that no reinforcements would be permitted; that their supply would have to be negotiated between West Berlin and the GDR; and that communications from the West by air would be curtailed.[22]

On 16 February Washington and its allies—minus Paris—finally responded by agreeing to negotiate at foreign minister level in Geneva on 11 May–19 June. Moscow was worried, nevertheless, seeing the offer to talk as a delaying tactic. "They are drawing us into an adventure," Khrushchev warned. "They expect the Russians to retreat." Mikoyan, as usual, expressed concern lest Russia look as though it were seeking to avoid negotiations.[23] Only Britain sought to appease. In anticipation of elections later that year, Prime Minister Harold Macmillan took himself to Moscow from 21 February to 3 March. There, behind the backs of the allies, Foreign Secretary Selwyn Lloyd hinted at recognition of the GDR on the condition that West Berlin retained its status. Adenauer was understandably furious. De Gaulle referred contemptuously to Macmillan as "*ce vieillard lachrymose*."[24]

"The imperialists are split on what to do," boasted a spokesman at Central Committee headquarters. "Adenauer opposes any talks. De Gaulle backs Adenauer. Macmillan, much to the annoyance of Adenauer, de Gaulle and the U.S., has another view."[25] But Khrushchev was also under pressure to deliver and responded with bluff directed as much at rivals as against other governments. He told the Central Committee plenum on 29 October 1957: "We have bombers that are not bad—long distance and medium range; they say that they are not worse than those of the Americans. But flying to America on bombers is currently a difficult task. The intercontinental ballistic missile (ICBM) is another matter. This is an absolute weapon. The ballistic missile will hit a targeted grid reference. This missile will carry out the basic requirement of destroying the enemy's bases at any point. As I already mentioned, we have a European missile. Now we must build them and pile them up. However, we need to perfect missile weaponry."[26] But this cost a great deal. Khrushchev had to trim expenditure elsewhere. And one of the key reasons for disposing of Zhukov had been because he had no enthusiasm for missiles and even less for reducing other capabilities to make way for them.

His mind made up, on 8 December 1959 Khrushchev wrote to members of the Presidium calling for "far-reaching cuts in armaments . . . even without conditions for reciprocity from other states, and for a significant reduction in numbers of men under arms." The latter could be cut by one million or one and a half million. "I believe that such a major reduction would not undermine our defense capability," he insisted. The reasons he gave included the claim that "we are in excellent condition with respect to missile construction; as a matter of fact, we have a range of missiles that can resolve any military problem, short or long-range, 'ground-to-ground,' 'air-to-ground,' 'air-to-air,' atomic submarines, etc., and in respect of explosive power we also have a wide range. Moreover, we have successfully set in place serial production of these missiles." Given possession of such fearful weapons, what need was there for "the large army that we have? It is crazy."[27]

Khrushchev had increasingly focused on the fact that in the intercontinental nuclear arms race, the USSR was rapidly lagging behind the United States. France was well on its way to acquiring a nuclear capability, a process begun under de Gaulle's socialist predecessors; West Germany, too, was now looking in the same direction. Adenauer insisted that unilateral renunciation of building the bomb made in 1954 no longer counted: "They [the Americans] have to hand over to us atomic weapons in one form or another," he told de Gaulle.[28] Yet Western Europe was by no means a serious military threat to Russia. With its medium- (R-12) and newly deployed intermediate-range (R-14) ballistic missiles, Moscow could destroy the region several times over.

Khrushchev, however, had yet to acquire a truly intercontinental capability, whereas Washington possessed a bomber force fully capable and was now enhancing an enormous advantage in killing power. The Single Integrated Operational Plan (SIOP-62) was intended as an all-out assault on the Sino-Soviet bloc with atomic strike forces amounting to 2,258 delivery vehicles carrying 3,423 weapons, regardless of the conditions prompting general war. It came into effect on 1 April 1961.[29] Yet the edge held by the United States was a matter of debate in Washington, which hitherto had no conclusive proof of Soviet backwardness in engineering ICBMs. Khrushchev was thereby able to conduct a tough policy of bluff against Eisenhower. This strategy had a limited time horizon, however: until Washington discovered the truth. Moscow clearly hoped to be able to make up the distance before that happened.

ABORTING THE PARIS SUMMIT

Khrushchev had insisted on a summit between the Great Powers (excluding China).[30] He and Eisenhower met at Camp David in late September 1959. But Khrushchev wanted more. He was therefore vulnerable should Washington resist. Eisenhower also hoped to meet, particularly to hasten a ban on nuclear tests. But Moscow was always fiercely averse to any inspection regime that would make arms control or disarmament meaningful. Had the two Superpowers trusted one another sufficiently to do without such a regime, there would have been no need for such measures in the first place. But mistrust ruled both sides. Espionage was therefore vital: both human intelligence ("humint") and national technical means ("sigint"). After Moscow launched the world's first artificial satellite orbiting the earth, Sputnik, on 3 November 1957, CIA embarked upon Operation Lincoln: the use of humint for gathering information, inter alia, on the state of Soviet rocketry. In 1959 alone seventy such agents were trained and dispatched to the USSR, followed by one hundred in 1960.[31]

National technical means were already available. The first US U-2 spy flight at high altitude took place on 7 April 1956.[32] The problem for Khrushchev was that his supposed superiority in intercontinental ballistic missiles was a fiction. "At that time," Khrushchev since confessed, "we were substantially behind in the accumulation of nuclear weapons and did not have the necessary number of missiles for delivery. Our aircraft could not reach US territory and we therefore remained weaker."[33] Yet he mounted a reckless foreign policy on a fragile fiction of superiority. "We are all alive thanks to your missiles," Mao assured Khrushchev in July 1958. "Yes, to a certain extent this is so," Khrushchev replied, "one can say so without being modest. It deters [our] enemies."[34]

But these exaggerations could be uncovered at any moment. Downing the U-2 was therefore top priority for the Air Defense Forces (*Voiska PVO*). Hitherto the flights took place out of range at 21,000 meters, whereas Soviet interceptor aircraft could reach only 19,000 meters.[35] Surface-to-air missiles (SAMs) were, however, now in mass production and although the first generation in 1952 could never reach such a target,[36] the next generation (1957) could in principle do so.[37] The problem was that a spy plane had yet to be brought down.

Finally on 1 May 1960 a SAM-2 (V-75) missile battery in the Urals under the command of First Lieutenant Bukin succeeded.[38] It was not a direct hit. The plane flew slightly to one side of the battery, which threw up a defensive barrage that clipped the tail and wing assembly of the aircraft, thus saving the life of the pilot and making possible his capture (when he failed to destroy himself and the aircraft) and that of the plane.[39] That day Malinovsky had telephoned to warn that a U-2 was en route from Pakistan to Sverdlovsk. Khrushchev was reviewing the May Day parade on Lenin's mausoleum in Red Square when Marshal Sergei Biryuzov reported that the U-2 had been downed and its pilot was in Soviet hands. From outset, Khrushchev decided to publicize the coup; that was why he had Biryuzov appear in full uniform to give the news.[40] Khrushchev said that they had followed the first flight on 9 April, but that on 1 May, when Malinovsky told him of the second run, "he had given orders to shoot [the] plane down."[41] The aircraft was then displayed in Moscow's favorite playground, *"neskuchny sad"*—the Gorky Park of Rest and Culture—in the very center of the city. But in case Washington wished to retaliate, Khrushchev halted all ongoing espionage operations for the time being.[42]

Khrushchev "was sure Eisenhower knew of the overall plan for such flights," but he was equally "sure . . . that he had no knowledge of that individual flight of [Gary] Powers. That was," he said, "something Allen Dulles cooked up. I just can't conceive of Eisenhower sending over a plane on the eve of the Paris Conference."[43] Khrushchev was wrong. But the press sustained the fiction and reported that the flight had been authorized by Dulles rather than Eisenhower. That suited Khrushchev, since he intended to use it as leverage in the summit forthcoming. He also hoped to keep secret the fact that the pilot was alive and in custody. But Deputy Foreign Minister Malik unwittingly leaked that fact in conversation with the Swedish ambassador, thus depriving Khrushchev of surprise at a moment chosen for maximum effect.[44] Up to this point approaches by Soviet ambassadors to clarify Western arrangements for the summit indicated that before 1 May Moscow was still serious about negotiations. Only on the eve did trouble appear. The planned visit to the United States by Chief of the Air Staff Marshal Konstantin Vershinin was abruptly cancelled on 13 May.

When Eisenhower let it be known that he had, indeed, personally authorized the flight, Khrushchev was baffled. "It was obviously a senseless statement, to say the least. A stupid statement. But it was made."[45] Khrushchev took personal prestige seriously. Yet, as Erofeev (now number two at the Paris embassy) points out, Khrushchev at the same time "when necessary . . . knew how to restrain his own emotions." Erofeev, a cautious witness, notes that in respect of the U-2, "Khrushchev was led not so much by feelings as by sober calculation." He points out, and this is confirmed by Western sources,[46] that at Vnukovo airport just prior to departure for Paris "Khrushchev unexpectedly lingered in the departure lounge with members of the Presidium seeing him off, in order, I suggest, to discuss in principle the question of the value of conducting the meeting in the light of a situation generally unfavorable to us arising from the German question. Then, during the period of the flight, with Gromyko and other main members of the delegation he prepared our possible tactics, though he did not disclose his thoughts until the last minute."[47] Khrushchev had consulted Gromyko and Malinovsky, who both agreed with him (it would have been most unwise to have disagreed too strongly and certainly out of character for Gromyko). A typist and stenographer were aboard. The brief was redrafted "180 degrees" and was, of course, not yet seen by the leadership as a whole.[48] When Moscow was then fully consulted, not everyone was pleased. According to an unconfirmed account from Russian sources, it was as ever Mikoyan who tried to persuade Khrushchev to relent.[49]

Erofeev commented: "It had become clear to Khrushchev from his talks with de Gaulle that his proposals on German matters would not make progress and, moreover, would be publicly and unanimously rejected by the Western participants to the meeting; he would be isolated, in a losing position. The summit had for him become unnecessary; more than that, undesirable."[50] It opened on 16 May and collapsed in vituperation two days later with Khrushchev's suggestion that they reconvene in six to eight months and that Eisenhower postpone his visit to Moscow scheduled for June. After its collapse, Khrushchev told those gathered around him in the embassy: "Well, what's the matter? Why are you so downhearted? For us it were better the meeting never took place."[51]

Mikoyan believed that by his intemperate behavior Khrushchev had "buried détente." "He simply spat at everyone, including de Gaulle, who had taken up a position independent of the USA. Thus he is guilty of setting détente back fifteen years, which cost us massive amounts thanks to the arms race."[52] A proud man, de Gaulle was personally affronted by Khrushchev's disruptive and boorish antics. But Khrushchev was contemptuous of his self-importance. "De Gaulle has nothing," he said; "de Gaulle is as poor as a church mouse; he could not even dispose of his own trousers. He doesn't represent any real capability at all." He "doesn't have a significant voice because he has no missiles, no bombs." And as for de Gaulle acting against Washington, he would not be able to, "otherwise the bourgeoisie of France will oppose him and won't support the government."[53]

Thus at the Soviet Embassy in Paris Erofeev saw the collapse of his own and his ambassador's laborious efforts to bring about a Franco-Soviet rapprochement. "Deeply wounded by Khrushchev for the disruption of a meeting so important to him (the first in Paris since the war), de Gaulle abruptly and for five years turned his back on us over an array of international issues. He stood decisively on the side of the United States during the Cuban [missile] crisis; signed a treaty of cooperation with West Germany in 1963, that met with an extremely negative response in Moscow; recalled his ambassador Dejean from the USSR; and indicated to his favorite, S. A. Vinogradov, the desirability of leaving for Moscow for consultations after the Soviet Union recognized independent Algeria de jure in 1962 and expressed its readiness to establish diplomatic relations. Thus the level of interstate ties was lowered to that of chargé d'affaires, and political contacts between the two countries were in effect curtailed. De Gaulle never met Khrushchev again and only after his removal agreed to visit the USSR officially in June 1966. Almost six years were lost in the development of Franco-Soviet relations."[54]

THE CONGO CRISIS

A most implausible area for Soviet intervention was sub-Saharan Africa by reason not only of distance but also unfamiliarity. Until 1960, senior KGB officer Vadim Kirpichenko recalls, "the attitude toward African problems in the organs of state security was relatively quiescent, as our intelligence and counter-intelligence interests were concentrated on the USA, Europe, and China. In respect of Africa we were obviously behind the times. In the USSR Foreign Ministry there were two African departments already at work, and in the Ministry of Foreign Trade already three; but in the KGB, only a small directorate of five people, of which I became the head immediately after my return from Cairo in the spring of 1960." In Cairo, Kirpichenko had "maintained business contacts with almost all the representatives of the African national liberation movements which found hospitable refuge on Egyptian soil."[55]

The crisis in the Congo, a country enriched by copper and uranium, followed directly from rapid decolonization by Belgium, leaving a population uneducated past the age of eleven with no security other than that provided by Belgian troops, with large mining companies determined not to lose their assets. The main aspirant for power, Patrice Lumumba, was volatile, alternately idealistic, ruthless, and vengeful. In mid-April 1959 he made his way secretly to Brussels, having made initial contact with the Soviet ambassador in Guinea to express interest in diplomatic relations with Moscow on independence and in visiting the USSR beforehand.[56] He also met the General Secretary of the Communist Party for a five-hour meeting. Subsequently the Belgian communist leader told first secretary Savinov at the Soviet embassy that "conditions for the spreading of Marxism in the Congo are more favorable than in the other countries of Africa."[57]

After bloody uprisings, Belgium finally granted independence on 30 June. Moscow immediately established diplomatic relations. But, Keith Kyle recalls: "The Belgians were . . . counting on continuing to run the country in the name of the new African rulers."[58] To Belgium, Lumumba was already a marked man.[59] Belgian commercial interests held an enormous £1,000m in Congolese assets. Union Minière was the most powerful; 15 percent was British owned.[60] On 23 March head of Union Minière Herman Robiliart warned, "There is no doubt that on 1 July these men will open wide the doors of the Congo to their friends in the East."[61] It is not surprising that they sought to hinder Lumumba's progress from the start. Moreover Victor Nendaka, a close associate of Lumumba, had been briefing CIA and the Belgians on his subventions from Moscow.[62]

Lumumba and his party, the MNC (Mouvement National Congolais), won only 33 seats out of 137 in the assembly but, larger than any other grouping, had sufficient support to form an administration in Léopoldville. Belgium, however, unilaterally changed the Loi Fondamentale, allowing Lumumba's rival Moïse Tshombe to form an autonomous administration in Katanga, the southern and richest part of the country. Tshombe served Belgian commercial interests. In a matter of days after independence, the Force Publique mutinied against an entirely white officer corps that treated them with contempt. Belgian civilians panicked and fled the country, threatening the economy.[63] On 9–10 July Belgium decided to invade,[64] and by mid-July it had retaken the key towns. Katanga seceded on 11 July after the directors of the Societé Generale passed a unanimous resolution for its independence.[65] Tshombe was duly rewarded with financial assistance by Union Minière.[66] And the Société Générale prevailed upon the King not to take action against Katanga.[67] On 12 July Lumumba called for UN intervention against "foreign aggression." Two days later the Congolese government broke off relations.

At the KGB, Chairman Alexandr' Shelepin was horrified to discover that the committee lacked a full department to cover Africa. Head of the tiny Africa section, Kirpichenko was immediately recalled from holiday, promoted to be head of the new department and given additional personnel. But though able to form plans, he had no one to carry them out.[68] A small group of KGB officers then arrived in the Congo during July under diplomatic cover headed by Leonid Podgorny to form an embassy.[69]

The UN Security Council demanded withdrawal but did not condemn Belgium for aggression because Washington, London, and Paris were anxious to avoid complicating relations. The Security Council decided on intervention to provide "such military assistance as may be necessary until . . . the national security forces may be able . . . to meet fully their tasks." Belgium, however, withdrew only to Katanga. That day Lumumba turned to Moscow, incautiously asking them "to follow hour-by-hour the development of the situation in the Congo." The telegram also contained a phrase—doubtless intercepted by the NSA, fixing thereby US hostility toward Lumumba: "It is possible we will be obliged to ask for the intervention of the Soviet Union, should the Western camp not cease aggression against the sovereignty of the Congolese Republic."[70] Moscow responded promptly on 15 July: "The government of the Congo can be assured that the Soviet government will render the Congolese Republic the assistance necessary that may be required for the victory of our just cause."[71] At this stage only food aid was sent, but soon five Ilyushin-18 aircraft were offered for the transportation of Ghanaian troops into Léopoldville; then one hundred lorries and a group of Soviet instructors. Doctors were also dispatched. From Belgium former members of the Congo Sûrété were now recalled to their former hunting grounds.[72] The crocodiles were circling.

Lumumba's request to Moscow hardened UN Secretary General Dag Hammarskjöld against him. Under Secretary Ralph Bunche had told Hammarskjöld that Tshombe was nothing but a "puppet" manipulated by Belgium, so high-sounding talk of the "legitimate" objectives of Tshombe were, to say the least, insincere.[73] British officials were warned that he "had conceived the United Nations operation as a means of preventing the Soviet penetration of Africa. And he had set about removing the elements of danger one by one."[74] UN neutrality was fatally compromised.

On 5 August Moscow repeated a demand for Belgian withdrawal. The Russians called for replacement of the UN command in the Congo if it failed to observe the decisions of the Security Council and demanded resolute measures to end the occupation of Katanga. They also called for the replacement of contingents in the country with those effective in fighting the interventionists.[75] Lumumba accused Hammarskjöld of refusing to send troops into Katanga. On 27 July King Badouin met privately with Hammarskjöld and asked him not to

damage the Tshombe regime.[76] On 8–9 August the Security Council weakened its demand that Belgium withdraw by simultaneously declaring the UN
would not be party to the conflict between two halves of the Congo. Reflecting
Hammarsjöld's opinions and contradicting the resolution of 14 July, the latest
resolution instructed UN forces not to be "used to influence the outcome of
any internal conflict, constitutional or otherwise." This bizarre reinterpretation
of Congolese sovereignty naturally had Belgian approval. Thus Hammarskjöld
negotiated directly with Tshombe to secure the entry of UN troops into Katanga in place of the Belgians, as a result of which Lumumba broke off relations on 14–15 August. The Security Council backed Hammarskjöld. Moscow
could not overturn the previous UN resolution without facing a US veto. At
Belgian bidding Lumumba was dismissed by the president[77] on 5 September
in collusion with the UN. By then Hammarskjöld was unalterably convinced
not only that Lumumba "was already clearly a Communist stooge" but also
that "no stable settlement could be envisaged unless his powers could be further reduced."[78] Lumumba's disastrous attempt to reach Katanga with remnants
of the Force Publique ended in bloody massacres when they were distracted
by and embroiled in preexisting ethnic strife between Luluas and Balubas in
South Kasaï.

On 16 September, with US support, the officer commanding the Force Publique, Joseph Mobutu, paid by Belgium, seized power and broke off relations
with Moscow. Deputy Prime Minister Antoine Gizenga fled to Stanleyville
with the rest of the government. Lumumba was captured in Léopoldville and
placed under house arrest. His assassination was precipitated by a mutiny of
Congolese forces and fear that Lumumba would return to power.[79] Even British officials incautiously speculated on "ensuring Lumumba's removal from
the scene by killing him."[80] Oleg Nazhestkin, a KGB officer stationed under
diplomatic cover, claims CIA sent in a "Michael Malroney" (Larry Devlin)
from operations. His job was to lure Lumumba out into the open. This was
done through an agent in Lumumba's entourage.[81] Lumumba escaped from
his residence and headed for Stanleyville only to be detained by Major General
Henry Templer Alexander, officer commanding the UN Ghanaian contingent,
and handed over to Mobutu's men on orders from New York. Lumumba was
flown back to Léopoldville where he was assaulted in front of the press and then
sent to Thysville barracks.

On 15 January Belgium insisted Tshombe take Lumumba. He was transported to Katanga by plane and murdered with Belgian collusion on 17 January
1961. It was a disastrous performance by the UN, tainted by the Cold War as
was every institution that had come into contact with it. Moscow was effectively

helpless—grandstanding was all Khrushchev accomplished. Khrushchev found he had no naval power nor airlift capacity worthy of the name and that the former would take at least five years to build and with money he could not afford.[82] In the end he was reluctant to create a crisis with the United States for such a remote return. A new administration was in the offing.

KHRUSHCHEV CONFRONTS KENNEDY

The end of the Eisenhower administration left Khrushchev guessing. What he certainly did not want was victory for Nixon, a hard-line anticommunist with whom Khrushchev had a bruising encounter in a "miracle kitchen," a US exhibit, on the vice presidential visit (23 July–2 August 1959).[83] But the ineptitude with which Khrushchev attempted to influence the election in favor of Kennedy, via the candidate's brother Robert, cannot have impressed the Democrats that Moscow had any real understanding of the United States.[84]

Cuba had been a thorn in America's side since Fidel Castro took power in 1959. From 1959 blatant infringement of US commercial interests made a collision between Havana and Washington inevitable. Whether Cuba also became a Soviet base area in the Caribbean with immediate reach into the heart of Latin America was more a matter of choice. Cuba had long been the playground of American millionaires and the Mafia. It had little claim to fame except cigars, rum, and, less well known, pharmacology. While profits were safe, no US government worried about the dictatorship established by Batista in 1952; it was only when US interests were jeopardized that democracy suddenly became high priority.

The Cuban revolutionaries who seized power in January 1959 decided to hold military forces in reserve while the facade of constitutionalist government was set up under a respectable lawyer brought in from exile for that purpose by Castro. From March 1959 "el Che" (Guevara), in particular, was restless to pursue that more distant goal of bringing the revolution to Argentina and the rest of the subcontinent.[85] Yet these activities cut directly across the strategy favored by Moscow formulated under the influence of the Chilean Communist Party, which favored constitutionalism above insurrection.[86] Cuba's hasty moves to export revolution in the Caribbean inevitably made Moscow cautious, especially when conducted by such independently minded revolutionaries.

The US-sponsored invasion of Cuba at Playa Girón with the bombing of airfields on 15 April 1961 and landings by exiles two days later showed Khrushchev that Kennedy could be swayed by hawks. The invasion failed. The bland assumption that the population would rise up and aid the invasion was shown to be false. "When you take a job like this, you simply have to depend on the judgement of the men around you. And you don't know them at first," Kennedy later lamely confessed.[87]

Khrushchev then backtracked in his determination to reduce conventional forces. Calling on Malinovsky, Zakharov, and Grechko to stiffen forces in Germany in late May 1961, Khrushchev emphasized, "If we wish to carry on our policy and that this policy is recognized and respected and feared, we have to be resolute." He added: "One has to bolster [one's forces] because words have to be bolstered by acts."[88] Suddenly Khrushchev was overwhelmed with nostalgia for the dull predictability of the 1950s. "The most intelligent politician in the USA in recent years was Dulles. With him we always knew what we could count on. And Dulles would not go to war." Kennedy, however, was different. "The events in Cuba indicate that he is not very intelligent."[89] But Khrushchev appears to have forgotten his comment about Dulles to Mao in 1958: "It is better to do business with a fool than an intelligent person."[90]

Kennedy's failure over Cuba encouraged Khrushchev's disparagement, a view reinforced by ambassador Mikhail Menshikov. He misleadingly predicted that Kennedy would "mount the high horse" but would be the first to give way. Yet this is certainly not the entire story.[91] If Kennedy were, indeed, weak, then on the face of it he was equally if not more susceptible to pressure from hawks within the United States as the Cuban fiasco suggested. The Vienna summit of 3–4 June certainly did not resolve this conundrum.

Kennedy was strongly advised not to get involved in tortuous debates about general principles—for which he had neither talent nor training—but he did precisely that and came off badly, ineptly acknowledging the value of peaceful coexistence without understanding the full significance of the concept (peace between states but class war between societies). In turn the condescending tone adopted by Khrushchev prompted icy politeness: Kennedy "had not assumed office to accept arrangements totally inimical to US interests."[92] He stormed out of the Soviet embassy. He had "expected this summit to open the way to the relaxation of tension that he had promised in his inaugural . . . instead it had turned into a bewildering showdown for which he had not been prepared."[93] Indeed, the Presidium's subsequent report on the summit crowed about Khrushchev's "extensive mastery of the subjects [under discussion] and his aggressive spirit."[94]

"This is a man who dreams but decides which way to go on a day-by-day basis," Khrushchev said scornfully, adding, more significantly, "The man himself has very little authority among those that decide and direct the policy of the United States."[95] Kennedy was, in his words, "too young. He lacks the authority and prestige to settle this issue [Berlin/Germany] correctly."[96] Taking advantage of Kennedy's failure over Cuba in order to bolster the Soviet position in Europe, on 29 July Shelepin outlined a strategy "to create circumstances in different areas of the world which would assist in diverting the attention and forces of the United States and its allies, and would tie them down during the settlement of the question of a German peace treaty and West Berlin." This was approved by the Presidium on 1 August.[97]

Moscow did not get its way, however. It settled instead for an interim solution that further damaged Soviet standing. The decision to build the Berlin wall was Khrushchev's alone. During a long conversation with Ulbricht on 1 August he announced his decision "to encircle Berlin with a steel ring." His offer to reinforce the number of Soviet divisions in Germany only made Ulbricht nervous, however.[98] Anxious lest Bonn react by implementing trade sanctions, Ulbricht wanted prior warning, but Khrushchev was having none of it.[99] Preparations were conducted in the tightest secrecy. Nothing was communicated to East Berlin in code or even by the Kremlin's special telephone line.[100] "Naturally, the GDR would not close the border without us," Khrushchev told ambassador Kroll. "Of course, we shut the border; this was done at our request, though technically it was carried out by the GDR as it is a German issue."[101]

The Berlin wall went up during the night of 12–13 August, effectively making East Berlin a part of the GDR and cutting off West Berlin.[102] Western intelligence had been caught napping.[103] This ugly scar threatened allied rights in the city and raised the political temperature considerably as those seeking to escape were shot dead. The potential for miscalculation on either side was real. Yet, and this increasingly became a source of anxiety, Khrushchev had persistently ridiculed the very notion of miscalculation at the Vienna summit.[104] It would take a crisis bringing both sides to the brink of war for Moscow as well as Washington to realize the importance of very real dangers in the thermonuclear era.

Khrushchev still thought war remote, however. At Pitsunda on 17 August he assured Ho Chi Minh: "At present, in our opinion, the real danger of war breaking out is about 3–5 percent. But war may break out by accident, and we are ready for it." The appointment of Marshal Ivan Kon'ev Commander-in-Chief of the Group of Soviet Forces in Germany buttressed this firm line. The policy described to Ho allowed for a measure of threat. It was one of "logic and a big stick." Should a German settlement be secured, the ultimate prize lured him on: "Regulation of the German question will create a completely new situation in Western Europe. . . . It is currently scarcely possible to presuppose that West Germany would dare attack socialist countries. It has not got the strength to do it. At the same time it is sufficiently powerful to try to improve its position at the expense of its western neighbors. The main avenger now in Europe is West Germany. It is worth the Western Powers thinking about this."[105]

To discourage agitation about the Wall, Moscow decided on 31 August to resume nuclear testing and to implement a range of measures buttressing its position in Eastern Europe. "This reminded the Western Powers of the real balance of power and the need to take it into account," recalls Petr Abrasimov, quondam ambassador to the GDR.[106] Moreover, Khrushchev did not drop the German question with the erection of the Wall. The Belgian representative to NATO was told that Khrushchev "would continue to use Berlin as a means of pressuring [the] allies and in this connection quoted Chekhov's story of [a] fisherman who was called before [a] judge for having stolen spikes and ties from [a] railroad which he used to weight his fishing line. [The] accused in defense offered [the] fact that he had never removed enough spikes or ties to put [a] train off balance."[107]

The aim was entirely as foreseen and the very reason why de Gaulle adamantly refused even to negotiate on the subject of Berlin: if Moscow succeeded in decoupling Berlin from the allies, then Bonn would draw the lesson that they could no longer rely on NATO. Having read deciphered dispatches belonging to the other side, in October 1961 Khrushchev assured Britain's ambassador that if Bonn lost faith in the West, "they will turn to us. They have no place else to go."[108] But when? To Kennedy's press secretary Pierre Salinger in Moscow, Khrushchev vilified Adenauer as "a dangerous and senile old man. The only way Adenauer could reunite Germany," he insisted, "is through war, and he hasn't got the courage to do that."[109] This anger indicated severe stress from growing pressure to obtain results. The new British ambassador, Sir Frank Roberts, did not differ from his predecessor Sir Patrick Reilly in concluding that "Khrushchev had staked his prestige entirely on settling the Berlin question."[110] Sulzberger interviewed Khrushchev in early September and was struck by his "continual use of the word 'prestige.'" He sensed that "Khrushchev really wants informal contact—not through diplomats—and he would like to circumvent his own foreign office and government and save his own prestige."[111] That is precisely what comrades feared.

In January 1961 Khrushchev had reasserted the Party's commitment to national liberation movements. But this was essentially a rhetorical flourish designed to appease critics, and not just dissentient China, with whom relations had been deteriorating. When Khrushchev held talks with Mao in 1954 he said, "A conflict between China and ourselves is inevitable." At root Mao could not bear the thought that any other Communist Party stood above China in the hierarchy.[112] Thus Moscow never placed Beijing's claim to a permanent seat on the UN Security Council ahead of other, more pressing priorities: the German question and the creation of a modus vivendi with Washington. Mao became the ever more irate backseat driver in the Soviet car, forever chiding Khrushchev for attempting to seek détente with Eisenhower. Kennedy seemed a soft target of opportunity. For Moscow, facing West rather than East, Asia was always a secondary priority.

Nothing underscored Khrushchev's priorities more than his statement to Ho on 19 August 1961 that "the German question is now more important than that of Laos and takes up all our time." In Laos the communist Pathet Lao had been engaged in an insurgency since July 1959. What Ho sought was aid for the Pathet Lao that would enable the creation of an army of 10,000 men. By taking and holding neighboring Laos, Hanoi could assure lines of supply to forces fighting in the South. Khrushchev instead favored "a more flexible policy" of sustaining the more neutralist Souvanaphouma in power. Souvanaphouma was unstable but he "already fears us more than the imperialists." He was not a communist any more than was Castro, but he had his uses. Ho needed to rectify his line, Khrushchev insisted. "We send weapons for Laos via Vietnam; you redistribute them, but you redistribute them wrongly. This has to be corrected."[113]

Warned by Eisenhower that this was the key to peace in Southeast Asia, Kennedy had expressed his concerns about Laos with Khrushchev in Vienna. Both had agreed that the country was, in Kennedy's words, "of no strategic importance and was not vital to either side."[114] Some kind of deal was feasible. But Hanoi never found it advantageous to observe any such accommodation; and this was Vietnam's backyard, whereas Moscow was working from a tremendous distance that made enforcement well nigh impossible. Moreover, Kennedy was as reluctant as Dulles and Eisenhower to risk the domestic fallout of coming to terms with Beijing. Thus the problem of neutralizing revolution in Indochina as a whole was bound to persist because China had every interest in causing trouble for Washington, there and elsewhere.

THE SINO-SOVIET SPLIT

Washington had known of cracks in Sino-Soviet unity for some considerable time. But policy making and execution under Eisenhower from 1952 to 1959 lay in the hands of Assistant Secretary of State Robertson. A Virginia Democrat and businessman, Robertson had served in Chungking from 1945 to 1946 as minister-counselor. He felt strongly that Chiang had been betrayed by not granting him $500 million in aid and by letting Russia into Manchuria. His notoriously strong personal ties with Chiang and the China lobby in Congress gave him special status. Mindful of public opinion, Dulles always worked through him on Far Eastern matters. Robertson also maintains that "there was never any division on any basic issue. We worked together in complete harmony." Robertson loathed Britain, whose recognition of Communist China he considered "a fatal mistake." Worse than that: "the British were opposed to taking any action in Asia to stem the Communist aggression," he later reflected. "They gave a token support in Korea, but only a token support." And they failed to join the United States in propping up the French in Indochina.[115]

On Robertson's watch, no attempt was countenanced to exploit Sino-Soviet differences that accepted continued communist control of China. In May 1955, asked "if he had heard any reports about difficulties between Russia and China or shooting on the border," Robertson said "he had heard none. Furthermore, he added, even if there were difficulties on a local basis, they would be unimportant. The interests of the two countries lie together. Robertson claims that already in 1940, Mao Tse-tung was writing that he wanted to support world communism under Soviet leadership. . . . Robertson said he recently told Dulles there is no hope whatsoever of Mao Tse-tung becoming a 'Titoist.' He told Dulles that Mao is as loyal to his own principles as Dulles is loyal to the principles taught him by his father, a Presbyterian preacher."[116] The problem for US intelligence reading an ever-growing number of increasingly large tea leaves was to convince the administration that differences were genuine and growing apace.

On 28 February 1957 proposals even reached the NSC to recognize Beijing in return for good behavior. But Dulles argued strongly against, with Eisenhower's support.[117] It took over a decade and in much worse circumstances for Washington to return to the issue. Meanwhile, in June 1959 with a US summit ahead, Khrushchev told Mao that Moscow would not be donating the prototype for atomic weapons because of the test-ban negotiations. Later that year, a Sino-Indian border clash prompted a TASS statement regretting the incident in view of the forthcoming US-Soviet summit at Camp David. China took offense. Mao argued, "The Khrushchev people are very naïve. He does not understand Marxism, and is easily fooled by imperialism." Mao still hoped to avoid a breach but believed, even after the abandonment of the Paris summit, "that the basic thinking of Khrushchev of dominating the world through US-Soviet cooperation has not changed."[118] Chou, for example, described the withdrawal of Soviet experts in 1957 as Khrushchev lifting a rock "only to drop it on his own feet."[119] Indeed, it was fear of the United States that kept China within the Soviet bloc: as Liu Shao-Ch'ih indicated after returning from a major collision with Khrushchev at the Moscow conference of Communist Parties in November–December 1960.[120]

In August 1961 Moscow expelled troublesome and self-obsessed Tirana from the Warsaw Pact, prompting Chinese accusation of killing the chicken "to frighten the monkeys."[121] But China's criticism alienated Khrushchev still further: "We used to be in great need of your support. But now it's different, now we're in a much better position, and we'll walk our own way."[122] Nonproliferation was in the air: Moscow aimed at Bonn; Washington, at Beijing. But what finally killed the relationship was the border war between China and India on 22 October 1962. The manner in which Khrushchev switched positions within a matter of days from a relatively pro-Chinese to a pro-Indian position in parallel with the shift from confrontation with Washington over missiles in Cuba and agreement on withdrawal was just too much for Beijing to swallow.[123]

No change was made until Nixon came to power after voicing a major reconsideration. The inflexibility of the Democrats was further to be seen in respect of Vietnam and also Cuba. It was never entirely clarified whether the process of containment was containment of the Sino-Soviet bloc or of communism in general. If it were merely containment of Soviet and Chinese power, then a differentiated and nuanced approach to the rest of the world communist movement made sense. But if, of course, it were fundamentally ideological, then concessions to any burgeoning communist movement was detrimental to the cause. Failure to face up to this question and clarify policy confined US foreign policy making to a straightjacket inherited from the past and exacerbated the irritation of NATO Europe at US priorities.

The contrast with military strategy is striking. Here there was greater readiness to review policy; yet even here changes in doctrine were cosmetic rather than substantial and the result somewhat muddled. A consequence of the Berlin crisis was reappraisal of the "massive retaliation" strategy under SIOP-62. Democrats sought to improve on the inflexibility of the Eisenhower administration, criticized by Professor Henry Kissinger from Harvard, in respect of nuclear war planning. SIOP-62 was essentially a second-strike strategy responding to a Soviet attack. The question raised by Berlin was what would be appropriate to a Soviet attack not on the United States but on a more limited objective, such as West Berlin. All-out nuclear war was scarcely a credible response. In trying to defend Berlin with conventional forces on the ground, an escalation of the level of force deployed by the other side was likely, and this could rise at some stage to approximate general war.

The execution of SIOP-62 would kill an estimated 37 percent of the Soviet population. "Is this really an appropriate next step after the repulse of a three-division attack across the zonal border between East and West Germany? Will the President be willing to take it?" Instead, Professor Carl Kaysen, an economist and deputy to Kennedy's national security adviser MacGeorge Bundy, advocated what became known as "flexible response," including the initiation of a nuclear first strike planned for the occasion, focusing on the smallest possible list of targets. These targets were Soviet long-range systems that could hit the United States. Having ruled out B-47 and B-52 bombers because they could easily be detected and hit by SAMs, Kaysen stated that what were needed were relatively small numbers of planes with low-altitude penetration because "at present, the USSR has little capability for active defense against very low altitude attacks" (NIE 11-3-61, July 1961). The chosen instruments of delivery were therefore most obviously "overseas-based or carrier-based aircraft."[124]

Although USAF procurement followed suit, little came of this strategic reappraisal in terms of an alternative strategy to all-out nuclear war. France resolutely opposed the idea. Only after it left the integrated military structure of NATO was Washington able to obtain acceptance of "flexible response," in 1967. And by the end of that decade it had an array of dual-capable aircraft (the F-111, F-111A, A-4s, and A-6s) that could accomplish counterforce missions. Because of its potential for a first strike against Soviet command, control, and communications, Moscow became increasingly obsessed with their removal. Both American and Russian officers thought in terms of the possibility of a first strike, launching missiles before the enemy's missiles reached their targets. In this sense the distinction between preemption and launch-on-warning was marginal. This was certainly not what the military on each side wished to hear discussed beyond the closed circle. Indeed, during the strategic arms limitation talks (SALT) that began at the end of the decade a Soviet general complained to his US counterpart that the subject of launch-on-warning should not be raised with civilians present and that, "as a military man," General Allison "should have known the answer to that question."[125]

OVERCOMING US STRATEGIC SUPERIORITY

Diplomatic relations between Havana and Moscow were opened on 7 May 1960. Under American eyes on 10 September the first significant shipment of armaments arrived via Czechoslovakia.[126] Subsequent to the abortive US-sponsored invasion at Playa Girón, between 4 August and 30 September 1961 Moscow signed two agreements pledging more armaments over the following three years. Growing Cuban-Soviet cooperation was paralleled by Havana's transition toward a Soviet-style regime. On 16 April, the day after the Americans started bombing Cuban airfields, Castro declared the Cuban revolution to be socialist. On 2 December he proclaimed his government Marxist-Leninist.

Cuba, however, remained on the periphery of Khrushchev's vision. At the Presidium on 8 January 1962 he made clear that compromise on Berlin was unacceptable. "It would be better not to have an agreement and to preserve for ourselves the initiative of exerting pressure at the necessary moment and the necessary place on the question of West Berlin than to have an agreement that does not satisfy us." He insisted that "now we must prepare for the final showdown over West Berlin."[127] And when Anatoly Dobrynin was briefed by Khrushchev prior to taking charge of the Washington embassy in March 1962, the conversation focused on Germany. Khrushchev was primarily preoccupied with gaining leverage over the West to secure a satisfactory settlement. He then complained of the emplacement by the United States of missiles in neighboring Turkey "under the very nose of the Soviet Union" and said of US nuclear capabilities, "It's high time their long arms were cut shorter."[128]

For Khrushchev the failure to make progress on Germany underlined the importance of catching up. In an off-the-record meeting at the height of the crisis on Cuba, 16 October 1962, Secretary of State Dean Rusk commented, "Berlin is . . . very much involved in this . . . for the first time, I'm beginning really to wonder whether maybe Mr. Khrushchev is entirely rational about Berlin."[129] Indeed, a CIA assessment subsequently argued that in his frustration Khrushchev "made a final, unsuccessful attempt in 1962 to break the East-West deadlock over the German question with a badly miscalculated venture to place strategic missiles in Cuba."[130] Talks on Germany between Russians and Americans had continued since the construction of the Berlin wall on 13 August 1961 but made no progress.

In March 1962 discussions began between Gromyko and Rusk, though it immediately became clear that substantial progress through mutual compromise was unlikely. France refused to participate because of Khrushchev's barefaced blackmail at a time he had twenty divisions in the Soviet group of forces in Germany.[131] Poland, not wishing to see postwar frontiers change or Germany reunited under any regime, misled the United States into believing that concessions could be found. It was only a month later, however, that Khrushchev persuaded the leadership to accept the insertion of missiles in Cuba.

New evidence suggests that one major motivation behind Khrushchev's decision was realization that the West now knew he had insignificant strategic nuclear forces. What utterly undermined Khrushchev's bluff was a piece of luck for British intelligence which, given the nature of things, meant a welcome gift to Washington. In Moscow MI6 was headed by Roderick (Ruari) Chisholm, who had worked in Berlin focusing on members of the Soviet armed forces until his sudden withdrawal at short notice in June 1955.[132] Under cover as visa officer, he and his wife, Anne (Janet), second secretary, arrived in Moscow on 1 July 1960. In December a disillusioned colonel in the GRU, Oleg Pen'kovskii, then forty-one years of age, met British businessman Greville Wynne, part of a larger delegation, at the Leningradskaya Hotel. The following month the KGB first observed suspicious behavior by Pen'kovskii during an operation conducted against the Canadian commercial attaché and a representative of the National Research Council.[133] This resulted in no action, however; just a note in the file. At a follow-up meeting in the restaurant at the Natsional Hotel in April 1961 Pen'kovskii told Wynne about himself, his work in the GRU, and the wish to cooperate with MI6. On 20 April in London at the Mount Royal Hotel he met senior members of both MI6 and CIA. His recruitment was secured and he was given the code name "Young."[134]

Pen'kovskii had access to military secrets that was unusual. He was married to the daughter of Lieutenant General Gapanovich (1896–1952), officer commanding the Kiev military district. He was also a protégé of Marshal Sergei Varentsov (1901–1971), commander-in-chief of artillery and onetime lead candidate to head the Strategic Missile Forces, demoted to major general following Pen'kovskii's execution. After further training in missile technology Pen'kovskii worked at the State Committee on the Coordination of Scientific Research work on Gorky Street (now Tverskaya) headed by Kosygin's son-in-law Dzhermen Gvishiani.[135] A "vengeful person" who liked the good life but was denied further promotion when the KGB discovered that his father died an officer opposed to the Bolsheviks, Pen'kovskii provided key insights into the state of Soviet defenses.

At his first debriefing on 20 April 1961 Pen'kovskii insisted that Kennedy should be "firm," that Khrushchev was "not ready for any war."[136] Subsequently he revealed what Gvishiani had told him in confidence: "You know . . . with respect to ICBMs, up to now we don't have a damn thing. Everything is only on paper, and there is nothing in actual existence."[137] Problems had arisen with electronics that complicated construction of effective guidance systems.[138] Furthermore Pen'kovskii reported that there was "a difficult situation in the country right now. Everything is subordinated to the armaments race. . . . Everything is going for rockets [*sic*]."[139] This intelligence proved critical. In 1961 three pieces of evidence intersected to provide cross-confirmation: first, the discovery that Moscow was testing second-generation ICBMs, which, so soon after the first-generation tests, suggested limited deployment of first-generation weapons; second, two satellite reconnaissance missions in June–July 1961 clearly identified individual ICBM deployments in the field; and, lastly, the information from Pen'kovskii. It turned out that the USSR had only four operational ICBM launchers as of 1 September.[140] And it was not until 1964 that any submarine-launched intercontinental ballistic missiles (SLBMs) were deployed.[141] Washington was thereby finally capable of assessing the true balance of power vis-à-vis Moscow with a high degree of accuracy. Khrushchev was evidently bluffing. There was no missile gap against the United States; rather the reverse. At Kennedy's request on 21 October 1961 Deputy Secretary of Defense Roswell Gilpatric publicly refuted the myth.[142] Thus Khrushchev's declaration to atomic physicists that the Presidium had agreed on renewed testing of the 100-megaton superbomb to place "the sword of Damocles above the imperialists" was a futile gesture and he knew it.[143]

Chisholm had been careful not to be seen with Pen'kovskii, who was able to travel abroad for his work and thus extensive debriefing. In Moscow Anne, with her three small children and baby as cover, was the liaison. At the first meeting he had reportedly placed seven rolls of Minox microfilm on missiles in the pram.[144] All went well until the afternoon of 30 December 1961 when agents trailing Anne saw her come out of a courtyard on Maly Sukharevskii Pereulok. Moments later a man whom the agents could not readily identify also emerged. Suspicions were aroused when precisely the same sequence of events occurred on 19 January 1962. Instead of following Anne, the men followed her apparent contact to his place of work and then to his apartment at 36 Maxim Gorky Naberezhnaya along the Moscow River. They were astonished at what they found. Telescopic observation into Pen'kovskii's flat from the opposite side of the bank then determined that he was photographing material taken home. As soon as it became known that Pen'kovskii was GRU, the case, hitherto handled by head of the KGB's second department (counterintelligence) Ivan Markelov, was handed over to Oleg Gribanov, head of the second chief directorate.[145]

Thus by the end of March 1962, when Pen'kovskii attended a reception at the British embassy in the company of colleagues and Anne thereafter broke off all direct contact,[146] it was already too late. Khrushchev will have realized that Washington now knew the truth about the inadequacy of Soviet intercontinental missile capabilities. Indeed, the R-16 was, in the words of missile engineer Sergei Khrushchev, "in no way comparable to the 'Minuteman' missile. . . . The nitrogen acid corroding the missile tanks made it impossible for missiles to be kept in launch readiness, filled with fuel." As a result of such problems, the first R-16s were not deployed until "just prior to the Cuban Missile Crisis."[147] Even then, its inaccuracy (circular error probable) was two to three kilometers.[148]

The public statement by Gilpatric on 21 October 1961 describing US nuclear superiority was clearly based on inside knowledge. At the Presidium on 8 January 1962 Khrushchev complained that ambassador Thompson had found out Dobrynin was destined as the next ambassador to Washington. Other leaks also worried him: "I think the Americans have someone in our intelligence, because certain materials are leaking out that are quite close to the truth."[149] MI6, too, appeared "exceptionally informed about our state's decisions and government directives." This was attributed to advances in eavesdropping technology.[150] To avoid indicating that Soviet counterintelligence had discovered who was spying for the West, Pen'kovskii was allowed to continue unhindered except for any foreign travel (which may well have alerted him to something unusual). The damage had anyhow been done.

The paucity of intercontinental missiles on land was more than matched by the absence of a comparable capability at sea. Hitherto the Soviet navy was the orphan of the fighting services. It amounted to little more than a submarine fleet designed to protect coastal waters: 465 vessels deployed between 1947 and 1960.[151] Khrushchev had refused to implement plans for aircraft carriers that could alone provide air cover for a blue-water fleet that Navy Minister Admiral Nikolai Kuznetsov was promulgating.[152] From January 1954 missile-builder Sergei Korolev had been experimenting with submarine-launched ballistic missiles, beginning with D-1.[153] The proposal to build SLBMs originated with Admiral Lev Vladimirskii, chairman of the Naval Scientific and Technology Committee, in a memorandum to Khrushchev and Bulganin in February 1956. On 18 May 1957 the Politburo sanctioned work to that end and on 6 December defined the manner of its implementation.[154] A key problem was launching from beneath the surface. Finally, in February 1962 the R-21 missile was successfully tested from under water, but not until March 1963 did the D-4 missile system finally came into service.[155] Even then, according to General Makhmut Gareev, "SLBMs only had an accuracy for use against economic potential and industrial infrastructure and therefore were very poor weapons for anything but retaliatory strikes. Communications to SSBNs were not sufficiently responsive to rely on in an initial response or a retaliatory-meeting strike."[156] The submarine fleet was predominantly diesel, which meant these vessels also had to surface to recharge their batteries and were thereby further exposed to attack from the Americans.

The worst of it was that Khrushchev had pivoted his security policy on Russia's ballistic missile strength. The US capability for massive destruction made it ever more urgent that Moscow catch up. And Soviet military planners had formulated a new doctrine to meet the American threat. This amounted to focusing on preemption given that retaliation was impracticable. Rethinking had begun in 1960 and was virtually acknowledged by the summer of 1961. The dilemma faced was ably outlined by US intelligence:

> They see a rapidly expanding nuclear attack force in the United States and feel the blanket of secrecy over their own strategic forces gradually receding. They are faced with the prospect of not being able to deliver an effective second strike in a nuclear war and they are aware of this. They seem to reason in drawing up a doctrine for the start of war, that only by striking first, by blunting much of the enemy's attack forces, can the USSR survive the first nuclear phase of the war.

This doctrine was enunciated by Malinovsky at the Twenty-second Party Congress in October 1961. By that time, Washington learned, Moscow had "already taken steps to speed up the process of making the decision to go to war as well as the implementation of that decision. These steps include the assignment of the strategic missile forces to a Supreme High Command, which exercises exclusive control over their deployment and use, and the placing of Khrushchev at the head of the country's strategic arm in the post of Supreme High Commander." It was believed that this post "enables Khrushchev personally, without prior consultation with the ruling collegium [sic], to push the war button." Preemption necessarily meant targeting the enemy's forces rather than population centers. To succeed in preemption the Russians added up the enemy's targets to calculate force needs.[157] The pressure on Khrushchev was thus accentuated by a new doctrine evolved by the military that required an ability to target successfully as much of the US intercontinental capability as practicable. In the circumstances an attempted shortcut to the solution was inevitable.

CRISIS OVER CUBA

Meanwhile Khrushchev desperately sought to make up the strategic imbalance with the Unites States. According to Mikoyan's younger son, just before Khrushchev embarked on a trip to Bulgaria toward the end of April 1962, he took a walk in the garden with First Deputy Chairman Mikoyan (their datchas being close). This was how Khrushchev tried out most of his "hare-brained" foreign policy initiatives. Given Mikoyan's personal knowledge of Havana, Khrushchev raised the idea of putting medium- and intermediate-range nuclear missiles in Cuba. Mikoyan was opposed, not least because he felt Washington would find out before they were installed, though Khrushchev intended putting them in under cover, to reveal them only after the congressional elections in November. Mikoyan also thought Castro likely to object because it might prompt rather than deter an invasion.[158] Khrushchev found support, however, from Malinovsky and his deputy Biryuzov ("a not very intelligent person" on Mikoyan's view).[159]

During a trip to Leningrad on 3–4 May, having dismissed the need for a surface fleet, Khrushchev now saw it as a real possibility as a consequence of missiles in Cuba to rectify the imbalance. He told representatives of the military-industrial complex and the fleet: "The Americans often send squadrons of their ships to other countries and by this means exert influence to a certain extent on the policies of these countries. It wouldn't be bad if we also had such a navy that could be sent to those countries where in the circumstances it could be of use to us, for example, in Cuba, in the countries of Africa, etc." He added: "It is well nigh time 'to put on long trousers.' Now we are still living through a period of transition. For the time being there exists a balance of our military power with the enemy. But soon this balance will be broken to our advantage and we will have to activate ourselves. And here at some time the leading role will be played by the navy."[160]

The decision to put missiles into Cuba inevitably had implications for resolution of the German question, the imbalance to US advantage proving decisive. Khrushchev's reasoning was: "If we took an extreme position on this question then we would refrain from taking the offensive. And this would be wrong. We have to take the offensive, we must do so having thought it through: in this game we must not be like the gambler who stakes everything in his pocket and then grabs his revolver and shoots himself. We shouldn't ever be like the gambler; we haven't the right to be so; nothing would prompt us to this."[161] Martha Mautner, covering Germany at the US Bureau of Intelligence and Research (INR), found the administration initially reluctant to see the connection. But, she notes: "Those of us who were familiar with the German scene were always convinced that the Cuban missile crisis had very little to do with Cuba per se. We saw it as a Khrushchev ploy to create a military equation which would allow him to put pressure on us to force negotiations on Berlin."[162]

General Anatoly Gribkov, then head of the Operations Department of the General Staff and deputy secretary to the Defense Council chaired by Khrushchev, has insisted that the dominant idea was "never said in public, but everybody understood it very clearly: that the ratio of forces was by far [*sic*] not in favor of the Soviet Union. In terms of nuclear warheads, we had a 1-to-17 disadvantage against the US. . . . As for delivery vehicles that could hit the continental United States from the Soviet Union, we only had 25 delivery vehicles."[163] What he did not say was how ill informed the rest of the leadership were about the state of Soviet missile capabilities. In justifying to the Presidium a sharp cut in the army announced in January 1960 — prompting resignations in protest from Chief of the General Staff Sokolovskii and Commander-in-Chief of the Warsaw Pact Marshal Ivan Kon'ev — Khrushchev had argued that these unilateral measures did "not undermine our defense capability," because "we are in an excellent situation with missile construction: strictly speaking, we now have a range of missiles for the resolution of any military problem whether long or short range." And, he claimed, "We have much improved the serial production of these missiles."[164] Khrushchev was therefore not in a position to clarify the true rationale for missiles in Cuba to the others whom he had systematically misled about the state of the country's defense capability.

Inevitably swift enhancement of the Soviet nuclear capability vis-à-vis the United States, outflanking its early warning system — BMEWS — that faced north, promised Khrushchev dividends in the event of another crisis over Berlin. France had pressed ahead with developing its own atomic bomb in the belief that the United States could not be trusted to risk its own security for Europe if Russia had matching nuclear firepower. Since 1957 Bonn had increasingly acted on this same supposition, and Adenauer by no means felt bound by the unilateral declaration made in 1954 to renounce the development of the bomb or the acceptance of such weapons for his own forces. Initially France had offered to share. When this became impracticable, Bonn pressed for its own from 1957. If Khrushchev could demonstrate publicly a checkmate in the strategic military balance, would not Germany hesitate in its reliance upon the United States and turn, perhaps, to Russia for a final settlement? From December 1961 this could not be ruled out. Under Adenauer's instructions his ambassador in Moscow encouraged belief that a settlement was possible. On 27 December Khrushchev took the bait and issued Bonn with a long memorandum opening with the flattering suggestion that "the Soviet Union and the Federal Republic are the largest states in Europe."[165] But by March 1962 Moscow had decided that Bonn was merely flirting. A calculated risk thus seemed worthwhile. Boosted by the apparent practicality of the Cuban scheme, on 12 May Khrushchev told Salinger that he could not recognize the right of the allies to station troops in Berlin. He rejected the recent US compromise of establishing an "access authority" to safeguard allied access in the event of the threatened Soviet-GDR peace treaty while maintaining formal nonrecognition of the East German regime.

It was only a little after a week later, on 20 May, heading home from Bulgaria, that Khrushchev finally broached the idea of missiles in Cuba with Foreign Minister Gromyko. He, however, warned that this could cause a political explosion in Washington—of this he was "absolutely certain, and this had to be taken into account."[166] Gromyko was, however, not a member of the Presidium, so his opinion could safely be disregarded, as it frequently was. Undeterred by advice to the contrary, on 21 May Khrushchev presented the Presidium with his scheme, plans for which came to another meeting on 24 May. It would be "an offensive policy." Only along the subheading and not in the record of what was decided appear the words "aid to Cuba."[167] In the discussion Mikoyan was the first to voice objections; others also expressed doubts but tried to avoid committing themselves. He later described the plan as "pure adventure," but he also counted on Castro rejecting the proposal.[168] The majority agreed, however, and according to tradition since 1929, the final result was that all members present signed their assent.[169] The leadership thus resolved: "1. To approve operation 'Anadyr' in its entirety and unanimously. (On receipt of F. Castro's agreement.) 2. To send a commission to Fidel Castro for negotiations."[170]

Colonel General Semyon Ivanov, secretary to the Defense Council, told his deputy, Gribkov, of the decision taken in the strictest secrecy to send Soviet forces to Cuba, ironically named operation Anadyr (the name of an Arctic river). Generals Gribkov, Eliseev, and Kotov were to plan the operation. The initial proposal was ready after two days and came to the Party leadership ambiguously entitled "On the creation of a group of forces in Cuba."[171] Under the plan a group of forces, including all types of weapons under joint command, was to be dispatched. The strategic missiles were those of the 43rd division, consisting of three regiments of medium-range SS-4s (the R-12) in 24 silos and two regiments of SS-5s (the R-14) in 16 silos, with ranges from 2.5 to 4.5 thousand kilometers.[172] The R-12s would be able to reach the southern United States; the R-14s would be in a position to attack the entire country with the exception of the northwest coast. And since BMEWS faced north to Canada, not south to Central America, Washington would have no advance notice of attack. Instructions to attack could come only from Moscow. The commander's orders ran: "The missile forces constituting the basis of the defense of the Soviet Union and the island of Cuba must be in readiness on a signal from Moscow to deliver a nuclear strike against the most important targets in the United States of America."[173] In addition, four separate motor rifle regiments would accompany these forces. The total number of men would amount to 44,000. Tactical nuclear weapons would also be deployed.[174] The request from Marshal Zakharov that the officer commanding, General Pliev, be given the right to deploy these independently of Moscow in the event of invasion was blocked by Malinovsky.[175]

A delegation left for Cuba on 28–29 May, including a candidate member of the Presidium overseeing the Third World, Sharaf Rashidov, along with Biryuzov, Deputy Chief of the Air Staff Lieutenant General Ushakov, and Major General Ageev (representing the Operations Directorate).[176] Their report giving details of the operation was then accepted formally by the Presidium on 10 June.[177] Biryuzov assured one and all that "the terrain allows for concealment of all the work" undertaken.[178] Two days later Pliev arrived in Cuba to decide on the deployment details.[179] At the end of June Raúl Castro came to Moscow and initialed a treaty.[180] After changes, including removal of the misleading assertion that Havana had requested the missiles,[181] the treaty was finally signed by Guevara in Moscow on 27 August.[182] By then shipment of equipment and men had already begun—on 12 July, continuing for the next three months.[183] The *Maria Ul'yanova* docked with the first crates on 26 July; a further nine shipments arrived in the four days following.[184] The R-12s were scheduled to be ready for launch on 28 October; the R-14s on 15 December, the date now set for Khrushchev's appearance at the UN.[185]

Much has been made of the assertion that the missiles were installed purely to defend Cuba. But Khrushchev told Alekseev, Moscow's new ambassador to Havana, that once the missiles were installed, "we will be able to talk to the Americans as equals."[186] And Havana remained resolutely skeptical of Khrushchev's purported motivations. They too believed that the global power balance was at stake. The larger strategic purpose was clear to Biryuzov while in Cuba.[187] It was also what Castro told Mikoyan on 5 November 1962.[188] Alekseev said that the Cuban leadership, above all Castro, "did not believe or understand that, in connection with the Caribbean crisis, the Soviet Union's aim was to ensure Cuba's independence and her rescue from invasion" despite "all the Soviet efforts."[189] And Castro told *Le Monde* in March 1963: "It was explained to us that, in accepting them [the missiles], we would be reinforcing the socialist camp on a world scale. . . . This was not to assure our own defense, but above all to reinforce socialism on an international level. This is the truth even if other explanations are furnished elsewhere."[190] As he revealed many years later, Cuba could equally have been protected by a treaty of mutual assistance. "The United States," he pointed out, "has many of these pacts throughout the world, and they are respected."[191] Something else was afoot, and that was Germany.

Khrushchev was still actively pressing Washington on the German question. Ambassador Thompson had come to the end of his term. Two days before departure, on 25 July, Thompson called on Khrushchev to bid good-bye. In a thinly veiled threat he asked "whether it would be better for him [Kennedy that the] Berlin question [were] brought to a head before or after our Congressional elections. He did not want to make things more difficult for [the]

President—and in fact would like to help him."[192] No particular concern was expressed for the defense of Cuba.

Nuclear warheads began reaching the island mid-August 1962. The following month missiles, bombers, and tactical nuclear missiles appeared.[193] On 6 September at Pitsunda, unable to contain himself, Khrushchev complained to US Secretary of the Interior Stuart Udall that Kennedy did not have the courage to resolve the German problem. The situation was "no longer tolerable. A treaty will inevitably be signed. If we and the President can agree," he added, "then there will be great opportunities for cooperation in science, technology, and outer space. Without a solution to this problem, our relations will continue to be cancerous and exacerbated. So we will help him solve the problem. We will put him in a situation where it is necessary to solve it. We will give him a choice—go to war, or sign a peace treaty."[194] His throwaway comment that "out of respect for your President we won't do anything until November" again looks alarmingly pointed in retrospect given the simultaneous timing of missile readiness and the congressional elections.[195] A TASS statement on 11 September then hinted at a direct connection between events in Cuba—as yet unknown to Washington—and in Berlin.[196] That day Soviet forces went into their highest state of readiness since the start of the Cold War. It included "some unprecedented activity among offensive forces." The alert ended ten days later. But the day after the crucial U-2 overflight that identified the missiles in place (15 October), Soviet forces "went into a preliminary . . . stage of alert."[197]

The deadline set by Khrushchev was hard to meet, given the intense scrutiny by Western intelligence of these protracted voyages from the Barents Sea, the Baltic, and from the Black Sea where these heavily laden vessels had to pass through the tight mouth of the Dardanelles into Mediterranean and past Gibraltar before the Atlantic crossing. One sergeant on board, Alexei Maslov, recalls his trip on the *Bavier.* "West German intelligence, for instance, was interested in the cargo that we were carrying while sailing through the Dardanelles Strait. Also, British intelligence tried to inspect our ship's cargo when we passed Gibraltar, but the energetic response of our crew stopped them."[198] The soldiers—in total 42,000 men—had to be kept mostly in stifling heat below decks to be rotated out only in numbers sufficiently small to avoid suspicion. And once on land missiles were even harder to hide. "They need launch pads, blast shields, cable troughs, control buildings; they need bunkers for storing the warheads, trailers for fuel and oxidizers. All those things come first. Rockets don't creep about in the night; they move like a travelling fair."[199] Indeed, they had to be stored in hangars before siting on launch pads for action, which, plus fueling, "encouraged one to strike first" rather than deploy while the enemy attacked.[200] "The first R-12 missile was ready on 4 October; ten were ready by 10 October; and a further ten by 20 October.[201]

In a private three-hour exchange at the UN on 6 October with Secretary of State Rusk, Gromyko argued that a German settlement "must be made." "Only a madman would talk of revising frontiers today, or could think that a revision of the frontiers could be achieved by calls for revanche. Those who were making such calls would only break their necks." At a further meeting, on 18 October, Rusk underscored the bottom line of the American stance: "At present we were in West Berlin and we would not be driven out. We were a great power and we would not accept defeat unless the U.S.S.R. fought a war and attempted to defeat us." Gromyko insisted that "United States security interests were certainly not among those motives [in clinging to West Berlin]. Thus the conclusion had been drawn that the United States wished to retain West Berlin as a hotbed of tension."[202] What Gromyko said at his meeting with Kennedy would carry a more ominous meaning once Washington was sure that Moscow had installed ballistic missiles in Cuba. He "said that the Soviet Government had already indicated that it would do nothing with regard to West Berlin before the US elections unless it was compelled to do otherwise by the activities of the other side. However, the Soviet Government proceeded from the fact that it was necessary to hold an active dialogue in November to bring about concrete results with regard to a German peace treaty and to the normalization of the West Berlin situation on the basis of such a treaty."[203]

Finally, on 14 October a U-2 was observed flying over R-12 emplacements. Operating from as much as 14 miles up, it had an HR-73B camera with a 36-inch lens loaded with two 6,500-foot rolls of nine-and-a-half-inch film. More than 4,000 frames could be produced from one mission; a single frame could capture 5.7 square nautical miles.[204] Not all shipments had yet made port. The final loads were expected to arrive between 3 and 5 November. The last units of the R-12 regiments would not get in until 25 October. Those of the R-14 would not be there until 5 November.[205] And the preparations for siting the R-14 were much more demanding than for the R-12. They required "complex permanent launch sites, with troop quarters, missile shelters, warhead bunkers and a large logistics train."[206] When news of the U-2 flight (the eighth since 29 August)[207] was published in *Time*, Gribkov, heading Operations at the Soviet General Staff, realized that masking techniques were inadequate.[208] Moreover, "not a single missile that was deployed in Cuba was in a vertical position. . . . Not a single missile was fueled. It didn't have any oxygen. . . . It didn't have any flight plan. . . . And not a single missile had a nuclear warhead attached."[209]

Rumors that Russia was constructing missile bases in Cuba had in fact been circulating for some months. Republican Senator Kenneth Keating had alluded to the possibility. But, as reports of the enormous increase in the size of shipments materialized, officials resolutely refused to believe the worst. Only CIA Director John McCone stuck to his guns in the belief that ballistic missiles were, indeed, being shipped. He "simply did not believe that Khrushchev would commit the newest version of his highly successful surface-to-air missiles, the SA-2, to Castro unless there was something vital to be protected. As McCone saw it, only the need to protect the medium-range ballistic missile sites would balance this equation."[210] Unable to convince his employers, however, he disappeared on a lengthy honeymoon. Bulky deck cargo was explained away, as was heavy equipment set on eight-wheel trailers traveling down Cuban roads.[211] Indeed, as late as 19 September a national intelligence estimate on "The Military Buildup in Cuba"—NIE 85–3-62—ruled out missile deployment on the plausible grounds that this "would be incompatible with Soviet practice to date and with Soviet policy as we presently estimate it. It would indicate a far greater willingness to increase the level of risk in US-Soviet relations than the USSR has displayed thus far."[212] Moreover, throughout, "Soviet communications security was almost perfect."[213]

Now, however, with photo reconnaissance ("photint") results on the table, the US government could no longer avoid the obvious. A U-2 flight of 14 October by Major Rudolph Anderson was prompted by human intelligence and knowledge that the surface-to-air missile (SAM-2) sites near San Cristobal in western Cuba formed a trapezoid, a point defense, to protect some other installation. With photos from Pen'kovskii to set against what lay on the ground beneath the U-2, the specialists had one more crucial advantage. Gribkov has acknowledged: "We foresaw, naturally, the possibility that U.S. intelligence might discover us. As it turned out, on October 14 they photographed areas that we had not been able to camouflage . . . there were white slabs of concrete. Naturally, they could be seen quite well from the air and were very difficult to disguise, . . . Some of our comrades . . . thought that the missiles could be placed in such a way that they could not be distinguished from palm trees, but that was a stupid conclusion, because all the missile sites had to be prepared, cables hung, launching pads built—in other words, everything was complicated."[214] Indeed, the day after the flight the Pentagon was told R-12s had been identified. The camera had captured a convoy an instant before it moved safely under tree cover.[215] A further mission on 17 October revealed the installation of a fixed R-14 site at Guanajay, west of Havana.[216]

Missiles discovered, the connection with events in Central Europe was immediately drawn to Kennedy's attention. At a meeting on 16 October Rusk expressed the opinion that "Berlin is . . . very much involved in this . . . for the first time, I'm beginning really to wonder whether maybe Mr. Khrushchev is entirely rational about Berlin."[217] Reluctantly but inexorably a week later Kennedy announced the alarming news. The last deliveries had been loaded for shipment on 20 October and were due on 3–5 November.[218] The R-12s would be ready for launch on 28 October. The crisis had begun.

The problem was summarized by Rusk:

> These bases have special significance since missiles based in [the] USSR and targeted on US nuclear forces are still relatively few in number. In addition, we have radar systems which pick up missiles coming over [the] ice-cap from [the] Soviet Union. The limitations on Soviet intercontinental ballistic missile capability provides [the] West with [a] margin of nuclear superiority which is [the] heart of [the] Western deterrent. If [the] Soviets had been permitted to complete [a] substantial missile program in Cuba, [the] balance of nuclear power could have been significantly shifted. IRBMs in Cuba would be free of radar detection and with zero alert time both ICBM sites and SAC bases could come under attack without warning and with greater accuracy due to short range. This could seriously prejudice [the] US nuclear posture and with [the] first strike from Cuba [the] Soviets could seriously impair [the] US capability to cover all necessary targets.[219]

This would obviously jeopardize the ability to stand behind West Germany, and West Berlin in particular.

For the next week twenty further U-2 missions flew over Cuba for confirmation.[220] The US military, the USAF in particular, wanted to deal a fatal blow. William Kaufmann, then advising McNamara, recalls that the Commander-in-Chief of the Strategic Air Command, General Thomas Power, "insisted that the only way to deal with these barbarians [the Russians] was to blow them all up and I said, 'But who's going to win that?' And he said, 'I would be satisfied if there were just two Americans left and one Russian—that would be . . . we would have won.' And I said, 'Well there'd better be one of them a woman.'"[221] When Kennedy issued his ultimatum on 22 October, announcing a naval blockade, the Kremlin became intensely anxious lest Washington strike the island from the air. Thirty minutes before the televised speech, after warnings came in from the KGB resident in Washington, tipped off by ABC correspondent John Scali,[222] Malinovsky instructed Pliev to "take immediate steps to raise combat readiness and to repulse the enemy together with the Cuban army and with all the power of the Soviet forces, except Statsenko's means and Beloborodov's cargoes [nuclear weapons]."[223] Moscow also reacted with "an extraordinary high state of alert, similar to the September event." But defensive forces, air defense, and tactical air capability were to the fore this time.[224] Meanwhile, beginning on 23 October Washington launched a series of low-level aerial reconnaissance missions by the navy and air force, soaring in at targets below line of horizon radar from across the Gulf of Mexico some 500 feet above ground at 600 mph.[225] Early that day Washington intercepted a message to Soviet ships en route. Merchant ships stopped and some now turned back.[226]

The blockade presented severe problems for Moscow, not least because, although it had originally planned to send in substantial elements from the Northern Fleet to reinforce their presence in Cuba and safeguard the shipments, on 25 September it was agreed to cancel the sending of surface vessels in support for fear that it "would attract the attention of the entire world." Instead only submarines were dispatched.[227] But these submarines were diesel-powered and had to surface to recharge batteries. This the First Deputy Minister of Defense Marshal Andrei Grechko did not know; he assumed that they were atomic submarines.[228]

At this stage Castro had no idea that Moscow would back down. It is claimed that before the blockade could be effective, the *Alexandrovsk* docked at Isabela de Sagua with the rest of the warheads.[229] Yet by no means all R-12s and R-14s were in place. In Moscow, therefore, the atmosphere was one of alarm. The Presidium sat overnight in Khrushchev's datcha at Novo-Ogarevo, a residence in the classical style reconstructed by Malenkov in the mid-fifties to the west of Moscow.[230] The wires to the Washington embassy fell silent.[231] Dobrynin had not been forewarned and was now in the dark as to Moscow's thinking.

At the Pentagon, where plans were laid for the possibility of direct military action, the mood was upbeat. Major General Jack Catton (USAF) recalls: "We had absolute superiority. Khrushchev was looking down the largest barrel he had ever stared at . . . the value of superiority was so obvious that it couldn't be missed."[232] Without any instructions from above, the USAF "were able . . . from the JCS [Joint Chiefs of Staff] on down (without involving the politicians) to put [the] SAC [Strategic Air Command] on a one-third airborne alert, to disperse part of the force to civilian airfields, with nuclear weapons, to arm . . . air defense fighter forces with nuclear weapons and disperse them, and to take all the ICBMs we had, including those still in the contractors' hands, and count them down."[233] This entire display was intentionally visible to the Russians. On 24 October Moscow intercepted the order en clair placing SAC on Defcon 2— readiness for war—for the first time since 1945.[234]

The Russians did not even have a ballistic missile early warning system to detect and track incoming missiles until the mid-sixties.[235] They were so intimidated that "they did not increase their alert; they did not increase any flights, or their air defense posture. They didn't do a thing, they froze in place."[236]

Although Malinovsky proposed mobilization, Khrushchev ruled it out.[237] The most he did was to cancel leave.[238] After sustained tension and diplomatic soundings, exhausted and at times confused,[239] Khrushchev finally backed down on 28 October, but taking from the crisis two lesser prizes: a US commitment not to invade Cuba and a further commitment to withdraw its missiles from Turkey—scarcely worth bringing the world to the brink of nuclear war.[240]

An important catalyst forcing the decision may have been information on US countermeasures intercepted and deciphered in Moscow. Code breaking at the KGB was concentrated in the eighth directorate from 16 March 1961 under Lieutenant General Serafim Lyalin. This was a very successful unit. The previous year it claimed to have decrypted some 209,000 secret telegrams from the USSR's adversaries.[241] Washington was naturally the priority; and its codes and ciphers the hardest to crack. But Moscow had been assiduously searching for a back door into the systems of the National Security Agency (NSA) at Fort Meade, Maryland, thirty miles north of the capital. First they recruited William Martin and Bernon Mitchell, who defected in great publicity in June 1960 and told what they knew to Moscow. Both had worked for the NSA since 1957.[242] They were, however, more of a propaganda victory compared to the fortuitous acquisition of a major prize that provided the keys to entire systems. From 1958 Jack Dunlap carried "raw" messages in sealed packets to and from Major General Garrison Coverdale, chief of staff of the NSA, and for his successor, General Watlington, from August 1959. His clearance enabled him to drive off base in order to enable the Russians to copy the material. He was discovered only in 1963 through a polygraph test that he was finally obliged to take when he sought reemployment as a civilian.[243] According to Russian intelligence sources, Dunlap procured for them "various manuals, mathematical models, and research and development plans for the most secret deciphering machines at the NSA."[244] From these sources Soviet cryptographers could reverse engineer US systems of encryption and decryption. An array of those at the eighth main directorate of the KGB involved in this cryptographic breakthrough were given medals; the most outstanding were secretly awarded the coveted Lenin Prize when their work gave Khrushchev direct access to secret US communications during the missile crisis that convinced him just how serious the situation had become.[245]

CONSEQUENCES

Pen'kovskii had finally been arrested on 22 October. Head of the GRU General Ivan Serov was then dismissed on 2 February 1963 and replaced by General Petr Ivashutin. More significant was what a leading Soviet diplomat had to say on the longer-term impact of the crisis. Vasilii Kuznetsov was a safe pair of hands. Formerly a metallurgical engineer, he had been transformed by taking a master's degree in the United States before the war. He had risen to the post of deputy chairman of Gosplan under Stalin and from 1944 to 1950 chaired the central council of trades unions, also chairing the council of nationalities of the Supreme Soviet, which had oversight of foreign policy from the Party viewpoint. Soviet ambassador to China in 1953, he was "tall, a little round-shouldered, a kind man"[246] of great charm and excellent English.[247] He became First Deputy Foreign Minister in 1955. Throughout the crisis he had headed a special staff on Cuba at the MID.[248]

His comment to John McCloy at the UN amounted to a direct threat: "You Americans will never be able to do this to us again."[249] And in summing up, General Nikolai Detinov, then deputy head of the air defense section of the Party's powerful Military-Industrial Sector, noted: "The Caribbean crisis demonstrated that the attainment of superiority in the nuclear sphere is important also because the very level of these armaments have not only a military impact but also an effect on political influence, including upon the countries of the 'Third World.'"[250] "Lack of armaments and the weakness of the Soviet Union came as a shock to the Soviet leadership," Detinov reflected. "It was like a cold shower for the government, which realized that these weaknesses had to be overcome."[251] But it also added a further priority prompted by Kennedy's command of the seas to blockade Cuba. Hitherto the Russian fleet was almost entirely subsurface. At the Vienna meeting with Kennedy, "Khrushchev referred to the obsolescence of naval surface ships such as cruisers and carriers. He said that the Soviet Union had switched to the production of submarines."[252] Sokolovskii used to say, "Ships! In the next war they will be food for fishes!"[253] No longer. A blue-water surface fleet now became the order of the day. Prior to this it had been a Khrushchevian daydream, a luxury affordable once parity had been secured. Now it had become a dire necessity.

AN OPENING TO WEST GERMANY

The State Department concluded that the "Soviet action was probably primarily geared to [a] showdown on Berlin, intended to be timed with Khrushchev's arrival in [the] US [late November] and completion of [the] installation of nuclear missiles in Cuba."[254] This was also very much what Kennedy had suspected.[255] Well after the Cuban crisis, Khrushchev continued to obsess about the German question. Dobrynin recalls that the First Secretary "was still stubbornly trying to have his own way on Germany and Berlin despite the fact that he came out of the Cuban crisis with his position weakened."[256] When Khrushchev saw British ambassador Sir Frank Roberts in November before his new posting to Bonn, he emphasized that the key question was Germany. "If we could find some solution here many other things would fall into place."[257]

Khrushchev even sought to revive the notion with which he began the Berlin crisis. On 26 July 1963 he warned Harriman of the possibility of an alternative approach to the question that was to prove deeply worrying to his own subordinates. Khrushchev suggested US policy was effectively driving Bonn into Moscow's arms. The "reason for this was the Germans becoming convinced [the] US, France and other allies could do nothing to [the] GDR and [were] unable [to] reestablish [a] united capitalist Germany." The Wall would not come down until there existed a united socialist Germany. He then added that "from time to time [the] Sov[iet]s would step on [the] president's foot so he could realize he should cut out his corns."[258] This was also the tenor of Khrushchev's discussions with Spaak in Moscow on 13 July.[259]

The failure to break out of containment and the exacerbation of relations with Beijing had boxed in Khrushchev to an extent that left him utterly exasperated. What diehards feared was lest he find an opportunistic way out of his difficulties through an overture to Bonn unencumbered by commitments previously made to the Poles, Czechs, and East Germans. Earlier references to Rapallo and the Nazi-Soviet pact indicated as much. And, as Khrushchev's son relates, his father "more than once returned to the necessity of the Soviet Army's departure from Hungary, Poland, and possibly even from East Germany."[260] The military also feared arms control agreements with the United States. On 6 August 1963 Moscow signed a treaty banning the testing of nuclear weapons above ground. This met with sullen silence on the part of Malinovsky throughout the period of ratification, during which some supportive comment could have been expected had all been well. Similarly, speculation inevitably arose when Malinovsky's orders of the day for the Soviet armed forces—which highlighted the aggressiveness of Western imperialism—were temporarily embargoed from publication in the press. But the issue of relations with Germany proved the turning point.

That summer the *Ruhrnachrichten* of Dortmund, the *Rheinische Post* of Düsseldorf, and the *Münchner Merkur* invited Khrushchev's son-in-law Adzhubei to visit. But no response was forthcoming. In June 1963 Khrushchev reverted to old threats: "We will have a new August 13th. On August 13th, we put up a wall between East and West Berlin. Next time, we shall put locks on the doors."[261] In mid-October, however, Ludwig Erhard succeeded Adenauer as Chancellor. He activated a "policy of movement" toward the Soviet bloc. Khrushchev therefore found it difficult to stand still. On 5 February deputy chairman of the KGB

Nikolai Zakharov reported US moves toward closer cooperation with Bonn on the German question, impelled by the worsening of Washington's relations with Paris.[262] On 8 May the KGB indicated that Bonn was nervous about meetings with Khrushchev as they would increase pressure to recognize the GDR and the postwar territorial status quo.[263] There was therefore good reason for Khrushchev to press ahead with a summit. Moreover, the KGB reported that NATO was about to acquire by the end of the year a multilateral nuclear force (MLF) which would allow Bonn a finger on the trigger. This gave added incentive.[264]

Britain's ambassador noted that after Cuba "a period of uncertain leadership" followed, "during which Khrushchev appeared to be taking personal initiatives, perhaps with the idea of recovering the ground lost by the Cuban gamble."[265] At the beginning of June 1964 Khrushchev implausibly argued that "West Germany had now become a problem for the West and not for the East. It was leading NATO by the nose."[266] This was followed by the bald assertion that "real German interests lay in friendship with the Soviet Union not with the West, because of trade and 'things might happen which you do not imagine.' Asked if he was thinking of a Rapallo-type agreement he replied 'this may be so' and dismissed the argument that this was impossible with East Germany in the way."[267] With the prospect of engaging Bonn in a dialogue, the invitation to Adzhubei was finally taken up in the summer of 1964, resulting in a visit from 20 July to 1 August.

The visit inaugurated an abrupt shift in tone from Khrushchev. The week before, he told the West German ambassador of his interest in a summit with Erhard, and the day after Adzhubei's departure, at anniversary celebrations in Poland, he marked out his position from Gomułka, Novotný, and Ulbricht by ignoring the issues of frontier recognition in Eastern Europe, the MLF, German revanchism, and the need for a peace treaty.[268] Meanwhile in Dortmund, Adzhubei directed the attention of the West German press to Khrushchev's remarks in Warsaw.[269] Adzhubei also went one step further.

On 10 August Dr. Shulte-Strathaus from the German embassy in London visited the Foreign Office to read extracts from private conversations between Adzhubei and newspaper publishers. Khrushchev, of course, had sent his son-in-law to Bonn, "but the Germans must not suppose that everyone in Russia approved of this visit. There was even more objection to it in Pankow [the GDR]." The issue of an all-German federation had been raised by Adzhubei: "It seemed to him the idea contained more dangers for the DDR than for the Federal Republic. If you associated a strong partner with a weak one, who was likely to benefit most in the long run? The West Germans should think opinion about federation. As to Ulbricht personally, he was getting old and Adzhubei thought he only had a couple of years ahead of him in office." "It seems that in these talks Adzhubei invoked the spirit of Rapallo very freely. He said that after all it had always been the Russians who had protected Europe against the Mongols. The Europeans had no conception of how large a part relations with China now played in Soviet thinking and no idea how many frontier violations the Chinese were perpetrating along the Sino-Soviet borders."[270] These sentiments were echoed by General Talenskii at a Pugwash meeting in Karlovy Vary, Czechoslovakia, in September, where he said that Moscow "was eager to have the Chinese Communist nuclear potential smashed." He is also reported as having said that Moscow could not yet disengage from the embarrassing Ulbricht regime, but the decades ahead were another matter.[271] Further evidence that something serious was afoot emerged in November and December from Soviet and East European sources traced by CIA which "privately stated that Khrushchev had favored a deal with Erhard at the expense of Ulbricht."[272]

Adzhubei's indiscretions yielded nothing from Bonn but formed part of the indictment drawn up against Khrushchev on 13–14 October by the rest of the Presidium.[273] It is an irony that Khrushchev had paved the way for his ascendancy through exposing and denouncing Beria for seeking to solve the German problem by aborting the Ulbricht regime, and that having stumbled through crisis after crisis seeking an alternative solution, he finally began converging on the same position only to lose power as a result. On 2 September Khrushchev had accepted an informal invitation from Erhard to visit Bonn. It was announced two days later (but not within Russia). Apparently someone important did not want it to go ahead. On 6 September an electrician at the West German embassy, Schwirkmann, was assaulted with mustard gas while visiting Zagorsk. No proper apology was given until Khrushchev was voted out the Central Committee. Other telltale signs emerged of dissonance, between Adzhubei's *Izvestiya* and the Party paper *Pravda*.

Khrushchev was overthrown in a constitutional manner according to Party rules. The era of reckless behavior and ill-considered initiatives thereby drew to a close. Most of the world now breathed a sigh of relief. But the dilemma for the West between accepting détente, and standing up to Soviet global ambitions at the price of enduring tension in relations had by no means disappeared with Khrushchev. It was about to reappear in more complex form and in circumstances by no means as favorable to the capitalist world as in the 1950s. This first became apparent when the United States became bogged down in Vietnam.

8

DÉTENTE

Under Brezhnev . . . détente could not have become irreversible or transformed into something more.

—*Anatoly Chernyaev*

Khrushchev's overthrow ushered in a colorless new regime led by First (later General)[1] Secretary Leonid Brezhnev, Chairman of the Council of Ministers Alexei Kosygin, and President Nikolai Podgorny. Primus inter pares, Brezhnev was initially uninterested in foreign policy.[2] Names appeared in alphabetic order rather than by rank. The leadership as a whole was thereafter ostentatiously collective: "In the Politburo there was . . . an unwritten rule: by all means have a discussion, but don't poke your nose into the business of others. Each to his own."[3]

Behind this ostentatious display of collectivism, there lay "persistent disagreements" over economic priorities and between politicians and the military.[4] The tendency was "to dodge a number of painful decisions simply by assigning high priorities to a broad variety of competing goals, including defense, heavy industry, agriculture, and the consumer."[5] In the short to medium term, therefore, relaxation of international tension was the most obvious way of reducing the strains on the economy that resulted. But to accomplish this, Moscow was entirely opposed to sacrificing its ideological commitments abroad. On the contrary, détente led to the reinforcement of them as if to reassert Soviet identity against Western hopes of convergence.

A Minindel memorandum for the Politburo argued: "In the conditions of detente it is easier to consolidate and broaden the positions of the Soviet Union in the world." What had to be avoided was "a situation where we have to fight on two fronts—that is, against China and the United States. Maintaining Soviet-American relations on a certain level is one of the factors that will help us achieve this objective." The policy of détente also envisaged "weakening US positions in Western Europe." Overall it was represented as a continuation of Lenin's policy of peaceful coexistence; which meant that the class war would continue but open warfare would have to be avoided. This dualism was to be followed using the traditional distinction between Party and government. Gromyko explained: "We should not cut off the possibility of diplomatic maneuver for ourselves in relations with individual Western countries, including the United States, by adhering to a one-sided view on imperialism. In certain cases it is necessary to draw a more distinct line between the activity of Comintern [*sic*] and that of the foreign ministry, the difference stressed by Lenin."[6]

Central to this process was Brezhnev. He was born on 19 December 1906 to literate working-class parents in Kamenskoe, the Ukraine. Above average height, strong, youthful looking, exuding good health, with lively blue eyes, a friendly manner and "softness of character,"[7] Brezhnev was not gifted except as a bold organizer and a master of intrigue.[8] He was intellectually lazy; he read little and scoffed at Kosygin for reading a book on a free evening when they were together on a foreign trip.[9] "Uneducated, ignorant. Lazy about reading even what was put in front of him," recalls his interpreter Viktor Sukhodrev.[10] That said, Alexander Bovin insists that he was "far from stupid."[11] Brezhnev could be boorish, authoritarian, narrow-minded and anti-Semitic; and anyone proved untrustworthy was ruthlessly discarded. Détente under way, he received top-of-the-line cars from the United States, Germany, and Britain, rapidly acquiring the reputation of Mr. Toad for reckless driving.[12]

Brezhnev had been responsible for defense industries from 27 February 1956 to 16 July 1960. He joined the Presidium on 29 June 1957 and became second secretary (de facto) on 22 June 1963. He was a safe choice for comrades fearful of others—notably *zheleznii shurik* (Alexander Shelepin, head of the KGB from 25 December 1958 to 13 November 1961)—who might have been tempted by Stalin's methods.[13] Shelepin's manner was "harsh." He had no idea how to approach matters other than head-on.[14] This mattered. He had a seat in the Presidium and in the secretariat; he was deputy chairman of the Council of Ministers and headed the Party-state control apparatus. Protégé Vladimir Semichastny controlled the KGB. In December 1965, however, Shelepin lost the Party-state control apparatus and soon also lost a direct role in Party appointments.[15] Shifted to responsibility for Party organization, Shelepin was then removed to consumer goods and light industry: not much of a fist for a hawk.[16] Yet he remained a threat to Brezhnev's position.

Brezhnev "could not take a step without his assistants."[17] Leading on foreign policy was Andrei Alexandrov-Agentov, handpicked for Brezhnev's presidential staff in 1961.[18] Brezhnev valued his "phenomenal capacity for work, the sharpness of his trained mind, his quickness, precision and accuracy at the job." He "liked" Alexandrov "and was certain of his reliability."[19] Alexandrov would sit, lap piled high with ciphered telegrams and various other documents, summing up contents with critical precision while Brezhnev struggled to hold his attention.[20] Dressed like an American preppie in tweed jacket, his nervous, fussy manner gave rise to his nickname *Vorobyshek* (little sparrow) which Alexander Bovin called him to his face, as Alexandrov's tiny bald head honed in on a document (he was extremely shortsighted).[21] His other sobriquet was *Tiré* — haggard.[22] He could be cantankerous, had a very high opinion of his own abilities, and once in the Kremlin he showed open disdain for his intellectually inferior former mentor, Gromyko, as well as everyone else he used to depend upon.[23]

Andropov became KGB Chairman on 18 May 1967,[24] a most unexpected development that provoked considerable comment.[25] Within the KGB, however, it was clearly understood as a safe substitution for Semichastny. Also a nonvoting member of the Politburo from 21 June, Andropov was Jewish in origin; born in Stavropol province on 15 June 1914, the son of a teacher, Evegniya Feinshtein, whose father had been a wealthy merchant, and railway employee Vladimir Andropov (originally Lieberman, so it is said). Andropov's father died when the boy was just five years old; his mother passed away when he was only thirteen.[26] He was "complex"[27] and "a man of many parts,"[28] ascetic to the point of fanaticism (no gifts were ever accepted; his apartment as bare as that of the average citizen), highly intelligent, a patient listener, though of strong beliefs, and extremely well organized. He was also, in the words of a subordinate who worked closely with him on the invasion of Czechoslovakia in 1968, "thoughtful, decisive, self-critical."[29] "It was interesting to work with Andropov," Bovin recalls. "He had the ability and loved to think. He loved to fence with arguments."[30] But to rivals he appeared "haughty, arrogant" as well as personally distant, if not actively unfriendly.[31]

Andropov was a fundamentalist. Having served in Hungary throughout the revolt, he was exceptionally alert to the need for violence to preserve the bloc. It was, indeed, rumored that the screams making for sleepless nights in Budapest had driven his wife into a trauma from which she never recovered.[32] A former subordinate reports that in December 1956 Andropov suffered a heart attack and was airlifted to Moscow.[33] During the early sixties he succumbed to hypertension and diabetes — which required regular hospitalization (in the suburbs at Kuntsevo where the KGB had special housing): hence the perpetual pallor that marked him out within the leadership.[34] After Hungary he headed the department dealing with socialist countries from the third floor of the massive gray Central Committee building at Staraya Ploshchad'. Here on 25 December 1963 he requested and on 3 January 1964 received permission to set up a "think tank" within his department, into which he recruited young talent, such as Arbatov, Bovin, Shakhnazarov, Delyusin, and others.[35] When he moved to head the KGB, leading aides Arbatov and Bovin wrote a piece of verse expressing the wish for his speedy return. Also in verse, Andropov's response was illustrative. He admitted that the transition was made "with difficulty." But "the sad lesson of Hungary" gave him to understand that "the truth" could not be defended merely with "word and pen" but also, "if needs be, with the hatchet."[36]

Andropov had "friendly" relations with all ministers of defense, from Malinovsky to Ustinov.[37] Indeed, he and Ustinov became "very close."[38] He "often argued even with Leonid Ilych,"[39] but he was always tactful and became "one of the closest and most vital of Brezhnev's subordinates."[40] At a Central Committee plenum on 27 April 1973 Shelest was ejected from the Politburo. Andropov, Grechko, and Gromyko were elevated to full membership. Brezhnev went out of his way to applaud the fact that "the KGB under the leadership of Yuri Vladimirovich renders enormous help to the Politburo in foreign policy. It is usual to think that the KGB amounts to arresting and imprisoning people. That would be a profound mistake. The KGB is first and foremost a matter of vast and dangerous work abroad. This takes ability and character. Not everyone can resist selling out and treachery in the face of temptation."[41] Andropov also set up a system of institutes vital to the KGB that were no less scholarly than their academy of sciences counterparts, notably in computer science, electronics, communications, and cryptography.[42] Among these was the Institute for the Economics of the World Socialist System under economist and Hungarian specialist Oleg Bogomolov, a former adviser.

Initially on good terms with Brezhnev was the physically imposing (six feet six) Defense Minister Andrei Grechko, who succeeded Malinovsky on 13 April 1967 at the age of sixty-three. A Party member from 1928, once a friend of Khrushchev's, he commanded the Soviet Group of Forces in Germany from 1953 before becoming a Marshal (1955) and then first deputy defense minister in 1957. He seemed a natural successor to Malinovsky. Yet it took nearly a fortnight after Malinovsky's death to secure the post; most likely due to resistance from such as Chairman of the Council of Ministers and Politburo member Kosygin, who focused on the budget and was unlikely to welcome a known hawk. It is also suggested that Suslov sided with the military in opposing a civilian defense minister.[43]

The rival candidate was Dmitrii Ustinov. A member of the Party since 1927 and of the Central Committee since 1952, he had headed the defense industries since World War II. But resistance to the prospect of a civilian from within the military made itself effective, for the time being at least.[44] A Party member since 1928 and a formidable personality, Grechko had commanded the 47th and 18th armies at Novorossisk in 1942–43 when Brezhnev served as the head of the political section of the 18th army. Likewise Admiral Gorshkov, Commander of the Soviet fleet from 1956 and Deputy Minister of Defense, had been deputy commander of Novorossisk regional defense and for a time also commander of the 47th army.[45] It was Grechko who was responsible for reversing Khrushchev's dismissal of the value of conventional warfare, and under his leadership land and air forces were reinforced to gain the upper hand in any nonnuclear encounter with NATO.[46] And he proved ruthlessly successful in holding out against any restrictions on the growth of Soviet submarine-launched ballistic missiles at the strategic arms limitation talks (SALT).[47] Relieved of the climate of fear under Stalin, the military had finally come of age. Nasser told Sir Humphrey Trevelyan "that he found dealing with the Russians very different from ten years before. The Marshals had recently started to give their own opinions and did not always conceal their disagreements with the civilians."[48]

Grechko is said to have warned the Politburo that the very idea of negotiating with the United States on strategic forces was criminal.[49] And during the strategic arms limitation talks which opened in September 1969, he is said to have "remained permanently apoplectic. . . . His incurable distrust of, and violent opposition to, the talks, so well known to all of us involved in the negotiations, affected even the more realistic and sophisticated generals and politicians in a negative way. Grechko would repeatedly and irrelevantly launch into admonitory lectures on the aggressive nature of imperialism, which, he assured us, had not changed. There was no guarantee against a new world war except a continued buildup of Soviet armed might."[50] Detinov recalls that "Grechko was against any accords with the United States" and "that we had no right to enter into agreement with the imperialists . . . that we would be had, we would be cheated, we had to stay away from them."[51] He was certainly not an isolated voice. "All the decisions" on arms control made at SALT and later START "were strongly opposed by the military," according to Colonel General Danilevich, assistant to the Chief of the Main Operations Directorate of the General Staff in the 1970s.[52] A number of generals took great exception to articles by Bovin, now at *Izvestiya*, suggesting that a global nuclear war could not be won. In 1973 they invited him to the main political directorate of the armed forces where they tried to convince him that a nuclear missile exchange with the United States could be won by the USSR and accused him of "defeatism."[53]

Interpreter Sukhodrev considered that Kosygin "surpassed all our leaders" "intellectually." A literate man with good Russian marking him out above the rest,[54] Kosygin could handle a press conference with ease.[55] He was seen as "perhaps more temperamentally disposed than any of the others to take a calculated risk in going some way to meet the other chap's point of view when he judges that it would be to the long term advantage of the Soviet Government to do so."[56] Yet Brezhnev was not unalterably ideological like Suslov. During a meeting at Zavidovo the General Secretary said he had once been offered the job of Dnepropetrovsk regional Party secretary for ideology but turned it down because he did "not like engaging in this ceaseless waffle."[57] Kosygin, on the other hand, was one of the leadership most committed to supporting Hanoi. He had Stalinist instincts in domestic politics, strongly favoring the suppression of dissent;[58] and in the first major discussion on foreign policy after Khrushchev's downfall, he sided with Shelepin in attacking a draft prepared for a Warsaw Pact meeting because it conceded too much to "imperialism" (the West) and was insufficiently grounded in "a class position." He also took Brezhnev to task for not visiting China, which now presented itself as a new Bolshevik Rome (or Avignon Papacy), to heal the breach created under Khrushchev.[59] Moreover, and in striking contrast to Brezhnev, Kosygin had the "best" understanding of military technology of all the civilian leaders except Ustinov.[60]

Brezhnev did not stamp his personal authority on relations with the West until 9 April 1971 with the Twenty-fourth Party Congress. Thereafter statements were made in private to the effect that henceforth he was taking personal responsibility for relations with Washington and Bonn.[61] Dobrynin noted: "The infighting between them [Kosygin and Brezhnev] continued for the first two years of Nixon's presidency."[62] But Brezhnev was a predictable victor given the structure of Party and state, even if he continued to respect Kosygin's expertise and expected no show of deference on his part.[63] Nevertheless Brezhnev remained envious of Kosygin who was far more popular both in the Party and the country.[64]

Known among his staff as "gloomy" (*khmurii*),[65] Gromyko stood at awkward disadvantage vis-à-vis Ponomarev, head of the Central Committee's International Department, given Ponomarev's elevation as a candidate member of the Politburo on 19 May 1972. Even after Gromyko's promotion as a voting member a year later, personal relations were appalling. But Brezhnev disliked Ponomarev and went out of his way to show it, apparently because, at the crucial moment when Khrushchev was overthrown, Ponomarev made the critical mistake of not switching loyalties sufficiently quickly.[66]

Gromyko's greatest asset was a phenomenal memory. A significant problem was lack of confidence in delegating to subordinates;[67] that left him "basically a rather frightened man—in the sense of being frightened to take final responsibility for major decisions." It was also rightly suspected by London "that he is . . . rather obsessional—particularly about the Germans; and that he spends a great deal of time wondering how he can 'destroy NATO' (as he once put it . . .) without really expecting that he will succeed and perhaps even doubting whether he could cope with the consequences if he did!"[68] He felt a new confidence after Khrushchev's fall. Soon after Brezhnev's accession, Gromyko told a meeting of subordinates: "A new balance of power has formed in the world. If previously before taking a major initiative we had above all to calculate closely the possible reaction of the other side, now we can allow ourselves to do what is considered necessary, and then see how the other side reacts."[69] Yet, hidebound though Gromyko was, relations with the hawkish Grechko were "never good."[70] And in his bounded vision the United States *was* world politics. Falin recalled that "Gromyko . . . for some reason was inclined to believe Washington more than Paris, London and especially Bonn."[71]

THE VIETNAMESE OBSTACLE

The drift toward an understanding with Washington was already under way as a result of intermittent American contacts with Kosygin from 1965, culminating in the summit at Glassboro, New Jersey, in late June 1967. But a key obstacle arose: US military intervention in Vietnam.

The regime ruling South Vietnam broke the Geneva accords by reversing land reform with US encouragement,[72] making title dependent on approval from Saigon, and refusing to abide by the agreement to hold elections nationwide. Moscow was inclined to accept the status quo. Indeed, on 24 January 1959 it had proposed that both states be accepted into the UN. But Hanoi passed a resolution in May: "The time has come to push the armed struggle against the enemy."[73] The point of no return came in September 1960 when Le Duan was approved as the new Secretary General of the Party. On 19 December the National Liberation Front (NLF) of South Vietnam was proclaimed. A diplomatic initiative was simultaneously launched to canvass it as a neutralist movement.[74] Yet a Lao Dong circular noted: "The People's Revolutionary Party has only the appearance of an independent existence. Actually the party is nothing but the Lao Dong Party of Viet-nam unified from north to south under the central executive committee of the party, the chief of which is President Ho . . . take care to keep this strictly secret . . . especially in South Viet-Nam, so that the enemy does not perceive our purpose."[75] Moscow was nervous, asking "whether the transition toward an open armed struggle against the Ngo Dinh Diem regime would not put the revolutionary forces of South Vietnam under threat and, on the other hand, whether this would not lead to an even deeper U.S. intervention in South Vietnam that is fraught with the complication of the political situation in that region and could lead to the transformation of South Vietnam into a sharp ganglion of international tension."[76] It was thus not merely because of the critical situation in Berlin, in August 1961, that Khrushchev declined Ho's invitation to visit Hanoi.[77]

Between 1961 and 1965 Moscow supplied weapons of German manufacture to minimize the impact on relations with Washington.[78] And when Le Duan led a delegation to Moscow in January 1964, pressing the importance of the national liberation movement across the Third World in language no different from that of China, Moscow brusquely warned of the consequences for relations with the USSR.[79] Thus whereas Beijing favored increased military aid to Hanoi, Moscow refused.[80] By then Diem, who had flirted with the idea of negotiations with the North, had been ousted and assassinated in a coup backed by Washington (1 November 1963), leaving a chaotic scramble for power among the military.[81] Hanoi thus saw an opportunity for decisive action. The NLF delegation in Moscow in the summer of 1964 met with a cool reception, however, when they asked for increased military aid and a permanent mission in the Soviet capital.[82] Britain's ambassador noted: "Khrushchev had decided to have nothing to do with Vietnam . . . and virtually signed off."[83] Denied help from Moscow, Hanoi turned to Beijing. Having given Russian military advisers their papers, Hanoi signed a treaty with Beijing in December 1964 envisaging the advent of support troops into the North.[84] Sobering news simultaneously came into Washington that China was rapidly building an air base at Ningming just beyond the border with North Vietnam.[85]

US intervention began under Kennedy but grew into a major commitment under Lyndon Johnson. Contemptuous of Kennedy, Johnson was determined to succeed where his predecessor had failed. It was no accident, he believed, that the communists became more warlike in Vietnam after Kennedy's accession. From then on, "they saw that we were getting weak. They looked around and saw what Castro did and they saw that young man sit here in the White House. And when Khrushchev talked like war to Kennedy in Vienna we just didn't do very much. We called up the reserves but that didn't scare Khrushchev. He put his missiles into Cuba and all that young fellow here did was to say to Khrushchev: 'Please, sir, take your missiles out and we won't trouble you any more. Yes, you can go ahead and propagate Communism in Cuba and we won't touch you if you will just take those missiles out.'"[86]

The overthrow of Khrushchev completely altered Soviet policy. Hanoi soon acknowledged that it brought the Lao Dang "closer to the CPSU."[87] Kosygin was vigorously supportive of a more radical shift in policy toward a rapprochement with China and in antagonism with the West. The attempt failed and ultimately exacerbated tensions between the two major communist Powers. But the net effect was to drive Beijing and Moscow into competition for Hanoi; thus growing US pressure on North Vietnam merely stimulated that rivalry to Hanoi's advantage. Between 1953 and 1964 Moscow supplied 200 million rubles worth of aid, of which 70 percent was industrial (including training).[88] CIA estimated total Soviet military aid to the North between 1953 and 1964 at $70 million, half the total given by the entire communist bloc, which meant about half came from China. Between January 1965 and March 1967 it delivered about $670 million.[89] And all military aid was gratis. Between the autumn of 1964 and April 1965 aid totaled 486.5 million rubles, of which 300 million had been given since January.[90] Moscow was returning to Leninism in international relations. World revolution was back, with Washington an unknowing catalyst in exerting ever more force against Hanoi.

Perhaps because of rather than despite the Sino-Vietnamese agreement, Moscow began delivery of SAM-75 missiles for air defense to Hanoi in December 1964 before the US bombardment had even begun, evidently as a result of intelligence information.[91] Some signs of hesitancy on the part of Hanoi naturally emerged nevertheless when 49 US Navy jets proceeded with reprisal attacks on North Vietnam (7 and 8 February), leading to operation Rolling Thunder, a sustained bombing campaign of gradual escalation begun on 2 March. McGeorge Bundy had recommended this as "the most promising course available." But his lack of confidence in the operation and the use of bombing to cover the government's domestic political flank were betrayed in the remark added that "even if it fails to turn the tide—as it may—the value of the effort seems to us to exceed the cost."[92] The cost in one year alone included 351 aircraft and the loss of their pilots.[93] Malinovsky's reports of "the widening of the scale of the military conflict in this region"[94] were read with heightened concern. Moscow was committed to Hanoi, however, despite regarding them as a "bunch of stubborn bastards."[95]

When bombardment began, Kosygin visited Beijing to concert assistance and heal the rift. The visit was carefully prepared. Some were pessimistic about prospects. The proposal from the Politburo's foreign policy committee (Suslov, Andropov, Ponomarev, and Il'ichev) considered that there was no need to focus on areas of acute disagreement but to highlight what was held in common against imperialism.[96] Leading the arguments in favor were Brezhnev, Shelepin, Kosygin, and Suslov. Brezhnev's working assumption was that "Khrushchev did a lot of damage in foreign affairs."[97] But no one was interested in opening the question of territorial claims, and good Soviet relations with India, including arms supplies, were justified in terms of denying India to the United States.[98]

Kosygin visited Hanoi from 6 to 10 February, stopping off in Beijing on 5–6 and 10–11 February en route. Although Chou acknowledged that "the positions of the CPC [China] and CPSU [Russia] were either very close or completely coincidental" in respect of Vietnam, Beijing refused a joint declaration condemning Washington for breaching the Geneva accords. Mao, ever suspicious of Soviet motives, coolly displayed little interest in any direct confrontation with Washington. He offered no further aid to Hanoi: "The people of South Vietnam," he said, "fight well enough even without us. It will on its own drive out the Americans." As to the bombing, Mao considered this the "stupidity of the Americans." He also delivered a lecture on the world situation. "We are truly a warlike people . . . ," he emphasized, "tension will grow. There is obviously no détente at all; this is also an illusion . . . we need to prepare for war."' All was not lost for Sino-Soviet relations, however. "In 10–15 years, when the imperialists raised their hand against you or ourselves, we will fight together. War will unite us."[99]

Moscow moved more resolutely in support as a consequence of US bombing with the enthusiasm of the military.[100] On 6 July 1965 the Council of Ministers resolved on the dispatch of instructors to train North Vietnamese in the use of surface-to-air missiles.[101] About 2,500 went in.[102] A total of more than 10,000 to 12,000 men on strict rotation served over the course of the war. Between 1965 and 1970 North Vietnamese air defenses absorbed more than 85 percent of Soviet military aid.[103] Along with air defense, Moscow offered a squadron of fighter-interceptor aircraft with crew. Beijing was asked to accept overflights to supply them to Hanoi and base areas on Chinese soil while Vietnamese bases were in preparation. China refused point blank. Hanoi also preferred to have its own pilots trained in Russia for use of the MiG-21. Moscow agreed.[104]

Beijing conveyed to Washington (via an intermediary) a four-point statement emphasizing that China would not provoke war but would support anyone against US aggression and "fight to the end" should Washington retaliate.[105] In the event of US forces landing in North Vietnam, Beijing agreed to send in troops as strategic reserves.[106] Ho announced that Hanoi would "take the main burden of the war by themselves," but from Mao he also asked for and obtained "whatever support was needed by the Vietnamese."[107]

Balancing between Moscow and Beijing became increasingly difficult, however, as relations between the two became more acute. Le Duan, the leading figure in the North Vietnamese party—aside from Ho, who was fatally ill— took a detached view of Soviet "revisionism": "The Soviet Union is like the sun. I would compare revisionism to the clouds. Clouds may perhaps for a time cover the sun, but it always reappears."[108] That this relaxed attitude irritated Beijing in the heat of the so-called Cultural Revolution was apparent when Le Duan visited in November 1966 and was refused access to Mao.[109] By then China had more than 200,000 soldiers controlling the strategic routes to South Vietnam and Laos handling air defense along the line from Dien Bien Phu–Hanoi–Honghai to the Chinese border.[110] Inevitably with Hanoi's forces simultaneously concentrated to the south, fears naturally arose that the Chinese presence could give rise to "a potential coup d'état."[111]

Beijing's presence worked to Hanoi's advantage: Johnson was thereby inhibited from the most extreme options that others favored by the daunting prospect of reliving 1950–51.[112] Washington was therefore driven to seek help from Moscow. Kosygin was, however, content to wait upon events. He repeatedly said that he had "no authorization whatever from our Vietnamese comrades" to negotiate. Kosygin also emphasized that "the Vietnamese comrades do not exclude a political settlement, even one bypassing the Chinese (*Pomimo Kitaitsev*)." That settlement "would be on the basis of the retention of the 17th parallel." The advice he offered was to respond directly to Chairman of the Council of Ministers Pham Van Dong's four points. He insisted Washington could never win through force. Instead the Americans would be chased out as they had been elsewhere.[113]

The bombing of the North at the time of Kosygin's visit in February 1965 had been humiliating. It ensured that any talk of Johnson visiting Moscow was completely scotched. "It showed to them that there had never been any serious intention of such a visit," Dobrynin told Harriman, Governor of New York and Johnson's intermediary. "His remarks exposed again the sensitivity and feeling of inferiority which I have noted over the years, but which has not been as marked recently," Harriman concluded, entirely missing the point.[114] In his first round of conversations with Harriman in Moscow during July 1965, Kosygin had said that the Vietnamese problem was "an impediment to the solution of many important problems such as disarmament, nuclear weapons and the like."[115]

HAWKS IN MOSCOW SPEAK OF WAR

Escalation of the war exacerbated rivalry within. Brezhnev and Kosygin were not securely in place. Others, such as the younger Shelepin, who believed Brezhnev's post should have been his for the taking,[116] were advancing on the basis of more assertive policies. At the celebrations of the October Revolution anniversary in the Kremlin on 7 November 1964 Shelepin, "tough and generally on the attack," launched a verbal assault on the British ambassador and two other envoys concerning Johnson's recent speech on aid to Saigon. Shelepin compared it to Churchill's iron curtain speech. He also said of Khrushchev, by way of warning, that the "old man used to blather away, but we are not bound by what he said." Before this could be clarified, Kosygin appeared and he sheepishly confessed to having expressed his personal opinion.[117]

Shelepin lost his position as Deputy Chairman of the Council of Ministers in 1965 but retained membership of the all-important Politburo. Bovin, working under Andropov in the Central Committee apparat, recalls: "Toward the middle of 1966 within the Soviet leadership there began to develop a determination to stamp their feet, to intimidate the Americans, to put them in their place. It was proposed to have a tough conversation on the 'hot line,' to recall the ambassador from Washington, to organize military exercises in the Far East etc." This prompted a memorandum to Andropov for discussion in the Politburo. The measures suggested, Bovin argued, made sense only in the event that "we are prepared to go to war with the United States of America and . . . if, although we are not prepared to fight, the Americans believe in our readiness to start military action against the USA." But, Bovin continued, none of these conditions held good. Instead he recommended encouraging Hanoi to negotiate and at the same time increasing military assistance in the form of armaments.[118]

Thus when Kosygin and Soviet diplomats warned of the Vietnam War escalating to general war, the attitudes of the more hawkish could not have been far from their minds. In mid-May the bombing of Hanoi in progress and US intervention in the Dominican Republic a public spectacle, Grechko addressed the leadership, evidently with Brezhnev's support. He represented these two events as provocations against Moscow that could lead to action against Cuba. Active measures were therefore required, such as mobilization of the armed forces in Germany and Hungary as a demonstration effect. And were Cuba threatened, then Moscow had to be ready to hit West Berlin. They should not fear the risk of war. Mikoyan, witnessing this display of belligerence, was completely "taken aback."[119] A week later, when the matter was opened to extended discussion, Mikoyan, Kosygin, Podgorny, and Suslov dismissed the proposals, Kosygin pointing out the manner in which both Stalin and Khrushchev were eventually forced to back down after creating a crisis over Berlin.[120]

The Shelepin faction was not removed until 1967 when approaches were made to Mikoyan to have Brezhnev supplanted.[121] What Kosygin told Harriman in July 1965 was also to have great significance in the next few years for the emergence of détente: "One possibility would be for a meeting to be held—not necessarily in the USSR or U.S., it doesn't matter where—prior to a disarmament conference where a fundamental understanding could be reached on these important issues." In essence he wanted a summit. "Naturally, progress could be made by conventional methods as well, but faster progress might be made by adopting unconventional ones. However nothing can be done today because of the Vietnamese problem. Thus, the Vietnamese problem—which is a small problem—becomes large and influences all other important issues."[122] By then, however, Washington had slipped ineluctably into combat operations on the ground.

Kosygin had good reason to believe that Washington and Hanoi would ultimately be obliged to negotiate a peace, but as a result of the pressure from events alone. This much was confirmed when on 6 October the Russian military attaché in Hanoi reported that "among part of the officer corps of the Vietnamese army feelings of discontent are apparent with respect to the course being pursued by the leadership of the DRV, which to please the Chinese is conducting a policy not meeting the interests of the Vietnamese people. The Vietnamese people are tired of protracted war and the sacrifices entailed and see no real prospect of any improvement in the situation. The people show indifference toward the political tasks undertaken under the slogan 'a decisive struggle to the end.' These feelings are deepening given that, with weak military-economic capabilities of its own, the DRV is giving assistance to Laos." Thus "officers of the Vietnamese People's Army are strengthening in the belief that the political line of the leadership of the DRV and the VWP directed at refusal to search for means of resolving the Vietnamese question by means other than direct military struggle is wrong."[123] Opinion in Hanoi shifted, however, and Soviet understanding was often little more than inspired guesswork.

COMMUNISM IN INDONESIA ABORTED

Elsewhere in Asia US interests were also threatened at another crossroads where Moscow and Beijing competed for dominance, notably in the most populous country of Southeast Asia, where China already wielded significant influence: the former Dutch East Indies. After gaining independence for Indonesia on 27 December 1949, President Hatta had recognized China only a few months later. An irredentist state, claiming territory from Malaya, and in search of a major role in Asia commensurate with its massive population, Indonesia had hosted the first conference of nonaligned countries in Bandung in 1955. And in October 1956 President Sukarno became only the second head of state after Ho to visit Beijing in a fanfare of publicity. Thereafter the two states increasingly swam the same waters. Thus in Indonesia the Unites States faced "a nation-wide, gov[ernmen]t sanctioned leftist effort to remove [the] American presence."[124] In January 1965 Sukarno withdrew from the UN. The normally taciturn Soviet ambassador, Mikhailov, expressed his anxiety at Indonesia's drift toward war with Malayia and at its orientation away from Moscow toward

Beijing.[125] And Sukarno was no friend of Washington. CIA had tried and failed to overthrow him in 1958.[126] He had long engaged in a delicate balancing act mixing nationalism with socialism and anti-Americanism in order to outflank the powerful Communist Party (PKI) oriented more toward Beijing than Moscow. The conflict with Malaysia had driven him ever closer to the Eastern bloc, which gave the PKI ever-growing influence.

The PKI had a remarkable General Secretary in Aidit, born in Insel Sumatra of Malay extraction on 30 July 1923. Aidit rose rapidly through the ranks of the communist youth movement, then underground, from 1939 to 1945, before becoming leader of the Party proper in 1951 at the early age of twenty-eight. Membership then stood at a mere 7, 910. By 1963, however, the PKI numbered some 3.5 million,[127] with a further 1.5 million in the youth wing and another 25 million in front organizations.[128] The PKI pressed Sukarno to arm the peasantry and dismiss the more moderate ministers. And in a TV interview on 4 February Sukarno said he did not mind the PKI taking power as long as it did not harm the country.[129] CIA then reported that President Sukarno had "given instructions for [the] sustained harassment of American officials in Indonesia."[130] In an unusual message of greetings to the PKI on 20 May, Mao congratulated the Party on having "indonesianized Marxism-Leninism with outstanding success." On 23 May Aidit called for the confiscation of US property. Britain concluded that "Indonesia is slipping steadily into the Communist sphere."[131] "Perhaps like Castro he [Sukarno] will in due course discover that he has been a Communist all the time," a diplomat noted sardonically.[132]

Preoccupied with Vietnam, strategically far less important than Indonesia, Johnson was initially inclined to appease Sukarno. But in the early hours of the morning on 1 October Lieutenant Colonel Untung of the air force launched a savage coup and nearly succeeded in wiping out the entire leadership of the army, which was largely anticommunist. According to PKI Politburo member Sobsi, Sukarno's illness prompted fears in the Party leadership that the council of generals would take the helm. A coup was first discussed in July and settled on in August.[133] Aidit's visit to Beijing on 3–4 August may have played a contributory role. Untung later acknowledged the role of the PKI, though that was under interrogation, where doubtless he could have been induced to say anything.[134] But Japan also learned that Untung was a PKI member and speculated that the Party leadership were unusually absent from the 1 October festivities in Beijing—celebrating the People's Republic anniversary—because they were too busy preparing to seize power.[135]

A secret report from *Pravda*'s local correspondent Shurygin on 10 October reluctantly acknowledged that "it is quite possible that the communists prepared something similar to the events of '30 September'; they wanted to draw

Sukarno and the most sympathetic elements of the air force into these events; however, for some reason or other, events took them by surprise, and the move took place prematurely. Here it is possible that at the critical moment the leadership split. One of the reasons which could have driven them to act might have been a serious deterioration in Sukarno's health on the night of 1 October. It is entirely possible that in these circumstances Lieutenant Colonel Untung decided to play the role of Boumedienne."[136] Aidit's worry over Sukarno's health also emerged from the interrogation of PKI Politburo member Njono.[137]

Conspirator Major Bambang of the parachute regiment said the coup involved more than the PKI and that some 2,000 volunteers had been brought in from various parts of the country for training by the air force at a base near Djakarta.[138] The aim was said to be the formation of a supreme revolutionary council that would lead to a national government under the PKI. General Nasution, however, escaped the purge by clambering over his garden wall. He then orchestrated a devastating onslaught against those responsible for the bloodthirsty murder of his friends and colleagues with some assistance from Washington. Robert Martens from the US embassy's political section had spent the previous two years compiling a comprehensive list of PKI members. The list was handed over piecemeal to Tirta Kentjana ("Kim") Adhyatman, an aide to Adam Malik, Suharto's ally. "It really was a big help to the army," Martens recalled. "They probably killed a lot of people, and I probably have a lot of blood on my hands, but that's not all bad. There's a time when you have to strike hard at a decisive moment." "No one cared as long as they were Communists, that they were being butchered," Howard Federspiel, Indonesian expert at INR, commented. "No one was getting very worked up about it."[139] Within a week, Sukarno still clinging to office, and a parallel government in being, the military were rounding up and shooting PKI members en masse. In total around 300,000 were killed over the subsequent four and a half months.[140]

The reaction in Beijing, where insurrections overseas were strongly advocated, shows how far out of touch with reality the Maoist leadership was. In 1964 Mao pressed both the Indonesians and the Japanese to launch uprisings. And on 28 March 1966 Mao told a delegation from the Japanese Communist Party of two errors committed by the PKI. First, "they blindly believed in Sukarno, and overestimated the power of the Party in the army"; second, the Party "wavered without fighting it out."[141] The precise role of CIA is still murky. In Djakarta, however, the deputy chief of mission "made clear that [the] embassy and USG[overnment] generally [were] sympathetic with and admiring of what [the] army [were] doing."[142]

The extinction of the PKI came as a shock to Moscow. But it represented a body blow to China. Testifying on 10 February 1966, from retirement, Kennan argued that China had "suffered an enormous reverse in Indonesia . . . one of great significance, and one that does rather confine any realistic hopes they may have for the expansion of their authority."[143] Russia, though broadly sympathetic to the PKI, was nevertheless prepared to carry on as though nothing had happened. Talks between Washington and Moscow were still a real possibility, though Russia was inclined to hold progress elsewhere hostage to progress (on their terms) regarding Vietnam. Chinese activism was also apparent in South Asia. There, in September 1965, Beijing had encouraged Pakistan in its longstanding confrontation with India over the latter's continued possession of Muslim Kashmir. The resultant border war was mediated by Moscow, anxious to restore stability to a region where trouble could only benefit rival China. The Tashkent agreement of 10 January 1966 succeeded in holding the line for a few years more. The image of the Brezhnev-Kosygin regime was thus at this early stage a good deal more reassuring than that of Maoist China, now succumbing to the misnamed Cultural Revolution, a brutal and xenophobic display of loyalty to Mao.

DÉTENTE WITH THE UNITED STATES?

When Harriman mentioned China, Britain, and France as likely interlocutors on nuclear nonproliferation, Kosygin was typically brusque. On his view, Washington and Moscow were "the only real owners of nuclear weapons. Others have some capability . . . but are not now of any importance. However, science is making great strides and is the property of all states. Cheaper bombs, which do not require the present tremendous amount of electric power for their manufacture, will be developed, Kosygin said. Many states will thus be able to possess nuclear weapons and when this happens, there will be no guarantees as to who might take these weapons into their hands." Here Germany reared its head. What if another Hitler arose? "These weapons are terrible," Kosygin said. "We must do all in our power to prevent proliferation of these weapons. That is why the American proposal to pool nuclear weapons [in NATO under MLF]—which amounts to giving weapons to the Germans—arouses such emotional opposition in the USSR."[144] Of course, Moscow had yet to sign a nuclear nonproliferation treaty; neither had Bonn, for whom it was primarily envisaged (in Moscow). This turn in the discussion with Harriman led Kosygin on to a related issue: "The U.S. pretends the GDR does not exist, but it does exist . . . We will not let down the East Germans and turn them over to your hands. . . . As I see it, let there be two Germanies for a while until they come together by themselves. You are none the worse off for this."[145]

Kosygin was emotionally swayed by Vietnam but had to accept that Hanoi would not submit to mediation (after the precedent of Geneva in 1954–55). The dilemma was spelt out in a Foreign Ministry memorandum presented to the Politburo on 13 January 1967:

> As regards the American aggression against Vietnam and its effect on bilateral relations, we should go on rendering comprehensive assistance to the DRV in consolidating its defense capacity to repulse the aggression, without getting directly involved in the war. We must give the Americans to understand that further escalation in the military actions against the DRV will compel the Soviet Union to render its assistance to this country on an ever-growing scale, and that the only way out of the present situation is reaching a political solution on the basis of respecting the legitimate rights of the Vietnamese people. Nevertheless, putting an end to the Vietnam conflict would undoubtedly have a positive effect on Soviet-American relations and open up new possibilities for solving certain international problems.[146]

Handling negotiations for Johnson, Harriman continued to fret over the failure of a recent British initiative to make progress. "Somehow the Soviets had to be induced to assume responsibility for bringing Hanoi to negotiations."[147] Yet this wishful thinking matched a lack of realism about Vietnam as a whole. Harvard professor Henry Kissinger "was never against the war in Vietnam."[148] As such he interceded with the Russians on behalf of the Johnson administration. Director of the Czech Institute of International Affairs Anton Snejdarek, an intelligence officer, who had headed the Czech military mission in Germany in the late 1940s and was a member of the foreign policy collegium of the Czech Council of Ministers, told him that Moscow believed "the United States was getting stuck deeper and deeper in the muck of Vietnam. Sooner or later, the United States would get tired of it and then accept terms going far beyond anything now being conceived." Moscow was counting on "American psychological exhaustion. A North Vietnamese victory would then enable the Soviet Union to strengthen its influence in Hanoi as a counterweight to China."[149] Indeed, on 21 February an assessment for the Politburo took heart from the evident fact that Chinese leaders were worried by the tendency of the North Vietnamese toward greater independence of action from China.[150]

As the war showed no signs of ending, Moscow dropped its reservations and adopted a resolutely favorable view of communist prospects in South Vietnam. The US troop commitment had reached its upper limit of 650,000 to 750,000 without mobilization. Armaments were flowing southward in a "broad stream."

In these circumstances Hanoi was uninterested in negotiations. "It can be estimated," the Soviet ambassador told colleagues, "that the entire armed forces of the FLN are almost as powerful as the American, Saigon, and allied forces put together. The Saigon army merely functions as police, its morale is at rock bottom. The officer corps is corrupt and is thus disintegrating." Desertion was at an all time high; some 100,000 were lost to Saigon in 1967. Without US aid the regime could not continue. "The Vietnam War and the negro problem are weighing Johnson down," the North Vietnamese noted. "For this reason they intend to use military means up to the start of the election period to bolster Johnson's position."[151] The only bad news for Moscow and its allies was that of Ho's illness, which inevitably complicated decision making. But Southeast Asia was not the only theater of direct confrontation. The Middle East was now at boiling point and, as with Vietnam, the diehards in Moscow considered its policy too conciliatory.

THE SIX DAY WAR 1967

The perpetual threat from the Arab states to drive Israel into the sea turned it into a garrison state which, without natural frontiers, exercised the traditional right of preemptive war whenever its security was jeopardized. Nothing was done, however, to find a humanitarian solution for the Palestinian refugees driven from the lands now settled. In 1967 Nasser took up refugee rights as the banner to unite Arab opinion by challenging Israel. Yet in the Arab world cacophony rather than harmony reigned. This made Israel no more secure, however. From 23 February 1966 the new radical Baathist government in Syria allied to Cairo began backing terrorist attacks against Israel from Fatah, the burgeoning Palestinian movement. Moscow had been approached by the Palestine Liberation Organization several times but held them at arms' length.[152] They turned instead to China.

Moscow insisted the Arab-Israeli dispute was an extension of global class struggle, with Israel an instrument of US power, ironically at the very time Washington refused to sell arms directly to Tel Aviv. Britain and France remained the primary sources once West Germany had dropped out under Arab pressure. So sentiment within Israel became increasingly unilateralist. The announcement from London in 1966 that it would pull out from bases east of Suez, which would leave Aden open to the insurrectionist forces backed by Cairo and Moscow, added to anxieties.

Soviet ambassador in Tel Aviv Dmitrii Chuvakhin described Israel as occupying "an important place in the strategic plans of the imperialist Powers, having as their aim the struggle with the world socialist system," and in their tactics, "directed at sucking the blood out of and breaking down the anti-imperialist front of nations, at 'casting off' the national-liberation movement." The West was blamed for trying to use Israel as "a standing source of tension in the Near and Middle East" to justify the "theory of the balance of power in this region." Yet Chuvakhin looked upon the more flexible foreign policy of Prime Minister and Defense Minister Levi Eshkol as a significant improvement upon that of his predecessor, hardliner David Ben-Gurion, and understood that Israel's interests were not always furthered by Western policy which was dictated by more global, anti-Soviet considerations. He highlighted the disputes between Israel and the other capitalist Powers—including US pressure on France to desist from aiding the construction of the nuclear reactor at Dimona. Chuvakhin also saw "little Israel" with its limited resources as unlikely to be able to sustain military rivalry with the Arab countries over the long term. But his proposals for a major Soviet peace initiative fell on deaf ears.[153] In this he appears to have been influenced by lobbying from the Israeli Communist Party (Maki), chairman Moshe Sneh in particular.[154]

As terrorists continued to strike across the west bank of the Jordan River, Eshkol, a native Russian speaker, approached Chuvakhin in late October 1966 asking for pressure on Damascus to avert a conflict. Eshkol expressed his willingness to meet the Soviet leadership at any time and in any place. Gromyko dismissed the proposal out of hand.[155] On 9 November Deputy Foreign Minister Vladimir Semyonov warned the Israeli ambassador that his country should be cautious and take the longer view.[156] But three days later an Israeli patrol was struck by a mine, losing three dead and six injured. The following day reprisals were launched against Fatah at Es-Samu in Jordan, which by then formed part of a united military command with Egypt and Syria.

Moscow now paid serious attention. Concern was apparent in Gromyko's comment to the Politburo that "extremist elements among the Palestinians are also trying to take advantage of the deterioriation in the Arab-Israeli conflict. The leader of the 'Palestine Liberation Organization,' Ahmed Shukeiri, linked to China, has recently significantly increased its activity in Arab countries, openly calling for war with Israel. Shukeiri stated at a press conference in Algiers in November this year that 'instead of words, speeches, conferences, protests, we have armed struggle' and that the 'Palestine Liberation Organization' has the support of the Chinese People's Republic, which supplies it with weapons and is training military personnel for it with the aim of solving the Palestinian problem by military means." Given that Fatah's attacks on Israel "may lead to serious complications in this region," the Soviet ambassador to Syria had made representations to the prime minister in Damascus. "However,"

Gromyko continued, "there are signs that the Palestinian organization headed by Shukeiri has supporters within influential circles in Syria, Iraq, and Jordan and may precipitate the occurrence of even more serious incidents." In the rear lurked China, "aiming at the opening of 'a second Vietnam' in the Near East."[157]

The fact that even the more moderate kingdom of Jordan would not accept the idea of UN troops along the border to forestall further incidents showed Moscow how far out of line with Arab opinion it had come. Naturally an unrepresentative monarchy that had annexed the west bank of the Jordan River (Palestine) in collusion with Israel had a precarious basis for legitimacy. Ambassador in Amman Petr Slyusarenko was nonetheless surprised to be told in confidence by the foreign minister that "the presence of UN forces on the Jordani-Israeli demarcation line will deprive the Palestinians of the possibility of resolving the Palestinian problem by the only means available to them— through armed struggle." The UN presence in Gaza after all prevented Egypt helping the Palestinians.[158]

Having failed to restrain Arab opinion, Moscow instead decided to follow. The Central Committee plenum in December resolved to pursue "unswervingly" a policy designed to strengthen the forces of national liberation. Here the hawkish influence of Shelepin and his followers made itself felt. Whether Moscow was reading Israeli ciphers is not known, but if its leaders saw Chief of Staff Yizhak Rabin's telegram to the military attaché in London, it would have fed hostile sentiment in Moscow and completely neutralized Eshkol's earnest efforts to keep the peace: "An escalation with Syria is not against Israel's interest," wrote Rabin, "and in my view there is no better time than now for a confrontation with Syria. I prefer to go to war rather than allow this continuous harassment, especially if the Syrians persist in their efforts to facilitate the activity of Fatah on our border."[159]

While Israeli ambassador to the UN Gideon Rafael was in Moscow updating them on his country's conduct, Semyonov handed the Israeli ambassador a note warning "that the Soviet government was in possession of information about Israeli troop concentrations" along its borders.[160] On 13 May at a meeting with Anwar Sadat, chairman of the Egyptian National Assembly, Gromyko insisted that Moscow would stand firm alongside Damascus. And when Sadat stressed that in the next few years Egypt would have to conduct a greater struggle than in 1956, Gromyko answered: "We well understand this and on this question we can only agree. We have interests in common."[161]

It was at around this time, mid-May, that Moscow "received reports that Israel was preparing a military attack against Syria and other Arab countries."[162] This was passed on to Cairo and Damascus. Yet if this information was as poor as that which prompted Semyonov's note of 26 April, little reliability should have been placed on it. Nevertheless on 16 May ambassador to Egypt Dmitrii Pozhidaev accompanied military attaché Fursov to see Defense Minister Shams A-Din Badran at his request. Pozhidaev was told of Egyptian information from Syria that Israel had indeed concentrated twelve brigades along the border. As a result the Egyptian Chief of Staff had left for Damascus. Syria had been assured that in the event of attack Egypt would immediately come to its assistance. Egyptian forces were moving into position in the Sinai. It was, however, agreed that mere frontier incidents would not be construed as an invasion from Israel. Badran wanted armaments from Moscow at short notice. From 1955 until 1966 Moscow had supplied military equipment to Egypt worth $1.16 billion, just over half gratis and the rest as low-interest credit.[163] On 14 May Badran wrote to Grechko for more fighter aircraft: MiG-21s, Sukhoi-7s, and various other items.[164]

What came as a shock to Moscow as well as Tel Aviv was when Egypt demanded that the UN emergency force (UNEF) be withdrawn from the cease-fire line along the border with Israel.[165] As tension rose, Johnson, tempted to back Israel overtly but dissuaded by Walt Rostow, his national security adviser, made it known that he could not "accept responsibilities on behalf of the United States for situations which arise as a result of actions on which we are not consulted."[166] But on 16 May Fawzi, Chief of the Egyptian General Staff, told commander of UNEF General Rikhye to withdraw and simultaneously placed all forces on full alert. At noon on 17 May Rafael heard that the UN had issued a statement saying that if Egypt insisted, the Secretary General would have to pull out UNEF completely.[167]

The Egyptian ambassador to the UN did not even know whether the pullout was to be partial or whether the Secretary General would receive a formal request. Yet both U Thant and his deputy, Ralph Bunche, rapidly agreed, despite the fact that it conflicted entirely with the understandings reached in 1957 when UNEF was formed and the fact that they knew there to be no concentration of Israeli forces along the Syrian frontier.[168] Interestingly, Egypt indicated that Bunche had actually opposed the idea of pulling out UNEF but that U Thant, who seemed not to understand the likely consequences, insisted.[169] U Thant thereby breached the undertaking given to Israel in March 1957 in return for evacuating the Straits of Tiran and Gaza, augmented by a letter from his predecessor dated 5 August 1958.[170] Whatever the motives for this ineptitude, the sequel was tragically predictable.

Even Moscow regarded Egypt's demand as "ill-advised."[171] Cairo explained its reasoning variously: an attempt to deter Israeli military action against Syria;

a means of bolstering policy on the Palestinian question by showing that its forces were capable of acting against Israel; and an effort to foil Anglo-American plans to bring down the Syrian government. Vice President Marshal Amer insisted they were not about to attack Israel but added that Egypt had to be prepared for any eventuality "right up to a serious military conflict." He also asked that Moscow speed up delivery of the MiG-21s due for 1968 so that they reach Egypt before the end of 1967. They also needed 100–150 armored troop carriers.[172]

If Moscow saw this saber rattling as risky, its passivity did nothing to cool the atmosphere. It appeared to be a situation that could be exploited at little or no expense. At the UN Sinologist and anti-Semite Fyodorenko, the Soviet ambassador, was instructed to sustain close contact with Egypt and Syria, and that should they, as before, oppose bringing the situation to the Security Council, Fedorenko should support them. If the question arose as to Egypt's right to have UNEF withdrawn, he should also back them up.[173] Yet Moscow was never told beforehand what Cairo was expecting to do. On 20 May a paratroop battalion and an infantry brigade of the Egyptian army reached Sharm el-Sheikh. Long-range 130-mm guns from the USSR were emplaced. Two days later Pozhidaev was informed by Nasser of another fait accompli while U Thant was en route to Egypt to mediate.

Nasser thanked Fyodorenko for detail on the numbers and location of Israeli forces. He claimed that on 12 May certain political figures had directly threatened Syria with war and the occupation of Damascus, evidently counting on Egypt's embroilment in the Yemen to deter it from offering effective support. Subsequent measures had sobered Israel, he claimed. They were now calling for peace. Speaking to Egyptian forces in the Sinai that same day—22 May— Nasser announced the "decision of the UAR government [Egypt] to close entry to the Gulf of Aqaba to all Israeli vessels and also to vessels of third countries bringing strategic goods to Israel. By taking this step, the president said, the UAR wishes to reestablish the position prevailing prior to the aggression of 1956." "Israel always threatened," he continued, "that if the Gulf of Aqaba was closed, it would unleash a war. The UAR is not determined to complicate the situation any further, in Nasser's words. But should Israel have recourse to war, then the UAR will reply by every means at its disposal." And, having taken this risky step without prior consultation, Nasser now asked that Moscow issue the same kind of declaration as it had issued in October 1956 against Britain, France, and Israel. Not only would this not complicate its relations with Washington, but it would fully clarify the situation.[174]

The same day it was announced that Iraq would join Egypt in the event of war. King Feisal of Saudi Arabia added his country to the list on 23 May, followed by Jordan on the 24th, and four days later general mobilization was announced in the Sudan. On 29 May Algeria said units were to go to the Middle East to help Egypt. A further menacing omen was the signature by King Hussein on 30 May of a pact with Nasser which placed of Jordan's forces under Egyptian command. Nasser foolishly stated: "Today we tell the Israelis we are facing you in the battle and are burning with the desire for it to begin."[175] On 31 May the Iraqi air force moved to its most western base, closest to Israel.

Meanwhile Badran had come to Moscow to ask the Russians for their agreement to a preemptive strike against Israel. Kosygin led the talks along with Deputy Minister Vladimir Semyonov and the head of a Near Eastern department. Arabist Pogos Akopov was present as an adviser. Kosygin was adamantly against the idea, repeating his refusal on the following day. Nasser backed down.[176] Clearly uninformed of the change, on 3 June Egyptian commander General Mortajii issued an order of the day: "Our forces are arrayed in accordance with a clearly defined plan. We are completely ready to carry the war beyond Egypt's borders. The outcome of this great hour will be of historic importance to our Arab nation and to the Holy War. This is the day we have been waiting for—to restore the plundered land to its rightful owners. I have been asked, when will the time come for the Jihad? The time is now!"[177] Two days later Nasser circulated governments with the assertion that a blockade was now in force, justified by the "state of war with Israel." Israel was entirely encircled. In the face of all this, U Thant's timid and tentative attempts to sustain the peace proved futile.[178]

Rostow explained to Johnson the importance of "dealing with Nasser not on a rising trend but in somewhat the same as Khrushchev in the Cuba missile crisis; Nasser is trying to achieve a quick fix against an underlying waning position."[179] The blockade of Tiran necessarily drew Washington into the game. Eisenhower had, as a quid pro quo to ensure Israeli evacuation of the Sinai, agreed on 11 February 1957 to keep the straits open. But Washington—now bogged down in Vietnam—refused to step up to the line, despite repeated personal entreaties from Tel Aviv. For Rostow there was no way of coming out ahead, whether by challenging Egypt or deserting Israel. "Whoever is the bigger winner, we are the sure loser," he quipped.[180] Washington had on 20 May brought elements of the Sixth Fleet to within two days' steaming time of the eastern shore of the Mediterranean, near Crete and Rhodes.

Rostow wrongly believed that Moscow feared an Arab-Israeli war because if Israel won, "after more than 10 years of pouring Soviet arms into the Middle East, the whole Soviet arms game will be profoundly degraded. It has already been substantially degraded by the outcome in Indonesia."[181] But Moscow's greater fear was of alienating Nasser. Unwilling to sanction preemptive war, it nevertheless made no attempt to restrain him from blockading the gulf.[182] At the Soviet embassy in Cairo, Sergei Tarasenko and his colleagues knew that in the event of war Israel would win. But, he recalls, "We thought that Egypt would stick it for two-three weeks or a month; then the Superpowers would interfere and find their way to a settlement." They certainly "didn't think it would be so short."[183] Moreover, Gromyko always assumed Israel would do what it was told by the United States.[184] The US Joint Chiefs of Staff predicted a swift Israeli victory.[185] Rostow thus advised a nod and a wink to Israel, leaving to it the decision on the action to be taken. On his view, if Israel took more Arab territory, it could hold its return hostage to full diplomatic recognition. With an unofficial hint to Israel from Johnson's confidant, Supreme Court Justice Abe Fortas, Washington thus effectively gave Tel Aviv an amber light for preemptive war.[186] By then, Syria was dangerously complacent that no war would take place.[187] Moscow, however, saw war as now inevitable, and there were no illusions about its likely outcome. The fleet—with a total of 25 warships, 9 submarines (2 of which were atomic), 1 training cruiser, 4 destroyers, 2 large antisubmarine vessels, 6 protection vessels, and 2 trawlers—was instructed to keep out of the way of the Americans and their allies.[188]

Israel struck at 7:45 a.m. on 5 June. The first reports came in to the White House situation room at 2:38 a.m. eastern standard time; at 5:00 a.m. the log recorded: "All HELL broke loose." The US ambassador at the UN proposed a cease-fire and informally suggested to the Russians that both Israel and Egypt be asked to remove their forces to the territorial status quo ante bellum.[189] To entangle Moscow, Cairo and Damascus falsely claimed that Washington and London were giving Israel air cover. Kosygin, however, refused to credit this and resisted Nasser's persistent pressure.[190] The Soviet delegation at the UN stalled, still awaiting instructions and Egypt hoping for a miracle. Finally at around noon on the following day, Semyonov telephoned on an open line telling them to await instructions. These were to accept the proposal informally proffered by US ambassador Goldberg; that unavailing, then acceptance of the cease-fire. Gromyko added that this should be done even in the face of Arab opposition.[191] At 4:00 p.m. Fyoderenko called for a resolution for a cease-fire on the assumption that the original Goldberg proposal was still on offer. This misunderstanding was evident in Kosygin's message to Johnson received on 7 June.[192] By instinct pro-Israeli, Johnson persuaded Rostow that a mere cease-fire would then put the onus on the Arabs to come to terms. "This would mean that we could use the de facto situation on the ground to try to negotiate not a return to armistice lines but a definitive peace in the Middle East," Rostow noted.[193]

Moscow airlifted spares for Egyptian tanks and aircraft but did nothing further.[194] The airlift took more than 120 Ilyushin-27 transporters flying 350 sorties and was accomplished by the end of 8 June.[195] Moscow also provided air cover with MiG-25s and manned antiaircraft batteries: "Our missile men were on the front line of the Suez Canal," Tarasenko recalls.[196] A US emissary reported from Tel Aviv that Israel did not intend to repeat the experience of 1956–57, "to withdraw within their boundaries with only paper guarantees that fall apart at the touch of Arab hands."[197] Israel was this time going to hold out for all it could get before withdrawal. The problem for Washington was how to make Israel more pliable when Eshkol insisted he "isn't going to pay any attention to any imperialist pressures."[198]

On 10 June Kosygin once again contacted Johnson to complain that Israel was ignoring the UN resolution on a cease-fire. Moscow, anxious lest Israel seize Syria, now issued a direct threat: "A moment of great responsibility has now arrived," the message read, "which obliges us, if military action does not cease within hours, of taking independent decisions. We are prepared for this. However, such action may bring us to blows, which would lead to a great catastrophe. Apparently there are forces in the world for whom this would be advantageous."[199] Under cover at the Soviet embassy in Washington, KGB officer Boris Sedov warned CIA that Moscow would intervene militarily to protect Damascus if the Israelis continued to refuse a cease-fire.[200] From Washington the order immediately went out to bring elements of the Sixth Fleet to within 100 miles of the coast. Amphibious units were, however, held back south of Crete. "It wasn't Dayan that kept Kosygin out," Johnson later insisted.[201]

PROSPECTS FOR ARMS LIMITATION

Kosygin's presence at the UN also afforded an opportunity to discuss arms control at a higher level. Washington was alarmed at deployment of an antiballistic missile (ABM) system around Moscow. The Vietnam War was straining the budget, given that raising taxes was not an option without jeopardizing electoral hopes for 1968. Thus Washington approached Moscow with a view to mutual abnegation of ABM systems. At the urging of Dobrynin, the Politburo agreed to sound out Washington on negotiations to restrict both defensive *and* offensive systems. This was done on 18 March 1966. But doubtless because it still held the advantage in offensive systems, the United States did not respond, instead pressing once again merely for ABM restrictions without, however, curbing research and development.[202] The Soviet side repeated its offer on 6 December.[203] But Moscow was in no great hurry. Washington responded in mid-February 1967[204] and prompted confirmation in a letter from Kosygin to Johnson on 27 February.[205] As became rapidly evident, Moscow was not interested in freezing the existing balance of strategic power which lay to US advantage.[206]

Once clear that both sides were willing to proceed, it also became evident that progress would splinter both governments. Whereas McNamara was looking to the long term and the impossibility of sustaining superiority without breaking the budget, the military naturally wanted to keep the high margin of advantage they already possessed. Chairman of the Joint Chiefs of Staff General Earle Wheeler naturally insisted that he "wanted a plan that would maintain the strategic superiority of the U.S. at all times."[207] It is also striking that early in October Dobrynin said that the reason why Moscow did not respond to more detailed US proposals "was not lack of interest nor lack of attention . . . but was because of the differing points of view within the Soviet Government on it. . . . unlike the U.S. Government where there appeared to be ready means of coordination on both the political and military aspects of such a proposal, in the Soviet Government the Foreign Ministry dealt primarily with political questions and all military matters were the responsibility of the Defense Ministry. In the Foreign Ministry," Dobrynin emphasized, "there were few, if any, individuals having experience and competence in a subject of this sort and the military were unwilling to let the Foreign Ministry discuss the question in any way except what he characterized as 'meaningless general terms.'" Dobrynin added that US boasting of a two to three margin of superiority created severe difficulty "for those in the Soviet Union who felt that such talks might be useful to convince the military that any serious discussion of limitations and possible reductions was in the Soviet interest."[208]

The Shelepin faction had to be purged from the leadership for the road to be cleared. Semichastny was removed from the KGB on 18 May. Then, first secretary of the Moscow city Party organization, the young militant Nikolai Yegorychev, spoke out at the Central Committee plenum after the Six Day War, expressing anxiety at the state of Soviet defenses. On 27 June he was promptly and unceremoniously replaced by the reliable Viktor Grishin.[209] Shelepin was moved over to Grishin's old job as head of the trades unions. On 26 September he lost his post as a secretary of the Central Committee.

Although initially skeptical about US proposals for banning ABM systems and by inclination suspicious of Washington, in 1968 Kosygin clashed with the Soviet military in commissioning a study of the arms race.[210] He was the first Politburo member to endorse strategic arms limitation that July and at a meeting in November requested with former Defense Secretary McNamara, he described disarmament as an "imperative necessity."[211] The opening of the treaty on the nonproliferation of nuclear weapons (NPT) for signature on 1 July 1968 finally paved the way for talks to be scheduled. The Czech crisis then delayed a decision on timing from Moscow. It was, however, on 20 August—the very eve of the Soviet invasion of Czechoslovakia—that Kosygin wrote to Johnson proposing talks in Geneva on 30 September. Although, perhaps, lightening the blow to East-West relations of restoring by force the dominance of Soviet socialism in the Warsaw Pact, it meant that Johnson was effectively in no position to sanction arms control negotiations before presidential elections that November. This delay gave Moscow more time to build up its offensive missile capability prior to talks. It therefore may have resulted from a compromise between doves and hawks to put off until tomorrow the disruptive bickering involved in hammering out an agreed negotiating position.

AN OPENING IN EUROPE

Concerns mirrored in Washington and Moscow about the need to slow down the spiraling arms race had been reinforced by mutual antipathy to Bonn's acquisition of nuclear weapons.[212] In this respect Bundy told Dobrynin on 23 November 1965 "that we understood the Soviet concern with Germany and that indeed we shared it."[213] A key incentive for Moscow was the MLF allowing Bonn access to atomic weapons without actually possessing them.[214] The skepticism of Bundy and others had already done much to undermine plans. Nonproliferation thus paved the way to a larger discussion of strategic nuclear issues and the potential of arms control.

China was of some significance. Worsening relations confronted Moscow with the prospect of a war on two fronts. Washington also attributed Russian willingness to limit the arms race to falling GNP and failure to decide on a five-year plan, which was, in 1967, already two years overdue. Kosygin, the leader most centrally concerned with the economy, told the Poles that the arms race and commitments overseas were stretching the economy too far.[215] He complained to Johnson of "the conflicting demands for resources" and that "he was under great pressure to devote more of the resources of his country to . . . peaceful pursuits, that many people came to him with requests for more money and that he was hard put to explain why not all these requests could be granted."[216] The same needs also militated in favor of détente in Europe.

Several years earlier Moscow had proposed a collective European security system encompassing "all the countries of Europe with the participation of the USA."[217] This originated with Polish Foreign Minister Adam Rapacki and reflected the longstanding aim to secure international recognition of the Polish-German frontier as immutable, not merely inviolable. Rapacki repeated the request at the UN on 14 December with a call for a European security conference.[218] The proposals were subsequently ratified by the political consultative committee of the Warsaw Pact on 19–20 January 1965, emphasizing their Polish origins.[219] The idea of a European security conference contained within it a trap, however: the GDR could expect to attend, yet the NATO Powers refused to recognize its existence. In other words the proposed conference was a roundabout way of securing recognition of East Germany. And since NATO could not commit to that without prior permission from Bonn, the initiative remained stillborn. Thus sooner or later Moscow had to win over Bonn, though without the disruptive tactics of Khrushchev: loose talk of another Rapallo merely unsettled Poland, against whom the original treaty (April 1922) had been aimed. Not until 1967, as we have seen, did the tide begin to turn.

France had always promised much but delivered little. Khrushchev brusquely dismissed de Gaulle as "king in [a] fairy tale with no clothes."[220] Illusions nevertheless arose, not entirely discouraged by de Gaulle and furthered somewhat overenthusiastically by senior members of the Soviet embassy in Paris, seduced by the great man and the resurgence of French prestige.[221] Ambassador Sergei Vinogradov, onetime professor of history before unexpected dispatch to Ankara in 1940, openly admired de Gaulle as "a very great man—even greater than Churchill."[222] Moreover, de Gaulle kicked the Americans out of France and abandoned NATO's permanent organization in 1966, but—despite the material costs to French interests (notably access to US intelligence)—this was no prelude to a Franco-Soviet pact.

The Franco-Soviet honeymoon ended badly when de Gaulle toured the USSR in the summer of 1966 with his tiresome reiteration of "La Russe" instead of "L'Union Soviètique." Even though France continued to display unusual solicitude for Soviet feelings,[223] de Gaulle was resigned to staying within NATO when the treaty came up for renewal in 1969, albeit outside the integrated military structure. Johnson acknowledged to Chancellor Kurt Kiesinger his appreciation of the fact that NATO could be abandoned only if the threat from Moscow were removed, and that this had yet to be done.[224] Thus the worst fears expressed by Rusk, refracted in Moscow's hopes, that "President de Gaulle's growing fear of Germany, plus his desire to cast France in a leading world position, may induce him to go to unusual lengths to reach an understanding with the Soviet Union" were never realized.[225] Indeed, de Gaulle began to follow Bonn's *Osteuropapolitik* in pursuing a policy of divide and rule between East Europeans and Russians. Speaking to the Polish assembly in September 1967, he insisted he had done all he could. "I left the military organs of NATO and now I expect that you, in your own sphere, will follow my example."[226]

Paris a disappointment, it made good sense turning to Bonn. Soviet policy had hitherto been almost entirely negative because the CDU sought reunification on its own terms: it denied recognition to East Berlin, ostracized any states that granted such recognition, and continued to argue for direct access to nuclear weapons. But this strategy proved fruitless. Hopes for reunification had to await détente.[227] Neither Adenauer nor Erhard accepted concessions to Moscow in advance of withdrawal from the "zone." Bonn had a veto over NATO recognition of the GDR. This resulted from being the army second only in size and effectiveness to the United States within the alliance. London was too fixated on entry into the European Economic Community (EEC) against French wishes to risk delicate relations with Bonn. Having failed to convince Kennedy to back out of Berlin, Moscow saw nothing to lose from encouraging de Gaulle to extract France from NATO. While this enticing illusion prevailed, it had little or no incentive to reach out to Bonn.

Andropov was keen to make progress in Germany, "the main strategic bridge-head of NATO" as well as the leading state, both economically and militarily, in Western Europe.[228] Germanists within the Foreign Ministry were not a speedy route to that objective. Prior to SALT they inched ahead under the leadership of Semyonov, while Gromyko focused on Washington. Falin said Gromyko scorned the Germans as about as important as "a Central African tribe."[229] When, for instance, Gromyko finally met former mayor of West Berlin Willy Brandt in October 1968, he appeared completely uninformed and relied entirely on Semyonov.[230] And this mattered, because the Erhard administration had unrolled a "peace initiative" for the mutual renunciation of force on 25 March 1966.[231] It was a counter to "communist propaganda against Germany,"[232] so it cannot have been a great surprise when the Soviet response of 17 May proved "intransigent and without any sign of a readiness to compromise."[233] But this habit of closing ranks whenever an initiative came in from Bonn ultimately proved unsustainable.

Due to Gromyko's characteristic stubbornness, Moscow insisted once again on its own terms: signature of the NPT; denuclearization of Germany (which meant withdrawal of US forward-based nuclear-capable systems); a European security conference; and a German peace settlement based on recognition of the territorial status quo, including recognition of West Berlin as an entity entirely independent of the Federal Republic. Bonn's access to nuclear weapons tended to arouse the sharpest feelings in Moscow. The USSR, Kosygin warned, "would use force to prevent it. This was a categorical position."[234] It is argued strongly by some that by rejecting Bonn's proposals for partnership in nuclear weapons and by demanding greater payments for military equipment pressed upon reluctant West Germans, Johnson inadvertently precipitated the downfall of Erhard after his visit to Washington at the end of September 1966. "Thus in 1966," recalls Helmut Schmidt, "the American lack of international experience and the egoistical lack of consideration on the part of the American President helped bring down the Chancellor and led to a change of coalition in Bonn."[235] Conditions were thus ripe for a fundamental reappraisal of Soviet-German relations.

Progress had to await emergence of the Grand Coalition under Kiesinger in December 1966. Even then attitudes such as Kosygin's required delicate footwork. For the first time the SPD was in office, though not fully in power, with Brandt as Foreign Minister. Born in Lübeck on 18 December 1913 as Herbert Ernst Karl Frahm to a working-class mother, Brandt joined the SPD during the battle against both the Nazis and the communists in 1930. From there he moved to the Trotskyist Socialist Workers' Party and fled to Norway in 1933, under the nom de guerre Willy Brandt. After detention by German occupation forces, who failed to identify him, he fled to Sweden and took Norwegian citizenship. He resumed German citizenship and rejoined the SPD after the war in Berlin, where he worked for Mayor Reuter. After his own service as mayor, he became chairman of the SPD in 1964. Described as "a massive fellow, about six foot one, about 215 pounds, handsome, possessed, standing very straight," he is said to have evinced no great intelligence but acted with "decency and integrity."[236] His great assets were charm—a great man for the ladies—and toughness.

The arrival of the socialists in office caused a stir in Moscow, which now divided as to how to proceed. The new State Secretary at the Ausamt, Klaus Schütz, "said that the Federal Government were determined to see what could be done in Eastern Europe. Their immediate task was to convince the Soviet Union that the improvement of West German relations with the Soviet Union's European allies was not directed against Moscow and also to prevent Ulbricht lining up the other Warsaw Pact members behind his own hard line."[237] To avert a split, what Brandt and Kiesinger had agreed upon was to pursue diplomatic relations with Romania and Czechoslovakia, in expectation of isolating the GDR within the Warsaw Pact. Here Romania presented little problem, in that its dictator Nicolae Ceauşescu, rather like de Gaulle in respect of the Americans, welcomed any and every opportunity to spit in the face of Moscow. Stalinism at home and nationalism abroad was uncomfortable but ultimately acceptable to the Kremlin; the reverse, as the Prague Spring came to show, was anathema. The key to the success of the Eastern policy did not lie here, however. "Importance was attached to approaching Czechoslovakia simultaneously in order to break into the more inflexible northern tier within the Warsaw Pact.

While no one in Germany would oppose diplomatic relations with Rumania," Schütz pointed out, "the government would have serious differences from the Sudeten Germans and others over Czechoslovakia. This was one reason why they did not want discussion in the Cabinet now."[238]

A Russian diplomat, Aleksandr' Zinchuk, said Moscow was waiting with an open mind to see what the Grand Coalition signified. Ulbricht would, he acknowledged with an ironical laugh, have his own views. But Germany "would no doubt be re-unified one day in a federation or in some other way, but in the meantime there were two German states."[239] The first fruit of the new *Osteuropapolitik* appeared with diplomatic recognition of the Federal Republic by Romania (1967). Hitherto France had made it a working assumption that the states of Eastern Europe could be lured away from Moscow. Couve de Murville had assured Rusk that "these countries as a whole now have more freedom to act."[240] Yet France had nothing to offer as an incentive. Bonn, however, now had the largest and fastest growing economy in the region. But the elephant could scarcely move in the room without causing alarm.

The consequences of the new *Osteuropapolitik* were predictable. "The Zone [the GDR], frightened by the success of our East European policy, threatened by isolation, at first placed on the defensive, has begun a counteroffensive," noted Egon Bahr.[241] As ambassador-at-large, and later head of policy planning at the Ausamt, this man—viewed by Moscow as a German Talleyrand—now ran Brandt's office. Much affected by the Berlin uprising and the refusal of the allies to act, a feeling reinforced by the allied reaction to erection of the Berlin Wall, it was Bahr who conceived and enunciated a novel philosophy on 15 July 1963: that of *Wandel durch Annäherung*—change through rapprochement: "The prerequisites for reunification," he had told the Evangelical Academy in Tutzing, "can only be worked out with the Soviet Union. They are not to be found in East Berlin, nor against the Soviet Union, nor without it."[242] Only in 1969 with a new government could this fundamental truth at last fully implemented by Brandt, though Bahr insists that between himself and Brandt "there were no differences of opinion."[243]

Brandt had also made informal overtures to the GDR in the first half of 1966 on the issues of human exchange and technology that encouraged him. Indeed, he was struck by just how porous the East German monolith turned out to be: "Behind this monolithic facade, there are groups and particular interests," Brandt marveled.[244] And this was critical to his belief that inner-German relations could be improved through détente. Dominated by Christian Democrats, Bonn was, however, still unwisely assuming that better relations with Moscow were not the absolute prerequisite to progress in Eastern Europe. This policy had to be pursued to destruction before an alternative was accepted. Bahr now moved on Prague. Czechoslovakia was a crucial link in the northern tier of the Warsaw Pact. It was also the country that had suffered most from sovietization since 1948, since its technological level before absorption into the Eastern bloc placed it on a par with Germany.

East Berlin was disturbed that "the various tactical and demagogic maneuvers of West German imperialism were not always sufficiently speedily recognized. . . . The Czech reaction to the concrete actions of the Bonn government in the form of its 'new Ostpolitik' together with the Czech interest in improving relations with West Germany, above all in the economic field, offers thereby from the West German side a starting point for sustaining it expansionist aims and in pursuit of their gradual realisation."[245] The results were inevitably disappointing because Moscow also loomed in the background ready to veto progress. On 12–13 June 1967 willingness to reach an accommodation proved insufficient to surmount the distance still separating the two sides.[246] The invasion of Czechoslovakia in August 1968 then demonstrated conclusively that a policy of divide and rule would fail.

CZECHOSLOVAKIA 1968: ILLUSIONS DISPELLED

In Moscow reasons of state had yet to predominate. The "reflex of international duty" weighed heavily on policy making.[247] And Brezhnev was not inclined to drop his guard: "The reasons that the imperialists do not dare attack Czechoslovakia, Poland, and the other socialist countries, is that they are aware of the immense military strength of the Soviet Union," he insisted. "The Americans leave in peace those countries with whom the Soviet Union has concluded a treaty because they know only too well that we are superior. They constantly talk about a balance of forces, but they are fully aware of the actual disposition of forces."[248] This was stated in Prague the day after Brezhnev arrived, on 9 December 1967. He had been called in by First Secretary and President of the Republic Antonín Novotný to halt a revolt within the Central Committee.[249] He soon left in despair: "It appears . . . that the main cause of these difficulties is the fact that . . . Novotný is incapable of cooperating with the comrades," Brezhnev told Hungarian leader János Kádár on 13 December.[250] The issues at stake were not merely economic (Czech backwardness relative to its prewar status and therefore every national expectation) but also ethnic, in that Novotný had reneged on Slovak autonomy and was attempting to marginalize Slovak politicians.

Moreover, under Novotný Prague had, since Khrushchev's removal, behaved with a degree of independence that irritated Moscow. Discussions had been opened with West Germany for financial credits despite Bonn's nonrecognition of East Germany and its continued refusal to abrogate the Munich agreement of September 1938 that had stripped Czechoslovakia of the Sudetenland. CIA learned that in the summer of 1967 Novotný also pleaded with Moscow to cut the Czech share of aid to the Arab states. Moreover the regime had decreed that Czechs no longer needed to study Russian. And Washington also understood that the majority of the Party favored granting diplomatic recognition to Bonn.[251] Novotný thus looked like he was moving in the direction of Ceauşescu, combining authoritarian personal rule over Party and state with an increasingly assertive nationalism. But what was tolerated in the Balkans was less acceptable on the front line facing Bonn.

Slovak, Alexander Dubček, replaced Czech, Novotný, as First Secretary. Dubček had grown up in the USSR, his father's place of exile, and was therefore regarded with a degree of trust. In Moscow, however, he met blank incomprehension when he told Soviet leaders of plans for renewal and revival.[252] Brezhnev cautioned: "We are adamant that we cannot lose the GDR and that we cannot fritter away the results of World War II; we must insist on stable European borders. These principles cannot be abandoned in exchange for money."[253] At a meeting with the aging and increasingly reactionary Gomułka on 7 February he was warned "that all this [Czech reform] would bring about uncontrollable political consequences. It could undermine the position of the Party."[254]

On 9 February *Rudé Právo* published an article by senior member of the Presidium and Dubček supporter Josef Smrkovský on the conclusions of the Central Committee plenum. Here Smrkovský irritated Moscow by announcing the "search for a Czechoslovak road to socialism" and talking of "equal rights principles" in relations between socialist countries.[255] This prompted Soviet ambassador Stepan Chervonenko to claim in a dispatch that Smrkovský was calling for a "more independent" foreign policy, putting relations with the USSR on "an entirely new basis."[256] At a meeting in Dresden scheduled for leaders of the Warsaw Pact to discuss economic cooperation, Brezhnev launched the accusation that "a wave of public and political activities of an entire group or of entire centers has come into existence which has brought the entire public life of Czechoslovakia to counterrevolution." Among those assembled only Kádár was unwilling to use the term "counterrevolution."[257]

What the KGB feared was a "soft" takeover "by dissidents and bourgeois elements."[258] The brunt of the attack, however, was led from East Berlin and Warsaw. If Prague expected, because of the past, to find Gomułka as understanding as Kádár, it was to be sorely disappointed. Unrest led by students was shaking the ground in Poland. During demonstrations signs appeared with a pun on the word "wait" [*czeka*] also sounding like "Czech": "Poland is awaiting its own Dubček" (*Polska czeka na swego Dubczeka*). Gomułka took the view that Czechoslovakia was already en route to becoming "a bourgeois republic." He "once again expressed the need for us to intervene immediately, arguing that one cannot be an indifferent observer when counterrevolutionary plans are beginning to be implemented in Czechoslovakia."[259]

On 8 April a directive to General Vasilii Margelov, commander of the paratroops, stated that "the Soviet Union and the other socialist countries, true to their international duty and the Warsaw Pact, must send in their forces to render assistance to the Czechoslovakian people's army in defense of the motherland from the dangers hanging over it."[260] Yet Prague continued to act as if military intervention by their allies were impossible. Bahr paid a visit to Prague in secret from 17–19 April, raising the prospect of a treaty renouncing the use of force (as proposed to Moscow). "By concluding such treaties, the FRG would in fact take a positive and sufficiently convincing stand regarding the existing borders of Europe, including the Oder-Neisse border as well as the borders between the FRG and the GDR."[261]

Bahr was thereby pressing Prague to open diplomatic relations beforehand with Bonn in a blatant threat to the cohesion of Moscow's negotiating position. The offer was bound to evoke suspicion given Bonn's *Osteuropapolitik*. Dubček's subsequent claim to Moscow that the Czechs "decided not to receive him" (Bahr) will not have convinced them of anything other than his deviousness, since Russia had its own sources.[262] Nor did his explanation that in offering trade credits Bonn was merely looking to open new markets ring true to Soviet ears. "There's no such thing as a free lunch," Podgorny retorted.[263] On or around 20 May Moscow moved one step closer to intervention. The Politburo set up a group of five chaired by Brezhnev—Andropov, Gromyko, Grechko, and Suslov. They in turn created a working group of subordinates: Vice Admiral Leonid Bekrenev (deputy head of military intelligence, the GRU), Blatov, Shishlin, and Sergei Kondrashev (deputy head of KGB foreign intelligence).[264]

"We believe," Brezhnev told Dubček, "that the events at present are being organized and directed by forces linked to the West. The thread that controls them clearly leads to France, to West Germany, in a word, you yourselves know where."[265] Anxiety about subversion led the KGB on 8 May 1968 to issue a directive highlighting the fight against "ideological diversion" by foreign intelligence as one of the most important tasks of state security.[266] Kosygin, for one, was too intelligent, however, to believe claims about German spies. It was clear to him that Dubček and his followers were seeking to establish social democracy, "something along the lines of Austria."[267] He had no illusions, however. Brezhnev continued to try to persuade Dubček to purge his Party. But procrastination and deceit became too blatant to ignore.[268] Chervonenko wanted Soviet troops on exercise in Czechoslovakia withdrawn, but the majority attending the Politburo objected, influenced among others by Andropov. Moreover, Gromyko argued that time was working against them. "It is now clear, obvious, that we cannot avoid military intervention." Kosygin shared this view.[269]

On 18 August, after months of delay prompted by concerns to obtain signature of the nuclear nonproliferation treaty and agreement from the Americans on strategic arms limitation talks, plus the need to convince a grudging Brezhnev that no alternative existed,[270] the Politburo finally took the decision to invade.[271] "This decision will be carried out," Grechko was quoted as saying, "even if it leads to a third world war."[272] It was a massive operation codenamed "Dunai" (Danube). The Czech armed forces were not to be trusted. General Miroslav Vacek, minister of defense in 1989, recalls that as a young captain he and his fellow officers were also influenced by public opinion "marked by the striving for the freedom of the country and its citizens." Since he and his comrades believed "that our society could sort out its contradictions independently," the Russian-led invasion came as "a shock."[273]

The first KGB special forces were delivered to Prague on troop transports the night of 20–21 August. The basic military objectives were rapidly achieved. By 11:00 p.m. on 20 August units of the Soviet 24th air army had taken the main airports in Czechoslovakia and arranged for the arrival of hundreds of Antonov transporters loaded with men and tanks. Soviet forces also began entering Czech territory from the north, the south, and the east and blocked off the border with West Germany. By the morning of 21 August the entire communications system was under Soviet control.[274]

A NEW OSTPOLITIK

Sir Percy Cradock noted the shock the invasion produced in military and intelligence circles: "The fact that the Russians could achieve tactical surprise within this framework of strategic alert and launch major forces at such short notice was worrying and raised serious questions, not only of Soviet sincerity in the matter of détente but also of NATO's readiness and the efficacy of the Alliance's warning system."[275] In Prague bitter despondency took hold. "Which is the most neutral country in the world today?" asked a Czech diplomat. "Czechoslovakia—because its government doesn't even dare to intervene in its own affairs."[276] Moscow felt it could live with this. "At the time we were not afraid of taking action against counterrevolution in Czechoslovakia . . . we managed to survive," Brezhnev remarked with sangfroid half a dozen years later.[277] Success so easily obtained inevitably encouraged a certain arrogance.

The subsequent haughty assertion on 12 November 1968 of Moscow's "right to intervene, by force if necessary, to protect socialism"—penned, it is said, by Gromyko[278]—shocked those who hoped that détente would break down the opposing blocs, that Soviet-style socialism had the capacity to mellow into social democracy and allow for the free choice of government in Central and Eastern Europe. Crucially, it also rendered the Grand Coalition's *Osteuropapolitik* entirely inoperable. Indeed, the secret Soviet assessment drew a much starker picture than that:

> In respect of Czechoslovakia, the Warsaw Pact demonstrated . . . the ability at comparatively short notice to put into effect successfully operations on a major strategic scale that, on Bonn's evaluation, NATO's military organization is currently incapable of doing. The leadership of the FRG was particularly alarmed by the fact that the forces of five countries could enter the CzUSR [Czech Union of Socialist Republics] in a situation where the USA and other allies of West Germany did nothing and were passive and that to NATO as a whole such an action turned out to be, in respect of timing and effectiveness in implementation, completely unexpected. Judging from everything, in the first days after the forces of allied states entered CzUSR, the possibility was not excluded in Bonn's political and military circles of the Soviet Union taking certain measures even in relation to the FRG itself, as the country rendering the most active support to counterrevolution in Czechoslovakia.[279]

Although claiming no change of principle in Bonn's foreign policy, Moscow noted "certain correctives": "In Bonn it is recognized that the entry of allied states' forces into the CzUSR [Czechoslovakia] dealt a serious blow to the plans of the FRG, which aimed at the internal disintegration of the socialist countries, at wrenching them away from the Soviet Union and isolating the GDR; that, as a result of this, the possibilities of the 'new Ostpolitik' have been significantly reduced."[280] Thus whereas the invasion set back the clock on US-Soviet détente, it could plausibly be presented as having advanced the process of European détente. Ponomarev later argued in private that "had there been no Czechoslovakia, there would have been no Brandt in Germany, nor Nixon in Moscow, nor détente."[281]

Soviet leaders nevertheless worried lest the new *Ostpolitik* become more effective by becoming more flexible. The most gloomy prognosis was that "the rulers of the FRG, including the right-wing leadership of the SPD, as before are counting on the fact that links between socialist countries will gradually weaken, that in the final analysis nationalist tendencies will come out on top in their policies, that one by one socialist countries will be 'neutralized' and move away from the Soviet Union. As a result, sooner or later, the situation will arise when the USSR, with China to the rear, will see the benefit of resolving the German problem on FRG terms." In the short term Moscow faced the prospect that Bonn would activate a greater degree of military readiness within NATO "and sabotage the treaty on the nonproliferation of nuclear weapons"[282]

The invasion shattered the Grand Coalition and, in combination with a generational shift to the left, eventually led to severe punishment for the CDU at the polls. In May 1969 London noted "a growing feeling in Germany that the Federal Republic must at the least come to de facto terms with the existence of East Germany."[283] "After the invasion of Czechoslovakia," Bahr recalled, "the CDU's ability to make a real advance dropped to next to nothing and became less substantial among the population as the elections of 1969 approached."[284] The CDU, the CSU, and the rising minority party of neo-Nazis (the NDP) were the target. For its part Moscow was determined to do all it could to encourage the GDR to exert "such influence on the outcome of the election campaign in the FRG as to weaken these parties and prevent them from taking the dominant position in the political arena and suppressing the more realistically inclined groups." Moscow felt it had, indeed, already had a salutary effect on the mentality in Bonn. A memorandum from Moscow to East Berlin underlined the fact that "the forms and methods of struggle between socialist and capitalist states are changing. Our defense capability is severely curtailing the military influence of imperialism over the countries of the Warsaw Pact."[285] A rising young Germanist at the third European department of the Soviet Foreign Ministry, Yuli Kvitsinsky, was explicit: "The situation in respect of Germany after the Czech events became ever more favorable in the sense that Bonn and the West as a whole increasingly came to the firm conclusion that they must come to terms in Europe and reach some kind of détente on the basis of recognizing the status quo."[286]

An electoral setback for the CDU (193 seats) and CSU (49 seats) as against the SPD (224 seats) on 28 September 1969 made possible the formation of a new coalition between the SPD and the FDP (30 seats) on 22 October. Foreign Minister Brandt had proposed a nonaggression pact to Moscow on 3 July, but Gromyko thought it "not very realistic."[287] On the other hand, Andropov was emphatic in briefing Vyacheslav ("Slava") Kevorkov at the Lubyanka: "We have to build our home in Europe . . . and here there is no way of avoiding Germany."[288] He wanted a back channel to Bonn that circumvented the foreign ministries who would only slow things up. Gromyko's people were moving in the same direction—notably Falin, head of the third European department—

but under the minister's nervous leadership it would take too long. With Brandt now Chancellor and Bahr, several days later, States Secretary at the Federal Chancellery, the wheels turned swiftly. (Scheel of the FDP became Foreign Minister but effectively foreign policy was made by Brandt under Bahr's close advice.) Bahr was similarly seeking a back channel: "a tremendously useful instrument to gain trust . . . to say what one wants, what one doesn't want and what one really wants without prestige."[289] In Moscow Bahr was given the code-name "David," later more affectionately, "Dodik."[290]

Even before the elections the logjam was broken on 12 September when Semyonov handed the West German chargé d'affaires a note agreeing to a proper dialogue.[291] Although the note was a response to soundings from the United States, Britain, and France, its timing and content were primed for events in Bonn. It spoke of the renunciation of force between the FRG and GDR as well as between the FRG and the USSR and respect for the "special position of West Berlin."[292] Bonn naturally noted the connection between growing alarm in Moscow at Beijing's growing power and the "heightened intensity" of Russia's search for full recognition of its sphere of influence in Europe. The "careful" approach of the Kremlin to the issue of Berlin was symptomatic.[293] Moscow was already shifting ground in anticipation of Brandt's victory.

Bahr laid out his notion of a package of negotiations encompassing the USSR, Poland, the GDR, Czechoslovakia, and the status of West Berlin. Negotiations with Eastern Europe would be set within the context of what the USSR would "tolerate." For these reasons Bonn would have "to strive for an improvement in relations with the Soviet Union."[294] These proposals were outlined by Bahr to Kissinger who was "very mistrustful." "I have not come here to Washington in order to consult but to brief you," he told Kissinger. "We know what we want and we are going to do it!" As he admitted later, the Americans could have made problems, but they did not.[295] A back channel was set up between them to ensure no misunderstandings,[296] though when negotiations moved rapidly forward in the following spring Kissinger did express fears lest Bonn concede "essentials."[297] Some feared "the beginning of a possible national German foreign policy. We shared that suspicion at first," he later acknowledged.[298]

Bahr knew to expect that not all would run smoothly in the East. Sharp differences were apparent between members of the Warsaw Pact over dealing with Bonn: Ulbricht was hostile, but Poland and Czechoslovakia were eager to improve relations. And Romania wished to overthrow the postwar division of Europe entirely.[299] Yet in contrast to the previous *Osteuropapolitik*, the new *Ostpolitik* followed Bahr's conception to the letter. It was explicitly focused on Russia rather than its satellites. "The USSR and the FRG have no frontiers in common, but the USSR is interested in all frontiers," Gromyko insisted.

Ambassador Allardt noted: Moscow was bent on "the consolidation and legalization of the hegemonic position of the Soviet Union in Eastern Europe."[300] Gromyko had also instructed him firmly that "the FRG's conception of representing all Germans must be dropped."[301] Brandt's statement, a week after assuming office, that Bonn was now prepared to sign the NPT had removed further uncertainty in Moscow. But Brandt also insisted on sustaining the ultimate prospect of German reunification (although preferring the term "unification" in order not to arouse anxious memories of the first three empires): "It is a question of leaving a door open," he said.[302]

"There will be no European security conference without the Federal Republic. This is our lever," Bahr pointed out.[303] He met Gromyko in Moscow on 30 January 1970. "Détente in Europe without a positive stance from the Federal Republic would be very difficult," Bahr insisted. He anticipated an understanding between Bonn and Moscow, an agreement between Bonn and Warsaw recognizing the Oder-Neisse frontier, and the establishment of diplomatic relations between the FRG and GDR. But he also emphasized that Berlin had to contribute to détente in Europe: "Berlin must not remain an island of Cold War. That is the main thing," whether it was settled by the wartime allies or "by the Germans themselves." The latter was bound to set off a rebuttal from Gromyko. The West Germans, he insisted, should have no say at all on West Berlin. "You want to negotiate directly with the GDR, to expound your position, but," he warned, "the fundamentals of the position also interest us, and you know why. Do you see how contradictory FRG policy, your policy, is?"[304]

The marathon of negotiations began—Bahr later estimated the meetings with Gromyko to number somewhere between fifty-two and fifty-six.[305] A high point was reached on 6 February when Bahr outlined the details of his "package." The presentation and debate continued relentlessly for four hours and forty minutes in English. "These negotiations were complicated from beginning to end. On each clause, each formulation in the treaty there was a long and intense struggle and, of course, a struggle not only at the negotiating table," Brezhnev recalled.[306] Bahr was pressing the pace relentlessly in order to secure a bilateral agreement before talks on a European security conference snatched his negotiating position from under him by general recognition of the territorial status quo. He argued that Bonn recognize the inviolability of the territorial status quo and therefore recognize the existence of the GDR until peaceful change was feasible. But he also insisted that Bonn would nevertheless retain its legal claims to the whole of Germany.

"The hope was advanced from the Soviet side that Bahr reconsider the developing situation and, if it were true that the FRG really wished to come to terms, then he should seek out within the West German position the possibility of moving closer to reality." They met again four days later, and Moscow once again insisted Bahr withdraw his "reservations" or a deal would prove impossible.[307] "As Gromyko refused to give way, Bahr was given to regular outbursts of hysteria in front of Falin. It appears that, faced with this situation, Falin, with the help of the KGB, gradually obtained access to Brezhnev, through whom influence could be exerted on the minister in his rigidity. . . . In those days Falin more than once said: if the minister is not restrained, he may through his hard-line posture bring negotiations to a dead end."[308]

In the hope of breaking the deadlock, Bahr met Kosygin on 13 February and confronted him on the issue of potential German unity. "The unification of Germany," Bahr asserted, "is the business of the future. When this takes place—in 10–15 years or within several generations—now no one can answer. The current government of the FRG, however, cannot tell the people that a rapprochement with the Soviet Union has been attained at the price of the final division of the country. It is necessary, Bahr insisted, to allow the Germans a unification with which all Germany's neighbors are agreed, which would not lead to destruction of the balance of power in Europe and would not present a threat to the security of anyone." This prompted resistance from Kosygin. "Attempts to force the GDR into concessions would be adventurism. Any such attempt could not produce anything good in the past and will not succeed in the future."[309] Kosygin could sound tough, but he was much more restrained than Gromyko, who, in one five-hour marathon, expressed an "unusually acidic" reaction to Bahr's views on the question of Berlin.[310] Kosygin could take the larger view. He was a realist: "The central problem for détente in Europe is relations between the Soviet Union and the Federal Republic of Germany," he readily acknowledged.[311] He hinted, for example, at other possibilities by playing the anti-American card, pointing out "the need for the FRG to conduct a more independent policy and not to look all the time to the West."[312]

Agreement was finally reached after heated debate in which Andropov and Gromyko held to a common line. (Gromyko had only been brought on board after his officials let him insist that the letter accompanying the treaty which spoke of possible German unity would have no legal status as part of the treaty.)[313] This was apparently Falin's ingenious device.[314]

East Berlin was unhappy, however, because Bonn refused to concede explicit recognition of the GDR in the treaty. Brezhnev had to telephone Ulbricht to explain that nothing could be done.[315] Bonn did, however, commit to a separate agreement concerning negotiations with the GDR, Poland, and Czechoslovakia (which they envisaged anyway) to facilitate the entry of the GDR as well as

the FRG into the UN and the convening of an all-European security conference.[316] They had, after all, finally agreed to recognize the postwar borders of
Europe as inviolable and to accept the existence of the GDR, though still as
part of the German nation. And they effectively made implementation of the
Soviet-German treaty dependent on a Four-Power agreement on the status of
West Berlin. Yet even those predisposed to settle by compromise, such as Kosygin, found it hard to overcome their prejudices. Brandt arrived in Moscow to
initial the treaty on 11 August. As he landed, Kosygin asked Falin what the mark-
ings on the aircraft meant: "Air force," said Falin. "Did Adenauer also fly in
[1955] on a Wehrmacht plane?" parried Kosygin. He was then duly corrected—
"Luftwaffe," not "Wehrmacht." Undeterred, however, he reflected: "The Germans are amazing [*Chudnye nemtsy*]. Why do they love playing soldiers?"[317]

The treaty affirmed the inviolability but not the permanence of postwar frontiers and the territorial integrity of all states in Europe; it made no explicit reference to the status of West Berlin; and Bonn's aspirations to future unity were
restricted to a letter from Foreign Minister Scheel to Gromyko devoid of legal
authority.[318] Moscow continued to underline the importance of the GDR in occupying "a vital position" in the socialist camp. And Brezhnev had been blunt
in enforcing the new line. He warned Honecker, Ulbricht's heir apparent: "I
often say to you, Erich: do not forget, the GDR cannot exist without us, without
the Soviet Union, its power and strength. Without us there is no GDR."[319]

Negotiations toward a final Quadripartite agreement settling the autonomous status of West Berlin (in which Bahr and Brandt also played a role behind the scenes, infuriating Ulbricht) ended in a treaty on 3 September 1971,[320]
supplemented on 3 June 1972 by a final protocol that brought into effect inner-
German settlements involving both the GDR and FRG.[321] Together with the
Polish–West German treaty of 7 December 1970, recognizing the Oder-Neisse
border between the GDR and Poland,[322] the Basic treaty between Bonn and
East Berlin on 21 December 1972,[323] and the Czech-West German agreement
of 11 December 1973,[324] the entire package amounted to a settlement of the territorial status quo for the first time since the end of World War II. Throughout,
Bonn tried to hold ratification of the Moscow treaty hostage to a satisfactory
and final settlement of West Berlin, but finally it had to concede in May 1972.[325]
Only Washington could secure that objective.

TROUBLE IN POLAND

Even as negotiations proceeded for a West German treaty with Poland, the
latter began to succumb to the inevitable consequences of economic retarda-

tion, accelerated by a fierce winter and a summer drought that provoked strikes and demonstrations in Katowice into the autumn. After food price hikes dockers erupted in unrest on 14 December 1970 at the shipyards in Gdańsk, Sopot, Gdynia, and, two days later, in Szczecin. Whereas students and intellectuals could be suppressed in the streets in open violence, a party that ruled in the name of the workers was not to find it so easy to apply such methods to its nominal guardians. Moscow trod carefully throughout. The Politburo had sent a letter to Gomułka warning not to use force against the workers; "but," as Suslov noted later, "in fact our voice was not listened to, the Polish leadership then resorted to arms."[326] After draconian measures on 17 December Gomułka was soon forced to resign in favor of Edward Gierek three days later. Food prices were immediately frozen for two years. Yet this was but a taste of things to come. From 16 to 19 December the Soviet Politburo was in session. Brezhnev, now deeply anxious, introduced the Polish crisis. Before this there had been much reading of diplomatic and Party dispatches, news reports, and evaluations of the situation in Poland: "All of this alarmed us considerably," noted Pyotr Shelest in his diary.[327] Shelest's reading of the situation was that Party and government had failed to work with the people and "satisfy the lawful demands of the people—the working class."[328] In this Shelest, an opponent of détente, also spied the sinister hand of NATO.

"There is no doubt that the imperialists' intelligence services, with backing from domestic reactionaries, have attempted in Poland to take revenge for defeat in Czechoslovakia," Shelest editorialized, while acknowledging that "there is more than enough 'fuel' for this in Poland itself." The grievances initially concerned food prices but spread to encompass attacks on the Party and Gomułka himself. Shops were robbed, policemen and secret policemen killed, regional Party headquarters burned to the ground. But there were deaths on both sides. As protest grew, it also became more political. By the time of the Politburo meeting one key demand called for complete freedom of the press. It rapidly became clear to Shelest that Brezhnev would use the occasion to dispose of Gomułka, whose manner, not least during the Czech events, had caused him considerable personal grief.[329]

On the telephone to Gomułka during the Politburo sessions, Brezhnev suggested restraint. Gomułka was incensed. "There can be no question of sorting this out politically," he insisted. "It is impossible to retreat and, if they set fire to regional committees, then measures have to be taken. To countermand our decisions, as you, comrade Brezhnev, recommend, means acknowledging the defeat of the Party." And when Brezhnev suggested he write a letter to Warsaw to express these views, Gomułka lost his temper entirely: "And what can you write? We are the people really responsible and it is clearer to us what has to be done in our own country." Gomułka was certain this was a counterrevolution, as a result of which Poland could leave the Warsaw Pact. He could not understand why Brezhnev was "so blatantly and tactlessly interfering in Poland's internal affairs," pointing out that "you have enough in your own country to think about and busy yourself with; we can take care of ourselves." In that case there was no question of sustaining the regime in Poland, Brezhnev retorted; did he seriously expect Moscow to bring in troops to establish order? It would be "better for the safety of the work of socialism for you to step down from the post of First Secretary of the PUWP." Gomułka was duly relieved of his duties at a Central Committee plenum on 21 December.[330]

NIXON'S EXPECTATIONS

Détente in Europe was incomplete without Washington. From Nixon, Moscow expected "a tougher and less flexible" regime that would essentially continue past policy. In a carefully balanced assessment delivered to fraternal Party leaders in Eastern and Central Europe, Moscow stated that it expected Nixon would be prepared to improve relations with Beijing "as a counterweight to the USSR" but not at the cost of "major concessions." And to the degree that the United States managed to extract itself from Vietnam, they expected further reinforcement of NATO at the expense of its European members; a "far-reaching rapprochement with the FRG"; an improvement in relations with post–de Gaulle France; and a certain cooling of the special relationship with Britain. Western Europe would face harder bargaining on tariffs with the Americans. In the Middle East they foresaw better relations with the Arabs. In Africa and Latin America they expected greater emphasis on backing military regimes and a hardening of pressure on Cuba. Moscow also expected greater attention to the USSR and increased expenditure on new weaponry, "especially if the war in Vietnam were over."

"Taking into account sentiments enumerated," Moscow reasoned, "it appears that under Nixon it will be more difficult to obtain agreement on the weighty questions of disarmament, although he will enter into negotiations on these questions, taking everything into account, this will be in order to sound out our positions and to pay his dues to the public opinion of his country." Nixon would nevertheless recognize Russian importance "in the resolution of international problems or at least in relaxing tension around them (Vietnam, Middle East, etc.)," not least in the hope of a second term. Another plus was the expectation that Nixon would seek to cut the mounting tax bill, and that could only be done by cutting the military budget. Thus Moscow hoped these sentiments would offset the obvious desire "to hold back the economic growth of the Soviet Union by the arms race." "In short, the American economy, for all its strength, has its limits." Lastly the Russians accepted the evaluation of those close to Nixon, that, although with a strongly right-wing and anticommunist past, he was deep down "quite a cautious man, disinclined to precipitate international crises, understanding, like his predecessors in the White House, the need to sustain a certain degree of mutual understanding with the USSR and to follow a course that would make possible the avoidance of nuclear war with it."[331]

MOSCOW AND BEIJING EMBATTLED

Soon after Nixon's inauguration a brief but bloody border war broke out between China and Russia. This limited Moscow's room for maneuver, wrecked any cooperation in the vital shipments of aid to Hanoi, and raised false hopes that the terms for peace in Vietnam could be obtained short of open defeat. The frontiers between China and the Russian empire were fixed by treaty and the threat of force. Although Lenin had declared these to be unequal treaties, once Soviet Russia became more preoccupied with security than revolution Moscow did all it could to ensure treaty observance and respect as the legatee of empire. On 25 January 1969 China prepared a plan of attack on border guards (KGB) patrolling Damansky/Zhenbao island on the river Ussuri that separated China from the USSR. This island lay to the Chinese side of the river that formed the boundary, as the maps of 1861 make clear and as has since been officially acknowledged.[332]

The plan was confirmed by China's general staff on 19 February. Mao named the operation "Retribution," which gives one a clear idea of its purpose. On the night of 1–2 March some three hundred soldiers traversed the Ussuri to the island and dug in. They had "special equipment and special training," according to Chinese military sources.[333] On engaging an investigating patrol, reinforcements came in from the Chinese side and left thirty-one Russians dead and fourteen wounded. The disfigured corpse of one prisoner was thrown from a helicopter onto Soviet territory. Moscow immediately issued a note of protest, to which Beijing failed to react. Moscow sent in more troops but further fighting forced them off the island. Only when the 135th motorized rifle division arrived did the balance shift. They opened up on the island with a heavy artillery barrage wiping out almost all Chinese and took possession with only seven Russians dead and nine wounded as against some six hundred losses to the adversary. The ensuing bloodshed led Beijing to cut off the direct communication line by phone to the Kremlin[334] and prompted rumors of a possible preemptive strike by Soviet forces. Mao called a halt on 15 March.[335]

The fighting ended by 16 March. Thereafter Moscow reinforced the borders with divisions of tanks. About a week later the Beijing embassy received a telegram from Moscow suggesting the evacuation back home of women (thirty) and children (five) from the compound. Although in no hurry to comply, on the grounds that he did not expect war, chargé d'affaires Alexei Elizavetin sent in the requisite passports to China's Foreign Ministry for processing exit visas. The Chinese were visibly disturbed.[336] In turn embassy personnel endured the kind of harassment and indignities experienced by Western missions during the so-called Cultural Revolution. Summer saw the political temperature rise with Soviet maneuvers encompassing the Far Eastern, the Trans-Baikal, Siberian, and Central Asian military districts.[337] Moscow did not believe Beijing was prepared to risk "a major war" but would instead create "endless armed clashes" for political purposes.[338] However, it is apparent from the circulation of various *ballons d'essai* that some Russians contemplated the prospect of a drastic solution. Arkady Shevchenko, a senior diplomat who worked directly for Gromyko and acted as go-between with Andropov, asserts that Grechko wanted very much to get rid of the threat from China "once and for all" (a colleague of Shevchenko attended the Politburo where this was said).[339]

In late March or early April visitors to Boston, including Gvishiani, suggested that China's nuclear facilities were a target for Moscow. And at the World Communist Conference in June a senior Soviet figure asserted that the USSR could destroy China but would not do so except in extremis.[340] On 18 August Boris Davydov, second secretary at the embassy in Washington, took lunch with William Stearman, special assistant for North Vietnam at INR. "Davydov asked point blank what the US would do if the Soviet Union attacked and destroyed China's nuclear installations." Two objectives would thereby be served: "First, the Chinese nuclear threat would be eliminated for decades. Second, such a blow would so weaken and discredit the 'Mao clique' that dissident senior officers and Party cadres could gain ascendency in Peking." He went on to rephrase his question: "What would the US do if Peking called for US assistance in the event Chinese nuclear installations were attacked by us? Wouldn't the US try to take advantage of this situation?" Thus, on the one hand, Moscow wanted to know whether they would find Washington sympathetic. On the other hand, Davydov echoed fears of a Sino-American détente followed by entente. "Specifically he wanted to know if recent US moves to improve relations with the CPR were aimed at an ultimate Sino-American collusion against the USSR."[341]

Russian attempts to draw China to the negotiating table failed until Kosygin headed the delegation to attend Ho's funeral early in September. There he asked his Chinese counterpart, Chou, for talks. Disappointed, Kosygin flew back home. But at 10:00 p.m. on 11 September Elizavetin was called into the Chinese Foreign Ministry and told Chou had agreed to meet Kosygin at Beijing airport. Kosygin, still en route to Moscow, flew back to Beijing from Tashkent. Talks thus opened that night with the Soviet ambassador present. Kosygin emphasized that a Sino-Soviet conflict played into the hands of their enemies. Chou appeared to agree on the need "to reduce tension and not give imperialism the possibility of taking pleasure from the complications in Sino-Soviet relations." But the central question was that of borders. Chou suggested the areas be demilitarized. He went on to express concern at the rumors of a possible preemptive strike against Chinese nuclear installations. Everything should instead be resolved through negotiation. Both assured one another that neither side was interested in war. But Kosygin refused to admit to "regions in dispute" between the two parties. "Treaties exist between our countries," he insisted, "and they must be respected." And as to Chou's suggestion that both sides withdraw their forces, Kosygin was having none of it: "We have inhabitants there and we cannot leave them defenseless."[342] They nonetheless agreed on talks. But when Kosygin boarded his plane back to Moscow that evening, the ambassador learned that the agreed communiqué had been unilaterally altered by the Chinese side: ill will and mistrust were still the order of the day in Beijing in respect of their former allies.[343] Abortive negotiations were conducted from 20 October. These were led by Kuznetsov and included the chief of staff of the border forces Colonel General Matrosov, Elizavetin, and Tikhvinskii (KGB).[344]

The obvious occurred. "On our side," Kosygin noted, "it was also emphasized that disagreements between the USSR and the CPR play into the hands of world imperialism, weaken the socialist system and the rank-and-file fighting for national and social liberation. It was pointed out that in the entire history of the struggle with communism, imperialism had never received a greater gift than that resulting from the deepening, not due to us, of differences between the CPR and the Soviet Union and other socialist countries."[345] But all that resulted was a cease-fire rather than a settlement. This gave Washington hope. Hanoi sat uneasily between two heavily armed camps. It was natural for Nixon to believe that he had more bargaining power as Moscow had to defend its rear against an erstwhile ally.

LINKAGE

Nixon's main aim in Vietnam was to retreat with honor.[346] But Moscow made plain that the US attempt to make détente contingent on forcing Hanoi to concede was a nonstarter.[347] As Nixon's national security adviser, Kissinger had approached Hanoi in January 1969 with a proposal for meeting secretly in Paris but received a decisive rebuff; equally so from Moscow, which would have nothing to do with the idea.[348] Meanwhile both Secretary of Defense Melvin Laird and Secretary of State "Bill" Rogers were pressing Nixon for an early withdrawal. But they met with fierce opposition from Kissinger. Even before coming to office, he believed strongly that "as a practical matter I might try to drag on the process for a while because of the international repercussions."[349] Thus Kissinger now insisted that they "can't preside over [the] destruction of [the] Saigon government."[350] Dobrynin concluded that "Nixon has not yet any kind of clear-cut program of his own on Vietnam that differs from the Johnson line." He went on to suggest that "the Vietnamese question and our role in negotiations remain, in our hands, an important weapon for exerting pressure on the new administration in the United States."[351]

Moscow concluded "that Nixon is above all concerned about his own political reputation and the question as to how sorting out Vietnam may affect his political fate into the future."[352] The insecurity of the new administration appeared baffling,[353] all the more so because Kissinger seemed so "extraordinarily vain."[354] Nixon and Kissinger shared the robust view of "the need for military strength as a basis for successful negotiating." "It's only us non-intellectuals who understand what the game is all about," the president boasted.[355] But Nixon—to Kissinger an impenetrable personality—initially seemed content with merely a show of toughness while negotiating in private to withdraw from Vietnam. This rendered attempts at "linkage" hopeless.

In a memorandum to Nixon of 18 October 1969 Kissinger insisted on the importance of linkage.[356] It was therefore entirely to be expected that instructions to the delegation negotiating strategic arms limitation included the proviso that, to be meaningful, progress must be accompanied by progress on critical political problems.[357] Moscow had, however, already publicly dismissed any hope "that the USSR is more interested than the USA in putting an end to the uncontrolled arms race and that therefore, they say, the USA can in return be granted some concessions in other areas."[358] And CIA had repeatedly warned Nixon and Kissinger that this strategy "would not work."[359] A briefing paper produced in November 1969 illustrates well just how far apart were US hopes from Russian realities. Prime Minister Pham Van Dong led a delegation to Moscow (13–20 October). Not since Le Duan's trip in April 1965 had North Vietnamese leaders been openly received in Moscow. The very fact of the visit indicated a hardening of the Soviet line. Pham Van Dong emphasized that this was a good moment to pursue the struggle, including the war. It was "indicative," Moscow noted, "that the Americans had without any conditions halted the bombardment of North Vietnam and were obliged to go from the offensive to the defense." Nixon's policy of "vietnamization" was also seen as evidence. Hanoi was bent on the unconditional withdrawal of US forces and a coalition government in the South. Pham Van Dong was confident that in the end Nixon would have no choice but to discuss these proposals seriously. American bombing had done "serious damage" to North Vietnam and its economy. But Moscow assured the prime minister that the USSR would fully support them in the "successful completion of this struggle." Hanoi was told that Moscow considered "correct" the continuation of the fight on all fronts, including military. Moreover it was warned to be "vigilant against Washington's political and diplomatic maneuvers insofar as the actions of the Nixon administration do not testify to its intention to end aggression in Vietnam."[360] At almost that very time Kissinger wrote a memorandum to Nixon blandly assuming that Washington could hold the forthcoming strategic arms limitation talks with Moscow hostage to progress on Vietnam.[361] The White House was deluded.

Finally, having failed to gain Soviet acceptance of linkage, Nixon moved to the idea that Washington would act without external restraint elsewhere on the globe as its interests dictated: chiefly but not exclusively this meant freedom to bomb Hanoi to the conference table. Relations between Moscow and Washington thus deteriorated.[362] The reaction showed just how uncomfortable this made the Russians: "The imperialist theory of so-called selective coexistence, envisaging the possibility of relations of peaceful cooperation with some socialist countries and freedom to conduct aggressive wars against other countries and nations, does not meet the interests of strengthening peace and international security."[363]

SALT

The Soviet team at Helsinki on 17 November 1969 was led by Semyonov, who knew nothing about armaments.[364] When Brezhnev was advised of this, he retorted, "All the better; then at least no secrets will be betrayed." At the briefing Brezhnev asked point blank, "What is your preference comrade Semyonov, the Lubyanka [KGB prison] or the place of execution, if the delegation breaches these instructions?" Luckily for Semyonov he could count on acquaintance with Andropov.[365] As late as April 1973, SALT an accomplished fact, the Kremlin remained coy about revealing details even within the Party hierarchy. Grechko later boasted to the Central Committee that his ministry estimated Chinese nuclear capability to be well below that of Washington; that China possessed a mere 200 delivery vehicles. Grechko joked, "And we have . . ."

and broke off, turning to the chair, "What do you think, Leonid, how many do we have?" "No need to frighten everyone," Brezhnev retorted.[366] Head of the US department at the Foreign Ministry and, since 1968, member of the ministry's ruling collegium, Georgii Kornienko was also a delegate. Reference to the Lubyanka, he recalls, had "a paralytic effect" on the group.[367] And as Semyonov was leaving, Brezhnev told him not to hasten with the talks; instead draw them out and keep him posted.[368] Facing potential criticism at the very least from Grechko, Podgorny, Shelest, and Shelepin, Brezhnev blandly expected the team to negotiate the limitation of armaments without any classified Soviet figures placed on the table. This fitted in with Brezhnev's notion of the division of labor. According to Danilevich, he "ceded control over military decisions to the Minister of Defence. . . . He also gave *carte blanche* to the Ministry of Defence in terms of defining force requirements."[369]

The first round thus resulted in nothing of substance. Washington hoped that moving toward Beijing would have a salutary effect. Indeed, on 13 February 1970 Moscow drew attention to the "fact that the rulers of the USA are swiftly transforming their policy in relation to China, trying to further exacerbate Soviet-Chinese disagreements and make use of them for their own ends." Washington had reduced its trade embargo, ended the Seventh Fleet patrols in the Taiwan Straits, and was reconsidering arms supplies to the Nationalists. The State Department had also reopened contacts with Beijing broken off in 1968. "It is clear," Moscow concluded, "that by such measures the rulers of the United States are giving the Beijing leadership to understand that, in becoming more anti-Soviet, it need not experience any difficulty from the US side."[370]

When the delegations reconvened in Vienna on 16 April 1970 comprehensive formulae finally emerged. A key issue was Soviet insistence that strategic arms be defined as all nuclear delivery vehicles and loads capable of reaching the USSR: that is to say, including all US forward-based systems, on land and at sea (carrier-based dual-capable aircraft and medium-range bombers based in Europe). This stumbling block was overcome only by a compromise to agree upon limiting ABM systems and freezing ICBM levels, but allowing Moscow what amounted to free rein in building up their submarine ballistic missile forces (SLBMs). Indeed, thanks not least to Kissinger's dismissive attitude toward "the usual nitpicking over the level of nuclear weapons required for 'equal security,'"[371] rather than slow down the nuclear arms race, SALT merely channeled it in selective directions. James Schlesinger, US Secretary of Defense (1973–75), notes that "there was an explosion after the agreement of research and development activities in the missile area by the Soviets. We saw new missiles going—being tested, and in particular the SS-18 and the SS-19, which were substantial improvements over the earlier generation of missiles, the SS-11, the SS-13 and the like."[372] And under Schlesinger the Pentagon certainly did not sit still.

Finally, both sides were keenly anxious to show they had pressed their case on Vietnam. Moscow had increased the supply to Hanoi of the most up-to-date weaponry from 1971 as fourteen divisions drove south.[373] Having thus failed to secure the substance of linkage, Kissinger tried for its appearance. Thus on his visit to Moscow (20–24 April 1972) to pave the way for Nixon's arrival and signature of SALT I, Kissinger "insisted that from the communiqué it was at least obvious that the Vietnam problem had occupied a significant place in his negotiations in Moscow." This, however, prompted resistance from some members of the Soviet leadership.[374] And no explicit reference to Vietnam was included. Nixon duly arrived and the agreements were signed. The interim agreement "on certain measures with respect to the limitation of strategic offensive arms," as its rather deflating title suggests, provided only a makeshift framework for containing the arms race.[375] The importance was symbolic and political rather than military and substantial. Given the extent of concessions made to secure even this agreement (which were made against the wishes of the US delegation), Nixon sought to play up other advantages, namely, hastening an end to the Vietnam War. In a lengthy briefing given by Moscow to fraternal ruling parties, however, the language was designed to leave no doubts. "We made use of the negotiations to exert strong pressure on Nixon on this question [Vietnam]," Moscow argued. "Our position in relation to American aggression in Vietnam and, particularly, the bombing of the Democratic Republic of Vietnam was expressed as frankly as possible, without diplomatic niceties."[376]

With respect to China, Brezhnev saw SALT as a demonstrable success in blocking the route to an anti-Soviet alliance. In the talks, Moscow noted, "the question of China was not specifically discussed. We did not consider it necessary to do this so that the Americans did not think that Nixon's trip to Beijing worries us." "However," the briefing paper continued, "as a whole we think that the results of the talks, our agreements with the USA, objectively create a serious obstacle with which to disrupt the activities of the Maoist leadership in foreign policy toward a Sino-American rapprochement on an anti-Soviet basis and lessen the likelihood of such an outcome."[377]

The European and American treaties were celebrated by ousting hard-liner Shelest from the Politburo on 27 April 1973 and the elevation of candidate members Andropov, Gromyko, and Grechko to the Politburo as full, voting members. This represented a significant adjustment to the prevailing balance of power within the leadership. Yet it did not represent a wholehearted endorsement of détente, as events were to show.

CSCE AND BASKET THREE

Western hopes of changing the Soviet system, certainly of overthrowing it, had abated in all but the most extreme circles. Optimism was possible only for the dedicated who adhered to the "Lyautey" principle much favored at MI6 in the early fifties. Marshal Louis Lyautey had been résident général of French Morocco (1912–25) when he decided to plant an avenue of palms as a grand approach to headquarters. When challenged by a young subordinate as to whether it was worth the effort, given Lyautey's advanced age and the time required for the palms to mature, Lyautey responded with Olympian disdain that this was all the more reason to make an early start. The means of implementing the principle against Moscow included broadcasting from the BBC (funded by the Foreign Office), Radio Free Europe (controlled by CIA and directed to Eastern Europe), Radio Liberty (to the Soviet Union), Voice of America, and Deutsche Welle. Moscow jammed reception, but this was not a foolproof defense. Other means had proven disappointing. The dropping of propaganda by balloon failed miserably. A promising option emerged, however, after Khrushchev's secret speech early in 1956.

The strategy thereafter became more discriminating, since the speech demoralized many within the communist elite. The expansion of cultural contacts, including academic exchanges, was one very limited means to that end. It is notable that both Alexander Yakovlev, Gorbachev's éminence grise, and Oleg Kalugin, a very senior KGB officer who later defected, were two out of three on the first postwar exchange to the United States. A further measure was designed to reach the greatest number within the nomenklatura. And this, conceived in April 1956 at Free Europe Press, became known rather grandly as the "Marshall Plan of the Mind."[378]

Overseen and funded by CIA through dummy foundations, initially under Cord Meyer and Emmons Brown, the program targeted individuals behind the Iron Curtain with free books, articles, and pamphlets mailed from a variety of Western addresses. After Hungary it came under the direction of one man, a Romanian exile, George Minden. Literature mailed was not explicitly political. "The ideas, forms of entertainment, works of art, fashions, sources of varied information, and our general welfare—all these things that will help us feel independent and fill our lives—have a real fascination for our targets,"

Minden wrote. "It is common knowledge that the Russians have completely failed in substituting anything for the banned Western sources of intellectual, spiritual or aesthetic life, not to mention sources of information." And what began as a campaign in Eastern Europe soon expanded with a parallel operation to encompass the USSR under Isaac Patch from Radio Liberty. The two enterprises—Liberty and Free Europe—merged under Minden at Radio Free Europe in 1974, as negotiations for a conference on European security, in which the West pressed the issue of human rights and access to information, came to a climax. Five years later, to provide further cover, the organization was removed from Radio Free Europe to the International Advisory Council, also a CIA front. The books and magazines were purchased from the publishers but mailed as gifts therefrom. By 1991 more than a quarter of a million titles were dispatched annually.[379] Yet in the early seventies prospects were bleak.

Following the invasion of Czechoslovakia, NATO was obliged to assume that communist regimes were here to stay. But only the shift in Bonn's policy made possible NATO recognition of the postwar territorial status quo and the summoning of a European security conference for that purpose. The Conference on Security and Co-operation in Europe (CSCE), which Moscow had been seeking since the autumn of 1964, universalizing recognition of postwar frontiers, was thus tabled with vigor throughout the negotiations with Bonn and Washington. The West in turn procrastinated until both the German and US talks had concluded. NATO also argued for negotiating mutual and balanced force reductions (MBFR) in Europe parallel with the European security conference, though, in the face of Soviet obduracy, it was agreed not to insist on their interdependence.

Negotiations on CSCE thus opened on 22 November 1972; it took four months for the agenda to be agreed. The Warsaw Pact countries sought to restrict talks to vague declarations of principle relating to security—most of which were breached by the invasion of Czechoslovakia. Soviet commitment to détente was viewed as purely "tactical." Richard von Weiszäcker of the CDU referred to the proposed CSCE as "the intellectual disarmament of the West."[380] But NATO had already agreed to broaden the agenda to encompass "freer movement of people, information, and ideas" and asserted that the conference should go beyond the status quo "by initiating a process of reducing the barriers that still exist."[381] This was a startling innovation emanating from the Foreign and Commonwealth Office (FCO) attributable to those bridling at the thought of further concessions to Soviet sensibilities.

Wedded and glued to spheres of influence, Washington had no understanding of or sympathy for the disruptive and potentially explosive value of human rights as leverage against Soviet hegemony in Eastern Europe and wanted none of it. Nixon blamed London for initiating CSCE because the Foreign Secretary, Sir Michael Stewart, a weak man, had been reluctant to rebuff Russian insistence because of public opinion.[382] Kissinger pointed out at the time that the Russian aim was twofold: "to sustain a mood in Europe in which Defence became progressively less important, and gradually to insinuate the idea of alternative security organisations."[383] He later said, "CSCE was never an element of US foreign policy. We never pushed it and stayed a half step behind our allies all through the process."[384]

"Unpalatable though it may be to have to admit it," the FCO noted, "Western countries have had to accept it [a European security conference] largely because of domestic political pressure: they have had, in effect, to accept the Soviet thesis that support for a Conference is the only acceptable evidence of willingness to work for *détente*." As the chilling events of August 1968 receded into the distance and after negotiations on Germany lessened the Soviet sense of urgency for such a conference, London reckoned that Moscow's motives were now more long term in nature and extent. They were attempting to "undermine the Atlantic link" and "to weaken NATO." The British had thus searched for a means of counterattack while maintaining allied unity and frustrating Soviet aims "without appearing to sabotage *détente*."[385] They found it in what soon became known as "Basket Three"—human rights. So soon after the liquidation of the Prague Spring, with bloody suppression of unrest in Gdańsk a recent memory and with repressive measures taken against such writers as Andrei Amalrik and Alexander Solzhenytsin, Moscow was hypersensitive to anything that further exposed the tyrannical elements of their system. Indeed, in advice to the East Germans back in July 1969 the Russians had cautioned that "the opponents of détente in Europe will in their own way attempt to use idea of an all-European conference to pursue their policy of 'building bridges.'"[386]

A keen-eyed hawk determined to gain something from the forthcoming conference was George Walden, first secretary in the East European and Soviet department of the FCO, and already a veteran of the brutal Cultural Revolution in China: "in our aim to secure genuine improvements in reducing barriers within Europe and 'generally to spread the contagion of liberty' we should not shrink from asserting Western beliefs in the freedom of movement, information, and cultural contacts." He suggested drafting

hardheaded proposals which:
(a) it would be difficult for the Russians to decline;
(b) can be agreed with our allies;
(c) appeal to the popular imagination;

(d) are workable in practice;

(e) involve a minimum of Government finance;

(f) will attract sufficient numbers of Western participants (e.g., in any increased exchanges);

(g) introduce another germ of freedom into the East.[387]

Moscow fought against admitting this Trojan horse within the walls of the conference but had to concede on 8 June 1973.[388] Otherwise it was doubtful whether they would have had a conference at all. The issues lay in three baskets: (1) security, (2) economic cooperation, and (3) humanitarian and other fields. At Helsinki on 5 July Foreign Secretary Alec Douglas-Home insisted that "Basket I will be empty unless there are plenty of eggs in Basket III."[389] But, from initially dragging their feet, the Americans led by Kissinger soon dragged his feet on these core issues. There was no love lost between Kissinger and European statesmen. Britain's ambassador to Washington, Lord Cromer, noted Kissinger's "astonishing intellectual arrogance," "the highly devious nature of Kissinger's intellectual make-up" and "his general scorn for 'the Europeans.'"[390] Kissinger expressed "serious doubts about the proposition that the proliferation of human contacts will produce peace." It had "become an intellectual fashion." "We have a strange combination," he told the Belgian Foreign Minister, "composed of people who want to transform Soviet society but at the same time want to reduce our defenses." He also much resented the fact that from June to October 1973 "no European would talk to us while the European countries were formulating their position. This is," he asserted, "really worse than the situation we have in dealing with our adversaries."[391]

The entire CSCE process loosened the bonds of trust—already strained by SALT and Bonn's *Ostpolitik*—that tied the United States and Western Europe together. "As many predicted when the Nixon-Brezhnev summit was first mooted," British official Anthony Elliott noted in late July 1974, "it was swiftly followed by efforts on the part of Dr. Kissinger to persuade his NATO allies to adopt precipitately what he judges to be a more realistic stance on the CSCE negotiations. . . . In recent months . . . it appears that he has come to see the Conference as a positive obstacle to his task of developing Soviet-American cooperation." "It sometimes seems," the telegram continued, "that Dr. Kissinger misunderstands the significance of the CSCE to the West. He often gives the impression that *détente* is primarily a matter of inter-governmental accommodation and that the human aspect is secondary."

Yet British officials could not "see how *détente* will have any real meaning or will last" without a progressive relaxation of restrictions imposed by communist regimes on person-to-person contact with the outside world.[392] And when challenged, Elliott retorted: "If they [the Russians] thought that they would be able to circumvent them [articles in Basket Three] completely, it would hardly have been necessary for them to devote so much time and care to criticising our textual formulas; they could simply have accepted texts (and thus moved towards their aim of bringing the Conference to an early end without having any intention of doing anything about them."[393] Britain's ambassador to Moscow, Sir Terence Garvey, agreed.[394] Russia was hamstrung in the end by Brezhnev's desperate concern to achieve agreement in "negotiations that the world forgot." This was, Sir Michael Alexander recalls, Brezhnev's "major mistake." In May Alexander therefore instructed the British delegation to persist on Basket Three to extract the highest price. If Russia refused to accept it, then everything would be renegotiated piece by agonizing piece.[395]

The agreement was hammered out and the Helsinki Final Act was duly signed on 1 August 1975 by all the states of Europe, plus the USSR and United States. This was no treaty and had no force of law. It is fair to say, though, that the degree of attention paid to the formulation of its provisions and later to its enforcement meant that it was treated subsequently no less seriously than legally substantive agreements.

The agreement blasted a breach in the security wall that Andropov had cemented across the communist bloc in Europe. The USSR, however, was considered fairly secure. After Helsinki Andropov presented the Politburo with a memorandum on dissidents. The number confined added up to 850, of which 261 were held for anti-Soviet propaganda. But as many as 68,000 had been told to report to the KGB, where due warning was given about the unacceptability of their behavior. The secret police also claimed to have penetrated 1,800 anti-Soviet groups and associations.[396] These numbers gave Andropov a specious reputation for tolerance; liberalism, indeed. Yet this was not all: on 29 April 1969 he proposed confining dissidents to psychiatric hospitals.[397] This was accepted. In January 1970 the Politburo instructed the relevant organizations to bring forward proposals for putting the idea into action.[398] By the time the system was closed down in 1988 the astonishing figure of 800,000 patients had to be released.[399] Even so, in a country of 250 million this was still a tiny proportion of the population. Of greater concern in Moscow was the possible impact of Helsinki on the rest of the Warsaw Pact, Russia's Achilles' heel.

Senior Soviet diplomat Yuli Kvitsinsky later lamented: "The formulation of the third basket was considered by the West as its victory. This view was also shared by many in Moscow, looking with mistrust on the fruits of the work of our delegation headed by A. G. Kovalev."[400] Anatoly Kovalev, a Deputy Minister of Foreign Affairs from 1971, had been part of the Zavidovo group working for

Brezhnev. He was close to Andropov. This was also because at CSCE Kovalev had been instructed by Gromyko to deal directly with the KGB chief on Basket Three. In the end, however, it was Brezhnev who dictated the terms acceptable, and these meant overruling the KGB. Andropov told Kovalev: "You will understand that this is a game with more than one goal: the Foreign Ministry wins and the KGB loses. The inviolability of frontiers is fine, very good; but the frontiers will be transparent."[401]

Indeed, they proved to be. By way of postscript: in the summer of 1991, the Soviet empire in ruins, the Berlin Wall down, and socialism in Eastern Europe for most an unpleasant memory, Sir Michael Alexander came to dine at the embassy in Moscow. The issue of Basket Three came up in rhetorical form: "Did our participants at the time imagine the consequences of their activity?" Alexander's answer was that some certainly were farsighted. "I don't think that he was wrong," lamented Kvitsinsky.[402]

9

THE IMPACT OF VIETNAM

However, we must not let ourselves become self-satisfied, as imperialism will use every means of pressure at its disposal. The struggle between the two systems is still going strong.

—*Boris Ponomarev, 27 February 1973*

The Third World was the sphere that held out the greatest hopes for progress against the West. In 1958 Khrushchev boasted of winning "the hearts of the people of these countries."[1] Such naïveté wasted resources and bought Moscow little influence. And in October 1964 the Party roundly condemned Khrushchev for his ignorant and profligate approach. "One has to look at things realistically," the indictment ran. "And the reality is that for hundreds of years the Americans, the French, the English, and the Germans held the dominant position in Asia, Africa, and Latin America. There they established their bastions—economic and military; they were very well acquainted with the situation, customs, laws, and living conditions of these peoples; they had their civil servants there. The people in these countries used their language. We, in no sense knowing anything about such countries, from time to time render them extensive financial, technological, military, and other forms of aid." To what effect? "The results in many cases have been lamentable: having swallowed what we gave them, the leaders of some of these countries turned their backs on us."[2]

Yet Khrushchev's successors were to match his mistakes repeatedly on an even greater scale. This was the impact of Vietnam. On 27 January 1973 the accords signed in Paris effectively ended the longstanding US military commitment to Saigon. By March 1975 the slogan for the renewed offensive from Hanoi in concert with Moscow and Beijing was "Achieve a victory like Dien Bien Phu." A month later the Americans were gone, leaving Hanoi in complete control. At the time Kissinger cautioned that "we should not characterize our role in the conflict as a disgraceful disaster."[3] But nearly twenty years later, he acknowledged it to be "a debacle."[4] "It is doubtful that Castro would have intervened in Angola," Kissinger notes, "or the Soviet Union in Ethiopia, had America not been perceived to have collapsed in Indochina, to have become demoralized by Watergate, and to have afterward retreated into a cocoon."[5] Former CIA director Robert Gates agrees: "Spring 1975 marked an ending and a beginning of the superpower struggle in the Third World. It saw the end of the Vietnam War for the United States, and final communist victory and American defeat there. . . . The perception quickly grew that it would be a cold day in hell before the United States again involved itself militarily in a Third World struggle."[6]

Once Moscow had acquired the means of airlifting military supplies across the globe, opportunity and capability created a new basis for rivalry with the West. The total number of transports stabilized at 600 by 1984. They showed their value in the 1967 and 1973 wars in the Middle East, when they operated round-trips of up to 6,000 nautical miles (given the problem of overflights) at short notice. Within three days of war breaking out in 1967 Moscow managed 350 sorties in twenty-seven days. Invading Czechoslovakia the following year, 500 flights in one night constituted a fine-tuned operation. Moreover, the acquisition of a blue-water fleet (a 40 percent increase in large surface warships between 1965 and 1981)[7] marked a coming of age for the Soviet navy, perhaps more significant for showing the flag than in terms of the overall global balance. Of greater material import was the emergence of an amphibious assault capability and heavy lift transport aircraft, including the Antonov-12 (similar to the American C-130), Antonov-22 and the Iyushin-76 (similar to the American C-141). This transformed Moscow's capacity for projecting power during the 1970s. A decade before, it had no heavy transports for long-range operations.

THE YOM KIPPUR WAR

By 1973 Moscow was congratulating itself on advancing its cause in the Middle East. Despite warnings from knowledgeable KGB, GRU, and Foreign Ministry Arabists, the Kremlin deluded itself into believing that despite the death of Nasser on 28 September 1970 and his replacement by Sadat, Egypt would never desert the USSR. On 30 April 1971 Cairo's KGB resident Kirpichenko delivered a particularly blistering prediction of Sadat's likely treachery which had the extraordinary effect of stinging Podgorny into saying that Kirpichenko had no business talking about presidents in such a disrespectful manner.[8]

Delusions went much further. Egypt, Iraq, Syria, and Algeria were all seen as potential converts to communism. The Baathists ruling Syria and Iraq were cooperating with local communists; the former even had two such ministers. Ponomarev claimed Moscow had "given him [Nasser] to understand that it is not possible to sustain good relations with the Soviet Union while at the same time persecuting communists." Indeed, Russia had "to take into consideration that in the Arab world the great social question remains, which road such states as Egypt, Iraq, and Syria are to take, the socialist or the capitalist one."[9] And military aid was seen as one promising route enticing such countries in the direction of socialism.

On the Soviet view, therefore, no fast distinction was drawn between the policy of the state toward Third World countries and the revolutionary proselytism of the International Department. The assumption was that victory in Vietnam would facilitate a Middle East solution to Israel's disadvantage. Washington would now have to decide whether to have "Israel as a satellite" and have millions of Arabs as enemies or become more reasonable. "Vietnam has set the Arabs a good example," Moscow reasoned. "It shows how necessary it is to combine military action with political discussion."[10]

Russia was not alone in seeing the Middle East as a neuralgic point in the Cold War. The region's oil was critical to Western Europe, even though Washington could, if determined, source strategic requirements in its own hemisphere. "If we consider Vietnam," Kissinger wrote, "our most anguishing problem, certainly the Middle East, constitutes our most dangerous problem." "In the Middle East," he added, "the ingredients included the Arab states poised against Israel but with both sides backed by the super-powers which do not finitely control the actions of their clients. Therefore a relative triviality in a global context could lead to the kind of confrontation which neither of the super-powers would want but which neither could prevent."[11] Moreover by August 1973 Watergate had proved "a disaster" for US foreign policy. "Everything is harder now and takes a little longer now," complained Kissinger.[12]

In late April Moscow had agreed to "measures for the strengthening of Egypt's military potential."[13] But it wanted to use this as leverage for negotiation rather than as prelude to war. This is apparent from conversations with Sadat in February 1972.[14] Unrealistic in his assessment of Egypt's capability, however, Sadat was decided on war. To keep Moscow in line, he terminated Soviet access to air and naval facilities; the exception, Alexandria was not closed to Soviet naval vessels—submarines in particular—until relations with Moscow were completely broken, in 1976.[15] These losses were irreplaceable and marked a notable success for Kissinger's diplomacy in luring Egypt westwards.

Without consulting Moscow, Sadat and Hafiz al-Assad (for Syria) attacked Israel on 6 October 1973 to reverse the results of the Six Day War. There was little prior warning, despite the presence of more than a thousand military advisers in Syria. Relations had cooled with Cairo since the expulsion of the Soviet contingent from Egypt following on Sadat's long-term aim of turning toward the United States. Moscow was no better informed than Washington which, prior to hostilities, "made a serious effort in the short time available to stop it."[16] Sadat arranged for Assad to convey the bad news to Moscow on 4 October, which promptly led the Russians to airlift their remaining (civilian) personnel out of Egypt.[17] On 6 October US ambassador Kenneth Keating told Prime Minister Golda Meir that the Syrians and Egyptians were coordinating an attack on Israel late that afternoon.[18] Kissinger was convinced that Moscow had not urged the Arabs to attack.[19]

Thus after informing Israel at 6:00 a.m. (EST), Kissinger called Dobrynin before 9:00 a.m. telling him to notify his superiors immediately that Washington and Moscow held a special responsibility to prevent war.[20] It soon became clear, however, that Moscow would not stand back. Bill Quandt, in charge of the Middle East at the NSC, noted: "When it became clear that the fighting might be prolonged and the Soviets began a massive resupply effort, we had to act to prevent the Soviets from tilting the military balance against Israel. This past weekend, therefore, we began a program of resupply to Israel."[21] Russia sent in at least twenty-six transport aircraft fully laden to Cairo, Damscus, and Baghdad.[22] They also dispatched two missile destroyers and a cruiser en route to the eastern Mediterranean.

The problem was less one of Soviet intervention[23] than that, although incapable as ever of beating Israel, Egypt and Syria would conduct a low-level war of attrition. Since 1967 Washington had generously bankrolled Tel Aviv just as Moscow underwrote Havana. Israel owed the United States $1.7 billion on cash and credit purchases with a twenty- to thirty-year repayment schedule. Yet this has to be set against the cost of the war, which worked out at $250 million per day.[24] Washington therefore came up with an additional $2.2 billion.[25] It was "the view of the US intelligence community, that superior Israeli combat effectiveness would be able to turn the tide and reverse initial setbacks"[26]— even though the Arabs were more equipped. The ratio of Arab to Israeli fighter aircraft was 2.45 to 1, tanks 2.52 to 1. Yet the Arabs lost four times as many troops as the Israelis.[27] Moscow tried to enhance the odds for Damascus by deploying a SAM-6 brigade on a temporary basis. But this made little difference to the outcome of the conflict.

"The Soviets may be putting us to the test in the larger context of our overall relations," wrote one aide at the White House. "We certainly want to show that we are not immobilised and have not opted out of the Middle East because of energy, Watergate, detente, or Soviet power." The conclusion was that "the Soviets will be less likely to become involved if it is clear that we mean business about their staying out and that larger interests are at stake."[28]

The real problem for Washington, however, was entirely unexpected: mobilization of the Arab oil-exporting states. In Saudi Arabia, Feisal, who had seized power from his brother a decade before, rejected US demands for a reversion of Arab and Israeli forces to the status quo ante, which would leave Israel with the gains made in 1967. Feisal was prepared to cut output to 7.2 million barrels per day and then at the rate of 5 percent each month until the Israelis withdrew.[29]

The American aim to stare down the Russians was thus further complicated by the need to avoid a collision with the entire Arab world. Kissinger was most aware of the corrosive effect of Watergate on the international standing of the United States and therefore even more predisposed than subordinates to show the flag backed by the threat of force to deter Russia from intervention. Similarly, he was aware of the possible threat of escalation. Kissinger told the Belgian Foreign Minister "that if the Soviets were to involve themselves directly in the Middle East hostilities, then we would react very sharply."[30]

Brezhnev was under pressure from not only Sadat and Assad to neutralize Washington and thus expose Tel Aviv, but also from the irascible Grechko, now a voting member of the Politburo, who wanted both to punish the Arabs for their disobedience and to reinforce the Soviet military presence in the Middle East. But Brezhnev initially held firm: "We have already made a principal [principled?] decision not to be involved in the Middle East war, and there are no reasons to change our decision."[31] The final decision, however, was to threaten intervention in order to persuade the United States to rein in Israel, which was as usual continuing to fight on despite a UN Security Council resolution calling for a cease-fire. Soviet credibility was reinforced by the presence of 96 warships and auxiliaries deployed to the Mediterranean.[32] Resupply of Egypt and Syria in the 1973 war began four days after hostilities opened and required 40 percent of all Soviet medium- and long-range troop transports. In all, 850 sorties were conducted in twenty-five days, averaging 50 per day without losses. In that same conflict 400,000 tons of supplies were also delivered to Egypt, Syria, and Libya in thirty-five days by the Soviet navy. Moreover, from the mid-1970s Moscow could rely on a global communications system to underpin operations across the world via AWAC and satellites.[33] Inevitably possession of a long-range heavy lift capacity tempted Moscow to operate further afield. And the Middle East was never far from Soviet gun sights.

It matters that Moscow assumed Washington was paralyzed. The maintenance of détente appeared to be Nixon's top priority, Watergate was inflicting continuing damage, and the grim prospect of Arab oil sanctions darkened the situation room. "President Nixon is probably also interested in not letting the Near East events disturb the process of détente under way," Moscow judged. "The crisis in the American government does not help, and their interests in the region have to take into account for the time being the Arab oil coalition."[34] From those false premises, Moscow was emboldened into pressuring Washington to ease away from wholehearted support for Israel. And it is not impossible that the United States had intercepted and decrypted this assessment in transmission and therefore understood the urgent need to dispel Moscow's perilous illusions.

Kuznetsov drafted a message threatening unilateral action. It had been he who warned Washington in October 1962 that Moscow would never allow another humiliation. He evidently believed that now the shoe was on the other foot. Signed by Brezhnev, the message threatening unilateral action was sent to Washington late in the evening of 24 October (EST). After calling on the United States to join the USSR in the sending of military forces to implement the Security Council resolution, Brezhnev threatened unilateral military action: "I will say it straight that if you find it impossible to act jointly with us in this matter, we should be faced with the necessity."[35]

At the same time "Soviet actions signaled the buildup of the capability for rapid introduction of forces into the Middle East" that afternoon and evening. The NSC convened from 10:00 p.m. on 24 October to 3:00 a.m. on 25 October along with the chairman of the Joint Chiefs of Staff and the director of CIA. Kissinger took the chair.[36] With Nixon's assent, Defcon III was declared. In his reply to Brezhnev, Nixon assured Moscow that "we are already in close contact with the government of Israel aimed at ensuring its full compliance with the provision of the Security Council decisions,"[37] but he also insisted that "we must view your suggestion of unilateral action as a matter of the gravest concern involving incalculable consequences."[38] The motives for the alert have been clarified by Schlesinger: after the first calls in Congress for Nixon's impeachment "we feared that the Soviets might be concluding that the American Government was paralyzed, that it could not act, and it was for that reason, amongst others, that we responded to Brezhnev's note with the so-called nuclear alert, which incidentally was not just nuclear, it was our forces all over the world."[39]

The Kremlin was naïvely surprised. "The Americans had no right to put their troops on alert all over the world," Brezhnev whined.[40] But the alert had the desired sobering effect: "It is not reasonable to become engaged in a war with the United States because of Egypt and Syria," Kosygin said. We will "not unleash" a "Third World War," Andropov added. "We do not need another war," Ponomarev concluded. Others repeated as much.[41] Only hothead Grechko suggested sending troops to the Middle East in retaliation. Kosygin, however, made strong objection to the dangers of escalation and restated his remark to Sadat that "we would not become engaged in the war."[42] In early November Brezhnev expressed the wish to facilitate a border settlement, including a guarantee for Israel, arguing that diplomatic relations with Tel Aviv should be reestablished at the appropriate moment. When Gromyko protested at this upsetting the Arabs, Brezhnev lost his patience and insisted that the Arabs had got nowhere despite military assistance given by Moscow. "We won't fight for them. The people would not understand. And above all we don't have any intention of being dragged into world war because of them."[43]

Nixon took the view that the US airlift "saved Israel" over the objections of Defense and State. He had told Moscow "we would never have a conflict with them over Vietnam and definitely would over Europe." The Middle East, however, was "a maybe."[44] The war in the Middle East was nevertheless, in the opinion of the NSA's official history, "the closest that the United States and the Soviet Union came to war between the Cuban Missile Crisis and the end of the Cold War."[45] Moscow's response was to firm up assistance to Palestinian terrorism. Since 1968 the KGB had maintained contact with the People's Front for the Liberation of Palestine (PFLP) headed by George Habash. In April 1974 the PFLP outlined its operational plans including destruction of "oil storage tanks in various regions of the world (Saudi Arabia, the Persian Gulf, Hong Kong, etc.), the destruction of tankers and supertankers, actions against American and Israeli representatives in Iran, Greece, Ethiopia, Kenya; an attack on the diamond center in Tel Aviv, etc." It was seeking both training and equipment. On 23 April Andropov sought Brezhnev's agreement to this and received it.[46]

LATIN AMERICA IN REVOLT

Whereas the Middle East was ground clearly disputed, Latin America lay squarely within the US sphere of influence. This meant that Moscow would take a back seat to Havana. Pursuing a policy favored by Kennedy[47] on 31 March 1964 Washington—courtesy of military attaché Colonel Vernon (Dick) Walters—orchestrated the overthrow of the leftist João Goulart regime in Brazil with the US fleet standing offshore. The year before, in September 1963, a military coup had overturned the populist but incompetent government of Juan Bosch in the Dominican Republic. Thereafter a guerrilla campaign broke out with training and backing from the Cuban Dirección General de Inteligencia (DGI). On 24 April 1965 a revolt broke out against the regime among junior and middle rank officers.

The White House responded. Brushing aside McNamara's skepticism, Johnson sent in US Marines to seize power on 27 April, reinforcements following two days later, and reinstall a reliable dictatorship.[48] The message was clear: Washington would secure their sphere of influence from ideological infection through preemptive use of force. Moscow raised neither Brazil nor the Dominican Republic to the level of *cause célèbre*. Greece suffered a like fate. Wholly within the US sphere of influence since Stalin abandoned the KKE's struggle, Greece stood at the crossroads of the eastern Mediterranean and the Middle East and served the needs of the US Sixth Fleet. The resurgence of the left under George Papandreou resulted in a coup d'état by the military on 21 April 1967. There were good reasons to suspect American involvement. The seizure of power was by means of the Prometheus Plan, a NATO contingency in the event of a communist takeover. It was effected by Colonel George Papadopoulos, in the pay of CIA since 1952.[49] He had served as liaison between the agency and the KYP (its Greek equivalent) since 1960. Opposition politicians, who in the run-up to the coup approached deputy chief of station in Athens James Potts, were advised to turn instead to Papadopoulos: "He's my boy," Potts used to say. Meanwhile, after the coup, old hands at the US Military Aid Assistance Group jokingly referred to the colonel as "the first CIA agent to become Premier of a European country."[50]

This coup was not, however, quite what Washington expected. "Dick" Lehman, then in CIA's Office of Current Intelligence, recalls this as an unusual instance of Director Richard Helms losing his temper. "What happened was that the Greek generals had been planning a coup against the elected government," he recalls, "a plan we all knew about and was not yet ripe. But a group of colonels had trumped their ace and acted without warning." Helms had assumed the generals had gone ahead without telling him first.[51] As was the case with Brazil, the coup was relatively bloodless; it was only after that torture reared its ugly head.

Chile was treated no better. On 4 September 1970 Marxist Salvador Allende, presidential candidate for a socialist-communist coalition, won by a tight margin the greater proportion of votes cast. "A friend of the Party" who once seriously contemplated joining, Allende then managed to secure the majority in congress necessary for taking office. This was achieved in the face of a frantic and chronically mismanaged attempt by the White House to deny him office.[52] At this stage a close friend to Allende, Castro, advised caution. However, instead of attempting to propitiate the middle ground in Chilean politics in order to reduce the effectiveness of US interference, Allende embarked full speed on the nationalization of private property using existing legislation that allowed him to circumvent elected representatives. Property seized without compensation included that of many US multinationals whose investments had been encouraged by Kennedy in order to build an alternative model to Cuban socialism through the Alliance for Progress. The economic chaos resulting from Allende's actions was exacerbated by the falling price on world markets of Chile's staple export, copper. It took more than a year to take effect, but once apparent it laid the regime open to further attempts by Washington to subvert the socialist experiment.

On 21 August 1972 a shopkeepers' strike broke out that soon spread the entire length of the country and took in the drivers of heavy goods vehicles, gradually strangling the entire economy. Washington bankrolled the owner-drivers, but the political strike failed when Allende incorporated the military into his cabinet on 2 November in order to outflank the right. Emboldened by the willingness of senior officers to defend the new order, the communists suggested that Allende seize power from within—an *autogolpe*—before power was taken from them all. This was also Castro's advice. But Allende could be extremely stubborn; firm convictions were easily and all too frequently underestimated because he had the reputation of being a great parliamentary tactician, the master of *muñeca* (the flexible wrist). Allende adamantly refused the advice given because he remained committed to a constitutional order, even while his devious nationalization program undermined its spirit and credibility.

Meanwhile, having despaired of ever ridding the subcontinent of Allende when the strike failed, Nixon, with active encouragement from the US military advisory group in Chile, resolved on a coup. But because CIA was generally averse to this option, he turned instead to the Pentagon for implementation of operations independently of CIA station in Santiago and of the US ambassador, now Nathaniel Davis. On 29 June a putsch took place. It failed because the army around Santiago refused to rally round. The US role was hidden. But MI6 had to be called in from London to exfiltrate US agents unable to obtain help from the unknowing Santiago station. Nixon nevertheless became ever more determined, as the Watergate scandal ate away at his political credibility, to bring Allende down at whatever cost. Finally, the desired result was achieved courtesy of Walters, an old friend as well as Deputy Director of CIA, on 11 September. The timing was brought forward to forestall a referendum by Allende that could have ended the regime by peaceful means since few conclude that he would have won. But that would have taken time and the results could have proved insufficiently conclusive for Nixon. Throughout, in contrast to Havana, Moscow acted with restraint, failing to give Allende the kind of blank check they gave Havana. The KGB, for one, viewed the regime's economic policies as folly and their diplomacy as amateurish. Détente was certainly not viewed as expendable for such an uncertain and potentially unrewarding outcome.

REVOLUTION OF THE CARNATIONS

The events in Chile hung like a pall over the Communist parties of Western Europe. Since the invasion of Czechoslovakia the PCI under Luigi Longo and then Enrico Berlinguer had led the way toward greater autonomy from Moscow: the *compromesso storico*, compromising with the existing institutions of the Italian state—what was later generalized as Eurocommunism.

To some it altered nothing. In Bonn, Foreign Minister Hans-Dietrich Genscher expressed it crisply. "There is not one single Western Communist Party that has given up its final objective," he said. "They still want the dictatorship of the proletariat. This is the decisive point. The danger is that they become more attractive to the voters. It is easier for us to accept orthodox parties than parties that give the appearance of being independent." Even though the advanced economies were fairly secure, having tiny and unpopular Communist parties, elsewhere in NATO, notably its southern tier, matters were very different. Referring to Britain and Germany as safe, Foreign Secretary James Callaghan pointed out, however, that "we should recognize they are still the true enemy and not let them increase their appeal." He favored flushing them out by trying to make these parties "try harder to prove their independence." Yet, as Kissinger rightly observed, the problem was that "if we stress their independence, we create the impression that that's the only obstacle." And he found it particularly irritating that the Italian communists were "making themselves respectable" by reaching out to the broader opinion in the United States. "To the extent they become respectable in the U.S., they can use this in Italy to prove their respectability." Whereas the Russians, to his relief, were "so clumsy."[53]

Détente brought to the fore the issue of aid to foreign Communist parties and national liberation movements. Portugal's revolution raised both in the most acute form. The potential for overturning capitalism in Lisbon and for Soviet bloc expansion to encompass Angola and Mozambique was too tempting to pass over. Yet these opportunities were thrown up at a crucial moment in the evolution of détente. Moreover, events in Portugal taken together with the fall of the Greek dictatorship and the imminence of Franco's death prompted larger questions as to the future of southern Europe as a whole.

In Moscow the timing could not have been worse. The challenge to détente, suppressed hitherto, now reemerged. Andropov, Gromyko, and Grechko were voting members of the Politburo. Committed rather more to détente with

Washington than Western Europe, Gromyko was cautious. But Grechko was aggressively anticapitalist and Andropov staunchly committed to Leninism, as was Suslov, Brezhnev's number two. The very locus of power wavered with the grave decline in Brezhnev's health and therefore his capacity to control policy. In these conditions the newly acquired stability in East-West relations, upon which so much hope had been loaded, was jeopardized not by any change in the balance of power but by the degree of commitment on both sides to sustain that balance, come what may. Washington appeared less certain to maintain it; Moscow, more willing to risk its fracture for unilateral advantage.

Portugal succumbed to a coup when army officers backed by General António de Spínola seized power in Portugal as of 5:00 p.m. on 25 April 1974. The open question was whether this was prelude to communist revolution. Self-described as the Movimento do Forças Armadas (MFA), the officers, though largely apolitical, were under the sway of Marxist-Leninists. The initial motivation of all, including the vast majority of the MFA, was to end the futile struggle to sustain a colonial empire in Africa—Cape Verde, Guinea-Bissau, Angola, and Mozambique—against the wishes of its inhabitants. But others went far beyond that.

A respectable four-star general, six-year governor, and commander-in-chief of Portuguese Guinea, Spínola had fought on Franco's side in the Spanish civil war. But he revolted against the government's failure to see that colonial wars were bleeding the country white, and went public with a book in 1972 that elsewhere would scarcely have stirred much interest but which in Portugal created a veritable sensation. The MFA had emerged from among the young officers, mainly captains. Here there were many people of whom it could be said were not communist but were aligned with the theses of the Communist Party. Leader of the Portuguese Communist Party (PCP) Álvaro Cunhal remarked that "the victorious military movement of 25 April did not fall from the sky." A controlling hand directed contacts with the military.[54] Within the MFA some had been in touch with the PCP long before the 25 April.[55] By the end of March 1974 a coup was expected.[56] Indeed, it was estimated that the young officers' movement dominated by captains and majors was viewed sympathetically by some 50 percent of the population.[57]

On 15 May Spínola became President in an atmosphere still uncertain. Two days later the PCP was legalized but remained insecure nevertheless. The Party, strong among the professional middle classes, including artists, writers, and journalists, had long been forced underground by dictatorship; it was also dogma-driven; and it was slavishly loyal to Moscow, not unlike the Communist parties of Latin America. Cunhal, who was in his own right an impressive figure, had led infiltration of Portuguese political life for quite some time. Visiting Berlin on 16 May representatives emphasized that the "danger of a coup by reactionary forces is great."[58] Only a month after the coup a senior member of the PCI meeting PCP officials found them reluctant to give their names or reveal the fact of Party membership. Journals published by the Party did not make clear their origins; and small local newspapers referred to their identity only in terms of the front, MDP (Movimento Democrático Portugues). The leaders of trades unions were "almost exclusively communists, while in local councils, especially in small constituencies and in the towns, representatives of the MDP (therefore communists and friends of the communists) prevailed."[59]

The PCP was subsidized from East Berlin as well as Moscow.[60] Spain discovered in November 1974 that Portuguese escudos were being bought at a discount in Swiss money markets, apparently to finance the subsidies.[61] Due to clandestine activity and its elevated reputation as antifascist, the PCP held more residual organizational power than any rival. By the end of the year the communists boasted of the fact that "the MFA maintains the best relations with the PCP." The Portuguese comrades "judge the alliance between the MFA and the people's movement (the PCP and other forces) as a fundamental fact in the political situation of the country."[62] This was in large part due to one senior officer emerging from the coup who advanced his job to further the interests of the PCP: Colonel (soon to be General) Vasco Gonçalves.

Whether or not a secret member of the Portuguese Communist Party (PCP), as some have claimed, Vasco Gonçalves embodied communist influence within the leadership of the MFA. If not, then it is almost certainly true of him, as was said of another such figure, Ramalho Eanes: "They say he is a catholic but does not practise. They say he is not a communist but does practise." Socialist leader Mario Soares described him as "Cunhal's man, the man on whom Cunhal counted to install a communist dictatorship."[63] Indeed, after the Council of Ministers ran on until three or four in the morning, Cunhal used to leave the official residence to be seen, after an interval, surreptitiously retracing his steps for secret conversations with Vasco Gonçalves.[64] British intelligence, so well informed that it could operate in Portugal from London, certainly considered him either a Party member or committed to support the Party.[65]

The PCP and Vasco Gonçalves were not interested in turning Portugal into a democracy. Cunhal, who supported suppression of the Prague Spring, stated "that up to 24 April, in the forties and fifties and sixties, even we would have been more than happy to take part in a bourgeois democracy. But now history is offering another opportunity and we do not intend to lose it, and we will not lose it." He was not banking on success at the polls: "We do not accept the game of elections! You are mistaken to rely on such an idea. No, no, no: for me elections mean nothing. Nothing!" What interested him was that the MFA retain its own power within the state, that any future constituent assembly remain only one part of that state structure, without legislative power: "What I promise is that in Portugal there will be no Parliament." "There will be a constituent assembly and that is all, of limited importance and that is all. It will operate within a framework determined completely and conditioned completely by the agreements signed with the MFA ."[66]

Spínola thus feared the extreme left with good reason. It soon became evident that he was losing control.[67] Despairing of the future, on 19 June he met Nixon at the US air base in Lajes on the Azores. Nixon was accompanied by his friend Walters (interpreting). Spínola expressed "anxiety at the fact that the Soviet Union is subsidizing communist subversion in Portugal. This is irrefutable and is proven by the fact that the CP has just received from Russia substantial assistance in cash to prepare for its electoral campaign." He warned "that Portugal will turn into a communist country and the impact of this on neighboring Spain, whose structures, as he understood them, had been much shaken by the Portuguese revolution." He concluded by asking for assistance.[68]

Portugal, however, was merely "a sleeping partner in NATO." Its value was essentially geostrategic.[69] William Colby, Director of CIA, recalled: "We did not follow Portugal in detail because at that time [before the coup] it wasn't important."[70] For the British, however, MI6 was so immersed in it that no local residency was necessary; everything could be done from London.[71] Portugal also had the distinction of belonging to NATO's nuclear planning group—with access to the associated secrets—and hosted a NATO command (COMIBERLANT) linked to that in Norfolk, Virginia. With the Azores island chain off northwest Africa, Portugal stood at the mouth of the Mediterranean, a crucial stepping stone from the United States to the Middle East. In the airlift to Israel during the Yom Kippur War, more than 2,500 metric tons of fuel was required in the Azores to refuel US transport aircraft because it took 5 metric tons to deliver just 1 metric ton of aid.[72] As Portuguese politics drifted out of US control, Washington thus considered detaching the Azores from the mainland.[73]

PRESSURE BUILDS

Spain now looked uncertain as Franco succumbed to senility (he died on 24 November 1975). Kissinger's instinct was to shore up relations with Spain as a safeguard against the loss of Portugal. On 6 August 1970 Washington and Madrid had agreed a treaty of friendship and cooperation.[74] And until the assassination of Franco's first anointed successor, Washington had every expectation of continuity rather than change. Tension, however, grew throughout 1974 between those favoring fundamental change and fascist diehards including Franco. After the collapse of fascist and military dictatorships in Portugal and Greece, Spanish traditionalists began to look and feel increasingly isolated. Any such government friendly with Moscow would therefore not only jeopardize NATO security on its flanks but also breach alliance security at the core.[75] London was concerned lest Lisbon turn to Moscow and allow it to establish naval bases on its territory.[76]

The incentive to sort out the western Mediterranean was enhanced by events further east. On 15 July the Greek military dictatorship established in 1967 overthrew Archbishop Makarios in Cyprus as the prelude to a takeover of the island. This prompted a Turkish invasion five days later and a cease-fire on 21 July. But the plight of Greek refugees was keenly felt on the mainland. This desperate gamble on the part of the Greek military then brought down Karamanlis on 24 July. Given widespread suspicion of covert US complicity in the 1967 coup, it was inevitable that a price was now paid in terms of US influence. With a new Turkish offensive in Cyprus on 14 August, Greece withdrew from the military structure of NATO. Large anti-American demonstrations flooded Athens and US ambassador Davies was assassinated in Nicosia, capital of Cyprus.

Thus the White House looked to a coup against the left by Spínola and the more conservative elements within the MFA as the best hope. Not until this proved futile was Washington prepared to consider tactics already favored in Western Europe. These hinged upon the social democratic alternative to communism; something for which Nixon held little hope.

On 9 August 1974 Nixon finally resigned after complicity was clearly established in a break-in at Democrat campaign offices in Washington. Kissinger, now serving former Vice President Gerald Ford, did his best to sustain continuity of policy. The United States was still reluctant to back a leftist alternative to the PCP untried by elections: an option favored by allies in Europe but which Nixon and Kissinger personally had found unattractive. "The problem in Portugal," Kissinger stated, "is very serious, because it could be taken as a test case for possible evolutions in other countries, and not only if the Communists take over. It could also be the case if the Communists become the sinews of non-Communist government, and perhaps especially so."[77]

Given White House aversion to social democrats, it was inevitable that Spínola was talked into attempting a bloodless coup. Three days after Carlos resigned, Kissinger spoke out. On 1 August, Walters returned to Portugal. The streets then filled with demonstrators protesting against economic dislocation caused by the radicalization of society. Behind this ferment stood the architect Almeida Araújo and Coca-Cola's man in Portugal, Sérgio Geraldes Barba; and in the shadows lurked the Americans.[78] The counterattack had begun. On 21 September, Spínola announced that he would take personal control over negotiations toward colonial independence.[79] The putsch from the right gave a great boost to the far left, however. The PCP reported that "the antifascist democratic forces among the people and within the MFA were strengthened." Moreover, the main assault on private enterprise could begin "in the near future" with the support of "the decisive elements of the MFA" on the basis of the PCP's economic program, amounting to further nationalization and the creation of an effective state sector, including a monopoly of foreign trade.[80]

Generals conspiring with the President were forced out while Spínola himself was supplanted by Costa Gomes on 30 September. As commander in chief of the armed forces in 1972 he had approved Spínola's book, which then cost both of them their jobs. Thus it was that he had agreed on the coup in April and hitherto had acted as something of an éminence grise. Costa Gomes later showed himself to be closer to the socialists than the communists, though that was only when they were obviously gaining the upper hand.

MENSHEVISM DEFEATS BOLSHEVISM

The destruction of revolutionary socialism in Portugal then had to await decisive action from European social democracy backed by Washington. Forced to resign as chancellor on 7 May 1974 after it became known that his assistant Gunter Guillaume was an East German spy, Brandt remained chairman of the SPD and retained a good deal of authority at home and abroad. He visited Portugal at the invitation of Soares on 19–21 October to meet the president and prime minister. Brandt took the view that priority should be given to economic aid, but only after elections. This could be done by classifying Portugal as a "receiving nation" at the Organization for Economic Cooperation and Development assistance committee.

Brandt found the socialists had the greatest electoral support but that the communists had the best organized party. The MFA, in turn, "could turn 'peronist' should they become impatient with civilian political rule."[81] An EEC summit of socialist leaders on 1–2 November in The Hague approved Brandt's aid proposals. Chancellor Schmidt, "concerned about the potential political disintegration of the southern tier of Europe," and regarded as pro-American unlike his predecessor, sought greater US cooperation. The SPD leadership was "prepared to cooperate with other West European social democrats to try to assist their colleagues in Portugal from being swept aside by the communists." For its part Washington had no precise idea what Schmidt had in mind.[82] The SPD and the German trades unions were already assisting Soares organizationally and financially.[83]

A former defense minister, Schmidt agreed with Kissinger geopolitically, but their respective readings of Portugal diverged. Convergence seemed possible with the arrival as ambassador on 17 January 1975 of Frank Carlucci. He spoke the more melodic Portuguese of Rio de Janeiro and arrived accompanied by men who had served alongside him in Brazil.[84] Carlucci believed that the way forward was via the socialists.[85] His instincts were, however, not those of Kissinger. Indeed, they had "differences in views," as a result of which "some sharp exchanges" took place. Only "eventually" did Kissinger come around to accepting Carlucci's arguments.[86] Soares subsequently boasted that Portugal "proved Carlucci right against Kissinger."[87] This was possible only because the Secretary's star was on the wane. At Princeton, Carlucci and Ford's chief of staff Donald Rumsfeld had become close friends as fellow members of the university wrestling team, where quickness of mind and ingenuity were as important as physical fitness. He could therefore exercise a degree of autonomy that few others at State possessed.

London was forever pressing Washington to back Soares.[88] Despite this, a last desperate attempt was made to restore the old regime. On 11 March 1975 two companies of paratroops from an air base at Tancos helicoptered into Lisbon and took up positions close to the airport near the barracks of an artillery regiment, which was then assaulted by trainer aircraft. Meanwhile in the city center officers at the headquarters of the republican national guard imprisoned their commanding officer but were forced to surrender. Spínola fled the country and the head of the Christian Democratic Party disappeared. Washington was now short of alternatives. With this Kissinger had effectively shot his last bolt in Portugal.

The putsch was badly conceived and poorly implemented. Moreover, it gave the PCP its opportunity. Without pausing for elections, Gonçalves launched a series of measures to seize the commanding heights of the economy. The regime lurched to the left, the Prime Minister announcing his intention to increase the number of communists in the government (some under nominal guise of the MDP, including the Minister of the Interior). Alarmed, Soares called for help. Believing a Prague coup possible, he made a direct appeal to European socialists on 21 March. President Gomes no longer had the army in hand. The economic situation was critical. Preparations for the ballot forthcoming were being manipulated. Communists were taking charge of the secret police (PIDE) to suppress journalists critical of the PCP. "Soares asks us for influence to be exerted swiftly on the states of the EC [EEC], Moscow and the Vatican: the mobilisation of public opinion and pressure on President Gomes."[89]

When news reached Genscher, Schmidt contacted Ford and Wilson.[90] He warned: "The socialist party will be eliminated." Schmidt said that Costa Gomes was no longer in control. He suggested a meeting after the NATO Council meeting in Brussels.[91] This was agreed along with a series of measures to concert pressure on Lisbon. Typically the French government refused to cooperate, and although other members of the Council were sympathetic, they were reluctant to join any action that could be seen as interference in the internal affairs of another alliance member.[92] Britain had no such misgivings. Callaghan declared that the situation in Portugal was "potentially dangerous," the MFA "unpredictable," and all were heading toward "a totalitarian regime controlled by the Communists."[93] Schmidt seized the initiative and summoned Soviet ambassador Aleksandr' Tokovinin on 21 March and addressed him on the "alarming" news from Portugal, where the "chaotic" situation was in danger of "getting out of control." Tokovinin was advised to bring it to Brezhnev's attention.[94]

Once alerted, Kissinger—now trying to undo the damage wrought—instructed Carlucci to make a number of points to Costa Gomes on 23/24 March.[95] These included a warning against appointing additional communist ministers, the impression of a military dictatorship coming into being, and keen disappointment "should Portugal move from the tyranny of the right to a deeper tyranny of the left."[96] In Cabinet, Callaghan declared that the situation in Portugal was "potentially dangerous," the MFA "unpredictable," and all were heading toward "a totalitarian regime controlled by the Communists."[97]

MOSCOW OVERREACTS

Since 1919 Moscow had been unfailingly punctilious in preserving outward separation between sponsorship of foreign Communist parties via the Party and relations with noncommunist states conducted by government. In this instance, however, action was taken precipitously that can only be described as panic, leading to risk taking normally associated with Khrushchev rather than his hitherto more cautious successors.

Even though Gromyko is said to have worried more about Portugal falling into chaos than seduced by visions of Soviet gains,[98] what was at stake for Moscow was the chance of luring Portugal into the Soviet camp and, at the very least, ensuring the emergence of its colonies in Africa as states under communist auspices. This would have secured an unexpected windfall. In late March, François Mitterand, head of the French Socialist Party (PSF), had an unexpected visit from the Soviet ambassador. At this time the PSF was in coalition with the PCF in opposition to Giscard d'Estaing (who, like Kissinger, thought there was no hope of rescuing Portugal). But the PCF were firmly in support of the PCP as fellow diehards. The PSF and PCF were thus completely at odds over Portugal. The ostensible reason for the ambassador's visit was to discuss the details of Gromyko's visit. Mitterand told his fellow socialist leaders what happened next:

> He had hardly mentioned the visit at all and had spoken entirely about Portugal. He had started, as if he had been calling on the Foreign Ministry, by stating that the USSR could not accept any external interference in Portugal. M. Mitterand had replied that this was very interesting, and it was particularly interesting that a protest should be made in Paris in the offices of the French Socialist Party by the Soviet ambassador. The ambassador had not liked this at all and had hardened his attitude exactly as if he were making an official approach and repeated with emphasis what he had said about interference. During the visit to Moscow, which had lasted for two days during which Suslov was in the chair, the Russians had spent quite three hours talking about Portugal, as compared with a bare 20 minutes about the Middle East, and had again spoken in almost threatening terms about interference.[99]

Mitterand came away absolutely convinced that the PCP was firmly under Moscow's control and that instructions to it from Moscow were relayed by the PCF. Schmidt was himself equally certain that the PCF was financially entirely dependent on aid from the USSR.[100] When Tito and Berlinguer met on 29 March, they instantaneously found common ground in opposition to PCP rigidity which, Tito said, the "USSR not only supports but also encourages."[101] The only straw in the wind from Moscow was the demotion of Shelepin from the Politburo on 17 April, indicating that the struggle for power there had become bound up in the prospects for revolutionary change in the West.

European socialists were disappointed at the failure to exert greater pressure in Portugal. On 10 April Schmidt asked Kissinger for firmer action, including direct subsidies to political parties, government-to-government aid through defense contracts, and capital investment and direct assistance from the EEC. He made a key point: "For me, one consideration is decisive: can the policy of détente continue once one part of the Western alliance system is broken off? Would not forces in the West that have always taken a negative view of détente force it to an end? And would not the corresponding forces in the East say, when faced with the decay of NATO, that it is wrong for the USSR to make concessions on global issues to the USA?" He urged, "We will all have to face the consequences of an imprudent policy!"[102]

At the general election in Portugal on 25 April the PSP secured 37.87 percent of the votes; the PPD, 26.38 percent; the PCP a mere 12.53 percent; and its front, the MDP/CDE, just 4.12 percent. Yet instead of the ballot resolving the situation, a constitutional crisis now broke out. Cunhal's attitude was scarcely a secret. "We communists don't accept the game of elections!" he told Oriana Fallaci. "No, no, no: the elections mean nothing to me."[103] Similarly, former frigate captain, now rear admiral, Rosa Coutinho was shocked at the failure of the far left to obtain a majority. When asked what would happen as a result of the elections, he said that they need not have any impact at all. "It was impossible for the Armed Forces to allow the parties to govern alone."[104] This was presumably what Costa Gomes meant when he talked about "a pluralist socialist system."[105]

Thus, having granted the elections demanded, the MFA proceeded to nullify the impact of the results. It worried Schmidt that Washington concluded Portugal could not develop democratically. He was determined that NATO and the EEC ensure that it did so.[106] Schmidt confronted Vasco Gonçalves in Brussels on 30 May. The bizarre boast that Portugal was now "the freest country in Europe, perhaps even the freest in the world" prompted Schmidt to ask why, then, the journal *República* had been closed. The answer he found unconvincing; so too Vasco Gonçalves's arguments in favor of a legislature incorporating the military, which Schmidt protested as being "unacceptable abroad."[107]

On 5 June East Berlin noted increased pressure on Portugal from the West. "Their aim is thereby to bind Portugal more strongly to NATO and the EEC, to slow down the revolutionary-democratic process, and to preserve the capitalist economic order in Portugal. Increased influence has been obtained with political, ideological, and material support and through the application of open and covert political and economic pressure."[108] This view was reinforced by the meeting of EEC heads of government on 17 July which focused on the Portuguese problem.

Meanwhile both Cunhal and Soares became ministers without portfolio. The push to the left continued. But Soares fought back using every international connection at hand. At length, following the Stockholm declaration of solidarity with the Portuguese Socialist Party from the Second International on 2 August, and statements by Kissinger (14 August) and Ford (19 August), Moscow became seriously alarmed at the growth of anticommunist sentiment. Now it was the turn of the PCP to feel threatened. At headquarters the Italian communists noted a "continuous state of vigilance. Dozens of comrades in the day and hundreds at night. The leadership no longer meets at Party headquarters." An open struggle for power was taking place focused on capturing opinion within the MFA polarizing around Antunes (to the right) and Gonçalves (to the left). The PSP was becoming ever more anticommunist while the PCP was "isolating itself dangerously."[109]

"International imperialist forces continue to build up pressure on Portugal," Moscow noted, adding in some alarm, "They are manifestly aiming to create in Portugal a situation similar to that in Chile on the eve of the coup." "With the participation of the socialists," they observed, "an anticommunist campaign is being whipped up and is increasingly expressing itself in the form of a po-grom against the organizations of the Communist Party and of other democratic forces." "Now all the achievements of the Portuguese revolution, the freedom and lives of Communists and other democrats in Portugal are under threat," Moscow concluded. The Soviet authorities thus authorized a campaign of sup-port for their allies, including propaganda, commercial contracts, and "other measures."[110] In September Vadim Zagladin from the International Depart-ment was sent out to Portugal. The British and Americans suspected that "long-range control of Cunhal was no longer enough for the Russians."[111]

At a ministerial meeting on 6–7 October 1975 the EEC agreed on credit for Portugal: 180 million units of account, plus food and medical assistance. Then on 10 October Foreign Minister Melo Antunes met Ford and Kissinger, resulting in $55 million for 1976.[112] Costa Gomes tried hard to sustain a bal-ance between East and West. In Moscow on 14 October he emphasized the importance of stabilizing society but defined his country's future in terms of socialism. "However," Moscow noted, "judging from everything, socialism for Costa Gomes means a political course of a liberal nature and quite unclear." Using the opportunity to criticize the PCP, Gomes then backed away when Moscow defended it. "The President openly said that the normalization of the situation in Portugal hinders pressure from the Western countries which is con-nected with not only the participation of communists in the government, but also with NATO's mistrust of Portugal's policy of decolonization." Costa Gomes then went on to say how important was Soviet oil, "especially considering that the West is de facto boycotting Portugal economically."[113]

The drift away from Soviet anchorage continued. In July 1976 when Soares formed a new minority government he dropped Antunes. This pointed to down-grading the military in political life and, as Antunes suspected, the increasing abandonment of socialist control over industry.[114] The problem remained of avoiding direct support from the right-wing Popular Democratic Party and at the same time conceding nothing to the communists. But the announcement by Washington in mid-November that it was prepared to loan Portugal a further $300 million underlined the American commitment to Soares's regime.[115] The subsidy to the PCP also increased, by a factor of ten to $600,000 for the coming year, alongside existing subsidies from East Berlin.[116] But to no avail. Its fortunes continued to decline. A further announcement from Washington in mid-November that it was prepared to loan Portugal a further $300 million underlined the US commitment to Soares.[117]

Although the situation remained uncertain for at least a year, the battle for Portugal's future had effectively been won by the West. André Malraux said in one of his last interviews: "The Portuguese socialists are showing the world for the first time in history that the Mensheviks can defeat the Bolsheviks."[118] But this had been achieved only through a concerted effort from the leaders of Europe's main socialist parties, which managed to convince Washington that they had the answer. The same applied to the Spanish succession in November 1975 and thereafter. Moscow had to look elsewhere to undermine NATO. It had more luck in Portugal's ex-colonies, where matters were resolved before Soares's predominance was established.

THE REVOLUTION IN SOUTHERN AFRICA

Spínola had offered independence to the colonies and here, too, Moscow was vitally concerned. The leaders of the various resistance movements in Angola gathering at Alvor on 15 January 1975 agreed to form a coalition government to take power on 11 November. The Movimento Popular de Libertaçao de Angola (MPLA), the Uniã Nacional para a Independência Total de Angola (UNITA), and the Frente Nacional de Libertaçao de Angola (FNLA) had, however, been embroiled in a struggle for power for a decade, and in so doing they found support from the opposing parties to the Cold War. The largest group, MPLA, was self-consciously Marxist-Leninist, rooted in urban Angola and focused largely within one tribe: the Mbundu of the central-northern region. Within a week the Committee of Forty which supervised US intelligence operations resolved to aid the rival FNLA, led by Holden Roberto, based among the Bakongo in the east. On 18 July Ford approved $30 million for that purpose, and on 24 July he sanctioned the airlift of US armaments from San Antonio, Texas, to Kinshasa, in the Congo.[119] A large group of CIA advisers, including propaganda teams, also turned up in Kinshasa.[120] CIA drew in South Africans for raids on the MPLA. Yet when, in November, the administration asked Congress—kept in the dark about the previous assistance rendered—for another $28 million, it was refused.

The MPLA was the target of US hostility because, as the largest resistance movement, it had been founded by Agostinho Neto with assistance from the PCP.[121] Thereafter Neto had been backed by both Cuba and Russia. Known to Moscow since 1956, a doctor by profession and a poet by vocation, poor-sighted, Neto was neither warrior-like nor decisive in manner. But appearances were deceptive.[122] Daniel Chipenda had been deputy head of MPLA, but he had been ousted by Neto. He was an Umbundu (as was Savimbi who headed UNITA). At the beginning of 1974 the Soviet ambassador in Zambia, Dmitrii Belokolos, was tricked by Chipenda into insisting that Neto and Chipenda form a coalition. When, shocked at the request, Neto refused to do so, the ill-informed Russians withdrew their support in retaliation.[123]

Desertion by Moscow left the MPLA largely dependent on Cuba at the time of the Alvor agreement and its intended implementation. What had begun to turn the situation around was, with US support for FNLA a reality, at the beginning of October 1974 KGB Deputy Chairman Viktor Chebrikov sent an analytical memo to the Politburo warning of US intervention to forestall the takeover of the Angolan administration by the MPLA in November 1975. An additional spur was direct intervention by South African forces. Yet Moscow was slow to translate reassuring words into material assistance.

Deprived of Soviet support, in February 1975 Neto therefore asked the Cubans to make up the shortfall. Cuba had been active in the liberation of Africa from European colonialism since aiding Algeria against the French in 1961. This was followed by an ill-fated expedition to Zaire led by Che in 1965. But even after Che's death in 1967 at the hands of the Americans, African contacts remained strong, though attempts to provide military aid elsewhere proved unsuccessful. Not until the revolution in Portugal did an opportunity arise to demonstrate communist internationalism in a region remote from US predominance.[124] Neto's overture to Havana was made, he said, "despite our understanding that such a move would inevitably prompt a negative international reaction and provide grounds for reinforcement of interference from the West."[125] Cuba was at this time receiving the equivalent to about one-third of their GDP from the USSR in aid and all its military supplies. Military aid stood at $95 million in 1977 and rose to $652 million by 1983.[126] It might therefore be thought that in taking foreign policy initiatives with serious military consequences, Havana would consult Moscow beforehand.

It was only in August 1975, however, that Castro officially informed Soviet ambassador Alexeev of the request for Cuban military advisers. Cuba then held talks with Portuguese generals of the noncommunist revolutionary left, Saraiva de Carvalho and Rosa Coutinhou, who backed the idea. When Moscow found out, however, it was none too pleased. "It appeared excessively radical, if not smacking of adventurism; dangerous for Cuba itself," recalls Karen Brutents, then deputy head of the International Department responsible for liaison with foreign communist parties and national liberation movements. "As a result of a Politburo decision Castro was even sent a telegram recommending that he refrain from such risky behavior, but it arrived in Havana when the planes with Cuban troops had already crossed the Atlantic Ocean."[127] But Brutents may not have been fully informed. Unofficial contacts with the KGB, for example, may also have been in play.

Moscow was left with the invidious choice of backing Havana, which threatened to steal a march in revolution, or holding back for fear of upsetting Washington. Its decision to go in was thus spontaneous rather than the product of advanced planning. Nevertheless it indicated foreign policy priorities: was the continuation of détente more important than outflanking the West in southern Africa or not? "At Zavidovo, Brezhnev's residence, in the mid-seventies," Brutents recalls, "I witnessed a conversation from which one could conclude that Brezhnev was against the USSR being drawn to any extent into tropical Africa."[128] The decision went the other way, however. The KGB's first directorate came out strongly in favor of action, and Andropov would not have ignored the advice. "Africa has turned into an arena for a global struggle between the two systems for a long time to come," the directorate reported.[129] Detinov recalls that this was "ideology at work: the idea of spreading . . . socialism in the whole world."[130] Moreover Andropov saw himself as a true Bolshevik and thought highly of Castro.[131] CIA learned that Ponomarev "was a major advocate of the joint Soviet-Cuban involvement in the Angolan civil war, in opposition to Foreign Minister Gromyko." The agency believed Suslov would also have been associated with this decision. It noted that at the height of the war in February 1976 "Suslov approved for publication in Pravda an article that strongly affirmed Soviet support for the MPLA and made the first authoritative admission that the Soviet Union was supplying it with military aid. It was on Suslov's suggestion that the article was signed 'Observer,' presumably to lend greater weight to its message. At the 25th CPSU Congress [24 February—5 March] Suslov rose to his feet before other Soviet leaders to lead applause for the Angola speaker's call for 'down with imperialism.'"[132]

Echoes of Brezhnev's defeat were later to be heard mid-February 1976 at Zavidovo where his team was drafting his foreign policy speech for the Twenty-fifth Party Congress (24 February). Out of action through the greater part of 1975 when fateful decisions were reached on Angola, Brezhnev began reminiscing about the Cuban missile crisis and the bravura displayed by Khrushchev and his number two, Frol Kozlov. It was "a disgrace," Brezhnev asserted. "And nuclear war all but broke out. . . . I am genuine in wanting peace and will not retreat for anything. You can believe me. However, not all like this line. Not everyone agrees." Alexandrov protested that this was not so. Brezhnev persisted: "They aren't propagandists of one sort or another from a regional committee, but also people like myself. Only they think differently!" Witnessing this, Chernyaev was shocked. And Brezhnev repeated as much in front of Brutents from the International Department whom he had known for only a couple of days.[133]

Moscow had had no intelligence presence in Angola. Information came from Lisbon and other African capitals. Nazhestkin, a KGB officer, was sent to Luanda as a contact with Neto in the late autumn of 1975. But by the time he reached Brazzaville (Congo Republic) en route to Luanda, Moscow had decided to back the Cuban venture. Nazhestkin was briefed by ambassador Yevgenii Afanasenko that Moscow was ready to recognize Angola as independent as soon as the MPLA made the declaration on 11 November. Neto was astonished to learn of this when Nazhestkin arrived in the capital. "Finally, finally we have been understood. It means we will cooperate, cooperate and fight together," he declared with obvious enthusiasm. He added, "The Portuguese are going to cooperate with MPLA and are prepared to give us power even though among them are many who would prefer a Roberto or Savimbi government." What he required in the face of Western intervention was military assistance at an official level. "Our Cuban friends are doing everything that they can. But do not have enough armaments."[134] He did not need troops (Cuba already had a special forces battalion there), only weapons. And the Portuguese in Luanda would close their eyes if Soviet arms arrived before 11 November.[135]

To preserve form, however, Moscow cautiously awaited proclamation of the Angolan republic before sending arms. On the morning of that day, 11 November, General Vasilii Makarov was briefed on the upcoming dispatch of 20 military specialists to assist the MPLA in the use of Soviet weapons. Makarov was to go with the group to represent the General Staff (the tenth main directorate) in dealings with Neto, but also to keep Moscow informed in detail as to what was going on.[136] By the end of the month Moscow had 90 men in situ; the following year 344, including 96 advisers with 5 support staff, 159 specialists, 26 interpreters, and 58 from special units.[137] In the course of four months Russia ferried in aid through seventy flights with a maximum of seven per day over the course of 6,250 nautical miles one way.[138] In August 1976 KGB residencies were instructed:

One of the main requirements which SVIRIDOV [Andropov] has demanded for our work in Africa consists of directing the residencies towards major political problems. This means working more persistently to undermine the position of the Americans and British in Africa, and to strengthen

Soviet influence on the continent. It is necessary to establish firm positions and channels of influence within the ruling circles, governments and intelligence services, in order to obtain reliable prognoses concerning the situation in the country and the region as a whole, and on the activities of the Americans, the British and the Chinese, and to carry out wide-ranging measures against them.[139]

By the autumn of 1976 Moscow was rather pleased with developments. "A range of national revolutionary parties and movements are drawing close to Marxist-Leninist positions," Ponomarev reflected, adding, "A great deal of work in this sense is being done by the CPSU" in such countries as Angola, Mozambique, Somalia, etc.[140] What had yet to be added to the bill, however, was the cost of these operations in the accounting for détente.

DÉTENTE FAILS

The Soviet Union is not merely talking about world revolution but is actually helping to bring it about.

—*Andropov, October 1980*

A comforting but unsupported assumption underpinning Washington's policy of détente was that Moscow was becoming less revolutionary. CIA's Special National Intelligence Estimate for July 1969 asserted that "nonideological considerations are playing an increasingly important role in the formulation of Soviet foreign policies. The USSR tends to behave more as a world Power than as the center of the world revolution. Thus the Soviets are inclined to establish international priorities in accordance with a more traditional view of Russian security interests and a more realistic view of Russian security interests and a more realistic view of the possibilities for expanding their influence."[1] Similarly in allied Britain we also find the wish fathering the thought, even among hard-bitten diplomats. The man who shortly thereafter became the Permanent Under-Secretary at the Foreign Office, Sir Dennis Greenhill, announced that in the new atmosphere of détente following the Cuban crisis the KGB's golden age was drawing to a close, its influence about to diminish.[2]

This rationalist fallacy had occurred repeatedly in the past. It assumed that the commitment to international revolution was merely a matter of choice for Soviet leaders and in so doing underestimated the very point that Trotsky insisted upon; namely, that however reactionary in preferences, Soviet leaders were driven by the nature of the system to pursue the expansion of the revolution. But the rationalist fallacy was popular among liberal Sovietologists in the United States. The delusion perhaps had less to do with Moscow than the fact that the Americans were exhausted. They wanted détente. Liberal voices drowned out at the height of McCarthyism and its aftermath under Kennedy could now be heard loud and clear.

Events, however, ultimately made clear that Moscow had no intention of ending the Cold War through compromise in either the struggle over the balance of Europe or the larger ideological conflict over the shape of the international system. A backlash thus occurred at the end of the 1970s separately from both directions—Europe and the United States. If one did not write off the American will to power and German fear of the Red Army, it was utterly predictable. Yet it undoubtedly caught the elderly Soviet leadership entirely by surprise.

THE CORRELATION OF FORCES

Moscow became ever more optimistic about global transformation with the advent of détente. Though hard to credit, it did not rule out the introduction of Soviet-style socialism even in Italy and France. The "revolution of the carnations" gave false credence to such hopes even though it was effectively neutralized by West European social democracy. Ponomarev scolded the East Germans for saying "that today no revolutionary situation exists in any West European country. In the classical sense," he insisted, "this is correct; but in some countries 'there is something in the air.'" Much hinged upon the policy of Communist parties in their respective countries. Italy, Ponomarev insisted, "objectively had a great deal of inflammable material. We have said to the Italian Communist Party: you stand on the threshold of important events; but so much depends on you."[3]

The Kremlin blandly assumed that the capitalist world had no choice but to accept these new realities brought into play by the shift in the correlation of forces worldwide. It seriously underestimated the robustness of capitalism and failed to understand the weakness of its own position: the consequences of dismal economic growth that few at the top other than Kosygin understood. Looking back nostalgically, Andropov noted that "the 1970s were a time of far-reaching growth in the power and influence of the socialist community. . . . Critical losses were suffered by imperialism in wide areas of the so-called Third World. The prosperity of the West has hitherto depended on control over the resources of the Third World. The revolutionary changes in Angola, Ethiopia, Nicaragua, and other countries—and these conditioned by objective factors—were taken by Washington, and not without reason, to be a defeat for American policy."[4] It was all a matter of ideology. "It would be a mistake to seek an intelligent basis for this policy," argues Colonel Vitaly Shlykov, then serving in the GRU.[5]

AMERICOCENTRISM

The assumption that the shifting correlation of forces could not be halted let alone reversed lay behind the Soviet stance at SALT II. Moscow had failed to remove dual-capable US forward-based systems (FBS) under SALT I. These included F-111 fighter-bombers based across East Anglia in Britain with reinforcements in New Hampshire on the other side of the Atlantic (F-111A), having proven their deadly effectiveness in raids on North Vietnam, flying below radar level impervious to surface-to-air missiles. Dual-capable A-4s and A-6s could be launched from aircraft carriers in the Mediterranean and the Pacific. Soviet air defense had no means of dealing with these threats adequately.[6] In advance of the Geneva round of SALT II (24 September–16 November 1973) Moscow determined to remove FBS: "resolution must also be found for the question of the withdrawal of strategic, offensive means which, as a result of their geographical location, are capable of reaching the territory of the other side, and of the liquidation of the corresponding bases on the territory of third countries." On this view all FBS would go within five years.[7]

This stance ignored the fact that these systems underwrote the security of NATO Europe; were Washington to dispose of them, in a limited war Western Europe would face conventional superiority without sufficient countervailing force. Indeed, in 1977 Washington believed that "In Central Europe, the chance of NATO stopping a Warsaw Pact attack with minimal loss of territory and then achieving its full objective of recovering that land which had been lost appears remote at the present time."[8] Colonel General Danilevich at the Soviet General Staff freely acknowledges "that in the early 1970s the Soviet Union enjoyed a significant quantitative advantage in conventional forces over NATO."[9] But it was not merely a matter of numbers. At the Voroshilov General Staff Academy the officer corps were comforted by the assertion "that Socialist countries are situated in a more advantageous position vis-à-vis Western countries" through occupying the heart of Eurasia. Moreover, the depth of NATO Europe was "limited to 400–800 km, while many . . . rear bases and important targets are located near the borders of Socialist countries." "The most important weakness of NATO," Moscow emphasized, "is the separation of the European allies from their major ally, the United States, which constitutes the vital military and economic basis for the alliance. European NATO members are separated from the U.S. by the Atlantic Ocean, while naval supply routes to Europe, the Near East, and the Middle East are subject to direct threat."[10]

Thus to West Europeans, deterrence purely from American soil was not entirely credible, particularly if the United States negotiated away its superiority in warheads to reestablish parity at SALT II. Psychologically and politically, therefore, conceding removal of FBS might reassure Moscow at the price of retreating from obligations assumed under Truman to counterbalance Soviet power in Europe. A report from Britain's Joint Intelligence Committee on 6 May 1974 pointed out that the "threat derives as much from Western inaction and divisions as from Soviet design; but we doubt whether these shortcomings will be remedied. We therefore foresee a period of danger in the immediate future and fear that the Soviet Union may significantly improve its position in Europe in the period under review."[11]

Moscow was invariably Americocentric. This Superpower conceit was reinforced by détente insofar as it pivoted on SALT and insofar as arms control was entirely a Soviet-American affair, lulling Moscow into overlooking the separate security concerns expressed in Western Europe, a tendency equally evident in Washington. Just as in 1945–47, the European response demonstrated its influence over US policy to Moscow's disadvantage. Western Europe was a subject and not merely an object of the Cold War. Moscow paid highly more than once for neglecting this fact.

NATO Europe was unsurprised by Washington's position. Sir John Killick, Britain's formidable ambassador to the United States, argued that

> the familiar tendency to intellectual high-handedness in US policy, the conviction that the US Government is the best judge of the overall Western interest and a corresponding inclination to take the Alliance for granted are no less real in the age of détente than in the age of confrontation. In the present circumstances it must be tempting for the Americans to square the Soviet Government in private in advance, without waiting to consult their Allies, in the hope of de-fusing possible disputes before they become tiresome. Taken with Dr Kissinger's predilection for secret diplomacy, this can lead to bilateral understandings based on the American side on insufficient knowledge of the complications of the subject. With the best will in the world it then becomes bureaucratically difficult—and in the short term even important—to secure any change in the American position, involving as this must a potentially embarrassing reopening of the subject in question with the Russians.[12]

Not all were equally vulnerable, however. France enjoyed the luxury of being anti-American while living under US protection; and it, at least, had a handful of nuclear weapons to call its own. Not so Bonn. Having foresworn development and possession of nuclear weapons in 1969, the West Germans depended entirely on Washington for security. The slightest hint that the United States was not wholly committed to their defense was bound to rekindle anxieties; and

Soviet attempts to remove US forces drew sufficient draught into the cinders to set them ablaze.

BREZHNEV'S ILLNESS IMPAIRS DÉTENTE

Brezhnev's sickness created a further problem. According to Kremlin doctor Yevgeny Chazov, Andropov was the first to be informed officially of the deterioration—in 1972; followed by Suslov; finally, from 1978, the remainder of the Politburo.[13] Brezhnev had suffered a severe attack of angina in 1957.[14] He collapsed in mid-August 1968, the eve of the invasion of Czechoslovakia.[15] A further seizure occurred—which proved a turning point—immediately after the negotiations at Okeanskaya, Vladivostok, 23–24 November 1974.[16] Brezhnev was then said to be working only a three-day week.[17] Thereafter until the middle of February 1975, when he received the British Prime Minister, Brezhnev was absent from the Politburo.[18] He met Harold Wilson only because of "a whole wave of rumors of various kinds" in the Western press. "Questions and talk of one kind or another also arose at home; people had to be reassured," Brezhnev later told allies.[19] Unable to meet Gierek and Honecker in mid-March, Brezhnev made excuses: "Nothing special was wrong with me," he said, "simply exhaustion, ennervation, and the doctors began insisting on a certain period of rest. A genuine rest was unobtainable; it was interrupted by work . . . but all the same. . . . I had to refrain from trips, meetings, long sessions in the office."[20]

The abrupt removal of Shelepin from the leadership on 16 April 1975 signaled the need to bolster Brezhnev's policy, as the unprecedented intrusion of the Soviet ambassador to France into socialist policy on Portugal indicated. During the state dinner at Helsinki for signature of the Final Act of CSCE in August, Brezhnev had to leave during the first course. Subsequently, at a meeting scheduled with Genscher, conversation staggered forward. After only one hour Gromyko led Genscher into another room to explain that dinner was cancelled because of Brezhnev's deteriorating condition.[21] Falin concluded that he must have had another heart attack.[22] Head of the FCO East European and Soviet department, Sir Bryan Cartledge, saw Brezhnev in Helsinki. He appeared "rather like a convalescent after a long illness."[23] In London "secret sources of particular sensitivity"[24] confirmed as much.

Thereafter Brezhnev's capacity to concentrate diminished with progressive arteriosclerosis leading to onset of senile dementia, doubtless hastened by beta-blockers taken to lower blood pressure for relief of the heart.[25] Growing dependence on sleeping pills made matters worse. Even removal of Brezhnev's personal nurse failed to staunch the stream of opiates now cadged from friends and colleagues. And when he then forgot to turn on his hearing aid the result was disastrous. Concealment at meetings with foreign statesmen proved impossible. President Giscard d'Éstaing had already noticed the problem in 1974,[26] as had Gierek, who was on first-name terms.[27] Thereafter Politburo meetings on Thursdays lasted no more than one and a half hours at most.[28]

A TROIKA EMERGES

Kornienko, first deputy to Gromyko, asked Alexandrov-Agentov whether Brezhnev intended retiring at the Twenty-fifth Party Congress. He responded by pointing at the telephone (which normally contained a secret listening device), giving Kornienko to understand that such matters were not to be aired out loud.[29] In 1977 Foreign Secretary David Owen visited the Kremlin. His interpreter[30] was taken to one side by Alexandrov-Agentov, who bluntly asked that Owen ignore anything the General Secretary had to say.[31] The culminating point occurred during negotiations with the Americans not long before his death in 1982, when Brezhnev eventually turned up, read the prepared text with difficulty and promptly fell silent. To the amazement of all he turned to his assistant and asked out loud: "Have I read it all correctly?"[32]

Although decisions still required Brezhnev's assent, the substance of power tacitly passed to a troika: Andropov, Gromyko, and Ustinov, who met in the *orekhovaya* room (paneled in walnut) where the entire Politburo foregathered on Thursdays.[33] "They had at their disposal the kind of information and intelligence of which the other members of the Politburo knew nothing."[34] More precisely, Brochure No. 1 from the fourth department of the KGB's sixteenth directorate, now responsible for analyzing foreign decrypts, went only to Brezhnev, Andropov, Gromyko, Kirilenko, Suslov, and Ustinov.[35]

"A range of questions were in general beyond the control of the Politburo. Certain organizations, departments, parts of the country, and individuals were, so to say, untouchable, beyond criticism,"[36] Gromyko recalled. Of the three, Andropov, though cautious, was the more dynamic but also the greater fundamentalist. More pragmatic, Gromyko could also be too rigid, and advancing old age made him more cautious than ever. Dmitrii ("Dima") Ustinov, who became Defense Minister on Grechko's death (26 April 1976), Alexandrov-Agentov notes, "was far and away tougher and more resolute."[37]

A missile engineer, Khrushchev's son highlighted Ustinov as "one of the fathers of missile technology" whose authority was "of enormous weight." Brezhnev and Ustinov came to know one another soon after the war when Brezhnev was secretary of the Dnepropetrovsk regional Party committee and Ustinov was minister for armaments. He drove forward war production relentlessly and thereafter pioneered the development of missile technology.[38] Their paths crossed frequently through the late 1950s and after Brezhnev succeeded Kozlov, following the second secretary's heart attack, on 22 June 1963 and reacquired responsibility for the defense industries. "Business-like and purposeful, Ustinov subjected Brezhnev, known for his pliant character, to his will. Everyone knew of this."[39]

Ustinov had overseen defense industries as a Central Committee secretary from 26 March 1965[40] until, after joining the Politburo on 5 March 1976, finally he became defense minister. Although initially benefiting from his power over the military-industrial sector, which meant he could ruthlessly cut through red tape, by 1982 Ustinov had fallen out with the man he selected as Chief of the General Staff, Nikolai Ogarkov, with whom there had been an initial honeymoon.[41] His immediate subordinates—at what became "the center of the military-industrial complex"[42]—then found little to respect in a man past his peak; though unrivaled on technological matters, he wasted inordinate amounts of time at lengthy meetings. Moreover, when any specifically military question arose, "it was a problem for him."[43] Something of a political dinosaur from Stalinist times, and without the status of military command, he was incapable of meriting the kind of respect granted Grechko.

The troika reinforced tight interdependence between the KGB, the Foreign Ministry, the Ministry of Defense, the General Staff, and the Military-Industrial Committee of the Council of Ministers (VPK). The latter, set up in the early fifties, had mainly "to keep an eye on foreign defense technologies using our research institutes, design bureaus, etc., and make sure that our domestic weapon systems are at least as advanced as theirs." It determined the procurement budget and oversaw pilot projects. But it was not supposed "to manage the actual production process." In turn, the Central Committee Defense Sector oversaw the VPK. "They were our bosses," the former deputy director of the VPK recalls. They "dealt with individual items." And "they had more authority and none of the responsibilities."[44] The system made any policy change threatening to unravel the interdependence between interested institutions entirely impracticable. Meetings of the "five," attended by first deputy ministers on questions of exceptional importance came under the direct responsibility of the First Deputy Chief of the General Staff.[45] This did not mean state control over the Party, however, since the latter pervaded all departments through Party cells in each sector. Moreover, Brezhnev chaired the Defense Council that effectively made the final decisions, and he was served by the Military-Industrial Sector of the Central Committee apparatus. But in this case the chair was vacant much of the time.

At Okeanskaya near Vladivostok on 23–24 November 1974, just before a severe heart attack, Brezhnev stretched consensus on arms control to breaking point in agreeing a compromise for SALT II with Ford. Prior to this, Semyonov insisted on the inclusion of FBS under SALT II. Brezhnev agreed to drop this demand.[46] This appears to have raised a furor in Moscow. According to Kornienko, Grechko protested against the compromise agreed by Brezhnev and had Podgorny weigh in on his side; but Brezhnev wheeled in support from Kosygin, Ustinov, and Andropov.[47] It did not end there, however. CIA picked up a rumor deemed plausible that "at a Politburo meeting preceding a Central Committee plenum in December 1974, Suslov and Shelepin sharply criticised Brezhnev's handling of Soviet-US relations." Moreover Suslov "is said to have charged Brezhnev during this period with having exceeded Politburo instructions for negotiating on SALT at Vladivostok in November 1974."[48] And when talks renewed at Geneva on 1 February 1975, Semyonov's full draft treaty "took extreme positions incorporating every past Soviet contention and some new ones too: limiting our Trident submarines, making FBS an automatic part of future SALT negotiations, and others."[49] This was the first sign that what Brezhnev said was not the final word. Moscow also went ahead with a phased array radar at Krasnoyarsk in Siberia. "The establishment of a phased array radar system in Krasnoyarsk does in fact contradict article 6b of the ABM treaty," deputy head of the Military-Industrial Sector of the Central Committee apparatus Vitaly Kataev acknowledged later.[50]

Decisions worked against the grain of détente even while policy remained formally unchanged. The system of five originally established to advance the cause of détente, notably through arms control, by creating and sustaining a tight political grip over weapons building, turned into a system by which the military and allies in industry maintained a stranglehold over policy by vetoing developments favorable to détente. This was a natural development once force planning was integrated with arms control strategy. From being diplomats suspicious of military reasoning, Americanists (Gromyko and deputy ministers Viktor Komplektov and Kornienko) transmuted into negotiators fronting for the military. Deployment of the SS-20 missile (the RSD-10, or *Pioner*) epitomized this Faustian bargain.

THE SS-20 CRISIS

"I am against the [arms] race," Brezhnev told advisers at a meeting on 16 December 1975, "this much goes without saying, in all sincerity. But when the Americans talk about building up, the Ministry of Defense says to me that they cannot therefore guarantee our security. And I am chairman of the Defense Council. How can that be? Give them 140 or 156 million? The Americans are crafty; they say that these missiles are not strategic, yet they have the advantages given by geography."[51] Ivan Serbin, head of the Central Committee's Military-Industrial Sector, argued in 1975 that "the fundamental means by which strategic missile weapons will develop in the future is by qualitative improvement and, above all, the accuracy of targeting and the effectiveness of the military equipment." Moscow also expected Washington "to raise significantly the quality of military equipment . . . and by these means partly compensate for the quantitative superiority of the total usable capability of the USSR's missiles." Soviet design bureaux had exhausted their technical lead in warheads and had fallen seriously behind in the ratio between the power of a warhead and its weight. To make up the distance with Washington required fundamental research and concentrated effort across a range of requirements.[52]

The decision on the SS-20 was thus taken against a background of perceived relative weakness exacerbated by uncertainty over the removal of FBS under SALT II. Schmidt later asked Gorbachev why the decision had been taken. "That was never decided in the Politburo," he replied. "The old man did that on his own with the army." Schmidt was unclear whether this was because it was thought too unimportant or too important.[53] It also indicated Ustinov's extraordinary influence over Brezhnev. Ustinov was "inordinately proud" of the deployment.[54] "The decision to deploy the SS-20s was made in total secrecy," recalls Nikolai Leonov, chief analyst at the KGB. "Even our intelligence didn't know about it. The military-industrial complex was out of control, including the army. We in intelligence learnt about it from American sources."[55] Kataev recalls that, as with the Krasnoyarsk radar, the SS-20 decision was made in a small circle.[56] It had Gromyko's blessing, however.[57] It enhanced the ability to bargain over FBS.

The SS-20 (RSD-10) originated with the Nadiradze construction bureau in 1971. Since it was based on the mobile SS-16 (Temp-2) ICBM, which was discontinued, it made rapid progress.[58] Testing began at Kapustin Yar on 21 September 1974.[59] Even before testing had been completed, it went into serial production at Votkinsk near Kazan' in Siberia.[60] The first were commissioned on 11 March 1976, combat ready on 30 August.[61] On December 1976 NATO defense ministers pronounced on the dangers they presented.[62] Deployment allowed Moscow to redeploy heavy ICBMs hitherto targeting Western Europe to other tasks and to retire R-12s (SS-4s) and R-14s (SS-5s) from the force. Three divisions were based in Byelorussia; three in the Ukraine; and four more beyond the Urals.[63] The speed, accuracy, and maneuverability of the mobile SS-20 permitted Moscow to deliver timely blows at targets in Western Europe and the Far East, in the words of General Valentin Varennikov.[64]

It is not clear whether the emergence of the SS-20 gave rise to doctrinal rethinking or vice versa. But that such rethinking accompanied the mass deployment of the SS-20 is a fact. Lieutenant General Batenin, who worked for Akhromeyev when the latter was Chief of the Main Operations Directorate at the General Staff and then as First Deputy Chief of the General Staff under Ogarkov from January 1977, said, "The SS-20 was being deployed and Danilevich and others in his collective [within the Main Operations Directorate] were developing concepts."[65] These concepts led to the writing of a three-volume *Strategy of Deep Operations (Global and Theater)* published in a closed edition between 1977 and 1986. This work completely transformed the periodization of war according to principles not unlike the staged escalation in the US doctrine of flexible response. "I believe the SS-20 made it possible, that the SS-20 created the environment in which strategists could think about war on such a large scale," Batenin recalls. "Under the roof of the SS-20 it was possible to think about deep operations."[66] Indeed, Danilevich saw the SS-20 as "a breakthrough, unlike anything the Americans had. We were immediately able to hold all of Europe hostage."[67] The shift from massive retaliation to extended conventional war and then limited nuclear war had been blocked by Grechko, who disliked it, as did Marshal Vladimir Tolubko in charge of strategic missile forces.[68] The move toward the new strategy was thus gradual but assured by Ustinov's appointment and that of Ogarkov, who was, according to Batenin, his deputy, "very actively" fostering this new line.[69] Flexible response was thus seen in terms of "dosage" strikes.[70] Moreover, and on this Danilevich is adamant: "At some point in the 1970s there were offensive, as well as defensive plans, i.e., a pre-emptive strike" against NATO.[71] Danilevich tells us that such planning took place strictly within the General Staff Main Operations Directorate. Major commands and institutes were not consulted. As for the Politburo and Central Committee, "they had no idea of what we were doing."[72]

Not surprisingly, deployment raised a specter that caused particular alarm in Bonn, whose relations with Washington had reached their nadir. Relations with Jimmy Carter were worse than between any chancellor and US president since the war. Schmidt "the lip," whose reputation in the United States was high, had all but openly backed Ford for election in statements published during the summer of 1976.[73] At the height of campaigning vice presidential candidate Walter Mondale fretted at the impact of his outspokenness.[74] And for the first few weeks in office, no one dared even to mention Bonn in the presence of Polish-born National Security Adviser Zbigniew Brzezinski.[75]

Carter held to a firm stance on human rights in criticizing Moscow. This inevitably made matters worse for Schmidt, threatening arrangements for the repatriation of Germans living in the East.[76] The new line was an easy compromise: between the new White House chief of staff Hamilton Jordan, who had marched with Martin Luther King, and Brzezinski, ably assisted by former student Colonel William Odom.[77] Schmidt and Brezhnev thus found common ground. In an indiscreet letter to Brezhnev on 2 June 1977 Schmidt went so far as to boast that at the London summit Carter had been convinced of how "unwise" and "unrealistic" it was to raise human rights issues in absolute terms.[78]

Even greater complications arose because Carter was anxious to secure genuine nuclear disarmament. Since Bonn's security rested on the US nuclear deterrent, the new line was bound to arouse anxieties. These coincided with opposition to détente within the United States. Aside from the ABM provisions, SALT marked an agreement only temporary in nature, covering the number of missiles (and bombers) arrayed against each side, that left Moscow with a numerical advantage at intercontinental level. It was unlikely that this Soviet advantage could be expected to continue, however. The military on each side looked less at the advantages particular to its own force structure and instead focused on the unique opportunities afforded the adversary.

A radical and unattractive offer on SALT II made by Secretary of State Cyrus Vance in Moscow during April 1977 met with consternation. It came out of Presidential Directive NSC-7 of 23 March 1977. Moscow claimed that it was a complete revision of the understandings reached at Okeanskaya, to which the Russians had now become attached. Strong objection was raised against the "demagogic and provocative campaign by the US on human rights."[79] Carter had no comprehension that combining both was unwise.[80] But press spokesman Jody Powell took the view that backing the cause of dissent in the USSR—pressed not only by the Republican right but also by Democrat Senator Henry "Scoop" Jackson—outflanked conservative criticism of arms control and disarmament. Moreover, Jordan noted in June 1977, "To challenge the Soviets is 'conservative.'"[81]

The abrupt shift in US policy therefore met with uncomprehending hostility in Moscow, no less than in Bonn. Yet, for all the rhetorical fallout, both sides continued negotiating SALT II. Moscow was anxious lest the United States deploy cruise missiles.[82] NATO Europe was in turn anxious lest Washington forego the opportunity to modernize the theater nuclear arsenal to win a second SALT treaty. On 28 May Bonn was reassured that cruise missiles were indeed viewed in Washington as "an essential counter to the Soviet medium-range capability" that could prove significant were there negotiations on the "gray zone" of nuclear weapons systems.[83]

At NATO's Nuclear Planning Group meeting in Ottawa on 8–9 June 1977, US Secretary of Defense Harold Brown broke the news that five SS-20s were now deployed (two in the western USSR). Nevertheless he asked all to bear in mind that cruise missiles could become "a critical factor" in respect of SALT II: "In this case, the military benefits [from their deployment in Europe] had to be weighed against the SALT side [of the equation]." This came as a shock to the allies. Brown, indeed, acknowledged "concern at the possible splintering of political interests within the alliance on account of underlying geostrategic positions."[84] But this meant little if Washington was bent on sacrificing cruise to obtain SALT II. For its part Bonn had little reason to trust Brown. Thus to complicate his position, a counterweight was sought in the State Department.

Genscher expressed his concerns to Vance on 4 July. He reinforced Defense Minister Georg Leber's comments to Brown concerning the "vital interests" of NATO Europe. By negotiating on cruise, Washington was opening up FBS for trading. On this view nothing should be conceded that affected the nuclear balance at the regional level. In particular, any limitation below the range of 1,500 kilometers "was unacceptable to the Federal Government," and any limitation had to be balanced against Soviet medium-range missile capabilities. Otherwise there was a real possibility that "a wedge could be driven into the alliance" (*zum anderen könnte sie in der Cruise-Missile-Frage eine Chance sehen, einen Keil in die Allianz zu treiben*).[85]

At the Petrignani group of European experts on SALT in Brussels, where the issue of cruise was debated once more on 12 July, the British reiterated the concerns of Leber lest the fate of cruise split the alliance should Washington sacrifice deployment in Europe to obtain cuts in Soviet ICBMs.[86] And Bonn was not about to be fobbed off with patronizing platitudes, however well meant. The suggestion subsequently offered by Assistant Secretary of State for Politico-Military Affairs Leslie Gelb that the issue of cruise missiles was "more a psychological and less a military resource" was not even dignified by comment from Bonn.[87] When, however, Gelb subsequently repeated the point and told the Germans that Cruise would not appear in the SALT II agreement proper but in an additional protocol, he was bluntly "corrected" and had the military rationale explained to him.[88]

In late September and then mid-October Gromyko finally met Carter. Gromyko complained that US policy was contradictory. Anxious to appease, Carter showed eagerness to compromise: he agreed to the inclusion of air-launched cruise missiles (ALCMs) with a range of over 600 kilometers and undertook not to limit heavy Soviet missiles. These missiles were of major concern to Moscow. Cruise missiles flew below line-of-horizon radar and, though relatively slow compared with ballistic missiles, it was extremely hard to see them coming. And Soviet air defense had been shown by US bombardment of Hanoi in the early 1970s to be incapable of successfully coping with low-flying aircraft such as the F-111, let alone missiles.[89]

Gromyko thus left Washington delighted, though doubts remained concerning "the fierce struggle on the concrete substance of the new treaty."[90] The compromise obtained was, however, bound to throw NATO into disarray. The argument repeated from Washington was that what mattered was the global balance, not a regional or theater balance. Yet Moscow was planning for limited war. Crucially, Brezhnev's letter to Schmidt of 26 October attacking proposals for a US neutron bomb in Western Europe—designed to overcome massed Soviet tanks—was predicated on the possibility of limited war.[91] "By 1979," Danilevich recalls, "the General Staff began to contemplate the possibility of limited nuclear use or of limited nuclear war."[92] Moreover, until the early eighties the General Staff still assumed that the USSR's vast expanse guaranteed survivability in a nuclear war.[93]

Just two days after receiving Brezhnev's letter, on 28 October 1977 Schmidt went public at the Institute for Strategic Studies in London. Usually his speeches were carefully prepared with his subordinates. But on this occasion, he recalls, "I was seething; I spoke freely."[94] The problem was an additional, emerging imbalance of nuclear power in Europe: "Strategic arms limitation confined to the United States and the Soviet Union," he emphasized, "will inevitably impair the security of the West European members of the Alliance vis-à-vis Soviet military superiority in Europe if we do not succeed in removing the disparities of military power in Europe parallel to the SALT negotiations."[95]

One reason for hardening attitudes was growing recognition that Moscow had no need to enhance military superiority in Europe. One senior Soviet diplomat was certain in his own mind "that our extraordinary military potential in Europe is politically unjustified."[96] Schmidt said later: "These new Soviet medium-range missiles were perfectly suited to upset the military balance; most of them were aimed at West Germany. . . . Probably nothing would have happened under Brezhnev. He was actually afraid of war, I knew that. But I realized that things might look different later on, under another Soviet leadership. . . . I also gave some thought to how an American administration would react if only Germans were at risk."[97] Schmidt told the Federal Security Council that from the safety of their own territory Moscow and Washington maintained a balance of power, neutralizing each other's capability. Clearly with SALT II those in

Washington and Moscow "can sleep more quietly," but in Europe existing disparities were worsening. "The danger grows that Europe is decoupled from the USA-USSR sanctuary."[98]

Leber demanded suitable compensation for Soviet superiority in medium-range nuclear forces. But Washington was unconvinced. A hard-nosed scientist and practitioner but not a natural communicator and certainly no politician, Brown coolly took the view that Bonn need not worry given US nuclear superiority overall.[99] Any separation of the balance in the European theater from the global balance was thus artificial. Though technically true, this lofty appreciation was more easily maintained on the distant American continent than across the broad Atlantic. It was unsustainable politically, given Bonn's dependence upon Washington for its security against the Moscow; and the fact that, in overlooking European defense requirements, Russia sought predominance on the continent to counterbalance the United States globally. This was the very same problem that sparked the Cold War: Soviet assertion of the right to hold the balance of Europe, if not to prevail entirely.

From the embassy in Bonn, ambassador Falin conveyed concerns to Moscow. But Gromyko was not listening. When Schmidt proposed that the number of SS-20s be limited to those actually replacing the SS-4 and SS-5s, Moscow did not reply. "Our attempts to persuade Brezhnev to react positively had no result," Falin recalls. "Brezhnev said: persuade Gromyko; I agree in advance. But persuading Gromyko was impossible."[100] Schmidt also claimed that in 1979–80 Brezhnev made an attempt to cut SS-20 deployments but no longer had the power to do so.[101] Brzezinski remembered "being somewhat startled when Chancellor Schmidt started making a big issue out of the SS-20s, but then I came to realize that in a sense he was right: namely that the SS-20, while perhaps not a decisive military weapon, posed the risk of decoupling Europe's security from America's."[102] Schmidt was nevertheless convinced that Washington "still didn't push the Soviets strongly enough. . . . I remember Soviet Prime Minister Kosygin with undisguised triumph said, 'The Americans aren't mentioning the SS-20s at all. So you're completely isolated.'"[103]

Indeed, not until 1979 was Washington fully convinced that it faced a serious problem. A memorandum from Brown and Vance to Carter on 9 May 1979 outlined Schmidt's concerns. The recommendation resulting was deployment of Pershing II or Cruise missiles in Europe or a combination of both. NATO's High Level Group looking into the issue had independently concluded as much. Bonn insisted that all share the burdens of deployment equally for obvious reasons: opposition within the SPD. "Each Ally confronts major political problems, both domestically and vis-a-vis the Soviet Union. Nuclear issues provoke strong reactions among European publics. The certain Soviet propaganda campaign against deployments will find resonance in many countries because of this, and because of interest in protecting détente." Failure to follow through was spelled out in strong terms: "doubts" about "US political will and commitment to European security" would increase. "The ultimate outcome could be a weakened NATO and a Western Europe more independent of the United States." It would also harm the likelihood of SALT II ratification.[104]

Naturally, had Schmidt convinced Moscow to withdraw deployments, none of this would have been necessary. For long he remained convinced that Ogarkov led hard-line opposition to concessions.[105] Yet this was plausible only as long as Ogarkov held command. An officer with a good reputation intellectually as well as operationally, Ogarkov had taken up the post in January 1977 but he soon came into conflict with Ustinov.[106] Varennikov recalls that fighting started when Ogarkov repeatedly appealed over Ustinov's head, and he did so because Ustinov ignored advice offered by the General Staff.[107]

The impression that the blockage over the SS-20 was attributable solely or even largely to Ogarkov was inaccurate. A colleague told senior diplomat Adamishin: "Schmidt warned us: let us talk about the SS-20, when they were only beginning to be deployed; enter into talks; do not act unilaterally." Instead Moscow sent him away empty-handed. But it was Gromyko who held the decisive word.[108] And it was most unlikely that grandfather of all nuclear weapons systems Ustinov would willingly ignore pressures from the defense sector to sustain deployment. Moreover, the assumption that the Chief of the General Staff alone held a veto over defense policy oversimplified the situation. It seriously underestimated other interests: the level of inertia prevalent within the Brezhnev regime; the true extent and depths of Gromyko's "absurd, stupid stubbornness";[109] as well as the firm axis established since SALT between Foreign Ministry Americanists and the heads of the military-industrial sector. Respect for the military at Smolenskaya was deep-seated and difficult to dislodge later, when Shevardnadze took control. Kovalev, Deputy Foreign Minister and head of policy planning, recalls that "in the Ministry of Defense and especially in the General Staff there were educated people staunchly defending positions that, as they believed, had to be defended."[110]

One illustration of the manner in which the military could operate without interference can be found in Brezhnev's speech at Tula on 18 January 1977. Even his speechwriters were at a loss to explain the source of Brezhnev's renunciation of military superiority.[111] In these circumstances, too much was made of it in the West by those concerned to show how Russian military doctrine mirror-imaged our own. Odom recalls: "Gorbachev took pains to say that the change [in military doctrine] occurred only in 1986 at the Twenty-seventh Party Congress, and even then the language was ambiguous. According to several former senior Soviet officers whom I interviewed in June and July 1995, it did not change in reality even then because they still believed that like Brezhnev, Gorbachev was merely trying to mislead the imperialist powers."[112]

Furthermore, from a handful of SS-20s, Moscow stubbornly proceeded with mass deployment. This was, after all, a core element within the new planning for limited war options within the General Staff. Simultaneously Russia sought to sustain conventional military superiority and rid itself of the neutron bomb.[113] In mid-December 1977 the Politburo took a decision to put into effect additional active measures for the launching of a protest campaign against the determination of the US administration to produce the neutron bomb and deploy it in Western Europe. "[With] this aim in mind," Moscow informed its allies, "appropriate steps are being made at the present time, such as the use of Party links as well as via non-Party organizations [the Red Cross, the UN Association, the World Peace Committee, etc.]. All these manifestations are an important factor in the struggle against the arms race, in preventing the creation of new varieties and types of weapons of mass destruction. However, one must recognize that we are now at a turning point. The provision of the US Army with the neutron bomb and its deployment in Western Europe has created a new and quite dangerous situation."[114]

Moscow succeeded, while Carter and Schmidt played a mutually destructive game of pass the parcel. Carter emphasized to increasingly baffled and demoralized subordinates that "he did not wish the world to think of him as an ogre."[115] On 26 March 1978, having failed to obtain ever more explicit statements from his allies backing deployment and in the face of the highly effective Soviet-organized campaign against the weapon, Carter "said, in effect, that he did not wish to go through with it; that he had a queasy feeling about the whole thing; that his Administration would be stamped forever as the Administration which introduced bombs that kill people but leave buildings intact; and that he would like to find a graceful way out."[116] Carter then decided in April to postpone deployment sine die, which effectively undercut Schmidt and buttressed opposition from the left within the SPD, which had secured rejection of the neutron bomb at the party congress in Hamburg.

Bonn thus remained exposed to Warsaw Pact military predominance: most notably a two-to-one advantage in the number of tanks (61,084 to 30, 692), for which the neutron bomb had been seen as an effective antidote.[117] During his visit in May, Brezhnev was told by Schmidt that the West could not put up with ever more SS-20s deployed[118] and was persuaded into countersigning a statement underlining the importance of sustaining the existing military balance. Nevertheless, continued deployment rendered the statement worthless. One year after the Bonn declaration a further 50 missile systems (150 warheads independently targeted) took to the field.[119]

Moscow had every reason to celebrate. Not only was deployment of the neutron bomb averted but the president's "standing in the alliance received a strong blow."[120] The Russians nevertheless grumbled that "those circles within the USA that are opposing détente" were primarily responsible for the "zigzags and lack of resolution" in the administration's Soviet policy.[121] By mid-June 1978 Moscow recognized that in the divided US administration those advocating a "hardening" of policy toward the Soviet Union now predominated.[122]

In the face of this, continued Kremlin complacency was partly attributable to difficulties Schmidt faced seeking domestic support for rearmament. Herbert Wehner, SPD Chairman, friend of Honecker, and a pro-Soviet ex-communist, argued forcefully that it was more important to sustain détente against opposition.[123] The two chief veterans of détente, Brandt and Bahr, took a similar stance, though with greater circumspection. The battle joined thus jeopardized the future of the ruling SPD-FPD coalition, not least because Schmidt could also never be sure that Genscher (FPD) would stand loyally behind him if an advantage were to be had elsewhere.[124] Genscher did, after all, subsequently serve as Kohl's foreign minister in alliance with the CDU.

The success of the KGB's neutron bomb campaign promised to repeat itself—and on a greater scale with even more momentous consequences. Anxieties thus grew in Bonn. It sought deployment of the extended-range Pershing II, which could directly threaten Soviet territory not as a bilateral arrangement but multilaterally within NATO. Widening the compass of deployment to take in countries such as Belgium, the Netherlands, and Denmark naturally required considerable effort at persuasion from Washington. Brown, for one, would not risk another neutron bomb fiasco, brusquely insisting no decision be taken on Pershing II production until deployment was firmly agreed by all.[125]

At the Guadeloupe economic summit in January 1979 Schmidt secured agreement from Carter, Giscard d'Éstaing, and Prime Minister Callaghan for a dual-track solution: threatened deployment of new systems to counter the SS-20 combined with a deadline for agreed withdrawal through negotiation. In February Leber's successor Hans Apel discussed deployment with Brown. At the end of April the High Level Group ironed out technical details during a marathon twenty-five-day stay at a country club in Florida. Meanwhile the number of SS-20s multiplied as the dual-track decision moved to the top of the agenda on 12 December.

Schmidt made an abortive attempt to halt deployment when, in the summer of 1979, he stopped off in Moscow en route to Tokyo. At the airport he asked Kosygin that the numbers of SS-20s deployed be limited to the existing number of SS-4s and SS-5s or, if possible, to a lesser number given their superior characteristics. Kosygin suggested the Politburo think about this. Normally anything he proposed was dismissed by Brezhnev. On this occasion an uneasy silence ensued. Ustinov then broke in protesting on the grounds that it required revealing plans to NATO. At which point Brezhnev, bewildered, turned to Gromyko, who kept his counsel, and not merely to avoid a clash with Ustinov.[126] Detinov, long a key figure in missile building, also recalls Ustinov's resistance at the Politburo to Schmidt's idea.[127] The proposal thus proved stillborn. Schmidt met Ustinov and Ogarkov together on another visit to Moscow at the end of June 1980 in a last, desperate bid to halt further deployments.[128] To no avail: by October 1985 there were 243 deployed in Europe alone, each with three warheads.[129] Not until 1987 were the new plans for war attainable.[130]

Advice within Moscow from those who knew the West was ignored throughout from the mid 1950s. After the death of Stalin, Donald Maclean had settled in Moscow. Here he worked at the Institute of World Economy and International Relations initially under the name of Mark Petrovich Fraser—where he published on European security issues and on the EEC, under nom de plume Madzoevskii. He also defended dissentients in letters to Andropov, including Zhores Medvedev and Vladimir Bukovsky; and later young research workers who had fallen foul of the rules.[131] He warned that the SS-20 deployment was a mistake since it was certain to provoke US deployments in Western Europe, which would place the USSR in an even more disadvantageous position.[132] Such unsolicited advice was unwelcome, however. Deployment thus continued unhampered, and with it the underpinnings of détente steadily and predictably gave way.

ENTANGLED IN AFRICA

A further problem was the wave of Soviet-backed revolutions across the Third World following Vietnam. "An array of national revolutionary parties and movements are moving close to Marxist-Leninist positions," hailed Ponomarev on 20 October 1976.[133] This was the final campaign of the other Cold War.

Ponomarev's International Department was thus caught up in a spirit of "Third World optimism," which prompted "actions that were not thought through, major blunders even; though not entirely without reasonable cause. Part of the Party-government leadership still sustained an exaggerated impression of the potential of developing countries, of the incompatibility of their interests with the interests of the West, of the ability of the Soviet Union to draw some of them not just into its political but also its ideological orbit and, one could say, encircle the United States and its allies from the rear. An underestimation, to boot, of the readiness of the West to make a resolute defense of its positions in this world (and the decision of the developing countries themselves to define their own policies)."[134] Ponomarev's deputy Brutents adds: "In the second half and especially toward the end of the 1970s the weight of the military in the formation and conduct of our 'Third World' policy grew. The Soviet bid for a global presence, reinforced by the acquisition of strategic parity, facilitated by the possibilities of moving our forces great distances, by the construction and appearance on the open sea of 'the great fleet,' required the creation of strong points in various regions of the world."[135]

The initial focal point had occurred in Angola. Next came Ethiopia and Nicaragua. The military lobby had unusual strength, Brutents recalls. "At that time in a range of instances—although certainly not always—the approach of the military, their leadership, Ustinov for example, was tougher, made it easier for us more and more to be drawn in, if not locked in."[136] Indeed, military aid between 1955 and 1984 is estimated at around $85 billion; more than half was rendered from 1978 to 1984, accelerating the collapse of détente. Similarly the number of countries with more than one hundred military advisers doubled between 1975 and 1983. Some three-quarters of arms sales from 1978 to 1982 were exports for hard currency from the Middle East. And of the thirteen states almost totally dependent upon Moscow for weaponry, six provided extensive facilities for Soviet naval deployments, military aircraft, or signals intelligence: Vietnam, Cuba, Ethiopia, South Yemen, Syria, and Angola.[137]

The wars and civil wars that drew Soviet attention had their indigenous roots. The African view of the Ethiopian conflict with Somalia reflected the stance of the Organisation of African Unity circa 1964 that colonial borders, however badly drawn, should prevail. In siding with Ethiopia, Moscow was therefore safely with majority opinion. The fact that large numbers of Somalis lived in the Ogaden region of Ethiopia as a result of the Italo-Ethiopian treaty of 1908 nevertheless encouraged the Somali government into an irredentist war. On the same grounds the Somalis also claimed a section of northern Kenya.

Conflict between Ethiopia and Somalia, both now under radical military rule, had been simmering since 1964 with intermittent frontier incidents. Both had frequently called on Moscow to mediate, more recently in November 1976. Brezhnev had pleaded with the Somali dictator to avoid exacerbating the situation, but nothing came of this initiative.[138] On 3 February 1977 the revolutionary element in the ruling officer corps in Ethiopia had seized power from their more conservative colleagues. This convinced Castro that they were serious about socialism: it was, he said later, "a turning point."[139] Five days later, deprived of US arms supplies in view of the radicalization of the country, Mengistu Haile Miriam, the dominant figure in the military regime in Addis Ababa, asked José Peres Novoa, the Cuban ambassador, for military aid.[140]

Eager to displace Soviet influence in Mogadishu, Washington approached Somalia. Castro visited both countries. He was convinced "that there was a real revolution taking place in Ethiopia. In this former empire, lands were being distributed to the peasants." There was "also a strong mass movement," and the military leadership that had seized power from Emperor Haile Selassie was "considering creating a party. There is a harsh class struggle against the feudalists in the country," he added. "The petit bourgeois Powers are mobilizing against the Revolution. A strong separatist movement exists in Eritrea. Threats are coming from the Sudan, while Somalia claims 50 percent of Ethiopia's territory." Miriam struck him as "serious" and "sincere." Whereas Siad Barre, "a general educated under colonialism," "a chauvinist" for some socialism was "just an outer shell," had made a distinctly negative impression on him with "a map of Greater Somalia in which half of Ethiopia had been annexed." His "revolution was accomplished in a minute, with hardly a shot fired. He put on a socialist face and got economic aid and weapons from the Soviet Union. His country is important strategically, and he likes prestige." Castro told Siad Barre that his position "represented a danger to the revolution in Somalia, endangered the revolution in Ethiopia . . . these policies were weakening Somalia's relations with the socialist countries." The dilemma Castro outlined to Honecker in April was that if the socialist bloc helped Ethiopia, they would lose Siad Barre, but if they did not, "the Ethiopian Revolution will founder."[141]

Ethiopia was a priority. Castro had by April already made up his mind and was equipping Ethiopia (poorly provided for compared to the Somalis) with small arms and military advisers: "In Africa . . . we can inflict a severe defeat on the entire reactionary imperialist policy. One can free Africa from the influence of the USA and of the Chinese . . . it might even be possible that Sadat could be turned around and that the imperialist influence in the Middle East can be turned back."[142] As in Angola in 1975, Moscow followed impetuously in the wake of the Cuban man-of-war.

The effect soon made itself felt. On 1 May Ethiopia abrogated its security treaty with Washington. On 6 May Mengistu was received by Brezhnev and insisted, as he was to do repeatedly without acting on it, that he fully intended to set up a working-class party in Ethiopia. Moscow was not as enthusiastic as

Havana but clearly felt he was worth backing, while continuing to promote mediation between the two warring sides.[143] In July a delegation of officers under General Petrov visited Ethiopia to assess the situation. As a consequence, between November 1977 and April 1978 a total of 2,671 air shipments of munitions were delivered on Antonov-12s.[144]

"Soviet military transport aircraft overthrew Turkey, Syria, and other states en route . . . without asking permission." No one protested; even the United States. "The United States seemed to be acquiescing in a Soviet military buildup while denying new arms to its friends in the region," Brzezinski's military assistant General Odom recalls. "Some Middle Eastern and Southwest Asian governments feared that the United States would emulate Britain, which a decade earlier had decided to disband all its forces 'east of Suez.'"[145] Thus when US policy finally reacted, it had a hard time convincing others to fall in line.

A real problem nevertheless faced Havana and Moscow: "the level of political consciousness of the broad masses of the population (mostly illiterate) remains very low." General Arnaldo Ochoa, head of the Cuban military mission, suggested consolidating what had already been achieved in land redistribution, not pushing ahead with collectivization; instead assuring the bourgeoisie that they were not about to be dispossessed of land. However, he found Miriam "lightheaded" and irresponsible in requesting higher technology military assistance from Moscow without having the personnel trained sufficiently to deploy it. It was, in effect, like Afghanistan in the making.[146]

REVOLUTION IN NICARAGUA

Castro had trained revolutionaries from all over Latin America, especially the Caribbean. Among these were brothers Umberto and Daniel Ortega from Nicaragua, and it was Nicaragua that provided the main headache for Washington, because from Managua the revolution began spreading to neighboring El Salvador and Guatemala. The causes of revolution are not hard to see. A dynasty installed by Washington in 1927 to contain local radicalism meant that by the 1970s "the Nicaraguan government and armed forces have remained inherently the personal instruments of the Somoza family."[147] Economic backwardness, monopolies stifling business, a monoculture focused on the export of bananas, extensive corruption, all widened the gulf between governors and governed.

Nicaragua had been one of the soft spots pinpointed by Shelepin in July 1961. It was seen as worth exploiting through development of the Sandinista Revolutionary Front (Frente Sandinista de Liberación Nacional—FSLN), "creating a hotbed of unrest for the Americans in this area."[148] This was not least because leader Carlos Fonseca Amador worked for the KGB.[149] The strategy was approved, but hopes exceeded optimistic expectations and a desultory guerrilla campaign against Somoza slowly got under way. The 1972 earthquake, when substantial foreign aid was blatantly siphoned off into private bank accounts, brought matters to a head, however. The rigged presidential elections two years later, during which the opposition was suppressed—"Little distinction was made between criticism and subversion"[150]—then resulted in an attack on the regime by the FSLN, now in alliance with the non-Marxist opposition. It failed in its wider objectives.

In August 1977 a report surfaced that this alliance, the "Group of 12," had requested Cuban provision of $25,000 for arms to be smuggled in via Costa Rica, the favored place of exile for Nicaraguan rebels.[151] Attacks were launched against Somoza's government on 12 October, the largest since 1974. Assassination by the government of the respected conservative oppositionist Pedro Joaquín Chamorro in January 1978 only made matters worse. In August the FSLN audaciously captured the entire national assembly. Between 5 and 11 November Cuban arms reached the rebels via Panama.[152] And a more resolute offensive began once the leaders of the various factions within the FSLN— Umberto Ortega, Daniel Ortega, Víctor Tirado, Tomás Borge, Jaime Wheelock, and Henry Ruiz—had had their heads banged together by Castro early in March 1979.[153]

On 29 May the call for insurrection was heard. Aid arrived from neighboring Costa Rica, long alienated by Somoza, plus Panama, Venezuela, and Cuba. And on 18 June a junta led by the FSLN took power. This put Carter in difficulties, given that the revolution was spearheaded by Marxist-Leninists yet supported by US allies in the region.[154] Moscow soon recognized the new government on 20 July, but without unseemly haste. A network of agreements was put together, yet as Washington noted, economic assistance was both "sporadic and meager." Moscow channeled equipment via Havana, which took the lead. Although Russia treated the FSLN as the equivalent of a Communist Party, they were "not ready to shoulder any new economic burdens." From July 1979 supplies of arms had reached rebels in El Salvador, Honduras, and Guatemala.[155]

As in Angola, the Nicaraguan revolution illustrated an important effect not lost on CIA. "Cuba plays a central role in Soviet relations with Latin America," a National Intelligence Estimate for 1982 noted, "not only as a dependent client serving Moscow's interests but also as an independent actor influencing Soviet policies and tactics. Fidel Castro's vigorous support of Nicaraguan revolutionaries, for example, was originally a Cuban initiative, and the Sandinista victory had a marked impact on Soviet attitudes and policies. Soviet leaders came to share Castro's assessment that the prospects for the success of revolutionary forces in Central America were brighter than they had earlier calculated."[156]

Indeed, Washington noted that the Sandinista victory "caused the Soviet Union to reassess the prospects for revolutionary change through armed struggle in Central America." It "urged regional Communist parties, particularly those in Guatemala and El Salvador, to abandon their traditionally nonviolent tactics and join existing insurgent movements." During 1981 the Communist Party of Honduras was encouraged to revolt. Financial assistance and training was given to the Popular Vanguard Party within the coalition of communists in democratic Costa Rica.[157] Lawrence Pezzulo, US ambassador to Nicaragua, recalls the critical importance of Castro. They were "fascinated by the romantic idea that they were the new revolutionaries." Umberto said that Pezzulo was "fortunate to be here at this time, because you can see how things are going to play out all through Latin America" and that they, the Sandinistas, were from now on "to be the model all through Latin America."[158]

Washington was woefully ill informed. No one had approached the Sandinistas before the coup. Gates recalls: "The U.S. response was inhibited in part because of a lack of good intelligence on what actually was happening."[159] Director of CIA Admiral Stansfield Turner, ignorant of the intelligence world, effectively continued dismantling networks of undercover operatives here and elsewhere. Although a propaganda campaign was advanced and "a crash effort" began "to improve intelligence collection,"[160] making up the distance lost proved costly and time-consuming. And under Foreign Minister Miguel de Soto, a Catholic priest, Managua sustained a ruthlessly mendacious disinformation campaign in Washington which neutralized center and left of center opinion.[161]

Moreover, Washington did not even cut off aid to Managua until early April 1981 and then only when prompted finally by belated news of Sandinista arms shipments to support guerrilla operations in neighboring countries. Yet the Sandinista leadership had together with Castro in June 1980 secured unification of the communist factions in El Salvador as the Farabundo Martí de Liberación Nacional with the provision of training and base facilities. Untraceable Western arms were supplied by the Soviet bloc.[162] The removal of US aid under newly elected President Ronald Reagan indicated a much tougher approach to the problem of containing communism in the Americas. This then provoked the Soviet ambassador to announce the donation of some 20,000 tons of wheat; though Moscow was still careful to retain a modest public presence in Managua.[163]

The problem for Carter had been that, in focusing on distant East Africa, he turned a blind eye to a major security problem emerging in his own backyard.

BREAKING SOVIET CODES AND CIPHERS

The United States had been working on Soviet codes and ciphers for a considerable time. Aside from exploiting human error (most obviously the reuse of a onetime pad), word-frequency programs, and the issue of specimen statements in the hope that they would then be enciphered for dispatch to Moscow, further progress crucially depended on a revolution in computational hardware and software and that was to take a massive investment in manpower and machines over decades.

Sustained effort finally yielded extraordinary results during the Carter administration: a technological breakthrough enabled access to "traffic" in and out of Moscow. The capacity to cope with the number of characters or digits had to exceed the capacity of the enemy to produce them. Up to 1978 that had never been achieved, despite the fact that Moscow had fallen behind in computational technology in the late sixties and decided to buy IBM rather than continue to develop homegrown competitors (which then laid them open to a US embargo). Once the Jackson-Vanik amendment in 1974 denied most favored nation treatment in trade to the USSR, Moscow increasingly found itself at a serious disadvantage, not entirely compensated for by further KGB technology acquisition through covert operations, notably in Japan, which Andropov greatly expanded. The sixteenth directorate of the KGB had since June 1973 been responsible for electronic intelligence, radio interception, and decryption. The latter was specifically the job of the first department. They had to do most of their analytical work "by hand" despite the availability of a special computer system called "Bulat." "We did not even dare dream, like the Americans, of putting each interception through computer analysis," one former employee recalls. "I remember these long rows of cupboards packed with dusty files with intercepted but not deciphered material. In essence we worked with cupboards."[164]

The US breakthrough in engineering came with the advent of the Cray 1-A Computer. It cost more than eight and a half million dollars. It weighed five and half tons, it was transported in two refrigerated electronic vans, and more than thirty people were required to get it into a computer room. But it was more than worth the expenditure of money and effort. It provided "substantial increases with respect to both the number of data points and computations" so that the insoluble could now feasibly be solved.[165] Its design was simple relative to other computers; it could run for several days before failing (hitherto normal) and then only because of problems with the disks; and it outpaced all rival machines. The first to buy one was the Los Alamos National Laboratory. The second was the NSA under Admiral Bobby Inman in 1977.[166]

Those working on Soviet codes in A Group under the dogged tenacity of Ann Caracristi took full advantage of the new computer to break into hitherto impenetrable high-level systems, aided and abetted by errors made by Soviet cipher operators in the previous year.[167] They were further assisted when IBM announced for the first quarter of 1980 the 3033 attached processor complex, combining an auxiliary processor with a host 3033 computer, thus adding 80 percent more speed to the original 3033 and enabling the operator to handle up to 16 million characters under a single system control program with a 57-billionth of a second cycle time.[168]

These crucial advances enabled the NSA to open up a window onto Moscow's closely guarded political, diplomatic, and military secrets.[169] More important, for 1979, it gave those few with access in the US government the ability to read military and diplomatic traffic, and it was this—available only until betrayal by Geoffrey Prime who worked at the British code-breaking establishment in the spring of 1980—that enabled Brzezinski and Carter to trick Moscow into invading Afghanistan at the end of 1979 and to watch the process of intervention en clair.

LURING RUSSIA INTO ITS OWN VIETNAM

Afghanistan formed a buffer between the USSR and Western influence. It proved the graveyard of many an invading army, latterly the British in 1919. Its nonaligned status had long since turned upon the existence of a monarchy devoid of any principles that might jeopardize the country's impartial position between the two competing camps. That monarchy had collapsed with Mohammed Daoud's coup on 17 July 1973. Two years later the communist PDPA hoped to seize power but were discouraged by Moscow.[170] They were instead instructed to penetrate the regime. Finally, however, the PDPA had little choice. On 25 April 1978 Daoud arrested its leadership. Two days later, on 27 April 1978, those underground seized power with the fourth and fifteenth tank brigades and commando troops. Taraki made himself president and prime minister, Karmal his first deputy, Amin deputy prime minister and foreign minister.

The coup in progress had been reported to Moscow the day before by KGB resident Vladimir Osadchii and ambassador Aleksandr' Puzanov. The latter thought any attempted seizure of power would end in disaster. The KGB warned that Mossad could be behind an attempt to provoke a failed coup.[171] And Taraki reprimanded them for advising them against seizing power three years before.[172] As a fait accompli, however, the coup was greeted as an event of "extraordinary political importance": a rare instance in the Third World and, particularly, "the first social revolution in the lands of the Middle East." Not the least significant consideration was the extent of Afghanistan's 1,700-kilometer border with the Soviet Union.[173] Ten divisions joined the revolution—almost the entire army, or so it was claimed at the outset. All the key posts were held by leaders of the PDPA, founded only thirteen years before by merely 27 militants but now claiming as many as 50,000 in its ranks. They now held the capital of a country riven by tribalism, and they were bent on imposing socialism and secularism with speed and at any price. What made matters worse was internecine warfare that broke out within months of the coup. Soon rumors were circulating, on one hand, that Amin was an American agent under deep cover and, on the other hand, that Taraki was agent of both CIA and KGB.[174]

The most pressing problem was the need to restrain the south of Afghanistan, still loyal to the king. It was "above all vital" that their tribal chiefs were "won over." Taraki knew his Marxism well enough, Moscow noted, but he had now to learn his first words of Islam. Yet at a briefing on 10 May the new government spoke of radical land distribution. "The Ethiopian example of complete nationalization is not a plausible solution for Afghanistan," Moscow cautioned. Whereas in the north the land was farmed, in the south nomads wandered to and fro across the Pakistani frontier. There a different kind of solution had to be found.[175]

Head of the Afghan desk at the Soviet Foreign Ministry, Shumilov was not unduly pessimistic. Yet he too emphasized the importance of seeking a "pragmatic solution" to problems faced by the leadership, not least that of the economy. En route to Havana, Amin met Gromyko and requested economic assistance. Thus far the new regime still had a chance at succeeding. The United States, China, Pakistan, and Saudi Arabia opposed the revolution, and Iran had closed its borders for fear of infection. Thus far, late May 1978, they had adopted a stance of watchful waiting.[176] Yet the ruling group was badly divided between the Khalq and Parcham factions that had healed their longstanding rift barely a year before the seizure of power. Khalq—Amin and Taraki—thus turfed Parcham out of government. Through Soviet assistance to ensure his personal safety, Karmal was ignominiously exiled to the Prague embassy in July.[177] But the purge of his supporters continued despite Soviet advice. By September the Party Central Committee had yet to be convened and the rank and file continued to splinter.

Self-restraint did not last, and forcing the pace of change produced increas-ingly widespread revolt supported by the intelligence service (ISI) of Pakistan. 110,000 Afghans fled the country in 1978; between September and December 1979 alone the number grew to 750,000.[178] Pakistani support made geopoliti-cal sense. A communist Afghanistan drove a wedge between the revolutionary Islamic state of Iran and Pakistan. It therefore merited the "utmost attention and all-embracing sympathy" from the Soviet bloc for "strategic and political reasons."[179] This is what led to a decision in principle by the Politburo to under-write the security of the new regime.

Moscow thus fell hostage to its wayward protégés. Aid could not be denied despite the obvious "naïveté of our friends"[180] and lack of a "clear conception" on the part of Kabul as to "how to put into practice their Marxist-Leninist goals." Moreover, the situation was so bad that all ministries had an active Soviet ad-viser, and the number in the armed forces was so great that every unit had one of its own from the regiment all the way down. In the countryside, where the regime now faced joint opposition from feudal and tribal leaders reinforced by 260,000 mullahs, Kabul called for specialists in agriculture from Tadzhikistan. Moscow now backed forty to fifty projects at a cost of 400 million rubles each.[181] In a revealing conversation with the East Germans, Amin made two points indicating how far out of touch with reality he was. First, he claimed there was no need to be concerned about neighboring Pakistan: "It is an artificial creation that has no future" (as if Afghanistan were any different). Second, and this should have sounded even greater alarm in Moscow: "We will require the assistance of the socialist countries for fifteen years."[182]

When a serious uprising in Herat on 15 March 1979 left some 5,000 dead, including Soviet advisers, few in Moscow could have been taken entirely by surprise. On 18 March, the rebellion still in progress, Taraki phoned Kosygin to request direct military intervention (Kosygin was the point man handling Afghan matters). A parallel conversation took place between Ustinov and Amin. The real problem, which Taraki did not allude to but which Moscow knew full well, was that the regime's troops were deserting in great number. Half a division in Herat had crossed the lines and the other half were reluctant to fight. When Taraki suggested that the uprising be dealt with by raising troops from Kabul, Kosygin countered that they lacked officers and that the regime was facing troops from Iran and Pakistan in Afghan dress. Taraki wanted troops from Uzbek, Turkmen, and Tadzhik units from the USSR in Afghan dress: "No one will know." Kosygin was sympathetic but procrastinated, gently press-ing the Afghans to rely on their own resources. "It seems to me," he said, "that you need to try and create new units. You cannot count only on the strength of those that come from outside. You can see from the Iranian revolution how the people chucked all the Americans out of there and everyone else who tried to represent themselves as defenders of Iran."[183] The problem linked to the fundamentalist revolution in neighboring Iran. The Politburo had formed a committee on Iran chaired by Brezhnev and composed of Andropov, Ponomarev, and Ustinov. But it lacked information.[184] Andropov had some years before made up his mind that "there is no future for the Left in Iran."[185] If true, that presented the Afghan revolution with an additional problem to which no easy solution presented itself.

That day, however, debate in the Politburo demonstrated unanimous resistance to direct military intervention. Ustinov indicated that they there were no ethnically distinctive military units anyway, and he had no idea how many Tadzhiks could drive tanks. "The fact is that the leadership of Afghanistan has underestimated the role of the Islamic religion. In particular of the soldiers, an absolute majority, perhaps with rare exceptions believers, march under the banner of Islam. This is why they [the regime] call on us for help to beat back the attacks of the rebels in Herat." Andropov was characteristically even more outspoken, both as to principle as well as practice. He concluded: "We have to think very seriously indeed about the purpose of sending troops into Afghanistan. To us it is perfectly clear that Afghanistan is not now ready for a socialist solution. There, religion is a massive force, illiteracy among the rural population is all but complete, the economy is backward, etc. We know Lenin's teaching concerning a revolutionary situation. Whatever the situation in Afghanistan, no such situation exits there. I therefore consider that we can sustain the revolution in Afghanistan only with the aid of our own bayonets, and this is completely unacceptable to us. We cannot take that risk." This was not unlike the point made to Lenin by the pessimistic Radek in 1920.

Gromyko agreed with Andropov, and in a statement that no one then contradicted (quite the reverse in the case of Kosygin) he stated: "Our army entering Afghanistan will be the aggressor. Against whom will it be fighting? Above all against the Afghan people; and we will have to shoot at them. . . . We should ask ourselves: what would we get out of it? Afghanistan with its existing government, with a backward economy, with no weight of any significance in international affairs. On the other hand, it has to be borne in mind that from a legal point of view we would not be justified in introducing forces. According to the UN charter, a country can call for aid, and we could send in forces in the event of being subjected to external aggression. Afghanistan is not subjected to any aggression. This is their internal affair, a revolutionary civil war between one group of the population against another." They did, nevertheless, agree to prop up the regime with armaments. And Leonid Zamyatin said they would issue propaganda about Pakistani and Chinese aid to the insurgents to justify the shipments.[186]

The immediate crisis over, on 20 March Taraki flew in for talks with Kosygin, Gromyko, Ustinov, and Ponomarev, acting on behalf of the Politburo. Here, taking the bull by the horns, Kosygin warned that the entry of Soviet troops would result in a situation similar to that of the Americans in Vietnam.[187] It is not unlikely that other analogies were being drawn in Moscow; they certainly were in Washington, where this debate was intercepted by the NSA and read with fascination by Brown and Brzezinski.

On 23 August Amin raised with Moscow the possibility of transferring troops to Kabul so that one or two divisions from the Afghan garrison could be released to fight insurgents.[188] Moscow had good reason for mistrust. Amin was planning to seize power after Taraki left the country at the beginning of September to attend the conference of nonaligned countries in Havana. Attempts by Brezhnev and Andropov to warn Taraki fell on deaf ears, however. Instead Andropov arranged Amin's assassination. But the ambush failed when he took another route. At this point—on 13 September—Moscow then made a further attempt at persuasion. On the following day, after a shoot-out, in which it appeared Taraki hoped to dispose finally of his tenacious rival, Amin seized power for himself. On 8 October he had Taraki shot.[189] A wave of terror followed.

Meanwhile Washington was in disarray from the rapid evolution of events in Iran since the overthrow of the Shah: namely, seizure of the US embassy in Tehran by radical Islamist students on 4 November. Even allowing for ideological bias, Soviet intelligence benefited from lack of access to the highest levels in Iran, for which it compensated by frequenting the bazaar. This proved of inestimable advantage, placing Moscow one step ahead of Washington. Thus by September 1978 Moscow already considered the Shah's days numbered.[190] A KGB officer told an American that the Shah would soon be overthrown by "oppressed masses rising to overthrow their shackles."[191] Moscow was thrilled at the damage that could be done to US interests. This was the first real blow to the West in the region since the Suez debacle. It provided some compensation for Sadat's betrayal. "We could not have dreamed of such a turn in events," crowed Kornienko.[192]

Rumors soon reached Moscow from Teheran that Washington was planning to take military action. The Iranian revolution was not merely a Moslem fundamentalist manifestation, it was also violently anti-American. On 19 August 1953 by means of operation "Boot" MI6 and CIA had overthrown the nationalist government of Prime Minister Mossadeq to secure Iran's oil assets against nationalization on behalf of Anglo-Persian Oil (British Petroleum), "to reestablish the prestige and power of the Shah; and to replace the Mossadeq government with one which would govern Iran according to constructive policies." This meant "vigorously" prosecuting "the dangerously strong Communist Party."[193] It was therefore not to be expected in Moscow that Washington would lamely accept seizure of their embassy as a fait accompli.

Ustinov was particularly alarmed: "Are we expected to sit on our hands while the Americans deploy their forces on our southern borders?!"[194] Above Brezhnev's name a warning appeared in *Pravda* to the effect that intervention in Iran would be viewed by the USSR as touching on "its security interests."[195] Even though only Ponomarev appeared to believe the communists and their allies in Iran had any chance of taking power, Brezhnev, Ustinov, Gromyko, and Andropov were gratified that this was primarily an anti-American revolution. And after the Shah was forced out of Iran at the beginning of 1979, Andropov for one was convinced the communists had no future in the country: Khomeini and the Moslem clerics were in office for good.[196] By April, however, Moscow realized that this was also bad news for Soviet interests, particularly in Afghanistan. An appreciation by Deputy Chairman of the KGB Tsinev in October pointed out that Khomeini was set upon overturning the regime in Kabul and spreading Islam through the southern crescent of the USSR, not least in retaliation for Soviet supported attempts to spread communism in Iran.[197] The Iranian seizure of the US embassy on 4 November inevitably prompted mixed feelings in Moscow. "The Americans will not forgive such things," Andropov is quoted as saying.[198] It made retaliation all the more likely.[199]

One notable casualty was loss of NSA facilities in the north that enabled Washington to monitor the telemetry from Soviet missile tests and thereby ensure observance of the SALT treaties. It was entirely plausible to Moscow that Washington would seek to substitute facilities in Iran with facilities in Afghanistan; the Afghans, of course, willing. The attitude toward Washington had sharpened notably after the repeated confrontations over Cuba, Angola, and Ethiopia. Ogarkov told Varennikov of discontent within the Politburo, quoting Andropov as asking why Moscow should put its tail between its legs every time Washington sneezed.[200] Some were determined to act decisively.

On 3 July Brzezinski had persuaded Carter to offer direct aid for the rebels in Afghanistan. Washington was "well aware of Soviet concern over the situation. Beginning on September 10, intelligence reports to the president [deleted] began to discuss the possibility that the Soviet Union might be forced to act."[201] Moscow was already mistrustful of Amin. Within his circle, conversation about the Soviet Union and its leadership was both "arrogant and ironical," taken from the "American lexicon." He had also hitherto greeted news that Moscow would not send in troops with evident relief. Three ministers—Sarvari, Vatand-zhara, and Gulyabzoya—claimed Amin to be an American spy.[202] This was also the thrust of KGB assessments for the Politburo.[203] Moreover, Amin gave orders to the media to tone down attacks on imperialism and Pakistan, a sign he was moderating his hostility to them in favor of "a more balanced foreign policy course." This also meant confidential meetings with the US chargé d'affaires in Kabul, and on Amin's instructions they ceased operating against the US embassy.[204]

"We did not push the Russians into intervening," Brzezinski coyly confessed, "but we did knowingly increase the chances that they would do so."[205] Brzezinski planted the seeds of suspicion that would hopefully force Moscow to do precisely what it had set out to avoid: military intervention.[206] Thatcher's choice of ambassador to Washington was Sir Nicholas Henderson, who reminded the somewhat prickly Brzezinski of his prep school teacher. Talking to him over breakfast on 27 October, Brzezinski "gave a hint of their preparedness to do something to make life difficult for the Russians in Afghanistan."[207] This was only the beginning.

By 29 November 1979 Gromyko, Andropov, Ustinov, and Ponomarev had begun speculating on the two greatest dangers: "the victory of the counterrevolution" and "the political reorientation of H. Amin towards the West." Moscow had recently been picking up signs that the new leadership in Kabul was set on a more "balanced policy" in relation to the "Western Powers." "It is known, in particular, representatives of the USA on the basis of their contacts with the Afghans are drawing the conclusion that it is possible to change the political line of Afghanistan into a direction more favorable to Washington." They also noted, "Faced with facts testifying to the beginning of an about-turn by H. Amin in an anti-Soviet direction, we will bring forward additional proposals for measures on our part." On 8 December Andropov, Ustinov, Gromyko, and Suslov held a meeting in Brezhnev's study where they debated military intervention. It was here that Andropov and Ustinov presented incriminating evidence of Amin's shifting loyalties, including information as to "the efforts of the CIA resident in Ankara to build a 'New Great Islamic Empire' that would include the southern republics of the USSR."[208] Grishin recalls Andropov later telling the Politburo of evidence "that Amin is a CIA agent."[209] Philby, too, sustained the conviction that "there was more than a suspicion that Amin was dickering with the Americans."[210] Brezhnev, though still nominally General Secretary, was by this time failing fast—his condition, according to Kryuchkov, who attended the Afghanistan committee of the Politburo, as head of KGB foreign intelligence, "seriously deteriorated at the end of 1979."[211] Alexandrov-Agentov was completely cut out of the picture but later learned that ailing Brezhnev had been pressured into agreement.[212]

On 10 December Ustinov summoned Ogarkov. The Politburo had taken a decision to send 75,000 to 80,000 troops into Afghanistan. Ogarkov said this would be insufficient; it was foolhardy: rapid stabilization of Afghanistan required no less than thirty to thirty-five divisions.[213] Ustinov responded that it was not Ogarkov's job to instruct the Politburo but to obey orders. Later that day Ogarkov was summoned before Andropov, Ustinov, and Gromyko. That evening Ustinov told the collegium of the Ministry of Defense that they could soon expect a decision on intervention. The armed forces were issued with order No. 312/12/00133. Detailed instructions were handed out by Ustinov from 10 December. Two days later a meeting of the Politburo was chaired by Brezhnev. Here the decision to go in was finalized. Crucially, Kosygin, still resolute in opposition but his health deteriorating, was unable to attend.[214]

Privy to crucial information that Amin was suspected of betrayal to the United States but that the military leadership—Akhromeyev, Varennikov, as well as Ogarkov—had been overruled, Washington could lay a match to the fuse almost at will.[215] Disinformation played a critical role in triggering the Soviet decision. Head of the KGB's illegal intelligence—directorate "S'—Kirpichenko was told of facts that had come to light about Amin's "readiness to reorient his policy toward the USA." He was instructed to prepare Amin's overthrow with special forces from the GRU and KGB, the latter led by deputy head of foreign intelligence Major General Yuri Drozdov.[216]

Operations began on Christmas Day. In three days, largely at night and at four-minute intervals, 500 sorties of troop transports flew into Afghanistan. Two days after the invasion began, special forces disposed of Amin. When news reached Brzezinski in Washington, he shot a clenched fist into the air triumphally: "They have taken the bait!"[217] In his note to Carter that day Brzezinski jubilantly remarked: "We now have the opportunity to give the USSR its Vietnam War."[218] As the official history of the NSA notes: "This time there was no 'intelligence failure.' . . . After years of struggle, it was now possible to predict with some clarity and speed the intentions of the major antagonist."[219]

Moscow took the decision on Afghanistan knowing détente was dead but not buried. The dual-track decision by NATO early in December 1979 left Moscow stranded. But the Kremlin still hoped that NATO might break under the strain in implementing its decision; that Western Europe would sooner or later break ranks with Washington under pressure from domestic opinion; and that the sense of rivalry between European states would further weaken unity.

Moscow argued: "It is obviously necessary to strengthen still further pressure on the countries of Western Europe, on the widest variety of political circles, on society, in order as far as possible to hinder the implementation of the decision taken by NATO, raising against it an even broader wave of protests." The NATO leadership "now has had to maneuver. Furthermore, a certain degree of disarray has appeared within the bloc." Washington was equally certain that "even more noticeable has been the absence of mass public support in Western Europe for NATO policy."[220] Yet Soviet leaders simultaneously and falsely "continued to believe in the monolithic nature" of their own society—a fatal error.[221]

At a meeting with Axen, head of the SED's International Department, Ponomarev, Zagladin, Rachmanin, Ulyanovsky, Brutents, and Martynov reviewed the situation. "The Soviet comrades," noted Axen, "pointed out that one should analyze very carefully the different tendencies within the imperialist camp and take advantage of them. Adjustment to the USA today means renunciation of one's national interests. Except for the USA, no other imperialist Power can conduct a policy of force. Many capitalist countries are interested in the pursuit of relations with the socialist countries as a conscious counterweight to the USA. A breach in those relations would make subordination to the USA even greater." The dispute over attendance at the Moscow Olympics, forthcoming in 1981, which the Americans wished to boycott, illustrated the divisions within NATO. The Russians claimed they had not sought this; "We can, however, take advantage of it." And an instance of the disarray among the West Europeans themselves was blatantly apparent in an indiscretion from the president of the French National Assembly, Jacques Chaban Delmas, "that the states of Western Europe fear the increasing economic and political power of the FRG."[222]

The failure to come up with a realistic negotiating position was also due to the combined stubbornness of those such as Andropov, determined to maintain a military capability to meet the combined strength of NATO and China simultaneously; the General Staff, which required massed SS-20s to expand the options for limited war; Gromyko and like-minded Americanists, who stuck rigidly to a notion of balance that ignored West European security anxieties; and the military-industrial complex addicted to limitless rearmament. The failure ensured that Moscow would shortly face an imbalance in Europe to their disadvantage. In March 1981 Adamishin noted gloomily in his diary that US "medium-range missiles" were "a fatal danger for us, comparable to the Chinese; in 5–7 minutes they can wreck our cities and strategic missiles. None of this is being stated—the decision, taken because of our SS-20 programme which has added little, will, if put into effect, severely curtail our security."[223]

THE REAGAN PRESIDENCY

If one takes foreign policy, the period before Gorbachev's rise to power was a period amassed with lost opportunities.

—Valentin Falin

A trough in the economic cycle, runaway inflation, and rising unemployment on the back of stratospheric energy prices, plus a stagnant stock market, all contributed to Carter's political demise. But growing tension between the United States and the USSR, the storm in Europe over the SS-20, the abject failure of Carter to hold his own against fundamentalist Iran or contain the spread of revolution from Nicaragua, all ensured Reagan's election in November 1980.

On 17 January 1983 Reagan signed NSDD 75 setting the US government the task not only to contain but also "over time reverse Soviet expansionism" and to "promote" change within the USSR. Agreement with the Soviet regime was permissible only on the basis of "strict reciprocity."[1] Involved in its construction, Richard Pipes claims that in reality "subversion considerably exceeded the language of NSDD 75. Indeed," he adds, "at the December 1982 National Security Council meeting that reviewed NSDD 75, President Reagan insisted on the deletion from the document of certain points dealing with economic warfare lest they leak to the press and embarrass him."[2]

Moscow had reason to worry. According to the most authoritative estimates, national income fell from 3.4 percent average per annum for the period 1961–75 to 1.1 percent for the period 1976–90. And given a population increase of 13.9 percent in the latter period, per capita growth was less than 1 percent.[3] Oil and gas predominated as exports and for their growing contribution to GDP despite the fall in the dollar. Whereas in 1970 oil was valued at only 15.6 percent of exports, by 1984 it accounted for no less than 54.4 percent. In new western

Siberian fields production rose from 31 million tons in 1970 to 312 million in 1980. Similarly, natural gas output rose from 9.5 million cubic meters in 1970 to 156 million in 1980.[4] The real value of crude oil exports worldwide peaked in 1980 and dropped over 90 percent by 1988. Natural gas peaked in 1981 and dropped over 50 percent by 1988.[5] If this were not bad enough, instead of re-investing in productive capacity, most proceeds went to the military-industrial sector, Third World aid, and imports of grain that tripled between 1973 and 1981.[6] The trade balance thus faced a scissors in its foreign exchange position and threatened to lower even further national income and the standard of living. Moscow surreptitiously obtained the secret US assessment of this Soviet dilemma, National Intelligence Estimate 11–23–86, completed on 12 September 1986.[7] It predicted bleak prospects for domestic reform.

Moreover, the Russians were chronically weak in all areas of technology and the West knew it. The coordinated embargo launched by the Western alliance in 1950 did not end with détente. Issued on 14 March 1974, NSDM 247—"U.S. Policy on the Export of Computers to Communist Countries"—prohibited the sale of the most powerful machines to the USSR and its allies. The Russians worked relentlessly to evade the restrictions. On 19 July 1981 President Mit-terand revealed to Reagan the windfall of secret details on KGB technologi-cal espionage in the West obtained from Lieutenant-Colonel Vladimir Vetrov (agent "Farewell") during the previous year.[8] On 3 November 1982 Vetrov was found guilty of an horrific murder, however. Until that time, as deputy head of directorate T charged with scientific and technological espionage abroad, he handed over to the DST (*Direction de la surveillance territoire*) several thousand pages of documents, including the names of 450 intelligence officers and 78 traitors in OECD countries. As a result of a decision taken in January 1982, the Americans injected misleading data into the Soviet collection system which ultimately caused so much damage and chaos that Moscow began to distrust its own sources. From March 1983 the NATO countries, led by France, began winding up the Soviet network, as a result of which Vetrov's treachery became obvious to the authorities, who condemned him for betraying his country on 14 December 1983 and shot him on 23 January 1984.[9]

The Cold War appeared to be turning full circle. The Americans had no intention of negotiating except from a position of strength (superiority). Critical to this was the fact that Reagan was "a conviction politician," ideological to his fingertips. Ford had said that "détente must be—and, I trust, will be—a two-way relationship."[10] In contrast, Reagan argued that because of Moscow's unrelent-ing "promotion of world revolution," détente had been "a one-way street that the Soviet Union has used to pursue its own aims."[11] Moscow would no longer get away with it. "To me," Reagan recalled some years later, no problem was "more serious than the fact America had lost faith in itself."[12] In a series of radio broadcasts from the mid-seventies, he preached a homespun philosophy. A regular theme was bitter distaste for the "SALT-sellers": those insistent on arms control with Moscow, to Reagan a vivid symptom of decline. It was clear that the Russians "make promises, they dont [sic] keep them."[13] Reagan questioned the adequacy of defenses against incoming missiles, and he lambasted Soviet and Cuban subversion of the Western hemisphere.

No specific idea was ever offered as to what could be done, however. Carlucci, national security adviser in the second term, recalls: "Ronald Reagan clearly was not a detail person. He had a couple of issues he was interested in. He had a vision he liked to talk about. He had the jokes that he liked to tell, but he had uncanny instincts."[14] The argument pressed upon him, for example, by Pipes and veteran of net assessments, chairman of the National Intelligence Committee, "Harry" Rowen, was to force the transformation of the Soviet Union from within. This was anathema to the left and the old Republican right. It was something that Kennan, a liberal on the Cold War and something of a Cassandra, condemned as both immoral and impracticable. "It is," he believed, "improper, confusing to everyone, and usually ineffective when a government tries to shape its policy in such a way as to work domestic-political changes in another country." On Kennan's cold-blooded view it was wrong to allow dissentients such as Sakharov and Solzhenitsyn to manipulate the United States into "an instrument in their struggle with their own government."[15] Here, despite fundamental differences, two retirees from very different camps but looking down from the same Olympian heights, Kennan and Kissinger, coincided. In his deep conservatism, Kissinger expressed himself "not so foolish as to believe that we can pressure the USSR to change its internal order."[16] His was, after all, a major premise underlying the Nixon policy of détente. This premise had already been unthinkingly dislodged by Carter in his opportunist pursuit of human rights as an election winner. It was now jettisoned by Reagan.

THE PROBLEM OF NICARAGUA AND CUBA

If Washington took seriously the idea of ending communism in the USSR, it could hardly tolerate the expansion of communist influence on its doorstep. In Latin America Reagan reverted to covert operations prohibited by Congress since the downfall of Allende's Chile. This inevitably led to circumvention of the law (the Iran-Contra affair) and a collision with Congress, though these risks were deemed worth taking. Armed support for insurgents in El Salvador and the military buildup in Nicaragua had caused increasing alarm. "Cuba's generosity was total," recalls Sergio Ramírez, a leading Sandinista.[17] But Washington felt impotent. The incoming administration could prove to be all sound and no bite. In January the Sandinistas were warned that CIA had discovered a secret air strip in El Papalonal near Lago de Managua. A C-47 had been photographed airlifting arms to El Salvador.[18] Reagan had "absolute proof of Soviet & Cuban activity in delivering arms to rebels in El Salvador." "Intelligence reports say Castro is very worried about me. I'm very worried that we can't come up with something to justify his worrying."[19] Secretary of State Alexander Haig proposed normalizing relations in return for complete suspension of the arms traffic to El Salvador.[20] The Sandinistas then closed the runway but transported arms by other means—small wooden boats crossing the Golfo de Fonseca by night.[21]

Now head of the Latin American division at CIA, Duane Clarridge was sent in by the new director, William Casey, a veteran from operations, to get something done; which consisted of organizing an army—the Contras—that could operate across the Honduran border. It was conceived in cooperation with Argentina via the ruthless deputy director of military intelligence Colonel Mario Davico in the summer of 1981.[22] The problem was that the administration would have to go cap-in-hand to Congress to launch a serious insurrection.

Hitherto Moscow had been uninterested in further complicating relations with the USA, particularly under Reagan. This was about to change. During the revolution Ramírez had received someone calling himself "Gabo" at government house. "Gabo" asked that a visitor be received the following day. This was an official from the Soviet embassy in Mexico called "Vladimir." "Vladimir" immediately opened a mission in confiscated premises. The first Sandinista delegation reach Moscow at the end of May 1980 in search of arms, but the first shipments arrived via Algeria only after an agreement signed in 1981. Incoming Secretary of State George Shultz denounced the impending arrival of MiGs from the USSR in 1982. By then sixty pilots were already training in Bulgaria. They had to be withdrawn. Castro advised the Sandinistas to abandon their plans. Instead the Sandinistas ordered state-of-the-art attack helicopters—MI-25s—which actually proved more useful in counterinsurgency.[23]

Meanwhile Washington was receiving reports that "Soviet officers are advising the Nicaraguan general staff and have helped in the preparation of military plans." "Cubans are found in practically every Nicaraguan government agency," US intelligence advised. Rebels from El Salvador took flights via Managua for training in Cuba.[24] The number of Cubans in Nicaragua was estimated at 6,000, of whom some 1,750 were military or security advisers.[25] By the summer of 1983 the number of those advisers estimated had risen to 2,000 and included General Ochoa, deputy to Raúl Castro, Cuban Minister of Defense. Moreover, the GDR made available a massive $247 million in credit between 1980 and 1985. And the Russians under Gorbachev promised more.[26]

Ochoa had been credited with organizing the arms buildup in Angola in 1976 and in Ethiopia the year following.[27] Determined to put the Cuba in its place, Washington decided to act firmly through indirect means. Defying tough opposition on the Hill—the Boland amendment of 8 December 1982—early in September 1983 CIA Director Bill Casey authorized and received a proposal for covert action: "U.S. policy in Central America is to oppose the immediate and serious threat to Western Hemisphere peace caused by encroachments by the Soviet Union, Cuba, and their surrogates." It proposed arming and supporting the Nicaraguan counterrevolutionaries.[28] On 19 September Reagan issued a "finding" "as a means to induce the Sandinistas and Cubans and their allies to cease their support for insurgencies to the region; to hamper Cuban/Nicaraguan arms trafficking; to divert Nicaragua's resources and energies from support to Central American guerrilla movements; and to bring the Sandinistas into meaningful negotiations and constructive, verifiable agreement with their neighbors on peace in the region."[29]

MOSCOW'S FEARS

Reagan's more conservative colleagues, including Casey and Defense Secretary Caspar ("Cap") Weinberger, resolutely opposed negotiating with Moscow. Reagan, who disliked personal unpleasantness, dithered when the need arose to enforce policy. He wrote in November 1984: "I'm going to meet with Cap and Bill and lay it out to them. Won't be fun but has to be done."[30] By this time, Reagan realized that relations with Moscow were more complex than supposed. "Three years had taught me something surprising about the Russians," he acknowledged later. "Many people at the top of the Soviet hierarchy were genuinely afraid of America and Americans. Perhaps this shouldn't have surprised me, but it did. In fact, I had difficulty accepting my own conclusion at first."[31]

When members of the administration and selected outsiders gathered in a day-long session to prepare Shultz for a meeting with Gromyko, they "painted a picture of formidable Soviet military power, of an aggressive foreign policy, of intransigence on human rights, and of Gromyko as an unbending and often insufferable interlocutor."[32] Tension nevertheless persisted between those at State who like Vance and Kissinger wanted arms control to revive détente and those at Defense and the White House determined to break Moscow before substantive talks. Initially planning was accompanied by psychological warfare probing Soviet defenses worldwide through unauthorized penetration of air space— "exciter flights"—and sea space across the entire horizon for the purpose of intimidation.[33] It reinforced anxieties well entrenched in the Kremlin. Head of East German foreign intelligence Markus Wolf, on visiting Moscow in February 1980, was surprised at the extent of alarm. He and others met Andropov at the central clinical hospital—the so-called Kremlin hospital—in Kuntsevo, the Moscow suburbs.

Not only was Andropov seriously ill—his kidneys were failing—but Wolf had never seen him so seriously depressed. "He outlined a gloomy scenario in which nuclear war was a real threat."[34] That this was not merely a product of illness is evident from GDR Foreign Minister Oskar Fischer's "similar impressions" at meetings with Gromyko.[35] According to unconfirmed reports, after Reagan's election Kissinger had been dispatched to warn of decisive retaliation in the event of provocation. This, no doubt, and other factors led directly to the announcement of a new information-gathering program—RYAN—in May 1981 involving the KGB, GRU, and sister services from the Warsaw Pact issuing fortnightly reports on the immediate threat of nuclear war. The initiative came from the normally unexcitable Andropov and the more emotional Ustinov.[36] That this program was wound down by 1985[37] though not abolished until 27 November 1991[38] suggests it was a momentary expression of heightened alarm institutionalized well beyond its original purpose (a classic instance of Soviet bureaucratic inertia).

This was certainly the view of the National Intelligence Officer (NIO) for the USSR at CIA, Fritz Ermarth. He produced an intelligence estimate dated 18 May 1984. On "very strong evidence, we judge that the Soviet leadership does not perceive an imminent danger of war." Experts agreed "that there is currently a stable nuclear balance in which the United States does not have sufficient strength for a first strike. Moreover, the Soviets know that the United States is at present far from having accomplished all of its force buildup objectives."[39]

Ermarth subsequently confirmed "that what animated Soviet behavior and discontent was not fear of an imminent military confrontation but worry that Soviet economic and technological weaknesses and Reagan policies were turning the 'correlation of forces' against them on an historic scale." Oleg Gordievsky, deputy head of KGB station in London until defection, "noted, interestingly that intelligence professionals on the Soviet side did not take seriously the much ballyhooed warning system called VRYAN or RYAN; it seemed more like a political instrument to energize the geriatric Politburo."[40] The military did not take seriously the civilian understanding of war, and that included Andropov, who, even as General Secretary, in the words of Danilevich, "did not have time to get involved."[41] "No one believed there was a real likelihood (immediate threat) of a nuclear strike from the U.S. or NATO," Danilevich recalls. He "felt that the KGB may have overstated the level of tension because they are generally incompetent in military affairs and exaggerate what they do not understand."[42] Marshal Sergei Akhromeyev, then Deputy Chief of the General Staff, concurred that "war was not considered imminent."[43] Certainly Wolf doubted the premise behind RYAN. His key source within NATO, Rainer Rupp, made clear that there was, indeed, no danger of imminent nuclear war.[44]

Before long the Kremlin understood Washington to be bluffing; a view always held among the more hard-bitten Americanists: "We will always be able to turn out more missiles than you," an American diplomat was told. "The reason is that our people are willing to sacrifice for these things, and yours are not. Our people don't require a dozen colors of toilet paper in six different scents to be happy. Americans do now; for that reason you will never be able to sustain public support for military expenditures as long as you are not directly attacked."[45]

THE POLISH PROBLEM

The heightened alert coincided with a crisis in Poland predicted by the Institute for the Economics of the World Socialist System, set up by Andropov in the late sixties under Bogomolov.[46] After 1970 Poland was never quiescent. And the election of a Polish Pope on 16 October 1978 undoubtedly excited extravagant hopes. Industrial unrest had become politicized with the creation of the independent trades union Solidarność (Solidarity) on 17 September 1980. Its success was due not merely to the alienation of the working class under communist rule. It was also intimately bound up with the consequences of a disastrously short-sighted economic policy that turned Poland from a net exporter of agricultural produce in 1974 to a net importer within the decade. The country's trade turnover with the West increased over sixfold, entirely funded by credits, upon which payment fell due in the early eighties, when Poland was least able to afford it.

Strikes nationwide, on 28 August 1980 the Soviet Ministry of Defense had asked the Politburo "that in the event of military assistance being rendered to the PPR [Polish Peoples' Republic] a group of forces be set up and that three tank divisions . . . and one motor-rifle division . . . initially be brought to complete readiness for military action." It also requested bringing divisions within the Baltic, Byelorussian, and Trans-Carpathian military districts up to full complement for war "and, in the event of the core of the Polish army coming to the aid of the counterrevolutionary forces," the Defense Ministry also asked that Soviet troops in Poland be reinforced by five to seven divisions. For this purpose the ministry planned to call up as many as 75,000 men and requisition 9,000 automobiles. A further 25,000 men and 6,000 automobiles were also envisioned as part of the overall plan.[47]

Military action, though planned, was not taken, however,[48] despite Brezhnev's belief that this was "an entire orgy of counter-revolution" and Gromyko's insistence that they "must not under any circumstances lose Poland."[49] A show of force *was* required, however. Ustinov called in Chief of Staff of Warsaw Pact forces General Anatolii Gribkov and First Deputy Minister of Defense and Commander-in-Chief of Warsaw Pact forces Marshal Viktor Kulikov to arrange Warsaw Pact exercises—"Alliance"—to begin at short notice on 8–10 December. Given festivities in most of the allied countries, they tried in vain to dissuade him. But this was not merely Ustinov's idea: the exercises went ahead. The entire staff were flown into the Polish garrison at Legnitz, where they remained until March 1981. They were due to close with a review on 21 December. But at the last minute Ustinov asked for an additional exercise. "The aim of this maneuver was clear to all," Gribkov recalls "to continue the exertion of pressure on the Polish government and society." The exercises therefore lasted several months. The Warsaw Pact staff stayed on in Legnitz without any plausible explanation to give puzzled officers from the northern group of forces in the building opposite. Finally after rumors appeared in the Western press that the headquarters of the Warsaw Pact would be moving from Moscow to Legnitz, in late April an irritable Ustinov telephoned and demanded that they leave.[50]

Adamishin was told that the government was "gravitating towards the standard options, however much force had to be used." But it was reported that Brezhnev—in remission—was "resolutely opposed" on the grounds that this would be "a real tragedy." Defeating the Poles would take more than a year, and then they would have to be fed.[51] The memories of both Hungary and Czechoslovakia only too fresh, and Afghanistan an open wound, Andropov also robustly resisted Soviet military action. On 3 April 1981 a secret meeting was arranged in Brest, on the border with Poland, between Andropov and Ustinov on the one side and Prime Minister Stanisław Kania and General Wojciech Jaruzelski—Defense Minister and Foreign Minister—on the other. At a six-hour meeting the Poles were asked to sign plans for martial law. Jaruzelski said the documents would be examined on 11 April and signed.[52]

Despite the agreement, martial law was not effected, and by September the situation looked increasingly desperate. Gromyko pointed out that "now little power remains" in government hands.[53] In these circumstances Moscow instead on 19 October secured Jaruzelski as Kania's replacement in the expectation that he would institute martial law. When the general tried to find a middle way, as had Kania, he was promptly scolded: "We are not against agreements," the Soviet Politburo said, somewhat liberally, only to add somewhat less so: "But they must not contain concessions to the enemies of socialism."[54] To find a way out Jaruzelski, now also First Secretary of the Party, hinted that the USSR intervene. Ustinov contacted senior military officers but only Kulikov was explicitly and dogmatically in favor of intervention.[55] The Kremlin rejected that option outright. Gromyko led the chorus: "There can be no introduction of forces into Poland." Suslov pointed out Moscow was trying to lead a peace campaign in Europe and "world public opinion would not understand us." He dismissed the prospect of introducing troops as "a catastrophe."[56] From conversations with Andropov and Kryuchkov, head of KGB foreign intelligence, the clear impression given was that, after the invasion of Afghanistan, continued tension with China, and US belligerence, there was no question of military action.[57]

At a Politburo meeting on 10 December chairman of Gosplan Nikolai Baibakov reported on Poland's economic situation following his visit. The most serious problem was payment of debts owed to the West. He reported that Jaruzelski envisaged military intervention if the authorities could not handle resistance to martial law. Jaruzelski quoted Kulikov to the effect that if necessary the rest of the Warsaw Pact would aid them militarily. When Andropov heard this, he vented his anger at requests for economic insistence—"impertinent"—that if denied would heap the blame for failure on Moscow. Moreover, "if Kulikov actually talked of our forces going in, then I consider this incorrect!" It remained out of the question. They would have to find another way of safeguarding communications with the Soviet group of forces in Germany.[58] That afternoon at 4:35 p.m. Jaruzleski raised these questions directly with Soviet ambassador Averkii Aristov who contacted Konstantin Rusakov at the Central Committee. Jaruzelski was rebutted on each point. A day later Jaruzelski repeated his request for a commitment to intervene, a request directed at Kulikov, then in Poland. Finally, with nothing useful forthcoming, martial law was declared on 13 December.[59]

Reagan regarded the Polish situation as "the last chance in a lifetime . . . this is a revolution started against this 'damned force.'" But, since he did not want to abandon negotiations on theater nuclear weapons, options were limited.[60] Poland was, however, denied vital financial support from the IMF. And in February 1982 a CIA program of aid to Solidarność came into effect. Within months the union had received $8 million in aid.[61] Reversal of martial law would clearly take years rather than months, however.

ANDROPOV IN POWER

Brezhnev finally died on 10 November 1982 with détente in ruins, a crisis seething in Poland, and an interminable military commitment to sustain a regime almost universally loathed in Afghanistan. It appears that the first candidate for succession was none other than Konstantin Chernenko. Born on 24 September 1911, a former border guard who had made himself indispensable to Brezhnev as general factotum, Chernenko was a natural number two but a man entirely devoid of distinction. Since the early seventies, as an extrovert, he had made a reputation for himself as a skillful operator within the Party apparatus.[62] Adamishin understood from others—true or not—that Andropov was finally chosen as Brezhnev's successor only at the second vote and due to the combined efforts of Ustinov, Gromyko, and the young Mikhail Gorbachev; true or not, the fact of the rumors alone indicated a certain unease at the selection.[63]

Yet except for Gorbachev and Grigorii Romanov (born on 7 February 1923), these were old men, increasingly sclerotic, more in than out of hospital. Chernenko had liver and heart problems. Andropov was diabetic and by now had a gray, cadaver-like appearance. On 25 January 1982 Kirpichenko went to see him and found he could barely read.[64] Ustinov died not long thereafter, on 20 December 1984. Gromyko, at seventy-three and the key figure in any shift toward concessions to the West to forestall the arrival of US missiles in Europe, was more than due for retirement: "He gets very worked up especially when he tires and forgets what he has said," subordinates complained. Gromyko read few telegrams, rarely met ambassadors or heads of department, received "one-sided information," and his chief assistant briefed him in a biased manner; as a result of which the supporters of détente were stuck (*v zamazke*).[65]

These aging leaders were nervously awaiting US deployment of Cruise and Pershing missiles. Cruise was a particular danger because of its low visibility as Moscow still had "only limited effectiveness against low-altitude penetration."[66] The Pershing aroused special anxiety as a missile of enhanced accuracy with a counterforce capability and a range of up to 25,000 kilometers that could hit Moscow at great speed from West Germany. Against this, further developments had to be made in Moscow's ABM defenses to be completed only in 1987.[67]

Addressing the leaders of the Warsaw Pact on 4 January 1983, Andropov set the "turbulent situation" and the "inflammation of international tension" against the heady but illusory achievements of the previous decade. "The 1970s," he said, "were a time of the further growth of the strength and the influence of the socialist community." The attainment of "military-strategic parity" had given the bloc the possibility of dealing on equal terms with NATO. The "dynamic policy of détente" made for a transformation of international relations. Andropov celebrated "the critical losses suffered by imperialism in the furthest reaches of the so-called Third World," not least because "up to now the prosperity of the West has depended on control over the resources of the Third World." "The revolutionary changes in Angola, Nicaragua, and other countries—and these were conditioned by objective factors—meant for Washington, and not without reason, the acceptance of a defeat for American policy."

Andropov saw the "Reagan phenomenon" and his policy essentially as a product of the recession, inflation, and mass unemployment. "And the bourgeoisie as a rule seeks one way out of such situations by means of foreign policy adventures." So long as the Soviet bloc faced economic problems and domestic political complications of its own—Poland, in particular, was here assumed but not named—the "class enemy" would, Andropov warned, "create a political opposition in our countries, manipulate it, and destabilize the socialist system." Beyond this Washington also presented a military challenge. It had set as its "goal" the destruction of the balance of power. It was embarking on an arms race for qualitative improvements that would enable them to go beyond deterrence to war-fighting.

Andropov acknowledged that "it is hard to say what is blackmail and what is really a readiness to take calamitous steps. At any event we cannot, however, allow the USA military superiority and we will not allow them this. One must nevertheless reckon that the escalation of the arms race may make the military-political situation unstable and unsettled." It was "no exaggeration to say that we are faced with the greatest attempt by imperialism to put a brake on the process of social change in the world, to bring to a halt the progress of socialism and, at least in certain areas, press it into reverse."[68] Reagan had certainly made an impact where it mattered.

THE US STRATEGIC DEFENSE INITIATIVE

The threat posed came to be epitomized in the Strategic Defense Initiative (SDI). Both Washington and Moscow had been experimenting with space-based weapons systems since the 1960s. Neither made substantial progress. Soviet work on antimissile defenses from outer space—the D-20 program—was by the mid-eighties still at the stage of research and laboratory experiment. It remained squarely within the limitations imposed by the ABM treaty of 1972. But Moscow was working on an interceptor system—the S-550—which, if deployed, would contravene the treaty. The earliest expected target date for prototypes was the year 2000.[69] One promising area of focus had emerged: high-energy lasers. Much money had been expended attempting to develop systems that could both destroy communications satellites in space and intercontinental ballistic missiles (ICBMs) at the crucial boost phase after launch. This program began in 1965–66. By 1976, however, and after a great deal of costly expenditure, Moscow finally drew the unavoidable conclusion that high-energy lasers were no good for blowing up warheads on missiles.[70]

While the program was being pursued, scientific publication within the USSR reflected the slow state of progress, albeit obliquely in the form of pure science rather than engineering application. When the secret program was suddenly halted, publication naturally ceased. The unexpected disappearance of published papers inevitably aroused curiosity. A leading American scientist responsible for the H-bomb, anticommunist diehard Professor Edward Teller held joint appointments at the Hoover Institution (Stanford) and at the Lawrence Livermore Laboratory (part of the University of California, Berkeley). As a young scientist working on the atomic bomb he remembered what had happened at the end of the 1930s. That this might be repeating itself was drawn to Teller's attention by scientist George Chapline: "In 1977, I. I. Sobel'man and several other leading Soviet physicists published papers on a long wavelength X-ray laser of a novel and promising type." But "publications on the topic stopped abruptly the following year." Teller saw this as significant and attributed "recent Soviet efforts to ban further nuclear tests" to the possibility "that they may know important details about the X-ray laser that they hope we shall never learn."[71]

Teller sought significant funding for programs he headed at Livermore. But a tendency to oversell his project did not help get it off the ground. At Christmas 1982 Teller alleged that an X-ray laser had reached the "engineering phase," and in 1984 he asserted that the laser could become a space-based weapon which might destroy incoming Soviet missiles. The trouble was that the scientist who first alerted Teller to these possibilities, Chapline, withdrew his support; and the scientist at Livermore heading the research, Roy Woodruff, believed none of the claims made by Teller to be true.[72] Selling novel ideas in the face of skepticism thus required relentless persistence and tireless patience, characteristics Teller had in abundance.

Teller had recommended Dr George A. ("Jay") Keyworth for the post of Reagan's science adviser, and when Keyworth set up the White House Science Council he invited Teller to serve. Keyworth himself, however, was "rather doubtful, not only of the usefulness, but even of the very existence of an X-ray laser."[73] As of mid-1982, however, strategic defense technologies had yet to be discussed by the Council. Reagan had, however, received a briefing on Russian activities in outer space at the NSC. He noted on 28 June that Moscow had unquestionably "moved to a military priority in space. We must not be left behind."[74] Despite his skepticism, Keyworth agreed to hand Reagan a letter from Teller written on 23 July 1982, which Teller had been encouraged to write by right-wing columnist Bill Buckley.[75]

Teller drew Reagan's attention to developments in space weapons where there were "reasons to believe that the Soviet Union might be a few years ahead of us." It was, Teller wrote, "only recently that our understanding has advanced to the level where we could appreciate the significance of previously puzzling Soviet emphasis on the aspects of science and technology pertinent to the development of these weapons. Because of their extraordinary potential," he argued, "it seems likely that the Soviets would seek an early opportunity to employ such means to negate our offensive strategic capabilities, the more so as a 'bloodless' victory would be in prospect." Teller had already brought this to the attention of "all relevant people" in the administration, but "action," he wrote, "has yet to be taken which is commensurate with both the threat and the opportunity." Hence his own appeal to the President "for a mandate to vigorously explore and exploit the technological opportunities in defensive applications of nuclear weaponry." The stakes were high: "If the Soviets should be the first to develop and deploy these defensive nuclear weapons, the Free World is in the deepest trouble. However, if we act in this matter promptly and with the full vigor of which we are capable, we may end the Mutual Assured Destruction era and commence a period of assured survival on terms favorable to the Western Alliance."[76]

That autumn Teller asked Keyworth to create a study group on strategic defense. It duly reported in January 1983, arguing for the development of these technologies. At this point a chance encounter with Admiral James Watkins, Chief of Naval Operations, enabled Teller to expatiate on the subject of the laser; and although Watkins did not like its nuclear character, he supported the general idea and drew the Joint Chiefs of Staff in the same direction. They were particularly preoccupied with the vulnerability of silo-based missiles to preemptive attack from the new Soviet SS-18; the substitute mobile US ICBM system (MX) appeared to be going nowhere, now that the Joint Chiefs refused to accept a system of basing them closely together so that incoming missiles would collide with one another while homing in on densely packed targets. This would leave some US ICBMs untouched.[77]

On 11 February Reagan heard from the Joint Chiefs that strategic missile defense was a feasible alternative. Shultz was skeptical but "had absolutely no idea that the views he was expressing had any near-term, operational significance."[78] What occurred just over a month later therefore came as an unpleasant surprise. Reagan invited Teller to dine on 20 March 1983. Three days later the President delivered a speech announcing SDI.[79] This came as a severe shock to Moscow. It threatened to annihilate the balance of terror between the Superpowers, leaving the Russians vulnerable to an American first strike. If Moscow instead countered SDI, then it could be drawn into ever greater expenditure with an economy running out of steam. All Soviet proposals on nuclear arms control thereafter focused above all on removal of SDI as the ultimate if not the immediate goal.

Cut out of the decisions made, as a pragmatist Shultz nevertheless made the most of what SDI offered alongside the buildup in US capabilities worldwide and the deployment of Cruise and Pershing II in Europe.[80] "Of course," General Starodubov recalls, "far from everyone in the Soviet Union, including the top leadership in the country, took the information put out by Washington in relation to SDI at face value. Serious researchers understood that many of the American plans promulgated had a speculative, imaginary character. But this did not mean that the SDI program represented no danger. A wide-ranging antiballistic missile defense could be created even without putting into effect exotic programs."[81] Ogarkov inevitably took SDI seriously. In March 1983 he gave an off-the-record interview to Gelb, now *New York Times* correspondent. "Numbers of troops and weapons means little, he said. We cannot equal the quality of U.S. arms for a generation or two. Modern military power is based upon technology, and technology is based upon computers." In Moscow, unlike Washington, "we don't even have computers in every office of the Defense Ministry." Ogarkov went on to insist: "We will never be able to catch up with you in modern arms until we have an economic revolution. And the question is whether we can have an economic revolution without a political revolution."[82]

Britain's Prime Minister Margaret Thatcher was horrified. The idea that the United States would throw up a defense system to protect the subcontinent—fortress America—and leave Europe exposed to Soviet missiles did not exactly fit with NATO solidarity. She had assumed power on 4 May 1979 as détente slithered into oblivion. Reagan's accession in 1981 met her best hopes. But his invasion of Grenada, a former British possession, without securing her prior consent in October 1983 had, as he hurriedly acknowledged by phone, caused her acute embarrassment.[83] Offsetting this, Reagan's steadfast implementation of the dual-track decision by deploying Cruise and Pershing in Europe was heartening. The next shock, however, was also not foreseen: the unexpected proposal for an SDI.

Thatcher met Reagan at Camp David on 22 December 1984. Congratulating him on a second term with such overwhelming popular endorsement, she briefed him on Mikhail Gorbachev's recent visit to London, which had made such an impression. He was "unusual . . . much less constrained, more charming, open to discussion and debate, and did not stick to prepared notes." As a woman, of course, she had not overlooked the possibility that more charming could also mean more dangerous. But she was taken with his tolerance of criticism in contrast to Gromyko. "He also avoided the usual Soviet reaction of citing lengthy position[s] of principle." Then she subjected SDI to heavy skepticism, buttressed by scientific training, at a session including Shultz and National Security Adviser "Bud" McFarlane.

Thatcher "backed the U.S. research program." But "she understood that we will not know for some time if a strategic defense system is truly feasible. If we reached a stage where production looked possible we would have some serious and difficult decisions to take. There are the ABM and outer space treaties. Future technological developments and possible countering strategies must also be considered. She recalled, for example, that with the advent of heat seeking missiles the general view had been that there was no defense against them, but this proved erroneous. Avoidance devices were developed. It was her impression from talking to Gorbachev that the Soviets were following the same line of reasoning. They clearly fear U.S. technological prowess. However, Gorbachev suggested that the Soviets would either develop their own strategic defense system [which the Reagan administration always claimed they already possessed][84] or add additional offensive systems." There were, she observed, "all sorts of decoys, jamming systems and technological developments such as making the missile boost phase even shorter. All these advances," she warned, "make crisis management more and more difficult." She also voiced skepticism that the program was feasible on the grounds that if it were only 95 per cent successful, over 60 million would still die from what got through.

Unlike Reagan, Thatcher approved of the balance of terror which Reagan had condemned as "this horrible threat." "Nuclear weapons," she argued, "have served not only to prevent a nuclear war, but they have also given us forty years of unprecedented peace in Europe. It would be unwise, she continued, to abandon a deterrence system that has prevented both nuclear and conventional war. Moreover, if we ever reach the stage of abolishing all nuclear weapons, this would make conventional, biological, or chemical war more likely." As the discussion proceeded, it became increasingly apparent that what most disturbed Thatcher was the horrifying prospect that the threat of US superiority was destabilizing and yet the SDI system would actually prove all too imperfect as a defense. "Saying SDI as she understood it seemed to suggest inherent U.S. superiority, Mrs. Thatcher added that she was not convinced of the need to deploy such a system, particularly if it could eventually be knocked out by other technological advances."[85]

SDI threatened to reopen the very rift that Carter had inadvertently created. The alliance was persuaded to approve SDI, former Foreign Secretary Geoffrey Howe recalls, only "in order to bring constant economic and technological pressure to bear on the USSR."[86] Howe recalls: "when Margaret Thatcher visited Washington she insistently demanded that the USA remain loyal to the idea and practice of nuclear containment. Otherwise, the reliability of Europe's defense would have been undermined."[87] A battle thus began in Washington and between Washington and its allies between those who believed SDI worthwhile and practicable for its own sake and those who saw it as a means of breaking the back of the Russian economy or as a bargaining chip through which a rebalancing of power could be obtained.

THE CHERNENKO-GORBACHEV TRANSITION

The arrival of US Cruise and Pershing II missiles imminent by the end of the year, on 4 August 1983 Andropov told the Politburo: "Without wasting time, we must bring into action all the levers of possible influence upon the governments and parliaments of the NATO countries in order to create maximum obstruction against the deployment of American missiles in Europe." Whereupon the eager Gorbachev chimed in with a chorus on the "need to rebuff" Washington.[88]

A nasty incident that occurred on 31 August demonstrated the high cost in human life of the international tension mounting since the late seventies. That day a South Korean airliner was shot down by a nervous Soviet fighter-interceptor pilot when it flew directly over Kamchatka and Sakhalin, way off the course, its lights off, and unresponsive to the warning shots fired at it by the Russians. Air defense mistook the Boeing for a military aircraft of similar design used for high altitude electronic reconnaissance. This point was stressed by Ustinov. In that theater twelve such overflights had recently occurred. The pilot was thus under enormous pressure to put an end to the new intrusion. When disaster struck and Moscow was pilloried at the UN with the unwarranted accusation that a civil aircraft had deliberately been shot down, the Politburo convened with Chernenko in the chair to assess the political damage after Ogarkov, Kornienko, and Kryuchkov had assembled all relevant information.

The entire leadership rallied round, including Gorbachev, who was convinced that the Soviet response was "legal"—which entirely missed the point. He went on to advocate the adoption of "an offensive posture." Ogarkov, given to conspiracy as an explanation, suggested: "It is quite possible that this was a pre-planned provocation insofar as American intelligence on each occasion tried to determine where our air defense forces are arrayed and how they operate." Kornienko predictably took the same line.[89]

The last session of the Politburo chaired by Andropov was on 1 September 1983. Since the summer he had been on haemodialysis at the central clinical hospital.[90] He seemed exhausted and lifeless. That day he flew south to the Crimea and never reappeared.[91] He died at 4:50 p.m. on 9 February from kidney failure. This changed nothing of substance, however. In domestic affairs the impulse for change had been faint but audible; yet the corruption of Soviet society continued apace even while economic growth momentarily rose by a fraction. In foreign policy, he had anyway worked carefully within the established framework long fixed with Ustinov and Gromyko. His successor left foreign policy entirely to Gromyko.

Adamishin noted that the differences between Andropov and Chernenko effectively made no difference in practice. "Yuva liked one arguing with him, suggesting alternative decisions, even saying things that were scarcely patriotic. . . . But no practical consequences resulted." Whereas Chernenko was very different: "He completely depended upon position papers; he had no need of alternatives; and in matters of foreign policy he listened only to Andrei Andreevich [Gromyko]."[92] Meeting Gromyko in September 1983 and again in January 1984 Howe found him "absolutely uncompromising" on the issue of human rights. "And he didn't believe in the West's interest in arms limitation and peaceful coexistence. The position of the USSR at the time was hostile and defensive. It continued while Gromyko held the post of foreign minister."[93] Any change awaited the succession to Chernenko, whose failing health ensured the interval would be mercifully brief.

Under Chernenko Politburo meetings slowed down. He had been elected as a safe if shaky pair of hands. Vigorous Gorbachev became Second Secretary in charge of the Party secretariat, also taking control over the Politburo's political committee, while retaining the agricultural portfolio.[94] Foreign policy was paralyzed. When the Politburo met on 10 February 1984 to set the arrangements for Andropov's funeral, "the anti-war movement" that had "attained great reach" within Western Europe sustained high hopes. Members congratulated themselves on "the firm and unchanging" line held against the capitalist world.[95] Reagan thus had good grounds for holding back.

The SDI threatened the USSR in a number of ways. Above all it would require an enormous effort to raise the arms race to new technological levels, a further waste of scarce capital resources at a time when Moscow needed to divert military expenditure toward domestic investment. Washington was well aware of this; indeed, it was built into the advice the administration received from Rowen. Soviet labor productivity declined at an even faster rate in the last half of the seventies. Raw materials shortages, including fuel, transportation bottlenecks (rail), excess military expenditure, poor working incentives, financial conservatism in foreign trade (avoidance of debts to the West), and poor harvests all contributed to the problem.[96]

The SDI had a two-edged effect. It impressed upon hawks the need to accelerate further development of offensive missile capabilities to outflank antimissile defense. It thus buttressed rearmament. For the doves, on the other hand, it underlined the importance of negotiating concessions to forestall the realization of Reagan's dream.[97] Gorbachev found himself somewhere in between, though rarely equidistant between the two competing lobbies. He was strongly opposed to surrendering under pressure from SDI, which had in 1984 turned into an organization (the SDIO) under Lieutenant General James Abrahamson. It was in reaction to this that on 29 June Moscow under Chernenko proposed talks on prohibiting the militarization of outer space, with a moratorium on testing and deploying such weapons once negotiations began. Anxiety was thus hard to hide. "Considering the urgency and importance of the question, the Soviet government expects a speedy and positive response from the government of the USA," Moscow announced, revealing a nervous hand.[98]

Shultz and the allies had become impatient to start negotiating. Reagan appeared still in the hands of the diehards. Nevertheless a gut feeling began to emerge that he would "like to talk to him [Chernenko] about our problems man to man & see if I could convince him there would be a material benefit to the Soviets if they'd join the family of nations etc." On the other hand, Reagan did not "want to appear anxious which would tempt them to play games & possibly snub us."[99] The gut feeling was reinforced by Suzanne Massie, biographer of the last Tsar, when she lunched with Reagan on 1 March after her visit to Russia.[100] Reagan also now shared the view of Chancellor Helmut Kohl, who visited him on 5 March, that "the Soviets are motivated, at least in part by insecurity & a suspicion that we & our allies mean them harm." Kohl also thought Reagan should meet Chernenko.[101] Yet, paradoxically, on 6 March 1984 Reagan addressed the National Association of Evangelicals in Columbus, Ohio, bluntly stigmatizing the USSR as an "evil empire." Switching positions was a decision difficult for him to take.

This speech had not, of course, been cleared with the State Department. Shultz immediately insisted on a meeting. Two days later he found himself surrounded by faces some of which he did not even recognize, including academics specializing on Russia but not practitioners of equivalent expertise. "It is time to probe and test," Shultz insisted. In opposition stood National Security Adviser William Clark, whose outlook was accurately summed up by Shultz as that of dealing with the Russians only after they had changed. A further meeting on 11 March finally induced the President to agree that State move on Moscow. Shultz produced a memorandum, "Next Steps in U.S.-Soviet Relations," four days later.[102]

Shultz was thus ready for Chernenko's offer at the end of June. The US reply was cautiously ambiguous as to future negotiations. Both sides should "discuss and determine mutually acceptable approaches to talks on arms limitations in the areas that cause concern to each side." This threw Moscow into turmoil. Not until September did it agree to talks. Chernenko announced that an agreement banning space weapons "would not only prevent an arms race in outer space but, no less importantly, would facilitate the resolution of the questions of limiting and reducing other strategic weapons. I would particularly underline this."[103]

The unwritten Soviet agenda was that were Washington to drop SDI, Moscow would cut theater nuclear forces. Yet further attempts to draw Moscow out on this point met with silence and the press appeared reluctant even to endorse Chernenko's statement. The announcement on 6 September that Ogarkov had been removed from his post at a time when Ustinov was gravely ill suggested that the Kremlin faced insubordination from the military.[104] Moreover, Reagan's offer at the UN on 24 September of extending the arms control process met with an unyielding response from Gromyko three days later that effectively reneged on Chernenko's original proposal. The United States, he insisted, had to remove "the obstacles which they created" before talks on strategic and theater nuclear weapons could take place.[105] Change was in the wind, nevertheless, with Gorbachev the heir presumptive.

Like many statesmen of note, Gorbachev was something of a mystery. Born 2 March 1931 at the height of the forced collectivization of agriculture, he emerged rapidly from humble origins on a collective farm to become deputy secretary of the student Party organization at Moscow University under Stalin. His background and manner never suggested a man about to overthrow the established order that had done so much to advance him from the back of beyond. In the latter stages Gorbachev emerged due above all to patronage from Andropov, the ascetic diehard who increasingly saw himself as a true follower of Lenin. When Gorbachev's wife Raisa was visiting Pamela Harriman, grande dame of Washington, DC, and Churchill's former daughter-in-law, she was shown to the bathroom and passed at the bedside a photo of Averell Harriman with Andropov: "We owe everything to him [Andropov]," she said.[106]

Better educated than his predecessors, naturally intelligent, and of considerable charm, Gorbachev represented the kind of instinctive politician more often seen in the American Deep South. He reached out in a populist manner. When alert, he showed an uncanny ability to detect his interlocutor's feelings even without an interpreter. Gorbachev was not embarrassingly informal like Carter, but he certainly was *"kontaktny."*[107] Ambitious, he made full use of his bailiwick in Stavropol, the northern Caucasus, to develop a tourist area favored by the leadership in order to obtain direct access to Brezhnev, but in particular to Andropov, about whom he had heard so much.[108]

Once a suitable hotel complex had been built, Andropov—a native of the region—appeared more regularly in Kislovodsk to take the waters. But, a man of few words and significant understatement, Andropov gave little away when questioned for an impression of the young Gorbachev: "unusual" and "nice" were all he had to say initially.[109] He was, however, more forthcoming to his son Igor, who recalls a comment around 1977 to the effect that Gorbachev could develop into "an outstanding worker, an outstanding leader . . . if, of course, nothing happens."[110] Andropov later indicated that Gorbachev stood above the rest, of whom he held a low opinion—gossips, careerists, and rogues. He pondered aloud as to how Gorbachev might be brought to Moscow.[111] Indeed, he seriously considered making Gorbachev deputy chairman of the KGB in charge of personnel.[112] But he was pipped at the post. With the sudden death of Brezhnev loyalist Fyodor Kulakov, on 27 November 1978 Gorbachev was charged with the transformation of agriculture, which had always drawn the short straw in Soviet economic priorities.[113] He had evidently impressed others as much as Andropov: Brezhnev reportedly commented that he was "a worthy Party leader."[114] Gorbachev was thus picked up by the Kremlin to breathe some life into a moribund portfolio and an increasingly geriatric Politburo.

In the West many dreamed that someone such as Gorbachev would appear. This was, after all, despite everything a system capable of spawning Dubček, author of the Prague Spring. Thatcher, in particular, took the view that "great men" determined the affairs of the world. Whereas many Americans believed (nurtured by the wrong kind of political science) that the USSR was essentially a mighty machine of which the General Secretary was merely the most important cog, Thatcher was waiting for the right man to come along and end the Soviet system. At that stage, however, no one had any idea whom this might be. Downing Street thus set about inviting two or three possibilities to Britain.[115] The Foreign Secretary described it: "In the autumn of 1983 we came to the conclusion that the main thing was to begin a dialogue with the Soviet leadership. We faced the task to determine who would head the USSR in the near future, inasmuch as the life of Andropov was coming to an end, and Chernenko could be an interim figurehead."[116]

At around this time a John the Baptist emerged to herald the arrival of the secular Savior. Fyodor Burlatsky was the leading Soviet political sociologist, formerly part of the Andropov team. He toured various universities in Britain and the United States in 1984 telling those Sovietologists willing to listen that a new leader was on the way who would transform the Soviet Union and East-West relations.[117] In government note was taken because Gordievsky, who had been spying for MI6 since the early seventies, privately echoed Burlatsky's opinion. Moreover, others knew better than any that Gorbachev had reformist instincts. When Zdeněk Mlynář, an old friend from Moscow university days, visited Stavropol in June 1967, Gorbachev was still under the illusion that Brezhnev would prove a transitional figure, because reform was essential.[118]

Thatcher nevertheless had to find out for herself. When it turned out that of those invited only Gorbachev could come, she determined this was an opportunity to be seized. Once in Britain Gorbachev did not, of course, contradict Politburo policy. No one would seriously have expected him to do so. Yet his entire approach to dealing with the USSR's staunch adversary in person was refreshingly different: he argued endlessly and to all appearances enjoyed doing so. It was for this reason that at the end of the visit, when interviewed for television on 17 December 1984, Thatcher cautiously but controversially expressed her optimism in a phase that was to echo into the future: "I like Mr. Gorbachev. We can do business together."[119]

In Washington, DC, however, most believed she had lost her judgment.[120] Nevertheless Thatcher's endorsement was significant to Gorbachev for the longer term. Senior British diplomats openly joked that "she created him." It would, though, be more true to say that Thatcher gave his reputation more than a nudge in the right direction. Rosalind Ridgeway, who headed the European section at State, recalls "the importance on the U.S. side" of "the external validation of Gorbachev by Mrs. Thatcher. It was very much a part of what made it possible for those who wanted to work the relationship in a positive way to go forward."[121] Gorbachev had inadvertently gained access to the world stage and made full use of it, thereby outdistancing his peers by a wide margin. The relationship between Gorbachev and Thatcher thus became something like that of player and coach. A certain bond began to form between them which Thatcher's friend and adviser on anti-Soviet affairs, Robert Conquest, found very frustrating. The problem was, of course, that coach and player belonged to opposing teams.

As Chernenko moved into hospital, word had it, however, that the succession was between Gromyko and Gorbachev. In late January 1985 signs emerged that both sides were prepared to go *"va banque,"* and that if Gorbachev pressed his case at the Politburo, "they will not let him through." The decision would then have to go to a Central Committee plenum.[122] This would have been embarrassing for all. In the event Gromyko, statesman rather than Party man, realized he could not count on support beyond Moscow. In charge of the Central Committee's all-powerful general department, Yegor Ligachev had been slowly but surely amassing appointments with a view to the succession, so that the hinterland of regional Party secretaries from the provinces were to a greater extent Gorbachev men. Convinced of the need to take second best, Gromyko thus sent word through his son, the Africanist Anatoly, via Yevgeny Primakov, a mutual friend, to Alexander Yakovlev. Yakovlev had befriended Gorbachev during the latter's visit to Canada in 1983, another brief foreign visit that reinforced his sense of Russian backwardness. Yakovlev now headed the Institute of World Economy and International Relations in Moscow.[123]

The deal offered was that Gromyko propose Gorbachev as General Secretary and, on assuming office, Gorbachev would then give him the honorific post of President.[124] Chernenko died at 7:20 p.m. on 10 March, ultimately of heart failure following emphysema, chronic hepatitis, and cirrhosis. The Politburo met the following day and Gromyko duly spoke in support of Gorbachev as his replacement, pointing out that Brezhnev had consulted him about bringing Gorbachev to Moscow and in so doing referred to his "indomitable, creative energy."[125]

GORBACHEV IN POWER

However, Gromyko also thought he could then elevate his like-minded deputy at the Minindel, Kornienko, into the post of Foreign Minister so that he, Gromyko, could continue to run matters at one remove.[126] He won the presidency, but it became immediately apparent that Gorbachev was not about to let foreign policy stultify. On 15 March Gorbachev recounted his meetings with foreign leaders in Moscow for Chernenko's funeral: "We told the NATO Powers candidly that the Americans evidently wish to drag out the negotiations in

Geneva indefinitely, thereby lessening the degree of alarm among the nations of the world; sowing disunity in the peace movement. Of course, we cannot allow this. Therefore the focus on Europe in our diplomatic, political, and other activities is extremely important to us. Here we have to be considerably more resolute and flexible."[127] Given this overriding need, Americanist Gromyko had to go. The subsequent plenum of the Central Committee on 23 April emphasized the importance of activating foreign policy.[128] On 30 June Gorbachev telephoned a friend of like mind, Georgian Party Secretary Eduard Shevardnadze, a former Interior Minister, intelligent and open-minded but with absolutely no specialist knowledge of or experience in foreign affairs, to offer the Foreign Ministry. On the following day when this was announced to the Politburo, Gromyko returned to the ministry in fury; Kornienko was stunned.[129] The appointment of Shevardnadze went through on 16 July.

Shevardnadze was pragmatic. But his instincts were for change. The man closest to Gorbachev and with the greatest impact upon him was another enigma: this was the tiny, squat figure of Yakovlev, with the large tufts of dark hair on both sides of the bald cone of a head—he chaired meetings on a raised seat— but a man to be taken extremely seriously. Also of peasant stock, his mother entirely illiterate, his father barely literate, Yakovlev was born on 2 December 1923 in the village of Korolevo near Yaroslavl. Older than Gorbachev, a war veteran chosen for the higher Party school, Yakovlev was swiftly advanced to the Central Committee apparatus in Moscow at barely thirty years of age, where he witnessed the extraordinary proceedings of the Twentieth Party Congress from the balcony. Never an orthodox thinker, he reacted with ambivalence, being a young war veteran, yet at the same time part of a generation looking forward to a better life even under Soviet conditions.

One of three in the first cultural exchange with the United States, Yakovlev studied at Columbia University, where, in the more homely teaching library at the St. John's hostel nearby, he educated himself into a new understanding of the world. He was impressed. "There were not even such books in the special collection" of the Lenin Library, he noted.[130] He also attended Alex Dallin's classes on the Soviet Union and world communism alongside Serewyn Bialer.[131] During that period he spent a month traveling across the country, every three to four days with a different family. He never liked the West—indeed, at times he could sound viscerally xenophobic[132]—but he was sure the USSR lagged behind for lack of democracy. Yakovlev believed Stalin a Russian fascist. And his reaction to the destruction of the Prague Spring had to be kept to himself not least because of its cold ferocity: "After Budapest and Prague I understood that the notion of a [Soviet] commonwealth is a chimera and had not the slightest future."[133]

It was certainly true that the problem Moscow faced from Washington was far greater than anything elsewhere. And, given Reagan's strategy of economic pressure, the need to outflank him seemed self-evident—at least to the reformist camp. The interconnection between foreign and domestic policies was crucial, Yakovlev insisted: "A rational foreign policy that has been thought through will allow us to save substantial sums that will, for instance, reduce the cost of maintaining our defense capability."[134]

Initially, though, and on the usual bad advice, Gorbachev played with the idea of setting Western Europe at odds with the United States—the customary wedge-driving that had never led to anything productive in the past. Yakovlev followed this line in a memorandum on 12 March. Here he warned Gorbachev of the American *"aspiration to confine our relations with the West to the Soviet-American framework* (the USA is watching its allies with concern)."[135] Drawing on this brief, Gorbachev was determined to amplify his range of action beyond Washington. "We told the NATO people to their faces that the Americans evidently want to drag out the talks at Geneva to infinity; by this means making the people more anxious, disrupting the movement in the defense of peace. We cannot, of course, allow this. Therefore," Gorbachev concluded, "the European orientation of our diplomatic, political, and other activities is extremely important for us. Here we must be much more resolute and flexible."[136] Anatoly Chernyaev, soon to become Gorbachev's right-hand man in foreign policy, recalls that until 1986 "the prevailing tactic was 'the indirect approach' via pressure on Western Europe, by means of stimulating friction within the Atlantic alliance, through propaganda . . . that is in effect the traditional line though with novel aims—to attain *real* disarmament."[137]

At a conference of secretaries of the Central Committee held in his Kremlin office on 15 March, following Chernenko's funeral, Gorbachev "noted that our conversation with the Prime Minister of England, Thatcher, had a somewhat different character" from those with other leaders. The US delegation led by Vice President George Bush and Shultz left a general impression of mediocrity. In contrast, "she spoke quite decisively in favour of expanding bilateral economic, scientific and cultural ties between our countries. Thatcher also stated that she was in favour of energising the dialogue aimed at establishing better trust between member states of the Warsaw Pact and members of NATO." Gorbachev "told the NATO countries openly that the Americans, apparently, want to prolong the negotiations in Geneva indefinitely. . . . Of course, we cannot allow this to happen. Therefore, the European orientation of our diplomatic, political and other actions is extremely important for us."[138]

It became rapidly apparent, however, that Europe was just a matter of tactics within a traditionally Americocentric strategy. Adamishin was a member of the ruling collegium and head of the first European department. He noted: "Once again they focus everything de facto on the USA . . . once again they undervalue Europe's potential; they want to give nothing to it, throwing what little crumbs there are to the Americans. They quietly stuff them in their pockets and make no moves of their own, which just legitimises our hard-line stance." The Minindel was dominated by Americanists under Kornienko. "The Military Industrial Committee and its representatives in the Foreign Ministry are strong and in contrast to the liberal doves behave insolently," the embittered Adamishin wrote. Kornienko's recent conversation with him underlined certain features of their approach: "They think (or give that impression) in purely military categories: how many of these against how many of those. The political pluses are not taken into account as a result of their intangibility." Equally evident was "the burning desire to do nothing, for the legitimate question arises, why things weren't done differently before and who will answer for that. The dead clasp the living."[139]

The close bonds between the military-industrial complex and senior Americanists were longstanding. The substitution of Shevardnadze for Gromyko therefore promised change. The announcement was made in early July along with news that Moscow had agreed to a summit in Geneva on 19–20 November 1985. Not everyone was pleased. Unable to contain his irritation, Dobrynin indiscreetly confided to Shultz: "Our foreign policy is going down the drain. They have named an agricultural type."[140] And even Adamishin despaired at "new words in foreign policy and old deeds. The Military-Industrial Committee and its representatives in the Foreign Ministry are trying more than ever to engage those newly empowered in old behaviour and the old line. They also understand that if changes are made in politico-military questions, where the military would have to be whipped into line, then this will obviously not happen soon, not being among the top priorities." Adamishin shared these thoughts with Shevardnadze, but he responded conventionally that "in security questions the final word is with the military," "G.M. [Kornienko] knows about these questions; he has good contacts with the military" and so on.[141] Adamishin was appalled. He never understood "why G.M. [Kornienko] adopts such an uncompromising position in favour, let us be blunt, of the military."[142] This habitual approach guided Soviet policy in the run-up to the first summit with Reagan, at Geneva. And it failed utterly. Disillusioned, Shevardnadze's aide Sergei Tarasenko recalls, "In Geneva we were ashamed of our leader."[143]

"Geneva ended up a cul-de-sac," Gorbachev came to conclude.[144] The summit was held at the Maison Fleur d'Eau, Geneva, on 19 November 1985. Gorbachev astounded Aleksandrov-Agentov with the amount of time devoted to preparing his negotiating position. They were up until four in the morning and at work again at seven.[145] When they met, it soon became clear to Reagan that SDI was the core issue. While he asserted that it was purely defensive, even with respect to space-based missiles, Gorbachev insisted it made sense only "if it is to defend against a *retaliatory* strike."[146] Why would Washington want to introduce such a destabilizing system into the relationship? Gorbachev insisted he "could not ignore the importance of the problem." And he had difficulty on occasion in keeping his temper when confronted with Reagan's "banalities." The tone became threatening at times when Gorbachev complained that "the U.S. had the impression that the USSR was weak and could be painted into a corner."[147]

Most of what occurred had been prefigured in preparatory talks between Shultz and Gorbachev. "We know what's going on," Gorbachev insisted. "We know why you're doing this. You're inspired by illusions. You think you're ahead of us in information. You think you're ahead of us in technology and that you can use these things to gain superiority over the Soviet Union. But this is an illusion. . . . First, you believe that the Soviet Union is less economically powerful and therefore it would be weakened by an arms race. Second, that you have the higher technology and therefore SDI would give you superiority over the Soviet Union in weapons. Third, that the Soviet Union is more interested in negotiations in Geneva than you are. Fourth, that the Soviet Union only thinks of damaging U.S. interests around the world. And fifth, that it would be wrong to trade with the Soviet Union because this would just raise its capability."[148] And as to SDI, Gorbachev said no compromise was possible without some guarantee against the militarization of space. Without that, Moscow "will let you bankrupt yourselves. But also we will not reduce our offensive missiles. We will engage in a buildup that will break your shield."[149]

Much of this was bluff. "The Analysis of Work on the American SDI Program," which was produced by the Central Committee's Military-Industrial Sector in the late summer of 1989, warned that the Soviet Union was *"increasingly out of touch with the newest technologies"* in the face of the near-term American aim of "establishing the necessary scientific basis for the development and creation in essence of new means of armed struggle and security systems, including waging war in outer space."[150] Gorbachev nevertheless stubbornly sided with the military in believing SDI could be countered. "It is possible to create a system for the destruction of their SDI systems. One can deploy nuclear explosions in space for these purposes," he told the Politburo.[151] But at what cost? Gorbachev never made that clear. After further concluding that Soviet fears only encouraged the Americans to proceed with the program, Gorbachev emphasized that "we have to stop being afraid of SDI."[152] Moreover, when foreign policy adviser Chernyaev argued that he "personally never believed that we had an efficient response to SDI," Gorbachev "dismissed it, saying, 'You just don't understand that subject.'"[153]

Akhromeyev and Kornienko had opposed cutting the SS-20, though they were finally overruled by Gorbachev. Prior to the summit, with Kornienko in New York accompanying Shevardnadze, fellow Americanist Deputy Foreign Minister Viktor Komplektov smelled the whiff of conspiracy. He "attempted at the last minute to call [Colonel-General Nikolai] Chervov ('what are you deciding in secret?'—this given the fact that beforehand *everything* was actually decided by our Americanists in secret), but the train has already departed."[154] Moreover, at Geneva Kornienko typically almost sabotaged an agreed communiqué through a sleight of hand until his bluff was called at Shultz's instruction.[155]

Back in Moscow Gorbachev briefed the Politburo. He lambasted Reagan as "a product of the military-industrial complex, of its most right-wing, reactionary wing. The essence of his thought has not changed. But our pressure, our strength, and world public opinion are having their effect upon him. He was obliged to meet us. It was important to him because the USA is heading for elections. Our policy—broad, objective, constructive—has had a certain political and economic impact." Of course, he acknowledged, no fundamental changes in relations had occurred; "nothing good could be expected." Military confrontation would continue. His conclusion was that "Party organizations must hold firmly to the business of defense. Among the people doubts have arisen: is the United States fooling us? That is to say, we also need force, the reinforcement of defense. For us this is 'the holy of holies.'"[156]

GORBACHEV GRASPS THE ZERO OPTION

Yet it was only as a result of the failure at Geneva that Gorbachev insisted upon more radical change. It illustrates the fact that throughout negotiations with Washington from the time of Chernenko the abiding aim was to eliminate the SDI. First Deputy Chief of the General Staff from 1987 to 1989 was General Vladimir Lobov. When asked whether he did not realize that the Americans were bluffing with SDI, Lobov said: "I wish we did! . . . It is a good thing the U.S.'s allies refused to play along. In any event, as long as the possibility existed, we had to take some kind of countermeasures."[157] Deputy Foreign Minister and Americanist Alexander Bessmertnykh recalls the atmosphere in Moscow as having been "very tense for the first years of the Reagan administration especially because of the SDI program: it frightened us very much."[158] Similarly, Tarasenko recalls that "we were afraid of SDI." But did Moscow have no answer to it? Not so, according to Tarasenko: "We had no such answer!" At the Minindel "the idea was not taken seriously. . . . But Gorbachev didn't read this criticism. The generals kept feeding him all this information about the threat of SDI."[159]

Anxious for progress, in January 1986 Gorbachev was persuaded to move toward the zero option on theater nuclear forces—abandonment of both the SS-20 and the new US weapons in Europe—that Reagan had advocated back in 1981. This proposal was prepared by Akhromeyev and was hammered together by head of its Treaty and Legal Department Nikolai Chervov and first deputy Viktor Starodubov. Gorbachev was briefed on it in the Crimea before finalization by Chervov.[160] The general message Gorbachev was trying to convey was, as Chernyaev put it, *"there will be no war."*[161]

Had Akhromeyev not preempted, the military would have found Gorbachev increasingly unsympathetic. Adamishin noted that the military had already "begun to bristle. They are already beginning to feel under pressure from various sides . . . the Military-Industrial Committee is a state within a state, around 40 percent of productive capacity; no one knows what they are up to. . . . Everything has been fenced off with signs: 'the interests of security,' 'secrets,' and so on."[162] The movement toward serious change now gained momentum. Crucially, in February, realizing that he was no longer really well regarded, Alexandrov-Agentov stepped down and gave way to Chernyaev, Yakovlev's favorite for the post. Meanwhile in May Gorbachev came to Smolenskaya for the first time to address Shevardnadze's team. No record was ever released of what was said; however, Tarasenko recalls in particular Gorbachev's biting criticism of the "American abscess" that had developed at the Minindel. He wanted greater attention to Europe and the Third World.[163]

At the urging of Chernyaev, Gorbachev realized the need to force implementation of policy into line with the spirit and substance of his own statements. Doubtless the nuclear explosion at Chernobyl on 26 April alerted him to how little had changed in the Soviet Union and to the costs of failure. His outburst at the Politburo in the spring reveals the depth of frustration and irritation at the glaring gap "between our policy statements and the stance taken in negotiations. . . . Where is it that policy decisions get eroded and why? . . . Most likely it is inertia. But if it is resistance, then we cannot work with such comrades."[164] "Our Foreign Ministry has given up," Gorbachev told Honecker, "and doesn't believe in progress."[165] Thus in late April Kornienko was removed to the International Department as deputy head now under Dobrynin.

Gorbachev was more than ever convinced from "our sources" that the Americans "wish to allow negotiations to run up a one-way street. We have removed the one-way street," he claimed. "The NATO states are now well aware of this and have begun to exert pressure."[166] Writing to Reagan on 15 September, Gorbachev lamented the sorry fact that "in almost a year since Geneva there has been no movement" on the key issues. Rather than wait until he visited the United States, Gorbachev suggested that "we have a quick one-to-one meeting, let us say in Iceland or in London, may be just for one day, to engage in a strictly confidential, private, and frank discussion (possibly with only our foreign ministers present)."[167] Reagan rejected London as an option and insisted on the prior release of political prisoners. Dobrynin argued that only the Americans would benefit from a summit. But Gorbachev was insistent.[168] In Soviet tradition, Dobrynin was then tasked with heading a working group to prepare for the meeting. Gorbachev told him that "what we need is a breakthrough and not the usual shoddy goods under the slogan 'all or nothing.'"[169]

Washington was divided. Shultz pressed for "substantive progress" on arms control and human rights. "The American people are all for it," he encouraged Reagan.[170] The summit was thus scheduled for 11–12 October 1986 at Höfdi House in Reykjavik overlooking Faxflóe Bay. Reagan saw the meeting as no more than a means of accelerating progress in resolving differences. "I do not anticipate signing any agreements," he made clear on 7 October.[171] Reagan thus arrived unprepared. Reformists complained that Gorbachev was "still not acting very decisively."[172] There was good reason for this. Although Gorbachev sought "to draw Reagan into discussing substance," he also believed that "in general nothing can, in truth, be done with this administration." Thus the idea was "to knock Reagan off balance," to find out "what the real substance is; in what respect the USA is bluffing; what can be obtained; what can now be got from them." And if the summit collapsed, "then we can say: this is how far we were willing to go!"[173] Indeed, Gorbachev expected a "difficult" meeting and could "not exclude the possibility of a failure." Reagan was "holding a meeting for the sake of a meeting." But Gorbachev was counting at the very least on a publicity coup: "We will aid those forces that are represented by Genscher, for example."[174] In one sense he was decisive in being determined to outflank Reagan. He thus surprised the Americans with a radical package including a stunning 50 percent cut in strategic weapons—which Reagan had previously demanded—and complete elimination of all theater nuclear weapons in Europe excepting those of Britain and France (Reagan's zero option).

The offer caught Reagan off guard. Momentary panic ensued because NATO had not been consulted. Both Kohl and Thatcher would be alarmed, as, indeed, they were when they heard that Reagan succumbed to Gorbachev's siren call as a long-term aim to abolish nuclear weapons entirely. Then came the coup de grâce; Gorbachev insisted that the Americans renounce SDI in terms of development beyond the laboratory. But to Reagan "Gorbachev was asking him to give up the thing he'd promised not to give up."[175] After sustained argument, Reagan walked out of the meeting in fury. But it was clear to Shultz, at least, that SDI had given the USA the leverage that brought Moscow to the table. "If he had given in on SDI, all other progress we had achieved with the Soviets would have been problematic," he recalls.[176]

Gorbachev was still working very much within old structures beholden to the military-industrial sector and to a standard repertoire. Only the performance varied. As Starodubov noted: "Gorbachev for quite some time avoided entering into open conflict with the military."[177] From the General Staff Danilevich, too, remarked that from 1985 through 1986 Gorbachev "was still swimming with the stream."[178] That was why senior diplomats, who hoped for substantial change, were so depressed. Even Yakovlev was contemptuous of the whole process: each side was trying to deceive the other and part of the Soviet team of experts was trying to deceive its own side. At one time, Yakovlev recalls, Lev Zaikov—installed by Gorbachev as Party overseer of the defense industry—telephoned and asked how many delivery vehicles they had. Yakovlev replied, 39,000. No, said Zaikov, 43,000. But our briefing papers say 39,000, retorted Yakovlev. Zaikov had forced out of a senior figure at the Ministry of Defense the true figure. "In this way they deceived us about other types of weapons as well," Yakovlev recollected. On his view a fantastic 70 percent of Soviet industry was engaged in military production.[179]

Reykjavik was a failure. Indeed, it was followed shortly after by Reagan's abrogation of SALT II. It was misconceived to believe that any progress could be made by the approach taken in Iceland. It did, however, prove a turning point in one respect. Tarasenko—not unimpressed by what he deftly called Reagan's "judicious idealism"[180]—reflected years later that "after Reykjavik we grew up."[181] This was not immediately apparent, however. Indeed, Gorbachev returned ever more determined to outmaneuver Reagan. "I would in no respect call Reykjavik a failure," Gorbachev insisted. To the extent that it was "a setback," Gorbachev put it down to two misconceptions held by "certain circles in the West": "First, that the Russians fear SDI and will therefore make any concessions. And, second, that we are interested in disarmament more than the United States." At Reykjavik, Gorbachev said, they "very soon felt that they expect me to show 'my cards' in full. At the same time the President arrived without a specific program, merely to pick up the fruit and put it in his basket."[182] "The US administration is shedding its outer camouflage in favor of the military-industrial complex." Condemnation of the USSR for breaching SALT II was "a provocation, a means of legitimizing 'positions of strength.'" Gorbachev believed that "against the background of Reykjavik the true essence of Reagan's policy becomes all the more evident." But he was not about to give up: "Now what is expected of us is not only words but also deeds in response to this display."[183]

Summing up, Gorbachev insisted that "Reykjavik is a new beginning for our all-out peace offensive. We need to develop new approaches to our military doctrine, including the structure of our armed forces and defense industry, and possible retaliation to SDI."[184] Yet it was evidently a contentious meeting. Both Gorbachev and Shevardnadze had to emphasize to the remainder of the Politburo that they had conceded nothing vital. Shevardnadze insisted that, though Moscow had to fight its corner, contact with Washington should not be broken. There had been no concessions, he argued, disingenuously; at least, nothing essential — "These were diplomatic concessions."[185]

"The only thing I don't understand," wrote the ever-despairing Adamishin managing European affairs, "is why intermediate-range weapons are tied into the SDI; why this wasn't decided on the spot — Shevardnadze could have been called to the meeting; a break in the proceedings could have been called." And where had this package come from? The Military-Industrial Committee?[186] Yet it was Gorbachev's own idea to forge this linkage: "in a very authoritarian manner, no one objected, although earlier Shevà had tried, entirely accurately, to point out that it was not worth it." But no one backed him.[187] Gorbachev's thinking was that "With the help of the package, we will pull Europe to our side against the SDI through the issue of theater nuclear weapons, and tie up the Americans through [proposals on] strategic weapons."[188] Furthermore Gorbachev still felt the need to carry the Politburo with him. And both his number two Ligachev and Gromyko, now President, insisted that INF — especially the fate of the SS-20 — not be decoupled from SDI.[189] The old guard had prevailed.[190] The Foreign Minister remained isolated outside his own department.

After Gorbachev's return, on 14 October 1986 the Politburo took a dual-tracked decision that had him straddling two very different policies in the military-industrial sector. The resolution instructed the Ministry of Defense to bring forward proposals on the structure of strategic nuclear forces to anticipate an agreement with Washington on reductions. But it simultaneously provided for the acceleration of work on retaliatory measures against a multilayered antimissile defense system, above all in outer space. Then in mid-December an "evaluation of the politico-military situation" suggested that now the focus had to be upon Europe, "where the task awaits of renewing détente." The corollary was that Washington had lost influence. Reagan suffered defeat at the November congressional elections; the Iran-Contra scandal had damaged the reputation of the administration; the national debt was rising; no achievements had been attained in foreign policy; and Reagan was under attack for failing to consult his allies at Reykjavik and for acting "impulsively and having made a mess of things." The conclusion drawn was that the shift to the Right was over. Thus Reagan needed agreement on nuclear disarmament. "What was SDI after all—the American have yet to understand it themselves." SDI was "a façade," it was "a convenient flag," it was "a big American stomach for processing 'grey matter' for internal and external digestion."[191]

It took sustained US pressure to prompt Soviet concessions of substance. A negative assessment of the prospects of a deal on strategic arms reductions produced in January 1987 was purloined by Moscow soon thereafter. From this the only ray of hope for Gorbachev appeared to be removal of theater nuclear weapons from the package of proposals offered.[192] Evidently as a result of this reassessment Moscow launched an initiative on 28 February in order to set disarmament in motion by concluding a treaty to dispose of theater nuclear forces.[193] This was not easily done without losing face. Writing to Vitaly Kataev at the Party's Military-Industrial Sector on 16 March, Akhromeyev emphasized the asymmetries at work: "It has to be borne in mind that their creation and development in the Soviet Union and the USA in the postwar period proceeded differently. In the USSR they were developed in the light of their being cheaper relative to contemporary fighter planes, and we moved ahead of the Americans in their construction." Whereas the Americans focused on tactical aviation.[194] This could prove a recipe for failure to reach agreement, because it would once again raise the thorny issue of FBS that had been deliberately excluded from the talks hitherto.

A major incentive, however, to ensure agreement lay in the fact that "the SS-20s [RSD-10] were a nightmare for Europe, and the Pershing IIs were, of course, a nightmare for us."[195] Moreover, even Gromyko now acknowledged that SS-20 deployment had been a grave error.[196] Chernyaev's argument that Washington would concede on other matters of greater importance, such as SDI, only if Western Europe was drawn toward Moscow and world opinion made itself felt in Washington must have made the prospect of dumping the original all-inclusive package easier to accept; though not without a great deal of reluctance.[197]

THE FALLOUT FROM THE INF TREATY

Tensions within Moscow were hard to contain, however. The leadership were inaugurating a new five-year plan. The problem as stated by Gorbachev was that "we have to combine both 'guns and butter.' It is hard, very hard. . . . If we retreat, if we get swayed, the outcome will be the same as with the reform of 1956." It was deeply depressing. "We just think we govern. We're just imagining it."[198] The "guns" drew increasing criticism. Adamishin noted that those "on the left" believed it was "necessary to be more decisive with the military," but that Gorbachev "remains cautious."[199] In May Defense Minister Sokolov gloomily concluded that Washington would breach the ABM treaty and develop the SDI to the point of no return. Thus agreement on strategic arms reductions in the immediate future had "little prospect." The Ministry argued that restructuring proposals for negotiation was not a good idea. Instead they should move ahead with retaliatory measures against multilayered antimissile defense and creation of "an antisatellite capability for the destruction of the components of the outer space layer of the USA's antimissile defense."[200] This would certainly accelerate the arms race still further. Shevardnadze thus pressed ahead on theater nuclear weapons with no great prospect of success. It made him ever more critical of the military as a result. At a meeting of the Defense Council military doctrine came under discussion. Akhromeyev described the scenario if war broke out with twenty-three potential adversaries. Danilevich describes what happened. "His attitude enraged Shevardnadze, who said: 'Is this the basis for our defense strategy? You want to fight practically the entire world!'"[201]

A bolt from the blue then miraculously came to the aid of the beleaguered Shevardnadze and seriously undercut Gorbachev's confidence in the advice from the armed forces that had hitherto paralyzed his policy on disarmament. Relations were already strained between civil and military. Ogarkov, in retirement, was said to be "very upset." But "to him," Gorbachev snapped, "it is just the more the better." The Reykjavik summit had increased such "hissing" among the ranks. "It is the generals who are trying to scare us," he warned Politburo members on 1 December 1986, "they are afraid that they would have nothing to do. There is enough work left for four or five generations of generals."[202] Then, on 28 May 1987 Matthias Rust, a young West German with an unrestrained sense of adventure fortuitously flew a tiny Cessna plane across the Finnish frontier toward Moscow, where he circled the Kremlin before landing just off Red Square.

Nothing epitomized the underlying structural defects in the air defense system more than this embarrassing incident. The news broke while the allied communist leaders gathered in Warsaw on 29 May. Gorbachev could not conceal his amazement and fury. "It is even worse than Chernobyl," he exploded. "It is an absolute disgrace."[203] At the Politburo on the following morning Gorbachev did not mince words. "The Ministry of Defense has shown scandalous impotence." The leadership had to work out how to explain it all to the Party and public. Deputy Minister Marshal Pyotr' Lushev lamely argued by way of excuse that this was an atypical situation. "And how will we act in combat conditions when atypical situations arise?" Gorbachev interjected. Moreover, this was not the only instance of this kind. One such aircraft had been hijacked to Turkey only a decade before.[204] After merely a fifteen-minute break, Sokolov was summarily dismissed and replaced by a mediocrity with a background in personnel, Dmitrii Yazov.[205] Not only would he take a considerable period of time to understand what was going on, but his limited background ill-fitted him to his new role.

The incident provided an opportunity for establishing political control over the military. "For a long time," Nikolai Ryzhkov said, "the army was a kind of forbidden zone for inspecting what was going on in it. As a result of this a certain corrosion has taken place." Both Syria and Libya had complained at the poor quality of the air defense they had received. With more than one grievance to sustain him given military resistance to his disarmament proposals, Shevardnadze lunged without restraint. "I must say plainly that what we have done in the country for reconstruction did not have any fundamental impact on our army. But with respect to the army, it always had a certain autonomy which was argued on the basis of its special conditions. This served as a barrier for information about its circumstances. I think we must have complete information about the state of affairs in the army."[206]

"In the army," Shevardnadze continued, "we have beatings and even pillaging, plunder and other instances of law-breaking among our forces in Afghanistan, in Mongolia and Hungary. I fear that there is insufficient discipline in the army; instances of drug addiction have been observed. The people know this." The army was being "devalued." "We have been fighting for eight years in Afghanistan. And what has changed in this term? Why do 100,000 of our forces in this country show their impotence?" He concluded by calling for resignations. The meeting closed with Sokolov's resignation.[207]

Then on 6 August the Politburo resolved to declassify the defense budget over the course of the next two to three years.[208] The military were now visibly in disarray. The path was thus open for fundamental change in the disarmament negotiations. Chernyaev recalls that "it took a long time to convince them [the military] of the need to take the SS-20s out of Europe."[209] By late November, however, Shevardnadze had drawn Akhromeyev into his web. As negotiations proceeded it was, noted Adamishin, "pathetic to see how he [Akhromeyev] met his end; in certain situations he visibly suffered."[210] Finally, on 7 December 1987 Gorbachev arrived in Washington to sign the resultant treaty eliminating intermediate-range and shorter-range missiles on the following day.

The reasons behind the INF treaty were outlined by the Politburo committee responsible (Zaikov, Chebrikov, Shevardnadze, Yazov, Dobrynin, and Maslyukov): "to take the first step along the road to the genuine liquidation of nuclear arsenals . . . to remove from Europe the American Pershing II missiles (particularly dangerous to us because of their small flight time and high degree of accuracy) and ground-launched Cruise missiles; to exert serious pressure on European and world public opinion, demonstrating the initial results of our new approach on the world stage."[211] Similarly, Major-General Yuri Lebedev, deputy head of the General Staff Treaty and Legal Directorate argued that "the problem of eliminating medium-range missiles and operational-tactical missiles has, one might say, become the key to resolving other major problems in limiting the nuclear arms race, in disarmament, including such problems as forestalling an arms race in outer space."[212]

However, a Party meeting of the department on 29 December attacked the "mistakes that were permitted in the preparation of the treaty on intermediate-range forces, when we defended our positions with inadequate firmness and gave way to the Americans." In the written version of the criticism given by Subbotin, the words "gave way" were substituted for the words "gave in." Criticism was hedged around with agreement in principle and focused on preparation that linked to relations between members of the department and corresponding members of the Minindel. And criticism focused on the state of those relations not just in respect of the INF treaty. One officer, Tatarnikov, "said that for certain employees of the Foreign Ministry perestroika is a matter of surrendering positions to our adversaries." Others argued that the selection of the military element in the delegation was "done frequently on the principle of who was 'acceptable' and who 'unacceptable.'" The sentiment was expressed "that senior figures in the legal and treaty department [sic] of the General Staff directorate, who firmly hold to instructions given from the center and demand, if necessary, the right to communicate their particular point of view to the leadership, meet with a disapproving attitude on the part of Foreign Ministry employees. And vice versa."[213]

In response the corresponding Politburo committee, made up mainly from the Military-Industrial Sector, agreed that on occasion at Geneva some behavior could be explained by the "attempts of our diplomats to maneuver on their own account especially at high level meetings to avoid taking with them 'un-congenial' specialists whose opinion might complication discussions." But the committee would not countenance criticism that diplomats had been making concessions to the adversary "even on those questions that are the prerogative of the military section of the delegation," but it did agree that diplomats had a tendency "to aim solely at reaching results instantaneously as a result of which they frequently surrender positions on questions of principle." This was most evident in the negotiations on conventional armaments at Vienna. The committee also agreed that the Foreign Ministry tended to try to vet potential delegates from other ministries for their degree of sympathy with the diplomatic viewpoint.[214]

Thus the talks following on from the INF treaty were drawn back under the control of the military-industrial complex, and further progress on disarmament was held up. One attempt to break the logjam was made in instructions for negotiations with Shultz for the meeting on 20–23 March 1988. The guiding principle was to sustain the position that a 50 percent cut in offensive nuclear weapons was feasible if Washington agreed not to depart from the ABM treaty for nine or ten years: once again to block SDI. And the shadow of disputes over the INF treaty was visible in the concern expressed not to concede any unilateral advantage in respect of cuts in conventional defense, but to untangle everything else and treat individual issues in dispute between Moscow and Washington on their merits and in isolation. In particular, Moscow had in mind to explore "the possibilities of Soviet-American joint action in the regulation of existing conflicts and not allowing new ones."[215] The thorny issue of conventional weapons had therefore still to be grasped and there was every sign that this was an area in which Gorbachev was loath to make concessions, for that would carry serious implications for the entire Soviet cordon sanitaire in Eastern/Central Europe, where the issue of fundamental change had been evaded for far too long. And despite occasional outbursts to the contrary, one should not underestimate his deference toward military requirements. Even when the Soviet economy was on the verge of collapse, on 18 April 1991 Gorbachev signed presidential decree 1812 on "Urgent Measures to Improve the Country's Mobilization Readiness," compensating industry for the costs of maintaining the capacity for mobilization.[216]

DOWN COMES THE WALL

It was useless to point out that even though we had lived 45 years without a war, a war was actually going on—precisely because of the order established in Europe after 1945.

—Shevardnadze

Hitherto Gorbachev had openly acknowledged neither the conventional military imbalance in Europe (including the occupation of Central/Eastern Europe) nor the ideological conflict (including aid to national liberation movements) as the root cause of the Cold War.

Progress with respect to the ideological struggle came first. A fundamental reconsideration had occurred among Gorbachev's inner circle that is ultimately attributable to the confluence of several causes: the Marshall Plan of the mind; the deep disillusion resulting from the years of stagnation under Brezhnev, particularly among the young; the impact of "Basket Three" at the Helsinki conference that the KGB so much dreaded; and, last but not least, the very process of glasnost that exposed the depths of moral crisis within Soviet society. It was equally evident among such varied minds as Yakovlev, Chernyaev, and Colonel Vyacheslav Dashichev (of whom more below). An early attempt to shift the ground beneath Soviet foreign policy had failed on the eve of the Twenty-seventh Party Congress (25 February–6 March 1986).

Shevardnadze is reported to have "had an allergy to words like 'class struggle' and 'proletarian internationalism.'"[1] On 25 July 1988 he finally broke public silence in downgrading "the struggle between two opposing systems" as "no longer the decisive tendency of the present age."[2] His aide Tarasenko recalls this as the turn "away from the idea of class struggle and opposition to the West."[3] It prompted a sharp riposte from Party second secretary Ligachev who, with Gorbachev on holiday, told Party activists in Gorky: "The priority of resolving global problems, above all removal of the nuclear threat, in no way means any kind of artificial constraint [*primortazhivaniya*] on the social and national liberational struggle, neglect of class contradictions and antagonisms."[4] But Gorbachev was leaning in Shevardnadze's direction. Symptomatic of this was the handling of Nicaragua, long a thorn in the side of relations with Washington. "Clever" Ortega had been the recipient of generous Soviet aid "in spite of the difficulties in the Soviet economy, above all with oil."[5] But in the autumn of 1988 it was summarily cut off, to the fury of the Sandinistas, who now had little choice but come to terms with Washington.[6] And when Gromyko complained that Russian leaders were not taking into account "the class struggle," Gorbachev cut in peevishly: "We will think of the class struggle when we drive our people into famine."[7] "We are in no sense idealists," Gorbachev reminded Brandt.[8]

These events underline the fact that, compulsive even under Stalin, the revolutionary drive had since 1917 exerted its influence only through accepting minds. This required conscious acceptance of its legitimacy by those in power. Here Brezhnev was a relatively passive receptacle. Whereas figures such as Shelepin, Kosygin, Andropov, and Gromyko were men of conviction, as Gorbachev appeared at the outset. Yet within his circle and among its outliers, the revolutionary impulse had long lost overarching authority. Only Ligachev clung onto the "class character" of Moscow's international relations.[9] The costs were demonstrably excessive at a time of extreme financial stringency; it had been repeatedly oversold as an advantage in the Third World; it had failed in Afghanistan; and it hinged upon assumptions about progress that the Soviet domestic crisis had shown to be in doubt. Russia's own needs—at a time of domestic turmoil and economic stagnation—were the highest priority; so much so that for radical reformers no other priorities counted.

The brusque dismissal of proletarian internationalism under Gorbachev matters because the Cold War always amounted to more than a struggle over the balance of power. What weighed in the balance—the nature of society and the international system—was of no lesser importance. Gorbachev took time to become aware of this underlying problem. "Until a certain point in time," Chernyaev recalled, "Gorbachev continued to believe that scaling down the Cold War meant basically scaling down the arms race."[10] Weapons did, of course, matter, and nowhere was this more apparent than in the center of Europe. But Russia's vaunted "superiority in conventional weapons"[11] and their positioning on the front line in Central Europe had no purpose in the protection of Soviet-style socialism if core Leninist principles were being jettisoned. With no need of conventional military superiority, domination over Eastern Europe was pointless. This was not yet Gorbachev's view; he was instinctively more cautious. But it was the view of Shevardnadze and others more radical, such as Yakovlev. By the end of 1989 events conspired to make it a fait accompli.

"From a geopolitical point of view," the International Department noted, "the importance of European socialist countries for the Soviet Union was determined by the fact that from the very beginning they played the unique role of a security belt, which created a strategic umbrella [*prykrytie*] for the center of socialism."[12] By 1989 the Minindel, was alarmed at the "growth of nationalism in all East European countries, and a strengthening of centrifugal tendencies in their policies."[13] Their populations were ready to break free as soon as peacefully practicable. All that was required to awaken them was knowledge that no one would save the regime once challenged. Up to that point, founder of protest movement Charter 77 Václav Havel tells us: "People withdrew into themselves and stopped taking an interest in public affairs. An era of apathy and widespread demoralisation began, an era of gray, everyday totalitarian consumerism. Society was atomized, small islands of resistance were destroyed, and a disappointed and exhausted public pretended not to notice. Independent thinking and creation retreated into the trenches of deep privacy."[14] It was thus questionable whether mere reform was enough. At the same time even marginal change for the better within Russia would inevitably destabilize such rigidly controlled societies. It therefore proved impossible to open up Soviet society and leave the Warsaw Pact untouched. Yet that is what the proponents of Russian reform tried to do. They did so because even had the Party accepted the need for fundamental change at home, it was utterly unprepared to ditch longstanding policy toward the "near abroad."

At the outset, in May 1985 Gorbachev insisted on only one model, "Marxist-Leninist socialism." And although he allowed for tactical differences, he insisted upon "closer coordination. Otherwise each will look for its own model. What would remain of socialism if each withdraws into its own apartment? Then imperialism can pick off one after the other."[15]

Initially no deeds matched Moscow's rhetoric. "We needed results," Gorbachev recalled in later years. "I could feel the resistance inside the country. . . . People were telling me, 'We support your policy, but you should know that nothing is changing here. The Nomenklatura continues to run things here, and we continue not to mean anything.'"[16] Nevertheless on 28 June 1986 he announced an extension of perestroika to relations with the Warsaw Pact. Previously, Gorbachev noted, "the Soviet Union . . . all but led fraternal countries by the hand, and they considered it obligatory to follow our example, recommendations and advice on everything to the letter." Moscow was seen "as some kind of conservative force which hinders transformations whose time has

come. . . . Instead of together discussing the real problems of socialist development, we frequently took upon ourselves the function of unique guardians and
defenders of Marxist-Leninist learning. . . . All these shortcomings, accumulated over the years, have caused serious damage." Instead Gorbachev called
for the exertion of "ideological influence, constructive initiatives for deepening
cooperation, the power of example, creative and effective solutions to the problems of social change."[17]

It was alleged that Moscow's allies were now "mostly" secure in their socialist
foundations; the implication being that reform would not risk destabilization.
Yet, though arguing for change, Gorbachev railed against "centrifugal tendencies" and emphasized the importance of economic integration within the bloc
and close coordination in foreign policy. Most delicately, Gorbachev referred
obliquely to the fact that "in most of the countries the time has come, for *objective reasons*, for a change in leadership."[18] Thus Moscow's allies were supposed
to become more independent but change their leaders, as usual, when the Russians demanded.

By the autumn—evidently after further advice—Gorbachev had retreated
safely behind accustomed lines. "Our common standpoint is: the independence of each Party, the sovereign right to decide on the resolution of national
problems of development, its responsibility vis-à-vis its own people,"[19] he reassured the Comecon summit in November. But since the regimes in power
had been imposed by Moscow and reimposed with force where challenged, it
meant that Gorbachev effectively switched from a reformist to a permissive policy toward Eastern Europe. This raised awkward questions about the sincerity
of "new thinking" at home and abroad. Here as elsewhere, he had yet to think
through the logic of well-meaning but mutually contradictory ideas.

Meanwhile, the satellites were increasingly pulled westwards. "Honecker
and Kádár and Zhivkov are moving away from us," Gorbachev told the Politburo in January 1987. "Economic ties with the West have gone a long way. This
is a consequence of the fact that we have not succeeded economically. We have
been unable to make available technology at an up-to-date level and they have
become indebted to the West."[20] Gorbachev became increasingly critical of
fellow leaders for remaining so long in power—seventeen, twenty-five, or thirty-
five years in some cases: these old men found it "simply physically difficult to
cope."[21]

Czechoslovakia had yet to recover from the invasion of 1968. Gustáv Husák,
a weak individual who betrayed Dubček and the reformists for leadership of
the Party, ruled entirely through repression. The only figure remotely akin to
Gorbachev was Lubomir Strougal, the Prime Minister, who was pressing for

economic reform but was more than countered by the hard-liners in the Polit-buro. Romania was a despotism of the most primitive kind.

The Typhoid Mary of Eastern Europe, Poland, infected by the bacillus of a genuine workers' movement, had effectively been consigned to quarantine. East Germany had a leadership living a dream about supposed technologi-cal supremacy but in practice on subsidies from Bonn. And Erich Honecker planned to make himself a world statesman by advancing East Berlin's relations with Bonn and Beijing independently of Moscow in the manner of Romania's dictator Nicolae Ceauşescu. Greater heresy existed elsewhere.

A massive foreign debt contracted in the 1970s when loans were cheap and oil prices low (for Comecon) effectively ate into Hungary's economic potential now that repayment was due and Russian energy costly. Budapest had for long realized that its future lay to the West. In March 1987, detecting a new spirit in the air, the Hungarians approached Moscow with a request to withdraw its divisions, and not just from Magyar territory but from the entire bloc. If not, they argued, the demand might arise from below, with serious consequences to follow.[22] Shevardnadze jesuitically replied that the Red Army was there to deter internecine conflict.

RAISING THE GERMAN QUESTION

Other countries mattered, but the balance of Europe had hinged on Ger-many since 1871. Gorbachev's views were entirely conventional. He was, like other children of the Great Patriotic War, hostile to Germans. The official line was that the results of Soviet occupation could not be changed. Yet Gorbachev was sufficiently open-minded to listen to alternatives. His interest had been sparked on a visit to West Germany in May 1975 with interpreter Viktor Rykin.[23] Gorbachev had seen the grim, ravaged, and antiseptic visage of the East a de-cade before, and nothing he "discovered in the FRG fitted in with previous impressions."[24] When he came to power and looked for "understanding on the part of Western Europe,"[25] Bonn was the least responsive in contrast to London. Indeed, Gorbachev expressed deep frustration at Chancellor Kohl's close align-ment with Reagan, a view reinforced by the SPD, Bahr in particular; "the social democrats are cunning people," Gorbachev commented.[26] In turn Kohl was none too happy that the Russians maintained their contacts with the SPD.[27] Yet, Gorbachev noted, "West Germany—like it or not and whether its allies in NATO like it or not—is a massive weight in the balance of world power, and its role in international affairs will grow."[28] More than once in his inner circle and at the Politburo Gorbachev pointed out that "without Germany we can have no real European policy."[29]

As early as 1986 Werner Krolikowski in the GDR leadership confided to Soviet ambassador Vyacheslav Kochemasov, an Andropov appointee, that the state of the country was unbearable, that Honecker was completely out of touch with reality, and that he should be replaced.[30] Moreover Falin had that same year forwarded a memorandum from Rem Belousov predicting the economic collapse of Comecon by the end of the decade. A year later this was reinforced by a memorandum on conversations with Wolf, who had just resigned as chief of East German foreign intelligence, predicting the collapse of the GDR.[31] From Bonn Bahr reappeared and "spoke to Falin, using him as a confidential channel" to Gorbachev. And on 13–16 February Bahr and Falin discussed a range of issues in a tone reassuringly anti-American and the substance of which thrust Bonn forward (and within it the SPD) as a possible partner.[32] Despite the setback at Reykjavik, which could have been expected to turn him back towards Western Europe, Gorbachev was initially reluctant to respond. In February he instructed Foreign Ministry officials and the International Department "not to make haste."[33] Shevardnadze, however, spoke out: "The idea of one German nation is alive in the psychology and the thinking even of Communists," he told the Politburo. "The West Germans are flirting with it." He therefore suggested that "the idea of a united Germany demands serious, scholarly study."[34]

Shevardnadze appointed as consultant to the Foreign Ministry Germanist Vyacheslav Dashichev, but for Eastern Europe, not Germany. The Germanists led by Alexander Bondarenko, head of the third European department and member of the Minindel collegium, whose entire career since 1949—with one minor exception in Bonn (1969–71)—had been taken up with the GDR and who was held in some affection by Honecker, refused point-blank to accept him. The son of a Red Army general who had been sentenced to ten years in the camps in 1942, himself a war veteran, Dashichev had engaged in the fierce historical debate about Stalin's blunder in June 1941 two and a half decades later; for which, in the neo-Stalinist climate, he was forced into early retirement. A protégé of Zhukov, he had spent a number of years working on the confidential military journal *Voennaya Mysl'*. He was chosen to head the newly created international relations department of the Institute of the Economics of the World Socialist System (IEMSS) set up in 1972. A closed institute separate from the Academy of Sciences, created by Andropov under Oleg Bogomolov, it had become a haven for thinking the unthinkable. It received classified information from its agents in embassies throughout the socialist camp and wrote reports (always unpublished) for the Central Committee alone. The reports resulting criticized Soviet military assistance in and around Africa attacked deployment of the SS-20, predicted the rise of Solidarność, opposed the invasion of Afghanistan, and argued for Reagan's zero option.[35] These reports spun off from the work of a secret standing committee of Warsaw Pact specialists set up in the summer of 1974 and organized by the institute with Dashichev as its supervising secretary. Its brief encompassed all aspects of East-West relations. Here heretical ideas could be aired within the official framework and for the purpose of the enterprise IEMSS employees maintained close contact with officials from the International Department and the Department for Socialist Countries, such as Georgii Shakhnazarov and Nikolai Shishlin. The "new thinking" that emerged under Gorbachev thus was spawned through the preceding decade within closed Party circles.[36]

Dashichev had begun arguing—in private—for the reunification (with neutralization) of Germany.[37] In January 1987 he wrote a memorandum to Shevardnadze criticizing the conduct of Soviet foreign policy, which on 18 May 1988 became the first article in the Soviet press—*Literaturnaya Gazeta*—to attack what had hitherto been unassailable and may well have inspired Shevardnadze to speak out on 25 July. In April 1987 he was appointed chairman of the Foreign Ministry's Academic Consultative Committee set up by Shevardnadze. It consisted of leading figures from the Minindel itself, KGB, foreign trade, and the Central Committee International Department. At its sessions the most acute issues of foreign policy were broached and debated.[38] Encouraged by this degree of support, Dashichev immediately sought to table the German question for discussion in June. But the debate was put off more than once on the grounds that the matter was "closed and not open to discussion."[39] Finally a meeting chaired by him was held on 27 November 1987 after President Richard Weiszäcker's visit had broken the ice though not entirely dispelled the chill.[40] Dashichev wrote a twenty-six-page analysis innocuously entitled "Some Aspects of the German Problem," warning that socialism was eroding in the GDR and nationalism was on the rise.

Only one person presented supported him: Yuri Davydov from Arbatov's institute. Everyone else threw themselves at him, and at a further meeting—this time within the Central Committee International Department and taking in leading figures from various government departments including the military— head of the department Falin stormed out in fury.[41] Dashichev had broken a taboo. On his view the core problem of the Cold War was the division of Germany. The option of reunification and neutralization had to be reconsidered. His report was distributed in thirty copies. The reaction was "very negative." He "was accused of defeatism" and "very strongly attacked by all those attending with one exception." Although Dashichev understood thereby that he had "no support within the Foreign Ministry nor within the Central Committee," nevertheless he believed that he had "laid the ground for an eventual revaluation of Soviet German policy."[42] Shevardnadze appears to have seriously contemplated a change in policy.[43] But Gorbachev sustained a different order of priorities. Dashichev did not understand this and instead believed his message was simply not getting through. He therefore tried instead working through Chernyaev. Chernyaev later complained to Gorbachev that Shevardnadze had been "too feeble in resisting" his own officials' attachment to "an untenable policy" on the German question.[44] But Chernyaev, too, was ineffectual in influencing Gorbachev at this stage.

Gorbachev's priority was to seek a solution in perestroika for East Germany. But he met unyielding resistance. Typical was GDR Politburo ideologist Kurt Hager who, when asked on 9 April 1987 whether East Germany would adopt perestroika, replied: "Would you, when your neighbor puts up new wallpaper, feel obliged similarly to put up new wallpaper?"[45] That perestroika should be identified as decor was not exactly complimentary. In March 1988 Falin, who was no supporter of reunification, sent Gorbachev another up-to-date warning that the GDR was on the verge of destabilization.[46] Forcing the issue, on 8 June at the Soviet embassy in Bonn, Dashichev told journalists that the Wall was a relic of the Cold War. The statement was published in *Die Welt* on 9 June under the title "Mauer wird verschwinden müssen" (The Wall Must Disappear). It was discussed in the East German Politburo and raised with the Soviet ambassador before being promptly and roundly denounced in *Neues Deutschland*;[47] it also elicited a stiff protest by the Central Committee Secretary responsible for international relations and Politburo member Hermann Axen.[48] The rebukes gave Dashichev an inordinate sense of satisfaction.[49]

Georgii Shakhnazarov—a more junior Andropov protégé from the apparat— had risen with Gorbachev from being a consultant to the Central Committee to become deputy head of its department dealing with socialist countries before elevation to the Politburo with a watching brief on Eastern Europe. On 6 October 1988 he recommended mobilizing specialists and advisers on Eastern Europe for a meeting with the Politburo to thrash out the options. "The evident signs of crisis demand radical reform throughout the socialist world," he stressed. As was the case with Poland in the early 1980s, the idea of external suppression "through military means" had to be "completely excluded." "What will we do if the social instability which is now taking a more threatening character in Hungary coincides with the regular round of unrest in Poland, demonstrations by Charter 77 in Czechoslovakia, etc.? In other words, do we have a conception in the event of a crisis which may simultaneously overcome the entire socialist world or a significant part of it?" Shakhnazarov also raised the German question. "To what extent does the future maintenance of Soviet forces in the territory of a range of allied countries (including the GDR) meet our interests?"[50] He was to repeat his request for such a meeting a number of times.[51] Gorbachev, however, was waiting on events. It was impossible to know what the Sphinx was thinking.

Tension was heightened by Kohl's crudely insensitive references to Gorbachev as a propagandist worthy of Goebbels.[52] The visit of President Richard von Weizsäcker and Foreign Minister Hans-Dietrich Genscher in July 1987 promised better. Indeed, much earlier Gorbachev had expressed the view that now "we have to approach the FRG with something out of the ordinary. We have to lure this country toward us." He suggested that "it is even worth taking risks to bring about a rapprochement with the Germans." Yet these more radical views were still constrained by the "very friendly" relations with the people of East Germany. Indeed, were it not for the language barrier, "one would feel oneself almost at home" there.[53] This was the first presidential visit from West Germany. As a necessary gesture of appeasement, Gorbachev finally granted Honecker permission to visit Bonn a little later, having refused him permission more than once in the past.[54] A back channel was eventually set up through to Kohl's special assistant on foreign policy Horst Teltschik. The man chosen was formerly an officer in the KGB first directorate, Nikolai Portugalov, a leading Germanist in the Party's International Department (KGB membership and membership of the apparat were incompatible) who had served in Bonn as a "journalist."[55] Teltschik describes Portugalov, who had "good personal contacts in the SPD and CDU," as "crafty," a little too friendly, and "a very good German-speaker with a brilliant understanding of German politics."[56]

Weizsäcker's interminable references to reunification at formal occasions were censored from the mainstream press. The Germans protested. Shevardnadze, Ryzhkov, and Yakovlev argued for publication. Having lost the decision in relation to the official press, Yakovlev placed the verbatim record with *Nedelya* and *Moskovskie Novosti*.[57] Nevertheless, an important marker had been fixed. Gorbachev recognized relations with Bonn to be "one of the most important lines in our policy."[58] Kohl eventually visited from 24 to 27 October 1988 with an imposing delegation that included leaders of industry. His impending arrival raised Gorbachev's hopes that finally the missing piece in his European détente could be slotted into place. He judged "the situation to be such that the country (FRG) is ready to go a long way with us, but the Chancellor is not ready; and with us the opposite is the case—the leadership is ready but the country is still not quite [ready]."[59]

WEST GERMANY AS MEDIATOR

Kohl plausibly presented himself as the pathway to Washington under the incoming Bush administration because of Bonn's centrality to NATO and Western Europe.[60] It was at this summit that he too raised reunification. "We Germans say the division is not history's final word. We as realists consider that war is not an instrument of politics. The changes about which we speak are possible only by peaceful means and together with our neighbors. We might have to wait a very long time. However, it must be accepted that this is not a relapse into revanchism. When we say that the nation will unite, we envision a chance that might open up in several generations. . . . Naturally, this is not a task for our generation. But we must head for a rapprochement in Europe. And, perhaps, our grandchildren will be given the chance of which I speak."[61] Had any previous Soviet leader been addressed in this manner, the subject would have been abruptly terminated. But Gorbachev replied that Kohl had touched upon an important issue, the clarification of which was essential to opening a new chapter in relations. Critically, Gorbachev said that he was "ready honestly and openly to talk about all questions." But "one cannot rewrite history."[62] "When it is said that the question of unification is open, when the wish is to resolve it at the level of the political thinking of the 40s and 50s, this will prompt a reaction not only among us, but also among your neighbors to the West."[63]

Progress in détente had slowed elsewhere. Delays in disarmament since the "little steps, like the agreement to liquidate medium- and short-range missiles" left Gorbachev deeply dissatisfied. Moreover, he was fully aware now that the "military doctrine we announced differs from what we are actually doing in military expansion. If we publish how matters stand," he insisted, "that we spend over twice as much as the US on military needs, if we let the scope of our expenditure be known, all our new thinking and our new foreign policy will go to hell. Not one country in the world spends as much per capita on weapons as we do, except perhaps the developing nations that we are swamping with weapons and getting nothing in return." An additional element was that Budapest was still calling for a Soviet withdrawal. "Right now the issue is not very acute. But," Gorbachev realized, "it could become severe in a situation like the one in Hungary right now. And then we won't be leaving voluntarily; we'll be driven out of there."[64] This represented the first recognition that withdrawal from Eastern Europe was merely a matter of time.

The Russians were also under pressure to cut conventional forces following the change in military doctrine to one of sufficiency. Thus at the UN in December 1988 Gorbachev announced a withdrawal of six tank divisions from the GDR, Czechoslovakia, and Hungary (some 5,000 tanks) and a cut in the number of troops by 50,000 (a slice of his overall cut in the armed forces of 500,000 by the end of 1991). After the speech Kissinger, still in the mind-set of the Nixon era, boldly suggested an ordered Soviet departure from Eastern Europe by prior arrangement with Washington. Much to his dismay, Gorbachev rushed off to Moscow on news of the earthquake at Spitak.[65] Kissinger then pressed his idea on the incoming Bush administration, which took fright at the very thought. It seemed both too radical (the notion that the USSR retreat to its own borders) and too conservative (the Superpowers alone restitching the fabric of Europe).

The military were not consulted over the cuts; nor, of course, was East Berlin. And in the Politburo on 27–28 December, Ligachev insisted that they did not have to cut defense capabilities to meet economic needs.[66] Hermann Axen, secretary of the GDR Politburo for international issues, told Defense Minister Heinz Kessler that the proposals "endanger" both "the external and internal security" of the most western and smallest socialist countries (Czechoslovakia and the GDR).[67] But Gorbachev was by now moving in more radical directions. "To many," he said, "the army is a feeding trough."[68] In February 1989 he insisted Ligachev was wrong: "It is now clear that without significant reductions in military expenditure we will not solve the problem of perestroika."[69] He had already complained that "the military doctrine declared by us conflicts with what we are doing in military construction. If we were to publish how matters stand—we spend two and a half more times more than the USA on military requirements—then our new thinking and our new foreign policy in their entirety will go to the devil."[70] Gorbachev's problem was that the Americans were well aware of this. US ambassador Jack Matlock had already indicated a delay in the US drafting of proposals for reductions in strategic weapons—a straw in the wind, as it turned out.[71]

Moreover, it was unlikely that Washington would act promptly anyway. "We should take into account that Bush is a very cautious politician," Gorbachev told the Politburo. He did not expect Bush to take the initiative in further developing relations. Gorbachev noted that "much will depend on how we act."[72] Advising him on matters military, Akhromeyev believed that "toward the beginning of 1989 M. S. Gorbachev came to view the possibility of major changes in the alignment of forces and, perhaps, also more fundamental upheavals in the countries of Central Europe."[73] If true, then firm bridges had to be built with the incoming administration. What emerged from Washington, however, was a babble of discordant voices. Bush was attacked on both flanks: from Reagan on the right (for his "indecisiveness") and Kennan on the left (for being "unresponsive").[74] Meanwhile, as a former Director of CIA, Bush listened to Scowcroft's deputy, Russian specialist and formerly Deputy Director, Robert Gates, who was deeply skeptical of Gorbachev. And Scowcroft "relied heavily" on Gates, who ran the committee of other deputy heads "so efficiently that full meetings of the National Security Council were rarely needed to clarify issues before they were presented to President Bush."[75] Washington was on the defensive. It looked very much as though a paralytic fear of failure predominated over the will to succeed.

Then in March 1989 the NSC recommended "top priority" to the "fate of the Federal German Republic."[76] Washington was alarmed lest Gorbachev seduce Kohl as he had apparently also suborned German public opinion. As a result Bonn was valued in Moscow as much for privileged access to Washington as on its own merits.[77] For this purpose Thatcher—hitherto a key link with Reagan—was no longer of any value as the White House reoriented toward Bonn.

Yakovlev reached Bonn on 8 January 1989 to prepare a state visit for the summer. The Soviet economy was deteriorating rapidly. Of 275 types of consumer goods only 10 were freely available in the second half of that year. Strikes were increasing at an alarming rate. Although the money supply and wages had risen and were rising, reported sales of meat, butter, fish, potatoes, vegetables, and fruit had dropped. The mismatch between demand and supply was such that accumulated unsatiated demand was estimated at 165 billion rubles, which meant that were prices freed, they would rise by at least 40 percent.[78] Disarmament existed on paper only, Yakovlev declared. Now the bill was due for military expenditure that rested on dubious statistics.[79] This grim prognosis was shared by Chernyaev, who foresaw unemployment and a severe deterioration in health and education provision.[80] Indeed, the situation was so bad that even defense expenditure faced marginal cuts; something that Gorbachev had studiously avoided hitherto but was now possible thanks to the retirement of Gromyko and Solomentsev from the Politburo at the end of September 1988 and demotion of Ligachev as head of the Central Committee secretariat.[81]

EASTERN EUROPE UNRAVELS

The unravelling of Eastern Europe had already begun. When Marshal Jaruzelski came calling for financial assistance the previous autumn—Poland owed more than $38 million—Gorbachev suggested instead that he come to terms with Solidarność. Bogomolov's institute stated that the scope of the "new workers' movement" in Poland and Hungary was "such that it is impossible any longer to treat the strikes as sporadic excesses any longer or, as was the case of Poland, to write them off as the influence of antisocialist forces inside the country and abroad. The strikes are obviously escalating into an ongoing social conflict between the workers and the party and state techno-bureaucracy." As to maintaining the existing order, the outlook was bad. Despite reassurances, the chances of containing change within "the framework of socialist renewal" were "shrinking." In Poland the report looked to a mixed economy and political pluralism. Change was inevitable. Moreover, "direct intervention of the USSR into the course of events on behalf of the conservative forces that are alienated from the people" would "signify the end of perestroika, the crumbling of the trust of the world community in us," and simultaneously "will not prevent a disintegration" of the socioeconomic and political systems in the region. But the report was ultimately reassuring with respect to the future alignment of these countries. The Warsaw Pact faced no threat; certainly not from Poland or the GDR.[82]

On 23 September 1988 Gorbachev received Poland's ambassador Jozef Czyrek. The latter explained: "Our tactics are to divide the opposition, to drag it, along with Wałesa, into the realistic constructive mainstream, into the process of national reconciliation and revival." On 21 October Gorbachev insisted to Prime Minister Mieczysław Rakowski that the Poles not concede socialism to the opposition in these negotiations and was reassured that the roundtable discussions could be used to isolate those fervently opposed to the socialist system.[83] Thus the Foreign Ministry was by no means out of line with Gorbachev in its concern "not to permit the erosion of socialism in eastern Europe."[84] It was important at this stage to insist that this dimension would somehow remain untouched while reform proceeded.

After progress in nuclear disarmament, the achievement of more democratic elections in the USSR, and on the eve of significant change in Eastern Europe, "Germany and Germany alone stood at the side of the great highway of history," Gorbachev recalled. "They, the Germans, felt insulted, embittered. And I understood them."[85] On 19 April, his courage in his hands, and he had plenty of that, Dashichev sent both Gorbachev and Shevardnadze a memorandum recapitulating proposals for a reunified and neutralized Germany. It also proposed other heresies including evacuation of the Baltic states.[86] Unsurprisingly, for nearly six months he received no response. East Berlin was by no means so confident, however, that Dashichev would be rebuffed. It waited anxiously lest the issue of reunification arise during Gorbachev's visit to Bonn.[87] The East

Germans would certainly not have been relieved to learn of an invitation for Dashichev to brief the Soviet embassy in Berlin on 24 May.[88]

At this stage, intent on outflanking opposition to change within the Communist Party, and after persistent prompting from Yakovlev, Gorbachev was in the process of transforming the purely symbolic Supreme Soviet into a genuine legislative and debating chamber, a process completed in May 1989. A far cry from representative democracy, this was nevertheless a real advance on what had gone before. And it acted as a spur to the transformation of Eastern and Central Europe. Once the nettle of Solidarność was grasped, negotiations had opened and agreement reached between the parties in Poland for a bicameral assembly, the new chamber open for free election, the first chamber maintaining two-thirds of seats for the communists and their allies, an apparently secure one-way bet. The elections were set for 4 and 18 June.

Meanwhile the original coalition partners of the communists—pressed into a shotgun marriage after the war—split away, and some candidates on the communist list turned out to be closer to Solidarność, thus depriving the Party of a majority in the Seijm. Solidarność then won all seats but one in the Senate.[89] What was intended as a gentle and controlled evolution to democracy thus degenerated into a rout for the communists, who attempted to cling to power. Minister of Internal Affairs General Czesław Kiszczak described the elections as "a total disaster for us." And Rakowski was entirely correct in saying: "What has happened in Poland is going to have [a] tremendous impact outside (USSR, Hungary, other countries). This may lead to upheavals in the whole camp."[90]

Moscow was not pleased. "Banking on the attainment of national consent through cooperation with the opposition," the Soviet assessment ran, "the PUWP failed to maintain control over the progress of events. An unprecedented situation for a socialist country came about: the ruling communist party was incapable of convincingly winning parliamentary elections and was forced to concede the right to the formation of government to the opposition."[91] Kohl told the Poles, when the latter complained in November at the pace of change in the GDR: "Without the developments in Warsaw, there would not be these developments in the GDR."[92] The communist monopoly had finally been broken on 19 August when Lech Wałesa succeeded in forcing Jaruzelski to accept Tadeusz Mazowiecki, a moderate candidate for Solidarność, as Prime Minister. "The course of events in Poland," Moscow noted, "will exert a negative influence on European socialist countries; strengthen anxiety about the fate of socialism; and will on occasion lead to false conclusions about the mistaken nature of the perestroika process."[93] Yet for the optimists not all was yet lost.

Gorbachev took consolation from Jaruzelski's continued presence as President. Indeed, he was encouraged to do so by the latter who boasted on 7 October: "If not for our decision to create the Mazowiecki Government and to partici-pate in it, we would have been defeated hands down in half a year." He added: "metaphorically speaking, I have leopard-crawled around the elections into the position of president."[94]

IN SEARCH OF US SUPPORT

Without Poland it was hard to see how Soviet forces could hold East Ger-many. In case of doubt, on 9 June Honecker—with the most to lose—reminded Shevardnadze: Poland lay between the USSR and the GDR. Thus it "must not be lost to socialism."[95] Moscow, however, privately accepted that at the very least "the coming to power of Solidarność will create problems for the working of the Warsaw Pact."[96] Indeed, Commander-in-Chief of the Soviet Group of Forces in Germany Boris Snetkov, an overbearing figure of the old school,[97] anxiously pleaded lest his troops get cut off as Poland deserted socialism and the Baltic republics rose in rebellion.[98] Gorbachev, however, still harbored hopes for Po-land.[99] He deftly declined to be drawn into critical remarks about Honecker; though what he said indicated a certain distance. Gorbachev underlined the importance of the new link with Bonn in suggesting a direct telephone line between his office in the Kremlin and that of Kohl in Bonn. Foreign policy adviser Teltschik was to visit Moscow for this purpose.[100]

Gorbachev swept into Bonn on 12 June with an extravagant delegation of sixty-seven, replete with a fleet of massive Zil limousines, requiring at least seven Ilyushin-76 transports to ferry them in just as news broke that Poland was coming apart. He arrived partly to clarify the puzzling attitude of the Bush administration. The new Secretary of State, James Baker, euphemistically re-calls "a deliberate pause" after the Republicans came to power.[101] The pause in respect of Russia, however, lasted no less than nine months. Gorbachev's con-cern was justified. He was hoping for access to credit that could help the Soviet economy buy time, but the White House was having none of it. The National Security Directive on relations with Moscow (NSD 23) was not ready until September. Its hard-headed approach had been evident since the inauguration. Drafted under Scowcroft, the memorandum argued that "Containment was never an end in itself." But "a new era may now be upon us. We may be able to move beyond containment to a U.S. policy that actively promotes the integra-tion of the Soviet Union into the existing international system." Washington sought nothing less than the "transformation of the Soviet Union." The reason was simple. "Our concern about the character of the Soviet system . . . is at the heart of our difficulties with Moscow." Thus the aim was "institutionalization of democratic internal laws [*sic*] and human rights practices, political pluralism, and a more market-oriented economic structure."[102] What more is needed to confirm the ideological nature of the Cold War to the very end?

Gorbachev complained that his proposals on troop cuts, for example, had induced no positive response.[103] The answer was that rhetoric seemed at variance with reality. US intelligence noted that "other units—and almost all the artillery and armored troop carriers . . . are being used in the restructuring of the remaining divisions, each of which is losing two battalions of tanks as one tank regiment is converted to a motorized rifle regiment. Moreover, the tanks being removed from Eastern Europe are not being destroyed." Furthermore, "the artillery in the remaining divisions is being increased by the addition of one artillery battalion in tank divisions and . . . artillery battalions in divisions are being expanded from 18 to 24 guns." These measures flatly contradicted statements issued from Soviet military authorities over several months following Gorbachev's pledge at the UN and thus blunted the impact intended.[104] The General Staff were digging in their heels.

That summer Shevardnadze gave Gorbachev a memorandum asserting that "the military (like a decade ago with the SS-20) are deceiving the political leadership. They are creating new weapons systems; they are deploying powerful groups of forces near NATO; they are provoking the NATO people with their intelligence activities, etc."[105] Chernyaev acknowledged that "the military doctrine declared by us conflicts with what we are doing in military buildup." He went on: "We expend two and a half times more than the USA on military requirements. . . . If we put into the open the extent of our military outlays, all of our new thinking and all of our new foreign policy would go to the devil." "In the GDR we have a powerful tank strike group. Plus river-crossing equipment. When this 'hangs over them,'" he asked, "how can they believe in the defensiveness of our doctrine?"[106] Unsurprisingly, Washington concluded that "the Soviet military threat has not diminished."[107] A summit with Gorbachev was postponed until December 1989, while the administration bolstered relations with Bonn and encouraged the opening of Eastern Europe to representative democracy and the market.[108] Meanwhile, Deputy Secretary of State Lawrence Eagleburger warned Kohl: "The long-term future of General Secretary Gorbachev is questionable."[109]

In Moscow the behavior of Bush, a cautious bureaucrat unhappy at the way he had been treated as Vice President and determined to carve out a different path, "gave rise to suspicions that the new President might be about to consign to the archives everything achieved under Reagan."[110] It mattered that Kohl was suitably reassuring. The visit to Bonn afforded Gorbachev closer acquaintance and a flattering opportunity to exercise his charm on the German public.[111] But, however reassuring Kohl tried to be, Gorbachev's "mistrust of the USA" was "still unmistakeable."[112] His own experience with Gorbachev taught Kohl (as it had Thatcher before him) that for the General Secretary "a personal bond of trust" was "very important, the 'chemistry' must be right."[113] Gorbachev operated primarily by instinct. He had to know whom he was dealing with at first hand. Intuition then took over. Kohl also had to assure the Americans that West Germany was not tempted eastwards. He had forewarned Gorbachev "that there is no chance of driving a wedge between the USA and the German Federal Republic or of detaching the Europeans from the USA." Gorbachev in turn reassured Kohl. "Neutralism would lead to destabilization. This was also a danger for the Soviet Union."[114] Dashichev was to be disappointed.

Although Moscow focused on Washington rather than Bonn, and although Bonn was en route to Washington, Gorbachev also needed direct reassurance that no advantage would be taken of the reforms begun in Eastern Europe. The GDR was naturally panic-stricken. Minister of State Security Erich Mielke had, as early as 7 April, expressed his "deep anxiety at certain developments in some socialist countries" to the new head of the KGB's first directorate Major-General Leonid Shebarshin, whom he ineptly harangued about Soviet domestic developments, such as the attacks on Stalin's memory. The GDR was, he went on, also subject to "subversive assaults . . . under the misinterpretation of glasnost and perestroika." He warned that "one should not underestimate Kissinger's plan on the part of the USA and the Soviet Union for a new political engagement on Eastern Europe." And, as for the optimism expressed from Moscow, Mielke was brutally dismissive: there were "no grounds for euphoria about détente."[115]

From this standpoint Moscow was of greater concern than Warsaw. The Stasi considered that "the outcome of the elections in Poland are not without consequences for other socialist countries: the movements of the opposition must feel strengthened. The restraint of the Soviet Union in the face of what has taken place in Poland has made an essential contribution to what oppositional activity could obtain on its own."[116] The fact that the authorities in East Berlin (8 June) and Prague (14 June) defended the bloody suppression of dissent in China clarified where they stood on democratic change. In Bonn the obvious question was: how could Gorbachev reconcile the policy of an "all-European home" (Brezhnev's tired cliché) with the existence of the Berlin Wall? Gorbachev's reply indicated just how far he had traveled. After a meaningless preamble, he said, "nothing is eternal under the sun," and "the Wall can be removed when the preconditions that gave rise to it disappear. I do not see a big problem here."[117]

EAST GERMANY CRUMBLES FROM WITHIN

In East Berlin such statements were treachery.[118] Few realized how far Moscow had come in thinking the unthinkable. But suspicions ran deep. When Yakovlev visited Bonn in January the East Germans became unnerved at his talk in public of German reunification "under certain conditions."[119] "Our friends," wrote the minister-counselor at the Soviet embassy in Berlin, "suspect that we are preparing something behind their back. This explains their nervous state."[120] And they were already worrying about the direction of events in Warsaw and Budapest.[121] When Wolf arrived in Moscow on 17 July, he glimpsed the new Soviet thinking at an evening with two officials of the International Department, Portugalov—the go-between with Bonn—and Valentin Koptel'tsev. Conversation was completely unguarded, except that when potential replacements for Honecker—then already diagnosed with cancer—were aired, Wolf kept silent.[122] Both Russians, however, freely acknowledged that the GDR was "the weakest link in the socialist camp."[123] The theme continued two days later in meetings with Falin. The constant harping back to the issue of German unity in both discussions seemed to Wolf a mere "theoretical nuance."[124] But certainly not in retrospect.

Gorbachev had not accepted Dashichev's proposal for evacuation of the GDR—made public after conversations held with contacts in West Berlin and condemned by Honecker.[125] Nevertheless the underlying sentiments were meeting growing sympathy. Dashichev exerted influence through indirect means—via Shevardnadze and Gorbachev's right-hand man Chernyaev, whom he had known at Moscow University. "From the beginning," Shevardnadze's aide Stepanov says, "the idea was inserted into this scheme of a step by step movement" toward reunification.[126] Working at the Office of the Secretary of Defense for Policy Philip Petersen by chance obtained a copy of Dashichev's memorandum from a German intelligence officer under cover as a journalist. Although his boss, General Richard Stillwell, was head of Pentagon intelligence, Petersen took Dashichev's memorandum to Director of Net Assessment Andrew Marshall, who encouraged him to dig deeper and obtain more, which meant a trip to Moscow to see Dashichev and others. But despite this painstaking fieldwork and lobbying by Marshall at the very top, no one was interested.[127] Politically controversial intelligence was swept aside. It was not least for these reasons that Washington and London were unprepared for what subsequently occurred. The intelligence community noted that since the autumn of 1988 there were "signs of uncertainty and discordant opinions voiced about the German Question within the Soviet policy community," but "public or private hints by Soviet officials of flexibility on reunification were interpreted by the Intelligence Community . . . as tactical ploys intended to exploit West German desires for unity." Indeed, this view was sustained all the way through to the eventual collapse of the Wall.[128]

Moreover, Dashichev was only one voice in a veritable chorus, as we have seen, but of which he was disconsolately unaware. The point was that this chorus was accompanied by a motley orchestra playing variations on a theme without a proper conductor nor to an agreed score. In addition to warnings from Falin (who was simultaneously continuing to undermine Dashichev), in April 1989 Shebarshin returned from the GDR with dire predictions of imminent collapse.[129] By then, as his chief Kryuchkov wearily reminds us: "Not only in 1989 but even earlier there were many alarming reports about the situation in the GDR."[130] That such analyses reached Gorbachev there can be no doubt. But he appears to have chosen to keep them to himself.[131] With article six of the new constitution in place, KGB reports went solely to the president. Members of the leadership other than Kryuchkov were left entirely in the dark: it was for Gorbachev to decide otherwise.

Gorbachev was reluctant to act decisively, but the ground began to move beneath his feet. As late as March, he had emphasized that "important though relations with the USA and Western Europe were, relations with the socialist countries were the point of departure for our relations with other countries."[132] But even Hungary, the most sympathetic toward perestroika, was distancing itself. Here Miklós Németh, the Prime Minister, found the country so indebted that it was "close to an abyss." "Politically," he recalls, "the country, all, all the key players within the country realized that there is no way to get a better life by reforming the socialist model. It was not publicly said, but informally when you attended a meeting, be that a private one with your friends, or a quasi-official one."[133] He did, however, secure an important concession from Gorbachev: Soviet troops would withdraw, but this was not be publicized.[134] Party leader Károly Grosz, a reluctant reformer, met Gorbachev in Moscow on 23–24 March. Change was already accelerating too rapidly for comfort: the pace was "somewhat disconcerting." Gorbachev was supportive but anxious lest the Party lose control. The Soviet leadership had recently concluded from a study of the Prague Spring that this "was a counterrevolution, with all the idiosyncratic traits of such an event." Dubček had lost control. Although Hungary needed democracy, a line had to be drawn to safeguard "socialism and the assurance of stability."[135]

At the beginning of May the impending visit of Bush to Budapest and Warsaw was announced. The Hungarians expected to make a plea for long-term low-interest loans.[136] Pressure was thus rising to appease the West. Grosz had visited Bonn (7–10 October 1987) where he was offered credits of one million Deutschmark to underwrite Hungarian reforms.[137] Further aid from Bonn came at an even higher price, as the Hungarians discovered in 1989. The political consultative committee of the Warsaw Pact met on 7 July. By then Honecker's dread suspicions had peaked. He assailed a startled Gorbachev: "When are you going to dismiss your collaborator Dashichev?"[138] Gorbachev was emollient, denying all knowledge of Dashichev—whom he had carefully evaded. "We have no illusions," he assured Honecker. "Many in the FRG are as enthusiastic as ever for German reunification." But, he added, "We are not aiming at later playing the 'German card.'"[139] "Serious politicians," Gorbachev intoned, with obvious reference to Kohl in Bonn, "are above all clear that destabilization of Eastern Europe carries with it unimaginably serious consequences for the entire continent."[140] Before long the unyielding tension carried Honecker, already diagnosed with cancer, off to hospital.

Gorbachev's frustration was also fast reaching its limits. He loathed most allied leaders, with the notable exception of Jaruzelski.[141] Mazowiecki assured Jaruzelski that the country would remain within the Warsaw Pact; that, in the words of East German intelligence, "Polish reason of state would not be called into question."[142] But the ideological roots of the government were what worried East Berlin. It was no encouragement that Soviet embassies throughout Eastern Europe "had not been able to analyze, foresee, forecast, and inform" Moscow. Indeed, the minister-counselor in East Berlin confided to his diary the "lack of contacts" and the "inadequate understanding of the true situation" in the GDR.[143] As if to confirm this dire assessment, on 17 July Poland opened diplomatic relations with the Vatican, and at the end of the month five leaders of Solidarność—Michnik, Bujak, Janas, Lipinski, and Jasinski—met in Czechoslovakia with the leaders of Charter 77 plus Dubček, Havel, and František, Cardinal Tomášek. A day later 169 members of Solidarność in the Seijm and the Senate made a foreign policy statement calling for "more democracy in the CSSR."[144] Contagion was clearly a problem, though the East German leadership still held out more hope for Poland than Hungary, in the mistaken belief that "Jaruzelski will fight."[145]

EASTERN EXODUS

The watertight compartment of the Warsaw Pact nonetheless began to leak. East Germans had begun demonstrating in Budapest, calling for the Berlin Wall to come down. The numbers absconding via Hungary had already doubled from the previous year, which breached bilateral agreements between Budapest and East Berlin of 1963 and 1969. East German "tourists" began flocking to the Federal Republic's embassy to obtain papers enabling flight through Austria.[146] A trickle—hundreds per year—swelled into a stream. During August more than 3,000 had fled into Austria. The Soviet ambassador in Berlin concluded that the exodus was already the most acute crisis in GDR history. The collapse of the state "will completely alter the situation in the commonwealth [the Warsaw Pact]."[147] Around 50,000 had escaped the GDR between 1 January and 31 September; by far the greater number from 10 September.[148] Budapest was trying to staunch a rising tide to avoid a direct clash with East Berlin. But Washington was demanding a coalition in Budapest before acceding to aid. And a coalition was certain to be more receptive faced with requests to open the frontier.

Finally on 25 August Németh and Foreign Minister Gyula Horn secretly visited Schloss Gymnich near Bonn. Németh agreed to open the frontier with Austria for GDR citizens. The question was whether Moscow would consent. Not only were there 300,000 Soviet troops in Hungary, but the country also depended on Russia for oil and gas supplies.[149] In his defense Németh pointed out that developments in Poland "place Gorbachev in a difficult position; he is having a hard time in Moscow." He also claimed that Hungary was doing its best to reinforce Gorbachev's position.[150] Genscher had already agreed on 9 June that Hungary needed help with deeds and not just words. Kohl was understanding and promised to intercede and obtain more flexibility from Washington and the IMF. He also promised to talk to France concerning EU assistance.[151] The Hungarians left with 500 million Deutschmark credit.[152] Predictably, on 8 September East Berlin heard that the agreement of 1969 was void as of midnight on the tenth. That evening the floodgates opened.[153] Bonn knew very well what it was doing. "The opening of the Austro-Hungarian frontier in September had in principle signalled the end of the GDR," Kohl recalled.[154] The GDR protested to no avail.

Ironically, it was around this time that Dashichev despondently received rejection of his April memorandum. The GDR could not be deserted, he was told, and the Western Powers have no interest at all in reunification.[155] This was not entirely nonsense. In Moscow on 23 September Thatcher told Gorbachev in confidence that all West European leaders were worried by events in Germany and that this could lead to destabilization of the existing order. No one wanted German reunification: neither Britain, Western Europe, nor the United States. They would respect Russian interests and not seek to decommunize Eastern Europe.[156] Gorbachev received similar signals from Giulio Andreotti of Italy and François Mitterand of France.[157] Genscher—a rival to Kohl as well as his Foreign Minister—told *Der Spiegel* that Bonn "also does not want the

GDR's future destabilised." On the other hand, he added that West Germany could not remain "indifferent when we witness the GDR itself destabilizing the situation and isolating itself by its refusal to reform." Genscher rejected the notion of "reunification" but jesuitically argued that nation states were giving way to federalism, so much so that there could be no return to the "centralized state." What mattered was that the Germans were embedding their "national interests" in "European interests."[158] What he omitted, of course, was that Bonn increasingly determined the definition of those European interests and that re-unification would add further to its weight.

On the eve of his arrival in East Berlin Gorbachev assured ambassador Kochemasov that "the GDR is now such an important country for us that un-der no circumstances would it ever be allowed to disintegrate."[159] In Moscow, nevertheless, Ligachev was deeply disturbed and, according to some, briefing Honecker to Gorbachev's disadvantage. Later, at the Central Committee ple-num on 6 February 1990, he warned of "the acceleration of German reunifica-tion and, effectively, the absorption of the GDR. It would," he intoned, "be unforgivably shortsighted and mistaken not to see that a Germany faced with vast economic and military potential has begun to loom on the world horizon." He claimed concern above all "to prevent the question of revising the postwar borders from being raised and—let us be blunt and say it—prevent a prewar Munich."[160]

Not everyone could get out. At the diplomatic level the temperature rose. On 11 September Kohl called for "freedom and self-determination" for all Germans. On 29 September Soviet ambassador Kvitsinsky protested to Bonn. Kvitsinsky insisted on the status quo. Teltschik's tart retort was that this was for "the people of the GDR."[161] The Federal Republic had served notice that the German question had shifted from international relations to inner-German re-lations. But such discussions were redundant, as was further talk of arms reduc-tions between Moscow and Washington, while popular protest mounted. The closing of GDR frontiers increasingly triggered violent clashes.

From early September four anticommunist movements had come into being. Of these the *Neue Forum*, in the words of the Stasi, had "the greatest influence and the widest reach. They represent the greatest danger from the opposition." Church committees led by clerics such as Eppelmann (Berlin), Richter (Er-furt), and Schatemmer (Wittenburg) underpinned the forum.[162] The Catholic Church—with 1 million members—remained aloof. But the Protestant Alliance was active and counted over 5 million members.[163] This was significant because these churches had since the 1950s always looked to reunification and the Prot-estant churches were democratic institutions. With the special church-building program sanctioned by Honecker from December 1972 (in order to obtain hard currency from West German churches) these links were inevitably substantially reinforced.[164] From 1974 Bonn's envoy in East Berlin regularly met Manfred Stolpe, Secretary of the Protestant Alliance, in his offices on Auguststraße.[165] It was later discovered that Stolpe played both sides of the fence.[166] On 24 November 1987 the Stasi reported that the West German government increasingly saw the churches in the "role of a controlled opposition" to the East German regime. Bonn had thus become interested in strengthening contacts between the churches on both sides of the border and the "self-confidence" of the representatives of those in the GDR.[167]

In this febrile atmosphere, obliged to visit the GDR for the fortieth anniversary of its foundation, Gorbachev very much wanted to cancel.[168] Once there he "immediately realized that those in power had lost their links to the people."[169] He also had difficulty concealing his personal distaste for Honecker.[170] In the streets, not just in Leipzig but also East Berlin, Potsdam, and Dresden, police broke up the masses calling for reform. Gorbachev's comments to members of the German Politburo in Berlin-Niederschönhausen on 7 October left no doubt what he thought would be the fate of the GDR if his hosts did not act in time. "These are times that require courage and courageous decisions," Gorbachev argued. "I say this from my own experience. It is as Lenin said: in stormy revolutionary times people learn more in weeks and months than they would normally in a year." He went on: "We are at the juncture of the most important decisions . . . you must think them through thoroughly for them to bear fruit. Our experience and that of Poland and Hungary have shown us: When the Party fails to respond to life it is doomed."[171]

As if to underscore the deafness of the leadership in Pankow, the day following witnessed more brutal assaults on demonstrators. This culminated on 9 October in a turnout of 70,000—Stasi estimates—in Leipzig. The magnitude of the protest made the authorities wary of using force to break it up and from East Berlin the wires fell ominously silent. Security chiefs had sensed change was in the air. Honecker instinctively responded with the thought of repression. But the Politburo was divided. The night before—8 October—Egon Krenz, the "crown prince," phoned Soviet ambassador Kochemasov to say that Honecker had instructed him (Krenz) to fly out to Leipzig with the heads of the interior ministry and the army to investigate and take necessary measures.

Krenz was worried. It was most important, Kochemasov indicated, that "no blood be shed. That is my categorical advice: on no account take any repressive measures and least of all by the army."[172] Kochemasov then asked Snetkov, officer commanding the Soviet Group of Forces in Germany, "to issue the instruction that our troops stay in barracks." And they should not get involved or respond to provocation. No sooner was this said than done. Snetkov must have assumed this was on express orders from Moscow. But it appears Kochemasov was acting on his own authority, having "received no advice from anybody."[173] Happily for him, Moscow confirmed the instructions the day following.

The danger was that matters would get completely out of control, the Red Army would shoot protestors, and Gorbachev's foreign policy would be tainted irrevocably in the eyes of the West; let alone the fear that West Germany would itself be drawn in, bringing Europe to the brink of war. First Deputy Foreign Minister Kovalev, a Germanist favored by Gorbachev, was not alone in his anxiety: "All the time," he recalls, "we wrote instructions to ambassadors, prepared messages to heads of government, to expedite the main aim—not to allow the situation get out of control, not to allow any destabilization of the situation, not to allow our forces to be provoked. They could come out of the barracks, some commander or other could give an order, and the troops could appear on the streets."[174] Elsewhere in Moscow pressure was exerted to intervene militarily. Former first deputy head of the Central Committee's International Department and adviser to Gorbachev Vadim Zagladin recalls that demands for intervention "of course came from the military, but not only them. Valentin Falin [head of the International Department] . . . and Yuli Kvitsinsky [ambassador to Bonn] were against German reunification; they were in favor of sending in the tanks. The discussion became very heated." Gorbachev also faced resistance from within the Politburo, but Shevardnadze pulled no punches, arguing that "putting such proposals into effect would have meant world war."[175]

At the GDR Politburo on 10 October Honecker insisted that the "majority of the Party and the working class stands behind our policy; it was correct and is correct."[176] The placards carried by demonstrators that greeted Gorbachev, on the other hand, left him with a different message: "Do you understand what is happening? It is the end Mikhail Sergeevich!"[177] Honecker criticized the USSR with the "subtext: your problems are considerably more serious than ours."[178] Gorbachev nonetheless emphasized to Kochemasov that should the SED fail to show leadership, matters would get out of hand. "Others are taking the initiative for change." The destabilization of the GDR and the destruction of socialism within it was not to be permitted.[179] On 17 October Brandt visited Moscow as President of the Second International. He and Gorbachov had a heart-to-heart talk. They were at a turning point, Gorbachev pointed out. He had said to Mitterand, Kohl, and Thatcher that no one wants a bull in a china shop. It would have disastrous consequences. He "had become disturbed." The GDR was drifting back into old habits. It was losing time. The regime did not understand that it was not merely a question of material needs and welfare but personal development as well. "I told our German comrades in the discussions: we have only one problem with you! Life itself is sending you signals that your policy must change."[180] Having rejected resort to force, Moscow was now no more than a bystander, anxiously looking on and unable to dissuade West Germany to ease the pressure.

Gorbachev recalls that the collapse of the Wall came as no shock: "We were prepared for such an outcome."[181] Indeed, no friend of Gorbachev, Yazov tell us that "for us these events were not unexpected. We knew what the situation was day by day."[182] That may, indeed, be so. But Gorbachev did his level best to forestall it, short of the use of force, which would have destroyed his entire policy worldwide. Thatcher's private secretary and adviser on foreign policy Charles Powell vividly recalls Gorbachev's "various telephone calls and messages to Bush and Thatcher at crucial points, urging them to put pressure on Kohl not to inflame the situation."[183] Not only did Moscow attempt to dissuade Budapest and Prague from opening their borders, on 11 October Gorbachev spoke to Kohl by telephone. The Chancellor was reassuring: "The FRG is in no way interested in the destabilization of the GDR." It was important that "the evolution of events does not get out of control." All Bonn wanted was that the GDR move toward the Russian path of reform. He insisted that they keep in frequent contact by phone.[184] Precisely one week later Honecker was forced to resign, an event anticipated by Krenz two days earlier.[185] Even Mielke had agreed to this. "We cannot begin firing Panzers. Erich is finished: I accept that," he announced somewhat unexpectedly.[186] "Now, what they do is their choice, and one must take it into account," Gorbachev said, when Kochemasov phoned with the news.[187] "I beg you, call me and report to me as events unfold. At any time of day and me personally," the General Secretary said.[188]

Krenz was a grim figure, long associated with the forces of repression, one of those who welcomed the massacre by the authorities in Beijing that summer and therefore scarcely Moscow's preference, which ran to Hans Modrow, the reformist Dresden party chief. But Krenz was ambitious, sufficiently agile, and unscrupulous to adjust. It took all of three days for Gorbachev to congratulate him by phone: scarcely a rapid or enthusiastic endorsement. But Gorbachev did attempt to reassure. Kohl, he advised, "has mounted the horse of nationalism. That is dangerous. He wants reforms in Bonn's image. This is unacceptable to us." Krenz was therefore told "not to give in."[189] Two days later, on 23 October, Leipzig—matched by Magdeburg, Halle, Dresden, and Schwerin—witnessed a massive demonstration of 300,000, with slogans against Krenz.[190] In anticipation of disturbances, Snetkov had telephoned to request to meet Krenz for that very day. Kochemasov promptly telephoned Krenz to say this might send "a false political signal."[191] Moscow was not only divided; the divisions were for the first time outward and visible to its allies. Krenz noted that between Soviet diplomats and the armed forces "this mistrust as little as a month before would have been unthinkable."[192] Krenz, evidently curious and hoping to exploit these differences, went ahead with the meeting. Snetkov made the brief but gratifying statement: "Comrade Krenz, we stand ever ready to give the GDR every assistance. Notify me whenever you wish."[193]

The distance between Snetkov and Kochemasov could be measured by the fact that while the Commander-in-Chief—doubtless on instruction from his Minister—was offering military aid, Kochemasov was in touch with bishops Eppelmann and Ebeling, leaders of the *Neue Forum* (Boley, Hendrich, and Reich), and *Demokratie Jetzt*.[194] The arrival of Krenz in Moscow on 1 November took place against the certain expectation of protests even larger than before and with information reaching the KGB that extremists were looking to "storm the Brandenburg Gate."[195] In conversations lasting five hours that Gorbachev did not even think worth recalling a decade later, Krenz was duly lectured as to the need to keep Moscow fully informed. He gave an honest account of the situation, but he had no sense of how to deal with it. For that matter neither had Moscow.[196] As though a disinterested spectator, Gorbachev was apparently prepared to make allowances for Bonn: "Kohl is no intellectual beacon [*keine intellektuelle Leuchte*], but a petit bourgeois [*ein Kleinburger*]. These are the strata he knows best. He is thus a skillful and persistent politician. In any event he is as popular as Reagan once was and it has paid off for quite some time."[197] As to the domestic solution, Gorbachev merely offered "Egon, a piece of advice. It is important for the SED not to cede the initiative. When spontaneity takes the upper hand and political orientation is lost, that is a major disaster. Then it's possible that false solutions prove decisive and the situation works to the advantage of other forces."[198]

Even had Krenz any ideas of his own, he was obliged to drag his more reluctant colleagues with him. It required veteran Willi Stoph's support—conjured up by Moscow—finally to bring Modrow on board to head the state apparatus. In a curious but symptomatic reflection of the underlying source of power in East Berlin, Kochemasov informed Krenz on 3 November of Stoph's support for Modrow.[199] It was, however, far too little, much too late. That day the Soviet Politburo met. Kryuchkov warned that 50,000 would be out in the streets of East Berlin the following day. "Are you hoping that Krenz will stay?" Gorbachev asked. "We won't be able to explain it to our people if we lose the GDR. However, we won't be able to keep it afloat without the FRG [West Germany]." Shevardnadze, always more consistent and focused than Gorbachev, typically suggested that "we'd better take down the wall ourselves." Gorbachev clearly felt cornered. The West Europeans appeared to be counting on him to block reunification. The East German people would be "bought up whole . . . and when they reach world prices, living standards will fall immediately," Gorbachev added. "The West doesn't want German reunification but wants to use us to prevent it, to cause a clash between us and the FRG so as to rule out the possibility of a future 'conspiracy' between the USSR and Germany."[200] All this left "a bad taste in the mouth," Gorbachev recalled decades later.[201]

Kryuchkov had underestimated the turnout. On 4 November one million or so demonstrated in East Berlin, calling for free speech and elections. The much-feared assault on the Wall did not occur, but pressure for fundamental change was irresistible. On cue at the Soviet embassy celebrations two days later, Snetkov grandly announced that the "Western Group of Soviet Forces will fulfill its international duty in the GDR under any circumstances."[202] The following day the entire GDR Politburo resigned, which allowed Krenz to bring Modrow and others into the Party leadership. But it was again too late. Even the benighted Czechs—despite Russian entreaties—were now allowing East Germans through into the West. In just three days (from 3 November) 15,000 had crossed their frontier to the FRG.

As the East German state haemorrhaged its life blood, Gorbachev continued to refuse Shakhnazarov's repeated request for a summit of experts. Finally Shakhnazarov gave up and took a belated break in Japan, just as everything promptly fell apart.[203] Kohl arrived in Warsaw on 9 November for a five-day official visit. More than 20,000 refugees had fled across the GDR border since the beginning of the year. He was visibly uneasy, but no more so than Krenz. News came in that GDR Politburo member Gunter Schabowski had apparently spontaneously declared at a press conference in answer to a planted question,[204] that anyone who wished to could travel as they pleased.[205] And when tens of thousands surged toward the Wall, border guards gave up trying to check visas and let anyone through on presenting personal identification. Krenz and his colleagues were by then desperate to avert bloodshed. He contacted Kochemasov and the latter phoned Shevardnadze but failed to get through to him. He did, however, get through to Kovalev who, true to Foreign Ministry protocol, wanted a telegram. Not awaiting the reply, Kochemasov concluded that no objection in principle to opening the border would be forthcoming.[206] At 12:30 a.m. on 10 November Krenz was informed that all checkpoints on the border with West Berlin were open.[207] He did not ring Gorbachev, dispatching a telegram later that morning.[208] Meanwhile the first news came in that morning to the International Department in Moscow like "a lightning bolt from the sky." Portugalov first suspected that Krenz, who had assured Gorbachev in October that he had the situation in hand, had cooked it up with Kohl. But everyone in Moscow soon realized "that Krenz was capable of nothing, just flashing his teeth."[209] News had come through to Gorbachev from Kochemasov in a matter of hours and his response to this fait accompli was typically positive.[210] Later that day Kohl was officially informed of the fact via Kvitsinsky.[211]

Gorbachev recalled: "They didn't coordinate that with me. In the morning, I got a phone call and they said how matters stood."[212] But he certainly approved of what had been done in his name. Mindful of Gorbachev's warning not to meet Kohl without the Russians present, Krenz had rejected the idea and instructed that the barriers be raised.[213] This effectively meant that Bonn would also react unilaterally. The precedent had been set. Gorbachev's assumption, however, that the United States—nervous lest the entire alliance system come apart at the seams in the prospect of reunification—would restrain Bonn was ill-founded.

Heading the International Department, Falin wished force had been used. Portugalov recollects Falin prowling the corridors of Central Committee headquarters loudly proclaiming the need to establish "law and order" and send in the tanks.[214] Dashichev recalls: "Representatives of the hard line in policy considered it necessary to bring into action Soviet forces in order to restore the wall and save the GDR. Head of the CC International Department Valentin Falin held this viewpoint when, soon after the fall of the Wall, he visited Berlin and spoke before diplomatic personnel at the Soviet embassy."[215] But, as Portugalov recalls, although the General Staff and hard-liners in the Politburo, including Ligachev, pressed him to "bite into granite," Gorbachev "fenced it all off, so that there was no interference."[216]

Shevardnadze subsequently issued a characteristically defiant rebuke to the diehards: "One comrade, speaking at the [Central Committee] plenum [February 1990] said: until recently the USSR was a great Power that commanded authority; the entire world admired it. And there was Eastern Europe—the guarantee of our security. . . . What is implied is that we have destroyed all this, both our greatness and the guarantee" "And what was all this worth? . . . We brought troops into Czechoslovakia and liquidated progressive change. Do they think that the world admired this? In Hungary 'order was reestablished' in '56. Was Europe also delighted? We went into Afghanistan. How was this then described—as an international duty? But it was right to call this an invasion. But did the world admire us again? . . . And among us even now awkward questions are raised: how is it that such a massive Power with an army of 5 million was unable to cope with little Afghanistan?"[217]

The Wall had finally come down. What was so unexpected was not the fact that it eventually fell but that it did so within the lifetime of Gorbachev and the very speed of events that led to it. As Kohl told Teltschik, "the wheel of history" was "turning faster."[218] The Wall was a symbol and for this alone it had great significance, Gorbachev acknowledged: "It embodied the division not just of Europe but of the whole world, the confrontation and everything that resulted from it."[219] Reunification was merely a matter of months. Contrary to what Gorbachev told Kohl in 1988, history could be and was being "rewritten." Kohl himself had good reason to value luck in statesmanship, after Frederick the Great. He was proved right in his instincts. Kohl hurried to Berlin to avoid repeating Adenauer's fatal mistake of staying away in August 1961.[220] Exhilaration was, however, inextricably mixed with deep anxiety. What if matters got out of control and Gorbachev's subordinates in the military and the KGB decided to act on their own? Only two days after the Wall fell, Gorbachev called Kohl's office in Bonn, saying that the KGB and Stasi both claimed Soviet soldiers and installations in the GDR were under threat of popular attack. This appeared to be a desperate provocation to wreck the German revolution. Kohl, stuck in West Berlin's town hall, gave assurances via Teltschik that this was not true.[221]

Reunification did not follow until 3 October 1990, but with the collapse of the Wall the Cold War had effectively met an abrupt end. The world could now breathe a sigh of relief. Gorbachev paid the price, for the Soviet Union was about to collapse from within and the loss of the security cordon into Central Europe undoubtedly played its part in his downfall.

The amateur dramatic coup against Gorbachev in August 1991 that failed so ignominiously proved the tragicomic finale. Under Mitterand France alone among the Great Powers indicated willingness to deal with the new regime. A once mighty threat to the peace of Europe and the stability of the international system had collapsed in on itself with more than a little help, of course, from its adversaries. "I believe that the Soviet leadership had concluded that they could no longer compete with the West, not economically and not militarily," concluded James Baker, Secretary of State under Bush. "The steadfast leadership of former President Ronald Reagan had begun to pay off."[222] Former Deputy National Security Adviser Robert Gates has put it more strongly: "If Gorbachev's actions and decisions between 1985 and 1991 took the Soviet Union from worsening crisis to collapse, the United States between 1970 and 1985 played a significant role in intensifying the Soviet crisis and in forcing actions and decisions in Moscow that led ultimately to the collapse."[223] The dates may not be entirely accurate — 1970 is surely far too soon — but the thrust of the argument remains true.

CONCLUSIONS

It means nothing to win the cold war; it is absurd. How could one win the cold war?

—*Vincent Auriol, President of France 1947–54*

The end of the Cold War took everyone by surprise. Not surprisingly, therefore, and despite a mass of publication, interpretations of the conflict remain diametrically opposed. Arguably the most important works are as mutually contradictory as ever. This should scarcely occasion surprise. The Cold War itself polarized opinion. Universities are not ivory towers, and political allegiance was not extinguished with the Soviet Union's demise.

The causes of the Cold War have always formed the main battlefield. Most recently one leading American historian has loaded the blame on the person of one man: "as long as Stalin was running the Soviet Union a cold war was unavoidable."[1] In stark contrast, a staunch leftist has, predictably perhaps, sought to absolve Stalin entirely. On his view the conflict occurred "because Western politicians such as Churchill and Truman were unable to see that beyond the alleged communist threat was an opportunity to arrive at a postwar settlement that could have averted the cold war."[2] And yet even firebrand former communist Eric Hobsbawm, unlikely ever to excuse Washington and a staunch believer that Russia had every right to take over Eastern Europe, more charitably holds that it was the "cold war" that "turned the US into the hegemon of the western world."[3]

Others, weary of polemic but on uncertain ground, write with greater circumspection; not so much humbled, perhaps, as confused. A firm American "liberal," who formerly blamed the Cold War more on Washington than Moscow before evidence emerged from Russia,[4] tells us that "neither Truman nor Stalin wanted a cold war"; that both "were not inclined to tolerate opposition"

393

(a bizarre way of likening the two men and the regimes they ran); and that "they could not do otherwise in an international order that engendered so much fear and so much opportunity."[5]

Elsewhere it is confidently asserted that the "Soviet sense of insecurity . . . bred the Cold War."[6] This sounds clear enough until, that is, the author tells us that the "unbridgeable chasm between Stalinist and Western values was also the reason why the post-Stalin leadership could not be brought to entertaining the idea of genuine accommodation with the West even if the West had tried."[7] Are we therefore expected to believe that the abyss between national values made no difference in the 1940s when the Cold War actually began and the Zhdanovshchina was destroying all trace of Western influence, but that they were very important in the 1950s when it was well under way and the horrors of totalitarianism gave way to something marginally more tolerant?

This illustrates a conundrum faced by all attempting to lay blame exclusively on Stalin. If it were purely a matter of Stalin, then his death should have resulted in a speedy end to the Cold War. Manifestly it did not do so. So it cannot just have been him. Moreover, to focus exclusively on Stalin as a personality might be plausible in domestic affairs where the dictator does not face equals, where people can be arrested, transported, and shot at a whim. But by its very nature foreign policy involves Powers outside the arena of dictatorial control and is therefore by definition reactive as well as initiatory. One man is not a warrior, Plato said (and Stalin repeated).

Thus the focus chosen has been on *Russia's* Cold War rather than *Stalin's* because it is impossible to conceive of the Cold War other than with the Russian Revolution at its core, and yet Stalin was a necessary but not a sufficient condition to its occurrence and continuation. In referring to Russia, it is not intended to disclaim differences between Imperial Russia and the Soviet Russia. But Marxism-Leninism was peculiarly Russian and alien to partly Western parentage. It was not that the USSR was expansionist and Russia proper not so. Russia, of course, became an empire through abiding purpose. Yet, however expansionist it was, the West always found a route to accommodation. Imperial Russia was a distant and alien civilization for Europeans and Americans alike, oriental rather than Western; but even at its most self-consciously Slavophile, Russia never held itself up as a substitute model for capitalism and democracy in the very West itself. In direct contrast the nature of the Soviet system meant that where its troops marched, almost without exception the territory under occupation was utterly transformed, entailing the wanton destruction of representative democracy and its economic underpinning, the market. The Soviet Union was in this crucial sense truly revolutionary even under Stalin.

Due weight must of course to be given to the United States—its emergence as a Superpower with limitless commercial ambitions backed by command of the air and supremacy at sea. To ignore Moscow's perceptions of American strength and purpose under capitalism is to render much of its behavior senseless. Surely Stalin was not entirely wrong about the United States. Most if not all Powers behave badly, especially when they have a greater capability to inflict damage than others. In this respect too much literature on the Cold War treats Russia to a standard of conduct more demanding than that applied to the behavior of our own governments. The expansion of US power inevitably meant the projection of misbehavior as well as good behavior longstanding within the Western Hemisphere to other dimensions of the international system hitherto untouched because beyond reach. Washington's conduct had never been a model of propriety—witness, as instances, military intervention against Mexico in 1913 or Nicaragua in 1927. It would have been too much to expect otherwise—as in Chile in 1973—where Americans prevailed without countervailing power. Subsequent US behavior in the Third World, especially, has done nothing to change this view.

Stalin, however, was a latecomer to the notion that Washington would emerge into postwar leadership. He overcompensated by inflating the likely consequences of future American supremacy. Ironically, in so doing he hastened the emergence of the United States as a military giant. Here, however, Stalin was well ahead of his subordinates, including Molotov, rather than on a different trajectory. There was sound reason for this. He had invariably been the more suspicious, the more consistently vigilant, and therefore more purposefully proactive. To that degree personality certainly mattered. Molotov and others soon caught up, nevertheless, because the Manichean framework that made possible the Cold War was not an historical accident, an idiosyncrasy of one man, but a feature broadly shared. Stalin's reading of the international situation was intimately bound up in Marxist-Leninist ideology: most notably the assumption that war under capitalism was inevitable. As soon as one war was over, the next had to be anticipated. This doctrine went unchallenged until Malenkov raised the matter in 1955. Even then it was robustly reaffirmed and not merely by the military. The system had become so ingrained that when Brezhnev protested his commitment to no first use of nuclear weapons at Tula in 1977, the military simply ignored it as disinformation for the gullible West.

Stalin and his closest supporters had every intention of seeking dominance over Europe by positioning Russia as the pivotal Power in the region, with Germany under foot, France counted out, and Britain confined to the periphery (largely to empire overseas). Quite apart from the Marxist-Leninist impulse, the belief was firmly fixed that Russians had a right to dominate the Continent in its entirety after the enormous blood sacrifice of war. It is a theme reiterated at unexpected moments in subsequent years. And to those less ideologically committed, the notion of imperial expansion was attractive enough.

Predominance could in principle have been secured at the expense of Eastern Europe as it had in previous centuries without necessarily threatening Western Europe, but only if the expansion of Russian power did not necessarily also mean expansion of the communist system. It was this that so stirred Churchill, Litvinov, and later Bevin into rousing Washington from the drift back toward hemispheric isolation that had made World War II inevitable. It was this that made all the difference to being merely a struggle between empires, as some would have it.[8] In this sense ideology was important not just to the Russians in their assessment of the postwar world—as has rightly been emphasized[9]—but it was also critical to the assessment by the West of the threat they posed. It was no accident that the hysteria this aroused in late-forties America matched that in late-twenties Britain. The difference between the two was that whereas before the war the Soviet threat was entirely ideological backed by Communist parties established across the known world, that threat had been compounded by the might of the Red Army from 1945.

Despite its assertiveness in canvassing American values, the US elite in 1945 was far less proactive than either Moscow or London. But this was not so much because it was naïve about power—though some undoubtedly were and others, including Kennan, certainly believed naïveté to be the problem—as complacent about the capacity to assure ascendancy without needing to fight to obtain and sustain it. This delusion proved far harder to dislodge than plain innocence. For Stalin, on the other hand, pressure on Western Europe was essential to keeping the Americans out of the Continent and by blatant exertion of pressure through indirect and direct means—Cominform and the blockade of Berlin—he gravely miscalculated. This was acknowledged by several of his successors in 1953 and by Khrushchev in 1956. Moscow's actions had thereby ensured that the Americans were welcome. Stalin's grievous miscalculation over Korea in 1950 then ensured that they stayed and rearmed capitalist Germany to boot.

Even after Stalin, Soviet leaders rejected the option of settling the peace of Europe on the basis of compromise (Beria and Malenkov's preferred solution to the German question) and persisted in the aim of ejecting US power from the region. And even when Stalin ruled, the inspiration for some of the foolhardy policies came from others—notably the proposed occupation of Hokkaido; the decision of the Greek Communist Party to revolt; territorial claims against Turkey; the colonization of northern Iran; Yugoslav support for the Greeks revolt;

Bulgarian pursuit of a Balkan federation; French communist defiance that led to their ouster in 1947; pressure to create a new International; Mao's revolution; and, indeed, the Korean war itself.

Arguably, though, even had Russia come to terms in Europe, the tensions arising from ideological rivalry in the Third World would have continued to poison relations, above all with the United States. There had always been more than one Cold War: that over the balance of Europe was matched by a preexisting global struggle that went back to 1917. The revolutionary inheritance from Lenin was not so lightly cast aside despite Comintern's abolition. There was surely good reason. This was not just a matter of legitimacy but also self-interest. A clear advantage was to be had in mobilizing a fifth column of believers in the Soviet system in the rear of the adversary, and the Third World as a whole represented the unprotected flank of the Western domain. General Danilevich reminds us that "in the 1960s and 1970s, twenty-three countries were categorized as our potential enemies. Among our main allies, we counted the six countries of the Warsaw Pact and seven other countries. Forty countries were considered basically neutral, but their orientation, especially in case of war, was uncertain. It is often said that the USSR squandered its resources by helping all these countries, including extending them military aid. However, just consider the global balance of power—we had to do something about this lopsided situation. If the forty countries regarded as neutral joined the enemy, we would have to face sixty-three rather than twenty-three countries. So we had to convince these countries, or at least some of them, to come on our side."[10] Self-interest thus intermingled with revolutionary commitment. Soviet leaders undoubtedly differed over the degree to which they saw revolution serving self-interest—not least because it varied according to the ups and downs in the world revolutionary process abroad. Nonetheless a core synergy undeniably existed between the two.

Anglo-Soviet tensions in the 1920s illustrate this and anticipated the Cold War of the 1970s with the focus on revolution in the extra-European world. Against this perspective, the politics of the thirties proved a distraction from the main business that reasserted its primacy once fascism was defeated. Here all Bolsheviks—with the notable exception of Litvinov—stood as one. Figures such as Andropov and Suslov explicitly identified themselves with Lenin and his priorities. Brezhnev and the more cynical were, like it or not, driven along with the rest. And even in instances where Marxism-Leninism did not motivate behavior, it most certainly played a leading role in interpreting behavior. Thus domestic pressures all too often proved more immediate and definitive in the making of foreign policy than the system outside. Even the jettisoning of the most hawkish in the leadership—such as Shelepin—left the Politburo vulnerable to accusations from within of appeasing the West and betraying Leninism. The war in Vietnam brought this out most clearly. The naïve conclusion of some in the late sixties that Moscow had dropped its revolutionary ambitions in converging with the West was undermined by the collapse of détente in part over vigorous support for revolution in the Third World.[11] And criticism of Raymond Garthoff's encyclopedic work on Soviet-American relations by Richard Pipes — that "there are no contending values or even interests; there are only misperceptions and fears"[12] — surely has a point.

Yet it is a tall order to go from this to assert "that the most important aspects of the Cold War were neither military nor strategic, nor Europe-centered, but connected to political and social development in the Third World."[13] This is a gross distortion of perspective that highlights one element at the expense of the rest and ignores other factors also critical to the decline of détente, not least the crisis in Europe over the SS-20. It took all this as well as the battle over the Third World to drive East-West confrontation to a peak, while the oil price collapsed and with it the Soviet economy, leaving in its wake the tragic figure of Gorbachev baffled by what had unexpectedly occurred.

A great deal of debate has revolved around the role of Gorbachev in ending the Cold War. No less than with respect to its origins, political inclination has too often predetermined interpretation. Gorbachev's adversaries in Russia blame him entirely for the destruction of the Soviet Union. Some in the West argue that it was all due to the "new thinking." Others argue that Gorbachev as statesman purposefully brought the conflict to an end. Some argue that Reagan's SDI and military buildup forced Russia off the road. Still more point to the domestic economy, not least the parallel between the falling price for oil on world markets and Russia's overall decline, ensuring the regime's collapse. The history is, as usual, more complicated. Circumstance—domestic and international—and personality both matter.

Russia was in economic crisis well before Gorbachev came into office and the need to solve it without delay was a factor crucial to his rapid ascent. Gorbachev's wife and alter ego Raisa understood this better than he. Yet despite the rhetoric about "acceleration" and then "perestroika," change was never anything more than marginal. Gorbachev had no understanding of economics. Not surprisingly, he never got to the core of the problem: despite flirting with the New Economic Policy of the 1920s, he never grasped the inefficiency of central planning as a mechanism for allocating scarce resources. It had been a sacrosanct pillar of the regime since at least 1929. The precipitate fall in world oil and later natural gas prices ate into foreign exchange receipts and seriously raised Soviet indebtedness. The complete failure of state and collective agriculture to deliver the goods made matters even worse. And the explosion of the nuclear reactor at Chernobyl on 26 April 1986 epitomized the sheer incompetence that hid behind walls of secrecy in the Soviet regime. But the new thinking among radical economists, such as the two Nikolais, Petrakov and Shemlev, was never put into action. Instead Gorbachev focused on the world arena, which he found more compelling and more satisfying.

This priority was not entirely mistaken. International tension was at its height in the spring of 1985 and this, too, necessitated a leader who could be trusted if required to explore unorthodox ways out of the logjam Russia helped create. So in the language of priorities a more peaceful international system would enable resources to be reallocated from guns to butter. SDI would require more guns. Foreign policy thus had to take precedent over economic policy. The trouble was that in focusing on guns Gorbachev never really got around to the butter. Indeed, live on television amidst a crowd of onlookers in the Lithuanian capital, the obviously well-fed General Secretary dismissed the shortage of sausage—the most basic commodity for the common man—with arrogant contempt: "What! You would break up the union over sausage?"

The person of Gorbachev cannot be irrelevant. We know from his predecessors, including Andropov, and those who usurped him in the summer of 1991, that riskier alternatives were conceivable, even if ultimately disastrous. Have not Cuba and North Korea hung on for longer as communist regimes with far less resources despite horrendous problems? It did matter that Gorbachev was extremely confident of his tactile political sense; that he was naturally intelligent though still relatively uneducated; that he was far more open-minded than his predecessors; that he was disorganized and chaotic as an administrator, even as a chairman in committee; that he was all to easily flattered by public attention in the West; that he knew—and not just from Yakovlev but also from personal experience—that Russia had to catch up by selectively adopting Western practices in order to compete. And more effective competition, not surrender, was always his ambition.

These personality traits mattered because it is a fact easily verifiable from the record that Soviet concessions to the West at negotiation were impelled by pressure from outside, not least fear of SDI—the INF treaty is a prime example. In this critical sense, whether one likes to admit it or not, the Carter-Reagan buildup in counterforce systems, the anticommunist zeal within Reagan's administration, and the obsession with space-based defense played a key role in the unravelling of Soviet security policy across the board. Paul Nitze and George Shultz were not alone in firmly believing this to be the case, and the evidence supports them.

It is equally clear that there existed no prior plan of action and that Gorbachev sought to improve the Soviet system, not destroy it. Policy under Gorbachev was alarmingly improvisational at every stage and highly contingent on the Western response as it was driven by a desire to end tension with the capitalist world. The influence of his more radical advisers—notably Yakovlev but also Chernyaev and Shevardnadze—thus mattered. In turn Thatcher's endless berating of Gorbachev, untiring pressure from Kohl, and the hard line of the Bush administration when faced with requests for financial aid all played their part in forcing the Soviet leadership to reconsider past policy and move to ever more radical change so as to enable perestroika to advance at home.

The archives leave no doubt that Gorbachev was very reluctant to turn against the military until driven to it in order to forge progress in East-West relations. Time and again the more fervent supporters of perestroika found him wanting in this respect. The reasons for this lay within the regime itself and among the others within the leadership. Gorbachev always appeared the reluctant revolutionary in this sphere. It is this, but not this alone, that makes a personality-centred explanation for events favored by such as Archie Brown and Garthoff so difficult to justify. Ironically, their views are matched by diehards such as General Lobov, quondam Chief of the General Staff, who suggested that "we didn't collapse for economic reasons but because in 1985 we were placed under a weak political will."[14]

It took a considerable time for Gorbachev to realize that to end the Cold War nuclear disarmament alone was insufficient and that a fundamental revision of security policy in Central and Eastern Europe was also required. And although he expected a diminution of forward-based Soviet forces, with power partly and slowly redistributed within Eastern Europe to popular advantage, he never expected communism to collapse so abruptly and so totally, even in East Germany, let alone Russia. This was his penultimate illusion: that communism in the region actually had roots, an illusion shared in the West by many even on the noncommunist left, whose shock was all too visible at the time.

Yet this revolution in policy—whether on INF, conventional force reductions, or political reform in Eastern Europe—was self-evidently grudging, and in most instances it took far too long for the accelerated pace of events. Popular opinion at home and abroad ran far ahead of policy. Events in the end escaped Gorbachev's control. Viktor Chernomyrdin, later Prime Minister, once lamented: "We hoped for the best, but things turned out as they usually do." A worthy epitaph, indeed, if not on the entire Soviet experiment then certainly on the Cold War that emerged from it.

NOTES

Epigraph: *Rossiya XX Vek. Dokumenty: 1941 God*, ed. V. Naumov (Moscow 1998) doc. 437.

PREFACE

1. "You and the Atom Bomb," *Tribune*, 19 October 1945; G. Orwell, *"As I Please" and Other Writings, 1943–47*, ed. P. Anderson (London 2006) p. 249.
2. For the differences between the two, terms often conflated, see Haslam, *No Virtue Like Necessity: Realist Thought in International Relations since Machiavelli* (London 2002).
3. See, for instance, G. Lundestad from Norway, reviewing Melvyn Leffler in *H-Diplo Roundtable Reviews*, vol. 9, no. 4 (2008) pp. 11–15.
4. Lundestad on Leffler; also Lundestad, "Empire by Invitation? The United States and Western Europe, 1945–1952," *Journal of Peace Research*, vol. 23, no. 3, 1986, pp. 263–277.

CHAPTER 1. UNDERLYING ANTAGONISMS

Epigraph: F. Chuyev, *MOLOTOV: Poluderzhavnyi vlastelin* (Moscow 2000) p. 144.

1. G. Kennan, "Is the Cold War Over? (1989)," *At a Century's Ending: Reflections, 1982–1995* (New York 1996) p. 152.
2. Preface to the F. Sorge correspondence, Lenin, *Collected Works*, vol. 12 (Moscow 1962) p. 373.
3. The unity congress of the RSDLP, 1906, ibid., vol. 10 (Moscow 1965) pp. 277–309.
4. "Inflammable Material in World Politics," ibid., vol. 15 (Moscow 1973) pp. 182–188.
5. Lenin to Stalin, 23 July 1920, *Komintern i ideia Mirovoi revolutsii: dokumenty*, ed. I. Drabkin et al. (Moscow 1998), doc. 39.
6. Radek, 22 September 1920, ibid., doc. 48.
7. V. Genis, *Krasnaya Persiya: Bol'sheviki v Gilyane, 1920–1921* (Moscow 2000) p. 261.
8. Ibid., pp. 428–429.
9. The best account remains R. Ullman, *Anglo-Soviet Relations, 1917–1921*, vol. 3 (Princeton 1973).

10. 29 December 1920: Lenin, *Collected Works*, vol. 31 (Moscow 1966) pp. 461–534.

11. E. H. Carr, *The Bolshevik Revolution*, vol. 3 (London 1953), chapter 22.

12. Speech, 21 December 1920, to the 8th All-Russia Congress of Soviets, *Collected Works*, vol. 42 (Moscow 1969) p. 245.

13. "Oborona Soyuza Sovetskikh Sotsialisticheskikh Respublik," 26 December 1926 S. Minakov, *Stalin i ego Marshal* (Moscow 2004) p. 376.

14. 9 June 1925: *Leningradskaya Pravda*, 23 June 1925.

15. For the best analysis, see E. H. Carr, *Socialism in One Country, 1924–1926*, vol. 1 (London 1958) p. 139 (Trotsky) and pp. 174–186 (Stalin).

16. Diary entry, 7 November 1937: *The Diary of Georgi Dimitrov, 1933–1949*, ed. I. Banac (New Haven 2003) p. 65.

17. Stalin to Averell Harriman, 26 June 1944, Harriman Papers, Library of Congress (hereafter Harriman Papers), box 173.

18. J. Haslam, *Soviet Foreign Policy, 1930–33: The Impact of the Depression* (London 1984), chapters 6 and 9. See also E. H. Carr, *Twilight of Comintern, 1930–35* (London 1982) chapter 3.

19. Carr, *Twilight*, chapters 3–4 especially.

20. Quoted in Haslam, *The Soviet Union and the Struggle for Collective Security in Europe, 1933–1939* (London 1984) p. 182.

21. Lecture at the University of Leeds on the 200th anniversary of the Foreign Office, 3 November 1982.

22. Memcon by Preston, 24 November 1943, enclosed in Sir Reader Bullard to Eden, 29 November 1943, FO 371/36957.

23. See Haslam, *Soviet Union and the Struggle for Collective Security*, pp. 168–169.

24. Comments from Lev Helfand, interviewed by Nevile Butler in Washington, 12 September 1940, Butler (Washington) to Sargent, 13 September 1940, FO 371/24845. For his defection, KV 2/2681.

25. Molotov (Moscow) to Maisky, 10 June 1939: *Dokumenty Vneshnei Politiki SSSR 1939*, vol. 22, bk. 1 (Moscow 1992) doc. 361.

26. Entry, 29 August 1939: Maisky, "Dnevnik," p. 227, Arkhiv Vneshnei Politiki Rossii, Moscow (hereafter AVPRF). Copy obtained from the late Lev Bezymensky of *Novoe Vremya*.

27. Entry, 14 October 1939, ibid., p. 284.

28. Entry, 7 September 1939, *Diary of Georgi Dimitrov*, p. 115.

29. Entry, 22 September 1939, ibid., and 25 December 1939, pp. 256 and 368.

30. Dimitrov at a committee of the Comintern secretariat, 29 November 1939: RTsKhIDNI (Moscow), fond 495, opis' 18, protokoll nos. 515–525. Presidium IKKI 29/11/39–30/12/39.

31. Quoted in A. Feklisov, *Za okeanom i na ostrove* (Moscow 1994) p. 51.

32. Report from NKVD foreign intelligence, 14 May 1941, *Rossiya. XX Vek. Dokumenty. 1941 God*, vol. 2, doc. 467.

33. Report from NKVD foreign intelligence, 22 May 1941, ibid., doc. 485.

34. General Vadim Kirpichenko quoted in N. Zen'kovich, *XX Vek. Vysshii Generalitet v Gody Potryasenii* (Moscow 2005) p. 230.

35. From an explanatory memorandum by Sudoplatov to Sovmin, 7 August 1953, *Rossiya XX Vek. Dokumenty. 1941 God*, vol. 2, doc. 651.

36. Eden's memcon, 17 December 1941, Avon Papers, Birmingham University (hereafter Avon Papers), vol. 25A, SU.

37. 8 January 1942: W. Churchill, *The Grand Alliance* (London 1950) p. 616.

38. Quoted in I. Zemskov, *Diplomaticheskaya istoriya vtorogo fronta v Evrope* (Moscow 1982) p. 15.

39. Stalin (Moscow) to Maisky (London), 30 August 1941, *Sovetsko-angliiskie otnosheniya vo vremya velikoi otechestvennoi voiny, 1941–1945*, vol. 1 (Moscow 1983) doc. 36.

40. *The Times*, 3 September 1941. Reported to Moscow by Maisky three days later.

41. *Pravda*, 7 November 1941.

42. Standley (Kuibyshev/Moscow) to Hull (Washington), 14 May 1942, *Foreign Relations of the United States* (hereafter *FRUS*), *1942*, vol. 3, Europe (Washington 1961) p. 441.

43. Eden (London) to Kerr (Kuibyshev), 5 May 1942, Avon Papers, vol. 25A, SU/42/91.

44. Memcon of a meeting between Molotov and Churchill, 22 May 1942, *Sovetsko-angliiskie otnosheniya vo vremya velikoi otechestvennoi voiny*, doc. 101.

45. Litvinov (Washington) to Molotov, 12 March 1942, *SSSR i Germanskii Vopros, 1941–1949* (Moscow 1996) doc. 21.

46. 30 May 1942, *FRUS*, *1942*, vol. 3, Europe, p. 576.

47. A. Gromyko, *V labirintakh Kremlya—Vospominaniya i razmyshleniya syna* (Moscow 1997) p. 50.

48. At dinner, 30 November 1943, Harriman Papers, box 170.

49. Stalin (Moscow) to Maisky (London), 19 October 1942, *Sovetsko-angliiskie otnosheniya vo vremya velikoi otechestvennoi voiny, 1941–1945*, vol. 1, doc. 147.

50. V. Lota, "Tegeran—43: trudnyi put' k soglasiyu. Neizvestnaya istoriya uchastiya sovetskoi voennoi razvedki v podgotovke i provedenii Tegeranskoi konferentsii," *Krasnaya Zvezda*, 1 November 1993.

51. V. Lota, *Sekretnyi Front General'nogo Shtaba* (Moscow 2005) p. 449.

52. Minister of State (Cairo) to Foreign Office, 30 September 1943, FO 371/36957.

53. Quoted in Lota, "Tegeran—43."

54. C. Amort, ed., *Dokumenty a materiály k dějinám c̆eskoslovensko-sovĕtskýu˚*, vol. 4, doc. 324.

55. "Note on Declaration about Joint Responsibility for Europe," 26 October 1943, Harriman Papers, box 170.

56. "Summary of the Eighth Regular Session of the Tripartite Conference," 26 October 1943, ibid.

57. "Summary of the Twelfth Regular Session of the Tripartite Conference," 30 October 1943, ibid.

58. Ivy to J. Freeman, 19 January 1943, Freeman Papers, Hoover Institution Archives, Stanford University (hereafter Freeman Papers), box 175.

59. J. Carswell, *The Exile: A Life of Ivy Litvinov* (London 1983) p. 155.

60. *SSSR i Germanskii Vopros*, p. 665, endnote 74. The committee included Deputy Commissar Lozovskii, a fundamentalist formerly head of Profintern; Manuilsky,

formerly de facto head of Comintern; Surits, formerly ambassador to Berlin and to Paris, a close friend; Tarle, the historian of 1812 and a traditionalist in imperial foreign policy thinking; and the secretary—Saksin and later Yunin.

61. This was said to Eden and Clark. Maisky was also present: "Memorandum of Dinner at the British Embassy," 28 October 1943, Harriman Papers, box 170.

62. T. Johnson, *United States Cryptologic History*, series 6. The NSA Period, vol. 5, bk. 1, p. 158.

63. Ibid., pp. 158–159.

64. Fitin to Dimitrov, 18 May 1943, Comintern Archive (Moscow, RTsKhIDNI), f. 495, op. 74, d. 6.

65. Harriman's personal notes of the dinner, 30 October 1943: Harriman Papers, box 170.

66. Maisky disparaged Bohlen's ability as an interpreter at Yalta: diary entry for 4 February 1945, O. Rzhshevskii, ed., *Stalin i Churchill. Vstrechi. Besedy. Diskussii: Dokumenty, kommentarii, 1941–1945* (Moscow 2004) doc. 175. Soviet ambassador to Washington Novikov says his Russian was good: N. Novikov, *Vospominaniya Diplomata* (Moscow 1989) p. 269. But Novikov's English was by no means as good as that of Maisky.

67. "Memorandum for the Ambassador," no date but estimated at early November 1943, Harriman Papers, box 170.

68. B. Podtserob, "Iz istorii vneshnei politiki SSSR: Vospominaniya diplomatov: Tegeran-Potsdam," *Diplomaticheskii Vestnik 1983* (Moscow 1984) p. 239.

69. Memorandum for the Ambassador, no date but estimated at early November 1943, Harriman Papers, box 170.

70. *Wartime Correspondence between President Roosevelt and Pope Pius XII*, ed. M. Taylor (New York 1947) p. 61.

71. Harriman's record, 29 November 1943, Harriman Papers, box 170.

72. Ibid. Repeated after the end of the war in the celebrated *Conversations with Stalin* held by Yugoslav leader Milovan Djilas.

73. Quoted in Lota, "Tegeran—43.'"

74. Ibid.

75. Harriman's record, 29 November 1943, Harriman Papers, box 170.

76. 30 November 1943, ibid.

77. 29 November 1943, ibid.

78. Ibid.

79. 30 November 1943, ibid.

80. Ibid.

81. Memcon, Roosevelt, Harriman, and Bohlen, with Stalin, Molotov, and Pavlov, 1 December 1943, Harriman Papers, box 171.

82. Hopkins to Harriman, 29 December 1943, ibid.

83. Diary entry, 11 August 1941, *Diary of Georgi Dimitrov*, p. 189.

84. Harriman to Hull, 28 January 1944, Harriman Papers, box 170.

85. N. Lebedeva, *Katyn: Prestuplenie protiv chelovechestva* (Moscow 1994); also *Dokumenty Katynia Decyzja*, ed. J. Snopkiewicz and A. Zakrzewski (Warsaw 1992).

86. This must have occurred in 1943: Harriman to Hull, January 1944, Harriman Papers, box 170.

87. Ibid.
88. J. Ciechanowski, *The Warsaw Rising of 1944* (Cambridge 1974), and for a balanced summing up of recent research that supports Ciechanowski's findings, S. Jaczyński, "Armia Czerwona a Powstanie Warszawskie," *Przglad Historyczno-Wojskowy*, vol. 5 (56), no. 3 (203), 2004, pp. 5–26.
89. Letter from Mary Bundy to the author, 9 November 2001. The Kennans later encountered Ivy in Yugoslavia, where George was ambassador in the early sixties. Ivy asked that George contact Meyer with instructions to destroy the papers. Mary, Dean Acheson's daughter, went to see Kennan on the author's behalf to ask about the Litvinovs.
90. Memorandum, September 1944, *FRUS, 1944*, vol. 4 (Washington 1966) pp. 906–908.
91. Draft, c. 26 July 1944, Harriman Papers, box 173.
92. Comments on the Polish-Russian Question, 3 July 1944, ibid.
93. C. Sulzberger, *A Long Row of Candles: Memoirs and Diaries, 1934–1954* (New York 1969) pp. 239–241.
94. Harriman and Abel, *Special Envoy*, p. 329.
95. Quoted in Haslam, *The Vices of Integrity: E. H. Carr, 1892–1982* (London, 2000) pp. 102–103.
96. 9 October 1943, *SSSR i Germanskii Vopros*, doc. 62.
97. K. Anderson et al., eds., *Komintern i vtoraya mirovaya voina*, vol. 2 (Moscow 1998) p. 432.
98. For the best analysis by far, see S. Pons, "In the Aftermath of the Age of Wars: The Impact of World War II on Soviet Security Policy," in *Russia in the Age of Wars, 1914–1945*, ed. S. Pons and A. Romano (*Annali*, Fondazione Giangiacomo Feltrinelli, 1998, Milan) pp. 287–288.
99. A minute dated 19 August 1944 on Yakov Malik's report on Soviet-Japanese relations, AVPRF, S-t V. M. Molotova, op. 6, por. 803, papka 58.
100. Quoted in Pons, "In the Aftermath," p. 287.
101. Haslam, *Vices of Integrity*, p. 107.
102. Quoted from the Russian Foreign Ministry archives in V. Pechatnov, "The Big Three after World War II: New Documents on Soviet Thinking about Post War Relations with the United States and Great Britain," *Cold War International History Project, Working Paper 13* (July 1995) p. 9.
103. E. Snow, *Journey to the Beginning* (London 1958) p. 312.
104. Ibid., pp. 313–315.
105. M. Gilbert, *Road to Victory: Winston S. Churchill, 1941–1945* (London 1986) pp. 992–993.
106. Ibid., pp. 993–994. Gilbert quotes at length from Birse's verbatim account. The Russian account is more sparing, by Pavlov, arguably a less able interpreter: *Stalin i Churchill*, doc. 161.
107. Wright (Washington) to London, 14 November 1944, FO 371/38550.
108. Kennan to Bohlen, 26 January 1945, Kennan Papers, Princeton University (hereafter Kennan Papers), box 2, Correspondence.
109. Ibid.
110. Quoted in Gilbert, *Road to Victory*, p. 1154.

111. Ibid., p. 1157.

112. Dimitrov and Baranov to Molotov, 21 October 1944, *Komintern i Vtoraya Mirovaya Voina*, doc. 198.

113. Quoted in Gilbert, *Road to Victory*, p. 1086.

114. A. Shatilov, "Greece after the Ejection of the German Invaders," *New Times*, no. 2 (12) 1945.

115. Request forwarded to Molotov from Sofia, 8 December. Reply forwarded via Sofia on the day following, *Diary of Georgi Dimitrov*, p. 345.

116. 9 January 1945, *Vostochnaya Evropa v dokumentakh rossiiskikh arkhivov, 1944–1953gg.*, vol. 1, ed. T. Volokitina et al. (Moscow 1997) doc. 37.

117. Stalin to Dimitrov, 10 January 1945, ibid., pp. 352–353.

118. Molotov to Dimitrov, 9 February 1946, ibid., p. 396.

119. W. Harriman and E. Abel, *Special Envoy to Churchill and Stalin, 1941–1946* (London 1976) pp. 363–364.

120. General Ismay in a telegram to Attlee: Gilbert, *Road to Victory*, p. 1020.

121. Harriman and Abel, *Special Envoy*, p. 379.

122. Stalin's talks with Harriman, 14 December 1944, *Sovetsko-amerikanskie otnosheniya vo vremya velikoi otechestvennoi voiny, 1941–1945*, vol. 2, ed. A. Gromyko et al. (Moscow 1984) doc. 164.

123. Quoted in V. Erofeev, *Diplomat* (Moscow 2005) p. 412. Erofeev interpreted for Stalin in meetings with the French.

124. E. Kardelj, *Reminiscences* (London 1982) pp. 66–67.

CHAPTER 2. IDEOLOGY TRIUMPHANT

Epigraph: Comments on secret intelligence, November–December 1952, quoted in L. Shebarshin, *Ruka Moskvy: Zapiski nachal'nika sovetskoi razvedki* (Moscow 1992); also, *Istochnik*, no. 5, 2001, p. 132.

1. V. Erofeev, *Diplomat* (Moscow 2005) p. 113.

2. Erofeev MS, "I. V. Stalin i V. M. Molotov kak rukovoditelya vneshnei politiki SSSR v voennye i poslevoennye gody," written in the early nineties. In this author's possession.

3. Quoted from the archives in N. Egorova, "Soviet Perceptions of the Formation of NATO, 1948–1953," http://history.machaon.ru/all/number_02/analiti4/2/index.html.

4. Quoted in A. Utkin, *Ruzvel't* (Moscow 2000) p. 788.

5. The meeting lasted just over one hour. It was transcribed by Major-General Talenskii: *Voenno-Istoricheskii Zhurnal*, no. 3, 2007, p. 3.

6. Chuyev, *MOLOTOV*, p. 18.

7. This appeared in *Cahiers du Communisme* and was reprinted in English in W. Foster et al., *Marxism-Leninism vs. Revisionism* (New York 1946) pp. 21–35.

8. Dimitrov to Molotov, 8 March 1944, *Komintern i Vtoraya Mirovaya Voina*, doc. 176.

9. The documents can be found in the Russian archives. For excerpts, see *The Soviet World of American Communism*, ed. H. Klehr, J. Haynes, and K. Anderson (New Haven 1998) docs. 18, 19, and 20.

10. Kathleen Harriman to Mary, on the eve of Yalta, Harriman Papers, box 176.

11. "Each stage has its limits," Molotov remarked in later years: Chuyev, *MOLOTOV*, p. 126; see also his opposition to Stalin's demands on Turkey for the Dardanelles, ibid., p. 147.

12. A. Birse, *Memoirs of an Interpreter* (London 1967) p. 183.

13. Diary entry for 7 February, *Stalin i Churchill*, doc. 178.

14. Haslam, *Vices of Integrity*, chapter 4.

15. Interview with Lord Brimelow, 20–21 April 1982, *British Diplomatic Oral History Project* (hereafter BDOHP), Churchill College, Cambridge. Confirmed from an extended conversation with Wilson.

16. A retrospective reflection in Clerk Kerr (Moscow) to London, 3 December 1945, FO 800/501.

17. Communication from the London residency, 27 January 1945, *Ocherki Istorii Rossiskoi Vneshnei Razvedki*, vol. 4 (Moscow 1999) doc. 68. For Burgess as the source, *Ocherki*, vol. 5 (Moscow 2003) p. 93.

18. Johnson, *United States Cryptological History*, p. 165.

19. Memcon of a meeting between Stalin and allied military chiefs, 15 January 1945, Harriman Papers, box 175.

20. Quoted in M. Narinskii, *Sovetskaya vneshnaya politika i proiskhozhdenie kholodnoi voiny—Sovetskaya vneshnaya politika v retrospektive 1917–1991* (Moscow 1993) p. 122.

21. Diary entry by Maisky, 6 February 1945, *Stalin i Churchill*, doc. 177.

22. Record of a conversation between Sir Stafford Cripps and Stalin, Cripps (Moscow) to London, 1 July 1940, Premier 3, 395/1, National Archives, London.

23. Contained in a dispatch from Britain's ambassador to the United States, former Foreign Secretary Lord Halifax, dated 1 January 1944: A. Vasil'ev, Yellow Notebook #4, p. 119, Vasil'ev Papers. This is available on the Web site of the Cold War International History Project.

24. Speech to voters, 9 February 1946, *Pravda*, 23 February 1946.

25. N. Simonov, *Voenno-promyshlennyi kompleks SSSR v 1920–1950-e gody: tempy ekonomicheskogo rosta, struktura, organizatsiya proizvodstva i upravlenie* (Moscow 1996) p. 192.

26. "Memuary Nikity Sergeevicha Khrushcheva," *Voprosy Istorii*, no. 6, 1993, p. 80.

27. J. Haynes and H. Klehr, *VENONA: Decoding Soviet Espionage in America* (New Haven 1999) pp. 138–145.

28. Memcon, Harriman Papers, box 173.

29. 16 July 1947, M. Brosio, *Diari di Mosca, 1947–1951* (Bologna 1986) p. 90.

30. Morris Rosenthal, 25 October 1944, *Post-war Economic Policy and Planning, House of Representatives, Subcommittee on Foreign Trade and Shipping of the Special Committee on Post-War Economic Policy and Planning*, US Congress, House Committee Hearings, 79th Cong. 1944 (Washington DC 1944) p. 876.

31. Ibid., p. 927.

32. Ibid., p. 934.

33. Ibid., p. 942.

34. Chenea to Stimson, 1 February 1945, microfilm edition of the Papers of Henry Lewis Stimson, reel 112, Yale University Library.

35. US Treasury Secretary Fred Vinson's testimony, *Anglo-American Financial Agreement. Hearings Committee on Banking and Currency*, March 5–20, US Senate, 79th Cong., 2nd sess. (Washington DC 1946) p. 3.

36. Ibid.

37. *Post-war Economic Policy*, p. 943.

38. Erofeev, *Diplomat*, p. 122. Each issue gave Erofeev heartache: Erofeev, "Desyat' Let," loc. cit., p. 124.

39. J. Jones, *A Modern Foreign Policy for the United States* (New York 1944) p. 7.

40. Ibid., p. 14.

41. Ibid., p. 32.

42. *Voina i rabochii klass*, 15 November 1944.

43. H. Luce, *The American Century* (New York 1941) p. 11.

44. Ibid., p. 16.

45. Ibid., pp. 17–18.

46. Luce to Buell, 10 July 1941, Buell Papers, Library of Congress (hereafter Buell Papers), box 22.

47. Buell to John Jessup (editorial board, *Fortune*), 29 October 1942, ibid., box 22.

48. Buell to Robert Lovett, Assistant Secretary of War for Air, 31 July 1941, ibid., box 18.

49. Buell to John Jessup 18 February 1943, ibid., box 22.

50. From the KGB archives, delo 40961, vol. 1, "Vnutripoliticheskoe polozhenie SShA," Yellow Notebook #4, p. 116, Vasil'ev Papers.

51. A. Krock, *Memoirs* (London 1968) p. 207.

52. John Metcalfe, 31 December 1943, contained in Buell to Luce, 10 January 1944, Buell Papers, box 23.

53. Podtserob, "Iz istorii."

54. Buell to Luce, 14 February 1944, Buell Papers, box 23.

55. Quoted in R. Murphy, *Diplomat among Warriors* (London 1964) p. 259.

56. C. Bohlen, *Witness to History, 1929–1969* (New York 1973) p. 129.

57. Krock, *Memoirs*, p. 205; also, Oral History Interview with Elbridge Durbrow, 31 May 1973, www.trumanlibrary.org/oralhist/durbrow.htm. Durbrow was chief of the Eastern European Division of the department from 1944 to 1946.

58. C. O'Sullivan, *Sumner Welles, Postwar Planning, and the Quest for a New World Order, 1937–1943* (New York 2008) p. 207.

59. Bohlen, *Witness to History*, p. 166.

60. NKGB to Stalin, Molotov, and Beria, 12 December 1944, from the KGB archives, delo 40935, vol. 1. "Pravitel'stva SShA," Yellow Notebook #4, p. 38, Vasil'ev Papers.

61. Buell to Luce, 27 November 1944, Buell Papers, box 23.

62. Council on Foreign Relations Papers, Library of Congress, vol. 15 (1944).

63. Ibid.

64. *The Diaries of Edward R. Stettinius, Jr, 1943–1946*, ed. T. Campbell and G. Herring (New York 1975) p. 206.

65. Ibid., p. 208.

66. *Perepiska predsedadetlya soveta ministrov SSSR s prezidentami SShA i Prem'er-ministrami Velikobritanii vo vremya velikoi otechestvennoi voiny, 1941–1945gg.*, vol. 2 (Moscow 1986), doc. 248 passim.

67. "Politobzor: Yapono-sovetskaya otnosheniya za 1943 god," 6 March 1944, AVPRF, S-t. V. M. Molotova, op. 6, por. 803, papka 58, d. 020. Yaponiya.

68. Shigemitsu (Tokyo) to Sato (Moscow), 16 June 1944, intercepted and decrypted by Allied intelligence and filed as "Japanese-Soviet Relations: Shigemitsu's Conversations with Ambassador Malik," 24 June 1944, HW 1, 2998, National Archives, Kew, London.

69. Malik, "K voprosu o yapono-sovetskikh otnosheniyakh (v nastoyashchee vremya i v svete perspektiv voiny na Tikhom okeane mezhdu Yaponiei SShA i Angliei)," 21 July 1944, AVPRF.

70. G. Bidault, *D'une résistance à l'autre* (Paris 1965), p. 148.

71. See enclosure (2), "Spravka. O poslevoennykh planakh soyuznikov—SShA i Angliya—v otnoshenii Yaponskoi imperii," as note 174. For the role of Hiss, finally proven from the Venona intercepts, see Haynes and Klehr, *VENONA*, pp. 155–156 and 170–173.

72. Malik, "K voprosu."

73. "Zapis besedy glav pravitel'stv vo vremya zavtraka," *Sovetskii Soyuz na Mezhdunarodnykh Konferentsiyakh perioda velikoi otechestvennoi voiny, 1941–1945gg.*, vol. 2. *Tegeranskaya konferentsiya rukovoditel'ei trekh soyuznykh derzhav—SSSR, SShA i Velikobritanii, 28 noyabrya–1 dekabrya 1943: Sbornik dokumentov*, ed. A. Gromyko et al. (Moscow 1984) doc. 59.

74. Quoted in Harriman and Abel, *Special Envoy*, p. 398.

75. *Sovetskii Soyuz . . .* , vol. 4. *Krymskaya konferentsiya rukovoditelei trekh soyuznykh derzhav—SSSR, SShA, i Velikobritanii (4–11 fevralya 1945g.): Sbornik dokumentov*, ed. A. Gromyko et al. (Moscow 1988) pp. 254–55.

76. A. Gromyko, *Pamyatnoe*, vol. 1 (Moscow 1988) p. 189.

77. Harriman (Moscow) to Washington, 6 April 1945, Harriman Papers, box 178.

78. Soviet record of a meeting with Mikołajczyk, 9 August 1944, *Sovetskii faktor v Vostochnoi Evrope, 1944–1953*, vol. 1, ed. T. Volokitina et al. (Moscow 1999), doc. 11. This was also what he told Milovan Djilas.

79. Nichols to Warner, 29 January 1945, FO 817/13.

80. Harriman (Moscow) to Washington, 2 March 1945, Harriman Papers, box 177.

81. Henderson's notes of his meeting, 13 March 1945, ibid., box 271.

82. Harriman and Abel, *Special Envoy*, p. 444.

83. "Minutes of the 5th session of the Polish commission," 23 March 1945, Harriman Papers, box 178.

84. Information from the military intelligence department, 28 March 1945, Leahy Diaries, Library of Congress (hereafter Leahy Diaries), reel 4.

85. "Minutes of the 6th session of the Polish commission," 2 April 1945, Harriman Papers, box 178.

86. C. Sulzberger, *A Long Row of Candles: Memoirs and Diaries, 1934–1954* (New York 1969) pp. 252–253.

87. Serov to Beria, 27 March 1945, *Iz Varshavy. Moskva, Tovarishchy Beriya . . . Dokumenty NKVD SSSR o Pol'skom Podpol'e 1944–1945gg* (Moscow-Novosibirsk 2001) doc. 37, and Serov to Beria, 5 April 1945, ibid., doc. 44.

88. Communication to the London residency, 21 March 1945, *Ocherki*, doc. 71.

89. Quoted in Gilbert, *Road to Victory*, p. 1276.

90. Minute, 2 April 1945, *The Foreign Office and the Kremlin: British Documents on Anglo-Soviet Relations, 1941–1945*, ed. G. Ross (Cambridge 1984) doc. 35.

91. Communication from the London residency, 22 April 1945, *Ocherki*, doc. 74.

92. For the Soviet record of the negotiations, see G. Mamedov et al., eds., *Dokumenty Vneshnei Politiki, 1940–22 iyunya 1941*, vol. 23 (Moscow 1998), 2, bk. 1, docs. 502 and 511.

93. Diary entry, 25 November 1940, *Diary of Georgi Dimitrov*, p. 137.

94. Dzh. Gasanly, *SSSR-TURTSIYA: ot neitraliteta k kholodnoi voine, 1939–1953* (Moscow 2008) p. 199.

95. Chuyev, *MOLOTOV*, p. 147.

96. Gasanly, *SSSR-TURTSIYA*, pp. 193–195.

97. Ibid., p. 201.

98. Ibid., pp. 213–214.

99. Kheifets, *Sovetskaya Rossiya i sopredel'nye strany vostoka v gody grazhdanskoi voiny, 1918–1920* (Moscow 1964) and *Sovetskaya diplomatiya i narody Vostoka, 1921–1927* (Moscow 1968).

100. Gasanly, *SSSR-IRAN: Azerbaidzhanskii krizis i nachalo kholodnoi voiny, 1941–1946gg.* (Moscow 2006) pp. 50–51.

101. Ibid., pp. 66–67.

102. Gasanly, *SSSR-TURTSIYA*, p. 187.

103. Central Intelligence Group, "Developments in the Azerbaijan Situation," 4 June 1947, CIA Electronic Reading Room, at www.foia.cia.gov.

104. Stalin to Pishevari, 8 May 1946: I. Egorova, "'Iranskii krizis' 1945–1946gg.: vzglyad iz rossiiskikh arkhivov," *Kholodnaya Voina. Novye Podkhody. Novye Dokumenty*, ed. I. Gaiduk et al. (Moscow 1995) p. 309.

105. Weizman's account, told to a meeting of the Jewish Agency Executive, 30 January 1941, ibid., doc. 1. For Maisky's account, dated 3 February, *Documents on Israeli-Soviet Relations 1941–1953*, part 1, doc. 2.

106. Ben-Gurion's record, 9 October 1941, ibid., doc. 7.

107. Ben-Gurion's record, 4 October 1943, ibid., doc. 31.

108. Y. Roi, *Soviet Decision Making in Practice: The USSR and Israel, 1947–1954* (New Brunswick NJ 1980) pp. 62–63, footnote 114.

109. Ibid., p. 62, footnote 112.

110. Samylovskii (head of the Near East Department of the Narkomindel) and Shchiborin to Dekanozov (Moscow), 25 November 1944, *Documents on Israeli-Soviet Relations, 1941–53*, part 1 (1941–49) (London 2000), doc. 43.

111. Communication from the London residency, 26 April 1945, *Ocherki*, vol. 4, doc. 75.

112. Kennan to Elbridge Durbrow, 2 December 1963, Durbrow Papers, Hoover Institution Archives, Stanford University, box 51.

113. *FRUS, 1948*, Europe (Washington DC 1973) pp. 950–953.

114. Entry, 24 September 1948, *The Forrestal Diaries* (London 1952) p. 464.

115. M. Djilas, *Conversations with Stalin* (New York 1962) p. 114.

116. S. Holtsmark, "Sovetskaya Diplomatiya i Skandinaviya, 1944–1947gg. Po Materialam Arkhiva MID RF," *Novaya i Noveishaya Istoriya*, no. 1, 1997, p. 52.

117. "It must be realized," wrote Harriman on 22 November 1945, "Litvinov has been consistently during the past two years extremely disgruntled with his personal position, has been obviously antagonistic to Molotov, and his advice has evidently been disregarded by the Soviet Government." Harriman Papers, box 184.
118. Noted early April 1945, ibid., box 178.
119. Letter to Margaret Truman, 3 March 1948: M. Truman, ed., *Letters from Father: The Truman Family's Personal Correspondence* (South Yarmouth, Mass. 1981) p. 174.
120. Gilbert, *Road to Victory*, p. 1303.
121. Communication from the London residency, 5 May 1945, *Ocherki*, doc. 77.
122. Gilbert, *Road to Victory*, p. 1306.
123. It is apparent from the documents now available that Stalin had access to encrypted correspondence between Whitehall and the British embassy in Washington: Yellow Notebook #4, transcript, p. 121, Vasil'ev Papers. This is available on the Web site of the Cold War International History Project.
124. Communication from the London residency, 6 May 1945, *Ocherki*, doc. 78.
125. Gromyko (Washington) to Moscow, 21 April 1945, *Sovetsko-Amerikanskie Otnosheniya vo vremya velikoi otechestvennoi voiny, 1941–1945*, vol. 2 (Moscow 1984) doc. 224.
126. Memcon, 20 April 1945, Harriman Papers, box 178.
127. Erofeev MS, p. 8.
128. Memorandum of the meeting, 23 April 1945, Harriman Papers, box 178.
129. 23 April 1945, Leahy Diaries, reel 4.
130. Memcon, 23 April 1945, Harriman Papers, box 178.
131. Truman, *Memoirs*, p. 82.
132. 23 April 1945, Leahy Diaries, reel 4.
133. O. Troyanovskii, *Cherez gody i rasstoyaniya* (Moscow 1997) pp. 129–130.
134. Quoted in V. Pechatnov, *Stalin, Ruzvel't, Trumen: SSSR i SShA v 1940-kh gg.* (Moscow 2006) p. 339.
135. M. Truman, *Letters from Father*, p. 177.
136. Troyanovskii, *Cherez gody*, p. 130.
137. Communication from the residency in San Francisco, 10 May 1945, *Ocherki*, doc. 79.
138. Zhukov, "Bezogovorpchnaya Kapitulyatsiya," unpub. article, March 1965: *XX Vek. Dokumenty. Georgii Zhukov. Stenogramma oktyabr'skogo (1957 g.) plenuma TsK KPSS i drugie dokumenty*, ed. V. Naumov (Moscow 2001) p. 535.
139. Prime Minister to President Truman, 12 May 1945, Churchill Papers, Churchill College Archives, CHAR 20/218/109.
140. Editorial, "A Magnificent Victory," *War and the Working Class*, no. 10, 15 May 1945.
141. Quoted in D. McCullough, *Truman* (New York 1992) p. 399.
142. Murphy, *Diplomat*, pp. 319–320.
143. McCullough, *Truman*, p. 399.
144. Letter of 18 May 1945, in possession of Mary Bundy (née Acheson).
145. Conversation with Mary Bundy.
146. Oral History Interview, 23 June 1971, www.trumanlibrary.org/oralhist/battle.htm.
147. V. Falin, *Bez skidok na obstoyatel'stva* (Moscow 1999) p. 53.

148. Letter to Bess Truman, 20 July 1945: *Dear Bess: The Letters from Harry to Bess Truman, 1910–1959* (New York 1983) p. 520.

149. McCullough, *Truman*, p. 451.

150. Władysław Gomułka, in conversation with Georgi Dimitrov, 10 May 1945: *SSSR— Pol'sha. Mekhanizmy podchineniya. 1944–1949gg. Sbornik dokumentov*, ed. G. Bordyugov et al. (Moscow 1995) p. 121.

151. Selivanovskii to Beria, 10 June 1945, *Iz Varshavy*, doc. 61.

152. Churchill (London) to Halifax (Washington), 14 May 1945, FO 371/46462.

153. Quoted in Gilbert, *"Never Despair": Winston S. Churchill, 1945–1965*, vol. 8 (London 1988) p. 32.

154. Snow, *Journey to the Beginning*, p. 357.

155. *Ocherki*, vol. 4, doc. 82.

156. Johnson, *United States Cryptologic History*, pp. 14–15.

157. Ibid., p. 15.

158. "Strength of Russian Forces in the Far East." Annex to Joint Planning Staff of the Chiefs of Staff Committee Report on "Possible Russian Participation in the War Against Japan," 10 July 1945, JP (45) 140 (Final), FO 371/46462.

159. N. Eronin, "O strategicheskikoi peregruppirovke sovetskikh vooruzhennykh sil na dal'nevostochyi teatr' voennykh deistvii letom 1945g.," *Pobeda SSSR v voine s militaristskoi Yaponiei i poslevoennoe razvitie vostochnoi i yugo-vostochnoi Azii* (Moscow 1977) p. 45.

160. *Pobeda na Vostoke*, ed. O. Borisov et al. (Moscow 1985) p. 24.

161. *Istoriya vtoroi mirovoi voiny, 1939–1945*, ed. A. Grechko et al., vol. 11 (Moscow 1980) p. 193.

162. Lozovsky to Molotov, 10 January 1945, AVPRF, Fond S.-t. V. M. Molotova, op. 7, por. 898, papka 55.

163. *Pravda*, 6 April 1945; on 7 April an editorial in *Izvestiya*, "K denonsatsii sovetsko-yaponskogo pakta o neitraliteta," justified the move.

164. V. Baryn'kin, "Manchzhurskaya nastupatel'naya operatsiya," *Voenno-istoricheskii Zhurnal*, no. 5, 1995, p. 17.

165. Malik (Tokyo) to Moscow, 7 June 1945, *Vestnik Ministerstva Inostrannykh Del SSSR*, no. 19 (77) 15 October 1990, p. 48.

166. Petersen (Moscow) to Foreign Office, 28 May 1946, FO 371/56784.

167. State Department memorandum, 14 May 1945, enclosed in Halifax (Washington) to London, 17 May 1945, FO 371/46453.

168. Gascoigne (Budapest) to Howard (London), 7 June 1945, ibid.

169. Hopkins notes quoted in Sherwood, *Roosevelt and Hopkins*, vol. 2, pp. 554–555. See also H. Feis, *The China Tangle* (Princeton 1953) pp. 309–311.

170. Slavinsky, "The Soviet Occupation of the Kurile Islands and the Plans for the Capture of Northern Hokkaido," *Japan Forum*, vol. 5, no. 1, April 1993, pp. 97–98.

171. Ibid., pp. 98–99.

172. First quoted in Haslam, "The Boundaries of Rational Calculation in Soviet Policy towards Japan," in *History, the White House and the Kremlin: Statesmen as Historians*, ed. M. Fry (London 1991) pp. 43–44.

173. Murphy, *Diplomat*, p. 329.

174. *Sovetsko-amerikanskie otnosheniya*, vol. 2, doc. 286.

175. A letter, never sent, to Byrnes, 5 January 1946, Truman Library, quoted at www. doug_long.com/hst.htm.

176. Pavlov was the only other witness to this exchange: "Avtobiograficheskie zametki' V. N. Pavlova—Perevodchika I. V. Stalina," *Novaya i Noveishaya Istoriya*, no. 4, July–August 2000, p. 110.

177. Truman diary entry, 18 July 1945, *Off the Record: The Private Papers of Harry S. Truman* (New York 1980) p. 54.

178. 3 March 1948, M. Truman, *Letters from Father*, p. 177.

179. 23 July 1945, Gilbert, *"Never Despair,"* p. 90.

180. A. Gromyko, *Andrei Gromyko*, p. 65.

181. Ibid., p. 65.

182. Message from resident "Briand," Ivan Sklyarev, 10 August 1941: V. Lota, "Vklad voennykh razvedchikov v sozdanie otechestvennogo atomnogo oruzhiya, 1941–1945gg.," *Voenno-istoricheskii Zhurnal*, no. 11, 2006, p. 40.

183. For the full text and provenance, see V. Chikov, *Dos'e KGB no. 13676. Nelegaly*, vol. 1. *Operatsiya "Enormous"* (Moscow 1997) pp. 17–19.

184. Simonov, *Voenno-promyshlennoe*, pp. 210–213.

185. Lota, "Vklad," pp. 41–42.

186. *Pravda*, 3 September 1945.

187. "Priem posla Velikobritanii i posla SShA Garrimana," 11 August 1945.

188. B. Slavinskii, *SSSR i Yaponiya—na puti k voine: diplomaticheskaya istoriya, 1937–1945 gg.* (Moscow 1999) pp. 482–483.

189. Ibid., p. 483.

190. Memcon by Harriman, 27 August 1945, Harriman Papers, box 182.

191. Quoted in V. Galitskii and V. Zimonin, "'Desant na Khokkaido Otmenit'! (Razmyshleniya po povodu odnoi nesostoyavsheisya operatsii)," *Voenno-istoricheskii Zhurnal*, no. 3, 1994, pp. 8–9.

192. The tensions played out between the Unites States and its allies in the Pacific are detailed in C. Thorne, *Allies of a Kind: The United States, Britain and the War against Japan, 1941–1945* (London 1978).

193. To Stalin, Molotov, and Beria, 7 September 1945, *Ocherki*, doc. 83.

194. M. Djilas, *Conversations with Stalin* (New York 1962) p. 69.

195. Chuyev, *MOLOTOV*, p. 123.

196. Erofeev, "Desyat' Let v Sekretariate Narkomindela," *Mezhdunarodnaya Zhizn',* no. 8, August 1991, p. 121.

197. Testimony of Oleg Troyanovsky, a foreign policy aide: O. Troyanovskii, *Cherez gody i rasstoyaniya*, p. 135.

198. Erofeev, *Diplomat*, p. 166.

199. Conversations with Vladimir Erofeev.

200. Ibid.

201. Ibid.

202. Ibid.

203. "Do 90 let on ezdil v polokliniku na elektrichke," *Kommersant Vlast'*, 21 March 2000, p. 46.
204. Diary entry, 20 February 1941, *Diary of Georgi Dimitrov*, pp. 148–149.
205. Smirtyukov, in *Kommersant Vlast'*, 21 March 2000, p. 48.
206. Ibid.
207. "Memuary Nikity Sergeevicha Khrushcheva," *Voprosy Istorii*, no. 7, 1993, p. 77.
208. "Conferences: Old Rock Bottom," *Time*, 19 August 1946.
209. 24 June 1957, "Poslednaya 'anti-partiinaya' gruppa: Stenograficheskii otchet iyun'skogo (1957g.) plenuma TsK KPSS," *Istoricheskii Arkhiv*, no. 3, 1993, p. 87.
210. "Stalin used to say Russia; it is Molotov who used to say the Soviet Union," G. Bidault, *D'une resistance à l'autre*, p. 148.
211. *Kommersant Vlast'*, 21 March 2000, p. 46.
212. Chuyev, *MOLOTOV*, p. 116.
213. Bedell Smith to Washington, 5 April 1946, *FRUS, 1946*, vol. 6, p. 736.
214. S. Alliluyeva, *Dvadtsat' pisem k drugu* (London 1967) p. 182.
215. Chuyev, *MOLOTOV*, p. 362.
216. Conceded in conversation on 8 April 1948: Krock, *Memoirs*, p. 234.
217. Anderson to Harriman, 12 October 1945, Harriman Papers, box 183.
218. Troyanovskii, *Cherez gody*, p. 124.
219. "Soyuzniki nazhimayut na tebya dlya togo, shtoby slomit' u tebya volyu . . . ," *Istochnik*, 2, 1999, p. 73.
220. Ibid., pp. 74–75.
221. Sklyarov (London) to Moscow, 9 October 1943, quoted in V. Lota, "Tegeran—43: trudnyi put' k soglasiyu," *Krasnaya Zvezda*, 1 November 2003.
222. "Memuary Nikity Sergeevicha Khrushcheva," *Voprosy Istorii*, no. 6, 1994, p. 115.
223. Wilhelm Pieck's accounted supplemented by that of Anton Ackermann, quoted in M. Kaiser, "'Es muß demokratisch assehen . . .': Moskau und die Gleichschaltung des Parteiensystems in der Sowjetischen Besatzungszone Deutschlands 1944/45–1948/49," in *Gleichschaltung unter Stalin? Die Entwicklung der Parteien im Östlichen Europa, 1944–1949*, ed. S. Creuzberger and M. Görtemaker (Paderborn 2002) p. 270.
224. Erofeev MS, p. 8; also Erofeev, *Diplomat*, p. 153.
225. A. Bullock, *Ernest Bevin* (London 1983) p. 193.
226. Ibid.
227. *Cold War International History Project Bulletin*, no. 11, Winter 1998, p. 136.
228. Johnson, *United States Cryptologic History*, p. 16.
229. Harriman (Moscow) to Washington, 22 November 1945, Harriman Papers, box 184.
230. Quoted in Pechatnov, *Stalin*, p. 714, endnote 132.
231. Kennan (Moscow) to Washington, 22 February 1946, *FRUS, 1946*, vol. 6 (Washington DC 1969) pp. 696–709.
232. Speech to an electoral meeting, Moscow, 6 February 1946: V. Molotov, *Voprosy Vneshnei Politiki. Rechi i Zayavleniya* (Moscow 1948) pp. 24–25.
233. W. Bedell Smith, *Moscow Mission, 1946–1949* (London 1950) p. 41; also Smith (Moscow) to Washington, 5 April 1946, *FRUS*, pp. 732–736. Confirmed in the diary of Sulzberger, entry for 7 May 1946, *Long Row of Candles*, p. 312.

234. Gilbert, *"Never Despair,"* p. 202.
235. Stalin to the Polish leaders, 24 May 1946, *Vostochnaya Evropa*, doc. 151.
236. Johnson, *United States Cryptologic History*, p. 16.
237. "Notes on the Marshall Plan," 15 December 1947, Kennan Papers, box 23, file 50.
238. *Washington Post*, 21–25 January 1952.
239. Roberts (Moscow) to Bevin (London), 6 September 1946, FO 371/156731.
240. *Washington Post*, 22 January 1952.
241. Roberts (Moscow) to Bevin (London), 6 September 1946, FO 371/5673.
242. Daughter Tatyana Litvinova, in conversation with the author.
243. FO 371/156731.
244. Ivy to Eugene and Agnes Meyer, 14 November 1943, Eugene Meyer Papers, Library of Congress, box 34.
245. Ivy Litvinova to Freeman, 5 January 1946, Freeman Papers, box 175. Edward Carter, quondam head of Russian Relief, passed on the same request orally. The MS was about 250 pages and one chapter concerned the events surrounding the Nazi-Soviet pact. Freeman incinerated the MS in the furnace in the bank's basement.
246. *Washington Post*, 21–25 January 1952; also Smith (Moscow) to Washington, 21 June 1946, *FRUS*, vol. 6, pp. 763–765.
247. Molotov's conversations with Chuyev: *MOLOTOV*, p. 131.
248. Y. Modin, *My Five Cambridge Friends* (London 1994) pp. 158–159.
249. R. Pikhoya, *SSSR: Istoriya velikoi imperii* (Moscow 2009) p. 149.
250. *SSSR i Germanskii Vopros 1941–1949*, ed. G. Kynin and I. Laufer (Moscow 2000) p. 794, note 318. See also V. Pechatnov, "Na etom voprose my slomaem ikh, anti-sovetskoe uporstvo . . . (iz perepiski Stalina s Molotovym po vneshnepoliticheskim delam v 1946 godu)," *Istochnik*, no. 3, 1999, pp. 92–104.
251. Ibid., doc. 112.
252. Soviet record of Molotov's conversation with Byrnes, 5 May 1946, *Sovetsko-amerikanskie otnosheniya, 1945–1948* (Moscow 2004) doc. 110.
253. Durbrow (Moscow) to Washington, 23 August 1946, *FRUS*, p. 776.
254. Recollections of Tatyana Litvinova.
255. Ivy's recollections, Ivy Litvinov Papers, Hoover Institution Archives, Stanford University, box 3.
256. *Diary of Georgi Dimitrov*, p. 415; "Goodwill Mission to the U.S.S.R.," Labour Party Archives (now Manchester University Library).

CHAPTER 3. COMINFORMITY

Epigraph: Vasil Kolarov's record of a meeting with Stalin, 10 February 1948, reprinted in "Na poroge pervogo raskola v 'sotsialisticheskom lagere'—Peregovory rukovodyash-chikh deyatelei SSSR, Bolgarii i Yugoslavii. 1948g.," *Istoricheskii Arkhiv*, no. 4, 1997, p. 97.
1. Trotsky, "SSSR v voine," *Byulleten' Oppozitsii*, nos. 79–80, 1939, p. 8.
2. Unaltered version of what was said: *Rossiya XX Vek. Dokumenty: 1941 God*, ed. V. Naumov (Moscow 1998) vol. 2.

3. Ibid.

4. Such astute minds as Hugh Seton-Watson were taken in before working in the region as a correspondent for the *Times*. His attitude then changed abruptly. Private conversation.

5. Pavlov's record of Stalin's conversation with Churchill and Eden, 17 October 1944, *Stalin i Churchill*, doc. 171.

6. *Diary of Georgi Dimitrov*, p. 451. See also N. Ganchovski, *The Days of Dimitrov as I Witnessed and Recorded Them* (Sofia 1979) pp. 549–550.

7. Sudoplatov, *Spetsoperatsii*, p. 364.

8. Chuyev, *MOLOTOV*, p. 106

9. Record of Stalin's conversation with the head of the delegation from the national committee for the liberation of Yugoslavia, 9 January 1945, *Vostochnaya Evropa v dokumentakh rossiiskikh arkhivov, 1944–1953gg*, vol. 1, ed. T. Volokitina et al. (Moscow 1997) doc. 37.

10. From the archives: A. Taras, *Anatomiya Nenavisti: Russko-pol'skie konflikty v VIII–XX vv.* (Minsk 2008) p. 773.

11. Memorandum directed to Mikhail Suslov, head of the department, 5 April 1948, *SSSR—Pol'sha. Mekhanizmy podchineniya, 1944–1949gg. Sbornik dokumentov*, ed. G. Bordyugov et al. (Moscow 1995) doc. 46.

12. The Soviet record of the conversation, 24 May 1946, *Vostochnaya Evropa*, doc. 151.

13. Leeper (Athens) to London, 30 May and 5 June 1945, FO 371/48419.

14. Speech to the Central Committee of the KKE, 30 June 1945, ibid.

15. A. Shatilov, "Greece after the Ejection of the German Invaders," *New Times*, no. 2, 15 June 1945.

16. *Manchester Guardian*, 28 August 1945.

17. Entry, 9 February 1946, *Diary of Georgi Dimitrov*, p. 396.

18. This is what Molotov told Partsalidis and other KKE leaders in January 1950. P. Stavrakis, *Moscow and Greek Communism, 1944–1949* (Ithaca 1989) p. 94.

19. Entry, 2 April 1946, *Diary of Georgi Dimitrov*, p. 402.

20. Entry, 2 September 1946, ibid., p. 414.

21. From Bulgarian archives: G. Daskalov, *B''lgariya i G''rtsiya: ot razriv k''m pomirenie, 1944–1964* (Sofia 2004) pp. 135.

22. Ibid., pp. 136–137.

23. Ibid., p. 137.

24. Ibid., pp. 138–139.

25. Ibid., p. 142.

26. Ibid., p. 134.

27. Quoted in V. Zubok and C. Pleshakov, *Inside the Kremlin's Cold War: From Stalin to Khrushchev* (Cambridge, Mass., 1996) pp. 127–128.

28. Daskalov, *B''lgariya*, p. 134.

29. M. Truman, *Letters from Father*, p. 180.

30. For the best account, see J. Chace, *Acheson* (New York 1998) p. 167.

31. Minute dated 20 November 1947, FO 371/61077.

32. Thomas Brimelow at the Foreign Office concluded after a detailed survey based on intelligence sources: "In some countries the leaders of the local communist party do get instructions from Moscow. . . . But there is nothing to prove that the Moscow directives cover all fields of Communist activity, or that local initiative is discouraged," 12 April 1957, FO 371/66295, and F.O. Minute on "Communism Abroad," 11 October 1947, FO 371/66296.

33. Testimony, 28 March 1947, *Legislative Origins of the Truman Doctrine. Hearings Held in Executive Session before the Committee on Foreign Relations*, US Senate, 80th Cong., 1st sess. on S. 938, A Bill to Provide for Assistance to Greece and Turkey (Washington DC 1973) p. 66.

34. Minute by P. Pares, 18 January 1949, on a dispatch from Washington characterizing the president, FO 371/74174.

35. Chace, *Acheson*, p. 168.

36. 25 September 1947, speech to the first conference of Cominform: *The Cominform*, ed. G. Procacci et al., *Annali*, Fondazione Giangiacomo Feltrinelli (Milan 1994) p. 238.

37. G. Tabouis, *Les Princes de la Paix* (Paris 1980) p. 159.

38. Report, 1 January 1947, from the commander of the 92nd Carpathian Red Banner regiment, Col. Blumkin and regimental Chief of Staff Major Morozov, *Pogranichnye Voiska SSSR, 1945–1950* (Moscow 1975) doc. 21.

39. For the medical report, see I. Chigirin, *Belye i Gryaznye Pyatna Istorii: O taine smerti I. V. Stalina i o nekotorykh obstoyatel'stvakh ego pravleniya* (Moscow 2008) pp. 136–137.

40. *Vostochnaya Evropa*, doc. 213, enclosure.

41. Ibid.

42. Italian Communist Party Archive (Archivio PCI, Rome), Verbale di Riunione della Direzione del Partito, 5 May 1947, 272.

43. Ibid., 19 January 1947.

44. Ibid., Verbale, 4 February 1947.

45. Ibid., Verbale, 16 April 1947, 272.

46. G. Cerreti, *Con Togliatti e Thorez. Quarant'anni di lotte politche* (Milan 1973) p. 307.

47. Ibid., p. 308.

48. Archivio PCI, Verbale, 3–5 June 1947.

49. Rákosi to Baranov, quoting the statement, 21 May 1947, Volokitina, *Sovetskii faktor v vostochnoi Evrope, 1944–1953: Dokumenty*, vol. 1 (Moscow 1999) p. 15.

50. 24 May 1947, *Vostochnaya Evropa*, p. 648, footnote 4.

51. Oral History Interview with John D. Hickerson, 10 November 1972, www.trumanlibrary .org/oralhist/hicklerson.htm.

52. Vinson testimony, *Anglo-American Financial Agreement. Hearings Committee on Banking and Currency*, March 5–20 1946, US Senate, 79th Cong., 2nd sess. (Washington DC 1946) p. 2.

53. Ibid., p. 14.

54. Ibid., p. 64.

55. Ibid., p. 313.

56. Bohlen, *Witness*, p. 259.
57. "Weekly Political Summary," British Embassy, Washington, 3 March 1947, FO 371/61053.
58. Bohlen, *Witness*, pp. 262–263.
59. G. Kennan, *Memoirs, 1925–1950* (New York 1967) pp. 339–341.
60. Kennan to Harriman, 24 February 1945, Kennan Papers, box 23, file 35.
61. "Weekly Political Summary," 7 June 1947, FO 371/61055.
62. Recollections of Erofeev quoted in M. Narinskii, "SSSR i Plan Marshalla," *Kholodnaya Voina: Novye podkhody, novye dokumenty* (Moscow 1995) p. 174.
63. Varga, "Plan Marshalla i ekonomicheskoe polozhenie Soedinennykh Shtatov Ameriki," 24 June 1947, *Sovetsko-amerikanskie otnosheniya*, doc. 200.
64. "Dollar Shortage," *Wall Street Journal*, 6 June 1947.
65. Ibid.
66. "Notes on the Marshall Plan," 15 December 1947, Kennan Papers, box 23, file 50.
67. Chuyev, *MOLOTOV*, p. 118.
68. Erofeev, *Diplomat*, p. 140.
69. Ibid., p. 141.
70. *Vostochnaya Evropa*, doc. 218.
71. Ibid., p. 667, footnote 3.
72. Ibid., p. 668; and Sudoplatov, *Spetsoperatsii*, pp. 378–379.
73. Memcon by Peterson, 24 June 1947, *FRUS, 1947*, vol. 3 (Washington DC 1972) p. 268.
74. Erofeev, *Diplomat*, p. 143.
75. Quoted in Narinskii, "SSSR," p. 175–176.
76. Ibid., p. 177.
77. Interview in M. Charlton, *The Eagle and the Small Birds* (London 1984) p. 77.
78. Griffis (Warsaw) to Washington, 18 August 1947, *FRUS, 1947*, vol. 4 (Washington DC 1972) p. 442.
79. Volokitina, *Sovetskii Faktor*, p. 47.
80. Quoted in M. Korobochkin, "Soviet Policy toward Finland and Norway, 1947–1949," *Scandinavian Journal of History*, 1995, vol. 20, no. 3, p. 191.
81. Soviet record of the talks, 9 July 1947: *Sovetskii faktor*, doc. 166; *Vostochnaya*, doc. 227.
82. V. Dedijer, *Tito Speaks* (London 1953) p. 300. See also L. Gibianskii, "Kak voznik Kominform: Po novym arkhyvnym materialam," *Novaya i Noveishaya Istoriya*, no. 4, 1993, pp. 135–136. Also, Cavendish Bentinck (Warsaw) to Hankey (London), 28 October 1946, FO 371/56835.
83. Information from the Italian ambassador, Eugenio Reale, a member of the PCI's *direzione*: Cavendish-Bentinck (also MI6, Warsaw) to Hankey (London), 28 October 1946, FO 371/56835.
84. Baranov to Zhdanov, 15 August 1947, *Vostochnaya Evropa*, doc. 234.
85. M. Djilas, *Rise and Fall* (New York 1986) p. 134.
86. Ibid., p. 135.

87. From the minutes, republished in *The Cominform*, ed. G. Procacci et al. (Milan 1994) pp. 58 and 44.

88. Djilas, *Rise and Fall*, p. 137.

89. Mission in Warsaw to Rome, 9 February 1948, Italian Foreign Ministry Archive, Rome. AP 1946–1950. URSS. B 13 (1948). URSS 1.3.

90. *"Them": Stalin's Polish Puppets*, ed. T. Toranska (New York 1987) p. 282.

91. 26 September 1947, *Cominform*, p. 290.

92. Ibid., p. 300.

93. *"Them,"* p. 283.

94. Erofeev, *Diplomat*, pp. 179–180.

95. Quoted in Haslam, "Stalin's War or Peace," *Virtual History* (London 1997), ed. N. Ferguson, p. 355.

96. Ibid.

97. Politburo directive to the MID, 14 October 1947, *Vostochnaya Evropa*, doc. 245.

98. *Moskva i Vostochnaya Evropa: Stanovlenie politicheskikh rezhimov sovetskogo tipa, 1949–1953: Ocherki istorii*, ed. T. Volokitina et al. (Moscow 2002) p. 45.

99. Numbers given by Khrushchev in 1959: B. Kostin, *Margelov* (Moscow 2005) p. 175.

100. Simonov, *Voenno-promyshlennyi*, p. 192.

101. Ibid., pp. 198–199.

102. Kostin, *Margelov*, p. 154.

103. Simonov, *Voenno-promyshlennyi*, p. 329.

104. P. Knyshevskii, *Dobycha: Tainy germanskikh reparatsii* (Moscow 1994) pp. 20–21.

105. Simonov, *Voenno-promyshlennyi*, p. 193.

106. V. Zima, *Golod v SSSR 1946–1947 Godov: proiskhozhdenie i posledstviya* (Moscow 1996) p. 149.

107. Memorandum for the President, 20 September 1947, Papers of William L. Clayton, Harry S. Truman Library and Archive, Fulton, Missouri.

108. *United States Foreign Policy for a Post-War Recovery Program. Hearings before the Committee on Foreign Affairs*, US House of Representatives, 80th Cong., 1st and 2nd sess., pt. 1 (Washington DC 1948) p. 75.

109. Ibid., pp. 464–465.

110. Ibid., p. 506.

111. Acheson to Truman, 16 February 1950, Papers of Harry Truman, White House Central Files, Confidential Files, Truman Library.

112. M. Abelson, "Private United States Direct Investments Abroad," Department of Commerce, *Survey of Current Business*, vol. 29, no. 11, November 1949, p. 18.

113. C. Shepler, "Foreign Transactions of the U.S. Government in 1948," ibid., May 1949, pp. 18–19.

114. "Notes on the Marshall Plan," Kennan Papers, box 23, file 50.

115. "Memuary Nikity Sergeevicha Khrushcheva," *Voprosy Istorii*, no. 9, 1993, p. 92.

116. "Unamerican Americans," *Wall Street Journal*, 11 June 1947.

117. For details, see the memoirs of R. Pannequin, *Adieu, camarades*, vol. 2 (Paris 1977) pp. 86–102.

118. "Notes on the Marshall Plan," Kennan Papers, box 23, file 50.
119. PCF meetings were recorded by the French secret police: V. Auriol, *Journal du Septennat, 1947–1954*, vol. 1 (Paris 1970) p. 612.
120. Archivio PCI, Verbale, 17 September 1947.
121. Ibid., Verbale, 7–10 October 1947.
122. Ibid., Verbale, 10 October 1947.
123. In conversation with the Yugoslavs, 27 May 1946: Cold War International History Project, "Conversations with Stalin" (unpub.) p. 357.
124. Archivio Secchia, *Annali*, Fondazione Giangiacomo Feltrinelli (Milan, 1978) p. 626.
125. Ibid., p. 611.
126. *Pravda*, 28 January 1948.
127. Bullock, *Ernest Bevin*, pp. 518–519.
128. *Vostochnaya Evropa*, pp. 763–764, footnote 5.
129. L. Gibianskii, "Forsirovanie sovetskoi blokovoi politiki," in *Kholodnaya Voina 1945–1963gg: Istoricheskaya retrospektiva* ed. I. Yegorova et al. (Moscow 2003) p. 167.
130. Memcon in Y. Girenko, *Stalin-Tito* (Moscow 1991) p. 309.
131. Quoted from Tito's letter of 26 January 1948: E. Hoxha, *The Titoites* (London 1982) pp. 440–441.
132. Ibid., pp. 445–446.
133. Vasil Kolarov's record of the meeting, 10 February 1948, reprinted in "Na poroge raskola v 'sotsialisticheskom lagere': Peregovory rukovodyashchikh deyatelei SSSR, Bolgarii i Yugoslavii 1948g.," *Istoricheskii Arkhiv*, no. 4, 1997, p. 98.
134. Ibid., p. 101.
135. V. Dedijer, *Tito Speaks* (London 1955) p. 332.
136. "The Position of the United States with Respect to Greece," report to the NSC, 6 January 1948, *FRUS, 1948*, vol. 4 (Washington DC 1974) pp. 2–5.
137. "Na poroge . . . ," p. 99.
138. Ibid., p. 101.
139. Soviet record of the conversation, 19 February 1948, *Vostochnaya*, doc. 259.
140. Quoted in Korobochkin, "Soviet Policy toward Finland and Norway," p. 192, footnote 29.
141. From Aleksandrov of the fourth European department of the Foreign Ministry, 2 March 1948: *Sovetskii faktor*, doc. 191.
142. Quoted from the archives, in G. Murashko, "Fevral'skii krizis 1948g v Chekhoslovakii i sovetskoe rukovodstvo po novym materialam rossiiskikh arkhivov," *Novaya i Noveishaya Istoriya*, no. 2, March–April 1998, p. 54.
143. Bamburgh (Karlovy Vary) to London, 12 September 1946, FO 817/34.
144. Murashko, "Fevral'skii krizis."
145. Ibid.
146. Ibid., p. 55.
147. Ibid.
148. *Sovetskii faktor*, p. 551, footnote 2.
149. Murashko, "Fevral'skii krizis," p. 58
150. Ibid.

151. Ibid., pp. 59–60.
152. M. Truman, *Letters from Father*, pp. 179–180.
153. Smirnov to Molotov, 12 March 1948, *SSSR i Germanskii Vopros, 1941–1949*, vol. 3 (Moscow 2003).
154. To Molotov and Vyshinsky, 23 March 1948, AVPRF, f. 07, op. 21, p. 33, d. 497, l. 1: A. Filitov, "Soviet Perceptions of the Formation of NATO, 1948–1953," *Mezhdunarodnyi istoricheskii zhurnal*, no. 20, 2002. (At www. history. machaon. ru/all/number. _02; I have tightened up the English.)
155. Minutes of a Politburo meeting, 19 February 1948, "Nachalo sovetsko-yugoslavskogo konflikta. Protokoly zasedanii Politburo TsK KPYu 19 fevralya–7 iyulya 1948 g.," *Voprosy Istorii*, no. 8, 2008, doc. 1.
156. L. Gibianskii, "The Beginning of the Soviet-Yugoslav Conflict and the Cominform," *Cominform*, p. 476.
157. Ibid., p. 477; also Djilas, *Rise and Fall*, pp. 184–187
158. "Nachalo," doc. 2.
159. "Ob antimarksistskikh ustanovkakh rukovoditelei kompartii Yugoslavii v voprosakh vneshnei i vnutrennei politiki," 18 March 1948, *Vostochnaya*, doc. 267.
160. Archivio PCI, Verbale, 21 January 1948. 199.
161. Archivio PCI, Verbale, 11 February 1948.
162. Quoted in V. Zaslavsky, *Lo Stalinismo e la Sinistra Italiana* (Milan 2004) pp. 84–85.
163. From the close friend of a former MI6 officer involved.
164. Archivio PCI, Verbale, 26 April 1948.
165. Archivio PCI, Verbale, 24–25 May 1948.
166. Archivio PCI, Verbale, 6 August 1948.
167. 5 April 1948, *Vostochnaya*, doc. 272.
168. Djilas, *Rise and Fall*, p. 189.
169. Reported by the Bulgarian minister in Rome on returning to Italy on 7 July and conveyed to London by MI6 two days later: KV 2/11665.
170. P. Howarth, quoting the ambassador and MI6 resident in Warsaw, Cavendish Bentinck, in *Intelligence Chief Extraordinary: The Life of the Ninth Duke of Portland* (London 1986) p. 210.
171. Volokitina, *Sovetskii faktor*, p. 499.
172. Ibid., p. 510.
173. G. Murashko and A. Noskova, "Sovetskoe rukovodstvo i politicheskie protsessy T. Kostova i L. Raika (po materialam rossiiskikh arkhivov)," *Stalinskoe desyatiletie*, pp. 23–35.
174. Djilas, *Rise and Fall*, p. 198.
175. Hoxha, *Titoites*, p. 498.
176. Resolution, 23 June 1948, *Cominform*, p. 618; Erofeev, *Diplomat*, p. 188. Erofeev was in the delegation to interpret for Zhdanov.
177. National Archives, London, KV 2/11665.
178. Erofeev, *Diplomat*, p. 188; also Zubok and Pleshakov, *Inside the Kremlin's Cold War*, p. 136.
179. Pikhoya, *SSSR*, pp. 209–210.

180. Malenkov's statement, 23 June 1948, *Cominform*, p. 600.

181. "Memuary Nikity Sergeevicha Khrushcheva," *Voprosy Istorii*, no. 9, 1993, p. 91.

182. Ibid., p. 92.

183. 31 January 1947: W. Wolkov, "Die deutsche Frage aus Stalins Sicht, 1947–1952," *Zeitschrift für Geschichtswissenschaft*, 48, 2000, pp. 28–29. The notes were taken by Vladimir Semyonov.

184. Soviet record of the discussion, 26 March 1948, republished in "Za sovetami v Kreml'," *Istoricheskii Arkhiv*, no. 5, 2002, p. 24.

185. Ibid., pp. 36–37.

186. AVPRF, f. 82, op. 34, p. 146, d. 7, l. 1: quoted in M. Narinskii, "Berlinskii krizis 1948–1949gg. Novye dokumenty iz rossiiskikh arkhivov," *Novaya i Noveishaya Istoriya*, no. 3, May-June 1995, p. 18

187. Smirnov to Molotov: Narinskii, "Berlinskii," p. 20.

188. Ibid., p. 21.

189. Quoted in ibid.

190. Ibid., p. 22.

191. AVPRF, Fond Molotova, op. 10, papka 37, por. 491, quoted in J. Payne, "The Berlin Crisis, 1948–49" (undergraduate dissertation, Cambridge History Faculty, 1996).

192. D. Rosenberg, "The Origins of Overkill: Nuclear Weapons and American Strategy, 1945–1960," *International Security*, vol. 7, no. 4, 1983, pp. 14–16.

193. Harrison (Moscow) to Hankey (London), 6 December 1948, FO 371/77587.

194. Diary entry, 20 December 1948, Sulzberger, *Long Row of Candles*, pp. 427 and 432.

195. Bohlen, *Witness*, p. 269.

196. "U.S. Foreign Policy Strategy," *New Times*, no. 14, 5 April 1950.

197. Annual Review of Events 1948, 29 September 1949, FO 371/74159.

198. 24 November 1947, National Archives, London, CP (47) 313.

199. Told to Cyrus Sulzberger, diary entry 15 October 1948, Sulzberger, *Long Row of Candles*, p. 412.

200. Russia Committee. Report of the Subcommittee set up to examine the problem of planning in relation to policy toward the Soviet Union and the Soviet Orbit, 14 December 1948, FO 371/71632A. The Russian Committee was an interdepartmental committee set up in 1946 to coordinate policy toward Moscow. It was run from the Foreign Office.

201. Draft, "British Policy towards Soviet Russia," ibid.

202. Report, ibid.

203. Krock, *Memoirs*, chapters 2–3.

204. Report by D. Stewart, 7 February 1949, FO 371/76638.

205. V. Gobarev, "Soviet Military Plans and Activities during the Berlin Crisis, 1948–1949," p. 31; N. Naimark, "Stalin and Europe in the Postwar Period, 1945–53: Issues and Problems," *Journal of Modern European History*, vol. 2, no. 1, 2004 p. 43.

206. Obituary, *Daily Telegraph*, 10 January 2009.

207. Modin, *My Five Cambridge Friends*, pp. 226–227.

208. Chace, *Acheson*, pp. 274–278.

209. Oral History Interview, 23 June 1971, www.trumanlibrary.org/oralhist/battle.htm.

210. McCullough, *Truman*, pp. 741–742.

211. Krock, *Memoirs*, p. 262. Truman said this on 24 May 1951.

212. 11 January 1949, FO 371/74174.

213. Permanent Under-Secretary's Committee (laying down policy for MI6), "Future Policy towards Soviet Russia," 17 January 1952, FO 371/116116.

CHAPTER 4. ON THE OFFENSIVE IN ASIA

Epigraph: S. Goncharev, J. Lewis, and Xue Litai, *Uncertain Partners: Stalin, Mao, and the Korean War* (Stanford 1993) doc. 6, p. 232.

1. Speech to the 10th plenum of the 8th Central Committee, 24 September 1962, *Mao Tse-tung Unrehearsed*, p. 191.

2. Told to Soviet ambassador Yudin—"Zapis' besedy s tovarishchem MAO TSE-DUNOM," p. Yudin, 31 March 1956: *Problemy Dal'nego Vostoka*, no. 5, 1994, p. 105.

3. A. Ledovskii, *SSSR i Stalin v sud'bakh Kitaya: Dokumenty i svidetel'stava uchastnika sobytii, 1937–1952* (Moscow 1999) p. 43.

4. Ibid., p. 45.

5. M. Kapitsa, *Na raznykh parallelyakh. Zapiski diplomata* (Moscow 1996) p. 23.

6. Harriman and Abel, *Special Envoy*, p. 532.

7. Quoted from the Russian foreign ministry archive in D. Heinzig, *Die Sowjetunion und das kommunistische China, 1945–1950* (Baden-Baden 1998) pp. 85–86.

8. A. Shirokorad, *Rossiya i Kitai: Konflikty i sotrudnichestvo* (Moscow 2004) p. 401.

9. J. Lilley, *China Hands* (New York 2004) p. 54.

10. Ledovskii, *SSSR i Stalin*, p. 50.

11. Ibid., p. 51.

12. Ibid., pp. 52–53.

13. Orlov to Stalin, 14 July 1948, quoted in Heinzig, *Die Sowjetunion*, pp. 203–204.

14. Mikoyan's memorandum to the Presidium of the CPSU on his visit to China, 22 September 1960, reprinted in Ledovskii, *SSSR i Stalin*, pp. 54–65.

15. Ibid., pp. 53 and 55.

16. Ibid., p. 58.

17. The revelations of these contacts from US archives at the time of the Sino-American rapprochement in 1973 led to some misleading conclusions by those who believed there had been a lost chance in 1949. In fact Soviet documents reveal the deception in its entirety. See KGB veteran S. Tikhvinskii, *Put' Kitaya k ob"edineniyu i nezavisimosti, 1898–1949* (Moscow 1996) pp. 463–469.

18. Ledovskii, *SSSR i Stalin*, pp. 60–65.

19. Memcon, "Korean Situation," 26 June 1950, Truman Library and Archive.

20. Heinzig, *Die Sowjetunion*, p. 210.

21. Kapitsa, *Na raznykh*, p. 43.

22. Ibid., p. 102. The entire text is on pp. 88–103.

23. Wu Xiuquan, *Eight Years in the Ministry of Foreign Affairs—Memoirs of a Diplomat* (Beijing 1985) pp. 9–10.

24. Entry, 10 February 1948, *Diary of Georgi Dimitrov*, p. 443.

25. Goncharev, *Uncertain Partners*, doc. 7, pp. 232–233.

26. The attack on Nehru sent a clear message to the head of the Malayan Communist Party, Chin Peng: *My Side of History* (Singapore 2003) p. 202. For the political thesis adopted by the CPI Congress: *Documents of the History of the Communist Party of India*, vol. 7, ed. M. Rao (New Delhi 1976) pp. 1–117.

27. Quoted in a telegram from the US embassy in Paris, 23 February 1949: T. Markin, "The Calcutta Conference," a paper written at SAIS, Johns Hopkins University, 16 January 1986.

28. "Current Situation in Malaya," 17 November 1949, CIA Electronic Reading Room.

29. Rundall (Washington), Weekly Political Summary, 4 January 1947, FO 371/61053.

30. The figures as of 1 July 1948 were: total population 5,800,000, of which 2,200,000 were Malay, 2,600,000 Chinese, and 600,000 Indians. Ibid.

31. A. Guber, "Malaya: Geographical Sketch," *New Times*, no. 50, 8 December 1948. In *Stalin i Indonezia: Politika SSSR v otnoshenii Indonezii v 1945–1953 godakh. Neizvestnye stranitsy* (Moscow 2004) the Russian historian L. Efimova argues no instructions were actually given for insurrection. The problem with this is that she had no access to the presidential archive, including Stalin's papers. Only that would allow a definitive conclusion. The absence of evidence from lesser archives is not evidence of absence. Moreover, even the evidence she adduces indicates both a tightening of control over the parties in Southeast Asia and their closer subordination to the general line, which meant open confrontation with Western imperialism and its clients. A further factor not directly addressed is the degree to which instructions flowed indirectly from Moscow via the Vietnamese and the southern bureau of the Chinese Party.

32. Chin Peng, *My Side*, pp 182–207. Chin claims it was July, but planned for September. This is not an assertion borne out by the evidence, however.

33. "Current Situation in Malaya," 17 November 1949, CIA Electronic Reading Room.

34. Vyshinsky's record of the conversation, 30 July 1949: Ledovskii, *SSSR i Stalin*, p. 112.

35. Memcon, Khrushchev with Mao in Beijing, 31 July 1958, Volkogonov Papers, Library of Congress (hereafter Volkogonov Papers).

36. Speech of 30 June 1949: Mao Tse-tung, *Selected Works*, vol. 4 (Peking 1969) pp. 415.

37. Wu, *Eight Years*, p. 21.

38. Kapitsa, *Na raznykh*, p. 45.

39. *Pravda*, 3 October 1949.

40. 12 October 1949.

41. Ledovskii, *SSSR i Stalin*, p. 118.

42. Mao (Moscow) to the CCP Politburo (Beijing), 2/3 January 1950: Goncharev, *Uncertain Partners*, doc. 25, p. 244.

43. S. Tikhvinskii, "Proshloe: Golos ochevidtsa," *Problemy Dal'nego Vostoka*, no. 4, 1990, p. 104. Tilkhvinskii, Sinologist and intelligence officer, was serving under diplomatic cover in the Soviet embassy, Beijing.

44. Ledovskii, *SSSR i Stalin*, p. 120.

45. Quoted in Y. Glenovich, *Rossiya—Kitai: Shest' dogovorov* (Moscow 2003) p. 103.

46. Ibid., p. 776.

47. NSC 13/3 and NSC 49: JCS memorandum to Secretary of Defense Louis Johnson, 22 December 1949, *FRUS*, vol. 9, p. 923.

48. Tatyana Kirpichenko unearthed this local history: *Svenska Dagbladet*, 23 June 2003.

49. CIA, "Current Capabilities of the Northern Korean Regime," 19 June 1950, CIA Electronic Reading Room.

50. A. Torkunov, *Zagadochnaya Voina: Koreiskii konflikt 1950–1953 godov* (Moscow 2000) p. 30.

51. *New Times*, no. 13, 23 March 1949.

52. Conclusions drawn from his diaries: Hyun-su Jeon and Gyoo Kahng, "The Shtykov Diaries: New Evidence on Soviet Policy in Korea," *Cold War International History Project Bulletin*, nos. 6–7, Winter 1995/1996.

53. Torkunov, *Zagadochnaya*, pp. 35–36.

54. Ibid., p. 31.

55. Ibid., p. 32.

56. Ibid., p. 34.

57. Ibid., p. 36.

58. Ibid., p. 37.

59. Ibid., p. 38.

60. Ibid., p. 48.

61. Ibid., p. 51.

62. Record of Stalin's conversation with Mao, 16 December 1949, Volkogonov Papers.

63. Ledovskii, *SSSR i Stalin*, p. 125.

64. Ibid., p. 128.

65. Ibid., p. 125.

66. Ibid., p. 136.

67. *Problemy Dal'nego Vostoka*, p. 106.

68. Torkunov, *Zagadochnaya*, p. 51.

69. Ibid., p. 52.

70. Ibid., p. 53.

71. "Annual Review of Events 1948," 29 September 1949, FO 371/74159.

72. Sir Oliver Franks (Washington) to London, 29 June 1950, FO 371/84080.

73. Acheson, "Crisis in Asia," pp. 116 and 115.

74. Goncharev, *Uncertain Partners*, p. 103.

75. Broadcast on Moscow's domestic service, 21 January 1950 at 0400 hours, *BBC Summary of World Broadcasts*, 23 January 1950.

76. Goncharev, *Uncertain Partners*, doc. 38, pp. 254–256.

77. "The Mao-Stalin Meetings, December 1949-February 1950," *Stalin and the Cold War, 1945–1953: A Cold War International History Project Document Reader*, ed. C. Ostermann et al. (Washington DC 1999) pp. 477–479.

78. Torkunov, *Zagadochnaya*, p. 55.

79. Ibid., p. 56.

80. Wu, *Eight Years*, pp. 11–18.

81. For the text, see Goncharev, *Uncertain Partners*, doc. 45, pp. 260–261.

82. Ibid., p. 74.
83. Yudin (Beijing) to Khrushchev (Moscow), 30 October 1957: "'Operatsiya proidet me-nee boleznenno': Beseda Mao Tzeduna s sovetskim poslom," *Istochnik*, no. 4 (23) 1996, p112. That this is not found in C. Andrew and V. Mitrokhin, *The Mitrokhin Arkhiv II* (London 2005) chapter 15, is no doubt due to the fact that Mitrokhin had access only to KGB files. And China fell traditionally more within GRU jurisdiction.
84. Torkunov, *Zagadochnaya*, p. 58.
85. Ibid., p. 59.
86. Vyshinsky (Moscow) to Mao (Beijing), 14 May 1950, Volkogonov Papers; also Torkunov, *Zagadochnaya*, pp. 66–67.
87. Torkunov, *Zagadochnaya*, pp. 69–70.
88. Ibid., p. 70.
89. Ibid., pp. 74–75.
90. Shtykov (Pyongyang) to Vyshinsky (Moscow), 30 May 1950, ibid.
91. Ibid., p. 75.
92. Ibid., p. 67.
93. Ibid., p. 70. As reported at the time by Chou En-lai to the Soviet ambassador.
94. Kovalev to Stalin, 18 May 1949, ibid., p. 64.
95. Johnson, *United States Cryptologic History*, p. 39.
96. Acheson to Truman, 24 June 1950, Truman Library; Notes by George Esley describing communications on 24 June, 1950, based on Eben Ayers's chronology, ibid.
97. Memcon by Philip Jessup, "Korean Situation," 25 June 1950, ibid.
98. "Statement by the President," 26 June 1950, ibid.
99. Memcon by Philip Jessup, "Korean Situation," 26 June 1950, ibid.
100. "Resolution Concerning the Complaint of Aggression upon the Republic of Korea Adopted at the 474th Meeting of the Security Council on 27 June 1950," ibid.
101. *Zagadochnaya*, p. 79.
102. Ibid., p. 78.
103. Ibid., p. 81.
104. Ibid., p. 82.
105. Ibid., p. 106.
106. Ibid., p. 111.
107. Ibid., p. 84
108. Ibid., p. 91.
109. Ibid., p. 94.
110. Ibid., p. 113.
111. Ibid., p. 114.
112. Ibid., p. 115.
113. Ibid., p. 96.
114. Stalin (Moscow) to Mao (Beijing), 5 October 1949, Volkogonov Papers.
115. *Zagadochnaya*, p. 117.
116. Ibid., p. 97.
117. Ibid., pp. 117–118.
118. *Memoirs of Lord Gladwyn* (London 1972) p. 245.

CHAPTER 5. THAW

Epigraph: Churchill to Eisenhower, 12 April 1953: M. Gilbert, *Winston S. Churchill*, vol. 8 (London 1988) p. 814.

1. N. Yamskoi, "Smert' na ob"ekte 001," *Sovershenno Sekretno*, no. 3 (202), March 2006. The author disposes in detail with rumors of his murder.
2. From the notes in the medical journal: Chigirin, *Belye i gryaznye pytana istorii*, pp. 142–143.
3. Addressing a Central Committee plenum on 29 October 1957: *Rossiya XX Vek. Dokumenty. Georgii Zhukov*, p. 403.
4. "Memuary Nikity Sergeevicha Khrushcheva," *Voprosy Istorii*, no. 6, 1993, p. 87. Elsewhere Khrushchev refers to Stalin deriding them as "blind men": *Rossiya XX Vek Dokumenty. Georgii Zhukov*.
5. "Memuary . . . ," no. 4, 1993, p. 39.
6. Kohler (Moscow) to Rusk (Washington), 16 October 1962, John F. Kennedy Presidential Library and Museum (hereafter Kennedy Library), NSF, box 188.
7. D. Shepilov, *Neprimknuvshii* (Moscow 2001) p. 247. Shepilov attended occasionally on such matters as a propagandist for the Central Committee, later as chief editor of *Pravda*.
8. Kohler to Rusk, loc. cit.
9. "Memuary . . . ," *Voprosy Istorii*, nos. 8–9, 1992, p. 76.
10. Harriman to Rusk, 23 July 1963, Kennedy Library, NSF 187A.
11. Meeting of the Presidium, 9 February 1956: *Prezidium TsK KPSS, 1954–1964*, vol. 1, ed. A. Fursenko (Moscow 2003) doc. 32.
12. 7 November 1954: CIA, "Resignation of Malenkov," 12 September 1955, CIA Electronic Reading Room, at www.foia.cia.gov.
13. L. Moseley, *Dulles: A Biography of Eleanor, Allen, and John Foster Dulles and Their Family Network* (London 1978) p. 333.
14. Copy in the National Security Archive, George Washington University (hereafter National Security Archive), available on the Web.
15. Johnson, *United States Cryptologic History*, p. 179.
16. C. Friedrich and Z. Brzezinski, *Totalitarian Dictatorship and Autocracy* (Cambridge, Mass., 1956).
17. G. Wigg, *New Statesman*, 30 October 1954.
18. N. Zen'kovich, *Elita: Samye Sekretnye Rodstvenniki* (Moscow 2005) p. 248; L. Opekkin, "Na istoricheskom pereput'e," *Voprosy Istorii KPSS*, no. 1, January 1990, pp. 106–109.
19. Chuyev, *MOLOTOV*, p. 403.
20. Testimony of Dmitrii Sukhanov, Malenkov's chief of staff: "Stalin poshevelil pal'tsami . . . ," *Novoe Vremya*, no. 48, 1991, p. 33; also, Chuyev, *MOLOTOV*, ibid.; and R. Pikhoya, quoting from the resolutions, *Moskva. Kreml'. Vlast'. Sorok let posle voiny, 1945–1985* (Moscow 2007). Sukhanov, born 1904, was formally Malenkov's assistant until March 1953 and thereafter (1953–55) head of chancery of the Presidium.
21. *Istoricheskii Arkhiv*, no. 3, 1993, p. 92, footnote 73.

22. Dedijer, *Tito Speaks*, p. 321.

23. S. Beria, *Moi Otets—Lavrentii Beriya* (Moscow 1994) p. 253.

24. Zen'kovich, *Elita*, pp. 19–20.

25. Chuyev, *MOLOTOV*, p. 403.

26. "Plenum tsentral'nogo Komiteta KPSS—Yanvar' 1955 goda," 9th session, 31 January 1955, Communist Party Archives, Moscow (hereafter RTsKhIDNI/TsKhSD), f. 2, op. 1, d. 127.

27. Ibid.

28. Protocol reprinted in Zen'kovich, *XX Vek*, pp. 633–639.

29. Chuyev, *MOLOTOV*, p. 407.

30. Ibid., p. 408.

31. A. Mikoyan, *Tak Bylo: Razmyshleniya o minuvshem* (Moscow 1999) p. 597.

32. "Memuary . . . ," *Voprosy Istorii*, nos. 6–7, 1992, p. 81

33. Chuyev, *MOLOTOV*.

34. "Memuary . . . ," *Voprosy Istorii*, nos. 6–7, 1992.

35. W. Hayter, *A Double Life* (London 1974) p. 114.

36. C. Bohlen, *Witness to History, 1929–1969* (New York 1973) pp. 369–370.

37. Sukhanov, "Stalin poshevelil pal'tsami . . ."

38. Beria to the CPSU central committee, to comrade Malenkov, 1 July 1953: "Lavrentii Beria, 'Cherez 2–3 goda ya krepko ispravlyus' . . . —Pis'ma iz tyuremnogo bunkera," *Istochnik*, no. 4, 1994, p. 5.

39. Chuyev, *MOLOTOV*, p. 405.

40. A suggestion from Gladwyn Jebb: *Memoirs of Lord Gladwyn*, p. 277.

41. Chuyev, *MOLOTOV*, p. 401.

42. Mikoyan, *Tak Bylo*, pp. 586–587.

43. For the details of Khrushchev's life and work, see W. Taubman, *Khrushchev: The Man and His Era* (New York, 2003).

44. "Khrushchev and the Soviet Leadership," Current Intelligence Weekly Review, 20 April 1962, *FRUS, 1961–1963*, vol. 5, doc. 183.

45. H. Trevelyan, *Worlds Apart* (London 1971) p. 219.

46. Testimony, 10 November 1997, *Istoricheskii Arkhiv*, no. 3, 1998, p. 62, footnote 14.

47. D. Shepilov, *Neprimknuvshii*, p. 281.

48. Mikoyan, *Tak Bylo*, pp. 597–598.

49. "Poslednaya 'Antipartiinaya' Gruppa: Stenograficheskii otchet iyunskogo (1957 g.) plenuma TsK KPSS," 25 June 1957, *Istoricheskii Arkhiv*, no. 4, 1993, p. 37.

50. Recollections of Tatyana Litvinova to the author.

51. *Prezidium*, p. 391.

52. Chuev, *MOLOTOV*, p. 438.

53. Meeting of the Presidium, 14 October 1964: *Prezidium*, p. 869.

54. Background paper, "Khrushchev: The Man and His Outlook," White House Central Files, Russia (23), KHV B-5/51a, 11 September 1959. Dwight D. Eisenhower Library and Archives, Abilene, Kansas (hereafter Eisenhower Library and Archives).

55. Testimony, J. Blight and D. Welch, eds., *On the Brink: Americans and Soviets Reexamine the Cuban Missile Crisis*, 2nd ed. (New York 1990) p. 238.

56. Mikoyan, *Tak Bylo*, p. 598.

57. "Memuary . . . ," *Voprosy Istorii*, nos. 6–7, 1992, p. 82.

58. Ibid., *Voprosy Istorii*, no. 2, 1995, p. 78.

59. Chuyev, *MOLOTOV*, p. 402.

60. A. Alexandrov-Agentov, *Ot Kollontai do Gorbacheva* (Moscow 1994) p. 56.

61. 2 July 1953: "Plenum TsK KPSS: Stenograficheskii otchet": *Izvestiya TsK KPSS*, 1991, no. 1, p. 140.

62. Speaking on 24 June 1957: "Poslednaya 'Antipartiinaya' Gruppa: Stenograficheskii otchet iyunskogo (1957g.) plenuma TsK KPSS," *Istoricheskii Arkhiv*, no. 3, 1993, p. 23.

63. 28 June 1957, "Poslednaya . . . ," ibid., no. 2, 1994, p. 4.

64. The literature on the Note still lacks the evidence needed to support firm opinion. Filitov makes a convincing argument concerning Ulbricht, however: "Sovetskii Soyuz i germanskii vopros v period pozdnego stalinizma (k voprosu o genezise 'stalinskoi noty' 10 marta 1952 goda)," in *Stalin i Kholodnaya Voina* (Moscow 1998) p. 339.

65. Quoted in extenso: Wolkow, "Die deutsche Frage aus Stalins Sicht . . . ," pp. 45–47.

66. I. Wall, *The United States and the Making of Postwar France, 1945–1954* (Cambridge 1991) p. 265; also *Memoirs*, pp. 46–47.

67. Ibid.

68. Memorandum of a Discussion, 31 March 1953, *FRUS, 1952–1954*, vol. 2 (Washington 1984) pp. 265–266.

69. Larres, *Politik*, pp. 78–79.

70. Entry 7, March 1953, Moran, *Struggle for Survival* p. 403.

71. *Memoirs*, p. 49.

72. Pikhoya, *Moskva. Kreml'. Vlast'*, p. 234.

73. Ibid., pp. 234–235.

74. "Plenum Tsentral'nogo Komiteta KPSS—Yanvar' 1955 goda," 9th session, 31 January 1955, TsKhSD, f. 2, op. 1, d. 127.

75. Pikhoya, *Moskva. Kreml'. Vlast'*, p. 234.

76. Sukhanov testimony, *GB99 KCLMA*, Cold War documentary archive, 28/15.

77. Pikhoya, *Moskva. Kreml'. Vlast'*, pp. 234–235.

78. "Plenum."

79. Ibid.

80. *Uprising in East Germany, 1953*, ed. C. Ostermann (Budapest and New York 2001) doc. 18.

81. Ibid., doc. 19.

82. Semyonov and Grechko (Berlin) to Molotov and Bulganin (Moscow), 17 June 1953, ibid., doc. 25.

83. Semyonov and Grechko (Berlin) to Molotov and Bulganin (Moscow), 17 June 1953, ibid., doc. 26; Semyonov (Berlin) to Molotov and Bulganin (Moscow), 17 June 1953, ibid., doc. 28.

84. 150th meeting of the National Security Council, 18 June 1953, ibid., doc. 46.

85. NSC 158. Report by the NSC on "Interim United States Objectives and Actions to Exploit the Unrest in the Satellite States," 29 June 1953. Eisenhower Library and

Archives, WHO OSANSA, Special Assistants Series, President's Subseries 1, President's Papers 1953 (5).

86. *Command 9080: Documents Relating to the Meeting of Foreign Ministers of France, the United Kingdom, the Soviet Union and the United States of America. Berlin, January 25–February 18, 1954* (London 1954), annex A.

87. Speaking to the Central Committee, 2 July 1953: "Plenum TsK . . . ," p. 163.

88. *Command 9080*, doc. 14 and annex D.

89. Ibid., annex G.

90. C. Jackson (Berlin) to McCrum (White House), 10 February 1954: *FRUS*, vol. 7, pt. 1 (Washington DC 1986) doc. 456.

91. 26 February 1954, 186th meeting of the NSC, Eisenhower Library and Archives.

92. Sir Hubert Graves (Saigon) to London, 24 March 1954, FO 371/112048.

93. 22 April 1954: Sulzberger, *Long Row of Candles*, p. 1000.

94. Draft speech for a CC Plenum, enclosed in Molotov to Khrushchev, 24 June 1954, Harvard Project for Cold War Studies Web site.

95. *Selected Works of Govind Ballabh Pant*, vol. 12 (Oxford 1999) pp. 217–218.

96. Note to Secretary-General, Foreign Secretary, and Commonwealth Secretary, 12 October 1953, concerning a talk with Indonesia's foreign minister, Sunarjo, *Selected Works of Jawaharlal Nehru*, 2nd series, vol. 24 (New Delhi 1999) pp. 553–554.

97. *Agreement between India and China on Trade and Intercourse between India and Tibet Region of China* (New Delhi 1954).

98. See Nehru to Chettur, 9 May 1954, *Selected Works*, vol. 24, pp. 478–480; and Nehru to U Nu, 29 May 1954, ibid., pp. 480–482.

99. Minute by Tahourdin, 5 March 1954, FO 371/112048.

100. Hoang Van Hoan, *A Drop in the Ocean* (Beijing 1988) p. 324.

101. "Plenum Tsentral'nogo Komiteta KPSS—Yanvar' 1955 goda," 9th session, 31 January 1955, TsKhSD, f. 2, op. 1, d. 127.

102. Conversation with the US ambassador, 9 June 1955, Bohlen (Moscow) to Washington, 10 June 1955, Eisenhower Library and Archives, Ann Whitman file, International Series, box 45, USSR 1953–1955 (1).

103. *Izvestiya*, 27 March 1955.

104. MF BBC MON 2015 PME; MF BBC MON 2017 PME; MF BBC MON 2019 PME; MF BBC MON 2021 PME; END BBC MON 2051 15 6, Foreign Office Minute to Mr. Corcos, 3 July 1954, FO 371/111675.

105. Pikhoya, *Moskva. Kreml'. Vlast'*, p. 291.

106. Sukhanov, "Stalin poshevelil pal'tsami . . ."

107. Ya. Viktorov, "Vazhnye shagi na puti smyagcheniya mezhdunarodnoi napryazhennosti," *Kommunist*, no. 14, 20 September 1955.

108. "Plenum Tsentral'nogo Komiteta KPSS—Yanvar' 1955 goda," 9th meeting, 31 January 1955, TsKhSD, f. 2, op. 1, d. 127.

109. Alexandrov-Agentov, *Ot Kollontai*, p. 56.

110. 19 May 1955, 249th meeting of the NSC, Eisenhower Library and Archives, Ann Whitman file, NSC 6.

111. Allen Dulles, 12 May 1955, 248th meeting of the NSC, ibid.
112. 18 January 1956, ibid., 7.
113. Le Roy (Moscow) to Pinay (Paris), 19 August 1955, *Documents Diplomatiques Français*, 1955, vol. 2 (Paris 1988) doc. 125.
114. *Sovetsko-izrail'skie otnosheniya: Sbornik dokumentov*, vol. 1 (Moscow 2000) doc. 126; also, *Documents*, doc. 127.
115. Deputy Foreign Minister Zorin's record of a conversation with the Egyptian ambassador, 5 August 1948, *Rossiya XX Vek. Dokumenty. Blizhnevostochnyi Konflikt, 1947–1956*, vol. 1, ed. V. Naumkin et al. (Moscow 2003) doc. 24.
116. Eban (New York) to Shertok (Tel Aviv), 12 August 1948, *Documents on Israeli-Soviet Relations*, doc. 145.
117. Record of the conversation by Bakulin, head of the Near and Middle East Department of the Soviet Foreign Ministry, 24 November 1948, *Blizhnevostochnyi Konflikt*, doc. 40. For the complete list: Ben-Gurion (Tel Aviv) to Ratner (Moscow), 7 November 1948, *Documents Documents on Israeli-Soviet Relations*, doc. 194. The list was not given to Moscow until 24 November: *Blizhnevostochnyi Konflikt*, doc. 202. Presumably because it was so delicate a message it came via the diplomatic bag to avoid interception and possible decryption by the British.
118. Boris Shtein's conclusions on a declaration from Lemberg, 22 April 1948: *Blizhnevostochnyi Konflikt*, doc. 16. These volumes contain documents from the Russian Foreign Ministry archive.
119. The best informed was always Sasson. See, for instance, his appreciation in Sasson to Epstein (Washington), 28 June 1946, *Documents on Israeli-Soviet Relations*, doc. 63.
120. G. Meir, *My Life* (London 1975) pp. 205–208.
121. "Conferences: Old Rock Bottom," *Time*, 22 July 1946.
122. Quoted from the archives: G. Kostyrenko, *Stalin Protiv "Kosmopolitov." Vlast' i Evreiskaya Intelligentsiya v SSSR* (Moscow 2009) pp. 180–181.
123. From the Centre to Washington residency, 26 August 1950, KGB archives, Black Notebook, p. 95, Vasil'ev Papers.
124. Yershov (Tel Aviv) to Moscow, 29 November 1951: *Documents on Israeli-Soviet Relations*, doc. 92.
125. Memorandum from Vyshinsky and Men'shikov (Ministry of Foreign Trade) to Stalin, 17 September 1951, *Blizhnevostochnyi Konflikt*, doc. 90.
126. Kozyrev (Cairo) to Moscow, 29 January 1953, ibid., doc. 110.
127. Kozyrev (Cairo) to Moscow, 10 February 1953, ibid., doc. 111. Also see the explanatory note at the foot of the telegram.
128. Note from the Soviet government to the Israeli legation in Moscow, 11 February 1953, *Documents on Israeli-Soviet Relations*, doc. 458. Also, *Blizhnevostochnyi Konflikt*, doc. 112 and enclosure.
129. *Blizhnevostochnyi Konflikt*, doc. 113.
130. Kozyrev (Cairo) to Moscow, 13 October 1953, ibid., doc. 116.
131. Solod's record of a conversation with Al-Masri, Egyptian minister to the USSR, 1 February 1954, ibid., doc. 123.

132. Nemchina's record of a conversation with Syrian Minister of Defense Al-Dawalibi, 31 March 1954, ibid., doc. 125.

133. Solod's record of the conversation, 15 June 1954, ibid., doc. 131.

134. Solod's record of the conversation, 8 July 1954, ibid., doc. 133.

135. Zorin to the minister in Syria, 25 December 1954, ibid., doc. 151.

136. Ibid., doc. 159.

137. Solod's record of the conversation, 21 May 1955, ibid., doc. 169.

138. Abramov (Tel Aviv) to Molotov (Moscow), 31 May 1955, ibid., doc. 170.

139. Memorandum, 18 July 1955, ibid., doc. 184.

140. Memorandum from the Near and Middle East Department of the Minindel to Deputy Minister Semyonov, 3 September 1955, ibid., doc. 194.

141. Record of a conversation between the Egyptian ambassador to the USSR and the Soviet ambassador to Egypt, 18 July 1955, ibid., doc. 185.

142. Solod's record of a conversation with Nasser, 9 August 1955, ibid., doc. 189.

143. Solod's record of a conversation with Nasser, 15 September 1955, ibid., doc. 201.

144. Solod's record of a conversation with the head of Nasser's private office, Ali Sabry, 26 September 1955, ibid., doc. 204.

145. Solod's record of a conversation with Nasser, 29 September 1955, ibid., doc. 206.

146. Ibid.

147. It was Harold Macmillan, Britain's Foreign Secretary, who raised the spirit of Geneva in conversation with Molotov on 29 October: Molotov (Geneva) to Moscow, 30 October 1955, ibid., doc. 218.

148. Solod's record of a conversation with Nasser, 18 October 1955, ibid., doc. 210.

149. Molotov's conversation with Israeli Foreign Minister Sharett, 31 October 1955, Molotov (Geneva) to Moscow, 1 November 1955, ibid., doc. 220; letter from Solod to Moscow on "The Question of Arab-Israeli Relations," 4 December 1955, ibid., doc. 226.

150. Chargé d'affaires Gerasimov's conversation with Nasser, 23 January 1956, ibid., doc. 232.

151. Kiselev (Cairo) to Moscow, 14 April 1956, ibid., doc. 243.

152. *John Foster Dulles Oral History Project*, Firestone Library, Princeton University, Couve de Murville testimony, p. 13.

153. Citing Minindel archives: N. Abramov, "K 200-letiyu MID Rossii: SHEPILOV Dmitrii Trofimovich," *Diplomaticheskii Vestnik*, no. 8, August, 2002, p. 138.

154. Address to a conference of the heads of mission in Europe, 28–30 June 1955, Nehru, *Selected Works*, vol. 29 (New Delhi 2001) p. 250.

155. Nehru to Secretary-General, 18 December 1954, ibid., vol. 27.

156. Speech to a closed session, 22 April 1955, *Selected Works*, vol. 28 (New Delhi 2001) p. 101.

157. "Poslednyaya 'Antipartiinaya' Gruppa: Stenograficheskii otchet iyunskogo (1957 g.) plenuma TsK KPSS," third session, 24 June 1957, *Istoricheskii Arkhiv*, no. 4, 1993, p. 35.

158. V. Zubok, "Soviet Intelligence and the Cold War: The 'Small' Committtee of Information, 1952–53," *Cold War International History Project, Working Paper 4*, 1992, p. 12.

159. Löwenthal (Washington DC), 27 September 1952: A. Schilcher, ed., *Österreich und die Grossmächte: Dokumente zur österreichischen Außenpolitik, 1945–1955* (Wien-Salzburg 1980) pp. 167–168.

160. Erofeev, *Diplomat*, p. 163.

161. "Memuary Nikity Sergeevich Khrushcheva," *Voprosy Istorii*, no. 7, 1993, pp. 74–76.

162. Record by Dr Gleissner, November 1954: *Österreich und die Grossmächte*, doc. 98.

163. Bischoff (Moscow) to Vienna, 25 February 1955, ibid., doc. 101.

164. Memcon, Vienna, 13 May 1955, *FRUS, 1955–1957*, vol. 5, doc. 72.

165. S. Khrushchev, *Nikita Khrushchev: krizisy i rakety—Vzglyad iznutri* (Moscow 1994) pp. 82–83.

166. Bohlen, *Witness to History*, p. 382.

167. "Memuary . . . ," pp. 71–72.

168. Ibid., p. 75.

169. Ibid., pp. 72–73.

170. Memorandum of Discussion at the 249th Meeting of the National Security Council, Washington, May 19, 1955, *FRUS, 1955–1957*, vol. 5, doc. 117.

171. Sir Roger Makins (Washington DC) to London, 15 June 1955, FO 371/118218.

172. Geneva Conference of Heads of Governments—UK Delegation (Geneva) to London, 19 July 1955, FO 371/118234.

173. "Memuary Nikity Sergeevicha Khrushcheva," *Voprosy Istorii*, nos. 8–9, 1992, p. 75.

174. Ibid., p. 77.

175. D. Kosthorst, *Brentano und die deutsche Einheit: Die Deutschland-und Ostpolitik des Außenministers im Kabinett Adenauer, 1955–1961* (Düsseldorf 1993) p. 64.

176. Protocol of Presidium meeting, 6 November 1955: *Prezidium TsK KPSS, 1954–1964*, vol. 1 (Moscow 2003) doc. 16.

177. 289th meeting of the NSC, 28 June 1956, Eisenhower Library and Archives, Ann Whitman file, NSC 8.

178. Quoted in a minute by Rose on a dispatch from Sir Frederick Hoyer Millar (Bonn) to London, 1 October 1956, FO 371/124525.

179. *United Nations Treaty Series 1952*, vol. 136, pp. 45–146.

180. Reaffirmation of NSC 125/3, 7 August 1952, Eisenhower Library and Archives, WHO OSANSA, Special Assistants Series, Presidential Subseries, 1, President's Papers 1953 (5).

181. 228th meeting of the NSC, 9 December 1954, ibid., Ann Whitman file, NSC 6.

182. 177th meeting of the NSC, 23 December 1953, ibid., Ann Whitman file, NSC 5.

183. NSC 162/2, 30 October 1953. Eisenhower Library and Archives, White House Office, Office of the Special Assistant for National Security Affairs, NSC Series, Policy Papers Subseries, Basic National Security Policy (1).

184. Dulles to Dean Rusk at the Rockefeller Foundation, 29 December 1953, Eisenhower Library and Archives, Dulles, J. F., Chronological Series, box 6.

185. 210th meeting of the NSC, 12 August 1954, Eisenhower Library and Archives, NSC Series, loc. cit.

186. Secretary Kyes, at 185th meeting of the NSC, 17 February 1954, ibid., Ann Whitman file, NSC Series, 5.

187. *Keesing's Contemporary Archive*, vol. 10, 1955–56, pp. 14006–7.

188. "Postanovlenie plenuma TsK KPSS: Ob antipartiinoi gruppe Malenkova, G. M., Kaganovicha, L. M., Molotova, V. M.," 29 June 1957, *Pravda*, 4 July 1957.

189. *Izvestiya*, 17 December 1954.

190. Quoted in J. Osborne, "The Importance of Ambassadors," *Fortune*, April 1957, p. 151; repeated in J. Allison, *Ambassador from the Prairie* (Boston 1973) p. 292.

191. "U.S. Policy toward Japan," 9 April 1955, NSC 5516/1, Eisenhower Library and Archives, WHO OSANSA, NSC Series, Policy Papers Subseries, 15.

192. Dening (Tokyo) to Allen (London), 22 June 1955, FO 371/115233.

193. Minute by Higgins, 15 September 1955, FO 371/115234.

194. Minute by Bullard on Harpham (Tokyo) to London, 20 December 1956, FO 371/121041.

195. A. Bérard, *Une Ambassade au Japon* (Paris 1980) p. 67.

196. Skagen, labor attaché, for Allison (Tokyo) to Washington, end of August 1956, US National Archives, Department of State, 661.941/8–3156.

197. "US Policy toward Japan", (1), NSC 5516/1, Eisenhower Library and Archives, WHO OSANSA, NSC Series, Policy Papers Subseries, 15.

198. Quoted in Haslam, "The Pattern of Soviet-Japanese Relations since World War II, Russia and Japan: An Unresolved Dilemma between Distant Neighbors," in *Russia and Japan . . .* , ed. T. Hasegawa, J. Haslam, and A. Kuchins (Berkeley 1993) p. 17.

CHAPTER 6. SUDDEN FROST

Epigraph: Memcon, Khrushchev with Mao, 3 August 1958, Volkogonov Papers, box 23.

1. C. D. Jackson log entry, Monday, July 11, 1955, *FRUS*, vol. 5, doc. 155.

2. Original text first published in Russia under Gorbachev: *Izvestiya TsK KPSS*, no. 3, 1989, pp. 128–170.

3. Dejean (Moscow) to Paris, 12 March 1956: *Documents Diplomatiques Français*, 1956, vol. 1 (Paris 1988) doc. 163.

4. Toranska, ed., *"Them,"* p. 174.

5. Bohlen, *Witness to History*, pp. 398–399.

6. Guy Monod (Warsaw) to Paris, 4 July 1956: *Documents Diplomatiques Français*, 1956 (Paris 1989) doc. 9. The official Polish estimate was 48 dead and 260 wounded.

7. "Relazione della delegazione . . . al Direzione del Partito," 18 July 1956, Archivio PCI.

8. Numbers from the Ministry of Defense archives, cited in Yu. Abramova, "1957-i: vlast' i armiya," *Svobodnaya Mysl'*, no. 12, 1997, p. 95.

9. Ibid., p. 96.

10. *"Them,"* p. 63.

11. *Centrum*, docs. 62–65.

12. "The Solution": B. Brecht, *Poems, 1913–1956* (London 1976) p. 440.

13. *"Them,"* p. 65.

14. A. Orekhov, "K istorii pol'sko-sovetskikh peregovorov 19 oktyabrya 1956g. v Bel'vedere (po novym materialam)," *Konflikty v polsvoennom razvitii vostochnoevropeiskikh stran*, ed. Yu. Novopashin (Moscow 1997) pp. 130–156.

15. Presidium meeting of 20 October 1956, *Prezidium*, doc. 76.

16. Presidium meeting of 21 October 1956, ibid., doc. 77.

17. *"Them,"* pp. 67–68.

18. Politburo meeting of 23 October 1956, *Prezidium*, doc. 78.

19. Politburo meeting of 24 October 1956, ibid., doc. 79.

20. Soutou (Moscow) to Paris, 30 October 1956, *Documents Diplomatiques Français*, 1956, vol. 3, doc. 55.

21. Report from Kryuchkov 16 June 1989 from the Russian archives: www.wilsoncenter .org/index.cfm?topic_id=1409&fuseaction=va2.document&indent . . .

22. S. Kopásci, *Au nom de la classe ouvrière: le mémoire du préfet de police de Budapest en 1956* (Paris 1979) p. 123.

23. Written for the US Department of the Army, "Hungary: Resistance Activities and Potentials (C)," 5 January 1956, National Security Archive.

24. László Borhi, "Containment, Rollback, Liberation or Inaction? The United States and Hungary in the 1950's," *Journal of Cold War Studies*, vol. 1, no. 3, 1999, pp. 67–108.

25. CC CPSU analysis sent to Togliatti, 26 November 1956, Archivio PCI, Fondo Mosca, Lettere PCUS sui fatti d'Ungheria, 198.

26. From Soviet Ministry of Defense archives: A. Kyrov, "Sovetskaya karatel'naya aktsiya v Vengrii (Khronika sobytii 1956g. po materialam voennogo arkhiva)," *Konflikty v pos-levoennom razvitii vostochnoevropesikikh stran*, ed. Yu. Novopashin (Moscow 1997) p. 108.

27. Current Intelligence Weekly Review, 27 September 1956, F-1992–02171, CIA Electronic Reading Room, at www.foia.cia.gov.

28. Kyrov, "Sovetskaya karatel'naya," p. 109.

29. Current Intelligence Bulletin, 24 October 1956, CIA Electronic Reading Room.

30. Kyrov, "Sovetskaya karatel'naya," p. 110; and *Sovetskii Soyuz*, p. 322.

31. For the letter in draft predated 24 October 1956 and the attempts to get the Hungarians to sign it: *Sovetskii Soyuz*, doc. 109 and note 2.

32. Speech reprinted: *Sovetskii Soyuz*, doc. 81.

33. For a contemporary account by the BBC's special correspondent, see G. Mikes, *The Hungarian Revolution* (London 1957). Also, *Sovetskii Soyuz*, pp. 321–323. Current Intelligence Digest, 24 October 1956, CIA Electronic Reading Room.

34. A. Cavendish, *Inside Intelligence* (London 1990) pp. 97 and 103; also R. Garthoff, *A Journey through the Cold War* (Washington DC 2001) p. 16. Cavendish was in MI6, Garthoff, CIA.

35. Oral History Interviews with Andrew J. Goodpaster, OH-378, Eisenhower Library and Archives.

36. Mosley, *Dulles*, pp. 419–420.

37. Protocol no. 48a, 23 October 1956, *Prezidium*, doc. 78.

38. Kyrov, "Sovetskaya karatel'naya," p. 111.

39. Memorandum from Zhukov and Sokolovskii, 24 October 1956: *Sovetskii Soyuz*, doc. 84.
40. CIA, Chronology, 24 October 1956: CIA, "Late News from Hungary," NSC Briefing, 26 October 1956, both in CIA Electronic Reading Room.
41. CIA, Hungary, c. 25 October 1956, ibid.
42. CIA, Chronology, 24 October 1956, ibid.
43. Kyrov, "Sovetskaya karatel'naya," p. 111.
44. Ibid., p. 113.
45. Mikoyan and Suslov (Budapest) to Moscow, 25 October 1956: *Sovetskii Soyuz*, doc. 93.
46. Text: *Sovetskii Soyuz*, doc. 92; also, Eastern Europe, 26 October 1956, ibid. The claim that the two Soviet leaders left the country at noon is incorrect.
47. Ibid.
48. Kyrov, "Sovetskaya karatel'naya," p. 114.
49. To Deputy Director (Intelligence), CIA, 27 October 1956, CIA Electronic Reading Room.
50. To Deputy Director (Intelligence), CIA, 26 October 1956, ibid.
51. To Deputy Director (Intelligence), CIA, 27 October 1956, ibid.
52. Current Intelligence Bulletin, 28 October 1956, ibid.
53. Kyrov, "Sovetskaya karatel'naya," p. 115.
54. To Deputy Director (Intelligence), CIA, 29 October 1956, CIA Electronic Reading Room.
55. Kyrov, "Sovetskaya karatel'naya," p. 116.
56. Current Intelligence Digest, 29 October 1956, CIA Electronic Reading Room.
57. Protokol zasedaniya vengerskogo Natsional'nogo pravitel'stva, 30 October 1956, *Sovetskii Soyuz*, doc. 119.
58. To Deputy Director (Intelligence), CIA, 30 October 1956, CIA Electronic Reading Room.
59. "Deklaratsiya Pravitel'stva Soyuza SSR ob osnovakh razvitiya i dal'neishego ukrepleniya druzhby i sotrudnichestva mezhdu Sovetskim Soyuzom i drugim sotsialisticheskim gosudarstvami," *Pravda*, 31 October 1956.
60. Protocol no. 49, 31 October 1956, *Prezidium*, doc. 82, p. 191.
61. F. Bobkov, *KGB i vlast'* (Moscow 1995) p. 144.
62. Oral History Interview with Andrew Goodpaster, OH-378, Eisenhower Library and Archives.

CHAPTER 7. TAKING THE WORLD TO THE BRINK

Epigraph: O. Troyanovsky, "The Making of Soviet Foreign Policy," *Nikita Khrushchev*, ed. W. Taubman et al. (New Haven 2000) p. 236. Son of the former Soviet ambassador to the United States and brought up in Washington, Troyanovsky, effectively bilingual, was a foreign policy aide to Khrushchev.
1. From the record of a meeting, 16 December 1975: K. Brutents, *Tridtsat' let na Staroi Ploshchadi* (Moscow 1998) p. 270.

2. "Doklad Prezidiuma TsK KPSS," 14 October 1964, *Istochnik*, no. 2, 1998, pp. 113–114.

3. P. Shelest, . . . *Da ne sudimy budete: Dnevnikovye zapisi vospominaniya chlena Politburo TsK KPSS* (Moscow 1994) p. 235.

4. Khrushchev, addressing a Central Committee plenum on 29 October 1957: *Rossiya XX Vek. Dokumenty. Georgii Zhukov. Stenogramma oktyabr'skogo (1957g.) plenuma TsK KPSS i drugie dokumenty*, ed. V. Naumov (Moscow 2001) doc. 19, pp. 380 and 408.

5. M. Zhukova, *Marshal Zhukov—Moi Otets* (Moscow 2007) p. 141.

6. Oral testimony, Cold War Oral History Project, Hoover-Gorbachev Foundation, Hoover Institution Archives (hereafter Hoover-Gorbachev Foundation Oral History Project), box 3.

7. Meeting of the Presidium, 14 October 1964, *Prezidium TsK KPSS*, p. 869.

8. Quoted in Georges-Henri Soutou, *L'alliance incertaine: Les rapports politico-stratégiques franco-allemands, 1954–1996* (Paris 1996) p. 73.

9. Details of the plan were told to Feklisov in 1962 by the former deputy head of the KGB in the GDR: Feklisov, *Za okeanom*, p. 224, footnote 1.

10. V. Falin, *Bez skidok na obstoyatel'stva* (Moscow 1999) p. 79.

11. As expressed to the GDR ambassador to Moscow: König (Moscow) to Berlin, 4 December 1958, translated and reprinted from archives in the *Cold War International History Project Bulletin*, no. 4, Fall 1994, p. 37.

12. Zapis' besedy N. S. Khrushcheva s poslom SShA v SSSR Lluellinom Tompsonom, 9 March 1961, Ulbrichts Büro, DY 30/3663, Bundesarchiv, SAPMO (hereafter BA SAPMO).

13. "Secretary Dulles' News Conference of September 9," *Department of State Bulletin*, no. 1004, 1958.

14. From the Soviet archives: V. Zubok and Z. Vodop'yanova, "Sovetskaya Diplomatiya i Berlinskii Krizis, 1958–1962," *Kholodnaya Voina: Novye podkhody, novye dokumenty* (Moscow 1995) p. 263.

15. Memcon, Khrushchev with Mao, 3 August 1958, Volkogonov Papers.

16. Ibid.

17. Kornienko, *Kholodnaya Voina*, p. 89.

18. Quoted by Douglas Selvage, "New Evidence on the Berlin Crisis, 1958–1962": *Cold War International History Project Bulletin*, no. 11, Winter 1998, p. 200.

19. Quoted in Vaïsse, *La grandeur*, pp. 281–282.

20. *Documents on Germany, 1944–1985* (Washington DC 1985) pp. 552–559.

21. Meeting, 24 January 1959: *Prezidium*, doc. 186.

22. Meeting, 11 February 1959, ibid., doc. 187.

23. Meeting, 21 February 1959, ibid., doc. 188

24. P. Cradock, *Know Your Enemy: How the Joint Intelligence Committee Saw the World* (London 2002) pp. 147–148.

25. Fedor Oleshchuk, in a lecture on 17 March, Owen (Moscow) to Washington, 20 March 1959, US National Archives, Department of State, 661.00/3–2509.

26. *Rossiya XX Vek. Dokumenty. Georgii Zhukov*, p. 428.

27. "'Armiyu nado sdelat' . . . Bez izlishestv': Zapiska N. S. Khrushcheva o voennoe reforme. 1959 g.," *Istoricheskii Arkhiv*, no. 3, 1998, doc. 1, pp. 63–64.

28. Quoted in Vaïsse, *La grandeur*, p. 231.

29. Memorandum for General Maxwell Taylor, Military Representative to the President. Subject: Strategic Air Planning and Berlin, 5 September 1961, National Security Archive.

30. S. Ambrose, *Eisenhower*, vol. 2 (New York 1984) p. 576.

31. From a "most secret" history of Soviet intelligence, produced for training by the KGB: *Istoriya Sovetskikh Organov Gosudarstvennoi Bezopasnosti. Uchebnik* (Moscow 1977) p. 537.

32. Johnson, *United States Cryptographic History*, p. 180.

33. "Memuary Nikity Sergeevicha Khrushcheva," *Voprosy Istorii*, no. 6, 1993, pp. 86 and 87.

34. Memcon, Khrushchev with Mao, 31 July 1958, Volkogonov Papers.

35. "Memuary Nikity Sergeevicha Khrushcheva," *Voprosy Istorii*, no. 10, 1993, p. 47.

36. *Sovetskie vooruzhennye sily: istoriya stroitel'stva* (Moscow 1978) p. 285.

37. M. Armitage and R. Mason, *Air Power in the Nuclear Age*, 2nd ed. (Urbana 1985) pp. 157–158; also, *Executive Sessions of the Senate Foreign Relations Committee (Historical Series)*, vol. 12, 86th Cong., 2nd sess., 1960 (Washington DC 1982) p. 349.

38. *Istoriya ural'skogo voennogo okruga* (Moscow 1970) p. 285.

39. Colonel Pen'kovskii, spying in the GRU for MI6, claims to have been on duty that day and thus knew details at first hand: debriefing on 24 April 1961 in Leeds, UK: *The Soviet Estimate*, no. 00289; also in CIA Electronic Reading Room.

40. "Memuary . . . ," p. 48.

41. Thompson (Moscow) to Herter (Washington), 8 September 1960, Eisenhower Library and Archives, Ann Whitman file, Dulles-Herter Series, 11.

42. Pen'kovskii debriefing, 24 April 1961: *The Soviet Estimate*, 00289; also debriefing, 1 May 1961: ibid., 00295.

43. Diary entry, 5 September: C. Sulzberger, *The Last of the Giants* (London 1972) p. 797.

44. Erofeev, *Diplomat*, pp. 464–465.

45. "Memuary . . . ," p. 50.

46. "External and Internal Causes of the Soviet Attitude towards the Summit Conference: Provisional United Kingdom Official View," enclosed in Shattock (London) to Shuckburgh (NATO), 3 June 1960, FO 371/151922.

47. Erofeev, *Diplomat*, p. 467.

48. Ibid., pp. 51–52.

49. King (Moscow) to Foreign Office, 18 May 1960, FO 371/151922.

50. Erofeev, *Diplomat*, pp. 467–468.

51. Ibid., pp. 467–468.

52. Mikoyan, *Tak Bylo*, p. 605.

53. Record of a Presidium discussion, 1 February 1960, *Prezidium*, doc. 211.

54. Erofeev, *Diplomat*, pp. 468–469.

55. V. Kirpichenko, *Razvedka: litsa i lichnosti* (Moscow 1998) pp. 161–162.

56. Gerasimov to Foreign Ministry, Moscow, 28 April 1959: *Rossiya i Afrika: Dokumenty i materialy XVIIIv. –1960g.*, vol. 2 (Moscow 1999) doc. 135.

57. Savinov to the Central Committee, Moscow, 9 May 1959, ibid., doc. 136.

58. K. Kyle, "The UN in the Congo," Ciaonet.org/wps/kye01/.

59. Chambre des Représentants, *Enquête Parlementaire visant à determiner les circon-stances exactes de l'assassinat de Patrice Lumumba et l'implication éventuelle des re-sponsables politiques belges dans celui-ci. Rapport,* vol. 1. Doc 50 0312/006 (Bruxelles 2001) p. 86.

60. Scott (Léopoldville) to London, 22 June 1960, FO 371/146635.

61. Chambre des Représentants, *Enquête,* p. 86.

62. Kyle, "UN in the Congo."

63. Scott (Léopoldville) to London, 19 July 1960, FO 371/146639.

64. Chambre des Représentants, *Enquête,* p. 40.

65. Minute on the Situation in the Congo, 13 July 1960, FO 371/146639.

66. Chambre des Représentants, *Enquête,* pp. 51 and 56.

67. Ibid., p. 62.

68. Kirpichenko, *Razvedka,* p. 162.

69. V. Prokof'ev, *Aleksandr Sakharovskii: Nachal'nik vneshnei razvedki* (Moscow 2005) p. 108.

70. "O pomoshchi Sovetskogo Soyuza Afrikanskim Stranam," 20 September 1963, Arkhiv TsK KPSS, roll 4645, 423 (RTsKhIDNI, Moscow); for the full text, *Rossiya i Afrika,* doc. 138.

71. *Rossiya i Afrika;* for the full text, ibid., doc. 140.

72. Chambre des Représentants, *Enquête,* pp. 160–161.

73. From the archives of the UN: L. De Witte, *L'Assassinat de Lumumba* (Paris 2000) pp. 51–52.

74. Beeley (New York) to London, 31 August 1960, FO 371/146779.

75. "O pomoshchi."

76. Chambre des Representants, *Enquête,* pp. 67–68.

77. Ibid. p. 39.

78. Beeley (New York) to London, 31 August 1960, FO 371/146779.

79. For an instance of this: Foreign Ministry Pierre Wigny to Foreign Ministry, 26 Septem-ber 1960: Chambre des Represéntants, *Enquête,* p. 154.

80. Minute of 28 September 1960, FO 371/146650. Quoted in R. Louis and R. Robinson, "The Imperialism of Decolonization," *Journal of Imperial and Commonwealth His-tory,* vol. 22, no. 3, September 1994, p. 511.

81. O. Nazhestkin, "Gody Kongolezskogo krizisa (1960–1963gg.). Zapiski razvedchika," *Novaya i Noveishaya Istoriya,* no. 6, November–December 2003, p. 157; L. Devlin, *Chief of Station, Congo: A Memoir of 1960–67* (New York 2007) chapter 8.

82. S. Khrushchev, *Rozhdenie Sverkhderzhavy. Kniga ob ottse* (Moscow 2000) pp. 70–71.

83. Taubman, *Khrushchev,* pp. 416–417.

84. The approach was made by the KGB head of station Aleksandr Feklisov, under diplo-matic cover at the embassy: A. Feklisov, *Za okeanom i na ostrove,* pp. 200–201.

85. "Barbaroja" Manuel Piñeiro, *Che Guevara and the Latin American Revolutionary Movements* (Melbourne 2002) p. 43. At that time the red-haired Piñeiro, a graduate of

Columbia University, headed the liaison department dealing with foreign revolutionaries, having run Castro's intelligence operations during the revolt.

86. See Haslam, *The Nixon Administration and the Death of Allende's Chile: A Case of Assisted Suicide* (London 2005)

87. 10 November 1962, Sulzberger, *Last of the Giants*, p. 932.

88. 26 May 1961, *Prezidium*, doc. 235.

89. "'Lenin tozhe riskoval': Nakanune vstrechi Khrushcheva i Kennedi v Venne v Iyule 1961 g.," *Istochnik*, no. 3, 1983, p. 89.

90. Memcon, Khrushchev with Mao, 3 August 1958, Volkogonov Papers, box 23.

91. G. Kornienko, "'Upushchennaya vozmozhnost': Vstrecha N. S. Khrushcheva i Dzh. Kennedi v Vene v 1961 g.," *Novaya i Noveishaya Istoriya*, no. 2, 1992; also, Kornienko, *Kholodnaya Voina: svidetel'stvo ee uchastnika* (Moscow 2001) pp. 85–88; and Dobrynin, *In Confidence*, p. 44.

92. State Department. Memcon. "Meeting between the President and Chairman Krushchev in Vienna," 4 June 1961, Kennedy Library, NSF 187A.

93. H. Brandon, *Special Relationships: A Foreign Correspondent's Memoirs from Roosevelt to Reagan* (New York 1988) p. 169.

94. A copy in translation: *Revelations from the Russian Archives: Documents in English Translation*, ed. D. Koenker and R. Bachman (Washington DC 1996) doc. 336.

95. Meeting of the Presidium, 8 January 1962, *Prezidium*, doc. 243.

96. 5 September 1961, Sulzberger, *Last of the Giants*, p. 798.

97. C. Andrew and V. Mitrokhin, *The Mitrokhin Archive II* (London 2005) p. 40.

98. Quoted from the archives : A. Fursenko, *Rossiya i Mezhdunarodnye Krizisy seredina XX veka* (Moscow 2006) p. 238; also S. Khrushchev, *Rozhdenie Sverkhderzhavy. Kniga ob ottse* (Moscow 2000) pp. 400–402.

99. Fursenko, *Rossiya*, p. 239.

100. Ibid., p. 240.

101. 9 November 1961, ibid., p. 233. See also the ambassador's verbatim account: H. Kroll, *Lebenserinnerungen eines Botschafters* (Köln 1967) p. 526.

102. See also B. Bonwetsch and A. Filitov, "Chruschtschow und der Mauerbau," *Vierteljahrschefte für Zeitgeschichte*, vol. 48, no. 1, January 2000, pp. 155–171.

103. Foreword to John Le Carré, *The Spy Who Came in From the Cold*, p. 6. Le Carré was then working for MI6 in Bonn, having begun in MI5 at Oxford. *News Telegraph*, 9 December 2000.

104. Department of State, Memcon, "Vienna Meeting between the President and Chairman Khrushchev," 3 June 1961, Kennedy Library, NSF 187A.

105. "'Ya veryu v velichie starshego brata'—Besedy N. S. Khrushcheva s Kho Shi Minom," *Istochnik*, no. 2, 1998, pp. 77–78 and 85.

106. P. Abrasimov, *Zapadnyi Berlin: Vchera i segodnya* (Moscow 1980) p. 45.

107. Bohlen (Paris) to Undersecretary Harriman (Washington), 11 July 1963, Kennedy Library, NSF 187A.

108. P. Salinger, *With Kennedy* (London 1967) p. 225. Salinger was White House press secretary.

109. P. Salinger, *With Kennedy* (London 1967) p. 225.
110. Diary entry, 5 September 1961, Sulzberger, *Last of the Giants*, p. 799. For his predecessor's assessment: "Sir Patrick Reilly's Valedictory Despatch," 18 August 1960, PREM 11/3121, National Archives, London.
111. Entry, 4 September 1961, Sulzberger, *Last of the Giants*, p. 784.
112. "Memuary Nikity Sergeevicha Khrushcheva," *Voprosy Istorii*, no. 10, 1992, p. 66.
113. "'ya veryu v velichie starshego brata'—Besedy N. S. Khrushcheva s Kho Shi Minom," *Istochnik*, no. 2, 1998, pp. 88–89.
114. State Department, Memcon, "Vienna Meeting between the President and Chairman Khrushchev," 4 June 1961, Kennedy Library, NSF 187A.
115. *John Foster Dulles Oral History Project*, Firestone Library, Princeton University, Walter Robertson testimony, pp. 14–15, 53, 55, and 75.
116. Entry, 11 May 1955, Sulzberger, *Last of the Giants*, p. 172.
117. NSC 314th Meeting, 28 February 1957, Eisenhower Library and Archives, Ann Whitman files, NSC 8.
118. For the best analysis by far, see Dong Wang, "The Quarrelling Brothers: New Chinese Archives and a Reappraisal of the Sino-Soviet Split, 1959–1962." *Cold War International History Project, Working Paper 49*, pp. 29 and 34.
119. Ibid., p. 42.
120. Dong Wang, "Quarrelling Brothers," p. 52.
121. Ibid., p. 60.
122. Ibid., p. 61.
123. Ibid., pp. 63–65.
124. "Memorandum for General Maxwell Taylor." Some have argued that none of this was significant. But there may be more significance than allowed for when looked at it in the context of the strategic arms limitation talks in the 1970s and Soviet priorities therein. For the leading skeptic: M. Trachtenberg, *A Constructed Peace: The Making of the European Settlement, 1945–1963* (Princeton 1999) pp. 286–297.
125. R. Garthoff, *A Journey through the Cold War* (Washington DC 2001) p. 267. Garthoff was a member of the US delegation.
126. Dulles, also at the NSC, 29 September 1960: *FRUS*, vol. 15, doc. 583.
127. Meeting, 8 January 1962, *Prezidium*, doc. 243.
128. Dobrynin, *In Confidence*, p. 52.
129. *International Security*, vol. 10, no. 1, 1985, p. 177.
130. CIA, "Strains in Soviet-East German Relations, 1962–1967," CIA Electronic Reading Room, www.foia.cia.gov.
131. US National Archives, National Security file (NSF) 186.
132. *Lubyanka 2. Iz istorii otechestvennnoi kontrrazvedki*, ed. V. Sobolev et al. (Moscow 1999) p. 273.
133. *Istoriya sovetskikh organov*, p. 357.
134. A. Tereshchenko, *"Oborotni" is voennoi razvedki: Devyat' predatel'stv sotrudnikov GRU* (Moscow 2004) p. 50.
135. Debriefing, 4 May 1961, CIA Electronic Reading Room.

136. Debriefing, London, 20 April 1961, ibid.

137. Debriefing, Leeds, 23 April 1961, ibid.

138. Debriefing, London, 20 April 1961, ibid.; debriefing, 27 April 1961, ibid.

139. Debriefing, 20 April 1961, ibid.

140. G. Padlow and D. Welzenbach, *The Central Intelligence Agency and Overhead Reconnaissance: The U-2 and OXCART Programs, 1954–1974* (a study partially declassified on 4 March 2002), CIA Electronic Reading Room.

141. I. Bystrova, *Voenno-promyshlennyi kompleks SSSR v gody kholodnoi voiny* (Moscow 2000) p. 44.

142. R. Garthoff, *A Journey through the Cold War* (Washington DC 2001) p. 122. Also Dallek, *John F. Kennedy*, p. 433.

143. Zubok and Vodop'yanova, "Sovetskaya Diplomatiya i Berlinskii Krizis," p. 269.

144. "Janet Chisholm," *Daily Telegraph*, 6 August 2004.

145. L. Mechin, *Shelepin* (Moscow 2009) p. 144.

146. *Lubyanka 2*, pp. 274–275.

147. S. Khrushchev, "Defence Sufficiency and the Military-Political Conception of Nikita Khrushchev, 1953–1964," in *Personalities, War and Diplomacy: Essays in International History*, ed. T. Otte and C. Pagedas (London 1997) p. 22.

148. Testimony of Colonel General Andrian Danilevich, J. Hines et al., eds., *Soviet Intentions, 1965–1985*, vol. 2: *Soviet Post-Cold War Testimonial Evidence* (produced in 1995) p. 38.

149. *Prezidium*, doc. 243.

150. N. Brusnitsyn, *Kto podslushivaet prezidentov—ot Stalina do El'tsina* (Moscow 2000) p. 91.

151. I. Kasatonov, *Flot vyshel v okean* (Moscow 1996) p. 355.

152. G. Kostev, *Voenno-Morskoi Flot strany 1945–1955: vzlety i padeniya* (St. Petersburg 1999) pp. 7–8.

153. Ibid., pp. 119–120.

154. Ibid., p. 119.

155. Ibid., p. 124.

156. *Soviet Intentions, 1965–1985*, vol. 2, ed. J. Hines et al., p. 75.

157. CIA, "Soviet Strategic Doctrine for the Start of War," 3 July 1962 (but classified Soviet material used only into the autumn of 1961), CIA Electronic Reading Room, www .foia.cia.gov/browse_docs_full.asp.

158. J. Blight and D. Welch, *On the Brink: Americans and Soviets Reexamine the Cuban Missile Crisis*, 2nd ed. (New York 1990) p. 238.

159. Mikoyan, *Tak Bylo*, p. 606.

160. Unpublished, quoted in N. Simonov, *Voenno-promyshlennyi kompleks SSSR v 1920–1950-e gody: tempy ekonomicheskogo rosta, struktura, organizatsiya proizvodstva i upravlenie* (Moscow 1996) p. 299.

161. 8 January 1962, *Prezidium*, doc. 243.

162. Interview, 7 November 1995, *The Foreign Affairs Oral History Collection of the Association for Diplomatic Studies and Training: Selected and Converted*, American Memory, Library of Congress, p. 18.

163. Gribkov at the Carnegie Endowment, 2000, www.ceip.org/cuban-missile-crisis/transcript.htm.

164. Memorandum to members of the Presidium, 8 December 1959: "Armiyu nado sdelat' . . . bez izlishestv"—"Zapiska N. S. Khrushcheva o voennoi reforme. 1959 g.," *Istoricheskii Arkhiv*, no. 3, 1998, pp. 63–64.

165. Quoted in Vaïsse, *La grandeur*, p. 247.

166. A. Gromyko, *Pamyatnoe*, vol. 1 (Moscow 1990) p. 480.

167. Meeting of 21 May, *Prezidium*, doc. 249; and 24 May, ibid.

168. Mikoyan, *Tak Bylo*, p. 606.

169. A. Gribkov, "Karibskii krizis," *Voenno-istoricheskii zhurnal*, no. 10, 1992, pp. 41–42 and 45.

170. Quoted in full in D. Volkogonov, *Sem' Vozhdei: Galereya liderov SSSR*, vol. 1 (Moscow 1995) p. 421.

171. "'Voz'mem,'" *Ogonek*, no. 44–46, 1992.

172. B. Putilin, "Karikbskii Krizis," *Sovetskaya vneshnaya politika v gody "Kholodnoi Voiny,"* 1945–1985, ed. L. Nezhinskii (Moscow 1995) p. 287. Putilin cites documents from the Ministry of Defense archive.

173. "'Voz'mem, k primeru, prostuyu pushku . . . ,' ili 'meropriyatie 'Anadyr,'" *Ogonek*, no. 44–46, 1992.

174. Gribkov, "Karibskii," pp. 43–45.

175. Volkogonov, *Sem' Vozhdei*, p. 426.

176. Putilin, "Karibskii," p. 45.

177. Ibid., p. 46.

178. Mikoyan, *Tak Bylo*, p. 606.

179. Putilin, "Karibskii," p. 289.

180. Dobrynin, "The Caribbean Crisis: An Eyewitness Account," *International Affairs* (Moscow), no. 8, 1992; Putilin, "Karibskii," p. 46.

181. Jon Lee Anderson, *Che Guevara*, p. 528.

182. Putilin, "Karibskii," p. 34.

183. Ibid., p. 37.

184. Ibid., p. 40.

185. From US intelligence sources: J. Hughes and Denis Clift, "Cuban Missile Crisis: The San Cristobal Trapezoid," *Studies in Intelligence*, 1990–1994, pp. 149–165. Hughes was special assistant to Lt. General Joseph Carroll, director of the Defense Intelligence Agency, responsible for reconnaissance intelligence support for the Secretary of Defense and others during the missile crisis.

186. Alekseev testimony, *GB99 KCLMA*, 28/65.

187. Putilin, "Karibskii," p. 46.

188. The occasion was Mikoyan's visit to secure cooperation in resolving the crisis with the United States: "We knew that the deployment of missiles in Cuba had in sight [*sic*] the defense of the Socialist Camp. They were important not only in the military terms, but also from a psychological and political point of view." Reprinted from Cuban archives, *Cold War International History Project Bulletin*, nos. 8–9, Winter 1996/1997, p. 342.

189. János Beck (Havana) to János Péter (Budapest), 24 January 1963, Cold War History Research Center, Budapest, www.coldwar.hu.

190. C. Julien, "Sept heures avec M. Fidel Castro," *Le Monde,* 22 March 1963.

191. Quoted in Tomás Diez Acosta, *October 1962: The "Missile" Crisis as Seen from Cuba* (New York 2002) p. 101. Diez, a trusted historian of the regime based his account on interviews with Cubans and Russians involved in the events. Former intelligence analyst Ramond Garthoff cites other statements by Castro to the same effect: R. Garthoff, *Reflections on the Cuban Missile Crisis* (Washington DC 1987) p. 7.

192. Thompson (Moscow) to Washington, 25 July 1962, *FRUS, 1961–1963,* vol. 15, doc. 87.

193. Putilin, "Karibskii," p. 289.

194. Memcon, 6 September 1962, *FRUS,* vol. 15, doc. 112.

195. Ibid.

196. *Pravda,* 12 September 1962.

197. Johnson, *United States Cryptographic History,* pp. 330–331.

198. Diez, *October 1962,* p. 112.

199. John Le Carré, *The Looking Glass War* (London 1999) p. 76. He was here referring to the SS-4 (the R-12).

200. Danilevich testimony, *Soviet Intentions,* p. 61.

201. Putilin, "Karibskii," p. 293.

202. Ibid.

203. NSF 187.

204. Hughes, "Cuban Missile Crisis," p. 153.

205. Memorandum for the Presidium, 25 September 1962, from Zakharov and Fokin, Volkogonov Papers.

206. Hughes, "Cuban Missile Crisis" p. 155.

207. Flights took place on 29 August; 5, 17, 26, and 29 September; 5 and 7 October: ibid., p. 153.

208. Gribkov, "Karibskii," *Voenno-istoricheskii zhurnal,* no. 12, 1992, p. 32.

209. Gribkov statement at the Carnegie Endowment, 2000, www.ceip.org/cuban-missile-crisis/transcript.htm.

210. R. Helms, *A Look over My Shoulder: A Life in the Central Intelligence Agency* (New York 2003) p. 212. Also, Johnson, *United States Cryptographic History,* p. 324.

211. Brown (Washington) to Edmonds (London), 30 March 1962, FO 371/162372; and Marchant (Havana) to London, 17 August 1962, ibid.

212. Quoted in Hughes, "Cuban Missile Crisis," p. 152.

213. Johnson, *United States Cryptographic History,* p. 332.

214. Quoted in Diez, *October 1962,* p. 121.

215. Hughes, "Cuban Missile Crisis," p. 154.

216. Ibid., p. 155.

217. "Off-the-record meeting on Cuba," 16 October 1962, *International Security,* vol. 10, no. 1, 1985, p. 177.

218. Volkogonov, *Sem' Vozhdei,* p. 247.

219. Rusk to the mission to NATO and the European Regional Organizations, 28 October 1962, *FRUS,* vol. 15, doc. 145.

220. Hughes, "Cuban Missile Crisis," p. 154.
221. www.cnn.com/SPECIALS/cold.war/episodes/12/script.html.
222. Feklisov, *Za okeanom*, p. 219.
223. Quoted in Diez, *October 1962*, pp. 158–159.
224. Johnson, *United States Cryptographic History*, p. 331.
225. Hughes, "Cuban Missile Crisis," p. 157.
226. Johnson, *United States Cryptographic History*, p. 329.
227. Memorandum for the Presidium, 25 September 1962, from Zakharov and Fokin, Volkogonov Papers.
228. The arguments that took place after the crisis on this are detailed in G. Kostev, *Voenno-Morskoi Flot Strany, 1945–1995: Vzlety i Padeniya* (St. Petersburg 1999) pp. 149–150.
229. Diez, *October 1962*, p. 160. It had been expected to arrive between 22 and 25 October: Memorandum for the Presidium, 25 September 1962, from Zakharov and Fokin, Volkogonov Papers.
230. Dobrynin, *In Confidence*, pp. 88–89.
231. Kornienko, *Kholodnaya Voina*, p. 130.
232. Interview, 15 June 1984, *International Security*, vol. 12, no. 4, 1988, p. 92.
233. Ibid., with Major General David Burchinal: ibid., p. 93. He was then deputy chief of staff for plans and operations, USAF headquarters.
234. Kornienko, *Kholodnaya Voina*, p. 129.
235. US National Foreign Assessment Center, *The Development of Soviet Military Power: Trends since 1965 and Prospects for the 1980s*, 13 April 1981, p. 37, CIA Electronic Reading Room.
236. *International Security*, p. 95.
237. Diez, *October 1962*, p. 159.
238. Report to the Presidium from Defense Minister Malinovsky, 24 October 1962: *Cold War International History Project Bulletin*, no. 5, Spring 1995, pp. 73–74.
239. Evident from the text of his message to Kennedy of 26 October.
240. For a rather different but more detailed account of the crisis: A. Fursenko and T. Naftali, *"One Hell of a Gamble": The Secret History of the Cuban Missile Crisis* (London 1997).
241. D. Prokhorov, *Razvedka ot Stalina do Putina* (St. Petersburg 2004) p. 267.
242. For their statement and the record of their press conference in Moscow: "Eshche Odin Proval Amerikanskoi Razvedki," *Pravda*, 7 September 1960. For the background: A. Feklisov, *Za okeanom i na ostrove: zapiski razvedchika*, pp. 207–208.
243. www.edwardjayepstein.com/question_suicide.htm.
244. Prokhorov, *Razvedka*, p. 282.
245. L. Kuz'min, "GUSS—etap v razvitii sovetskoi kriptografii," *Agentura*, Istoriya spetssluzhb, 25 January 2002.
246. L. Tikhvinskii, *Vozvrashchenie k vorotam nebesnogo spokoistviya* (Moscow 2002) p. 199.
247. FO 371/105344.
248. www.peoples.ru/state/ambassadore/viktor_komplektov/.
249. Bohlen, *Witness to History*, pp. 495–496.
250. Oral testimony, Hoover-Gorbachev Foundation Oral History Project, box 4.

251. www.cnn.com/SPECIALS/cold.war/episodes/12/script.html.

252. Department of State, Memcon, "Vienna Meeting betweent the President and Chairman Khrushchev," 4 June 1961, Kennedy Library, NSF 187A.

253. Brigadier J. Davidson-Houston, *Armed Diplomat: A Military Attaché in Russia* (London 1959) p. 54.

254. Department of State to the mission to NATO and the European Regional Organizations, 28 October 1962, *FRUS*, vol. 15, doc. 145.

255. Despite the incoherence of Kennedy's disjointed comment on 19 October (a symptom of stress?), the meaning is clear: "If you take the view, really, that what's basic to them is Berlin and. . . . There isn't any doubt. In every conversation we've had with the Russians, that's what. . . . Even last night we [Gromyko and I] talked about Cuba for a while, but Berlin—that's what Khrushchev's committed himself to personally." *The Kennedy Tapes: Inside the White House during the Cuban Missile Crisis*, ed. E. May and P. Zelikow (Cambridge, Mass. 1998) p. 176.

256. Dobrynin, *In Confidence*, p. 98.

257. Sir Frank Roberts's Report on His Farewell Interview with Khrushchev, 13 November 1962, Kennedy Library, NSF 188.

258. Harriman to Secretary of State, 27 July 1963, US National Archives, NSF 187A.

259. Bohlen (Paris) to Secretary of State (Washington), 13 July 1963, Kennedy Library, NSF 187A.

260. S. Khrushchev, "Defence Sufficiency," p. 224.

261. Conversation with Harold Wilson, Patrick Gordon Walker, Khrushchev, and Gromyko, 10 June 1963, PREM 11/4894, National Archives, London.

262. Zakharov to Gromyko, 5 February 1964, *Ocherki istorii rossiiskoi vneshnei razvedki*, vol. 5 (Moscow 2003), appendix doc. 111.

263. From the KGB, 8 May 1964, ibid., doc. 113.

264. From the KGB, 8 August 1964, ibid., doc. 115.

265. Trevelyan, *Worlds Apart*, p. 219.

266. Trevelyan (Moscow) to London, 4 June 1964, PREM 11/4994.

267. Trevelyan (Moscow) to London, 11 June 1964, ibid.

268. CIA, "Strains in Soviet-East German Relations, 1962–1967."

269. Ibid.

270. "Adzhubei's Visit to West Germany," W. Ledwidge, 10 August 1964, PREM 11/4894.

271. CIA, "Strains in Soviet-East German Relations, 1962–1967."

272. Ibid.

273. "Doklad Prezidiuma TsK KPSS," 14 October 1964, *Istochnik*, no. 2, 1998, p. 117.

CHAPTER 8. DÉTENTE

Epigraph: A. Chernyaev, *Byl li u Rossii shans? On—poslednii* (Moscow 2003) p. 22.

1. The title changed on 8 August 1966.

2. Recollections of interpreter V. Sukhodrev, *Yazyk moi—drug moi: Ot Khrushcheva do Gorbacheva* (Moscow 1999) pp. 259–260; also L. Tikhvinskii, *Vozvrashchenie k vorotam nebesnogo spokoistviya* (Moscow 2000) p. 196.

3. Oral testimony from Aleksandr Yakovlev, Hoover-Gorbachev Foundation Oral History Project, box 4.

4. US National Intelligence Estimate, 28 September 1967, *FRUS*, vol. 14, doc. 248. At this time US intelligence was intercepting conversations between Soviet leaders held on their car phones as they left and arrived at the Kremlin. This material was called Gamma Guppy: M. Aid, *The Secret Sentry: The Untold History of the National Security Agency* (New York 2009) pp. 143–144. This is the main reason why information on the positions and disputes between Soviet leaders is so full for the 1960s.

5. Ibid.

6. Memorandum, 13 January 1967, reprinted in Dobrynin, *In Confidence*, pp. 640–642.

7. S. Khrushchev, *Pensioner Soyuznogo Znacheniya* (Moscow 1991) p. 103.

8. N. Zen'kovich, *Elita: Samye sekretnye rodstvenniki* (Moscow 2005) pp. 31–32; Sukhodrev, *Yazyk Moi*, p. 258; also, *Leonid Brezhnev v vospominaniyakh, razmyshleniyakh, suzhdeniyakh* (Rostov-on-Don 1998), chapter 3; A. Aleksandrov-Agentov, *Ot Kollontai do Gorbacheva* (Moscow 1994) p. 118.

9. Aleksandrov-Agentov, *Ot Kollontai*, p. 257.

10. "Bez popravki na segodnyashnii den," *Ogonek*, no. 10, 28 February 1989.

11. A. Bovin, *XX Vek Kak Zhizn': Vospominaniya* (Moscow 2003) pp. 252–253.

12. G. Murrell, Research Department, Foreign and Commonwealth Office (hereafter FCO), 31 May 1974, FCO 28/2563.

13. Bovin, *XX Vek*, pp. 161 and 255. Shelepin, formerly head of KGB, continued to plot: A. Yakovlev, *Sumerki* (Moscow 2003) p. 222.

14. Mechin, *Shelepin*, p. 322.

15. CIA, *Intelligence Report: Policy and Politics*, pp. 14–15, CIA Electronic Reading Room.

16. CIA, *Intelligence Report: Leonid Brezhnev: The Man and His Power*, 5 December 1969, pp. 11–12, CIA Electronic Reading Room.

17. *Leonid Brezhnev v Vospominaniyakh*, p. 308.

18. A. Shevchenko, *Breaking with Moscow* (New York 1985) p. 149. See also Aleksandrov-Agentov, *Ot Kollontai*, pp. 111–113.

19. Chernyaev, *Moya zhizn' i moe vremya* (Moscow 1995) p. 259.

20. Ibid., pp. 261–262.

21. A. Chernyaev, *Moya zhizn'*, p. 262.

22. K. Brutents, *Tridtsat' Let na Staroi Ploshchadi* (Moscow 1998) p. 167.

23. Afanas'ev, *4-ya Vlast'*, pp. 152–153.

24. The previous chairman, Semichastny, served from 13 November 1961 to 18 May 1967.

25. F. Bobkov, former first deputy chairman, "Yuri Andropov, Kakim Ya Ego Znal," *Rossiiskii Kto Est' Kto*, no. 1, 2004; also www. Fsb.ru/dmi/article/andropov.html.

26. *Rossiskii Kto Est' Kto*, no. 2 (41) 2004, p. 17; I. Ustinov, *Krepche Stali: Zapiski veterana voennoi kontrrazvedki* (Moscow 2005) pp. 169–171; Zen'kovich, *Samye sekretnye*, pp. 8–9.

27. G. Kornienko, *Kholodnaya Voina*, p. 317.

28. G. Arbatov, *Chelovek Sistemy: Nablydeniya i razmyshleniya ochevidtsa ee raspada* (Moscow 2002) p. 368.

29. I. Ustinov, "On ochen' uvazhatel'no otnosilsya k armii," *Krasnaya Zvezda*, 11 June 2004.

30. Bovin, *XX Vek*, p. 245.

31. V. Grishin, *Ot Khrushcheva*, p. 245.

32. V. Kevorkov, *Tainy Kanal* (Moscow 1997) p. 37; also, Arbatov, *Chelovek*, p. 371.

33. V. Kazimirov, "Sataninskaya predannost' delu . . . ," *Krasnaya Zvezda*, 11 June 2004.

34. Kirpichenko, *Razvedka*, pp. 148–149.

35. L. Mlechin, *Yuri Andropov. Poslednaya nadezhda rezhima* (Moscow 2008) pp. 92–93.

36. Bovin, *XX Vek*, pp. 245–246.

37. V. Petrov, "My ozhidali, chto on mnogoe sdelaet . . . ," *Krasnaya Zvezda*, 11 June 2004. Petrov was commander-in-chief of land forces and Deputy Minister of Defense from 1980 to 1985.

38. Boris Stroganov testimony, Hines et al., eds., *Soviet Intentions*, pp. 132–133.

39. Kryuchkov, in *Leonid Brezhnev*, p. 264.

40. Alexandrov-Agentov, *Ot Kollontai*, pp. 265–266; also, *Leonid Brezhnev*, p. 265.

41. Quoted in Chernyaev, *Moya zhizn'*, p. 294.

42. Bobkov, "Yuri Andropov."

43. CIA, National Foreign Assessment Center, *The Foreign Policy Views of Mikhail Suslov*, July 1978, p. 8, CIA Electronic Reading Room at www.foia.cia.gov/browse_doc_full .asp.

44. Minute by Longrigg (FCO Research Department), 1 November 1974, FCO 28/2563.

45. I. Kasatanov, ed., *Tri veka rossiskogo flota* (St. Petersburg 1966) pp. 308–309.

46. V. Makarov, *V General'nom Shtabe nakanune gryadushchikh peremen* (Moscow 2004) p. 327.

47. General Nikolai Detinov, oral testimony, Hoover-Gorbachev Foundation Oral History Project, box 4.

48. Trevelyan, *Worlds Apart*, p. 233.

49. Vladimir Semyonov, present as deputy foreign minister responsible for SALT, recalled this in conversation with Yuli Kvitsinsky: Y. Kvitsinsky, *Vremya i sluchai: Zametki professionala* (Moscow 1999) p. 342.

50. Shevchenko, *Breaking with Moscow*, p. 202.

51. Detinov testimony, GB99 KCLMA, 28/81.

52. *Soviet Intentions*, p. 29.

53. Bovin, *XX Vek*, p. 269.

54. Sukhodrev, *Yazik moi*, p. 190.

55. Ibid., p. 192.

56. Burke Trend to Palliser, 29 February 1968, PREM 13/2405.

57. Chernyaev, *Moya zhizn'*, p. 286. Chernyaev listened to the conversation on the telephone and then heard Brezhnev's retelling of the position to Podgorny, also on the phone.

58. Sukhodrev, *Yazik moi*, p. 256.

59. Arbatov, in *Leonid Brezhnev*, p. 263.

60. Testimony, *Soviet Intentions*, p. 28.
61. CIA, *Research Study: The Soviet Foreign Policy Apparatus* (1976) pp. 4 and 15, CIA Electronic Reading Room.
62. Dobrynin, *In Confidence*, p. 207.
63. Medvedev , *Chelovek za spinoi*, p. 119.
64. Testimony from Nikolai Yegorychev, first secretary of the Moscow City Committee (1962–67) and member of the Central Committee: *Neizvestnaya Rossiya. XX Vek* (Moscow 1992) p. 301.
65. Pyrlin, *Trudnyi i dolgii put' k miru: Vzglyad iz Moskvy na problemu blizhnevostochnogo uregulirovaniya* (Moscow 2002), p. 83.
66. Chernyaev, *Moya zhizn'*, p. 260. Chernyaev worked as Ponomarev's deputy.
67. Falin, *Bez skidok*, p. 194.
68. Burke Trend to Palliser, 29 February 1968, PREM 13/2405.
69. Recalled by Yuli Kvitsinsky, "Vneshnyaya Politika SSSR v gody Perestroiki," *Nash Sovremennik*, p. 186.
70. Shevchenko, *Breaking with Moscow*, p. 202. Shevchenko was a close adviser to Gromyko and acted as liaison with the KGB: Grinevskii, *Tainy sovetskoi diplomatii*, p. 89.
71. Falin's recollections, Hoover-Gorbachev Foundation Oral History Project, box 4.
72. R. Brigham, *Guerrilla Diplomacy: The NLF's Foreign Relations and the Viet Nam War* (Ithaca 1999) p. 5.
73. Ibid., p. 10.
74. Ibid., pp. 20–21-
75. Elbridge Dubrow Papers, Hoover Institution, box 40, August 1966.
76. Quoted: I. Gaiduk, *Confronting Vietnam: Soviet Policy toward the Indochina Conflict, 1954–1963* (Washington DC/ Stanford 2003) p. 187
77. Ibid., p. 193.
78. From Russian archive: I. Gaiduk and O. Marinin, "Voina vo V'etname i sovetsko-amerikanskie otnosheniya," *Kholodnaya Voina: novye podkhody, novye dokumenty* (Moscow 1995) p. 386, footnote 3.
79. *Kholodnaya Voina*, p. 370.
80. INR assessments: "Vietnam 1961–1968 as Interpreted in INR's Production," IV, p. 30, National Security Archive online, George Washington University.
81. "Vietnam 1961–1968."
82. Gaiduk and Marinin, "Voina," pp. 370–371.
83. Trevelyan, *Worlds Apart*, p. 193.
84. Gaiduk and Marinin, "Voina," p. 371.
85. "Vietnam 1961–1968," p. 43.
86. Entry, 1 March 1966, ibid., p. 234.
87. Quoted in a note from the Russians, after meeting North Vietnamese leaders, 24 February 1965, BA SAPMO, Walter Ulbrichts Büro, DY 30.3667.
88. *CIA Historical Review Program*, #496488.
89. Director, Economic Research, CIA, to John Warner, 7 March 1968, ibid., #48328.
90. For Ulbricht, 2 August 1965, BA SAPMO, loc. cit.

91. Ibid.

92. Quoted in "Vietnam 1961–1968," IV, p. 44.

93. Ibid., V, p. 1

94. Report from Malinovsky to the Politburo on the situation at 0800 hours 27 March 1965, Arkhiv TsK KPSS, Rolik 4661, Ed. Khr. 480.

95. Karnow, *Vietnam*, p. 427.

96. "'Zapiska vneshnepoliticheskoi komissii TsK KPSS o normalizatsii sovetsko-kitaiskikh otnoshenii,' 7 January 1965: 'Spor idet o slishkom bol'shikh veshchakh.' Neudavshayasya popytka sovetsko-kitaiskogo primireniya 1964–1965 gg." *Istoricheskii Arkhiv* p. 6.

97. 14 January 1965, Presidium Protocol 187, ibid., p. 14.

98. "Material k besedam s rukovodyashchimi deyatelyami KNR po voprosam mezhgosudarstvennykh otnoshenii," 28 January 1965, ibid., pp. 20–21

99. For Ulbricht, 2 August 1965, BA SAPMO, loc. cit.

100. Danilevich testimony, *Soviet Intentions*, p. 23.

101. N. Salmin, *Internatsionalizm v deistvii: lokal'nye voiny i vooruzhennye konflikty s uchastiem sovetskogo komponenta; voennogo, voenno-tekhnicheskogo, ekonomicheskogo, 1950–1989* (Ekaterinburg 2001) p. 117.

102. *CIA Historical Review Program*, #496488.

103. "Soviet Military Aid to North Vietnam," 13 October 1971, ibid., #483947.

104. Note for Ulbricht, 2 August 1965, BA SAPMO, Walter Ulbrichts Büro, DY 30.3667.

105. Quoted in Qiang Zhai, "Beijing and the Vietnam Conflict, 1964–1965: New Chinese Evidence," *Cold War International History Project Bulletin*, Issues 6–7, Winter 1995/1996, p. 236.

106. Agreed between Hanoi and Beijing, June 1965, ibid.

107. Chen Jian, *Mao's China and the Cold War* (Chapel Hill 2001) p. 219.

108. "Aktenvemerk des Genossen Bergold, Botschafter in der DRV mit dem polnischen Botschafter in der DRV, genossen Siedliecky, am 9.11.1966," BA SAPMO, Ulbricht, DY 30.3667.

109. Ibid.

110. Information from Zverev at the Soviet embassy in Hanoi, related to the East Germans: Winzer to Ulbricht, Stoph, Honecker, and Axen, 8 September 1966, ibid.

111. "Abschrift eines Aktenvermerkes unserer Botschaft in Hanoi über eine Information des Genossen Peschtscherikow, 3. Sekretär der botschaft der UdSSR in Hanoi" (no date but circa 1966–67), ibid.

112. Rostow to Dobrynin, June 1966: Dobrynin, *In Confidence*, p. 142.

113. Excerpts from the second conversation with Kosygin, Harriman Papers, box 481.

114. Memcon, 21 May 1966, ibid., box 586.

115. Ibid.

116. *Entsiklopediya sekretnykh sluzhb rossii*, ed. A. Kolpakidi et al. (Moscow 2004) pp. 770–771.

117. Trevelyan, *Worlds Apart*, p. 226.

118. Bovin, *XX Vek*, pp. 134–135.

119. Account dictated by Mikoyan, 1 June 1965: verbatim in V. Prybitkov, *Apparat* (St. Petersburg 1995) pp. 83–84.

120. Ibid., pp. 85–86.

121. Mechin, *Shelepin*, p. 346.

122. Memcon 21 July 1965, Harriman Papers, box 587.

123. A. Yepishev to the Politburo, 6 October 1965: Arkhiv TsK KPSS. Rolik 4661. Ed. Khr. 480.

124. US embassy (Djakarta) to Department of State, 10 September 1965, Lyndon Baines Johnson Library and Museum (hereafter LBJ Library), NSF, Country File, Asia and the Pacific, Indonesia, box 247.

125. Dorget (Djakarta) to Paris, 22 January 1965, France, Ministry of Foreign Affairs (MaE) Asie-Océanie, Indonésie 1956–1967, 121.

126. V. Marchetti and J. Marks, *The CIA and the Cult of Intelligence* (London 1974) pp. 166 and 299.

127. Telegram from General Hertzfeld, 24 March 1965, BA SAPMO, Abteilung Internationale Verbindungen. Information Nr. 24/65 für die Mitglieder und Kandidaten des Politbüros über die Meinung der KP Indonesiens zum konsultativen Treffen der Bruderpartein in Moskau.

128. Memcon, Marshall Green and the Vice President, 17 February 1967, LBJ Library, NSF, Country File, Indonesia, vol. 7.

129. FO Guidance Telegramme, 18 May 1965, FO 371/180326.

130. CIA Intelligence Information Cable, 1 March 1965, LBJ Library, loc. cit.

131. Minute by Holland, 26 May 1965, FO 371/180326.

132. Minute by Derek Tonkin, 28 May 1965, ibid.

133. Cambridge (Djakarta) to SEAD, 1 December 1965, FO 371/180325.

134. Cambridge (Djakarta) to Tonkin (London), 25 November 1965, ibid.

135. Toussaint (Tokyo) to Paris (no date), *MaE*, Indonésie . . . .

136. "O Politicheskoi Obstanovke v Indonezii v Svyazi s Sobytiyami 30 Sentyabrya 1965 goda," 10 October 1965, Arkhiv TsK KPSS, reel 4661, item 480.

137. Cambridge (Djakarta) to London, 1 December 1965, FO 371/180325.

138. Cambridge (Djakarta) to Tonkin (London), 25 November 1965, FO 371/180325.

139. K. Kadane, "Ex-agents Say CIA Compiled Death Lists for Indonesians," *San Francisco Examiner*, 20 May 1990.

140. Rostow to Johnson, 8 June 1966, LBJ Library.

141. From Japanese Party archives: J. Chang and J. Halliday, *Mao: The Unknown Story* (London 2005) p. 520.

142. US embassy (Djakarta) to Washington, 4 November 1965, LBJ Library, vol. 5.

143. Quoted in McNamara, *In Retrospect*, p. 215.

144. Memcon, 21 July 1966, Harriman Papers, box 587.

145. Ibid.

146. Quoted in Dobrynin, *In Confidence*, p. 157.

147. Memcon, meeting with Foreign Secretary George Brown, 19 April 1967, Harriman Papers, box 586.

148. Interview, November 1972: O. Fallaci, *Intervista con la storia* (Milan 2008) p. 31.

149. Memcon, 30 September 1966, Harriman Papers, box 481.

150. Major-General V. Zolotarev, *Rossiya (SSSR) v lokal'nykh konfliktakh vtoroi poloviny XX Veka* (Moscow 2000) p. 93.

151. Briefing for Warsaw Pact allies, Soviet embassy, Hanoi, 12 October 1967. Note for Walter Ulbricht, 24 October 1967, BA SAPMO, Walter Ulbrichts Büro, DY 30/3667.

152. Soviet ambassador to the Lebanon, Nikiforov, with representative of the PLO Ahmed Shukeiri, 9 August 1965, *Blizhnevostochnyi Konflikt*, doc. 214.

153. Chuvakhin (Tel Aviv) to Gromyko (Moscow), 21 March 1966, *Blizhnevostochnyi Konflikt*, doc. 220.

154. R. Teitelbaum, "What Now, Comrade Sneh?" *Haaretz* (magazine), 28 May 2009.

155. Memorandum from Gromyko to the Politburo, 31 October 1966, *Blizhnevostochnyi Konflikt*, doc. 235.

156. Semyonov's record of a conversation with Kats, 9 November 1966, ibid., doc. 237.

157. Gromyko to the Politburo, November 1966, ibid., doc. 238.

158. Slyusarenko's record of the conversation, 15 November 1966, ibid., doc. 239.

159. S. Ben-Ami, *Scars of War, Wounds of Peace: The Israeli-Arab Tragedy* (London 2005) p. 100.

160. G. Rafael, *Destination Peace. Three Decades of Israeli Foreign Policy: A Personal Memoir* (New York 1981) p. 122. The Russians omit this note from their published collection, no doubt from embarrassment.

161. Gromyko's record of the conversation, 13 May 1967, *Blizhnevostochnyi Konflikt*, doc. 248.

162. Brezhnev's address to the Central Committee 20 June 1967 reprinted from the SED archive: "The Cold War in the Middle East" collection, 13AE3DE5-A34E-31C5-3F18C938B1E61F91, Cold War International History Project, Washington DC.

163. CIA Report, March 1967, "Soviet Military Aid to the United Arab Republic, 1955–66," *CIA Historical Review Program*, #496350.

164. Pozhidaev's record of the conversation, 16 May 1967, ibid., doc. 249.

165. Brezhnev's address.

166. Middle East Crisis: Chronological Guide, May 12–June 20, LBJ Library, NSF 17.

167. Rafael, *Destination Peace*, p. 137.

168. Memcon, Fyodorenko and the Egyptian ambassador, 17 May 1967, *Blizhnevostochnyi Konflikt*, doc. 250.

169. Memcon, Pozhidaev and Vice President Marshal Amer, 19 May 1967, ibid., doc. 251.

170. A. Eban, *Personal Witness* (London 1993) p. 359.

171. Brezhnev's address, loc. cit.

172. Memcon by Pozhidaev, 19 May 1967, *Blizhnevostochnyi Konflikt*, doc. 251.

173. Gromyko (Moscow) to Fyodorenko (New York), 21 May 1967, ibid., doc. 252.

174. Memcon by Pozhidaev, 22 May 1967, ibid., doc. 253. "Unfortunately, our Government had not been informed beforehand of this action which had serious repercussions," Brezhnev acknowledged: Brezhnev's address, loc. cit.

175. Eban, *Personal Witness*, p. 408.

176. P. Akopov, "Blizhnii Vostok—1967 god," 17 May 2004: www.mirros.ru/politics/1967.

177. D. Ben-Gurion, *Israel: A Personal History* (London 1972) p. 771.

178. Fyodorenko (New York) to Moscow, 29 May 1967, *Blizhnevostochnyi Konflikt*, doc. 258.

179. Rostow to Johnson, 4 June 1967, LBJ Library, NSF, *NSC History*, Middle East Crisis, box 18, vol. 3, May 12–June 19, 1967.

180. 31 May 1967, ibid., box 17. Middle East Crisis: Chronological Guide, May 12–June 20.

181. Rostow to Johnson, 4 June 1967, Middle East Crisis, box 18, vol. 3, May 12- June 19, 1967.

182. E. Pyrlin, *Trudnyi i dolgii put' k miru: Vzglyad iz Moskvy na problemu blizhnevostoch-nogo uregulirovaniya*, p. 59.

183. Tarasenko testimony, *GB99 KCLMA*, 28/82.

184. Sukhodrev testimony, ibid., 28/71.

185. 3 June 1967, Middle East Crisis: Chronological Guide.

186. Eban, *Personal Witness*, p. 405. Also interview with Rostow.

187. Memcon, Pozhidaev with Nasser, 1 June 1967, *Blizhnevostochnyi Konflikt*, doc. 260.

188. From the Russian archives: M. Monakov, *Glavkom. Zhizn' i deyatel'nost' Admirala flota Sovetskogo Soyuza S. G. Gorshkova* (Moscow 2008) p. 548.

189. Shevchenko, *Breaking with Moscow*, p. 134.

190. Johnson, *United States Cryptographic History*, p. 431.

191. LBJ Library, Middle East Crisis, pp. 134–135. Agreement to cease-fire proposals also sent by hotline at 5:34 a.m. Moscow time, 6 June.

192. H. Saunders to Kissinger, 31 March 1970, Nixon Presidential Materials Project, NSC, Country File, Middle East, box 666. The message went out at 6:07 p.m. Moscow time on 6 June and referred also to a withdrawal of forces: LBJ Library, Middle East Crisis, vol. 7, appendices G–H, p. 14.

193. Note dated 6 June 1967: LBJ Library, NSF Country File, Europe and USSR, USSR, box 229.

194. President's Daily Brief, 7 June 1967: LBJ Library, NSC, Middle East Crisis, May 12–June 19, box 19, vol. 6, appendices.

195. CIA Archives, "Soviet Global Military Reach (NIE 11–6-84)," CIA Electronic Reading Room.

196. Tarasenko testimony, Hoover-Gorbachev Foundation Oral History Project.

197. Special Counsel Harry McPherson from Israel to Johnson, 11 June 1967, Middle East Crisis: Chronological Guide, LBJ Library.

198. Lyndon Johnson, 9 June 1967, ibid.

199. Dispatched 8:48 a.m., Moscow time, 10 June, NSC, ibid.

200. Garthoff, *Journey Through the Cold War*, p. 215.

201. Johnson at an NSC special committee, 12 June 1967, Middle East Crisis: Chronological Guide.

202. Dobrynin, *In Confidence*, pp. 149–150.

203. Memcon by Llewellyn Thompson, 7 December 1966, *FRUS, 1964–1968*, vol. 11 (Washington DC 1997) doc. 168 and footnote 2, p. 405.

204. Washington to the Moscow embassy, 15 February 1967, ibid., docs. 181 and 182.

205. Ibid., doc. 185.

206. Thompson (Moscow) to Washington, 28 February 1967, ibid., doc. 187.

207. Notes of a meeting, 14 March 1967, *FRUS, 1964–1968*, vol. 11, doc. 191.

208. Memcon, 4 October 1967, ibid., doc. 212.

209. Grishin, *Ot Khrushcheva*, p. 323.

210. Inside information obtained by the CIA Directorate of Intelligence, "Soviet Premier Kosygin's Foreign Policy Role," 3 October 1977, *CIA Historical Review Program*, #498511, p. 5, CIA Electronic Reading Room.

211. Ibid.

212. See P. Ahonen, "Franz-Josef Strauss and the German Nuclear Question, 1956–1962," *Journal of Strategic Studies*, vol. 18, no. 2, June 1995, pp. 25–51.

213. Memcon, 24 November 1965, LBJ Library, NSF 229.

214. TASS declaration: *Pravda*, 15 November 1964; followed by a Note warning of unspecified retaliation: *Pravda*, 19 January 1965.

215. Information from Gawewski, Polish ambassador to France until 1961, working on foreign relations for the Sejm: entry, 3 December 1968, Sulzberger, *Age of Mediocrity*, p. 484.

216. Memcon, Glassboro, 25 June 1967, *FRUS, 1964–1968*, vol. 14 (Washington DC 2001) doc. 234.

217. Memorandum: *Pravda*, 8 December 1964.

218. D. Salvage, "Poland, the German Democratic Republic, and the German Question, 1955–1967" (PhD diss., Yale University, 1998) p. 29.

219. *Pravda*, 22 January 1965.

220. Bohlen (Paris) to Washington, 11 July 1963, Kennedy Library, NSF 187A. The information came from André de Staercke, Belgian representative to NATO, who accompanied Spaak to Moscow.

221. A firm impression formed from extensive discussions with Erofeev.

222. Entry, 22 January 1964, Sulzberger, *Age of Mediocrity*, p. 60.

223. Noted by allied diplomats: Ledwidge (Paris) to London, 7 August 1967, FCO 33/111.

224. McGhee (Bonn) to Washington, 23 February 1967, *FRUS, 1964–1968*, vol. 13, doc. 292.

225. Circular telegram to NATO posts, 2 March 1966, ibid., doc. 135.

226. Erofeev, *Diplomat*, p. 412.

227. Erhard to de Gaulle, 4 July 1964: "The American thesis is that German reunification will come about thanks to détente," MaE, Archives du Sécretariat Général, 1945–1968, vols. 22–23.

228. A characterization later given by Kryuchkov (Moscow) to all residents, 26 July 1977: C. Andrew and O. Gordievsky, eds., *More "Instructions from the Centre": Top Secret Files on KGB Global Operations, 1975–1985* (London 1992) p. 39.

229. Quoted in "Bund mit dem Teufel," *Der Spiegel*, 13 February 1995.

230. Jackling (Bonn) to London, 9 October 1968, FCO 33/569.

231. *Akten zur Auswärtigen Politik der Bundesrepublik Deutschland* (hereafter *Akten*), vol. 1, 1966, ed., H-P. Schwarz (Munich 1997) doc. 58.

232. Ibid.

233. Von Walther (Moscow) to Bonn, 25 May 1966, ibid., doc. 166.

234. Meeting between Kosygin and Foreign Secretary George Brown, c. 15 February 1967, FCO 33/110.

235. H. Schmidt, *Menschen und Mächte* (Berlin 1987) p. 177.

236. Entry, 25 October 1969, Sulzberger, *Age of Mediocrity*, p. 583.

237. Roberts (Bonn) to London, 5 January 1967, FCO 33/110.

238. Ibid.

239. Stewart (Bonn) to London, 27 January 1967, ibid.

240. Memcon, 17 December 1964, MaE, Amérique 1964–1970, 575.

241. "Vermerk des Referenten Bahr," 22 February 1967, *Akten*, doc. 65.

242. The Tutzing speech can be found on the World Wide Web. For more, see D. Cramer, *Gefragt: Egon Bahr* (1975) p. 42.

243. Ibid., p. 39. For more: "Wir haben Freiräume geschaffen," a conversation with Bahr, *Spiegel Special* no. 3, 2008, pp. 88–92.

244. Memcon, Brandt and Couve de Murville meeting of 27 April 1967, dated 5 May 1967, MaE, Archives du Sécretariat Général, Entretiens et Messages, vol. 30.

245. "Einige Haputprobleme der innen-und außenpolitischen Entwicklung in der CSSR im Jahre 1967," Berlin, 20 February 1968, BA SAPMO, Walter Ulbrichts Büro, DY30. 3416.

246. "Aufzeichnung des Legationsrats 1. Klasse Wilke," 14 June 1967, *Akten, 1967*, vol. 2, doc. 218.

247. Kornienko, "*Kholodnaya Voina*," p. 212.

248. Brezhnev's remarks to a meeting of leading Czech Party officials, Prague, 9 December 1967: *The Prague Spring 1968: A National Security Archive Documents Reader*, ed. J. Navratil et al. (Prague 1998) doc. 3.

249. A. Dubček, *Hope Dies Last* (London 1993) p. 120.

250. *Prague Spring*, doc. 4.

251. Board of National Estimates CIA, Special Memorandum, "Czechoslovakia: A New Direction," 12 January 1968, Lyndon Johnson Library, NSF 179.

252. Dubček, *Hope*, p. 134.

253. *Prague Spring*, doc. 8.

254. Dubček, *Hope*, p. 136.

255. *Prague Spring*, doc. 9.

256. Ibid., note 19.

257. Ibid., doc. 14.

258. I. Ustinov, *Krepche Stali: Zapiski veterana voennoi kontrrazvedki* (Moscow 2005) p. 163.

259. *Prague Spring*, doc. 24.

260. A. Margelov and V. Margelov, *Desantnik No 1 general armii Margelov* (Moscow 2003) p. 410.

261. *Prague Spring*, doc. 26.

262. Ibid., doc. 28, footnote 12.

263. Ibid., doc. 28.

264. S. Kondrashev, "Yu. V. Andropov," *Komanda Andropova* (Moscow 2005) pp. 114–115.

265. Summit, 2–5 May 1968: *Prague Spring*, doc. 28.

266. *Istoriya sovetskikh organov gosudarstvennoi bezopasnosti*, p. 549.

267. V. Andrianov, *Kosygin* (Moscow 2003) p. 21. Also *Nezavismaya Gazeta*, 14 December 2000.

268. Telephone conversation, 13 August 1968: *Prague Spring*, doc. 81.

269. Pikhoya, *Moskva. Kreml.' Vlast'*, p. 545.

270. Chernyaev, *Byl li Rossii shans?* p. 27.

271. *Prague Spring*, doc. 94.

272. Ustinov, *Krepche*, pp. 163–164.

273. S. Neporada, "Faktor Sderzhivaniya," *Krasnaya Zvezda*, 27 August 2008.

274. Ustinov, *Krepche*, pp. 164–165.

275. P. Cradock, *Knowing Your Enemy: How the Joint Intelligence Committee Saw the World* (London 2002) p. 241.

276. Entry, 18 November 1968, Sulzberger, *Age of Mediocrity*, p. 479.

277. "Zasedanie Politburo TsK KPSS," 7 January 1974, Volkogonov Papers, box 24.

278. Falin, Hoover-Gorbachev Foundation Oral History Project, box 4.

279. "O reaktsii v FRG na sobytiya v Chekhslovakii," BA SAPMO, Walter Ulbrichts Büro, DY 30/3495.

280. Ibid.

281. Noted by Chernyaev, in preparing a draft resolution for a CC plenum in April 1973: Chernyaev, *Moya zhizn'*, p. 292.

282. Ibid.

283. Stewart (London) to Wilson (Moscow), 15 May 1969, enclosure: *Documents on British Policy Overseas* (hereafter *DBPO*), series 3, vol. 1 (London 1997) doc. 31.

284. Interview with Bahr, 26 November 1973: quoted in A. Vogtmeier, *Egon Bahr und die deutsche Frage: Zur Entwicklung der sozialdemokratischen Ost-und Deutschlandpolitik vom Kriegsende bis zur Vereinigung* (Bonn 1996) p. 119.

285. 26 July 1969, BA SAPMO, Walter Ulbrichts Büro, DY 30/3525.

286. Kvitsinskii, *Vremya i sluchai*, p. 267.

287. Comment to ambassador Allardt: Allardt (Moscow) to Scheel (Bonn), 8 December 1969, *Akten*, 1969, vol. 2 (Munich 2000) doc. 392.

288. Kevorkov, *Tainyi*, p. 24.

289. Interview, Metz, 10 June 2006: www.ena./lu/.

290. "Bund mit Teufel," *Der Spiegel*, 13 February 1995.

291. Falin, *Bez skidok*, p. 131.

292. *Akten*, vol. 2, doc. 293, footnote 3.

293. "Aufzeichnung des Ministerialdirektors Ruete," 17 September 1969, ibid., doc. 293.

294. Quoted in Vogtmeier, *Egon Bahr*, p. 121.

295. Interview with Bahr in Metz, 10 June 2006: www.ena./lu/.

296. The author's interview with Bahr.

297. Comment to French ambassador Lucet, 13 April 1970: G.-H. Soutou, "Le Président Pompidou et les relations entre les Etats-Unis et l'Europe," *Journal of European Integration History*, vol. 6, no. 2, 2000, p. 118.

298. Letter, *New York Review of Books*, 24 September 1998.

299. Bahr memorandum, 22 December 1969, *Akten*, vol. 2, doc. 406.

300. Allardt (Moscow) to Scheel (Bonn), 24 December 1969, ibid., doc. 413.

301. Allardt (Moscow) to Scheel (Bonn), 11 December 1969, ibid., doc. 398.

302. *US News and World Report*, 29 December 1969.

303. Memorandum, 14 January 1970, *Akten, 1970*, vol. 1 (Munich 2001) doc. 8.

304. Bahr's record of talks with Gromyko, 30 January 1970, ibid., doc. 28.

305. Cramer, *Gefragt: Egon Bahr*, p. 57.

306. Speech to the political consultative committee, Warsaw Pact, 20 August 1970, Polish Party Archives. *Posiedzenie doradczego Komitetu Politycznego Państw Układu Warszawskiego Moskwa, 20 sierpnia 1970 r.* Web site of the Parallel History Project.

307. Untitled memorandum from Moscow, 1970, BA SAPMO, Arbeitsgruppe Allgemeine Abteilung. DY 30/J IV. 2/20.6.

308. Kvitsinsky, *Vremya*, p. 274.

309. Falin, *Bez skidok*, p. 197. Also, Bahr's record, 13 February 1970, *Akten*, doc. 54.

310. Bahr (Moscow) to Brandt (Bonn), 14 May 1970, *Akten, 1970*, vol. 2, doc. 205.

311. Brandt's record of talks with Kosygin, 12 August 1970, ibid., doc. 387.

312. Falin, *Bez skidok*, p. 197.

313. Kvitsinskii, *Vremya*, p. 275.

314. "Bund mit Teufel," *Der Spiegel*, 13 February 1995.

315. Memoirs of Hermann Axen, head of the SED international division: *Ich war eine Diener der Partei* (Berlin 1996) p. 281.

316. Brezhnev's speech, 20 August 1970: Polish archives, PHP website.

317. Falin, *Bez skidok*, p. 187.

318. J. Grenville and B. Wasserstein, eds., *The Major International Treaties since 1945* (London and New York 1987) pp. 194–195.

319. Record of a conversation between Brezhnev and Honecker, 28 July 1970: *Tatort Politbüro*, ed. P. Przybylski (Berlin 1991), vol. 1, doc. 15.

320. Grenville and Wasserstein, *The Major*, pp. 196–198.

321. *Command 6201*, doc. 153.

322. Grenville and Wasserstein, *The Major*, pp. 195–196.

323. Ibid., pp. 198–199.

324. Ibid., pp. 199–200.

325. See Vogtmeier, *Egon Bahr*, pp. 146–152.

326. Record of a meeting of the Politburo, 29 October 1980, www.bukovsky-archives.net.

327. P. Shelest, . . . *Da ne sudimy budete: Dnevnikovye zapisi, vospominaniya chlena Politburo TsK KPSS* (Moscow 1995) p. 459.

328. Ibid.

329. Ibid., p. 460.

330. Ibid., p. 462.

331. "Informatsiya," 22 November 1968, BA SAPMO, Walter Ulbrichts Büro, DY 30/3496.

332. A. Elizavetin, "Trudnye Gody v Kitae," *Diplomaticheskii Ezhegodnik* (Moscow 1992) p. 196.

333. Quoted in Yang Kuisong, "The Sino-Soviet Border Clash of 1969: From Zhenbao Island to Sino-American Rapprochement," *Cold War History*, vol. 1, no. 1, p. 29. The

article is not entirely reliable, however, and contains simple errors with respect to the Russian side of the picture.

334. "Informatsiya o besede A. N. Kosygina s Chzhou en'-laem 11 sentyabrya 1969 g.": as 1507.

335. Quoted in Kuisong, "Sino-Soviet," p. 30.

336. "Informatsiya," p. 197.

337. The sources are from KGB records: I. Ustinov, *Krepche stali: Zapiski veterana voennoi kontrrazvedki* (Moscow 2005) pp. 147–151.

338. Briefing, Moscow to Berlin, "O polozhenii na sovetsko-kitaiskoi granitse," BA SAPMO, DY 30 J IV 2/2–1240.

339. Shevchenko, *Breaking with Moscow* (New York 1985) p. 165. Shevchenko was close to Gromyko and a friend of Gromyko's son, Anatoly: "Entrevista: El General Nikolai Leonov en el CEP," *Estudios Públicos* 73 (verano 1999) p. 81.

340. "The Possibility of a Soviet Strike against Chinese Nuclear Facilities." Rogers to Nixon, 10 September 1969, *FRUS, 1969–1976*, vol. 12, p. 268.

341. Memcon, 18 August 1969, reprinted on the National Security Archive Web site.

342. Elizavetin, "Trudnye Gody," pp. 203–205.

343. Ibid., p. 208.

344. L. Tikhvinskii, *Vozvrashchenie k vorotam nebesnogo spokoistviya* (Moscow 2002) p. 196.

345. "Informatsiya."

346. *Sovetsko-amerikanskie otnosheniya. Gody razryadki, 1969–1976. Sbornik dokumentov,* vol. 1. bk. 1, ed. S. Lavrov et al. (Moscow 2007) doc. 1.

347. Memcon by Dobrynin on a meeting with Kissinger, 14 February 1969, ibid., doc. 2.

348. "Ob amerikano-v'etnamskikh kontaktakh," 1 September 1971: "K vlasti mogut priiti novye sily": Dokumenty o voine vo V'etname, *Istochnik*, no. 1, 1997, doc. 4, pp. 54–57.

349. Kissinger to Morgenthau, 13 November 1968, Hans J. Morgenthau Papers, Library of Congress, box 33.

350. Entry, 9 March 1969, H. R. Haldeman, "Journals and Diaries," Nixon Presidential Materials Project, box 1.

351. Memcon of a conversation with Nixon, 17 February 1969, *Sovetsko-amerikanskie otnosheniya*, doc. 5.

352. Memcon of a conversation with Kissinger, 21 February 1969, ibid., doc. 8.

353. Dobrynin (Washington) to Moscow, 13 March 1969, ibid., doc. 14.

354. Memcon by Dobrynin on a conversation with Kissinger, 11 June 1969, ibid., doc. 23.

355. Entry, 19 March 1969, Haldeman, "Journals."

356. *Sovetsko-amerikanskie otnosheniya*, doc. 29.

357. G. Smith, *Double Talk: The Story of SALT I* (New York 1980) p. 76.

358. G. Arbatov, "SShA: Bol'shie raketnye debaty," *Izvestiya*, 15 April 1969.

359. R. Gates, *From the Shadows*, p. 39.

360. BA SAPMO, UdSSR-Vietnam. 10.0420.

361. *Sovetsko-amerikanskie otnosheniya*, doc. 33.

362. Dobrynin's memcon after meeting Nixon, 10 June 1970, ibid., doc. 59.

363. D. Tomashevskii, "Leninskii printsip mirnogo sosushestvovaniya i klassovaya bor'ba," *Kommunist*, no. 12, August 1970, pp. 101–113.

364. For a scathing account of Semyonov at SALT II before he was supplanted by Viktor Karpov: V. Starodubov, *Superderzhavy XX Veka. Strategicheskoe protivoborstvo* (Moscow 2001) p. 302.

365. W. Semjonow, *Von Stalin bis Gorbatschow: Ein halbes Jahrhundert in diplomatischer Mission, 1939–1991* (Berlin 1995) pp. 338–339.

366. Chernyaev, *Moya zhizn'*, p. 295.

367. Kornienko, *Kholodnaya voina*, p. 177; also Semjonow, *Von Stalin*, p. 341.

368. Ibid.

369. Testimony, *Soviet Intentions*, vol. 2, p. 23.

370. Briefing paper for the East Germans, 13 February 1970, Abteilung Internationale Verbindungen DY 30/IV, 1011.

371. H. Kissinger, *Years of Renewal* (London 1999) p. 277.

372. *US-Soviet Relations in the Era of Détente, 1969–1976*, transcript at www.state.gov/r/pa/ho/97373.htm.

373. Zolotarev, *Rossiya (SSSR) v lokal'nykh voinakh*, pp. 92–93.

374. Kornienko, *Kholodnaya voina*, p. 184.

375. *Department of State Bulletin*, vol. 66, no. 1722, 26 June 1972, pp. 918–921.

376. Briefing paper initialled by Honecker, 5 June 1972, BA SAPMO, DY/30/J IV 2/0202. 571.

377. Ibid.

378. J. Matthews, "The West's Secret Marshall Plan for the Mind," *International Journal of Intelligence and Counter Intelligence*, vol. 16, no. 3, July–September 2003, pp. 409–427. Also the obituary of George Minden, *New York Times*, 23 April 2006.

379. Ibid.

380. Quoted in a draft FCO position paper, February 1972, *DBPO*, series 3, vol. 2 (London 1997) doc. 1.

381. NATO Council meeting communiqué, 9–10 December 1971: *Command 6932* (London 1977) doc. 39.

382. Minute by Brimelow, 14 August 1972, *DBPO*, series 3, vol. 2 (London 1998) doc. 12.

383. Comment to Foreign Secretary Sir Alec Douglas-Home, 14 September 1972, ibid., doc. 13, footnote 1.

384. US cabinet meeting, 8 August 1975, Gerald R. Ford Library online, box A1, National Security Adviser.

385. Draft position paper, February 1972, *DBPO*, doc. 1

386. 26 July 1969, BA SAPMO, Walter Ulbrichts Büro, DY 30/3525.

387. Walden (London) to Staples (Brussels), 4 August 1972, *DBPO*, doc. 11.

388. *Command 6932*, doc. 52.

389. Ibid., doc. 53.

390. Cromer (Washington) to Brimelow (London), 7 March 1973, FCO 73/135.

391. Kissinger's memcon, 10 October 1973: NARA, Nixon Presidential Materials Project, NSC, Country File, Middle East, box 664.

392. Elliott (Helsinki) to Callaghan (London), 29 July 1974, *DBPO*, doc. 94.

393. Elliott to Tickell, 3 September 1974, ibid., doc. 95, footnote 2.

394. Garvey (Moscow) to Tickell (London), 20 August 1974, ibid., doc. 95.

395. BDOHP, 34, Churchill College Archives.

396. Chernyaev, *Moya zhizn'*, p. 321.

397. Mlechin, *Yuri Andropov*, pp. 176–177.

398. "Vypiska iz protokola no. 151 zasedaniya Politburo TsK KPSS ot 22 yanvrarya 1970 goda," Bukovsky Archive.

399. Mlechin, *Yuri Andropov*, pp. 176–177.

400. Kvitsinsky, *Vremya*, pp. 313–314.

401. Interview with Kovalev, Hoover-Gorbachev Foundation Oral History Project, box 4.

402. Kvitsinsky, *Vremya*, pp. 313–314.

CHAPTER 9. THE IMPACT OF VIETNAM

Epigraph: Axen's meeting with Ponomarev, 27 February 1973, BA SAPMO, DY/30/IV B 2/20. 157.

1. Memcon, Khrushchev and Mao, 31 July 1958, Volkogonov Papers.

2. *Istochnik*, no. 2, 1998, p. 115.

3. "Lessons of Vietnam," undated memorandum from Kissinger for President Ford, c. 12 May 1975: www.ford.utexas.edu/library/exhibits/vietnam/750512f.htm.

4. H. Kissinger, *Diplomacy* (New York 1994) p. 695.

5. Ibid., p. 698.

6. Gates, *From the Shadows*, p. 65.

7. CIA Archives, "The Development of Soviet Military Power: Trends since 1965 and Prospects for the 1980s," 4 January 1981, CIA Electronic Reading Room.

8. V. Kirpichenko, *Razvedka: Litsa i lichnosti* (Moscow 1998) pp. 113–115.

9. Axen's conversation with Ponomarev, 27 February 1973, BA SAPMO, Internationale Verbindungen, DY/30/IV B 2/20.

10. Ibid.

11. Memorandum for the Record, Kissinger's briefing of White House Staff on Jordan, 25 September 1973, NSC, Country File, Middle East, Nixon Presidential Materials Project, box 664.

12. Memcon, Kissinger and Scowcroft, 3 August 1973, ibid., NSC, box 1027.

13. Information, signed as read by Erich Honecker, no date, BA SAPMO, DY/30/J IV 2/202.

14. Information signed as read by Honecker, 9 February 1972, ibid.

15. From CIA Archives. "Soviet Global Military Reach (NIE 11–6-84)," CIA Electronic Reading Room.

16. Bill Quandt to Kissinger, 17 October 1973—"Talking Points for the President's Cabinet Meeting on October 18—Middle East," Nixon Presidential Materials Project, NSC, Country File.

17. A. Sadat, *In Search of Identity: An Autobiography* (London 1978) p. 295.

18. Quandt to Scowcroft, 6 October 1973, Nixon Presidential Materials Project, NSC, Country File.

19. Memcon, Kissinger and Renaat van Eslande, 10 October 1973, ibid.

20. Kissinger to the White House Situation Room, 9:00 a.m., 6 October 1973, ibid.

21. Ibid.

22. J. Howe to Scowcroft, 10 October 1973, ibid.

23. This was ruled out, ibid.

24. Quandt to Kissinger, 13 October 1973, ibid.

25. National Security Council Memorandum for Kissinger from D. Stukel, 17 October 1973, ibid.

26. To Scowcroft from McFarlane, 16 October 1973, ibid.

27. Ibid.

28. Howe to Scowcroft, 7 October 1973, ibid.

29. Quandt to Scrowcroft, 10 October 1973, following a conversation with Sheikh Yamani of Kuwait, ibid.

30. Memcon, Kissinger and Renaat van Eslande, 10 October 1973, ibid.

31. Quoted by Viktor Israelyan, who served as rapporteur during the crisis at the Politburo sessions: V. Israelyan, *Inside the Kremlin during the Yom Kippur War* (Pennsylvania 1995) p. 168.

32. CIA data, "Soviet Global Military Reach," NIE 11–6-84, CIA Electronic Reading Room.

33. CIA Archives, "Soviet Global Military Reach (NIE 11–6-84)," ibid.

34. Briefing from Moscow, 24 October 1973, BA SAPMO, DY 30/J IV 2/202.

35. Israelyan, *Inside*, pp. 169–170.

36. "The Decision to Alert U.S. Forces, October 24–25," paper in the files, National Security Council, Nixon Presidential Materials Project.

37. This phrase is omitted from Nixon's memoirs but can be found quoted from the Soviet documents in Israelyan, *Inside*, p. 186.

38. Ibid., p. 187.

39. *US-Soviet Relations in the Era of Détente*.

40. Quoted in ibid., p. 180.

41. Ibid.

42. Ibid., p. 181.

43. Noted in Chernyaev's diary: Chernyaev, *Moya zhizn'*, p. 301.

44. Memcon, Senator Javits and Nixon, 12 November 1973, US National Archives, NSC, Presidential/HAK Memcons. Nixon Presidential Materials Project, box 1027.

45. Johnson, *United States Cryptographic History*, p. 432.

46. Mlechin, *Yuri Andropov*, pp. 243–244.

47. Quoted in E. Gaspari, *A Ditadura Envergonhada* (São Paolo 2002) p. 60.

48. McNamara is quoted in O. Westad, *The Global Cold War: Third World Interventions and the Making of Our Times* (Cambridge 2005) p. 427, footnote 107.

49. *New York Times*, 2 August 1974.

50. *Observer*, 1 July 1973.

51. R. Kovar, "An Interview with Richard Lehman," www.cia.gov/library/center-for-the-study-of-intelligence/csi.
52. For the evidence: Haslam, *The Nixon Administration and the Death of Allende's Chile: A Case of Assisted Suicide* (London 2005).
53. Memcon, US ambassador's residence, Brussels, 12 December 1975, NARA. Reproduced on the National Security Archive Web site.
54. BA SAPMO, DY/30/IV.B.2/20.209.
55. Information from a meeting between the PCI delegation and the PCP, 16–19 November 1974—Sergio Segre to Berlinguer, Pajetta and secretariat, 17 December 1974, Archivio PCI, 084.
56. Huggan (Lisbon) to Ministry of Defence (London), 27 March 1974, FCO 9/2044.
57. Huggan (Lisbon) to Ministry of Defence (London), 12 March 1974, ibid.
58. Meeting with Axen, 16 May 1974, BA SAPMO, DY/30/IV.B.2/20.209.
59. C. Colombo, "Impressioni sul PCP," 10 June 1974, Archivio PCI, Portugal 1974–1976. 078. III volume 3° bimestre 1974; also, SAPMO, loc. cit.
60. H. Schmidt, *Die Deutschen und ihre Nachbarn. Menschen und Mächte II* (Berlin 1990) p. 438; also V. Riva, *Oro da Mosca* (Milan 1999) pp. 745 and 747.
61. Nuno Aguirre, head of European affairs at the Spanish Foreign Ministry—Amembassy (Madrid) to Secretary of State (Washington), 6 November 1974, NARA Web site.
62. Briefing for Axen in Berlin, 1–4 November 1974, BA SAPMO, DY/30/IV B 2/20.
63. Interview, September 1975: Fallaci, *Intervista con la storia*, p. 676.
64. Maria João Avillez, *Soares: Ditadura e Revolução* (Lisbon 1996) p. 428.
65. "The Outlook for Portugal and Its Relationship with the Western Alliance," 30 June 1975, JIC (75) 17, CAB 186/20 (National Archives, London).
66. Interview with Oriana Fallaci, *L'Europeo*, 13 June 1975.
67. Lt. Colonel Andrade Moura: Bernardo, ed., *Equívocos*, p. 77. Also, Lt. Colonel António Ramos: ibid., pp. 107–110.
68. Spínola, *País sem Rumo: Contributo para a História de uma Revoluçao* (Lisboa 1978) pp. 159–160; also, Pedro Pezarat Correia, *Descolonizaçao de Angola: A Jóia da Coroa do Império Português* (Lisbon 1991) p. 63.
69. "Outlook for Portugal," loc. cit.
70. Interview, March 1976: Fallaci, *Intervista con la storia*, p. 618.
71. Information from a former head of MI6.
72. CIA Archives, "Soviet Global Military Reach (NIE 11-6-84)," CIA Electronic Reading Room.
73. Schmidt, *Menschen und Mächte*, p. 207.
74. *Department of State Bulletin*, vol. 63, 1970, pp. 237–243.
75. "Visita in Italia del Mundo degli Affari Esteri del Regno Unito di Gran Bretagna e Irlanda del Nord James Callaghan (3–5 luglio 1975)," Archivio Centrale dello Stato, Rome, Aldo Moro Papers 56, fasc. 2; "Il Portogallo nell'Alleanza Atlantica," ibid.
76. Minute by Barrett, FCO South-West European Department, 17 March 1975, FCO 9/2269.
77. Quoted in Haslam, *The Soviet Union and the Politics of Nuclear Weapons in Europe, 1969–87: The Problem of the SS-20* (London 1989) p. 49.

78. Lt. Colonel António Ramos: Bernardo, ed., *Equívocos*, p. 111.

79. Ure (Lisbon) to London, 25 September 1974, FCO 9/2059.

80. Briefing by a PCP delegation led by Jaime Serra of the PCP Politburo and Carlos Aboim Ingles, in Berlin 1–4 November 1974, BA SAPMO, DY/30/IV B 2/20. 49.

81. Amembassy (Bonn) to Secretary of State (Washington DC), 25 October 1974, NARA Web site.

82. Amembassy (Bonn) to Secretary of State (Washington DC), 14 November 1974, ibid.

83. Schmidt, *Die Deutschen und ihre Nachbarn*, p. 435.

84. Admiral Rosa Coutinho: Bernardo, ed., *Equívocos*, p. 273.

85. Avillez, *Soares*, p. 407.

86. Quoted in H. Kissinger, *Years of Renewal*, pp. 631–632.

87. Ibid., p. 408. Kissinger's lack of belief in the socialists was also noted by Anthony Lewis in the *New York Times*, 26 January 1978.

88. Wiggin, Assistant Undersecretary of State at the FCO—Amembassy (London) to Secretary of State (Washington DC), 30 May 1974, NARA Web site.

89. Press spokesman for the socialist fraction of the European Parliament Ruthmann in Lisbon, *Akten zur Auswärtigen Politik der Bundesrepublik Deutschland*, 1975, vol. 1, p. 282, footnote 2.

90. "Aufzeichnung des Vortragenden Legationsrats I. Klasse Munz," 22 March 1975, ibid., doc. 55.

91. Schmidt, *Mensche und Mächte*, p. 283.

92. Report from Boss (Brussels), 22 March 1975, *Akten*, p. 284, footnote 11.

93. 25 March 1975, FCO 9/2269.

94. Record by Munz, *Akten*, p. 284, footnote 10.

95. Callaghan (London) to Lisbon, 24 March 1975, PREM 16/603.

96. *Akten*, p. 300, footnote 4.

97. 25 March 1975, FCO 9/2269.

98. S. Pons, *Berlinguer e la fine del comunismo* (Turin 2006) p. 66, footnote 141.

99. Record of a meeting between Wilson, Palme, Uyl, Brandt, Mitterand, and Soares, 5 September 1975, FCO 9/2287.

100. Schmidt, *Menschen und Mächte*, p. 207.

101. Pons, *Berlinguer*, p. 62.

102. Schmidt (Bonn) to Kissinger (Washington), 10 April 1975, *Akten*, doc. 75.

103. Interview June 1975: Fallaci, *Intervista con la storia*, p. 702.

104. Clark (Lisbon) to Baker (London), 9 May 1975, FCO 9/2270.

105 Meeting with Harold Wilson, 1 August 1975, FCO 9/2285.

106. Schmidt comments at a meeting of the SPD leadership, 12 May 1975: H. Soell, *Helmut Schmidt 1969 bis heute: Macht und Verantwortung* (Munich 2008) p. 410.

107. Memcon, Schmidt with Vasco Gonçalves, 30 May 1975, *Akten*, doc. 141.

108. "Information über die Haltung imperialistischer Staaten und Organisationen zur Entwicklung in Portugal," 5 June 1975, BA SAPMO, DY/30/IV. B 2/20. 209.

109. "Nota sugli incontri avuti a Lisbona con il P.C.P. e il P.S.P. il 25 e 26 Agosto 1975 dal compagno A. Rubbi," Archivio PCI, MF 208.

110. Briefing paper, 29 August 1975, BA SAPMO, DY/30/J.IV. 2/202. 562.

111. Reported to the British by Harry Gilman (Operations and Policy Research) and Leonard Parkinson (Office of Strategic Research) from CIA: Bishop (FCO Research Department) to Cartledge, 3 October 1975, FCO 28/2759.

112. "Visita a Roma del Presidente della Repubblica del Portogallo Francisco da Costa Gomes (22–23 ottobre 1975)," Moro Papers, fasc. 10.

113. Record of meeting, 14 October 1975, BA SAPMO, DY/30/J IV 2/202.

114. *The Times*, 30 July 1976. Melo Antunes became chairman of the constitutional committee of the Council of the Revolution.

115. *The Times*, 18 November 1976.

116. Riva, *Oro da Mosca*, p. 751.

117. Ibid., 18 November 1976.

118. Quoted by Soares, with some pride: Mario João Avillez, *Soares: Ditadura e Revolução* (Lisbon 1996) p. 407.

119. O. Nazhestkin, "Sverkhderzhavy i sobytiya v Angole 1960–1970-e gody," *Novaya i Noveishaya Istoriya*, no. 4, July–August 1975, p. 35. Nazhestin was a Soviet intelligence officer operating in Angola.

120. Ibid., p. 36.

121. Ibid., p. 32.

122. Kirpichenko, *Razvedka*, pp. 205–207.

123. Nazhestkin, "Sverkhderzhavy," pp. 33–34.

124. P. Gleijeses, *Conflicting Missions: Washington, and Africa, 1959–1976* (Chapel Hill 2002) pp. 160–249.

125. Nazhestkin, "Sverkhderzhavy," p. 37.

126. CIA Archives, "Soviet Global Military Reach (NIE 11-6-84)," CIA Electronic Archive.

127. Brutents, *Tridtsat' let*, p. 207.

128. Ibid., p. 214.

129. C. Andrew and V. Mitrokhin, *The Mitrokhin Archive II* (London 2005) p. 95.

130. Detinov testimony, *GB99 KCLMA*, 28/81.

131. Aleksandrov-Agentov, *Ot Kollontai*, p. 280.

132. CIA, National Foreign Assessment Center, The Foreign Policy Views of Mikhail Suslov, July 1978, p. 18: www.foia.cia.gov/browse_docs_full.asp.

133. Chernyaev, *Moya Zhizn'*, p. 316.

134. Nazhestkin, "Sverkhderzhavy," p. 39.

135. Ibid., p. 40. The two best accounts, Gleijeses and Westad, do not use Nazhestkin as a source, yet it is a vital firsthand record. One (Gleijeses, *Conflicting Missions: Havana*, pp. 270–271) takes the other to task (Westad, *The Global Cold War: Third World Interventions and the Making of Our Times*, pp. 224–225) for predating the arrival of Cuban soldiers by several months. In fact, as Nazhestkin shows, Cuban special forces were already in Angola by November 1975 in effective numbers. But Westad, unaware of the friction with Neto, does appear to overstate the degree of Soviet commitment in the earlier stages.

136. V. Makarov, *V General'nom Shtabe nakanune gryadushchikh peremen: Avtobiograficheskie zapiski ofitsera General'nogo Shtaba* (Moscow 2004) p. 380.

137. Salmin, *Internatsionalizm*, p. 40.
138. CIA Archive, "Soviet Global Military Reach (NIE 11-6-84)," CIA Electronic Archive.
139. Andrew and Mitrokhin, *Mitrokhin Archive II*, p. 456.
140. Axen's record of a meeting with Ponomarev, 20 October 1976, BA SAPMO, DY/30/IV B 2/20.

CHAPTER 10. DÉTENTE FAILS

Epigraph: Addressing Pham Hung from Vietnam, October 1980: quoted in Andrew and Mitrokhin, *Mitrokhin Archive II*, p. 471.
1. Washington, 17 July 1969, *FRUS, 1969–1976*, vol. 12, doc. 68.
2. Quoted from MI5 archives: C. Andrew, *The Defence of the Realm: The Authorized History of MI5* (London 2009) p. 565.
3. Meeting between Axen and Ponomarev, 20 October 1976, BA SAPMO, DY/30/IV B 2/20.157.
4. Speech, 4–5 January 1983: www.isn.ethz.ch/php/documents/collection_3/PCC_meetings/coll_3_PCC_1983.html.
5. Interviewed by Sergei Belanovsky in Ellman and Kontorovich, eds., *The Destruction of the Soviet Economic System: An Insiders' History* (London 1998) p. 42.
6. See Haslam, *Soviet Union and the Politics*, pp. 20–27.
7. "O sovetsko-amerikanskikh peregovorakh ob ogranichenii strategicheskikh vooruzhenii." Briefing paper signed as read by Honecker, 23 November 1973, BA SAPMO, DY/30/J IV 2/0202.571.
8. Presidential Review Memorandum/NSC-10, 18 February 1977, US National Archives.
9. Danlievich testimony, Hines et al., eds., *Soviet Intentions*, p. 24.
10. *The Voroshilov Lectures: Materials from the Soviet General Staff Academy*, vol. 1, ed. G. Wardak (Washington DC 1989) pp. 66–67.
11. "The Soviet Threat," 6 May 1974, JIC (A) (74) 17, CAB 186/18.
12. FCO 28/2574.
13. E. Chazov, *Rok* (Moscow 2000) p. 59.
14. Chazov, *Zdorov'e i vlast.' Vospominaniya "kremlevskogo vracha"* (Moscow 1992) pp. 11–13; also in *Leonid Brezhnev*, p. 316.
15. Chazov, *Zdorov'e*, pp. 74–76; *Leonid Brezhnev*, p. 317.
16. Chazov, *Zdorov'e*, pp. 127–128; *Leonid Brezhnev*, pp. 319–320.
17. William Hyland, head of INR—Simons (Washington DC) to Bullard (London), 17 December 1974, FCO 28/2563.
18. CIA, *Research Study: Brezhnev's Personal Authority and Collectivity in the Soviet Leadership* (1976) p. 10.
19. Alexandrov, "Zapis Besedy tov. L. I. Brezhneva s rukovoditelyami bratskikh partii sotsialisticheskikh stran v Budapeshte," 18 March 1975: copy at the National Security Archive.
20. Ibid.

21. Genscher, *Rebuilding a House Divided*, pp. 100–101 An extraordinarily misleading title which leaves the more modest German-language edition—"Memoirs"—in the shade.
22. Falin, *Bez skidok*, p. 333.
23. Cartledge to Killick, 5 August 1975, FCO 28/2761.
24. Cartledge to Sutherland (Moscow), c. 20 October 1975, ibid.
25. Information from his doctor, Evgeniya Chazov: A. Grachev, *Kremlevskaya*, p. 79.
26. *Leonid Brezhnev*, pp. 320–322.
27. Ibid., pp. 323–324.
28. V. Grishin, *Ot Khrushcheva do Gorbacheva: Politicheskie portrety pyati gensekov i A. N. Kosygina. Memuary* (Moscow 1996) p. 45.
29. Korninenko, *Kholodnaya voina*, p. 315.
30. Identified in the *Guardian*, 26 April 2004.
31. Information from Tony Bishop.
32. Sushkov, quoted in *Leonid Brezhnev*, p. 331.
33. Brutents, *Tridtsat' let*, p. 502.
34. Grishin, *Ot Khrushcheva do Gorbacheva*, p. 47. On domestic affairs, Grishin adds the names Chernenko and Tikhonov; but this may well refer to the early eighties rather than the period from the mid-seventies.
35. Prokhorov, *Razvedka*, p. 271. The directorate for codes and cyphers became the sixteenth in 1969.
36. Statements by Gromyko and Ligachev in the Politburo, 14 January 1986: Vorotnikov, *A Bylo Eto Tak . . . : iz dnevnika chlena Politburo TsK KPSS* (Moscow 1995) p. 84.
37. Alexandrov-Agentov, *Ot Kollontai*, p. 268.
38. I. Bystrova, *Voenno-promyshlennyi kompleks SSSR v gody kholodnoi voiny* (Moscow 2000) p. 243. Bystrova is mistaken with regard to Ustinov's age, however.
39. S. Khrushchev, *Pensioner Soyuznogo Znacheniya* (Moscow 1991) pp. 103–104.
40. Zen'kovich, *Samye Sekretnye*, p. 433.
41. Testimony of Lt. General Gelii Batenin, First Deputy Chief of the General Staff under Ogarkov, Hines et al., eds., *Soviet Intentions*, p. 9; also Gareev testimony, ibid., p. 75.
42. Makarov, *V General'nom Shtabe*, p. 435.
43. Varennikov, *Nepovtorimoe*, vol. 4 (Moscow 2001) p. 98.
44. Testimony from the deputy chairman of the VPK: Ellman and Kontorovich, eds., *The Destruction*, pp. 46–47; also Major General Larionov: ibid., p. 48.
45. Varennikov, *Nepovtorimoe*, 12.
46. U. Alexis Johnson, *The Right Hand of Power*, pp. 604–605.
47. G. Kornienko, *Kholodnaya voina*, p. 201.
48. CIA, National Foreign Assessment Center, *The Foreign Policy Views*, pp. 10–1: www.foia.cia.gov/browse_docs_full.asp.
49. Johnson, *Right Hand of Power*, p. 607.
50. "Spravka ob informatsii, izlozhennoi v vystuplenii pervogo zamestielya direktora TsRU R. Geitsa ot 25 noyabrya s.g.": Kataev Papers, Hoover Institution Archive, Stanford University (hereafter Kataev Papers), box 5.

51. Brutents, *Tridtsat' let*, p. 271.

52. Kataev Papers, box 7.

53. *Spiegel Special*, no. 3, 2008, p. 21.

54. Aleksandrov-Agentov, *Ot Kollontai*, p. 269.

55. www.cnn.com/SPECIALS/cold.war/episodes/19/script.html.

56. Kataev testimony, Hines et al., eds., *Soviet Intentions*, p. 98.

57. Information obtained from a reliable Washington-based diplomatic source in 1986.

58. I. Drogovoz, *Raketnye voiska SSSR* (Minsk 2007) p. 176.

59. DDR Ministerium für Staatssicherheit. Auskunft zum Erkenntnisstand des Gegners über das Potential sowjetischer Mittelsreckenraketen längerer Reichweite, 12 August 1986. B StU Archiv Berlin, ZA.HVA 48; also, Drogovoz, *Raketnye voiska*, p. 176.

60. P. Podvig, *Russian Strategic Nuclear Forces* (Cambridge, Mass., 2001) p. 225.

61. Ibid., p. 225; also A. Nedelin, "yadernyi vek otkryl dveri novomu periodu istorii . . . ," *Voenno-Istoricheskii Zhurnal*, no. 1, 2000, p. 58.

62. H. Apel, *Der Abstieg: Politisches Tagebuch 1978–1988* (Stuttgart 1990) p. 68. Apel became German defense minister in the spring of 1978.

63. Drogovoz, *Raketnye voiska*, p. 177.

64. V. Varennikov, *Nepovtorimoe*, p. 48.

65. Batenin testimony, Hines et al., eds., *Soviet Intentions*, p. 9.

66. Ibid., p. 8.

67. Danilevich testimony, ibid., p. 33.

68. Ibid., p. 40.

69. Batenin testimony, ibid., p. 9.

70. Danilevich testimony, ibid., p. 32.

71. Ibid., p. 49; also Gareev testimony, ibid., p. 75.

72. Danilevich testimony, ibid., p. 23; also, p. 49.

73. K. Wiegrefe, *Das Zerwüfnis: Helmut Schmidt, Jimmy Carter und die Krise der Deutsch-amerikanischen Beziehungen* (Berlin 2005) p. 71.

74. Ibid., p. 72.

75. Ibid.

76. Haslam, *The Soviet Union and the Politics of Nuclear Weapons in Europe, 1969–87: The Problem of the SS-20* (London 1989) p. 86.

77. Conversations with Odom.

78. Quoted in Haslam, *Soviet Union and the Politics*, p. 146.

79. "Informatsiya o vizite v SSSR Gosudarstvennogo sekretarya SShA S. Vensa," 6 April 1977, BA SAPMO, DY 30/J IV 2/202 572.

80. Evident from the earliest cabinet meetings: Wiegrefe, *Das Zerwüfnis*, p. 133.

81. Quoted in ibid., p. 134.

82. Memorandum by German ambassador von Staden, Washington, of a conversation with ambassador Dobrynin, 2 March 1977, *Akten zur Auswärtigen Politik der Bundesrepublik Deutschland*, 1977, vol. 1, ed. H. Möller et al. (Munich 2008) doc. 50.

83. Memorandum of a conversation by German ambassador Ruth with Leslie Gelb, director of the department for politico-military affairs at the State Department, 31 May 1977, *Akten*, doc. 140.

84. Memorandum by Dannenbing, 15 June 1977, ibid., doc. 155.
85. Genscher (Bonn) to Vance (Washington) 4 July 1977, *Akten*, 1977, vol. 2, doc. 173.
86. Ibid., vol. 1, p. 726, footnote.
87. Comment from Leslie Gelb, Assistant Secretary of State for Politico-Military Affairs: Ruth (Washington) to Bonn, 18 August 1977, ibid., doc. 220.
88. Hansen (Washington) to Bonn, 20 August 1977, ibid., doc. 224.
89. The evidence for this is easy to see from the "confidential" Soviet air defense forces journal then available in the Library of Congress: Haslam, *Soviet Union and the Politics*, pp. 20–27.
90. "Informatsiya SShA Dzh. Karterom i gossekretarem SShA S. Vensom," 13 October 1977, BA SAPMO, DY/30/J/IV. 2/202 572.
91. Soell, *Helmut Schmidt*, p. 717. This was researched from the private archive.
92. Danilevich testimony, Hines et al., eds., *Soviet Intentions*, p. 25.
93. Ibid., p. 29.
94. H. Schmidt/Giovanni di Lorenzo, *Auf eine Zigarette mit Helmut Schmidt* (Köln 2009) p. 194.
95. Haslam, *Soviet Union and the Politics*, pp. 90–91.
96. Entry, 24 September 1979, Adamishin Diary, Hoover Institution, box 1.
97. *Der Spiegel*, 26 August 2008.
98. Session of the Federal Security Council, 9 November 1977, *Akten*, doc. 318.
99. H. Apel, *Der Abstieg*, pp. 59–70, also p. 75.
100. Oral testimony, Hoover-Gorbachev Foundation Oral History Project, box 4.
101. H. Schmidt, *Weggefährten: Erinnerungen und Reflexionen*, p. 501.
102. www.cnn.com/SPECIALS/cold.war/episodes/19/script.html.
103. Ibid.
104. Memorandum for the President, 9 May 1979, Carter Presidential Library online.
105. Schmidt, *Weggefährten*, pp. 502–503.
106. V. Makarov, *V General'nom Shtabe nakanune gryadushchikh peremen: Avtobiograficheskie zapiski ofitsera General'nogo Shtaba* (Moscow 2004) p. 399.
107. Varennikov, *Nepovtorimoe*, vol. 4, p. 269.
108. Entry, 2 November 1982, Adamishin Diary, box 1.
109. Falin testimony, Hoover-Gorbachev Foundation Oral History Project.
110. Interview (no date), ibid., box 4.
111. Anatoly Chernyaev, "Bez ustali rabotayushchii intellekt," *Vospominaniya ob Aleksandre Bovine: politik, zhurnalist, diplomat* (Moscow 2006) pp. 69–70.
112. W. Odom, *The Collapse of the Soviet Military* (New Haven 1998) p. 443, footnote 91.
113. Haslam, *Soviet Union and the Politics*, p. 97, passim.
114. Briefing for East Berlin, 16 December 1977, BA SAPMO, DY 30/J IV 2/202.
115. Quoted in Haslam, *Soviet Union and the Politics*, p. 99.
116. Ibid.
117. Soviet numbers for 1989, unchanged in proportion from 1978: "1974–1989 gody, SSSR. Zapisi po problemam sozdaniya novoi tekhniki," Kataev Papers, box 8, 13.8.

118. Schmidt to Honecker, 11 December 1981: H. Potthoff, ed., *Bonn und Ost-Berlin, 1969–1982* (Frankfurt 1997) doc. 61.

119. Apel, *Der Abstieg*, p. 71.

120. Ibid., p. 100.

121. Briefing for East Berlin, 25 May 1978, BA SAPMO, DY 30/J IV 2/202.

122. "Informatsiya ob itogakh peregovorov A. A. Gromyko s prezidentom SShA Dzh. Karterom i gossekretarem S. Vensom," ibid.

123. For the controversy over Wehner's divided loyalties: C. Andrew and V. Mitrokhin, *The Mitrokhin Archive I*, pp. 590–592.

124. Apel, *Der Abstieg*, pp. 71–74.

125. Ibid., p. 76.

126. Kornienko, *Kholodnaya Voina*, pp. 293–294. Kornienko's claim that he spoke in support may not be entirely reliable given his identification with the military, evident in Adamishin's diary (quoted and cited extensively in the following chapters). Also mentioned in Starodubov, *Superderzhavy*, pp. 334–335.

127. Detinov testimony, GB99 KCLMA, 28/81.

128. H.-D. Genscher, *Erinnerungen* (Berlin 1995) pp. 421–422.

129. "1974–1989 gody, SSSR. Zapisi po problemam sozdaniya novoi tekhniki," 13.8, Kataev Papers, box 8.

130. Batenin testimony, Hines et al., eds., *Soviet Intentions*, p. 8.

131. S. Lekarev, "Konets 'Kembridzhskoi Pyaterki,'" *Argumenty. ru* 10 (96), 6 March 2008.

132. *Ocherki Istorii Rossiskoi Vneshnei Razvedki*, vol. 5, p. 86.

133. In conversation with Axen, BA SAPMO, DY/30/IV B 2/20. 157.

134. Brutents, *Tridsat' let*, p. 287.

135. Ibid., p. 307.

136. Ibid.

137. From CIA Archives, "Soviet Global Military Reach (NIE 11-6-84)," CIA Electronic Reading Room.

138. Abrasimov's report on East German delegation's visit to Somalia, 18 February 1977: reprinted, *Cold War International History Project Bulletin* 8–9, 1996–97, p. 54.

139. Castro to Honecker, 3 April 1977, ibid., p. 60.

140. Ratanov's record of a conversation with Peres, 10 February 1977, ibid., p. 53.

141. Castro to Honecker, 3 April 1977: CWIHPB 8–9, 1996–97, p. 60.

142. CWIHPB 8–9, 1996–97.

143. Report on the visit, 13 May 1977, ibid., pp. 62–63.

144. Salmin, *Internatsionalizm*, p. 217.

145. W. Odom, "The Cold War Origins of the U.S. Central Command," *Journal of Cold War Studies*, vol. 8, no. 2, Spring 2006, pp. 55–56.

146. Ratanov's conversation with Ochoa, 17 July 1977, *Cold War International History Project Bulletin*, pp. 65–66.

147. Testimony by Viron Vaky, assistant secretary of state for interamerican affairs to the Subcommittee on Interamerican Affairs of the Foreign Affairs Committee, US House

of Representatives, 26 June 1979: National Security Archive, *NICARAGUA: The Making of US Policy, 1978–1990*, microfiche. Document 00827.

148. Words of Sakharovskii, head of the first directorate: Andrew and Mitrokhin, *Mitrokhin Archive II*, p. 42.

149. Ibid. p. 41.

150. *NICARAGUA*.

151. DIA, Intelligence Appraisal, NICARAGUA: Challenge to Regime, 1 December 1977, ibid. doc. 00024.

152. US embassy, Guatemala, to Washington, 5 July 1979, ibid., doc. 00867.

153. S. Ramírez, *Adiós Muchachos : Una memoria de la revolución sandinista* (Buenos Aires 1999) p. 225.

154. Ibid., pp. 230–323.

155. "Nicaraguan Military Build-Up," 22 March 1982, *NICARAGUA*, doc. 01474.

156. "The Soviet Challenge to U.S. Security Interests," NIE 11–4-82, CIA Electronic Reading Room.

157. "The Soviet Union and Nonruling Communist Parties," SOV 82–10110X, ibid.

158. Pezzulo, "Nicaragua, 1979: Somoza Out, Sandinistas In," in D. Mak and C. Kennedy, *American Ambassadors in a Troubled World: Interviews with Senior Diplomats* (London 1992) p. 189.

159. Gates, *From the Shadows*, p. 150.

160. Ibid., p. 151.

161. Personal information from a relative given more than once at the time.

162. Andrew and Mitrokhin, *Mitrokhin Archive II*, p. 124.

163. State Department Bureau of Intelligence and Research, "Developing Soviet-Nicaraguan Relations," 24 June 1981, *NICARAGUA*, doc. 01346.

164. A. Sever, *Istoriya KGB* (Moscow 2008) p. 80.

165. Cray Research, Inc., *The Cray-1 Computer System* (1977); also, "SCD Supercomputer Gallery," www.cisl.ucar.edu/computers/gallery/cray/cray/1.jsp.

166. Admiral B. R. Inman, "Supercomputer Leadership: A U.S. Priority," ed. N. Metropolis, *Frontiers of Super-Computing* (Berkeley 1986) p. xvii.

167. M. Aid, *The Secret Sentry: The Untold History of the National Security Agency* (New York 2009) pp 164–165.

168. IBM history Web site: www-1.ibm.com/ibm/history/exhibits/3033/3033_TR03.html.

169. Aid, *Secret Sentry*, and a confidential source in a position to know.

170. Andrew and Mitrokhin, *Mitrokhin Archive II*, p. 386.

171. V. Mitrokhin, *The KGB in Afghanistan* (Washington DC 2002) p. 6.

172. Meeting with the ambassador and the rezident on 29 April, ibid., p. 7.

173. Points made by R. Ulyanovsky in conversation with Friedel Trappen at the Central Committee of the CPSU, 12 May 1978: "Information zur gegenwärtigen Lage in Afghanistan, Berlin 16 May 1978," BA SAPMO, SED ZK, *Internationale Verbindungen*, DY/30/IV B 2/20.229.

174. Mitrokhin, *KGB*, p. 9.

175. "Information zur."

176. GDR ambassador in Moscow, Vogl's record of a conversation with Shumilov, 23 May 1978: Vogl (Moscow) to Berlin, 25 May 1978, ibid.

177. A. Westad, "The Road to Kabul: Soviet Policy on Afghanistan, 1978–1979," in Westad, ed., *The Fall of Détente: Soviet-American Relations during the Carter Years* (Oslo 1997) p. 122.

178. Lyakhovskii, *Tragediya*, p. 48.

179. Record of a briefing from A. M. Puzanov, Soviet ambassador in Kabul, by Deputy Foreign Minister of the GDR, Klaus Willerding 11 July 1978, BA SAPMO . . . .

180. Vladimir Kryuchkov, reflecting on his visit of July 1978. He was then head of the first main (foreign) directorate of the KGB: A. Bondarenko, "Vladimir Kryuchkov: my vyigrali etu voinu," *Krasnaya Zvezda*, 13 February 2004.

181. Ibid.

182. Record of a conversation with Amin, 23 November 1978, BA SAPMO, loc. cit.

183. Lyakhovskii, *Tragediya*, p. 66.

184. L. Shebarshin, *Ruka Moskvy: Zapiski nachal'nika sovetskoi razvedki* (Moscow 1992) p. 133.

185. Ibid., p. 175.

186. Lyakhovskii, *Tragediya*, pp. 68–70.

187. Ibid., p. 71.

188. Ibid., p. 92.

189. Ibid., pp. 92–100.

190. O. Grinevskii, *Tainy sovetskoi diplomatii* (Moscow 2000) p. 168. Grinevsky was first deputy head of the Near East department.

191. Andrew and Mitrokhin, *Mitrokhin Archive II*, p. 181.

192. Grinevskii, *Tainy*, p. 170.

193. From the CIA history of the coup: D. Wilber, "Overthrow of Premier Mossadeq of Iran, November 1952–August 1953," Summary, pp. iii–iv, available from the National Security Archive; also obituary of Sir Dick Franks, *The Times*, 20 August 2008.

194. Grinevskii, *Tainy*, p. 170.

195. Ibid., p. 172.

196. Ibid., pp. 174–176.

197. Ibid., p. 177.

198. Ibid.

199. Ibid., pp. 174–175.

200. Varennikov, *Nepovtorimoe*, vol. 4, p. 99.

201. Johnson, *United States Cryptographic History*, p. 253.

202. Mitrokhin, *KGB*, pp. 41–42.

203. Dobrynin, *In Confidence*, p. 436.

204. Ibid., pp. 45 and 58–59.

205. Interview: *Nouvel Observateur*, no. 1732, 15 January 1998.

206. Off the record briefing from a source privy to the operation.

207. Sir Nicholas Henderson, Diary (with the permission of daughter Alexandra).

208. Lyakhovskii, *Tragediya*, p. 103.

209. Grishin, *Ot Khrushcheva*, pp. 50–51.

210. Quoted in Andrew and Gordievsky, *KGB* (London 1990) p. 482.

211. Bondarenko, "Vladimir Kryuchkov."

212. Aleksandrov-Agentov, *Ot Kollontai*, p. 246.

213. M. Gareev, *Afganskaya strada (s sovetskimi voiskami i bez nikh)* (Moscow 1999) p. 44.

214. Lyakhovskii, *Tragediya*, pp. 109–111. Also *Voprosy Istorii*, no. 3 1993, p. 5.

215. Conversation with Harold Brown, end of February 1984.

216. Kirpichenko, *Razvedka*, pp. 35–354.

217. Witnessed and related to me by the late General Bill Odom, then military assistant to Brzezinski. Odom died on 30 May 2008.

218. *Nouvel Observateur*, 15 January 1998.

219. Johnson, *United States Cryptographic History*, p. 254.

220. Initialled by Honecker, 21 December 1979, BA SAPMO, DY/30/J IV 2/202. 479.

221. *Ocherki istorii rossiskoi vneshnei razvedki*, vol. 6 (Moscow 2007) p. 92.

222. Axen's record, 23/24 January 1980, BA SAPMO, DY/30/IV B 2/20 157.

223. Adamishin Diary.

CHAPTER 11. THE REAGAN PRESIDENCY

Epigraph: Oral testimony, Hoover-Gorbachev Foundation Oral History Project, box 4.

1. NSDD#75, 17 January 1983: *National Security Directives of the Reagan and Bush Administrations. The Declassified History of U.S. Political and Military Policy, 1981–1991*, ed. C. Simpson (Boulder 1995) pp. 255–263.

2. *Foreign Affairs*, vol. 74, no. 3, p. 200.

3. Recalculations for Goskomstat, 1990–1993, under Moisei Eydelman: M. Ellman and V. Kontorovich, eds., *The Destruction of the Soviet Economic System: An Insiders' History* (London 1998) p. 76.

4. R. Pikhoya, *Moskva. Kreml'. Vlast': Dve Istorii Odnoi Strany. Rossiya na izlome tysyacheletii 1985–2005* (Moscow 2007) pp. 383–384.

5. US Energy Information Agency, *Annual Energy Review 2008*, table 3.8, p. 83.

6. Pikhoya, *Moskva. Kreml'. Vlast'. Sorok let posle voiny, 1945–1985* (Moscow 2007) p. 609.

7. "Implications of the Decline in Soviet Hard Currency Earnings," CIA Electronic Reading Room. Quoted in *Ocherki Istorii Rossiskoi Vneshnei Razvedki*, vol. 7, p. 11.

8. Gus Weiss, "The Farewell Dossier: Duping the Soviets," www.cia.gov/library/center-for-the-study-of-intelligence/csi-publications/csi-studi . . . ; "L'Espion Qui Venait du Froid," *Arte Magazine* no. 9, 21–27 February 2009 p. 11.

9. S. Lekarev, "Byvshii sotrudnik KGB po klichke 'Fervell' peredal frantszuskoi razvedke okolo 4 tysyach sekretnykh dokumentov. Podpolkovnik KGB Vetrov podorval ekonomiku SSSR," *Argumenty. Ru* 15 (49) 12 April 2007; Lekarev, "Frantsuzskii shpion v Moskve popalsya za popytku ubiistva lyubovnitsy. Podpolkovnik-shpion bezuspeshno pytalsya uiti ot rasplaty za predatel'stvo s pomoshchyu 'mokrukhi,'" ibid., 16 (50), 19 April 2007.

10. *Public Papers of the Presidents. Gerald R. Ford. 1975*, vol. 1 (Washington DC 1977) p. 179.

11. 29 January 1981: *Public Papers of the Presidents of the United States. Ronald Reagan. 1981* (Washington DC 1982) p. 57.
12. R. Reagan, *An American Life* (London 1990) p. 219.
13. 9 January 1978: *Reagan, In His Own Hand* (New York 2001) p. 152.
14. 28 August 2001, Ronald Reagan Oral History Project, Miller Center, University of Virginia, p. 28.
15. Kennan to Kissinger, 19 September 1973, enclosed in Eagleburger to Kissinger, 26 September 1973, NARA, Nixon Presidential Materials Project, NSC Files, Country File, Europe, box 722.
16. Meeting with Gromyko, 28 September 1973, ibid.
17. S. Ramírez, *Adiós Muchachos. Una memoria de la revolución sandinista* (Madrid 1999) p. 109.
18. Ibid., p. 134.
19. Entry, 11 February 1981: R. Reagan, *The Reagan Diaries*, ed. D. Brinkley (New York 2007) p. 4.
20. Ramírez, *Adiós*, p. 135.
21. Ibid., p. 135.
22. S. Kinzer, *Blood of Brothers: Life and War in Nicaragua* (Cambridge, Mass. 2007) pp. 142–143.
23. Ramírez, *Adiós*, pp. 147–148.
24. "Nicaraguan Military Build-Up," 8 March 1982, CIA Electronic Reading Room, doc. 01458.
25. Ibid.
26. "Vermerk über ein Gespräch des Gen. Erich Honecker, Generalsekretär des ZK der SED und Vorsitzender des Staatsrates der DDR, mit Gen. Michail Gorbatschow, Generalsekretär des ZK der KpdSU, am 5.5.1985 im Kreml im Moskau": *Honecker-Gorbatschow Vieraugengespräche* (Berlin 1993) p. 42.
27. Department of the Army, US Army Intelligence and Security Command, US Army Intelligence and Threat Analysis Center, *Army Intelligence Summary: NICARAGUA, May 1984.* Ibid., doc. 02078.
28. Memorandum for the Director of Central Intelligence, "Covert Action Proposal Concerning Central America," 9 September 1983, ibid., doc. 01813.
29. Ibid., doc. 01824.
30. Reagan, *American Life*, p. 606.
31. Ibid., p. 588.
32. G. Shultz, *Turmoil and Triumph* (New York 1993) p. 122.
33. Personal knowledge; also B. Fischer, "A Cold War Conundrum" (unclassified CIA study, 1997).
34. M. Wolf, *Spionagechef im geheimen Krieg. Erinnerungen* (Munich 1997) p. 326. This is an expanded version of the English edition published that same year in New York.
35. Ibid., p. 328.
36. Dobrynin, *In Confidence*, p. 523.
37. C. Andrew and V. Mitrokhin, *The Mitrokhin Archive: The KGB in Europe and the West* (London 2000) p. 512.

38. *Washington Times,* 28 November 1991.
39. "Implications of Recent Soviet Military-Political Activities: SNIE 10–11–84/JX," http://www.foia.cia.gov/browse_docs_full.asp.
40. F. Ermarth, "Observations on the 'War Scare' of 1983 From an Intelligence Perch," Parallel History Project on NATO and the Warsaw Pact, www.isn.ethz.ch/php.
41. Danilevich testimony, Hines et al., eds., *Soviet Intentions,* p. 43.
42. Ibid., p. 26.
43. Akhromeyev testimony, ibid., p. 6.
44. Wolf, *Spionagechef,* p. 322.
45. Directed at US chargé d'affaires Jack Matlock in the spring of 1981: J. Matlock, *Reagan and Gorbachev: How the Cold War Ended* (New York 2004) p. 29, footnote 1.
46. Informant: Vyacheslav Dashichev, then head of the international relations department of the institute.
47. Agreement to this signed by the Politburo's Polish committee formed on 25 August— Suslov, Gromyko, Andropov, Ustinov, and Chernenko, 28 August 1980: copy on the Harvard Project for Cold War Studies Web site.
48. Recollections of General Anatolii Gribkov, *Sud'ba Varshavskogo Dogovora: Vospominaniya, dokumenty, fakty* (Moscow 1998) p. 145.
49. Record of the Politburo meeting, 29 October 1980, copies in the Bukovsky Archive on the Web: 9.3 Pol'sha, 0403.
50. Gribkov, *Sud'ba,* pp. 145–146.
51. Entry, 24 March 1981, Adamishin Diary (Hoover Institution), box 1. Adamishin, born 11 October 1934, was head of the first European department and a member of the ruling collegium of the MID from 1978 to 1986, when he became first deputy minister of foreign affairs.
52. Gribkov, *Sud'ba,* pp. 134–136.
53. Record of a Politburo meeting, 10 September 1981, Bukovsky Archive.
54. Record of a Politburo instruction, 21 November 1981, Adamishin Diary.
55. Gribkov, *Sud'ba,* p. 147.
56. Record of a Politburo meeting, 10 December 1981, Bukovsky Archive.
57. M. Wolf, *Spionagechef,* p. 336.
58. Gribkov, *Sud'ba,* pp. 138–140.
59. Ibid., pp.140–141.
60. NSC meeting, 22 December 1981, Reagan Presidential Library.
61. *Ocherki istorii rossiskoi razvedki,* vol. 7, p. 22.
62. Vorotnikov, *A bylo eto tak . . . ,* p. 52.
63. Entry, 23 February 1985, Adamishin Diary, box 1.
64. *Ocherki istorii rossiskoi razvedki,* p. 123.
65. Entry, 9 April 1981, Adamishin Diary.
66. US National Foreign Assessment Center, *The Development of Soviet Military Power: Trends since 1965 and Prospects for the 1980s (U),* 13 April 1981, p. 14.
67. Kataev Papers.
68. Speech to Warsaw Pact leaders, 4–5 January 1983, www.isn.ethz.ch/php/documents/collection_3/PCC_meetings/coll_3_PCC_1983.html.

69. "SPRAVKA ob informatsii, izlozhennoi v vystuplenii pervogo zamestitelya direktora TsRU R. Geitsa ot 25 noyabrya s.g.," Kataev Papers, box 5.

70. "SPRAVKA o fakticheskom sostoyanii del v svyazi s pretenziyami SShA v otnoshenii soblyudeniya Sovetskim Soyuzom obyazatel'stv v oblasti ogranichenii vooruzhenii" (no date but after 1978 and prior to 1986), ibid. Dr. Key, on a grant from the Royal Society, specializing in laser technology, was in Moscow from 3 November 1976 for ten months and had reached the same conclusion, which must have reinforced the new skepticism. (I discovered this from him when in Moscow in the spring of 1977 on a grant from the British Academy.)

71. Edward Teller, "Invention of the X-ray Laser Gives a Major Boost to SDI Advocates," *New York Times*, 18 February 1988.

72. *San Jose Mercury*, 4 February 1988; also Teller.

73. Ibid.

74. Entry, 28 June 1982, Reagan, *Reagan Diaries*, p. 91.

75. Teller, loc. cit. Teller appeared on Buckley's television show *Firing Line* earlier that summer. Here he aired his views about defense from missile attack.

76. Teller to Reagan, 23 July 1982: Edward Teller Papers, Hoover Institution, box 282.

77. Teller, "The Ultimate Defense," www. hooverdigest. org/ 021/ teller.html. Also, Shultz, *Turmoil and Triumph*, p. 248.

78. Shultz, *Turmoil and Triumph*, p. 246.

79. *Vital Speeches of the Day*, 15 April 1983, vol. 49, no. 13.

80. Shultz, *Turmoil and Triumph*, p. 266.

81. Starodubov, *Superderzhavy*, p. 375.

82. L. Gelb, "Who Won the Cold War?" *New York Times*, 20 August 1992.

83. "Memorandum of a telephone conversation," 26 October 1983, Margaret Thatcher Foundation Archive (Reagan Library originals).

84. An acquaintance, then at the Office of the Secretary of Defense, described this as a "mickey-mouse system."

85. Memcon, 22 December 1984: ibid.

86. *Kommersant*, 9 May 2005

87. Ibid.

88. "Zasedanie Politburo TsK KPSS," 4 August 1983, Volkogonov Papers, box 25.

89. "Zasedanie Politburo TsK KPSS," 2 September 1983, ibid.

90. Chazov testimony: N. Zen'kovich, *Mikhail Gorbachev: Zhizn' do Kremlya* (Moscow 2001) p. 382.

91. Vorotnikov, *A Bylo eto tak . . .* , p. 31.

92. Entry, 15 January 1985, Adamishin Diary, box 1.

93. *Kommersant*, 9 May 2005.

94. "Zasedanie Politburo TsK," 23 February 1984, Volkogonov Papers, box 25.

95. Protokol 147, ibid.

96. CIA, *The Slowdown in Soviet Industry, 1976–82* (1983).

97. Wohlforth, *Witnesses*, p. 35.

98. Haslam, *Soviet Union and the Politics*, p. 144.

99. Entry, 22 February 1984, Reagan, *Reagan Diaries*, p. 220.

100. Entry 1 March, ibid., p. 222.
101. Entry, 5 March, ibid., p. 223.
102. Shultz, *Triumph and Turmoil*, p. 268.
103. Haslam, *Soviet Union and the Politics*, p. 144.
104. Ibid., p. 145.
105. Ibid.
106. Pye Friendly, then working as Pamela's personal secretary, was told this by her employer soon after the visit.
107. Tikhonov at a Politburo meeting on 11 March 1985, Volkogonov Papers, box 25. Confirmed on brief personal acquaintance.
108. V. Chazov, *Rok* (Moscow 2000) pp. 29–31. Chazov, one of Brezhnev's doctors, took a holiday in the area—Arkhyz—with the Gorbachevs, where this subject came up first in 1971.
109. Ibid., p. 39.
110. Zen'kovich, *Mikhail Gorbachev*, p. 198.
111. Chazov, *Rok*, p. 42.
112. Mlechin, *Yuri Andropov*, p. 348.
113. Chazov, *Rok*, p. 46.
114. Ibid., pp. 48–49.
115. Conversations with Lord Powell of Bayswater, Mrs. Thatcher's private secretary. Howe, see below, may have been wrong to suggest that along with other, more interested, parties they had already foreseen that Gorbachev was their man. It reads too much like unusual foresight. For another view: A. Brown, "The Change to Engagement in Britain's Cold War Policy: The Origins of the Thatcher-Gorbachev Relationship," *Journal of Cold War Studies*, vol. 10, no. 3, Summer 2008, pp. 3–47.
116. *Kommersant*, 9 May 2005.
117. The author met him at the time but, tired of repeated charm offensives, did not believe him.
118. Testimony, 13 October 1993: *Materialen der Enquete-Kommission . . .* , vol. V/1 (Baden-Baden 1995) pp. 137–138.
119. Thatcher Archive, COI transcript.
120. The author faced this wall of skepticism in Washington at the time.
121. W. Wohlforth, ed., *Witnesses to the End of the Cold War* (Baltimore 1996) p. 17.
122. Entry, 25 January 1985, Adamishin Diary.
123. A. Yakovlev, *Omut Pamyati* (Moscow 2001) pp. 442–443; also confirmed by others: R. Pikhoya, *Moskva. Kreml'. Vlast'. Dve Istorii . . .* , p. 14.
124. Ibid. Confirmed by Adamishin in his diary.
125. "Zasedanie Politburo TsK KPSS," 11 March 1985, Volkogonov Papers.
126. Matlock, *Reagan and Gorbachev*, p. 128.
127. "Soveshchanie Sekretarei TsK KPSS," 15 March 1985, Volkogonov Papers.
128. "Postanovlenie TsK KPSS. Nekotorye itogi deyatel'nosti Politburo i Sekretariata TsK za 1985g.," ibid.
129. Matlock, *Reagan and Gorbachev*, p.129. Matlock's informant is Bessmertnykh.
130. Testimony, 27 May 1999, Hoover-Gorbachev Foundation Oral History Project, box 4.

131. Information from Robert Legvold.

132. Personal acquaintance.

133. A. Yakovlev, *Sumerki* (Moscow 2003) p. 330.

134. *Aleksandr' Yakovlev: Perestroika, 1985–1991* (Moscow 2008) p. 295.

135. "About Reagan," 12 March 1985, National Security Archive.

136. "Soveshchanie sekretarei TsK KPSS," 15 March 1985, Volkogonov Papers.

137. A. Chernyaev, *Shest' Let s Gorbachevym. Po dnevnikovym zapisyam* (Moscow 1993) p. 78.

138. Minutes, National Security Archive.

139. Entry, 29 July 1985, Adamishin Diary.

140. Shultz, *Turmoil and Triumph*, p. 572.

141. Entry, 11 August 1985, Adamishin Diary.

142. Entry, 12 February 1986, ibid.

143. Interview: Oral History of the Cold War, Mershon Center, Ohio State University.

144. Comment made 14 October 1986 at the Politburo. For the minutes: *V Politburo TsK KPSS. Po zapisyam Anatoliya Chernyaeva, Vadima Medvedeva, Georgiya Shakhnazarova, 1985–1991* (Moscow 2006) p. 76.

145. Aleksandrov-Agentov, *Ot Kollontai*, p. 288.

146. Memorandum of Conversation, Reagan-Gorbachev Meetings in Geneva, November 1985—Second Private Meeting, 19 November, National Security Archive.

147. Ibid., Third Plenary Meeting, 20 November, National Security Archive.

148. Quoted in Shultz, *Turmoil and Triumph*, pp. 592–593.

149. Ibid., p. 593.

150. "Analiz Rabot po Amerikanskoi Programme SOI (1983–1989gg.)," Kataev Papers.

151. *V Politburo*, p. 29.

152. Chernyaev testimony: Wohlforth, *Witnesses*, p. 36.

153. Ibid., pp. 36–37.

154. Entry, 22 September 1985, Adamishin Diary.

155. Shultz, *Turmoil and Triumph*, pp. 604–605.

156. Verbatim, 28 November 1985: Vorotnikov, *A Bylo eto tak . . .* , p. 79.

157. Interviewed by Belanovsky: Ellman and Kontorovich, eds., *The Destruction*, p. 59.

158. Wohlforth, *Witnesses*, p. 14.

159. Interview: *Oral History of the Cold War*, Mershon Center, Ohio State University.

160. Starodubov, *Superderzhavy*, p. 396.

161. Letter to Kovalev, September 1986: Chernyaev, *Shest' let*, p. 107.

162. Entry, 7 January 1986, Adamishin Diary.

163. Interview, Oral History of the Cold War, Mershon Center, Ohio State University.

164. Chernyaev, *Shest' Let s Gorbachevym. Po dnevnikovym zapisyam* (Moscow 1993) p. 80.

165. "Vermerk über das Gespräch des Genossen Gorbatschow, Generalsekretär des ZK der KpdSU, mit den Genossen Erich Honecker, Generalsekretär des ZK der SED und Vorsitzender des Staatsrates der DDR, Herbert Mies, Vorsitzender der Deutschen Kommunistischen Partei, Horst Schmitt, Vorsitzender der Sozialistischen Einheitspartei Westberlins," no date but sometime in late September 1986: *Honecker-Gorbatschow Vieraugengespräche* (Berlin 1993), p. 125.

166. Ibid., p. 126.

167. National Security Archive.

168. Chernyaev, "Notes from the Politburo Session," 22 September 1986, National Security Archive.

169. *Honecker-Gorbatschow Vieraugengespräche*, p. 126.

170. Shultz to Reagan, 2 October 1986, ibid.

171. NSDD 245, 7 October 1986: *National Security Directives*, p. 723.

172. Entry, 15 September 1986, Adamishin Diary.

173. "Ustanovki Gorbacheva gruppe po podgotovke Reik'yavika," 4 October 1986: *V Politburo*, pp. 73–74.

174. A. Chernyaev, "Notes for the Politburo Session," 8 October 1986, National Security Archive.

175. Memcon, 16 October 1986, ibid.

176. Shultz, *Turmoil and Triumph*, p. 773.

177. Starodubov, *Superderzhavy*, p. 444.

178. Danilevich testimony, Hines et al., eds., *Soviet Intentions*, p. 43.

179. Testimony, 27 May 1999, Hoover-Gorbachev Foundation Oral History Project, box 4.

180. Interview, Oral History of the Cold War, Mershon Center, Ohio State University.

181. Testimony, Hoover-Gorbachev Foundation Oral History Project, box 1.

182. "Ob itogakh vstrechi v Reik'yavike," 14 October 1986: *V Politburo TsK KPSS*, p. 77.

183. Vorotnikov, *A Bylo eto tak . . .*, p. 113.

184. "Ob itogakh . . ."

185. Vorotnikov, *A Bylo eto tak . . .*, p. 115.

186. Entry, 19 November 1986, Adamishin Diary.

187. Entry, 5 December 1986, ibid.

188. Chernyaev, "Notes from the Politburo Session," 30 October 1986, National Security Archive.

189. Session of the Politburo of the CC CPSU, 14 October 1986, Volkogonov Papers.

190. Entry, 24 December 1986, Adamishin Diary.

191. "K otsenke voenno-politicheskoi obstanovki," 18 December 1986, Kataev Papers, box 1.

192. A summary of the US position, undated, appears in Kataev's Papers: ibid., box 6.

193. TsK KPSS. "O nashei dal'neishei takticheskoi linii na peregovorakh s SShA po yadernym i kosmicheskim vooruzheniyam," ibid., box 5.

194. "Predlozheniya po razvitiu nashei pozitsii v otnoshenii raket srednei dal'nosti i raket operativno-takticheskoi napravleniya," 15 March 1987, Kataev Papers, box 3.

195. Chernyaev testimony: Wohlforth, *Witnesses*, p. 48.

196. Chernyaev, "Notes from the Politburo Session," 8 October 1986, National Security Archive.

197. For Chernyaev's view: Chernyaev, *Shest' let*, p. 107.

198. A. Chernyaev, Notes from the Politburo session, 30 October 1986, National Security Archive.

199. Entry, 19 April 1987, Adamishin Diary, box 1.

200. Sokolov, "TsK KPSS. Po voprosam utochneniya struktury strategicheskikh yadernykh sil SSSR i protivodeistviya amerikanskoi programme sozdaniya mnogoeshelonnoi sistemy protivoraketnoi oborony," 17 May 1987, Kataev Papers, box 6.

201. Danilevich interviewed by Belanovsky: Ellman and Kontorovich, eds., *The Destruction*, p. 42.

202. Chernyaev, "Notes from a Conference with Politburo Members and Secretaries of the Central Committee," 1 December 1986, National Security Archive.

203. "Stenografische Niederschrift des Treffense der Generalsekretäre der Bruderparteien der Staaten des Warschauer Vertrages am Freitag, 29.5.1987," BA SAPMO DY 30/2354.

204. "Zasedanie Politburo TsK KPSS," 30 May 1987, Volkogonov Papers.

205. Starodubov, *Superderzhavy*, p. 444.

206. Ibid.

207. Ibid.

208. P78/UP, 6 August 1987: referred to in "Spravka" (1989), Kataev Papers, box 7.

209. Chernyaev, *Shest' let*, p. 137.

210. Entry, 26 November 1987, Adamishin Diary.

211. "Spravka," Kataev Papers, box 6.

212. Lebedev and Podberezkin, "Unikal'nyi shans dlya Evropy, dlya vsei planety," *Kommunist Vooruzhennykh Sil*, no. 22, 6 November 1987, p. 94.

213. TsK KPSS. "O kriticheskikh zamechaniyakh kommunistov, vyskazannykh na partiinom sobranii v Dogovorno-pravovom upravlenii General'nogo shtaba," Kataev Papers.

214. Ibid.

215. "Direktivy dlya peregovorov s gosudarstvennoi sekretarem SShA Dzh. Shul'tsem (Vashington, 20–23 marta 1988 goda)," Kataev Papers, box 1.

216. Cited in V. Shlykov, "Back into the Future, or Cold War Lessons from Russia," *Russia in Global Affairs*, no. 2, April–June 2006.

CHAPTER 12. DOWN COMES THE WALL

Epigraph: *The Future Belongs to Freedom* (New York 1991) p. 234.

1. Aide Sergei Tarasenko: R. English, *Russia and the Idea of the West; Gorbachev, Intellectuals and the End of the Cold War* (New York 2000) p. 209.

2. *Pravda*, 26 July 1988.

3. Interview with Tarasenko, Oral History of the Cold War, Mershon Center, Ohio State University.

4. Speech 4 August 1988—"Bez Raskachki—Za Delo": E. Ligachev, *Izbrannye rechi i stat'i* (Moscow 1989) p. 291.

5. Gorbachev to Honecker, 5 May 1985, *Honecker-Gorbatschow Vieraugengespräche*, p. 42.

6. "Abteilung. Internationale Verbindungen. Vermerk über ein Gespräch des Gen. Armeegeneral Heinz Keßler, Mitglied des Politbüros des ZK der SED und Minister

für Nationale Verteidigung, mit Gen. Daniel Ortega, Koordinator der Exekutivkommission der Nationalleitung der FSLN und Präsident der Republik Nikaragua, am 8.10.1989," 10 October 1989, BA SAPMO, DY 30/IV 2/2.035.

7. Quoted in the Stepanov-Mamaladze Papers (Hoover Institution), box 1, diary, p. 264.

8. "Aus der Aufzeichung des Gesprächs des Präsidenten der SI un Ehrenvorsitzenden der SPD, Brandt, mit dem Generalsekretär des ZK der KpdSU, Gorbatschow, in Moskau," 5 April 1988: Brandt, *Berliner Ausgabe*, vol. 10, doc. 43.

9. Politburo minutes, 27–28 December 1988: quoted in Pikhoya and A. Sokolov, *Istoriya Sovremennoi Rossii. Krizis kommunisticheskoi vlasti v SSSR i rozhdenie novoi Rossii. Konets 1970-x–1991* (Moscow 2008) p. 230.

10. Quoted in W. Wohlforth, ed., *Witnesses to the End of the Cold War*, p. 15.

11. Chernyaev's notes on a conversation with Gorbachev, 17 November 1986, National Security Archive.

12. Memorandum to Yakovlev, February 1989: *CWIHPB*, issue 12/13, Fall/Winter 2001, p. 64.

13. 24 February 1989, ibid., p. 69.

14. *Disturbing the Peace* (London 1990) pp. 119–120.

15. *Honecker-Gorbatschow Vieraugengespräche*, p. 45.

16. Interview: http:/edition.cnn.com/SPECIALS/cold.war/episodes/23/interviews/gorba chev/.

17. "V Politburo TsK KPSS: O nekotorykh aktual'nykh voprosakh sotrudnichestva s sotsstranami," 28 June 1986, Volkogonov Papers.

18. Ibid.

19. At the Comecon summit, 10 November 1986, as quoted from SAPMO, the East German Party archive, now part of the Bundesarchiv in Berlin: B.-E. Siebs, *Die Aussenpolitik der DDR, 1976–1989: Strategien und Grenzen* (Padeborn 1999) pp. 326–327.

20. Politburo minutes, 29 January 1987: *Mikhail Gorbachev i Germanskii Vopros: Sbornik dokumentov, 1986–1991*, ed. A. Galkin and A. Chernyaev (Moscow 2006) p. 29.

21. Ibid.

22. Diary entry, 27 March 1987: cited by Teimuraz Stepanov, a foreign policy aide to Shevardnadze, Hoover-Gorbachev Foundation Oral History Project, box 5.

23. "Ein Marschall auf meinem Sessel," *Der Spiegel*, 4 October 1999.

24. M. Gorbachev, *Kak eto bylo* (Moscow 1999) p. 75.

25. Ibid., p. 55.

26. "Information über das Treffen des Gen. E. Honecker mit Gen. M.S. Gorbatschow am 20. April 1986 im Berlin," *Honecker-Gorbatschow Vieraugengespräche*, pp. 98–99.

27. Ibid., p. 99; also, "Protokoll des Gesprächs des Vorsitzenden der SPD, Brandt, mit dem Generalsekretär des ZK der KpdSU, Gorbatschow, in Moskau," 27 May 1985: W. Brandt, *Berliner Ausgabe*, vol. 10 (Berlin 2009) doc. 20.

28. Gorbachev, *Kak eto bylo*, p. 59.

29. Ibid.

30. Kochesmasov's interview with *Der Spiegel*, 16 November 1992.

31. Falin's testimony, Hoover-Gorbachev Foundation Oral History Project, box 4.

32. Chernyaev to Gorbachev, 20 February 1987, and Falin to Gorbachev, 19 February 1987, Zelikow-Rice Papers, box 3.

33. Instructions, 2 February 1987: *Mikhail Gorbachev i Germanskii Vopros*, p. 31.

34. Politburo minutes, 12 February, ibid., p. 32.

35. Dashichev, 28 October 1993: *Materielen der Enquete Kommission . . .* V/1, p. 343; also conversations with Dashichev. After Dashichev published the first open attack on the bases of Soviet foreign policy, I invited him to spend a week with me at King's College, Cambridge, 14–20 May 1989, for extended private discussion.

36. V. Dashichev, "Proekt 'Zvezda'— v poiskakh pute'i vykhoda iz 'kholodnoi voiny,'" *Novaya i Noveishaya Istoriya*, no. 2, March–April 2010, pp. 120–132.

37. Dashichev, 28 October 1993: *Materielen der Enquete Kommission . . .* V/1, p. 343; also conversations with Dashichev.

38. Dashichev, *Materialen der Enquete-Kommission . . .* , p. 362.

39. Dashichev testimony, *Gorbatschow und die deutsche Einheit. Aussagen der wichtigsten russischen und deutschen Beteiligten* (Bonn 1993) pp. 20–21.

40. V. Dashichev, "On the Road to German Reunification: The View from Moscow," in G. Gorodetsky, ed., *Soviet Foreign Policy, 1917–1991: A Retrospective* (London 1994) pp. 171–173; also, conversations with Dashichev.

41. Interview: *Der Spiegel*, 21 January 1991.

42. *Gorbatschow und die deutsche Einheit*, p. 21.

43. Stepanov testimony, Hoover-Gorbachev Foundation Oral History Project, box 5

44. On working through Chernyaev: conversations with Dashichev. For the quote which appears in a memorandum from Chernyaev: M. Kramer, "The Collapse of East European Communism and the Repercussions within the Soviet Union (Part 3)," *Journal of Cold War Studies*, vol. 7, no. 1, Winter 2005, p. 18.

45. Quoted in the memoirs of Hans Modrow, *Die Perestroika: Wie ich sie sehe* (Berlin 1998) p. 55.

46. V. Falin, *Konflikty v Kremle: Sumerki bogov po-russki* (Moscow 1999) p. 148.

47. Dashichev, "On the Road . . ."; "Vermerk über ein gespräch des Gen. Hermann Axen, Mitglied des Politbüros und Sekretär des ZK der SED, mit dem Außordentlichen und Bevollmächtigen Botschafter der UdSSR in der DDR, Gen. Wjatscheslaw Kotschemassow, am 9. Juni 1988," BA SAPMO, DY 30/IV 3/2.035 60.

48. "Vermerk über ein Gespräch von ZK-Sekretär Hermann Axen mit Wjatscheslaw Kotschemassow, UdSSR-Botschafter in der DDR, am. 9 Juni 1988," *Countdown zur deutschen Einheit*, ed. D. Nakath and G.-R. Stephan (Berlin 1996) doc. 16.

49. Conversations with Dashichev.

50. Memorandum published in Shakhnazarov, *Tsena Svobody* (Moscow 1993) pp. 367–369.

51. Conversation with Shakhnazarov.

52. Interview, *Newsweek*, 27 October 1986. The backlash in Germany was no less severe: "Kohl hätte sich entschuldigen müssen," *Der Spiegel*, 10 November 1986.

53. Politburo minutes, 11 June 1987: *Mikhail Gorbachev i Germanskii Vopros*, p. 43.

54. R. Weizsäcker, *Der Weg zur Einheit* (Moscow 2009) p. 89.

55. "Bund mit dem Teufel," *Der Spiegel*, 13 February 1995.
56. From Teltschik's diary—entry, 21 November 1989: "De Bärn is geschält," ibid., 23 September 1991.
57. "Ob"edinenie Germanii. Kak eto bylo? (po materialam pomoshchnika prezidenta SSSR)," Zelikow-Rice Papers, box 3.
58. Politburo minutes, 16 July 1987: *Mikhail Gorbachev i Germanskii Vopros*, pp. 56–57.
59. Gorbachev, *Kak eto bylo*, p. 61.
60. Ibid., pp. 63–64.
61. Ibid., p. 68.
62. Ibid., p. 69; plus the briefing for Honecker by Bondarenko—"Aktennotitz über ein Gespräch des Gen. Erich Honecker, Generalsekretär des ZK der SED und Vorsitzender des Staatsrates der DDR, mit Gen. Alexander Bondarenko, Mitglied des Kollegiums und Leiter der 3. Europäischen Abteilung des MfAA der UdSSR, am 30.10.1988,V," BA SAPMO, DY 30/IV 2/2.035 60. See also K. Diekmann and R. Reuth, *Helmut Kohl: "Ich Wollte Deutschlands Einheit"* (Berlin 1996) p. 39. On this issue Kohl's memoirs are uninformative, however: H. Kohl, *Erinnerungen, 1982–1990* (Munich 2005) pp. 652–654.
63. Gorbachev, *Kak eto bylo*, p. 69.
64. Entry, 3 November 1988, Politburo discussion, Chernyaev's diary, National Security Archive.
65. Falin testimony, Hoover-Gorbachev Foundation Oral History Project, box 4.
66. Quoted in Pikhoya and Sokolov, *Istoriya Sovremennoi Rossii*, p. 230.
67. Axen to Keßler, 17 January 1989, BA SAPMO, DY 30/IV 2/2.035 60.
68. Quoted in Pikhoya and Sokolov, *Istoriya*, p. 231.
69. Quoted in Chernyaev, *Shest' Let*, p. 253.
70. Ibid., pp. 255–256.
71. Memcon, Yakovlev, 26 December 1988: *Aleksandr' Yakovlev*, doc. 55.
72. Politburo minutes, 27–28 December 1988: CWIHPB, 12/13, Fall/ Winter 2001, p. 25.
73. S. Akhromeev and G. Kornienko, *Glazami marshala i diplomata* (Moscow 1992) pp. 226–227.
74. Well-attested in M. Beschloss and S. Talbott, *At the Highest Levels: The Inside Story of the End of the Cold War* (London 1993) p. 50.
75. P. Zelikow and C. Rice, *Germany Unified and Europe Transformed* (Cambridge, Mass. 1997) p. 23.
76. Quoted but severely abridged in R. Hutchings, *American Diplomacy and the End of the Cold War* (Washington DC 1997) p. 31. Hutchings served as director for European affairs at the National Security Council.
77. This is apparent from Gorbachev's reflections: Gorbachev, *Kak eto bylo*, p. 76.
78. *FBIS, Daily report*, The Soviet Union, 1 February 1990.
79. H. Kohl, *Erinnerungen*; for a memcon by Yakovlev of talks with Kohl: *Aleksandr' Yakovlev*, doc. 57.
80. A. Chernyaev, "Na Staroi ploshchadi . . . ," *Novaya i Noveishaya Istoriya*, no. 3, May–June 2006, p. 97.

81. CIA, "Gorbachev's Strategy for Managing the Defense Burden: An Intelligence Assessment," April 1989, CIA Electronic Reading Room. Also, "The Soviet Economy in 1988: Gorbachev Changes Course," April 1989, ibid. Gromyko and Mikhail Solomentsev had long been identified as diehards: "'Pangermanisches Fieber'—bis in die DDR," *Der Spiegel*, 13 August 1984.

82. Translation in *CWIPB*, 12/13, 2001, pp. 52–61.

83. Quoting from classified Russian archives, Pavel Stroilov: *Front Page Magazine*, 9 September 2009.

84. Memorandum of 24 February 1989: *CWIPB*, p. 70.

85. Interview: "Gorbaciov: 'Così ho lasciato cadere il Muro,'" *La Repubblica*, 30 September 2009.

86. Conversations with Dashichev; also, *Gorbatschow und die deutsche Einheit*, p. 31.

87. Entry, 18 May 1989: Maksimychev, "*Narod ne prostit*," p. 37.

88. Entry, 24 May 1989: ibid., p. 38.

89. L. Walesa, *The Struggle and the Triumph: An Autobiography* (New York 1992) p. 214.

90. www. gwu.edu/~nsarchiv/news/19991105/Doc-57.html.

91. "Ob obstanovke v Pol'she, vozmozhnykh variantakh ee razvitiya, perspektivakh sovetsko-pol'skikh otnoshenii," 20 September 1989—Vyiska iz Protokola No. 166 Zasedaniya Politburo TsK KPSS, 28 September 1989, Zelikow-Rice Papers, box 3.

92. Memcon, Kohl and Walesa, 9 November 1989: www. gwu.edu/~nsarchiv/news/19991105/9nov89.html.

93. "Ob obstanovke . . ."

94. Quoted by Stroilov: *Front Page Magazine*.

95. Quoted in B-E. Siebs, *Die Aussenpolitik der DDR 1976–1989: Strategien und Grenzen* (Padeborn 1999) pp. 403–404.

96. "Ob obstanovke . . ."

97. H. Halter, "Am Rande des Bürgerkriegs," *Der Spiegel*, 2 October 1995.

98. E. Krenz, *Herbst 89* (Berlin 1999) p. 38.

99. "Telefongespräch des Bundeskanzlers Kohl mit Präsident Bush. 15 Juni 1989," *Dokumente zur Deutschlandpolitik. Deutsche Einheit. Sonderedition aus den Akten des Bundeskanzleramtes 1989/90*, ed. H. J. Küsters and D. Hofman (Munich 1998) doc. 5.

100. Kohl, *Erinnerungen*, p. 887.

101. Interview, www. gu.edu/~nsarchiv/cold war/interviews/episode-23/baker1.html.

102. NSD 23, 22 September 1989, George Bush Library Web site.

103. "Gespräch des Bundeskanzlers Kohl mit Generalsekretär Gorbatschow. Bonn, 13. Juni 1989," *Dokumente zur Deutschlandpolitik*, doc. 3.

104. National Intelligence Council Memorandum, "Status of Soviet Unilateral Withdrawals," NIC M89–10003, October 1989, CIA Electronic Reading Room.

105. Summed up by Chernyaev: "Na Staroi ploshchadi . . . ," p. 102.

106. Diary entry, 3 November 1989, ibid., pp. 100–101.

107. US National Security Directive 23, 22 September 1989, George Bush Library Web site.

108. Testimony from Condoleezza Rice, 17 December 1997: www. gwu.edu/~nsarchiv/coldwar/interviews/episode-24/rice 1.html.

109. "Gespräch des Bundesministers Seiters mit dem stellvertretenden Außenminister Eagleburger. Bonn, 7. September 1989," *Dokumente*, doc. 37.

110. Gorbachev, *Kak eto bylo*, p. 76.

111. Diekmann and Reuth, *Helmut Kohl*, p. 47.

112. Ibid., p. 49.

113. Ibid., p. 50.

114. "Telefongespräch . . . ," *Dokumente*, loc. cit. The fact that this was a private exchange is referred to in "Telefongespräch des Bundeskanzlers Kohl mit Premierministerin Thatcher, 15. Juni 1989," ibid., doc. 6.

115. "Notiz über die Besprechung des Genossen Minister mit dem Stellvertreter des Vorsitzenden des KfS der UdSSR under Leiter der I. Hauptverwaltung—Genossen Generalmajor SCHEBARSCHIN—am 7.4.1989 in Berlin," BstU, ZA, ZAIG 5198, Bl. 100–140.

116. ZAIG, "Monatsübersicht Nr. 6/89 über aktuelle Probleme der Lageentwicklung in sozialistischen Staten," 22 June 1989, BstU, ZA, ZAIG 5337, Bl. 96.

117. Quoted: Dikeman and Reuth, *Helmut Kohl*, p. 79.

118. Krenz, *Herbst*, p. 16.

119. Entry, 12 January 1989: I. Maksimychev, *"Narod nam ne prostit": poslednie mesyatsy GDR. Dnevnik sovetnika-poslannika posol'stva SSSR v Berline* (Moscow 2002) p. 21.

120. Entry, 20 February 1989, ibid., p. 24.

121. Entry, 14 February 1989, ibid.

122. M. Wolf, *Po sobstvennom zadaniyu* (Moscow 1992) p. 117. The book is based on diaries.

123. Ibid., p. 117.

124. Ibid., p. 118.

125. Conversations with Dashichev.

126. Stepanov testimony, Hoover-Gorbachev Foundation Oral History Project, box 5.

127. Interview with Petersen, 20 October 2009, whom I had known since 1985. I met him again on 20 May 1989 when he was en route back from Germany after obtaining the Dashichev memorandum. He was astonished to have missed Dashichev in Cambridge by a matter of hours and pressed me to get hold of him urgently, which I could not do. He then asked me to put in writing what I knew.

128. CIA, Directorate of Intelligence, 27 November 1989, *The German Question and Soviet Policy*. To be found in the Princeton Collection on the CIA Web site.

129. Cited in the interview with Yakovlev, Hoover-Gorbachev Foundation Oral History Project, box 4.

130. Kryuchkov testimony, ibid.

131. Ibid.

132. Entry, 28 March 1989: Maksimychev, *"Narod nam ne prostit,"* p. 32.

133. Interview: www. gwu.edu/~nsarchiv/coldwar/interviews/episode-23/nemeth 1.html.

134. Memcon of a later meeting, 24–25 July 1989: www. gwu.edu/~nsarchiv/news/19991105/24jul89.html.

135. Memcon: www. gwu.edu/~nsarchiv/news/19991105/29mar89.html.
136. *New York Times*, 5 May 1989.
137. Kohl, *Erinnerungen*, pp. 622–627.
138. Krenz, *Herbst*, pp. 16–17.
139. Ibid.
140. Ibid.
141. "Gespräch des Bundeskanzlers Kohl mit Staatspräsident Mitterand. Paris, 22. Juni 1989," *Dokumente*, doc. 8.
142. ZAIG, "Monatsübersicht Nr 8/89 über aktuelle Probleme der Lage entwicklung in sozialistischen Staaten," 23 August 1989, BStU, ZA, ZAIG 5338, Bl. 1–34.
143. Entry, 11 July 1989: Maksimychev, "*Narod ne prostit*," pp. 42–43.
144. ZAIG, "Monatsübersicht . . ."
145. Maksimychev, "*Narod ne prostit*," p. 44.
146. ZAIG, "Hinweise zum verstärkten Missbrauch des Territoriums der Ungarischen Volksrepublik durch Bürger der DDR zum verlassen der DDR sowie zum reiseverkehr nach der UVR," BStU, ZA, ZAIG 5352, Bl. 124–134.
147. Entry, 6 September 1989: Maksimychev, "*Narod ne prostit*," p. 54.
148. ZAIG, "Information über die Entwicklung und Lage auf den Gebieten des Reiseverkehrs, der ständigen Ausreisen und des ungesetzlichen Verlassens der DDR," 20 October 1989, BStU, ZA, ZAIG 7438, Bl. 77–80.
149. Kohl, *Erinnerungen*, p. 922.
150. "Vermerk des Bundesministers Genscher über das Gespräch des Bundeskanzlers Kohl mit Ministerpräsident Németh und Außenministers Horn. Schloß Gymnich, 25 August 1989," *Dokumente*, doc. 28.
151. Ibid.; and "Gespräch des Bundeskanzlers Kohl und des Bundesministers Genscher mit Ministerpräsident Németh und Außenminister Horn während des Mittagessens Schloß Gymnich, 25 August 1989," ibid., doc. 29.
152. Kohl, *Erinnerungen*, p. 923.
153. ZAIG, "Information über die Massenaktion zur Ausschleusung von Bürgern der DDR aus der UVR," 11 September 1989, BStU, ZA-Zentralarchiv, ZAIG 14398, Bl. 28–31.
154. Interview: H. Hertle and K. Elsner, eds., *Der Tag, an dem die Mauer fiel: Die wichtigsten Zeitzeugen berichten vom 9. November 1989* (Berlin 2009) p. 88.
155. *Gorbatschow und die deutsche Einheit*, p. 31.
156. Recalled from memory after the meeting: quoted by Stroilov from the memcon—"Zapadnye lidery svalyali duraka," *Radio Svoboda*, 14 September 2009.
157. Gorbachev interview: *La Repubblica*, 30 September 2009.
158. "Hier is Engagement gefordert," *Der Spiegel*, 25 September 1989.
159. Entry, 21 September 1989: Maksimychev, "*Narod ne prostit*," p. 58.
160. *Pravda*, 7 February 1990.
161. "Gespräch des Ministerialdirektors Teltschik mit Botschafter Kwizinskij. Bonn, 29 September 1989," *Dokumente*, doc. 50.
162. "Information über antisozialistische Bewegungen in der DDR," 30 October 1989: Erich Mielke, Wolfgang Herger, Friedrich Dickel u. Klaus Sorgenicht, "Vorlage für

das Politbüro des ZK der SED Betreff: Maßnahmen zur Verhinderung der weiteren Formierung und zur Zurückdrängung antisozialistischer Sammlungsbewegung," BA SAPMO, DY 30/ J. IV. 2/2A/3252. Bl. 151–162, 173–179.

163. I.-S. Kowalczuk, *Endspiel: Die Revolution von 1989 in der DDR* (Munich 2009) p. 197.

164. M. Hartmann, "Baustoff Hoffnung; Über Probleme mit dem Kirchbau," *Kirche im Sozialismus*, no. 3, 1987, p. 94.

165. H. Bräutigam, *Ständige Vertretung: Meine Jahre in Ost-Berlin* (Hamburg 2009) p. 211.

166. Weizsäcker, *Der Weg*, p. 78.

167. "Information des Ministeriums für Staatssicherheit über 'grundsätzliche Positionen der Bundesregierung zur Weiterentwicklung der Beziehungen BRD-DDR' vom 24. November 1987," *Countdown zur deutsche Einheit*, doc. 2.

168. Entry, 5 October 1989, Chernyaev's diary: *Mikhail Gorbachev i Germanskii Vopros*, p. 204.

169. Gorbachev interview: *La Repubblica*, 30 September 2009.

170. Comment from Chernyaev in seminar, Chatham House, confirmed with anatomical references by Stroilov, *Front Page Magazine*.

171. "Stenografische Niederschrift des Treffens der Gen. Des Politbüros des Zentralkomitees der SED mit dem Generalsekretär des ZK der KpdSU und Vorsitzenden des obersten Sowjets der UdSSR, Gen. Michail Sergejewitsch Gorbatschow, am Sonnabend, dem 7. Oktober 1989 in Berlin-Niederschönhausen. 1.00 p.m.," BA SAPMO, DY 30/IV 2/2.035. 60.

172. W. Kotschemasow, *Meine letzte Mission: Fakten, Erinnerungen, Uberlegungen* (Berlin, c. 1994) pp. 168–169.

173. Ibid., p. 169.

174. Kovalev testimony, Hoover-Gorbachev Foundation Oral History Project, box 4.

175. Luigi Ippolito, "1989, Mosca invade Berlino," *Corriere della Sera*, 8 March 1995.

176. Krenz, *Herbst*, p. 96.

177. Gorbachev, *Kak eto bylo*, p. 84. Former Polish Prime Minister Rakowski translated this for Gorbachev.

178. Entry, 8 October 1989: Maksimychev, "*Narod ne prostit*," p. 65.

179. Ibid.

180. "Aus der Aufzeichnung des Gespräch des Präsidenten der SI und Ehrenvorsitzenden der SPD, Brandt, mit dem Generalsekretär des ZK der KPdSU und Präsidenten der Sowjetunion, Gorbatschow, in Moskau," 17 October 1989: Brandt, *Berliner Ausgabe*, vol. 10, doc. 54.

181. Gorbachev, *Kak eto bylo*, p. 84.

182. Yazov testimony, Hoover-Gorbachev Foundation Oral History Project, box 3.

183. Lord Powell to the author, 29 October 2002.

184. Gorbachev, *Kak eto bylo*, p. 85.

185. Krenz, *Herbst*, pp. 109–110.

186. "Oktober 1989: offene Krise und Machtwechsel/Wortschaftslage": www.bstu.bund.de/cln029/nn_913306/DE/MfS-DDR-Geschichte/revolutionskale.

187. Kotschemasow, *Meine*, p. 179.

188. Ibid., p. 177.

189. Krenz, *Herbst*, p. 145.

190. Kotschemasow, *Meine*, p. 179.

191. Krenz, *Herbst*, p. 149.

192. Ibid., p. 150.

193. Ibid., pp. 149–150.

194. Kotschemasow, *Meine*, p. 172.

195. Krenz, *Herbst*, pp. 199 and 206.

196. Kotschemasow, *Meine*, p. 180.

197. Krenz, *Herbst*, p. 198.

198. Ibid., p. 200.

199. Ibid., p. 210.

200. From the archives retained by Stroilov, as quoted in *The Times*, 11 September 2009.

201. Interview in *La Repubblica*, 30 September 2009.

202. Ibid., p. 225.

203. In conversation with the author; also Hertle and Elsner, *Der Tag*, p. 110.

204. "Rückschau: Der Mauerfall—Zufall oder Plan?" *Mitteldeutscher Rundfunk*, 19 April 2009.

205. H. Teltschik, 329 *Tage: Innenansichten der Einigung* (Berlin 1991) pp. 11–12.

206. Kotschemasow, *Meine*, p. 186.

207. Ibid., p. 249.

208. G.-R. Stephan and D. Kuchenmeister, *"Vorwärts immer, rückwarts nimmer!"*: *Interne Dokumente zum Zerfall von SED und DDR 1988/89* (Berlin 1994) doc. 48.

209. Recollections in "Gorbatschow widerstand den Hardlinern," *Berliner Zeitung*, 9 November 1994.

210. Gorbachev, *Kak eto bylo*, p. 86.

211. "Mündliche Botschaft des Generalsekretärs Gorbatschow an Bundeskanzler Kohl, 10. November 1989," *Dokumente*, doc. 80.

212. Gorbachev, *Kak eto bylo*.

213. Krenz, *Herbst*, p. 247.

214. *Berliner Zeitung*.

215. Dashichev, "Ot totalitarnoi k demokraticheskoi politike v germanskom voprose," D. Proektor et al., *Rossiya i Germaniya v gody voiny i mira, 1941–1955* (Moscow 1955) p. 501.

216. *Berliner Zeitung*.

217. *Izvestiya*, 19 February 1990.

218. Teltschik, 329, p. 15.

219. Interview: "Schön, ich gab die DDR weg," *Der Spiegel*, 2 October 1995.

220. Kohl testimony: Hertle and Elsner, *Der Tag*, p. 102.

221. Kohl interview on *Hard Talk*, BBC, 16 November 1999.

222. "Ihnen ging alles zu schnell," *Der Spiegel*, 21 September 2009; for the original English: *Spiegel Online*, 23 September 2009.

223. Gates, *From the Shadows*, p. 535.

CONCLUSIONS

Epigraph: To Robert Schuman, 27 April 1950: *Journal du Septennat, 1947–1954,* vol. 4 (Paris 2003) p. 187.

1. J. Gaddis, *We Now Know: Rethinking Cold War History* (Oxford 1997) p. 84.
2. G. Roberts, *Stalin's Wars: From World War to Cold War, 1939–1953* (New Haven 2006).
3. E. Hobsbawm, "America's Imperial Delusion: The US Drive for World Domination Has No Historical Precedent," *Guardian,* 14 June 2003.
4. For a spirited but ill-judged defense of the Soviet interpretation of the Yalta provisions on Poland, see M. Leffler, "Adherence to Agreements: Yalta and the Experience of the Early Cold War," *International Security,* vol. 11, no. 1, Summer 1986, pp. 88–123. This article was explicitly driven by hostility to the Reagan accusations against the Soviet Union for breaking SALT, which in fact it did.
5. Leffler quoted by Lundestad: *H-Diplo Roundtable Reviews,* vol. 9, no. 4, 2008, pp. 13–14.
6. V. Mastny, *The Cold War and Soviet Insecurity* (Oxford 1996) p. 191.
7. Ibid., p. 194.
8. For example, C. Maier, "The Cold War as an Era of Imperial Rivalry," ed. S. Pons and F. Romero, *Reinterpreting the End of the Cold War: Issues, interpretations, periodizations* (London 2005), chapter 1.
9. V. Zubok, *A Failed Empire: The Soviet Union in the Cold War from Stalin to Gorbachev* (Chapel Hill 2007).
10. Quoted from an interview with Sergei Belanovsky in Ellman and Kontorovich, *The Destruction,* p. 41.
11. W. Zimmerman, *Soviet Perspectives in International Relations, 1956–1967* (Princeton 1969). He paid no attention to Soviet support for the war in Vietnam. To Zimmerman this was "tactical, and transitory": ibid., p. 236. In fact it indicated the thrust of policy well into the future.
12. The work: *The Great Transition: American-Soviet Relations and the End of the Cold War* (Washington DC 1994). The criticism: R. Pipes, "Misinterpreting the Cold War: The Hard-Liners Had It Right," *Foreign Affairs,* vol. 74, no. 1, p. 155.
13. A. Westad, *The Global Cold War* (Cambridge 2005) p. 396.
14. Interviewed by Belaovsky: Ellman and Kontorovich, eds., *The Destruction,* p. 52.

BIBLIOGRAPHY

PRIMARY SOURCES

ARCHIVES

Russia

Adamishin Diary, Hoover Institution Archive, Stanford University

Arkhiv Vneshnei Politki Rossiskoi Federatsii, Ministry of Foreign Affairs, Moscow (AVPRF)

Bukovsky Archive, Web site

Chernyaev's Diary, National Security Archive

Communist Party Archives, Moscow (TsKhSD, formerly RTsKhIDNI)

Gorbachev archive within the National Security Archive, George Washington University, Washington DC

Kataev Papers, Hoover Institution Archive, Stanford University

Ivy Litvinov Papers, Hoover Institution Archive, Stanford University

Stepanov-Mamaladze Papers, Hoover Institution Archive, Stanford, University

Vasil'ev Papers, Web site of the Cold War International History Project

Volkogonov Papers, Library of Congress

Published

Aleksandr' Yakovlev. Perestroika: 1985–1991 (Moscow 2008)

"'Armiyu nado sdelat' . . . Bez izlishestv': Zapiska N. S. Khrushcheva o voennoe reforme. 1959 g.," *Istoricheskii Arkhiv*, no. 3, 1998

A. Chernyaev, "Na Staroi ploshchadi . . . ," *Novaya i Noveishaya Istoriya*, no. 3, May–June 2006

Cominform, The, ed. G. Procacci et al., *Annali*, Fondazione Giangiacomo Feltrinelli (Milan 1994)

"Doklad Prezidiuma TsK KPSS," 14 October 1964, *Istochnik*, no. 2, 1998

Dokumenty. Georgii Zhukov. Stenogramma oktyabr'skogo (1957 g.) plenuma TsK KPSS i drugie dokumenty, ed. V. Naumov (Moscow 2001)

Dokumenty Vneshnei Politiki, 1940–22 iyunya 1941, ec. G. Mamedov et al., vol. 23, 2, bk. 1 (Moscow 1998)

"Iz Varshavy. Moskva, Tovarishchy Beriya . . . Dokumenty NKVD SSSR o Pol'skom"

Komintern i ideia mirovoi revolutsii: dokumenty, ed. I. Drabkin et al. (Moscow 1998)

Konferentsiyakh perioda velikoi otechestvennoi voiny 1941–1945gg., vol. 2: *Tegeranskaya konferentsiya rukovoditel'ei trekh soyuznykh derzhav—SSSR, SShA i Velikobritanii, 28 noyabrya—1 dekabrya 1943: Sbornik dokumentov*, ed. A. Gromyko et al. (Moscow 1984)

"'Lenin tozhe riskoval': Nakanune vstrechi Khrushcheva i Kennedi v Venne v Iyule 1961g.," *Istochnik*, no. 3, 1983

E. Ligachev, *Izbrannye rechi i stat'i* (Moscow 1989)

Mikhail Gorbachev i Germanskii Vopros: Sbornik dokumentov, 1986–1991, ed. A. Galkin and A. Chernyaev (Moscow 2006)

Moskva i Vostochnaya Evropa: Stanovlenie politicheskikh rezhimov sovetskogo tipa, 1949–1953: Ocherski istorii, ed. T. Volokitina et al. (Moscow 2002)

'Nachalo sovetsko-yugoslavskogo konflikta. Protokoly zasedanii Politburo TsK KPYu 19 fevralya–7 iyulya 1948 g.,' *Voprosy Istorii*, no. 8, 2008

"Ob amerikano-v'etnamskikh kontaktakh," 1 September 1971: "K vlasti mogut priiti novye sily," Dokumenty o voine vo V'etname, *Istochnik*, no. 1, 1997

Perepiska predsedadetlya soveta ministrov SSSR s prezidentami SShA i Prem'er-ministrami Velikobritanii vo vremya Velikoi Otechestvennoi Voiny, 1941–1945gg, vol. 2 (Moscow 1986)

Podpol'e 1944–1945gg (Moscow-Novosibirsk 2001)

Pogranichnye Voiska SSSR, 1945–1950 (Moscow 1975)

Pol'sha. Mekhanizmy podchineniya, 1944–1949gg. Sbornik dokumentov, ed. G. Bordyugov et al. (Moscow 1995)

"Poslednyaya 'Antipartiinaya' Gruppa: Stenograficheskii otchet iyunskogo (1957 g.) plenuma TsK KPSS," third session, 24 June 1957, *Istoricheskii Arkhiv*, no. 4, 1993

The Prague Spring 1968: A National Security Archive Documents Reader, ed. J. Navratil et al. (Prague 1998)

Prezidium TsK KPSS, 1954–1964, vol. 1, ed. A. Fursenko (Moscow 2003)

Revelations from the Russian Archives. Documents in English Translation, ed. D. Koenker and R. Bachman (Washington DC 1996)

Rossiya i Afrika: Dokumenty i materialy XVIIIv.–1960g., vol. 2 (Moscow 1999)

Rossiya XX Vek. Dokumenty: Blizhnevostochnyi Konflikt, 1947–1956, vol. 1, ed. V. Naumkin et al. (Moscow 2003)

Rossiya XX Vek. Dokumenty: Georgii Zhukov. Stenogramma oktyab'skogo (1957g.) plenuma TsK KPSS i drugie dokumenty, ed. V. Naumov (Moscow 2001)

Rossiya XX Vek. Dokumenty: 1941 God, ed. V. Naumov (Moscow 1998)

Sovetskii faktor v Vostochnoi Evrope, 1944–1953, vol. 1, ed. T. Volokitina et al. (Moscow 1999)

Sovetskii Soyuz . . . , vol. 4. *Krymskaya konferentsiya rukovoditelei trekh soyuznykh derzhav—Sovetsko-amerikanskie otnosheniya. Gody Razryadki, 1969–1976. Sbornik dokumentov*, vol. 1, bk. 1, ed. S. Lavrov et al. (Moscow 2007),

Sovetsko-amerikanskie otnosheniya, 1945–1948 (Moscow 2004)

Sovetsko-amerikanskie otnosheniya vo vremya velikoi otechestvennoi voiny, 1941–1945, vol. 2, ed. A. Gromyko et al. (Moscow 1984)

Sovetsko-izrail'skie otnosheniya: Sbornik dokumentov, vol. 1 (Moscow 2000)

SSSR i Germanskii Vopros, 1941–1949, ed. G. Kynin and I. Laufer (Moscow 2000)

SSSR i Germanskii Vopros, 1941–1949, vol. 3 (Moscow 2003)

SSSR i Stalin v sud'bakh Kitaya: Dokumenty i svidetel'stava uchastnika sobytii, 1937–1952, ed. A. Ledovskii (Moscow 1999)

SSSR—Pol'sha. Mekhanizmy podchineniya, 1944–1949gg.: Sbornik dokumentov, ed. G. Bordyugov et al. (Moscow 1995)

SSSR, SShA, i Velikobritanii (4–11 fevralya 1945g.): Sbornik dokumentov, ed. A. Gromyko et al. (Moscow 1988)

The Voroshilov Lectures: Materials from the Soviet General Staff Academy, vol. 1, ed. G. Wardak (Washington DC 1989)

Vostochnaya Evropa v dokumentakh rossiiskikh arkhivov, 1944–1953 gg., vol. 1, ed. T. Volokitina et al. (Moscow 1997)

V Politburo TsK KPSS. Po zapisyam Anatoliya Chernyaeva, Vadima Medvedeva, Georgiya Shakhnazarova, 1985–1991 (Moscow 2006)

"'Ya veryu v velichie starshego brata'—Besedy N. S. Khrushcheva s Kho Shi Minom," *Istochnik*, no. 2, 1998

"Zapis besedy glav pravitel'stv vo vremya zavtraka," *Sovetskii Soyuz na Mezhdunarodnykh konferentsiyakh perioda Velkoi Otechestvennoi Voiny, 1941–1945gg.: Sbornik dokumentov* (Moscow 1980)

"'Zapiska vneshnepoliticheskoi komissii TsK KPSS o normalizatsii sovetsko-kitaiskikh otnoshenii,' 7 January 1965: 'Spor idet o slishkom bol'shikh veshchakh.' Neudavshayasya popytka sovetsko-kitaiskogo primireniya, 1964–1965 gg.,'" *Istoricheskii Arkhiv*

Zhukov, "Bezogovorchnaya Kapitulyatsiya" (March 1965). Published in *Rossiya XX Vek. Dokumenty. Georgii Zhukov: Stenogramma oktyab'skogo (1957g.) plenuma TsK KPSS i drugie dokumenty*, ed. V. Naumov (Moscow 2001)

Britain

Avon Papers, Birmingham University

FO 800, National Archives, Kew

KV 2

FO 371

Sir Nicholas Henderson, Diary

Margaret Thatcher Foundation Archive on the World Wide Web

CP

Command 6201

Command 6932 (London 1977)

Command 9080: Documents Relating to the Meeting of Foreign Ministers of France, the United Kingdom, the Soviet Union and the United States of America: Berlin, January 25–February 18, 1954 (London 1954)

Documents on British Policy Overseas, series 3, vol. 1 (London 1997) and vol. 2 (London 1997)

United States of America

Presidential Papers

Truman (Missouri); Eisenhower (Kansas); Kennedy (Massachusetts); Lyndon Johnson (Texas); Nixon (Washington DC); Ford (World Wide Web); Carter (World Wide Web)

Other

Buell Papers, Library of Congress
Central Intelligence Agency Electronic Archive, World Wide Web
Council on Foreign Relations Papers, Library of Congress
Elbridge Dubrow Papers, Hoover Institution Archive, Stanford University
Eugene Meyer Papers, Library of Congress
Joseph Freeman Papers, Hoover Institution Archive, Stanford University
Harriman Papers, Library of Congress
George Kennan Papers, Princeton University
Edward Lansdale Papers, Hoover Institution Archive, Stanford University
Leahy Diaries, Library of Congress
Luce Papers, Library of Congress
Hans J. Morgenthau Papers, Library of Congress
Papers of Henry Lewis Stimson, microfilm edition, Yale University Library
State Department, National Archives, College Park MD
Edward Teller Papers, Hoover Institution Archive, Stanford University
Zelikow-Rice Papers, Hoover Institution Archive, Stanford University

Published

Anglo-American Financial Agreement: Hearings Committee on Banking and Currency. March 5–20. US Senate, 79th Cong., 2nd sess. (Washington DC 1946)
Dear Bess: The Letters from Harry to Bess Truman, 1910–1959 (New York 1983)
Documents on Germany, 1944–1985 (Washington DC 1985)
The Diaries of Edward R. Stettinius, Jr, 1943–1946, ed. T. Campbell and G. Herring (New York 1975)
Executive Sessions of the Senate Foreign Relations Committee (Historical Series), vol. 12, 86th Cong., 2nd sess., 1960 (Washington DC 1982)
Foreign Relations of the United States (FRUS)
FRUS, 1942, vol. 3, Europe (Washington 1961)
FRUS, 1944, vol. 4 (Washington 1966)
FRUS, 1946, vol. 6 (Washington DC 1969)
FRUS, 1947, vol. 3 (Washington DC 1972)
FRUS, 1948, vol. 4 (Washington DC 1974)
FRUS, 1952–1954, vol. 2 (Washington 1984)
FRUS, vol. 7, pt. 1 (Washington DC 1986)
FRUS, 1955–1957, vol. 5 (Washington DC 1989)
FRUS, 1964–1968, vol. 11 (Washington DC 1997)
FRUS, 1964–1968, vol. 14 (Washington DC 2001)

FRUS, 1969–1976, vol. 12 (Washington DC 2006)

Foreign Trade and Shipping of the Special Committee on Post-War Economic Policy and Planning. US Congress, House Committee Hearings, 79th Cong. 1944 (Washington DC 1944)

The Forrestal Diaries (London 1952)

The Kennedy Tapes: Inside the White House During the Cuban Missile Crisis, ed. E. May and P. Zelikow (Cambridge, Mass. 1998)

Legislative Origins of the Truman Doctrine. Hearings Held in Executive Session before the Committee on Foreign Relations. US Senate, 80th Cong., 1st sess., on S. 938. *A Bill to Provide for Assistance to Greece and Turkey* (Washington DC 1973)

National Security Directives of the Reagan and Bush Administrations: The Declassified History of U.S. Political and Military Policy, 1981–1991, ed. C. Simpson (Boulder 1995)

Off the Record: The Private Papers of Harry S. Truman (New York 1980)

Post-war Economic Policy and Planning. US House of Representatives Subcommittee on Public Papers of the Presidents. Gerald R. Ford. 1975. vol. 1 (Washington DC 1977)

Public Papers of the Presidents of the United States: Ronald Reagan, 1981 (Washington DC 1982)

M. Truman, ed., *Letters from Father* (New York 1982)

Truman Family's Personal Correspondence (South Yarmouth, Mass. 1981)

France

Ministry of Foreign Affairs (MaE), Paris

Published

V. Auriol, *Journal du Septennat, 1947–1954*, vol. 1 (Paris 1970)
Documents Diplomatiques Français, 1955, vol. 2 (Paris 1988)
Documents Diplomatiques Français, 1956, vol. 1 (Paris 1988)
Documents Diplomatiques Français, 1956 (Paris 1989)

Germany

Ministry for External Relations of the German Democratic Republic, Ministry of Foreign Affairs, Berlin
Ministry of Foreign Affairs of the Federal Republic, Berlin
Archives of the SED (East German Communist Party), Bundesarchiv, SAPMO, Berlin
BstU, ZA, ZAIG, Stasi Archive, Berlin, also World Wide Web

Published

Akten zur Auswärtigen Politik der Bundesrepublik Deutschland, 1966, vol. 1, ed. H.-P. Schwarz (Munich 1997)
Akten . . ., 1969, vol. 2 (Munich 2000)
Akten . . ., 1975, vol. 1 (Munich 2006)
Akten . . ., 1977, vol. 1, ed. H. Möller et al. (Munich 2008)
W. Brandt: *Berliner Ausgabe*, vol. 8, ed. B. Rother and W. Schmidt (Berlin 2006); vol. 9, ed. F. Fischer (Berlin 2003); vol. 10, ed. U. Mai et al. (Berlin 2009)
Bonn und Ost-Berlin, 1969–1982, ed. H. Potthoff (Frankfurt 1997)

494

Bibliography

Countdown zur deutschen Einheit: Eine dokumentierte Geschichte der deutsch-deutschen Beziehungen, 1987–1990, ed. D. Nakath and G.-R. Stephan (Berlin 1996)

Der Tag, an dem die Mauer fiel: Die wichtigsten Zeitzeugen berichten vom 9. November 1989, ed. H. Hertle and K. Elsner (Berlin 2009)

Dokumente zur Deutschlandpolitik. Deutsche Einheit. Sonderedition aus den Akten des Bundeskanzleramtes 1989/90, ed. H. J. Küsters and D. Hofman (Munich 1998)

Gorbatschow und die deutsche Einheit: Aussagen der wichtigsten russischen und deutschen Beteiligten (Bonn 1993)

Honecker-Gorbatschow Vieraugen gespräche (Berlin 1993)

Uprising in East Germany, 1953, ed. C. Ostermann (Budapest and New York 2001)

"Vorwärts immer, rückwärts nimmer!": Interne Dokumente zum Zerfall von SED und DDR 1988/89, ed. G.-R. Stephan and D. Kuchenmeister (Berlin 1994)

Italy

Ministry of Foreign Affairs (MAE), Rome
Archives of the Italian Communist Party, Archivio PCI, Istituto Gramsci, Rome
Aldo Moro Papers, Archivio Centrale dello Stato, Rome

Published

Archivio Secchia. Annali. Fondazione Giangiacomo Feltrinelli (Milan, 1978)

Miscellaneous

Agreement between India and China on Trade and Intercourse between India and Tibet Region of China (New Delhi 1954)

C. Amort, ed., *Dokumenty a materiály k dějinám československo-sovětských*, vol. 4

Chambre des Représentants. *Enquête Parlementaire visant à déterminer les circonstances exactes de l'assassinat de Patrice Lumumba et l'implication éventuelle des responsables politiques belges dans celui-ci. Rapport*, vol. 1

Documents of the History of the Communist Party of India, vol. 7, ed. M. Rao (New Delhi 1976)

J. Grenville and B. Wasserstein, eds., *The Major International Treaties since 1945* (London and New York 1987)

Mao Tse-tung, *Selected Works*, vol. 4 (Peking 1969)

Mao Tse-tung Unrehearsed, ed. S. Schram (London 1974)

Selected Works of Govind Ballabh Pant, vol. 12 (Oxford 1999)

Selected Works of Jawaharlal Nehru, 2nd series, vol. 24 (New Delhi 1999)

A. Schilcher, ed., *Österreich und Die Grossmächte: Dokumente zur österreichischen Außenpolitik, 1945–1955* (Wien-Salzburg 1980)

United Nations Treaty Series, 1952, vol. 136

MEMOIRS AND ORAL HISTORIES

P. Abrasimov, *Zapadnyi Berlin: Vchera i segodnya* (Moscow 1980)
S. Akhromeev and G. Kornienko, *Glazami marshala i diplomata* (Moscow 1992)
A. Alexandrov-Agentov, *Ot Kollontai do Gorbacheva* (Moscow 1994)

S. Alliluyeva, *Dvadtsat' Pisem k Drugu* (London 1967)

J. Allison, *Ambassador from the Prairie* (Boston 1973)

H. Apel, *Der Abstieg: Politisches Tagebuch, 1978–1988* (Stuttgart 1990)

G. Arbatov, *Chelovek Sistemy: Nablyudeniya i Razmyshleniya Ochevidtsa ee Raspada* (Moscow 2002)

"Avtobiograficheskie zametki' V. N. Pavlova—Perevodchika I. V . Stalina," *Novaya i Noveishaya Istoriya*, no. 4, July–August 2000

H. Axen, *Ich war ein Diener der Partei* (Berlin 1996)

W. Bedell Smith, *Moscow Mission, 1946–1949* (London 1950)

D. Ben-Gurion, *Israel: A Personal History* (London 1972)

C. Bentinck, in *Intelligence Chief Extraordinary: The Life of the Ninth Duke of Portland* (London 1986)

A. Bérard, *Une Ambassade au Japon* (Paris 1980)

S. Beria, *Moi Otets—Lavrentii Beriya* (Moscow 1994)

G. Bidault, *D'une résistance à l'autre* (Paris 1965)

A. Birse, *Memoirs of an Interpreter* (London 1967)

J. Blight and D. Welch, eds., *On the Brink: Americans and Soviets Reexamine the Cuban Missile Crisis*, 2nd ed. (New York 1990)

C. Bohlen, *Witness to History, 1929–1969* (New York 1973)

A. Bovin, *XX Vek Kak Zhizn': Vospominaniya* (Moscow 2003)

H. Brandon, *Special Relationships: A Foreign Correspondent's Memoirs from Roosevelt to Reagan* (New York 1988)

H. Bräutigam, *Ständige Vertretung: Meine Jahre in Ost-Berlin* (Hamburg 2009)

British Diplomatic Oral History Project, Churchill College, Cambridge

M. Brosio, *Diari di Mosca 1947–1951* (Bologna 1986)

K. Brutents, *Tridtsat' let na Staroi Ploshchadi* (Moscow 1998)

Z. Brzezinski, *Nouvel Observateur*, 15–21 January 1988

G. Cerreti, *Con Togliatti e Thorez: Quarant'anni di lotte politche* (Milan 1973)

M. Charlton, ed., *The Eagle and Small Birds* (London 1984)

E. Chazov, *Rok* (Moscow 2000)

——, *Zdorov'e i vlast'. Vospominaniya "kremlevskogo vracha"* (Moscow 1992)

A. Chernyaev, "Bez ustali rabotayushchii intellekt," in *Vospominaniya ob Aleksandre Bovine: politik, zhurnalist, diplomat* (Moscow 2006)

——, *Byl li u Rossii shans? On—poslednii* (Moscow 2003)

——, *Moya zhizn' i moe vremya* (Moscow 1995)

——, *Shest' Let s Gorbachevym. Po dnevnikovym zapisyam* (Moscow 1993)

Chin Peng: *My Side of History* (Singapore 2003)

F. Chuev, *MOLOTOV: Poluderzhavnyi vlastelin* (Moscow 2000)

W. Churchill, *The Grand Alliance* (London 1950)

D. Cramer, *Gefragt: Egon Bahr* (1975)

V. Dashichev, "On the Road to German Reunification: The View from Moscow," in *Soviet Foreign Policy, 1917–1991: A Retrospective*, ed. G. Gorodetsky (London 1994)

——, "Ot totalitarnoi k demokraticheskoi politike v germanskom voprose," in D. Proektor et al., *Rossiya i Germaniya v gody voiny i mira, 1941–1955* (Moscow 1955)

J. Davidson-Houston, *Armed Diplomat: A Military Attaché in Russia* (London 1959)

V. Dedijer, *Tito Speaks* (London 1955)

L. Devlin, *Chief of Station, Congo: A Memoir of 1960–67* (New York 2007)

G. Dimitrov, *The Diary of Georgi Dimitrov, 1933–1949*, ed. I. Banac (New Haven 2003)

M. Djilas, *Conversations with Stalin* (New York 1962)

——, *Rise and Fall* (New York 1986)

A. Dobrynin, "The Caribbean Crisis: An Eyewitness Account," *International Affairs* (Moscow), no. 8, 1992

——, *In Confidence* (New York 1995)

"Do 90 let on ezdil v polokliniku na elektrichke," *Kommersant Vlast'*, 21 March 2000

A. Dubček, *Hope Dies Last* (London 1993)

John Foster Dulles Oral History Project, Firestone Library, Princeton University

A. Eban, *Personal Witness* (London 1993)

A. Elizavetin "Trudnye Gody v Kitae," in *Diplomaticheskii Ezhegodnik* (Moscow 1992)

M. Ellman and V. Kontorovich, eds., *The Destruction of the Soviet Economic System: An Insiders' History* (London 1998)

"Entrevista: El General Nikolai Leonov en el CEP," *Estudios Públicos*, 73 (verano 1999)

V. Erofeev, "Desyat' Let v Sekretariate Narkomindela," *Mezhdunarodnaya Zhizn'*, no. 8, August 1991

——, *Diplomat* (Moscow 2005)

——, "I. V. Stalin i V. M. Molotov kak rukovoditelya vneshnei politiki SSSR v voennye i poslevoennye gody" (unpub. MS in author's possession)

V. Falin, *Bez skidok na Obstoyatel'stva* (Moscow 1999)

——, *Konflikty v Kremle: Sumerki bogov po-russki* (Moscow 1999)

O. Fallaci, *Intervista con la storia* (Milan 2008)

A. Feklisov, *Za okeanom i na ostrove* (Moscow 1994)

N. Ganchovski, *The Days of Dimitrov as I Witnessed and Recorded Them* (Sofia 1979)

M. Gareev, *Afganskaya strada (s sovetskimi voiskami i bez nikh)* (Moscow 1999)

R. Garthoff, *A Journey through the Cold War* (Washington DC 2001)

——, *Reflections on the Cuban Missile Crisis* (Washington DC 1987)

R. Gates, *From the Shadows* (New York 1997)

GB99 KCLMA, the Cold War television documentary archive

H.-D. Genscher, *Erinnerungen* (Berlin 1995)

——, *Rebuilding a House Divided: A Memoir* (New York 1998)

A. Grachev, *Kremlevskaya Khronika* (Moscow 1994)

A. Gribkov, "Karibskii krizis," *Voenno-istoricheskii zhurnal*, no. 10, 1992.

——, *Sud'ba Varshavskogo Dogovora: Vospominaniya, dokumenty, fakty* (Moscow 1998)

O. Grinevskii, *Tainy sovetskoi diplomatii* (Moscow 2000)

V. Grishin, *Ot Khrushcheva do Gorbacheva: Politicheskie Portrety Pyati Gensekov i A. N. Kosygina: Memuary* (Moscow 1996)

A. Gromyko, *Andrei Gromyko. V labirintakh Kremlya—Vospominaniya i razmyshleniya syna* (Moscow 1997)

——, *Pamyatnoe*, vol. 1 (Moscow 1988)

W. Harriman and E. Abel, *Special Envoy to Churchill and Stalin, 1941–1946* (London 1976)

W. Hayter, *A Double Life* (London 1974)

R. Helms, *A Look over My Shoulder: A Life in the Central Intelligence Agency* (New York 2003)

J. Hines et al., eds., *Soviet Intentions, 1965–1985*, vol. 2: *Soviet Post-Cold War Testimonial Evidence* (produced in 1995)

Hoang Van Hoan, *A Drop in the Ocean* (Beijing 1988)

Hoover-Gorbachev Foundation, Cold War Project, Hoover Institution

E. Hoxha, *The Titoites* (London 1982)

J. Hughes and Denis Clift, "Cuban Missile Crisis: The San Cristobal Trapezoid," in *Studies in Intelligence, 1990–1994*

R. Hutchings, *American Diplomacy and the End of the Cold War* (Washington DC 1997)

B. R. Inman, "Supercomputer Leadership: A U.S. Priority," in *Frontiers of Super-Computing*, ed. N. Metropolis (Berkeley 1986)

V. Israelyan, *Inside the Kremlin during the Yom Kippur War* (Pennsylvania 1995)

U. A. Johnson, *The Right Hand of Power* (New Jersey 1984)

Julien, "Sept heures avec M. Fidel Castro," *Le Monde*, 22 March 1963

M. Kapitsa, *Na raznykh parallelyakh: Zapiski diplomata* (Moscow 1996)

E. Kardelj, *Reminiscences* (London 1982)

G. Kennan, *Memoirs, 1925–1950* (New York 1967)

Kevorkov, *Tainyi Kanal* (Moscow 1997)

N. Khrushchev, "Memuary Nikity Sergeevicha Khrushcheva," *Voprosy Istorii*, no. 10, 1992

——, "Memuary Nikity Sergeevicha Khrushcheva," *Voprosy Istorii*, nos. 8–9, 1992

——, "Memuary Nikity Sergeevicha Khrushcheva," *Voprosy Istorii*, no. 6, 1993

——, "Memuary Nikity Sergeevicha Khrushcheva," *Voprosy Istorii*, no. 7, 1993

——, "Memuary Nikity Sergeevicha Khrushcheva," *Voprosy Istorii*, no. 9, 1993

——, "Memuary Nikity Sergeevicha Khrushcheva," *Voprosy Istorii*, no. 6, 1994

S. Khrushchev, "Defence Sufficiency and the Military-Political Conception of Nikita Khrushchev, 1953–1964," in *Personalities, War and Diplomacy: Essays in International History*, ed. T. Otte and C. Pagedas (London 1997)

——, *Nikita Khrushchev: Krizisy i rakety — Vzglyad iznutri* (Moscow 1994)

——, *Pensioner Soyuznogo Znacheniya* (Moscow 1991)

——, *Rozhdenie Sverkhderzhavy. Kniga ob ottse* (Moscow 2000)

V. Kirpichenko, *Razvedka: Litsa i Lichnosti* (Moscow 1998)

H. Kissinger, *Diplomacy* (New York 1994)

——, *Years of Renewal* (New York 2000)

H. Kohl, *Erinnerungen, 1982–1990* (Munich 2005)

A. Kolpakidi et al., eds., *Entsiklopediya Sekretnykh Sluzhb Rossii* (Moscow 2004)

S. Kondrashev, "Yu. V. Andropov," *Komanda Andropova* (Moscow 2005)

S. Kopásci, *Au nom de la classe ouvrière: le mémoire du préfet de police de Budapest en 1956* (Paris 1979)

G. Kornienko, "Upushchennaya vozmozhnost': Vstrecha N. S. Khrushcheva i Dzh. Kennedi v Vene v 1961 g.," *Novaya i Noveishaya Istoriya*, no. 2, 1992

——, *Kholodnaya Voina: svidetel'stvo ee uchastnika* (Moscow 2001)

W. Kotschemasow, *Meine letzte Mission: Fakten, Erinnerungen, Uberlegungen* (Berlin, c. 1994)

R. Kovar, "An Interview with Richard Lehman," www.cia.gov/library/center-for-the-study-of-intelligence/csi

Krenz, *Herbst '89* (Berlin 1999)

A. Krock, *Memoirs* (London 1968)

H. Kroll, *Lebenserinnerungen eines Botschafters* (Köln 1967)

Y. Kvitsinskii, *Vremya i sluchai: Zametki professionala* (Moscow 1999)

V. Makarov, *V General'nom Shtabe nakanune gryadushchikh peremen* (Moscow 2004)

I. Maksimychev, "Narod nam ne prostit": *poslednie mesyatsy GDR. Dnevnik sovetnika-poslannika posol'stva SSSR v Berline* (Moscow 2002)

A. Margelov and V. Margelov, *Desantnik No. 1 general armii Margelov* (Moscow 2003)

J. Matlock, *Reagan and Gorbachev: How the Cold War Ended* (New York 2004)

R. McNamara, *In Retrospect* (New York 1996)

Medvedev , *Chelovek za spinoi* (Moscow 1994)

G. Meir, *My Life* (London 1975)

G. Mikes, *The Hungarian Revolution* (London 1957)

A. Mikoyan, *Tak Bylo: Razmyshleniya o minuvshem* (Moscow 1999)

Y. Modin, *My Five Cambridge Friends* (London 1994)

H. Modrow, *Die Perestroika: Wie ich sie sehe* (Berlin 1998)

Moran, *The Struggle for Survival* (London 1968)

R. Murphy, *Diplomat among Warriors* (London 1964)

O. Nazhestkin, "Gody Kongolezskogo krizisa, 1960–1963gg.: Zapiski razvedchika," *Novaya i Noveishaya Istoriya*, no. 6, November–December 2003

——, "Sverkhderzhavy i sobytiya v Angole 1960–1970-e gody," *Novaya i Noveishaya Istoriya*, no. 4, July–August 1975

N. Novikov, *Vospominaniya diplomata* (Moscow 1989)

Oral History of the Cold War, Mershon Center, Ohio State University, Columbus

R. Pannequin, *Adieu, camarades*, vol. 2 (Paris 1977)

Pezzulo, "Nicaragua, 1979: Somoza Out, Sandinistas In," in *American Ambassadors in a Troubled World: Interviews with Senior Diplomats*, ed. D. Mak and C. Kennedy (London 1992)

M. Piñeiro ("Barbaroja"), *Che Guevara and the Latin American Revolutionary Movements* (Melbourne 2002)

B. Podtserob, "Iz istorii vneshnei politiki SSSR. Vospominaniya diplomatov: Tegeran-Potsdam," *Diplomaticheskii Vestnik 1983* (Moscow 1984)

E. Pyrlin, *Trudnyi i Dolgii put' k miru: Vzglyad iz Moskvy na problemu blizhnevostochnogo uregulirovaniya* (Moscow 2002)

G. Rafael, *Destination Peace. Three Decades of Israeli Foreign Policy: A Personal Memoir* (New York 1981)

S. Ramírez, *Adiós Muchachos. Una memoria de la revolución sandinista* (Buenos Aires 1999)

R. Reagan, *An American Life* (London 1990)

——, *The Reagan Diaries*, ed. D. Brinkley (New York 2007)

Ronald Reagan Oral History Project, Miller Center, University of Virgina, Charlottesville

A. Sadat, *In Search of Identity: An Autobiography* (London 1978)

P. Salinger, *With Kennedy* (London 1967)

H. Schmidt, *Menschen und Mächte II: Die Deutschen und ihre Nachbarn* (Berlin 1990)

——, *Menschen und Mächte* (Berlin 1987)

——, *Weggefährten: Erinnerungen und Reflexionen* (Berlin 1996)

H. Schmidt and Giovanni di Lorenzo, *Auf eine Zigarette mit Helmut Schmidt* (Cologne 2009)

W. Semjonow, *Von Stalin bis Gorbatschow: Ein halbes Jahrhundert in diplomatischer Mission, 1939–1991* (Berlin 1995)

G. Shakhnazarov, *Tsena svobody* (Moscow 1993)

L. Shebarshin, *Ruka Moskvy: Zapiski nachal'nika sovetskoi razvedki* (Moscow 1992)

P. Shelest, . . . *Da ne sudimy budete: Dnevnikovye zapisi vospominaniya chlena Politburo TsK KPSS* (Moscow 1994)

D. Shepilov, *Neprimknuvshii* (Moscow 2001)

A. Shevchenko, *Breaking with Moscow* (New York 1985)

G. Shultz, *Turmoil and Triumph* (New York 1993)

E. Snow, *Journey to the Beginning* (London 1958)

Spínola, *País sem Rumo: Contributo para a História de uma Revoluçao* (1978)

V. Starodubov, *Superderzhavy XX Veka: Strategicheskoe protivoborstvo* (Moscow 2001)

Sudoplatov, *Spetsoperatsii: Lubyanka i Kreml', 1930–1950* (Moscow 1997)

D. Sukhanov, "Stalin poshevelil pal'tsami . . . ," *Novoe Vremya*, no. 48, 1991

V. Sukhodrev, *Yazyk moi—drug moi: Ot Khrushcheva do Gorbacheva* (Moscow 1999)

C. Sulzberger, *Age of Mediocrity* (New York 1973)

——, *The Last of the Giants* (London 1972)

——, *A Long Row of Candles: Memoirs and Diaries, 1934–1954* (New York 1969)

G. Tabouis, *Les Princes de la Paix* (Paris 1980)

H. Teltschik, *329 Tage: innenansichten der Einigung* (Berlin 1991)

L. Tikhvinskii, "Proshloe: Golos ochevidtsa," *Problemy Dal'nego Vostoka*, no. 4, 1990

——, *Put' Kitaya k ob"edineniyu i nezavisimosti, 1898–1949* (Moscow 1996)

——, *Vozvrashchenie k vorotam nebesnogo spokoistviya* (Moscow 2000)

T. Toranska, *"Them"* (New York 1987)

O. Troyanovskii, *Cherez gody i rasstoyaniya* (Moscow 1997)

——, "The Making of Soviet Foreign Policy," in *Nikita Khrushchev*, ed. W. Taubman et al. (New Haven 2000)

I. Ustinov, *Krepche Stali: Zapiski veterana voennoi kontrrazvedki* (Moscow 2005)

Varennikov, *Nepovtorimoe*, vol. 4 (Moscow 2001),

V. Vorotnikov, *A Bylo Eto Tak . . . : iz dnevnika chlena Politburo TsK KPSS* (Moscow 1995)

L. Walesa, *The Struggle and the Triumph: An Autobiography* (New York 1992)

R. Weizsäcker, *Der Weg zur Einheit* (Moscow 2009)

M. Wolf, *Po sobstvennom zadaniyu* (Moscow 1992)

——, *Spionagechef im geheimen Krieg: Erinnerungen* (Munich 1997)

Wu Xiuquan, *Eight Years in the Ministry of Foreign Affairs: Memoirs of a Diplomat* (Beijing 1985)

A. Yakovlev, *Omut Pamyati* (Moscow 2001)

——, *Sumerki* (Moscow 2003)

P. Zelikow and C. Rice, *Germany Unified and Europe Transformed* (Cambridge, Mass. 1997)

M. Zhukova, *Marshal Zhukov—Moi otets* (Moscow 2007)

PERIODICALS

Annual Energy Review 2008
Arte Magazine
BBC Summary of World Broadcasts
Berliner Zeitung
Byulleten' Oppozitsii
Cold War International History Project Bulletin
Corriere della Sera
Daily Telegraph
Estudios Públicos
Department of State Bulletin
Foreign Affairs
Front Page Magazine
Guardian
Haaretz
International Security
Istochnik
Istoricheskii Arkhiv
Izvestiya TsK KPSS
Journal of Cold War Studies
Journal of European Integration History
Journal of Imperial and Commonwealth History
Keesing's Contemporary Archive
Kirche im Sozialismus
Kommersant Vlast'
Kommunist
Krasnaya Zvezda
Le Monde
Leningradskaya Pravda
Manchester Guardian
Mezhdunarodnaya zhizh'
Nash Sovremennik
New Statesman
Newsweek
New Times

New York Review of Books
New York Times
Nouvel Observateur
Novaya i Noveishaya Istoriya
Observer
Ogonek
Pravda
Problemy Dal'nego Vostoka
La Repubblica
San Jose Mercury
Der Spiegel
Survey of Current Business
Svenska Dagbladet
Svobodnaya Mysl'
Time
The Times
Voenno-istoricheskii zhurnal
Voina i rabochii klass
Voprosy Istorii
US News and World Report
Vestnik Ministerstva Inostrannykh Del SSSR
Viertel jahschefte für Zeitgeschichte
Wall Street Journal
Washington Post
Washington Times

SECONDARY WORKS

Yu. Abramova, "1957-i: vlast' i armiya," *Svobodnaya Mysl'*, no. 12, 1997

P. Ahonen, "Franz-Josef Strauss and the German Nuclear Question, 1956–1962," *Journal of Strategic Studies*, vol. 18, no. 2, June 1995

M. Aid, *The Secret Sentry: The Untold History of the National Security Agency* (New York 2009)

J. L. Anderson, *Che Guevara* (New York 1997)

K. Anderson et al., eds., *Komintern i vtoraya mirovaya voina*, vol. 2 (Moscow 1998)

C. Andrew and O. Gordievsky, eds., *More "Instructions from the Centre": Top Secret Files on KGB Global Operations, 1975–1985* (London 1992)

C. Andrew and V. Mitrokhin, *The Mitrokhin Archive I* (London 1999)

——, *The Mitrokhin Archive II* (London 2005)

V. Andrianov, *Kosygin* (Moscow 2003)

M. Armitage and R. Mason, *Air Power in the Nuclear Age*, 2nd ed. (Urbana 1985)

M. J. Avillez, *Soares: Ditadura e Revolução* (Lisbon 1996)

V. Baryn'kin, "Manchzhurskaya nastupatel'naya operatsiya," *Voenno-istoricheskii Zhurnal*, no. 5, 1995

S. Ben-Ami, *Scars of War, Wounds of Peace: The Israeli-Arab Tragedy* (London 2005)

M. Bernardo, ed., *Equívocos e Realidades* (Lisbon 2004)

M. Beschloss and S. Talbott, *At the Highest Levels: The Inside Story of the End of the Cold War* (London 1993)

F. Bobkov, *KGB i vlast'* (Moscow 1995)

B. Bonwetsch and A. Filitov, "Chruschtschow und der Mauerbau," *Vierteljahrschefte für Zeitgeschichte*, vol. 48, no. 1, January 2000

L. Borhi, "Containment, Rollback, Liberation or Inaction? The United States and Hungary in the 1950s," *Journal of Cold War Studies*, vol. 1, no. 3, 1999

O. Borisov et al., eds., *Pobeda na Vostoke* (Moscow 1985)

R. Brigham, *Guerrilla Diplomacy: The NLF's Foreign Relations and the Viet Nam War* (Ithaca 1999)

A. Brown, "The Change to Engagement in Britain's Cold War Policy: The Origins of the Thatcher-Gorbachev Relationship," *Journal of Cold War Studies*, vol. 10, no. 3, Summer 2008

N. Brusnitsyn, *Kto podslushivaet prezidentov—ot Stalina do El'tsina* (Moscow 2000)

A. Bullock, *Ernest Bevin* (London 1982)

I. Bystrova, *Voenno-promyshlennyi kompleks SSSR v gody kholodnoi voiny* (Moscow 2000)

E. Carr, *The Bolshevik Revolution*, vol. 3 (London 1953)

——, *Socialism in One Country, 1924–1926*, vol. 1 (London 1958)

——, *Twlight of Comintern, 1930–35* (London 1982)

J. Carswell, *The Exile: A Life of Ivy Litvinov* (London 1983)

J. Chace, *Acheson* (New York 1998)

Chen Jian, *Mao's China and the Cold War* (Chapel Hill 2001)

V. Chikov, *Dos'e KGB No. 13676: Nelegaly*, vol. 1: *Operatsiya "Enormous"* (Moscow 1997)

J. Ciechanowski, *The Warsaw Rising of 1944* (Cambridge 1974)

P. Cradock, *Know Your Enemy: How the Joint Intelligence Committee Saw the World* (London 2002)

Cray Research, Inc., *The Cray-1 Computer System* (1977)

G. Daskalov, *B"lgariya i G"rtsiya: ot razriv k"m pomirenie, 1944–1964* (Sofia 2004)

L. De Witte, *L'Assassinat de Lumumba* (Paris 2000)

K. Diekmann and R. Reuth, *Helmut Kohl: "Ich wollte Deutschlands Einheit"* (Berlin 1996)

T. Diez Acosta, *October 1962: The "Missile" Crisis as Seen from Cuba* (New York 2002)

Documents on Israeli-Soviet Relations, 1941–1953, pt. 1 (London 2000)

I. Drogovoz, *Raketnye voiska SSSR* (Minsk 2007)

I. Egorova, "'Iranskii krizis,' 1945–1946gg.: vzglyad iz rossiiskikh arkhivov," *Kholodnaya Voina. Novye podkhody: Novye dokumenty*, ed. I. Gaiduk et al. (Moscow 1995)

——, "Soviet Perceptions of the Formation of NATO, 1948–1953," http://history.machaon.ru/all/number_02/analiti4/2/index.html.

R. English, *Russia and the Idea of the West: Gorbachev, Intellectuals and the End of the Cold War* (New York 2000)

N. Eronin, "O strategicheskikoi peregruppirovke sovetskikh vooruzhennykh sil na dal'nevostochyi teatr' voennykh deistvii letom 1945g." in *Pobeda SSSR v voine s mili-*

taristckoi Yaponiei i poslevoennoe razvitie vostochnoi i yugo-vostochnoi Azii (Moscow 1977)

H. Feis, *The China Tangle* (Princeton 1953)

A. Filitov, "Sovetskii Soyuz i germanskii vopros v period pozdnego stalinizma (k voprosu o genezize 'stalinskoi noty' 10 marta 1952 goda)," in *Stalin i kholodnaya voina* (Moscow 1998)

——, "Soviet Perceptions of the Formation of NATO, 1948–1953," *Mezhdunarodnyi istoricheskii zhurnal*, no. 20, 2002

B. Fischer, "A Cold War Conundrum" (unclassified CIA study, 1997)

Foreign Affairs Oral History Collection of the Association for Diplomatic Studies and Training, selected and converted, American Memory, Library of Congress, Washington DC.

W. Foster et al., *Marxism-Leninism vs. Revisionism* (New York 1946)

C. Friedrich and Z. Brzezinski, *Totalitarian Dictatorship and Autocracy* (Cambridge, Mass., 1956)

A. Fursenko, *Rossiya i mezhdunarodnye krizisy seredina XX veka* (Moscow 2006)

A. Fursenko and T. Naftali, *"One Hell of a Gamble": The Secret History of the Cuban Missile Crisis* (London 1997)

J. Gaddis, *We Now Know: Rethinking Cold War History* (Oxford 1997)

I. Gaiduk, *Confronting Vietnam: Soviet Policy toward the Indochina Conflict, 1954–1963* (Washington DC/Stanford 2003)

I. Gaiduk and O. Marinin, "Voina vo V'etname i sovetsko-amerikanskie otnosheniya," *Kholodnaya Voina: Novye podkhody, novye dokumenty* (Moscow 1995)

V. Galitskii and V. Zimonin, "'Desant na Khokkaido Otmenit'!' (Razmyshleniya po povodu odnoi nesostoyavsheisya operatsii)," *Voenno-istoricheskii Zhurnal*, no. 3, 19

R. Garthoff, *The Great Transition: American-Soviet Relations and the End of the Cold War* (Washington DC 1994).

D. Gasanly, *SSSR-IRAN: Azerbaidzhanskii krizis i nachalo kholodnoi voiny, 1941–1946gg.* (Moscow 2006)

——, *SSSR-TURTSIYA: ot neitraliteta k kholodnoi voine, 1939–1953* (Moscow 2008)

Gaspari, *A Ditadura Envergonhada* (São Paolo 2002)

V. Genis, *Krasnaya Persiya. Bol'sheviki v Gilyane. 1920–1921* (Moscow 2000)

L. Gibianskii, "Forsirovanie sovetskoi blokovoi politiki," in *Kholodnaya Voina 1945–1963gg.: Istoricheskaya retrospektiva*, ed. I. Yegorova et al. (Moscow 2003)

——, "Kak voznik Kominform: Po novym arkhyvnym materialam," *Novaya i Noveishaya Istoriya*, no. 4, 1993

M. Gilbert, *Winston S. Churchill*, vol. 8 (London 1988)

——, *"Never Despair": Winston S. Churchill, 1945–1965*, vol. 8 (London 1988)

M. Gorbachev, *Kak eto bylo* (Moscow 1999)

Y. Girenko, *Stalin-Tito* (Moscow 1991)

The Memoirs of Lord Gladwyn (London 1972)

P. Gleijeses, *Conflicting Missions: Washington and Africa, 1959–1976* (Chapel Hill 2002)

Y. Glenovich, *Rossiya—Kitai: Shest' dogovorov* (Moscow 2003)

V. Gobarev, "Soviet Military Plans and Activities during the Berlin Crisis, 1948–1949," *Journal of Slavic Military Studies*, vol. 10, no 3, September 1997

S. Goncharev et al., *Uncertain Partners: Stalin, Mao, and the Korean War* (Stanford 1993)

J. Haslam, "The Boundaries of Rational Calculation in Soviet Policy towards Japan," in *History, the White House and the Kremlin: Statesmen as Historians*, ed. M. Fry (London 1991)

———, *The Nixon Administration and the Death of Allende's Chile: A Case of Assisted Suicide* (London 2005)

———, *Soviet Foreign Policy, 1930–33: The Impact of the Depression* (London 1984)

———, *The Soviet Union and the Politics of Nuclear Weapons in Europe, 1969–87: The Problem of the SS-20* (London 1989)

———, *The Soviet Union and the Struggle for Collective Security in Europe, 1933–1939* (London 1984)

———, "Stalin's War or Peace," *Virtual History*, ed. N. Ferguson (London 1997)

———, *The Vices of Integrity: E. H. Carr, 1892–1982* (London 2000)

J. Haynes and H. Klehr, *VENONA: Decoding Soviet Espionage in America* (New Haven 1999)

D. Heinzig, *Die Sowjetunion und das kommunistische China, 1945–1950* (Baden-Baden 1998)

S. Holtsmark, "Sovetskaya Diplomatiya i Skandinaviya, 1944–1947gg. Po Materialam Arkhiva MID RF," *Novaya i Noveishaya Istoriya*, no. 1, 1997

Istoriya Sovetskikh Organov Gosudarstvennoi Bezopasnosti: Uchebnik (Moscow 1977)

Istoriya vtoroi mirovoi voiny, 1939–1945, ed. A. Grechko et al., vol. 11 (Moscow 1980)

S. Jaczyński, "Armia Czerwona a Powstanie Warszawskie," *Przglad Historyczno-Wojskowy*, vol. 5 (56), no. 3 (203), 2004

T. Johnson, *United States Cryptologic History*, series 6. The NSA Period, vol. 5, bk. 1 (declassified 2006)

J. Jones, *A Modern Foreign Policy for the United States* (New York 1944)

M. Kaiser, "'Es muß demokratisch aussehen . . .': Moskau und die Gleichschaltung des Parteiensystems in der Sowjetischen Besatzungszone Deutschlands 1944/45–1948/49," in *Gleichschaltung unter Stalin? Die Entwicklung der Parteien im östlichen Europa, 1944–1949*, ed. S. Creuzberger and M. Görtemaker (Paderborn 2002)

I. Kasatonov, *Flot Vyshel v Okean* (Moscow 1996)

G. Kennan, "Is the Cold War Over? (1989)," in *At a Century's Ending: Reflections, 1982–1995* (New York 1996)

Kheifets, *Sovetskaya Rossiya i sopredel'nye strany vostoka v gody grazhdanskoi voiny, 1918–1920* (Moscow 1964)

———, *Sovetskaya diplomatiya i narody vostoka, 1921–1927* (Moscow 1968)

S. Kinzer, *Blood of Brothers: Life and War in Nicaragua* (Cambridge, Mass. 2007)

H. Klehr, J. Haynes, and K. Anderson, eds., *The Soviet World of American Communism* (New Haven 1998)

Knyshevskii, *Dobycha: Tainy germanskikh reparatsii* (Moscow 1994)

M. Korobochkin, "Soviet Policy toward Finland and Norway, 1947–1949," *Scandinavian Journal of History*, vol. 20, no. 3, 1995

G. Kostev, *Voenno-morskoi flot strany, 1945–1955: Vzlety i Padeniya* (St. Petersburg 1999)

Kosthorst, *Brentano und di deutsche Einheit: Die Deutschland-und Ostpolitik des Außen-ministers im kabinett Adenauer, 1955–1961* (Düsseldorf 1993)

Kostin, *Margelov* (Moscow 2005)

G. Kostyrenko, *Stalin protiv "Kosmopolitov": Vlast' i evreiskaya intelligentsiya v SSSR* (Moscow 2009)

I.-S. Kowalczuk, *Endspiel: Die Revolution von 1989 in der DDR* (Munich 2009)

M. Kramer, "The Collapse of East European Communism and the Repercussions within the Soviet Union (Part 3)," *Journal of Cold War Studies*, vol. 7, no. 1, Winter 2005

A. Kyrov, "Sovetskaya karatel'naya aktsiya v Vengrii (Khronika sobytii 1956g. po materi-alam voennogo arkhiva)," in *Konflikty v poslevoennom razvitii vostochnoevropesikikh stran*, ed. Yu. Novopashin (Moscow 1997)

N. Lebedeva, *Katyn: Prestuplenie protiv chelovechestva* (Moscow 1994)

J. Le Carré, *The Looking Glass War* (London 1999)

M. Leffler, "Adherence to Agreements: Yalta and the Experience of the Early Cold War," *International Security*, vol. 11, no. 1, Summer 1986

Leonid Brezhnev v vospominaniyakh, razmyshleniyakh, suzhdeniyakh (Rostov-on-Don 1998)

J. Lilley, *China Hands* (New York 2004)

V. Lota, *Sekretnyi front General'nogo Shtaba* (Moscow 2005)

———, "Tegeran—43: trudnyi put' k soglasiyu," *Krasnaya Zvezda*, 1 November 2003

———, "Vklad voennykh razvedchikov v sozdanie otechestvennogo atomnogo oruzhiya. 1941–1945gg.," *Voenno-istoricheskii Zhurnal*, no. 11, 2006

R. Louis and R. Robinson, "The Imperialism of Decolonization," *Journal of Imperial and Commonwealth History*, vol. 22, no. 3, September 1994

H. Luce, *The American Century* (New York 1941)

G. Lundestad: *H-Diplo Roundtable Reviews*, vol. 9, no. 4, 2008

Lyakhovskii, *Tragediya Lubyanka 2. Iz istorii otechestvennnoi kontrrazvedki*, ed. V. Sobolev et al. (Moscow 1999)

C. Maier, "The Cold War as an Era of Imperial Rivalry," in *Reinterpreting the End of the Cold War: Issues, Interpretations, Periodizations*, ed., S. Pons and F. Romero (London 2005)

V. Marchetti and J. Marks, *The CIA and the Cult of Intelligence* (London 1974)

V. Mastny, *The Cold War and Soviet Insecurity* (Oxford 1996)

J. Matthews, "The West's Secret Marshall Plan for the Mind," *International Journal of Intelligence and Counter Intelligence*, vol. 16, no. 3, July–September 2003

D. McCullough, *Truman* (New York 1992)

S. Minakov, *Stalin i ego Marshal* (Moscow 2004)

V. Mitrokhin, *The KGB in Afghanistan* (Washington DC 2002)

L. Mlechin, *Shelepin* (Moscow 2009)

———, *Yuri Andropov. Poslednyaya nadezhda rezhima* (Moscow 2008)

M. Monakov, *Glavkom: Zhizn' i deyatel'nost' Admirala flota Sovetskogo Soyuza S. G. Gor-shkova* (Moscow 2008)

L. Moseley, *Dulles: A Biography of Eleanor, Allen, and John Foster Dulles and Their Fam-ily Network* (London 1978)

G. Murashko, "Fevral'skii krizis 1948g v Chekhoslovakii i sovetskoe rukovodstvo po novym materialam rossiiskikh arkhivov," *Novaya i Noveishaya Istoriya*, no. 2, March–April 1998

G. Murashko and A. Noskova, "Sovetsoe rukovodstvo i politicheskie protsessy T. Kostova i L. Raika (po materialam rossiiskikh arkhivov)," in *Stalinskoe Desyatiletie Kholodnoi Voiny*, ed. I. Gaiduk et al. (Moscow 1997)

N. Naimark, "Stalin and Europe in the Postwar Period, 1945–53: Issues and Problems," *Journal of Modern European History*, vol. 2, no. 1

M. Narinskii, "Berlinskii krizis 1948–1949gg.: Novye dokumenty iz rossiiskikh arkhivov," *Novaya i Noveishaya Istoriya*, no. 3, May–June 1995

——, *Sovetskaya vneshnaya politika i proiskhozhdenie kholodnoi voiny—Sovetskaya vneshnaya politika v retrospektive, 1917–1991* (Moscow 1993)

——, "SSSR i Plan Marshalla," *Kholodnaya Voina: Novye podkhody, novye dokumenty* (Moscow 1995)

Ocherki istorii rossiiskoi vneshnei razvedki, vol. 4 (Moscow 1999)

Ocherki istorii rossiiskoi vneshnei razvedki, vol. 5 (Moscow 2003)

Ocherki istorii rossiiskoi vneshnei razvedki, vol. 6 (Moscow 2007)

W. Odom, "The Cold War Origins of the U.S. Central Command," *Journal of Cold War Studies*, vol. 8, no. 2, Spring 2006

——, *The Collapse of the Soviet Military* (New Haven 1998)

L. Opekkin, "Na istoricheskom pereput'e," *Voprosy Istorii KPSS*, no. 1, January 1990

A. Orekhov, "K istorii pol'sko-sovetskikh peregovorov 19 oktyabrya 1956g. v Bel'vedere (po novym materialam)," *Konflikty v polsvoennom razvitii vostochnoevropeiskikh stran*, ed. Yu. Novopashin (Moscow 1997)

J. Osborne, "The Importance of Ambassadors," *Fortune*, April 1957

C. O'Sullivan, *Sumner Welles, Postwar Planning, and the Quest for a New World Order, 1937–1943* (New York 2008)

G. Padlow and D. Welzenbach, *The Central Intelligence Agency and Overhead Reconnaissance: The U-2 and OXCART Programs, 1954–1974* (a study partially declassified on 4 March 2002)

J. Payne, "The Berlin Crisis, 1948–49" (undergraduate diss., History Faculty, Cambridge University, 1996)

V. Pechatnov, "The Big Three after World War II: New Documents on Soviet Thinking about Post War Relations with the United States and Great Britain," *Cold War International History Project*, Working Paper 13 (July 1995)

V. Pechatnov, *Stalin, Ruzvel't, Trumen: SSSR i SShA v 1940-kh gg.* (Moscow 2006)

Pedro Pezarat Correia, *Descolonizaçao de Angola: A Jóia da Coroa do Império Português* (Lisbon 1991)

R. Pikhoya, *Istoriya Sovremennoi Rossii: Krizis kommunisticheskoi vlasti v SSSR i rozhdenie novoi Rossii, Konets 1970-x–1991gg.* (Moscow 2008)

——, *Moskva. Kreml'. Vlast': Dve istorii odnoi strany. Rossiya na izlome tysyacheletii 1985–2005* (Moscow 2007)

——, *Moskva. Kreml'. Vlast': Sorok let posle voiny, 1945–1985* (Moscow 2007)

——, *SSSR: Istoriya velikoi imperii* (Moscow 2009)

R. Pipes, "Misinterpreting the Cold War: The Hard-Liners Had It Right," *Foreign Affairs*, vol. 74, no. 1

P. Podvig, *Russian Strategic Nuclear Forces* (Cambridge, Mass., 2001)

S. Pons, *Berlinguer e la fine del comunismo* (Turin 2006)

——, "In the Aftermath of the Age of Wars: the Impact of World War II on Soviet Security Policy," in *Russia in the Age of Wars, 1914–1945*, ed. S. Pons and A. Romano (*Annali*, Fondazione Giangiacomo Feltrinelli, 1998, Milan)

D. Proektor et al., *Rossiya i Germaniya v gody voiny i mira, 1941–1955* (Moscow 1995)

D. Prokhorov, *Razvedka ot Stalina do Putina* (St. Petersburg 2004)

V. Prokof'ev, *Aleskandr Sakharovskii. Nachal'nik vneshnei razvedki* (Moscow 2005)

V. Prybitkov, *Apparat* (St. Petersburg 1995)

Putilin, "Karibskii Krizis," in *Sovetskaya vneshnyaya politika v gody "Kholodnoi Voiny,"* *1945–1985*, ed. L. Nezhinskii (Moscow 1995)

V. Riva, *Oro da Mosca* (Milan 1999)

G. Roberts, *Stalin's Wars: From World War to Cold War, 1939–1953* (New Haven 2006)

Y. Roi, *Soviet Decision Making in Practice: The USSR and Israel, 1947–1954* (New Brunswick NJ 1980)

D. Rosenberg, "The Origins of Overkill: Nuclear Weapons and American Strategy, 1945–1960," *International Security*, vol. 7, no. 4, 1983

O. Rzhshevskii, ed., *Stalin i Churchill. Vstrechi. Besedy. Diskussii: Dokumenty, kommentarii, 1941–1945* (Moscow 2004)

N. Salmin, *Internatsionalizm v deistvii: lokal'nye voiny i I vooruzhennye konflikty s uchastiem sovetskogo komponenta; voennogo, voenno-tekhnicheskogo, ekonomicheskogo, 1950–1989* (Ekaterinburg 2001)

D. Salvage, "Poland, the German Democratic Republic, and the German Question, 1955–1967" (Ph.D. diss., Yale University 1998)

Sever, *Istoriya KGB* (Moscow 2008)

R. Sherwood, *Roosevelt and Hopkins*, vol. 2 (New York 1950)

A. Shirokorad, *Rossiya i Kitai: Konflikty i sotrudnichestvo* (Moscow 2004)

B.-E. Siebs, *Die Aussenpolitik der DDR, 1976–1989: Strategien und Grenzen* (Padeborn 1999)

N. Simonov, *Voenno-promyshlennyi kompleks SSSR v 1920–1950-e gody: tempy ekonomicheskogo rosta, struktura, organizatsiya proizvodstva i upravlenie* (Moscow 1996)

Slavinsky, "The Soviet Occupation of the Kurile Islands and the Plans for the Capture of Northern Hokkaido," *Japan Forum*, vol. 5, no. 1, April 1993

B. Slavinskii, *SSSR i Yaponiya—na puti k voine: diplomaticheskaya istoriya, 1937–1945 gg.* (Moscow 1999)

J. Snopkiewicz and A. Zakrewski, eds., *Dokumenty Katynia Decyzja* (Warsaw 1992)

H. Soell, *Helmut Schmidt 1969 bis heute: Macht und Verantwortung* (Munich 2008)

G.-H. Soutou, *L'alliance incertaine: Les rapports politico-stratégiques franco-allemands, 1954–1996* (Paris 1996)

——, "Le Président Pompidou et les relations entre les Etats-Unis et l'Europe," *Journal of European Integration History*, vol. 6, no. 2, 2000

"Soviet Perceptions of the Formation of NATO, 1948–1953," http://history.machaon.ru/all/number_02/analiti4/2/index.html.

P. Stavrakis, *Moscow and Greek Communism, 1944–1949* (Ithaca 1989)

A. Taras, *Anatomiya Nenavisti: Russko-pol'skie konflikty v VIII–XX vv.* (Minsk 2008)

W. Taubman, *Khrushchev: The Man and His Era* (New York, 2003)

A. Tereshchenko, *"Oborotni" is voennoi razvedki: Devyat' predatel'stv sotrudnikov GRU* (Moscow 2004)

C. Thorne, *Allies of a Kind: The United States, Britain and the War against Japan, 1941–1945* (London 1978)

A. Torkunov, *Zagadochnaya voina: Koreiskii konflikt, 1950–1953 godov* (Moscow 2000)

M. Trachtenberg, *A Constructed Peace: The Making of the European Settlement, 1945–1963* (Princeton 1999)

H. Trevelyan, *Worlds Apart* (London 1971)

R. Ullman, *Anglo-Soviet Relations, 1917–1921*, vol. 3 (Princeton 1973)

M. Vaïsse, *La grandeur: Politique étrangère du général de Gaulle, 1958–69* (Paris 1998)

A. Vogtmeier, *Egon Bahr und die deutsche Frage: Zur Entwicklung der sozialdemokratischen Ost-und Deutschlandpolitik vom Kriegsende bis zur Vereinigung* (Bonn 1996)

D. Volkogonov, *Sem' vozhdei: Galereya liderov SSSR*, vol. 1 (Moscow 1995)

I. Wall, *The United States and the Making of Postwar France, 1945–1954* (Cambridge 1991)

O. Westad, *The Global Cold War: Third World Interventions and the Making of Our Times* (Cambridge 2005)

——, ed., *The Fall of Détente: Soviet-American Relations during the Carter Years* (Oslo 1997)

K. Wiegrefe, *Das Zerwürfnis: Helmut Schmidt, Jimmy Carter und die Krise der deutsch-amerikanischen Beziehungen* (Berlin 2005)

W. Wolkov, "Die deutsche Frage aus Stalins Sicht, 1947–1952," *Zeitschrift für Geschichtswissenschaft*, 48, 2000

N. Yamskoi, "Smert' na ob"ekte 001," *Sovershenno Sekretno*, no. 3 (202), March 2006

Yang Kuisong, "The Sino-Soviet Border Clash of 1969: From Zhenbao Island to Sino-American Rapprochement," *Cold War History*, vol. 1, no. 1

V. Zaslavsky, *Lo Stalinismo e la Sinistra Italiana* (Milan 2004)

I. Zemskov, *Diplomaticheskaya istoriya votorogo fronta v Evrope* (Moscow 1982)

——, *Sovetsko-angliiskie otnosheniya vo vremya velikoi otechestvennoi voiny, 1941–1945*, vol. 1 (Moscow 1983)

N. Zen'kovich, *Elita: Samye sekretnye rodstvenniki* (Moscow 2005)

——, *Mikhail Gorbachev: Zhizn' do Kremlya* (Moscow 2001)

——, *XX Vek: Vysshii Generalitet v Gody Potryasenii* (Moscow 2005)

P. Zima, *Golod v SSSR, 1946–1947 Godov: proiskhozhdenie i posledstviya* (Moscow 1996)

W. Zimmerman, *Soviet Perspectives in International Relations, 1956–1967* (Princeton 1969)

V. Zolotarev, *Rossiya (SSSR) v lokal'nykh konfliktakh vtoroi poloviny XX Veka* (Moscow 2000)

Zubok, *A Failed Empire: The Soviet Union in the Cold War from Stalin to Gorbachev* (Chapel Hill 2007)

V. Zubok and C. Pleshakov, *Inside the Kremlin's Cold War: From Stalin to Khrushchev* (Cambridge, Mass., 1996)

V. Zubok and Z. Vodop'yanova, "Sovetskaya Diplomatiya i Berlinskii Krizis, 1958–1962," in *Kholodnaya voina: novye podkhody, novye dokumenty* (Moscow 1995)

INDEX